Visiting Picasso

The Notebooks and Letters of Roland Penrose

Elizabeth Cowling

with 72 black and white photographs, including over 40 by Lee Miller

 Thames & Hudson

This book is dedicated to John Golding and to the late Joanna Drew

Published in association with the Scottish National Gallery of Modern Art, Edinburgh, and the Roland Penrose Estate and the Lee Miller Archives, England

First published in the United Kingdom in 2006 by
Thames & Hudson Ltd,
181A High Holborn,
London WC1V 7QX

www.thamesandhudson.com

Visiting Picasso © 2006 Thames & Hudson, London
Photographs and text by Roland Penrose © Roland Penrose Estate, England 2006. All rights reserved.
Photographs and text by Lee Miller © Lee Miller Archives, England 2006. All rights reserved.
Text by Elizabeth Cowling © 2006 Elizabeth Cowling
Foreword by Richard Calvocoressi © 2006 Scottish National Gallery of Modern Art, Edinburgh
Works by Picasso © Succession Picasso/DACS 2006

Design by Sarah Praill

British Library Cataloguing-in-Publication Data
A catalogue record for this book is available from the British Library

ISBN-13: 978-0-500-51293-7
ISBN-10: 0-500-51293-0

Printed and bound in Singapore by CS Graphics

Endpapers A spread from Roland Penrose's 'Barcelona/Cannes' notebook, 1955

p. 2 'Picasso's notes, pinned up on the wall at La Californie when I was expected at the time I was writing his life, *c.* 1955': handwritten note by Roland Penrose on reverse of photograph. Photo Roland Penrose

Contents

8 Foreword

11 Introduction

17 A Note on Sources and Editorial Practice

Chapter 1 The Foundation of the Friendship, 1936–1939

22 Surrealism crosses the Channel
25 Visiting Mougins and Barcelona, August–December 1936
28 Penrose the 'collector'
33 Visiting Mougins with Lee Miller, Summer 1937
37 *Guernica* in England
45 Last months of freedom, 1939

Chapter 2 A Choice of Paths, 1939–1954

48 The War Years, 1939–1945
56 The 'Institute of Contemporary Arts', 1946
60 Picasso's play, *Le Désir attrapé par la queue*
63 Picasso visits England, November 1950
71 Visiting Paris, St Tropez and Vallauris, Summer 1953
76 In Vallauris with Georges Braque, June 1954

Chapter 3 Into the Vast Territories: The Novice Biographer, 1954–1955

82 A publishing offer accepted
96 Penrose launches his research campaign
101 Penrose and Lee Miller in collaboration: visiting France and
      Spain, February–March 1955
114 Visiting Paris, Barcelona and Cannes, June–July 1955
131 Visiting Paris and Cannes, October–November 1955

Chapter 4 The Biography Completed, 1956–1958

144 Visiting Paris and Cannes, February–March 1956
161 *Le Mystère Picasso* at the Cannes Film Festival, May 1956
165 Celebrating Picasso's seventy-fifth birthday, October 1956
175 Picasso and politics, Autumn 1956
182 Completing the biography
207 The biography published, October 1958

Chapter 5 The Story of an Exhibition, 1958–1960

210 The commission
216 Visiting Cannes and Vauvenargues, April 1959
223 Final preparations for the Picasso exhibition
231 'Picassomania'

Chapter 6 Three New Projects, 1960–1965

240 A new campaign: *The Three Dancers*
246 A second project: exhibiting Picasso's sculpture
248 A third project: a monument for Chicago
258 Visiting Mougins, March–June 1964
267 Françoise Gilot versus Picasso
271 *The Three Dancers*: a successful conclusion

Chapter 7   Picasso Sculptor, 1965–1967

282   The Chicago monument: second phase
288   The sculpture exhibition: obstacles and setbacks
290   Fundraising and petitioning
294   Visiting Mougins: Autumn 1966, Spring 1967
303   Picasso's sculpture in London
307   Inauguration of the Chicago monument

Chapter 8   Picasso's Last Years, 1968–1973

310   Visiting Mougins, 1968
316   The Penrose burglary, Spring 1969
318   *Suite 347* in London
321   Visiting Mougins, May–June 1970
330   Picasso at ninety
337   The last visits to Picasso and Jacqueline

344   Epilogue

349   Notes
394   Appendix 1   Biographical Dictionary
396   Appendix 2   Roland Penrose's Picasso 'Notebooks'
398   Appendix 3   Roland Penrose's Publications on Picasso
400   Further Reading
404   Acknowledgments
405   Picture Credits
405   Index

Foreword

Elizabeth Cowling's vividly written and masterfully compiled account of the long, complex and productive friendship between Pablo Picasso and Roland Penrose is the most significant publication based on material in the Penrose archive to have appeared since the acquisition of Sir Roland Penrose's library and papers by the Scottish National Gallery of Modern Art in 1994.

The Gallery's relationship with the Penrose family goes back to the early 1980s, when a number of important works of art from the Penrose collection, including several outstanding pieces exempted from Capital Transfer tax, were placed on long loan to the Gallery after the death of Lee Miller (Lady Penrose) in 1977. Further works followed on the death of Penrose himself in 1984.

Beginning in 1991 with the purchase of Joan Miró's early masterpiece *Maternity* (1924), the Gallery initiated a policy of acquiring as many of the paintings, sculptures and works on paper in the Penrose collection as it was able, with financial help from the National Heritage Memorial Fund, National Art Collections Fund and, from 1995, the Heritage Lottery Fund. In 1995, for example, a group of twenty-six paintings and drawings was bought, including work by Picasso, Salvador Dalí, Paul Delvaux, Max Ernst, René Magritte, Man Ray, André Masson and Yves Tanguy. Among the three works by Picasso was *Head* (1913), the most abstract of his Cubist collages, which had been a prized possession of André Breton, the founder of the Surrealist movement. Combined with the magnificent bequest of Gabrielle Keiller (1995), these acquisitions from the Penrose estate transformed the Gallery into one of the foremost centres in the world for the display and study of Dada and Surrealist art.

Penrose's archive consists of over 1,200 files chronicling his career as an artist, writer, collector, gallery owner and exhibition organiser. These files contain correspondence with major twentieth-century artists, in addition to notebooks, photographs, lecture notes, drafts of essays and books, diaries, press cuttings and other items. It is this extensive material that Elizabeth Cowling has drawn on for her 'biography of a friendship'.

As well as documenting Penrose's relationship with Picasso, the archive covers in depth his decisive role in bringing Surrealism to Britain, the acquisition of his superb collection of Cubist and Surrealist art, and the crucial part he played in founding the Institute of Contemporary Arts in London after the Second World War. Penrose's library of some 10,000 volumes contains not only a comprehensive collection of books and catalogues on Dada, Surrealism and modern art in general, but also a fine group of *livres d'artistes* by Picasso, Miró, Ernst and others, many with dedicatory drawings and inscriptions by the artists.

Penrose's library, together with that of Gabrielle Keiller, is housed in a special air-conditioned gallery where, through changing displays of books and archive material, visitors are invited to study and appreciate the twentieth-century book as a work of art in its own right – something that is not always possible in museums of modern art – as well as the history of Dada and Surrealism from its beginnings in the First World War right up to the 1950s.

I am delighted that Thames & Hudson showed interest in publishing the fruits of Elizabeth Cowling's research, and have done so in such a generous and imaginative form. This absorbing book – a major contribution to art history which also reads like a novel – marks a happy collaboration between the author, the Gallery, the Penrose family, the Lee Miller Archives (source of many of the illustrations) and the publisher. Given the riches of our archive, I have no doubt there will be more such projects.

Richard Calvocoressi
Director, Scottish National Gallery of Modern Art

Introduction

This book is the biography of a friendship that spanned almost forty years, from the time Roland Penrose and Pablo Picasso first met in 1936 until the latter's death in 1973. But since Penrose remained fascinated by Picasso for the rest of his life, it is with Penrose's death, not Picasso's, that the book ends. The course of the friendship was to a large extent shaped by the many projects Penrose undertook to promote Picasso's work in the English-speaking world: this is simultaneously their story. The chequered history of this particular relationship is also a paradigm because there were numerous other people whose devotion to Picasso was equally complicated by their urgent need for favours of some sort. One learns from Penrose's case how bruising, as well as exhilarating, it was to be Picasso's friend, but one also learns obliquely how hard it was to be Picasso, under siege from his legion of admirers.

The quality and depth of Picasso's feelings for Penrose can only be surmised. Their correspondence was extremely one-sided – a mere handful of letters and cards from Picasso or his wife Jacqueline, as against well over 200 from Penrose – and at best Penrose is given a walk-on part in books about Picasso. The documents published here reveal that on practically every visit Penrose paid to Picasso other people were also invited; evidently he was not treated as an especially intimate or privileged friend. Nevertheless, Picasso must have respected, trusted and been fond of Penrose, otherwise he would never have cooperated with him so frequently, given him so many presents of his work, or continued to welcome him year after year into his home. One curious and touching sign of Picasso's partiality is his account of a recurrent anxiety dream in which he arrived in England penniless and only felt calm again when he had 'decided to search for his friend Penrose'.[1]

By contrast, there can be no doubting the paramount importance of Picasso for Penrose. In *Scrap Book*, the charmingly informal memoirs he wrote when he was eighty years old, Penrose describes himself as 'spellbound'. On one of their first meetings he noted, 'I found myself transfixed by that pair of black eyes which seemed to burn through any obstacle.' Contact with Picasso was always thrilling and intensely stimulating:

Wherever one met him he had the effect of charging one's emotional batteries to the full, and the surprises and exaltation that arose when following the tempestuous flow of invention in his work were like being present at a fabulous banquet.

Before Picasso's work Penrose felt 'humility and wonder' and also an overriding sense of gratitude and privilege: 'I rejoice in my inestimable good fortune in having known him.'[2] No other artist Penrose wrote about or befriended – not even Joan Miró, Max Ernst or Man Ray – ever equalled Picasso in his eyes, or inspired such devotion and awe.

The passionate and obsessive nature of Penrose's love for Picasso is evoked by many of those who knew him best. This was a man who loved, and was loved by, many women and who enjoyed many profound and affectionate friendships with men, yet his love for Picasso seemed wholly exceptional to his friends. Dorothy Morland, director of the Institute of Contemporary Arts during its heroic early years, and a close friend and colleague, considered that Penrose 'was in love with Picasso, passionately, and he put Picasso before everybody and everything'. She added that Penrose's second wife, Lee Miller, 'suffered a lot from that'.[3] According to Terry O'Brien, another long-standing friend, 'There was no great passion in Roland, apart from Picasso.'[4] Joanna Drew, who worked with Penrose on both his great Picasso exhibitions for the Arts Council, was equally emphatic: 'Picasso was God and King for Roland.'[5]

A *leitmotif* of his friends' recollections is the suffering Penrose willingly endured at Picasso's hands. According to the painter and art historian John Golding,

[Penrose] talked endlessly about Picasso to me – in fact most of our talks were about Picasso. Roland revered Picasso. Picasso could be very cruel to Roland, I suspect, as he could be to all his friends, but Roland held him in such veneration that he was very patient about it.[6]

Rosamond Russell, one of Penrose's closest women friends, believed that the masochistic aspect of his fixation particularly irritated his wife:

Did you know Lee called herself a 'Picasso widow'? Roland was obsessed by Picasso. Often Picasso would keep him waiting for days, refusing to see him. Picasso enjoyed torturing those who loved him. That exasperated Lee.[7]

Penrose himself readily admitted that the enchantment was accompanied by pain. Thus in *Scrap Book* he recalled that Picasso's biographer and secretary Jaime Sabartès, who knew a fellow sufferer when he saw one, had once remarked to him: 'Ah! I see you too have caught the virus. I personally had no choice. I have suffered from it with pleasure all my life.'[8] The private notes and letters published here amply bear out these impressions.

Indeed, 'friendship' seems an inexact word for this fundamentally unequal relationship. In some respects it was more like medieval courtly love, for on one side there was adoration, constancy, the desire to serve and do honour, and long-suffering patience, and on the other, despite the many signs of partiality, a measure of aloofness and a tendency to caprice and cruelty. In this affair of courtly love Penrose was the Knight, Picasso the Lady – odd as it may seem to cast the notoriously macho artist in the female role. And as in tales of courtly love, it was Penrose, not Picasso, who was the active protagonist, Penrose who initiated the contact, did the travelling, the writing and the calling, and Picasso who received all these attentions – mostly in a gracious spirit but occasionally with a resounding 'No'. Yet although in this asymmetrical relationship Picasso was apparently all-powerful and Penrose prostrate at his feet, ultimately it was Penrose who triumphed through the sheer tenacity of his dedication. What might have been a sad tale of failure and humiliation is actually a tale of rare fulfilment and substantial rewards.

The *raisons d'être* of this book are the notes Penrose kept of the visits he paid to Picasso between 1954 and 1972 and the dozens of interviews he conducted with Picasso's lovers, friends and associates. All the notetaking and interviewing were prompted by the commission he received from the publisher Victor Gollancz for a 'definitive' biography of Picasso. The biography was first published in 1958, to almost universal acclaim, and Penrose revised and expanded the text for a new edition in 1971, the year of Picasso's ninetieth birthday. Throughout the whole of the intervening period he was embroiled in a succession of other Picasso schemes and so carried on keeping notes of their meetings, albeit less assiduously or consistently than at first.

Such is the fascination of these notes that one is bound to wish Penrose had started the practice when he and Picasso first met in 1936, for at that time Picasso was less of a celebrity, less surrounded by a pack of hangers-on, and correspondingly more accessible and forthcoming. Fortunately, however, there are other documents that go some way to compensating for the absent notes, among them Penrose's pocket-size appointments diaries, offering a tantalising glimpse of his superactive life.[9] His correspondence with Picasso spans their entire friendship and, although one-sided, is another invaluable resource. I have quoted from it liberally and occasionally used other correspondences, especially those with Lee Miller and Alfred Barr. Up to a point, and with due caution, one can also rely on *Picasso: His Life and Work* and on *Scrap Book* to fill in certain gaps, for in both Penrose drew on his fund of memories. This book is, then, primarily a collection of original documents, the great majority of which have never been published before. In the connecting chronological narrative I have attempted to make sense of the unfolding history of the relationship by supplying missing information and commenting briefly on the events described.

Another primary source has a very special place. Lee Miller may have complained about being 'a Picasso widow' but in fact she plays a leading role throughout this story and is second only in importance to the two principals. Penrose met and fell in love with her in 1937 and she was present – with her camera – during the holiday Penrose spent with Picasso and a band of Surrealist friends in the south of France that summer. The photographs she took during that idyllic interlude are the first of literally hundreds in which Picasso features, and those that predate Gollancz's commission are an invaluable visual record of the events she witnessed. As one would expect from Lee's character and her whole attitude to life, the tone of this record is not identical to Roland's. More hard-boiled, less awestruck, not driven by any overriding need, Lee could afford to be detached and there is sometimes an ironic or critical edge to her take on things, or a cool, no-nonsense appraising of psychological tensions that Roland missed or passed over in silence. After he started work on the biography, she often acted as his partner in the information-gathering expeditions, photographing the very scenes he was summarising in his notes. Her many portraits of Picasso 'at home' or in his studio reflect both her expertise in portraiture and also Penrose's determination to compile a complete visual as well as written narrative of the artist's life – a commitment that resulted in *Portrait of Picasso*. This came out in 1956, well ahead of the biography, but can be seen as its non-identical twin, and like the biography it was reissued in expanded form in 1971.

Lee was indispensable in another way. Picasso had been smitten by her during their first encounter and she continued to attract, intrigue and amuse him as they both grew older. She was adroit at dealing with Jacqueline Roque, who became the central figure in Picasso's life at the very moment Penrose embarked on research for the biography. When Lee accompanied Roland on his research trips to the south of France, things often went more smoothly and productively than when she was absent, partly because of Picasso's partiality, partly because Jacqueline grew fond of her, appreciated her shrewdly chosen gifts and liked confiding in her. Without Lee and Lee's photographs, this story would be paler, hazier and almost certainly less eventful.

I have described this book as a biography of the Penrose-Picasso relationship. It is in no sense the biography of either man – not even of Penrose, despite the fact that Picasso loomed so large in his life. Even leaving aside the whole period before he met Picasso, great tracts of Penrose's phenomenally full and active life are not at all, or barely, touched on in these pages: his own creative work, his far-flung travels, his leadership of the Surrealist movement in England, his involvement with the Institute of Contemporary Arts, his work for the British Council, the Arts Council and the Tate Gallery, the numerous exhibitions he devised and curated that did not revolve around

Picasso, the humming story of his love affairs, to mention only the most obvious omissions.

As for Picasso, what more do we learn about him from the documents gathered here? After all, taken together, they cover only minute fragments of his life or fill in small details of a picture that is already almost too well known. Since we have the biography itself and since Penrose's other writings on Picasso are obtainable with a modest effort, why should we bother with the raw material? John Richardson, author of what promises to be the definitive biography of the artist, provides an oblique answer in the handsome, but nuanced, tribute he pays to his predecessor in the first volume of his *A Life of Picasso*. Describing Penrose's biography as 'a book of incalculable value', he goes on: 'My only reservation stems from Penrose's fear of causing Picasso offense. For better or worse his portrait of the artist is without shadows.'[10]

Simply put, the 'shadows' are all in Penrose's private notes. Comparison between them and *Picasso: His Life and Work* reveals that Penrose drew heavily and constantly upon them, but also how much he omitted, what he toned down and who his informants were. As one would expect from an authorised biography written at a period when the secrets of a person's private life were considered off-limits, the toning down particularly affected the treatment of Picasso's love affairs, and there are many candid revelations and a good deal of indiscreet tittle-tattle scattered throughout the notebooks. Penrose also felt bound to omit anything that belittled Picasso, such as his childish tantrums and bouts of hypochondria, and anything likely to stir up a storm within his circle, such as the disparaging remarks he passed about his family and friends, or his caustic humour at the expense of the Communist Party, which he joined in 1944 and never left. And, naturally, the complaints against Picasso to which Penrose was privy were tactfully sidestepped. All these 'shadows' restore to Picasso his three-dimensional humanity so that, although throughout Penrose's notebooks he is the magnetic focus of everyone's attention and desire, he is never the unapproachable, quasi-mythic being of *Picasso: His Life and Work* – or the monster of pure egotism of certain popular narratives. The result is a picture that is at once far more complex and lifelike, and one can only regret that certain people who could undoubtedly have added many facets to this portrait were, for whatever reason, either never interviewed at all or not pressed a little harder.[11]

Apart from any tactful and necessary veiling or expurgation, in the arduous process of hammering out a text fit for publication Penrose sacrificed the fresh, light touch of his instantaneous reactions in the interests of a weightier effect. He used the first person singular when appropriate, but his normal mode is deliberately generalising, with the accent on full and balanced coverage, despite his own predilection for the erotic, mythic and expressionist aspects of Picasso's work. What the notes deliver, by contrast, is precisely that riveting sense of the personal voice and the particular moment, so that the reader feels as if he or she is 'really there', like the proverbial fly on the wall. Time and again one is, for example, the privileged viewer of Picasso's latest works and the privileged audience of Penrose's instinctive reactions to the parade he has just witnessed. So vivid and fluent is the effect of a scene actually unfolding before one's eyes that at times one absorbs the story, not as if one were reading it, but as if one were watching an unscripted home movie, with a convincingly flesh-and-blood Picasso wandering nonchalantly in and out of the frame. Uninhibited by the desire to write correctly, often adopting a form of telegraphese as he raced to get down his impressions, Penrose achieved a dramatic immediacy that eluded him in the biography itself.

It is indeed the authenticity of the notebooks that makes them so precious, even when the events recorded are in themselves trivial or the record itself highly elliptical. Other memoirs, such as those of Fernande Olivier and Jaime Sabartès,[12] not to mention Françoise Gilot's sensational *Life with Picasso*,[13] are based on first-hand experience and contain both striking anecdotes and vital information. But they were published years after most of the events they describe and the memories are filtered and diluted, just as Penrose's memories were when he converted them into publishable text. Even Brassaï's invaluable, but manifestly tidied-up, diary of his meetings with Picasso has less authenticity for the same reasons.[14]

This is not to say, of course, that Penrose was an ideally objective witness. The notebooks have the unmistakable ring of truth but it is *his* truth, not *the* truth. The events he describes would not have been experienced or recounted in identical terms by anyone else, and even when he resorts to the seemingly dispassionate mode of telegraphese, he is selecting and ordering and consequently interpreting. The biographical record always has, in short, an autobiographical shadow, and one of the most fascinating aspects of Penrose's notes is the uniquely unmediated insight they provide, not just into his personal vision and sensitivity, but into his motivation and psychology, as he catalogues his apprehensions, regrets and disappointments alongside his plans, hopes and moments of pure elation. In tracking Penrose on his visits to Picasso, we become more intimately acquainted with not just one remarkable man, but two.

A Note on Sources and Editorial Practice

Sources

I Original documents

The great majority of the original documents cited in this book are divided between the Roland Penrose Archive and Library at the Scottish National Gallery of Modern Art Archive in Edinburgh and the Archives Picasso at the Musée Picasso in Paris. Those cited *in extenso* are on one hand Penrose's notes of his visits to Picasso and his conversations about Picasso, on the other his correspondence with Picasso. Whereas relatively minor cuts have been made to the notes, the correspondence is cited very selectively.

The arrangement of all the documents is broadly speaking chronological, but chronology is occasionally broken in order to group closely related items and to make the narrative of events more coherent. Penrose often dismembered his notebooks in order, for example, to file the contents under thematic headings when he was drafting a text. This has confused the chronology of his notetaking at various points and I have reconstituted what I believe to be the original order when appropriate.

For convenience, Penrose's notes are all referred to as 'notebooks', although they take disparate forms, sometimes being written on loose sheets of paper, sometimes in pocket-size notebooks. In the Roland Penrose Archive (RPA), each 'notebook' has its own inventory number. These RPA numbers are given in Appendix 2, where the notebooks they refer to are numbered 1–65, listed in broadly chronological order and briefly described. Whenever the notebooks are cited in the main text or endnotes, the list number in Appendix 2 is given in square brackets at the end of the citation (e.g. [25]). By contrast, when letters and other original documents are cited, full details are given in the endnotes.

The Edinburgh Archive contains numerous plans and drafts for Penrose's books and essays on Picasso, as well as notes taken from the many secondary sources he consulted. Except for an abandoned 'Foreword' for the first edition of *Picasso: His Life and Work*, none of this material is reproduced here. Similarly, when, as occasionally happened, Penrose used his 'notebooks' to draft texts, this material is usually omitted entirely or a few short extracts only are cited.

Although Penrose cannot be described as an archivist *manqué*, he was fully aware of the historical importance of his papers. The sheer volume of documents now housed in the Edinburgh Archive suggests that, after 1945 at least, his attitude gradually took on the ultra-conservative complexion of Picasso's own – a policy of preserving everything, including, for instance, articles torn hurriedly out of newspapers, scrawled drafts of telegrams and visiting cards. Unlike Picasso, Penrose liked to live and work in a tidy, orderly environment, but according to Michael Sweeney, who was appointed to catalogue and organise his library and archive after his death, Penrose's attempts to file his papers in a systematic manner were at best sporadic. Thus, odd letters and original photographs might be used as bookmarks, and papers relating to a particular project might be scattered between as many as seven or eight different locations in his Sussex home, Farley Farm. (This was the case, for example, with the papers connected with the *Guernica* touring exhibition in England in 1938 and the Chicago monument in the mid-1960s.) The Picasso notebooks were also scattered: some had been put in the files dedicated to Picasso but others were stored in various pieces of furniture.[1] Although it is most unlikely that Penrose knowingly discarded any of his Picasso notebooks, we cannot rule out the possibility of unintentional loss. Notes have not been found for every visit Penrose made to Picasso after 1954 and it may well be that some records have gone missing.

One serious lacuna about which there can be no doubt concerns the correspondence between Penrose and Picasso. Comparison between the holdings in the Archives Picasso in Paris and the Edinburgh Archive reveals that the originals of many of Penrose's later letters to Picasso have disappeared. The Edinburgh Archive contains a few handwritten drafts and many carbon copies of typed letters dating from 1960. Losses from the Archives Picasso start to appear during the course of 1963 and become more common during 1964. The loss is total from the beginning of 1965 onwards. The word 'loss' may be inappropriate: perhaps the missing letters, cards and telegrams will eventually surface among the possessions of the artist's heirs. In the meantime, we are obliged to rely on the surviving drafts and carbon copies in Edinburgh, in the certain knowledge that postcards, greetings cards and telegrams sent after 1964, together with any handwritten letters that were not composed in rough first, are missing. The endnotes clarify the status of each letter cited, and where a carbon copy has been used no addresses (to or from) are given.

II   Published texts

Appendix 3 aims to be a complete list of all publications Penrose devoted entirely or substantially to Picasso. It is subdivided into sections – books, translations, exhibition catalogues, articles, open letters, book reviews and interviews – each of which is ordered chronologically. It is supplemented by a selective list of films. The general bibliography on pp. 400–403 consists of all publications, including those by Penrose, which are cited in abbreviation in the endnotes, plus other selected sources.

Editorial Practice

I 'Notebooks'

The style of Penrose's notes varies considerably, from quasi-literary discursive prose to *aide-mémoire* one-liners by way of his several forms of speed-writing. There has been no attempt here to edit the notes in order to soften the staccato shifts in style, and the layout adopted approximates to the layout of the text in individual notebooks. Some notebooks break into lists of names and addresses, titles of books, questions that need answering, and so forth. This material has been omitted, along with any notes that are so elliptical as to be incomprehensible and – as mentioned above – any chapter or essay drafts. Cuts made in citations, whatever their length, are indicated by means of omission marks within square brackets (i.e. [...]). The entries in Appendix 2 also indicate whether cuts have been made.

The notebooks are written in English with frequent short interjections in French, and very occasionally in Spanish, when Penrose is quoting verbatim. He wrote up the notes at speed and for his eyes only, but his English spelling was erratic at the best of times. His written French, while fluent and confident, was largely self-taught and is habitually littered with grammatical faults. Using both languages constantly, as Penrose did, compounded his problems with spelling. (Thus, for instance, 'subtle' is usually spelled, as in French, 'subtile', 'apartment' usually appears as 'appartment' and 'rhythmic' as 'rythmic'.) He often had difficulty with the spelling of unfamiliar proper names. (For example, the name of the Crommelynck brothers is hardly ever spelled correctly, Henri Clouzot was almost always 'Cluzot', and Pierre Baudouin was sometimes 'Beaudoin'.) The following short piece of untouched text gives a flavour of the original notebooks (an example of their physical appearance may be seen in the endpapers of this book):

P. sunburnt with his fringe of white hair round the back of his head, his never tyring black eyes, his red shirt is always the centre of everyones thoughts especially as everyone elses movements depend on his and no one not even he knows what it will be. As the children finish eating a move is made to the cars the Munoz say goodbye still uncertain if they have won and with the odds slightly against them. We return to Perpignan and after a last tieule with Toto & Rosita at a café P. reappears in Jac's car with P, having finally bedded down F & children and left Paolo and Pierre to go out on the town.[2]

In editing Penrose's notebooks and his letters written in English, the policy has been to make them accessible to the general reader, while at the same time respecting their original style. To this end, all spellings have been silently corrected and texts punctuated. Quoted speech and the titles of books and works of art have consistently been placed within single inverted commas – a practice Penrose used, but only sporadically. Where a text may be unclear because a word is missing, that word has been added in square brackets. Where Penrose has inadvertently used the wrong word or omitted the ending (e.g. 'where' for 'were'; 'end' for 'ended'), the correct word has been put in square brackets or the ending has been added in square brackets (e.g. '[were]'; 'end[ed]'). Where a word is illegible – a rarity – this is stated in italics in square brackets (i.e. [*illegible word*]). Any other editorial interventions are in square brackets (e.g. [*drawing of an eye*]). Where Penrose has used abbreviations that are in common currency (e.g. 'v' for 'very'; 'Sept' for 'September'), these have been retained but a full stop has been added after the abbreviation; where there is any possibility of doubt, square brackets have been used to complete the word (e.g. 'M' becomes 'M[onday]'). The same policy has been adopted for proper names, which Penrose frequently abbreviated. Except in the cases of Picasso and Jacqueline Roque (the second Madame Picasso), who appear constantly as 'P.' and 'J.' in the notebooks, when an abbreviated name appears for the first time in a citation it is completed in square brackets, but thereafter the abbreviation is respected, unless confusion could arise. A full stop is placed after the abbreviation of all proper names (e.g. 'AM' becomes 'A[na] M[aria Gili]' and on repetition 'A.M.'). First names and surnames are occasionally added in square brackets to facilitate identification.

Words that Penrose underlined have been italicised where they indicate emphasis or where they function as entry headings. For entry headings, the complete line (e.g. 'Vallauris visit Feb. 1954' or 'Dora Maar') has been italicised, whether underlined or not in the original note. Occasionally Penrose also capitalised individual words: these have been standardised in lower case. Penrose's own paragraphing has been adhered to but paragraphs have been indented and line spacings regularised for clarity.

Whenever Penrose used French or another foreign language in his notebooks, the citation is given in that language, without any corrections to the grammar, spelling or punctuation. An endnote supplies an English translation.

To acknowledge the strictly private and informal character of Penrose's notebooks, citations from them are presented with ragged line endings.

II Letters
All correspondence between Penrose and Picasso was in French, save for the very occasional inclusion of an English or Spanish phrase. The letters cited here are given in English translation in the main text, and the original French is given, uncorrected, in the endnotes. As mentioned above, Penrose's written French was fluent but faulty. From the late 1950s onwards he used a secretary to type up most of his letters and the French in the typed

letters tends to be noticeably more correct than his handwritten French, presumably as a result of the typist's interventions.

Penrose usually dated his letters to Picasso and Picasso usually kept the envelopes as well as their contents. Consequently, dating their correspondence presents few difficulties. Any problems are discussed in the main text or the endnotes.

All translations into English are by the author unless otherwise stated.

III Endnotes

These consist mainly of:

a) bibliographical details of original documents and published sources quoted or referred to in the main text, and abbreviated references to sources listed in the bibliography
b) the original version of texts quoted in translation in the main text
c) the title, date and, if in a public collection, present whereabouts of the great majority of the works of art by Picasso, or owned by Picasso, referred to in the texts cited, with, where relevant, a catalogue raisonné reference in square brackets
d) brief explanations of other allusions made in quoted documents, and occasionally references to secondary sources of information
e) evidence for dating if none is given in the framing narrative
f) occasionally, references to Penrose's published version of an anecdote recounted in a notebook
g) occasionally, references to accounts by other witnesses that parallel Penrose's account
h) brief information about persons mentioned who are not described in the framing narrative or who do not feature in Appendix 1 (see below).

IV Appendix 1: Biographical Dictionary

Brief biographical notes are provided about people mentioned repeatedly in the course of the book.

Chapter 1

The Foundation of the Friendship, 1936–1939

Surrealism crosses the Channel

Oddly enough, Roland Penrose's own account of the date and circumstances of his first meeting with Picasso is confused and unreliable. The fullest version appears in his memoirs, where he states that he was first introduced to Picasso by Paul Eluard, 'in 1935 when we were preparing the London Surrealist Exhibition', and that Eluard took him to Picasso's studio 'in the rue des Grands-Augustins'. The precipitating motive was, he says, his desire to buy *Woman Lying in the Sun on the Beach*[1] and the mission proved triumphantly successful.[2] It is a compelling story – and no one hitherto has challenged it – but the information simply does not add up, for although Penrose did have meetings with Eluard in 1935,[3] Picasso did not move into his studio in rue des Grands-Augustins until January 1937. To discover the actual sequence of events we need to go back.

Penrose's long love affair with Paris and its brimming community of writers and artists was shaped by his encounters with Roger Fry, Maynard Keynes and other members of the Bloomsbury group while he and his two elder brothers, Alec and Lionel, were undergraduates at Cambridge University between 1919 and 1922. Born in 1900, Roland was only a child when Fry's epoch-making Post-Impressionist exhibitions rocked the art establishment of pre-war London but as an undergraduate he became keenly interested in contemporary art and by the time he graduated with a first-class degree in Architectural Studies he had decided that painting, not architecture, was his true vocation. On the advice of Fry, but much against his father's wishes, in October 1922 Penrose set off for Paris and enrolled in the studio of André Lhote, who practised an accessible, academic form of Cubism and was renowned as an imaginative and effective teacher. Lhote was a great admirer of Picasso's work and among the most perceptive French critics to write about it during the 1920s and '30s, and one must presume that Penrose's first-hand knowledge of Picasso's painting increased dramatically under his teacher's guidance. But although he met Georges Braque during the 1920s, he did not meet his future idol.

A turning-point in Penrose's life was his chance encounter with the beautiful, temperamental, mystically inclined Gascon poet, Valentine Boué,

Opposite
Picasso and Roland
Penrose, Mougins,
August 1937. Photo
Lee Miller

during a long sojourn in Cassis-sur-Mer, where he had bought a villa in 1923 and set up a painting studio with the Greek artist, Yanko Varda. In 1925 Roland and Valentine were married. Under her and Varda's influence he began to take a deep interest in Surrealism and formed a close friendship with Max Ernst, through whom he was gradually introduced to the leading poets and painters. He made friends with both André Breton and Paul Eluard and through them met David Gascoyne in Paris in the autumn of 1935.[4] Gascoyne was only nineteen at the time but had already written, in French, a 'Premier manifeste anglais du Surréalisme', and in English a *Short Survey of Surrealism*, as well as completing a translation of Breton's popularising *Qu'est-ce que le Surréalisme?*[5] Together they decided to try to launch the Surrealist movement in England, agreeing that the best possible kick-start would be a comprehensive exhibition in London.

Breton and Eluard gave the venture their enthusiastic blessing and negotiations began in earnest in January 1936. The New Burlington Galleries in Piccadilly were selected as the venue and an English organising committee, headed by Penrose and the poet and critic Herbert Read, was formed. A rapid trawl netted a number of native recruits, including Henry Moore and Paul Nash. On 6 April 1936 the first of a series of meetings took place in Penrose's house at 21 Downshire Hill, Hampstead.[6] He had just returned from an intense week of meetings with the Surrealists in Paris and from his diary we know that he lunched with Eluard on Saturday 4 April. But he could not have visited Picasso since the latter had left Paris towards the end of March on a prolonged, clandestine visit to Juan-les-Pins with his lover, Marie-Thérèse Walter, and their six-month-old daughter Maya.[7] No one, except for his confidant and factotum Jaime Sabartès, knew where Picasso was or why he had made his sudden disappearance, for the affair with Marie-Thérèse had been kept secret even from intimate friends like Eluard.[8]

Somebody, however, had to persuade Picasso to allow his work to be included in the forthcoming London exhibition and there is no reason to doubt Penrose's word that the intermediary was Eluard.[9] It is unlikely that Picasso needed much persuading for he had inherited a soft spot for English furniture, English tailoring and English nineteenth-century painting from his father,[10] and would have seen the London Surrealist exhibition as the successor to Fry's historic Post-Impressionist exhibitions in which his work had featured prominently. Penrose's diary reveals that during his final, frantically busy trip to Paris before the exhibition opened, he met 'Sabartez' on 4 May 1936,[11] presumably in order to get some sort of official clearance for the works he planned to include, and perhaps in the hope of adding something new and unknown straight from the studio. In the event, all eleven of the Picassos included in the London exhibition were loaned either by private collectors (including Breton and Eluard) or by dealers (Paul Rosenberg in Paris and the Zwemmer Gallery in London).[12]

The Surrealist exhibition enjoyed a *succès de scandale* beyond anything Penrose, Read and the other members of the committee had dared to envisage.

On a sweltering June day around two thousand people packed the galleries during the elaborately stage-managed *vernissage* and by the time the show closed on 4 July some 23,000 people had paid to see it. A programme of lectures by Surrealist luminaries – Dalí gave his wearing a deep-sea diving suit – kept press interest at boiling-point and, to everyone's amazement, once all the expenses had been paid there was even a modest profit. For Penrose, one of the lasting benefits of the whole adventure was the blossoming of his friendship with Eluard, who had quarrelled violently with Breton shortly before the exhibition opened but continued to give Penrose his full support, exerting influence on friends like Dalí to ensure they too cooperated.[13] Wounded by his row with Breton, Eluard needed a new friend and was deeply touched by the warm reception he and Nusch, his waif-like and exquisite wife, received when they came to London at the end of June. On 15 July he wrote to Penrose: 'I want to tell you once again what magnificent memories I have of being with you in London, and how happy I am to have made a new, a real friend.'[14] He then pressed Roland and Valentine to join them in Mougins as soon as possible: other Surrealist friends would also be there and so too would Picasso – back in circulation after his long and mysterious absence. Penrose accepted with alacrity, shipped his Ford to France and motored south at the beginning of August. It was during this visit to Mougins that he met Picasso for the first time.

Visiting Mougins and Barcelona, August–December 1936

In Mougins, then a lovely unspoilt village tucked up among the hills above Cannes, there was a lively gathering. Apart from Picasso and the Eluards, the party included the painter and photographer Man Ray, the poet René Char, and Christian and Yvonne Zervos, publishers of *Cahiers d'Art* and currently at work on the second volume of the complete catalogue of Picasso's work. An occasional visitor was the photographer Dora Maar, then at the start of her long affair with Picasso. 'In such company,' Penrose wrote in *Scrap Book*, 'the long days passed with continuous delight undermined only by the sinister news of fighting in Spain which caused us all, especially Picasso, agonised misgivings.'[15] In *Picasso: His Life and Work* he recalled that Picasso, 'dressed in a striped sailor's vest and shorts', would entertain the assembled company 'with boisterous clowning' and his charming impromptu portraits made from anything that came to hand – 'burnt matches, lipstick, mustard, wine or colour squeezed from flowers and leaves'.[16] Dozens of photographs record the daily diet of sunbathing, swimming and beachcombing *en groupe* and the general air of good humour and lazy pleasure, and in his first ever letter to Picasso Penrose referred to the holiday in Mougins as 'an unforgettable dream of marvels'.[17]

Not everything went perfectly, however. Roland's marriage to Valentine had all but completely broken down several years before and in some of the photographs she looks tense, sullen and withdrawn in comparison to her

Roland Penrose, Nusch
Eluard, Valentine Penrose,
an unidentified friend,
Picasso and Man Ray
(holding his camera, far
right), Mougins, August
1936. Photographer
unknown

more hedonistic companions. Worse still, one day, with Penrose at the wheel of his Ford, there was a collision on the road from Cannes to Mougins.[18] Nobody was badly hurt except Picasso, who was flung violently against the side of the car and, convinced that he must have broken several ribs, had himself X-rayed.[19] The accident is referred to at length in the chagrined and solicitous letters Penrose sent him from England, for there was not only the question of Picasso's recovery but the medical costs to be paid by the insurance.[20] Over twenty years later Penrose was still trembling at the thought that he might have been responsible for Picasso's permanent maiming or – too terrible to contemplate – his death, and in his account of the drama in *Picasso: His Life and Work* he was at pains to blame the other driver for 'coming towards us on the wrong side of the road'.[21] This was hardly an auspicious beginning to so precious a relationship and perhaps we need look no further for an explanation for Penrose's curious lapse of memory about how and when he first met Picasso. However delightful it had been in other respects, that holiday in Mougins was forever clouded by humiliating feelings of alarm and guilt.

At the Hôtel Vaste Horizon everyone had followed developments in Spain with deepening anxiety, and Roland and Valentine decided to join the Zervoses on their forthcoming mission to Catalonia. This had a three-fold purpose: to take part in the effort to safeguard the artistic heritage; to gather evidence disproving reports that the Republicans and Anarchists were deliberately perpetrating acts of cultural vandalism under cover of the general chaos; and to assemble material for a pioneering study of Romanesque and medieval Catalan art and an exhibition to be held in Paris the following year.[22] Gascoyne, who had recently joined the Communist Party and was eager to make his contribution to the fight against Fascism, met the Penroses in London on their return from France and joined in the planning of the trip to Spain. In his journal he noted that the atmosphere at Downshire Hill was prickly and Valentine prone to ill-tempered outbursts against her husband's impeccable taste:

'How well I understand Rimbaud,' she said, 'and his hatred of perfection. That is what is the matter here,' – she indicated the room with a vague gesture – 'all these pictures. I should like to take a piece of chalk and scribble on them all!'[23]

Despite these marital tensions, the couple arrived in Barcelona as planned on 23 October 1936, with Gascoyne in tow.[24]

Sponsored by the Independent Labour Party and described as 'trustworthy Socialists' in the introductory letters they carried with them, the Penroses recorded what they saw, liaised with leading Republicans and worked on a news film whose purpose was 'to win support for the workers' struggle and to obtain material which will help us to arouse further support in this country [England]'.[25] Shortly before they left London, Penrose wrote offering his services to Picasso, who had been appointed Honorary Director of the Prado when the Civil War broke out but did not return to Spain himself.[26] At Picasso's request they visited his mother and his sister, Lola Vilató, in their flat near the centre of Barcelona. There Penrose was able to see for the first time a collection of pictures from Picasso's precocious boyhood. 'After elaborate greetings had been exchanged and many questions about her son answered,' he recalled,

the old lady took us to a window at the back saying: 'It's only today that I have been able to open this after so many days when the smoke and stench, from the convent over there that had been set on fire, nearly asphyxiated us all.'[27]

This direct contact with evidence of wilful destruction momentarily dented Penrose's conviction that 'democracy must and would survive in Spain', but he returned to London before Christmas in a relatively optimistic frame of mind and bearing a painting by one of Lola's painter-sons. He also collaborated with Zervos on a text staunchly defending the Republicans and Anarchists against persistent accusations that they had connived at, if not actually systematically perpetrated, acts of vandalism, and asserting that, 'in spite of the provocations of the insurgents [...] not a single monument of real value, not a single work of art had suffered irreparable damage'.[28]

Although he saw Eluard when he passed through Paris on his way home,[29] Penrose did not attempt to visit Picasso. Their relationship was still a fairly distant one and he had no real excuse for making an appointment since Gascoyne had already passed on the family news.[30] Nevertheless, the Catalan adventure was an important building-block in their fledgling relationship because it showed that Penrose was prepared to stand up against the British Government's policy and act decisively on behalf of the Spanish Republican cause – he was more politically *engagé* at this period than at any other in his life – and also that he was genuinely interested in the Catalan 'primitives' Picasso admired so much. And, of course, Picasso was not indifferent to Penrose's obvious veneration for his work or to the fact that he got on so well with some of his own best friends.

Penrose the 'collector'

1937 proved to be decisive in the history of their friendship not only because they saw more of each other but because Penrose's collection of Picasso's work increased dramatically. The death of his parents – his mother in 1930, his father two years later – had left Penrose with a substantial inheritance and he could afford to indulge his acquisitive instincts. One of several purchases made around the time of the London Surrealist exhibition was Picasso's great *Minotauromachy* etching, which he bought from the Zwemmer Gallery in February 1936.[31] Following the closure of the show he had tried to persuade Breton to sell him a Cubist *papier collé* depicting an abstracted triangular head, somewhat resembling a metronome, set on T-shaped shoulders.[32] But Breton had refused:

I am – insanely – determined to hang onto this little picture, which I pursued for years before I was able to contemplate it at my leisure. Also it's all I have left by Picasso and I fear that, having lost it, I shall feel even more impoverished. I know that you will understand my feelings perfectly.[33]

By February 1937, however, Breton was in no position to hold out any longer. His always parlous financial situation had become desperate and he wrote accepting Roland's original offer.[34]

In later life Penrose stoutly objected to being labelled a 'collector' because, he said, his approach was neither systematic nor driven by a predetermined scheme.[35] In saying this, he meant to distinguish his behaviour from that of his arch rival Douglas Cooper, who had come into his much larger fortune at the age of twenty-one in 1932 and, by the outbreak of the war, had amassed a truly spectacular, but also highly focused, collection of Cubist paintings.[36] Cooper unquestionably was a collector in the conventional sense. But such hair-splitting definitions aside, the process by which Penrose 'accumulated' works of art went on apace throughout the late 1930s and the house in Hampstead swiftly became thickly hung with contemporary European art of the highest quality. Like all his Surrealist friends, Penrose also 'accumulated' fine examples of tribal art and the kinds of heteroclite 'curiosities' which, in times past, packed the *Wunderkammern* of the aristocracy. All these objects were freely interspersed and juxtaposed with the contemporary works in the archetypal, deliberately provocative Surrealist manner.

We come now to the episode which Penrose later (mis)remembered as his first encounter with Picasso. On 11 March 1937 he wrote to Picasso from London. Partly, the letter was concerned with the embarrassing, tiresome and still unsettled issue of Picasso's doctor's bill and the insurance claim following the car crash in Mougins; partly its purpose was to announce his imminent arrival in Paris and his hope that Picasso would make time to see him.[37] Although he did not say so, his objective was to track down a painting of a female bather stretched out in the sun which he had seen illustrated in a recent issue of *Cahiers d'Art*.[38] The picture seemed, he later wrote, 'to contain magic of a kind I had never known before', and he was filled with 'longing to see and if possible own the original'.[39] Accompanied by Eluard, he visited Picasso in his new studio at rue des Grands-Augustins – *Guernica* would soon be painted there but Picasso had still not started on it – and asked outright whether he could buy the picture. Picasso was notorious for taunting would-be purchasers, stringing them along and playing them off against one another until they were haggard with frustration, but on this occasion he was uncharacteristically receptive: 'Well, first you must see it,' he replied, and,

Roland Penrose at 21 Downshire Hill, London, 1939, with part of his Surrealist collection. Photographer unknown

within a few minutes Marcel the chauffeur had been summoned and with all those present, Eluard, his wife Nusch, Dora Maar, Paulo (Picasso's son) and Picasso himself, I climbed into the spacious vintage Hispano and we set out for Boisgeloup.

Penrose was fascinated by this first visit to Picasso's country property in Normandy, with its spacious stables where so much sculpture had been made, its graduated stacks of paintings ranged in the upstairs rooms of the main house and its elegant entrance hall dominated, incongruously, by an enormous hippopotamus skull. He had expected the painting he had set his heart on to be 'impressive in size' and was amazed when Picasso pulled it out from a pile of the smallest works.

However, the magic was all there.[…] I had found my dream painting, my first acquisition of the great painter's work, and thanking Picasso profusely we all returned to Paris in the Hispano at great speed.[40]

A photograph shows the party, warmly dressed and gathered in the garden at Boisgeloup. Only Dora Maar is invisible: she was behind the camera.[41]

Why did Picasso agree so readily to the sale? The answer must be that he found Penrose *sympathique* for the reasons noted above and was seduced by the mixture of diffidence, enthusiasm and sincerity. Furthermore, in choosing *Woman Lying in the Sun on the Beach* Penrose had proved his discernment and daring for, without knowing it, he had picked a painting Picasso's dealer, Paul Rosenberg, had rejected outright with the immortal words: 'Non, je refuse d'avoir des trous de cul dans ma galerie.' ('No, I refuse to have any arse-holes in my gallery.') In *Scrap Book* Penrose claims that, until Picasso told him this story some years later, he had not even realised that the oval shape at the centre of the composition represented the bather's anus. For him the picture was simply a 'minute lyrical masterpiece'.[42] Maybe so. But he was not blind to the 'indecency' of the picture, as we learn from an entry in Gascoyne's journal for 8 April 1937 – the document, incidentally, which confirms once and for all in which year Penrose made this defining acquisition. After a 'gloriously funny' meeting of the English Surrealists in Downshire Hill, during which 'abuse flew from corner to corner of Roland's polite, sumptuously decorated drawing room', Gascoyne stayed on talking with his host,

and listening to his account of a recent visit to Paris and of going with Eluard, Nusch, Cécile and Picasso jr., to see Picasso's château out at Boisgeloup.[…] Roland has brought back a small new Picasso picture with him: very attractive, in blues and yellow, greys and white. Rosenberg had refused to show it in his gallery, because, he said, it was indecent; and when one looks at it closely one sees that part of the picture appears to be an underneath view of a woman with her legs stretched wide apart, with a sort of sun forming her head.[43]

Having obtained the coveted picture – to judge by his insurance records he paid a mere £90[44] – Penrose embarked on a major spending-spree. In May and June 1937 the Zwemmer Gallery was the venue for two exhibitions, the first devoted to Miró, the second to Picasso and De Chirico. Most of the works came from the collection of the Belgian businessman René Gaffé, who had asked his

compatriot, the Surrealist poet, collagist and entrepreneur E. L. T. Mesens, to arrange their sale. Mesens and Penrose had become friends during the run of the Surrealist exhibition in London and when all but a handful of Gaffé's pictures failed to sell Mesens advised Penrose to buy the rest *en bloc*. The cost of the entire haul of paintings by De Chirico, Miró and Picasso was set at £6,750 and in his letter to Penrose confirming his acceptance of the offer Gaffé did not forbear to point out that he had made a very astute investment:

I can tell you in all sincerity that from the artistic point of view you have made a truly masterly coup and from the business point of view an excellent deal. You will soon realise this. But I am delighted for you. You have shown more guts than the picture dealers who ought to have leapt at such an opportunity.[45]

The fourteen Picassos acquired from Gaffé ranged in date from 1903 to 1921 but came mainly from the Cubist period. Among them were some major works: a tough, 'Negro'-style oil of a crouching nude related to *Les Demoiselles d'Avignon* (for which Penrose paid £315); a refined 'analytical' Cubist painting of Fernande Olivier, which Penrose called *La Femme en vert* (*Woman in Green*, £720); the *Portrait of Wilhelm Uhde*, one of the three great

Cubist portraits of his dealers Picasso painted in 1910 (£675); and the famous *Girl with a Mandolin,* modelled by Fanny Tellier (£900) (see p. 49). The most important *papier collé* was *Man with a Violin* of late 1912 (£135), a highly abstracted work incorporating strips of newspaper on the scale of a largish oil painting.[46] At a stroke, Penrose had become the owner of the best collection of Picasso's work in Britain – and the target of anyone seeking to organise a retrospective or, for that matter, to buy a Cubist Picasso with a first-rate provenance. Picasso must have known what was going on and that the Englishman with the useful, if limited, private income was fast becoming an influential figure within the tight-knit community of aficionados of his work.

Shortly before concluding this deal with Gaffé, Penrose paid a visit to Picasso's studio at rue des Grands-Augustins with Henry Moore. They were part of a large lunchtime gathering that included Giacometti, Ernst, Eluard and Breton. Moore recalled that 'it was all tremendously lively and exciting', and that 'even Picasso was excited by our visit'.[47] Penrose knew, of course, about the vast mural the Republicans had commissioned for their pavilion at the Exposition Internationale and he was eager to see how Picasso had met the challenge to paint, for once, a picture with an overt political message. In *Picasso: His Life and Work* he reminisced about one particularly arresting moment during the viewing of the painting, which was still unfinished at the time:

The discussion between us turned on the old problem of how to link reality with the fiction of painting. Picasso silently disappeared and returned with a long piece of toilet paper, which he pinned to the hand of the woman on the right of the composition, who runs into the scene terrified and yet curious to know what is happening. As though she had been disturbed at a critical moment her bottom is bare and her alarm too great to notice it. 'There,' said Picasso, 'that leaves no doubt about the commonest and most primitive effect of fear.'[48]

About a month later, on 21 June, Penrose paid another visit to Picasso's studio.[49] By then *Guernica* was finished but had not yet been removed to the Spanish Pavilion. This time Penrose went in the evening and his main motive was surely connected with the rally and auction in aid of Basque refugee children which he was organising for 24 June at the Royal Albert Hall in London. Numerous artists, including Picasso, had agreed to donate works to the sale and Penrose must have gone to see Picasso in order to collect his offering since Picasso had reneged on his promise to attend the rally in person.[50] Maybe he also hoped to persuade Picasso to make the journey after all. If so he failed. But in any case, 21 June 1937 was a momentous day in Penrose's life for quite another reason. That night he accompanied Max Ernst to a fancy-dress party hosted by the daughters of the wealthy businessman Marcel Rochas. Looking like a crazed tramp in a pair of Ernst's dirtiest, most paint-bespattered trousers and with his right hand and left foot dyed blue, Penrose attracted the attention of the American photographer and fashion model Lee

Miller.[51] She had been Man Ray's assistant and lover some years before but was now married to Aziz Eloui Bey, head of the Egyptian National Railways. Smitten by her dazzling beauty and devil-may-care vivacity, Penrose contrived to meet Miller again the following day and by the time he left for London bound for the Albert Hall meeting they had become lovers and she had promised to join him and a party of his Surrealist friends at Lambe Creek, the house in Cornwall owned by his younger brother Beacus.

Visiting Mougins with Lee Miller, Summer 1937

Most of the Cornwall party – the Eluards, Man Ray and his girlfriend Ady Fidelin, the English Surrealist artist Eileen Agar and her husband Joseph Bard – regathered that August at the Hôtel Vaste Horizon in Mougins, where Picasso and Dora Maar were spending the summer.[52] The *bonheur de vivre* of the friends as they idled on the beach at La Garoupe or lunched in the shade of vines was captured in scores of photographs taken by Maar, Man Ray, Miller and Penrose himself, and in her memoirs Agar reminisced nostalgically about the free-and-easy sexual mores of that summer, when brief affairs were felt to cement, not jeopardise, both friendship and the central love relationship.[53]

To judge by the staging of several of her photographs, Miller herself was not so blinded by Penrose's passion for her to miss the signs of his infatuation with Picasso. In one that has become deservedly well known the two men are framed in the window of Picasso's Hispano-Suiza (see p. 23). Bull-necked, square-shouldered, smiling self-confidently at the attractive photographer, whose reflection glimmers mirage-like on the windscreen, Picasso is seated in the foreground, while Penrose, taller, thinner, weaker-looking, stands behind him, one arm resting against the roof of the car. Most striking, however, is the rapt devotion of Penrose's gaze, which is directed not at Lee but at Picasso. In that one shrewd take, she pinpointed the essential inequality of the relationship she was observing for the first time and the self-effacing fidelity of Penrose's love for Picasso – a fidelity which no woman, herself included, would ever inspire in him. Another portrait photograph in which Picasso turns to stare mesmerically at her captures his sheer, adamantine force (see p. 35). At the time Lee could have had no idea that the course of much of her life would be determined by the complex dynamic of the relations between Penrose and Picasso but, evidently, she did not underestimate the latter's merciless charisma.

Penrose's account of the holiday in *Picasso: His Life and Work* was necessarily more discreet than Eileen Agar's but he too paints a picture of high spirits and physical joy, with Picasso as the roguish master of ceremonies. The artist was, he says, 'seized with a diabolical playfulness' as a reaction against the strain of painting *Guernica* and produced numerous facetiously distorted 'portraits' of the assembled company. In the most notorious of these 'ludicrously recognisable' transformations, Eluard appeared in the traditional costume of an Arlésienne, green-faced and suckling a stripy kitten.[54] Unfortunately, Penrose never described the 'portrait' Picasso made of him, but it was conceived in the same iconoclastic spirit and was almost certainly another grinning, gaudily coloured Arlésienne.[55] The tall, blonde-haired Miller, with her racy wit and gap-toothed grin, fascinated Picasso and was the subject of several amusing, brilliantly coloured pictures that, skirting caricature, capture her piquant mix of classic, statuesque beauty and libertine sexuality (see p. 231). In *Scrap Book* Penrose described the best of them:

On a bright pink background Lee appeared in profile, her face a brilliant yellow like the sun with no modelling. Two smiling eyes and a green mouth were placed on the same side of the face and her breasts seemed like the sails of ships filled with a joyous breeze. It was an astonishing likeness. An agglomeration of Lee's qualities of exuberant vitality and vivid beauty put together in such a way that it was undoubtedly her but with none of the conventional attributes of a portrait.[56]

Picasso and Dora Maar,
Hôtel Vaste Horizon,
Mougins, August 1937.
Photo Lee Miller

In her memoirs Eileen Agar described 'le Peintre Soleil himself, Picasso
the Master' as 'indubitably boss of the roost, his thoughts and moods somehow setting the ruling temperature', and claimed he was the only person who
really worked that summer: 'I remember his cry of, "au travail, au travail!"
after lunch while we dozed or lay in the sun.'[57] But Penrose was not inactive
and, stimulated by the atmosphere of playful creative freedom, made a significant breakthrough by constructing the first of his postcard collages. Lee
photographed him squatting on the floor of their room in the hotel in the
process of assembling one. What made the collages unique was not the use
of popular postcards as such – other Surrealists including Ernst and Miró
had done that already – but the ingenuity with which Penrose exploited their
garish colours and the way he totally transformed their banal imagery by
arranging overlapping sequences of the same card into abstract shapes,
which, in combination with cut-outs of plain coloured paper and hand-
drawn elements, he ordered into surreal figurative compositions. With their
inventive visual puns and eye-catching decorative effects, the postcard collages are often considered Penrose's most original and entirely successful
contribution as an artist.[58] Indeed, this is ultimately how Penrose came to

think of them himself because when, aged eighty, he was asked what he felt he would be remembered for as an artist, he replied: 'I should think picture postcards stuck together.'[59]

To Roland's sorrow Lee kept to her plan of rejoining her husband in Egypt. Teardrops drawn in his diary and the two bald words 'Lee gone' register the fateful day, 4 October 1937.[60] As a love-gift, he bought their favourite portrait of her from Picasso, as he told her in his first letter after her departure:

In the afternoon I finally found Picasso and went with him and Dora to his studio. [...] As I thought my few words at Mougins had not been wasted and there was no difficulty in getting your 'portrait', which I took away with me in triumph; there was no time to get a frame or get it sent off so I have got it with me and will profit of its marvels while I look round for a suitable frame in London. It will then take the boat to you, darling, the inspiratrice of so many chef d'oeuvres.[61]

On the same day that he sold Penrose the portrait, Picasso dedicated a set of the *Dream and Lie of Franco* etchings to him.[62] Given their money-raising function, Roland must have bought, rather than been given, them, and he also bought a set for Lee, despatching it to her with the latest issue of *Cahiers d'Art*, which was almost entirely devoted to *Guernica* and its preparatory studies. As he remarked rather sheepishly in his letter: 'There seems to be rather a glut of Picasso in what I've sent, I hope you won't mind.'[63] There could hardly have been a more prophetic gift: almost from the first, Lee's and Roland's love affair was shadowed by Picasso.

The fate of Lee's portrait was a recurrent subject in Roland's subsequent letters to her. While he hunted for a suitable frame, it hung in Downshire Hill among the recently arrived Gaffé pictures:

'La jeune fille à la Mandoline', that very subtle cubist Picasso, hangs over the table in the living room with *your* portrait on the wall next to it, still waiting for its frame, making a strange contrast of past and present. Then there are Chiricos everywhere honeycombing the walls with metaphysical interiors. The hall is full of Picasso engravings and drawings and the dining room looks very impressive with the big Miró nude and 'La femme en vert' of Picasso.[64]

And he went on to beg her to allow him to include it in the Surrealist exhibition he was organising for the Gordon Fraser Gallery in Cambridge:

Being so recent a work and so good I would very much like all the little boys in Cambridge to take a squint at it. I shan't mention that it is *your* portrait. The exhibition closes on the 20 Nov. and I will have it packed at once and sent to you. I shall be terribly sorry to lose it as it reminds me of you and fills my room with your adorable presence. It is so gay, contains all Mougins, all the summer, the sea and your laugh.[65]

But once the Cambridge exhibition was over there was no excuse for further delay and on 13 December he wrote mournfully to confirm that the picture was on its way to Cairo:

I sent off your portrait last week, declaring its value as £30 for the customs and insuring it for £300 without them knowing. [...] So now you will be one degree more out of sight for me.[66]

When eventually Lee and Roland were married, the portrait was given a place of honour in their home. That it remained 'mysteriously a most convincing likeness' was, Penrose wrote, 'proved more than ten years later when I lifted our two-year-old son Tony in my arms to look at it for the first time. His instant cry of delight was "Mummy, Mummy."'[67]

Guernica in England

Meanwhile, on 29 October 1937, Penrose had gone into print on the subject of Picasso's work. It was a modest contribution – a letter to the Editor of *The Spectator* seconding Herbert Read's staunch defence of *Guernica* against Anthony Blunt's Marxist-inspired attack on its supposedly inaccessible, elitist symbolism and Picasso's ineffectual horror in the face of the atrocity. But it represented a significant step in that for the first time Penrose appeared publicly not just as Picasso's champion, but also as someone with inside knowledge of the artist's larger intentions. He now felt he could regard Picasso as a friend and visit him in his studio without being chaperoned by Eluard, and Picasso's name appears with increasing regularity in his appointments diaries.

That their relationship was on a new footing is underlined by Penrose's purchase of *Weeping Woman* from Picasso at the special, low price of £284.[68] Penrose had gone to Paris for the opening of the 'Exposition internationale du surréalisme' organised by Breton and Eluard at the Galerie des Beaux-Arts, and on 17 January 1938 he joined Picasso, Dora Maar and the Eluards for dinner. In a letter to Lee written the next day he described what had happened:

I bought a new picture off Picasso in a moment of enthusiasm, which I really ought not to have done if I had thought first of my overdraft, but still I'm very glad to have it. It is a very tragic one – a complete contrast to your portrait but in even brighter colours. We talked of you. Picasso asked after you a lot and wanted to know when you are coming back – so do I my darling.[69]

At some point Penrose also acquired copies of the third and seventh states of the closely related etching, also entitled *Weeping Woman*, which Picasso executed at the beginning of July 1937.[70] These purchases, like the purchase of the *Dream and Lie* portfolios and the letter to *The Spectator*, reveal how enthralled Penrose was by the impassioned works Picasso created in reaction to the tragedy of the Spanish Civil War.

By the time he came to write of the purchase of the oil of *Weeping Woman* in his memoirs, Penrose had convinced himself that he had done so when 'the paint was scarcely dry'.[71] But although this is an exaggeration – Picasso dated the canvas 26 October 1937 – there is no reason to doubt the rest of his account:

When he showed us [Eluard and Penrose] into his studio we were both astonished at the captivating power of a small newly painted canvas placed on an easel as though he was still at work on it. I have more than once been shaken by the emotional strength of a painting seen for the first time in an artist's studio, but this contained an unprecedented blend of realism and magic [...] For a while the impact of this small brilliant canvas left us speechless, but after a few enthusiastic exclamations I heard myself say to Picasso, 'Oh! May I buy that from you?' and heard in a daze his answer: 'And why not?' There followed the exchange of a cheque for almost nothing for one of the masterpieces of this century.[72]

In fact, Penrose made a down-payment of only £100 and sent the balance (£184) to Picasso with an effusive letter on 4 April 1938.[73] In that letter he also outlined his ambitions for the London Gallery in Cork Street, which had just reopened with Mesens in charge. Anton Zwemmer, proprietor of the Zwemmer gallery and bookshop, put up about a quarter of the money but Penrose himself put up the rest, selling farms he had inherited in Norfolk and Suffolk to do so. And he was prepared to sell some pictures from Gaffé's collection in order to keep the gallery and himself going.[74] Not that these purely commercial issues surfaced in his letter to Picasso, who might well have been resistant to selling to Penrose directly in future had he considered him a 'dealer' rather than a 'collector':

Dear Picasso,

The moment has at last arrived when I can pay my debts and I am therefore sending you the balance of what I owe you for your painting.

I am more and more delighted to own this magnificent canvas, which continues enormously to impress me and the dozens of people who have seen it. In these dreadful times when we live on a diet of atrocities, each worse than the next, this picture is like a drug and gives me courage. It misses nothing of this tragedy, but surpasses it.

In London an event of a very different order, but which touches me closely, has recently taken up a lot of my time – the arrival of my friend Mesens, who has taken on the management of a little picture gallery – the London Gallery. We've succeeded in gathering together a group of poets, painters, film-makers, critics and other enthusiasts and we hope to embark, despite the terrible situation at the moment, on a programme of activities the like of which

London has never seen. The first number of the Bulletin of the gallery, which Mesens plans to publish monthly, has been sent to you. I do hope you won't object to the inclusion of the photo of you with Eluard in Mougins. Your presence in the first number was a must and as we were very pressed for time I wasn't able to consult you in advance. In this bulletin our collaborators include Herbert Read, Eluard, Douglas Cooper, Breton – I'm citing these names just to give you an idea of the diversity – and several Belgians, all in all a very large collection of poets and critics from all over the world. In any case your support is of the essence for us. Imagine our delight if you were to send us a poem or a text!

I have no plans yet for my next visit to Paris but I very much hope to see you during the summer. In the meantime I send you my sincere best wishes.

Very cordially yours

Roland Penrose

I can't express the horror and disgust the news from Spain causes me. Please accept my profound condolences.[75]

Penrose's allusion to the latest dramatic events in Spain – Barcelona suffered severe bombardment and heavy loss of civilian life during March; Lérida was taken by the Nationalists on 3 April – was made against the background of preliminary negotiations to bring *Guernica* and 67 related studies to London as part of the continuing campaign both to raise funds for the beleaguered Republicans and to reverse the Chamberlain government's policy of non-intervention in Spain and appeasement with Hitler.[76] The project was supported wholeheartedly not only by the English Surrealist group but by the Artists' International Association, originally founded in 1932 with the express aim of defending contemporary art and culture against the threat of war and Fascism. A letter to Penrose from Juan Larrea, dated 12 February 1938, makes it clear that discussions had already begun by then and that both Picasso and Larrea, who was working for the Republican agencies in Paris and was one of those responsible for persuading Picasso to paint the mural in the first place, favoured sending *Guernica* to London, rather than to New York, once it had returned from an extended tour of Scandinavia. Since the closure of the Exposition in Paris, *Guernica* had been exploited as an effective propaganda tool, its fame increasing with each appearance: treated much like a theatre set, it was simply unstretched and rolled up after each showing.[77] 'Today matters stand like this,' Larrea wrote to Penrose:

We want the exhibition to happen with the maximum force and solemnity, both for Picasso himself, since the more admired he is the more useful he will be to our cause, and for our cause itself, since this is one of the rare means we have to reach that sector of the public for whom this kind of argument may prove convincing. The question of making money is only a secondary consideration.[78]

In May 1938 a small exhibition of works on paper by Picasso was held at the London Gallery. Perhaps this was intended partly as a warm-up. At any rate, plans for the London showing of *Guernica* were well enough advanced by July for an announcement to be published in *London Bulletin*.[79]

As Honorary Treasurer of the National Joint Committee for Spanish Relief,[80] Penrose was embroiled in the organisation of the *Guernica* exhibition throughout September 1938. On 16 September, writing from Paris, he described developments in a letter to Lee Miller, with whom he had just been on an adventurous tour of the Balkans:

Picasso & Dora arrived here yesterday in good form. They asked after you. Picasso has a wonderful Afghan hound who eats holes in his clothes and Dora a Persian cat. Having finished the arrangements for the exhibition I'm off home today. It seems quite likely, supposing things do settle down, that Picasso, Dora, Paul & Nusch will all come to London during the show.[81]

The dark reference to 'things' is an allusion to the current crisis in Czechoslovakia, and similar allusions appear in other letters relating to the *Guernica* tour in England, which coincided with a period of extreme political tension. Indeed, a letter Penrose sent to Picasso just before the exhibition was due to open at the New Burlington Galleries is postmarked 30 September, the day of the Munich Pact:

Dear Picasso,

Preparations for the 'Guernica' exhibition are continuing and public interest is growing daily in spite of the general consternation of the last few days. Because of the situation the pictures arrive only today, but we still hope to have everything ready for the opening next Tuesday at 3.30 p.m.

Sir Peter Chalmers Mitchell, who will open the exhibition with the Spanish Ambassador, is an elderly man who won great respect over here because of his admirable behaviour when he happened to be in Málaga at the time of its fall. He was also at one time Director of London Zoo. I hope you will approve of our choice.

I've already had two requests from provincial towns to exhibit the pictures after we close here. The cities of Leeds and Manchester would like to show the exhibition in their municipal galleries. We can arrange this under the same conditions as we've got here, if you like, but they do require a fairly rapid reply.

Both cities are very important centres and I think the exhibition might make a big sensation there.

I still hope that you will decide to come to London with Dora and the Eluards. If you can come for the opening next Tuesday so much the better, but if not you will be welcome at any time. Come when you can, my house will be at your disposal. There is a night train, which goes via Dunkerque without the need to change compartments – one sleeps just like a baby.

I was delighted to have your news through Larrea.

With very best wishes
Roland Penrose[82]

Indeed, so volatile was the situation that, at the last minute, Penrose cabled Picasso 'to find out if he was still willing to risk the loan and received an immediate reply saying that the purpose of the picture was to express the horrors of war and that it must take its chance'.[83]

As planned, the exhibition opened in the New Burlington Galleries on 4 October 1938. Picasso did not make the journey to England – with one notable exception, all Penrose's efforts in that direction were destined to meet with total failure – but Eluard did, and he wrote to tell Picasso that *Guernica* looked better in London than in the Spanish Pavilion because of the excellent top-lighting in the gallery.[84] By the time the exhibition closed on 29 October, some 3,000 visitors had paid the 1/3d admission charge: Penrose's diary for the period is crammed with calculations and notes of sales of the catalogue and of the meagre additional donations to the fund – 2/- was the norm.[85] On 6 November a rather disappointed Penrose sent a brief report to Picasso:

A spread from Roland Penrose's appointments diary, 24–30 October 1938, showing calculations relating to receipts at the *Guernica* exhibition

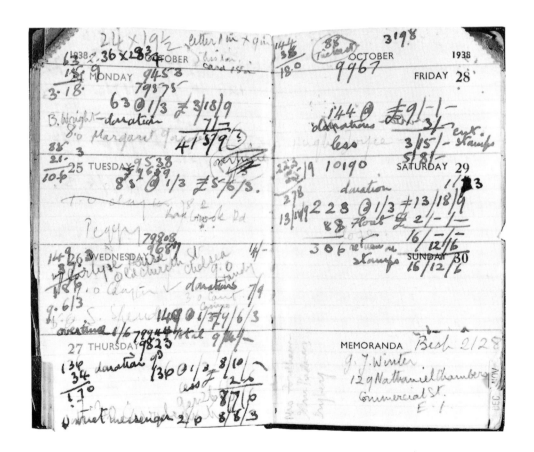

The 'Guernica' exhibition has closed in London. It has had an indisputable moral success but we didn't have the crowds of visitors I had hoped would come. I think that the crisis and the general feeling of demoralisation that ensued are in great part responsible.

The rest of Penrose's letter is mainly concerned with plans for repeat showings elsewhere: 'Two exhibitions seem to me definite, one in Oxford and the other in Whitechapel, a working-class district of London where there is very great sympathy for the Spanish cause.' And he closed by announcing his forthcoming visit to Paris, when 'I shall be very happy to see you again and tell you everything face to face'.[86] According to a diary entry for 15 November, they met for lunch at Brasserie Lipp, one of Picasso's and Dora's favourite haunts.[87]

No doubt Penrose was right about the principal reason for the public's relative indifference but lukewarm reviews cannot have helped. For instance, the well-known critic Eric Newton was dismissive of the mural itself, despite hailing some of the studies as 'the most expressive drawings Picasso has ever done'. 'One would guess from these preliminary studies,' Newton stated,

that Picasso was leading up to a stupendous essay in cumulative anguish. But no. After all this travail – lo, a mouse. True, 'Guernica' is a pretty big mouse, but it is disappointing after the elaborate preliminaries. [...] Whatever the explanation, the tight-rope walker's art failed him just when he needed it most.[88]

Nevertheless, the tour went ahead and was in fact extended quite significantly. *Guernica* and/or the related studies were shown in four other locations before being returned to Paris: in November 1938 at Oriel College, Oxford, where space restrictions meant that only the studies were shown; in December at Leeds City Art Gallery, where again the mural was absent but Penrose added *Weeping Woman*; in January 1939 at the Whitechapel Art Gallery, where the mural and studies were reunited; and finally – and improbably – *Guernica* and the studies hung for a fortnight in February 1939 in a car showroom in Manchester.

The showing at the Whitechapel Art Gallery was the most successful. With Penrose in attendance, it was opened by Major Clement Atlee, Leader of the opposition Labour Party and an ardent supporter of the International Brigade, and its avowed purpose was to help raise 'one million pennies' for a food-ship for Spain. Films about the Civil War were screened and Penrose, Read, the artist Julian Trevelyan and, despite his initial scepticism, Eric Newton gave regular guided tours explaining the meaning of the mural to anyone who would listen. These tactics and the barrage of press reports worked and some 12,000 visitors attended during the fortnight-long run.[89] In an enthusiastic letter Penrose wrote to Picasso of 'the profound impression your works have made on these simple people, whose responses are relatively

pure'.⁹⁰ He knew it would please Picasso to learn that his work had provoked so warm a response in the East End among the kinds of artisans with whom he always claimed to feel a special affinity.

Masterminding the *Guernica* exhibition had brought Penrose into much closer contact with his hero and he felt elated by this new form of collaboration. In contemporary letters to Lee Miller, however, he complained about the stresses and strains of organising the tour:

Picasso's exhibition is going round England – Oxford, Leeds, etc. and I have to keep track of it and write god's own quantities of letters – a bad change after living in a marble palace by the sea with you. But it seems to raise a lot of interest, and for Picasso and Spain one can do a lot of things that would be impossible otherwise.⁹¹

Of course, none of these grumbles found their way into his correspondence with Picasso. But in any case, although Penrose liked to pretend to a kind of aristocratic incompetence and fecklessness when writing to Lee – 'as you know I'm not used to jobs', 'appearing at a given place at a given time every morning doesn't fit in with my natural love of laziness'⁹² – he was actually energetic and resourceful, and had discovered in himself both a real flair for organising exhibitions and, crucially, all the necessary reserves of patience, tact and diplomacy. The *Guernica* tour was indeed the ancestor of all the great monographic shows he put on during the course of his career – not only those devoted to Picasso.

Just when negotiations to bring *Guernica* to London were reaching a climax, Penrose struck an exceptionally fortunate deal with Eluard. The poet was in financial difficulties and had decided to sell off the magnificent collection of modern art he had amassed since the Dada period. In June 1938 he approached Penrose. 'There was only one condition,' Penrose recalled:

[…] there must be no discussion about money. He would make out a list giving what he believed to be the market value of each item and all I had to do was to say 'yes' or 'no' and in either case we would remain friends.[93]

On 27 June 1938, in his apartment at 54 rue Legendre, Eluard drew up the agreement specifying the sum of £1,600 for 'le tout' (the lot), 'of which Roland Penrose still owes me £1,500, to be paid by 1 November 1938 at the latest'.[94] On the same day Penrose wrote to tell Mesens of this extraordinary new development: subject to the latter's agreement that this was a fair price, 'the sale will go ahead'. Penrose went on to explain that he planned to 'make a selection of 20 or 25 pieces that I like particularly' and put the rest into the London Gallery's stock, 'dividing it between you and me'. He would instruct Eluard that 'should he speak about the sale, he should simply say that the London Gallery is buying it'.[95]

The sum Penrose paid Eluard was remarkably little even by the standards of the day and even during a period of grave political instability. The greatest strength of the collection unquestionably lay in the work of Ernst, with whom Eluard had collaborated closely since the Dada period: there were forty of his works, many of great historical importance. But there were also exceptional works by all the other leading Surrealists. The ten works by Picasso were mostly recent drawings and prints, one being the richly coloured Surrealist drawing *The Pencil that Talks*, which Eluard had loaned to the London exhibition in 1936. There was also a small postwar Cubist painting of a glass, but Penrose gave that to Herbert Read.[96] The highlight of Eluard's Picassos was, however, a still life in carved and painted wood depicting a glass, knife, bread and salami on a table top decorated with a piece of real upholstery fringe – the only Cubist construction with which the artist had ever parted (see p. 49).[97] The acquisition of this uniquely inventive and witty piece strengthened Penrose's already important Cubist collection and, no doubt, contributed to his growing appreciation of Picasso's genius as a sculptor. From a typed list headed 'Ethnographical Objects and Sculpture' we learn that Penrose paid a mere 100 francs for it, whereas he paid 200 francs for a 'head' from the New Hebrides, 500 francs for a 'dragon' from Bali and 1,000 francs for a 'jade statuette' from Peru.[98] The surprising discrepancy may be explained by the fact that Eluard paid those sums for the ethnographic objects, whereas the Cubist construction was a gift from Picasso and had, in Eluard's eyes, only a nominal financial value.

Last months of freedom, 1939

The *Guernica* tour came to an end in Manchester in February 1939. But for two months afterwards the mural and all the studies were still in storage in London while Penrose tried to establish what Picasso and Larrea wanted to do next – have everything returned to Paris or shipped directly to New York, where there were various rival proposals for an exhibition. It was a terribly disheartening time for all Franco's opponents as the Civil War reached its last desperate stages – Barcelona had fallen to Nationalist troops on 26 January and the last Republican strongholds capitulated on 31 March – and the indecisiveness is not surprising. The fact that Penrose was ill at the time and feeling 'like a diseased hedgehog',[99] did nothing to help. On 28 March, in an attempt to settle matters once and for all, Picasso actually put pen to paper himself – a very rare event by this period and virtually the only occasion when he wrote Penrose a 'proper' letter. It had a mandatory function and began in peremptory style:

My dear Penrose
    As I told you I want 'Guernica' and the drawings and the other pictures which are in London to be sent to me in Paris as soon as possible, and I do not accept that anyone else has the right to decide where these works should be sent.

The second half of the letter, written on the other side of the sheet, was informal and friendly in tone:

    I was delighted to see you the other day and I hope that we will soon have the pleasure of spending more time together.
    Best wishes,
    Picasso[100]

Guernica and the studies were duly despatched to Paris in early April 1939 and thence, aboard the glamorous Art Deco liner *Normandie*, to the Valentine Gallery in New York for the first of a long string of fundraising exhibitions in North America. It was with palpable relief that Penrose wrote to Picasso on 15 April, expressing the hope that everything had arrived safely and including a few extra English press cuttings.[101] As this whole episode indicates, however great the personal gratification and however worthy the cause being served, there was a downside to playing the part of middleman and impresario, since at any minute 'business' matters might engender tension and misunderstanding and a friendship thus encumbered could never be simple. Nevertheless, this was the part Penrose was destined to play in future: in taking on the leadership of the English Surrealist group, buying into the London Gallery and collaborating with Mesens on *London Bulletin*, he had transformed himself into a highly effective, semi-professional intermediary between the British and Continental art worlds.[102]

One of the last exhibitions held at the London Gallery before the outbreak of war capitalised on the publicity generated by the *Guernica* exhibition. Entitled 'Picasso in Some English Collections', it opened on 15 May 1939 and proved so successful that the run was extended to the end of June. Over a third of the exhibits came from Penrose's collection and in the accompanying issue of *London Bulletin* he published a translation of one of Picasso's surrealist prose-poems.[103] It was only a short piece but it demanded verbal ingenuity and imagination on the translator's part and gave Penrose a taste for this unique form of mediation, anticipating his later more ambitious translations of Picasso's surrealist plays. Simultaneously, his own one-man show was held at the neighbouring Mayor Gallery and included a number of his recent postcard collages. It was an uplifting and satisfying note on which to end the season but the prelude to a complete cessation of activities: in July Penrose regretfully accepted Mesens's advice and closed down the London Gallery, which had been running at a loss and could not continue to function in the face of the escalating threat of war.

Penrose's last trip to France before war was declared took the form of a holiday with Lee Miller. They stayed first with Max Ernst and Leonora Carrington in Saint-Martin d'Ardèche, near Avignon, and then joined Picasso and Dora Maar in Antibes. It was a turning-point in Penrose's personal life as well as in the world at large. His divorce from Valentine had just been finalised and he was determined to establish his relationship with Lee on a more permanent footing, even though she remained married to the ever-tolerant Aziz Eloui Bey. Against this emotionally charged background the couple arrived in Antibes on 31 July to find Picasso working at 'incredible speed' on an enormous canvas depicting men spearing fish in the harbour at night by the light of glaring arc-lamps – a strange, premonitory scene executed in a funereal palette of black, indigo, purple and green.[104]

Although everyone tried to enjoy the Mediterranean holiday in the carefree spirit of previous years, it was impossible to maintain the fiction of normality, and the daily meetings on the beach and in the cafés were dominated by anxious speculation about the political situation. There was a momentary surge of joy when Picasso's two nephews, Fin and Javier Vilató, arrived suddenly in Antibes after crossing the Pyrenees with the defeated Republican army, but the sense of doom returned as more and more holiday-makers hurriedly left, to be replaced by troops of Senegalese soldiers setting up machine guns on the rocks close to the fashionable hotels and bathing pools. Still Picasso procrastinated, hoping for a miracle, and Penrose noticed that, although he managed to finish *Night Fishing at Antibes*, 'other large panels of canvas pinned to the walls remained untouched'.[105] On 26 August, following the French Government's announcement of a general mobilisation, the two couples bowed to the inevitable and said their farewells, little knowing that it would be five years before they met again.

While Picasso and his entourage headed for Paris, Roland and Lee set off for London. They arrived at Waterloo Station, 'just as the first air-raid alarm was sounding and the novel sight of barrage balloons rising into a clear blue sky greeted us'.[106] Penrose now faced a dilemma: fervently opposed to Fascism and to the policy of appeasement, he could not opt out, but as a committed pacifist he could not take up arms himself. His solution was to become involved in camouflage and, with his friends the painter Julian Trevelyan, the printmaker Stanley William Hayter and the engraver Buckland Wright, he set up the Industrial Camouflage Research Unit, which they ran from offices rented from the architect Erno Goldfinger.[107] The following year he was appointed a War Office lecturer on camouflage to the Home Guard.

Meanwhile, the fate of his collection was a pressing anxiety. Leaving everything unprotected in Hampstead would have been foolhardy and Penrose decided to send the most valuable items for storage in Bradenham Hall, the large country house in Norfolk belonging to his brother Alec, which had been requisitioned by the Army.[108] The only Picasso left in Downshire Hill during the war was *Grand air*, the etching on which the artist had collaborated with Eluard in 1936.[109] In a list drawn up for insurance purposes in 1943 *Grand air* is valued at a mere £2,[110] but Penrose may have kept it in Hampstead, not because it was worth less than everything else, but because in his mind it had talismanic power. It united the two men who had been indissolubly linked in his thoughts ever since his first meeting with Picasso, and keeping it in his home was a way of ensuring their safety and the resumption of the three-way friendship when at last peace was restored.

In the end, six of Penrose's remaining Picassos never went into storage at Bradenham Hall. Instead they were shown in the massive retrospective organised by Alfred Barr, which, in spite of the catastrophic turn of events in Europe, opened as planned at the Museum of Modern Art in New York in November 1939.[111] In a letter to Penrose dated 17 November Barr thanked him warmly for not reneging on his agreement to lend even during war time: inevitably, many European collectors had refused to allow their works to make the dangerous transatlantic voyage.[112] Calculating this might be a good moment to strike and Penrose in the mood to realise some of his assets, Barr then made the first move in what became a marathon campaign to buy *Girl with a Mandolin* – the most valuable of all Penrose's Picassos. On 15 December Barr cabled requesting 'lowest price our museum Femme Mandoline' and Penrose responded in the new year by demanding £3,000, or $12,000, three times the amount for which the picture had been insured during its transatlantic journey.[113] Penrose was chancing his arm: that August, when René Gaffé had attempted to buy the picture back from him through Mesens, he had set the price at £1,800.[114] Barr continued to haggle, cabling a raised offer of $6,000 at the beginning of April 1940 – an offer he repeated two years later.[115] Penrose held firm. He did not actually need the money and he did not want to part with the picture, which he knew was probably the single most important and valuable work of art he owned. Both men took their 'disagreement' in good part, not allowing it to sour their nascent friendship, and by the end of the war they were ready and keen to collaborate productively together.

Chapter 2

A Choice of Paths, 1939–1954

The War Years, 1939–1945

Penrose's direct contact with Picasso himself and with all his other Parisian friends effectively ceased with the signing of the armistice between Hitler and Pétain at the end of June 1940. Picasso was in Royan when the German army invaded France but returned to Paris in August, remaining there – on enemy territory as far as Britain was concerned – throughout the Occupation. For his part, Penrose became increasingly absorbed by his war work and in June 1940 *London Bulletin* followed the way of the London Gallery and ceased publication.[1] A few months later disaster struck when Taylor's Depository in Ranelagh Road, Pimlico, where the London Gallery stock was stored, was hit by a bomb: nothing by Picasso was there, but works by, among others, Ernst and Magritte were totally destroyed.[2] Camouflage must have seemed more essential than ever after that devastating event and Penrose's reputation as an expert on the subject was consolidated when his *Home Guard Manual of Camouflage* was published in 1941. Bizarrely, his experience of lecturing on camouflage was the foundation for his postwar career as a prolific lecturer on contemporary art.

Although Penrose lost touch with Picasso during the Occupation, he stayed indirectly in contact with Eluard by communicating with him via Louis Parrot, the writer, translator and Hispanist, who was based in Clermont-Ferrand, and the Brazilian painter-diplomat Cicero Dias, who was attached to the Brazilian Embassy in Vichy and was able, via Portugal, to pass correspondence between the French Resistance poets and London.[3] Thus towards the end of 1942 Eluard was able to get copies of *Poésie et Vérité* sent to Penrose at 21 Downshire Hill, and in 1944 Penrose and Mesens published their translation of the poems as *Poetry and Truth* under the imprint of the London Gallery.[4] An echo of these activities appears in the ardent letter Penrose wrote to Picasso on 27 August 1944, the day after De Gaulle entered Paris in triumph:

Dearest Friend,

At last the wall is breached – one can get back into contact with you and our friends whom we have missed so much throughout this interminable

Opposite
Roland Penrose at 11A Hornton Street, London, early 1950s. In the background is Picasso's *Girl with a Mandolin* (top left) and *Still Life* construction (centre). Photographer unknown

nightmare. The interminable has terminated. I hasten to write to you although I don't know where or when this letter will reach you, or in what state it will find you following all the privations you have had to endure. Quite possibly if you're in Paris you'll have had a visit from Lee before this reaches you. After a war of patience and work in London she got the chance to go to France as a War Correspondent attached to the American Army and I know that one of her aims will be to find you as soon as possible. As for me, I haven't been as lucky because, having joined the army with the idea that it would be the quickest way to get back to France, I find myself stuck in a provincial town without the least hope of getting to the Continent while I remain a soldier.

I am so longing to have news of you and of Dora, Paul, Nusch and so many other friends – one hardly dares ask after so long a silence and so much danger and I don't know how to get hold of them.

London has been in a state of total sterility since losing contact with Paris. Just one small exhibition of reproductions of your new paintings has taken place recently. Reproductions which have made me very eager to see the originals. After all the shouting and flag-waving, as soon as I can get out of khaki I shall come with incredible speed.

Mesens and I have translated and published Paul's poems, 'Poésie et Vérité' 42, and they have had quite considerable success. If you can give me his address I'll ask him belatedly for his permission to publish. I do hope that our gesture, which was so important for us in London, has done him no harm. Knowing that it was essential to avoid publicity, which might have delivered him into the hands of the enemy, we waited until the poems had already appeared [in the Algerian edition of Fontaine] before publishing them in London. I'd be relieved to know that nothing bad happened to him because of this.

It still seems almost incredible to be able to write to you – the war effectively killed off everything we hold dear. It will take time for life to begin again.

Tell me what you and our friends are lacking and I shall try to send it to you as soon as communications have been reestablished. For us, it is above all life, friends, poetry that we lack.

Dear friend and dear friends, I send you my most affectionate greetings
Roland Penrose[5]

He was right: Lee Miller had already been to see Picasso. Having joined British *Vogue* as a freelance photographer in 1940, she succeeded in getting accreditation as a US war correspondent in 1942 and following the D-Day landings she was often on assignment in France to record and report on the Allied advance. She witnessed the Liberation of Paris and, as Roland predicted, made Picasso's studio in rue des Grands-Augustins her first port of call, 'and between laughter and tears and having my bottom pinched and my hair mussed we exchanged news about friends and their work, incoherently, and looked at new pictures which were dated on all the Battle of Paris days'.

Picasso in his studio,
7 rue des Grands-
Augustins, Paris, August
1944. Photo Lee Miller

Having tried one of the tomatoes Picasso had been growing, and painting, in his studio – 'It was a bit mouldy but I liked the idea of eating a work of art' – she went off to a neighbouring bistro with him and Dora Maar: 'I added my K rations to their celebration chicken and we drank lots of wine, and *fine* and gossiped and held hands and cried some more.'[6] Lee's adventures and her freedom of movement as she pressed on with the army into Alsace, Luxembourg and Germany aggravated Penrose's sense of envy and frustration. In his next letter to Picasso, dated 16 September 1944, he referred to the 'superb' photograph of Picasso with Lee that he had in front of him: 'It makes me rage and groan to be in Paris too,' he added.[7]

Despite still being in uniform, on 28 September Penrose managed to get a week's leave in Paris and was reunited with Lee at the Hôtel Scribe, which the American press used as their headquarters. That evening they joined Picasso and the Eluards for dinner. In old age he remembered these joyous moments as 'unbelievable' and 'a miracle'.[8] Photographs taken by Miller show the four friends, together with Louis Aragon and his wife, the Russian writer Elsa Triolet, posing as a tight-knit group in Picasso's studio.

Roland Penrose, Paris 1944

with Jean Hélion Paris 1944
Liberation day

France 1944. Dilberstone, Hill

Preceding pages
A spread from Roland
Penrose's *Wartime
Scrapbook,* showing
photographs of Lee
Miller and Roland
Penrose at home, as
well as Paul and Nusch
Eluard on their wedding
day, 1945 (top left),
Picasso and Lee Miller
on Liberation Day (top
second left), Peggy
Bernier in bed (top
second right) and a
group photograph of
Lee Miller, Roland
Penrose and Louis
Aragon with Picasso,
Nusch Eluard, Paul
Eluard and Elsa Triolet,
Paris, 1945 (bottom
second right). Photos
by Roland S. Haupt,
Lee Miller, David E.
Scherman and an
unknown photographer

Significantly, Dora Maar is absent, but so is Picasso's new lover, the young painter Françoise Gilot. Penrose made contact with Dora while he was in Paris but if he heard about this new affair he may not have realised how serious it was or that Dora had been deposed.[9] Making up for the years of cultural isolation, he also embarked on an intoxicating round of visits to old friends: the pages in his diary bristle with their addresses and telephone numbers.

Before Penrose left for London, Eluard told him of Picasso's decision to join the Communist Party (the official announcement was made on the front page of *L'Humanité* on 5 October 1944). Penrose was neither surprised nor upset by this turn of events, although, despite his devotion to Eluard and his left-wing affiliations, he never seems to have meditated taking the same step himself. At no time did he question Picasso's own explanation of his idealistic motives – that he, Picasso, believed Communism was dedicated to making the world a better place for the greatest number of people, that the Communists had been the most resolute and courageous in fighting Fascism in France, that the *Parti communiste français* (PCF) provided him with a 'fatherland', 'while I wait for the time when Spain can take me back again', and that in joining the Party he had found 'brothers'.[10] Nor did Penrose ever presume, at this time or later, to criticise Picasso's political position – a stance which eventually brought him into (friendly) dispute with Alfred Barr.

Meanwhile the war dragged on and, even when it was over, Penrose had to wait for what seemed like an eternity before he was demobbed in February 1946. Not that he was inactive on the art front during that transitional period. On 5 December 1945 a Picasso-Matisse exhibition organised jointly by the British Council and the Direction Générale des Relations Culturelles opened at the Victoria and Albert Museum in London. Quite apart from its purpose of honouring the two most famous living painters, the exhibition had a propaganda function – on one hand a public expression of France's gratitude to Great Britain for her part in the Liberation, on the other a British celebration of the survival of high culture in France throughout the Nazi Occupation. It attracted enormous crowds in London – some 160,000 visitors during its five-week run – and then, with various adjustments to the content, toured to Manchester and Glasgow, and from there to Brussels and Amsterdam. In London, controversy raged in the media over the pictures Picasso was exhibiting, all of them executed between 1939 and 1945, whereas Matisse, who was having a mini-retrospective, was mildly criticised for being 'a little too effortless' and for verging on 'mere decoration'.[11] Eric Newton summed up the stark polarisation:

Poor Matisse has almost been ignored or treated as no more than a chocolate box painter in this storm in the British Council's teacup. Picasso is the villain. It is he who has debased the coinage of art and produced an 'insidious growth that will sap the roots of all that is fine in painting', a 'crazy guying of humankind' from which our schoolchildren must be protected.[12]

Matisse himself knew he had been eclipsed by his old friend and rival and, pointing to a fat wad of press cuttings, remarked ruefully to Brassaï: 'He [Picasso]'s the one who's getting most of the insults, not me [...]. They're courteous toward me [...]. Obviously, next to him, I always look like a little girl.'[13]

Inevitably, Penrose became involved in Picasso's defence. His one published intervention took the form of a 'debate' with William Gaunt, art critic of the *Evening Standard*, and in this too Matisse was totally ignored. It was all very gentlemanly in tone, the title 'Picasso: genius or hoax?' being punchier than the 'debate' itself, and Penrose, dubbed 'Britain's foremost authority on Picasso' in the lead-in remarks, was even allowed the last word. In response to Gaunt's suggestion that Picasso 'has led us into a cul-de-sac' and 'painters now are seeking a way out', he replied:

A young painter can no longer rely on a school. He has got to see and think for himself. In Picasso we have a masterly example of someone who has done this. Whether the younger generation can be as original and as dynamic is up to them to prove.[14]

Penrose also wrote a letter to *The Times* on 31 December 1945, but it was never published, either because he decided not to send it off or because the Editor decided that he had already given more than enough space to letters attacking and defending Picasso. The letter is none the less worth quoting because it gives insight into Penrose's preoccupations:

Sir,

Among the prodigious number of letters that have flooded the Press as a result of the Picasso Exhibition, no one can fail to notice the demand for further enlightenment. A demand which is to some extent a criticism of our current institutions. The fact that this is an exhibition only of Picasso's wartime paintings has produced a shock of horror to the public and the critics, few of whom have appreciated the immense and even tender understanding of life that his work reveals. Certainly it is asking too much, even of the most receptive, to expect them to understand this most recent and dramatic phase without knowledge of the background of the movement of modern painting which has been going on for over thirty years.

Shock tactics of this description may have the effect of reviving the interest of the public, but they also lead to superficial ranting from those who are offended and cheap imitations by those who admire. The right solution, now that we are able again to plan for a fuller life, should surely be more frequent retrospective exhibitions, such as the exhibition of Klee now at the National Gallery, combined with more comprehensive permanent collections of modern art.

Before the war other countries had developed institutions such as the Museum of Modern Art in New York and similar foundations in Paris and Brussels, which we would do well to study if we wish to catch up on the

habitual time lag in our artistic appreciation for which this country is notorious. If it is beyond the means of the State to meet this need, surely private
enterprise, inspired by the best traditions and this urgent demand, should
find a way to satisfy this necessity.

Yours etc.

Roland Penrose[15]

The reasoned plea for a 'museum of modern art' in Britain at the heart of
the letter reflects the shift in Penrose's perception of himself, which he described
with dignity and candour in his memoirs under the heading 'A choice of paths':

The war had disrupted the way in which I had hoped to develop, and even
before the war it had occurred to me that I would never attain the stature in
the arts of my brilliant surrealist friends [...]. I realised that one of the most
valid activities I had embarked on with some success was the encouragement
of others to understand and enjoy all that I had found most worthwhile for
myself. I felt an urge to bring about a wider appreciation of the poets and
painters who had inspired me. [...] [I]n future the pen was to take precedence
over the paintbrush as a means of expression and I was to join company with
friends in London and Paris in an effort to make the arts more accessible,
more appreciated and more an integral part of life.[16]

It was a characteristically generous and self-effacing decision and from this
period onwards, almost until the end of his life, Penrose put his own creative
endeavours a poor second. According to the journalist John Thompson, who
met Penrose in 1942, 'You wouldn't have known he was an artist,' so rare was
it for him even to mention his own work.[17] How much this cost Penrose emotionally we shall never know but some of those who loved him, including his
two wives, watched the eclipse of the artist with regret.[18] Practically speaking, Penrose's decision meant that immediately after the war he not only
began to write regularly about art but also became a prime mover behind the
groundbreaking art institution that set out to fulfil the educational programme sketched out in his unpublished letter to *The Times*.

The 'Institute of Contemporary Arts', 1946

When Penrose wrote that letter he, Mesens, Read and the other members of
the committee dedicated to the enterprise were still toying with the idea of a
'museum' of contemporary art loosely modelled on the Museum of Modern
Art in New York. But by May 1946 they had decided against forming a permanent collection on the grounds that it risked becoming static and would
require substantial sums of money from trustees, who might start meddling
in their projects and overturning their decisions. Accordingly, they adopted
the word 'institute' rather than 'museum'. By May 1946 they had also agreed
their basic policy: the institute would be international; it would embrace all

the arts, for demonstrating 'the unity of the arts' was one of their principal aims; it would lean towards the 'new and creative'; and it would have a broadly 'educative' role, striving to defeat the innate conservatism and philistinism of the British public.[19] For some four years after it was founded, the Institute of Contemporary Arts had no premises of its own, but the London Gallery, which reopened in Brook Street in November 1946 with Penrose as a director and Mesens as the manager, was often used for ICA events. So, by the time he hung up his army uniform for the last time, Penrose was actively involved in the resurrection of the London art scene – a role he found deeply absorbing and fulfilling.

At the same time great changes were occurring in his personal life. Lee Miller had been on assignment for *Vogue* in Central and Eastern Europe since the end of the war but at last agreed to resume her life with him in London in the spring of 1946. That summer they went to America together – Roland's first trip to the States – and a year later they married, having moved across the street to a larger house at 36 Downshire Hill. Their son Antony was born in October 1947. These domestic developments were not irrelevant to Penrose's new role as 'Britain's foremost authority on Picasso'. Lee with her camera became the indispensable collaborator on numerous 'missions' and Tony also – quite unconsciously – helped his father build a closer relationship with Picasso, who thrived in the company of young children and grew fond of the good-looking, lively child. By a happy chance Tony was also the perfect age to be a playmate for Picasso's children by Françoise Gilot: Claude was exactly the same age and Paloma a couple of years younger. Fatherhood seems, initially at least, to have created a new kind of bond between Penrose and Picasso.

But in 1947 fundraising for the ICA was a major preoccupation and, while Penrose's association with Picasso was to be of great help, in the early days of the institute most of the money was put up by Penrose himself and two other members of the committee, Eric Gregory and Peter Watson.[20] If they were to fulfil their large ambitions, they needed to attract a much larger public than the small coterie of like-minded art lovers that habitually foregathered at the London Gallery, and the programme of events moved up several gears in February 1948 with the opening of '40 Years of Modern Art' at the Academy Cinema on Oxford Street.[21] Penrose selected the works and loaned twenty pictures from his own collection, including two of the Picassos he had bought from Gaffé, the so-called *Negro Dancer* and *Woman in Green*. The avowed purpose of this quite conventional miscellany was to advertise the Institute, raise money and demonstrate through the selection that the founding members were 'not the partisans of some narrow clique'.[22] Far more adventurous and influential was Penrose's next exhibition for the ICA, '40,000 Years of Modern Art', which opened at the end of the year, again in the Academy Cinema.[23] In a letter to Picasso, he summarised the main purpose of the show, which reflected the Surrealists' conviction that there was an underlying affinity between 'primitive' artists and themselves, and the indisputable fact that many vanguard artists had been directly inspired by 'primitive' art of various kinds. But the chief point of the letter was to persuade Picasso to collaborate and as an early example of Penrose in his guise as silver-tongued exhibition curator it is worth quoting in full. It would not be the last time that he made use of an attractive emissary when requesting similar favours:

Dear Picasso,

No doubt you will remember Miss Gigi Richter, who will deliver this letter to you. As she was coming to France anyway, she has agreed to help me in my grand plans for an exhibition to be held this winter, organised by our Institute of Contemporary Arts.

Our idea is to make a confrontation between Primitive Art and Modern Art. To represent the primitive we shall have prehistoric, Oceanic and African objects loaned by the museums in Oxford, Cambridge, Brighton, etc., as well as the Musée de l'Homme. As regards modern art, the *pièce de résistance* will be 'Les Demoiselles d'Avignon', lent by the Museum of Modern Art in New York. We shall also include three or four of your important paintings and various sculptures and paintings representative of the modern period.

But in order to add another element of capital importance, what we really want is to be able to exhibit three or four of your ceramics, which I've seen reproduced in 'Cahiers d'Art'.

It's for this reason, and because I myself can't get away from London, that we're sending the lovely Gigi to you, in the hope that you will agree to confide to her a few pieces for our exhibition.

I must point out that the exhibition is not in the least commercial – nothing will be for sale – and I shall personally take care of the insurance and the return of the ceramics, if you are good enough to lend us any.

It would be a major coup for our Institute and for Londoners in general if we were able to have in the same show both 'Les Demoiselles' and examples of your latest works, which, judging by the photos, are really beautiful.

We should therefore be extremely grateful if you could see your way to granting this request. Lee joins me in sending you our most sincere best wishes. In any case we hope to see you once the exhibition is over.

Yours ever
Roland Penrose[24]

During the previous summer, Picasso had begun working intensively alongside the professional potters of the Madoura factory in Vallauris and by the end of 1948 had already produced an enormous and highly original oeuvre. Many of his pieces referred openly to pottery from the ancient cultures of the Mediterranean and Penrose was entirely justified in wanting to represent this latest aspect of Picasso's 'primitivism' in '40,000 Years of Modern Art'. Unfortunately, however, the show clashed with a major exhibition devoted to Picasso's ceramics in Paris,[25] and Penrose did not get the coveted loans.

Nevertheless, '40,000 Years of Modern Art' attracted large crowds and provoked a good deal of journalistic discussion as to the relative merits of the 'primitive' and 'modern' exhibits and the legitimacy of the show's thesis. For William Turnbull and other young artists, however, it was both a confirmation and a revelation, indisputably one of the high points in the early history of the ICA:

I thought it was a marvellous exhibition. I was ready for it; it was the first exhibition that I had seen that juxtaposed contemporary work with paleolithic and ethnographic art. I was thinking that way myself.[26]

Les Demoiselles d'Avignon was on show in London for the first time. The keystone to the entire argument of the exhibition, it would never have been loaned had Penrose not won Alfred Barr's trust and liking, and had he not kept his promise and allowed his Picassos to cross the Atlantic just after the outbreak of war. The two had first met before the war and their friendship was cemented during Penrose's trip to America in 1946. They identified each

Ewan Phillips, Director of the Institute of Contemporary Arts, and Roland Penrose, with Picasso's *Les Demoiselles d'Avignon*, London, December 1948. Photographer unknown

other as natural allies, with usefully different backgrounds but similar interests, aims and problems, and a valuable give-and-take collaboration was rapidly established. It proved to be a relationship admirably free of competitiveness, jealousy and egotism, and in its own way it was as important for Penrose as his friendship with Eluard, although its character was utterly different, for it was not as avant-garde artists and Surrealists but as exhibition curators and writers on art that Penrose and Barr found common ground. And it was, one might add, just the type of relationship Penrose needed given the change in direction of his career.

One might have thought that the ambitious, internationally oriented programme of the ICA would have taken all Penrose's time and energy. But, paradoxically, it was at this moment of maximum ferment that the deep-rooted, squirearchical side of his nature asserted itself. He began to yearn, he explained, for the 'green and pleasant countryside' of the Sussex Downs, which he had loved ever since 'the first world war when, harvesting in my uncle's fields, I had found nightjars' nests in the woods'.[27] One gets a touching glimpse of this unusual duality in the back pages of his diary for 1953 where a list of tribal objects and Melanesian islands follows a list of plants and shrubs and horticultural nurseries.[28] After searching for a suitable country property with Lee, who had serious reservations about the whole project, Penrose settled on a dairy farm with a rambling Georgian house and a large garden, and hired a manager. To raise the money, he was obliged to sell his house at Downshire Hill and take out the lease on a flat in Hornton Street, Kensington. The journey between the flat and Farley Farm was relatively easy and Penrose's week thereafter was usually divided between these two homes in the heart of London and the depths of the Sussex countryside.

Oddly enough, Picasso took an interest in this aspect of Penrose's activities, sometimes questioning him about the farm, sometimes putting aside for him cuttings about livestock he had happened upon when browsing through magazines. Probably this corresponded to some fantasy about England and the English landed gentry, for Picasso was proud of his father's reputation for looking like an English gentleman.[29] Maybe he thought of Farley Farm as Penrose's Boisgeloup and of himself as a countryman *manqué*: he once told Penrose that he had considered buying a farm and would have done so if only he were less busy and had more faith in the honesty of farm managers![30] At all events, it never seems to have occurred to Picasso to take Penrose less seriously as a writer and curator simply because he was also a farmer with crops and animals on his mind.

Picasso's play, *Le Désir attrapé par la queue*

In February 1946, when plans for the ICA were starting to take firm shape, Penrose had fitted in a short trip to Paris and visited Picasso several times. One topic we can be sure they discussed was his plan to translate Picasso's surrealist play *Le Désir attrapé par la queue*.[31] Written in January 1941, the play was performed for the first time on 19 March 1944 in the apartment of Michel and Louise Leiris, just a stone's throw from Picasso's studio. Friends, including Dora Maar, Simone de Beauvoir, Jean-Paul Sartre and the Leirises, took the parts, the performance was directed by Albert Camus, and the first audience was largely made up of distinguished artists such as Braque: a more star-studded line-up can hardly be imagined and it was duly immortalised in the photographs of Brassaï.[32] In being a play written in French by a Spanish painter, *Le Désir* represented a boundary-breaking ideal for the nascent Institute and Penrose conceived the plan of emulating the original readings in London. By the middle of January 1947 he was putting the finishing touches to his translation and checking it over with Picasso, and on 21 February, at 6.15 p.m., *Desire Caught by the Tail* had its first public performance at the London Gallery.[33] The artists Julian Trevelyan and John Banting were among those who took parts.[34]

Translating Picasso's first play was a considerable linguistic challenge but Penrose, who was steeped in French and English Surrealist writing and wrote Surrealist poetry himself, was equipped to meet it and did so with considerable verve. Other translations of Picasso's writings followed much later, so that he became in effect the artist's official English-language translator as well as his principal English-language biographer and interpreter. But it is unlikely that in 1946–47 he had formulated large ambitions of this kind. Probably what he wanted was quite simply to reignite, in a depressed, bomb-scarred, severely rationed London, the intellectual fire and ferment of prewar Surrealism, and to pay homage to the courage of the left-wing avant-garde in Resistance Paris, for those first performances of *Le Désir attrapé par la queue*, 'under the noses of the Nazis', were in themselves an act of daring and defiance.[35] The translation was also a step towards fulfilling the vow Penrose had inwardly taken to become a conduit for the creativity of those artists 'whose genius made the first decades of the twentieth century a period of unusual brilliance', as he expressed it in *Scrap Book*.[36]

In July 1949 the Penroses headed off for the south of France for their usual summer holiday and visited Picasso and Françoise in Vallauris. One topic of conversation must have been Bernard Frechtman's rival translation of *Le Désir attrapé par la queue*, which had dashed Penrose's hopes of publishing his own version. That September he wrote to report on the situation:

Dear Picasso,

I promised to give you news of the translation of your play, which is due to be published here. On returning to London I went to see the editor of Rider & Co. and he showed me the proofs. It's the same translation as was published in America under the title 'Desire'. The editor allowed me to compare this version with my translation and with the original and to make corrections. And they were sorely needed – there was a mass of mistakes. I corrected everything and insisted that the original title be restored – 'Desire caught by the tail' – and yesterday I saw the editor again and he accepted all my proposals.

So all I have to do is write the preface and I'm working on that now in the hope that I shall manage to do something worthy of such a marvellous play. I'll send you a copy as soon as it's ready.

We miss the Midi and the sunshine a great deal but we have such good memories of our visits to Vallauris. Lee and I send you, Françoise and Claude our warmest good wishes.

Yours ever
Roland Penrose[37]

It must have been galling, to say the least, to have to act as the copy editor of someone else's inadequate translation, and being invited to write a preface was not much of a consolation. Nevertheless, Penrose did what was required and at the end of October despatched a copy of his text to Vallauris for Picasso's approval.[38] Matters did not rest there, however, and early the following February the gentlemanly arrangements made with Rider & Co. came unstuck, leading the normally courteous Penrose to lose his temper. The tale is told with simmering fury in another letter to Picasso:

[…] at the last moment the big chief of the publishing house, who is a mortal enemy of all modern art, insisted that many passages be changed or cut altogether. I protested loudly but it seems that, according to the terms of their contract with the Philosophical Library of New York, who bought the rights from Gallimard in the first instance, they have the right to cut whatever they like. So I have withdrawn my preface – the only means I had to express my disapproval of this whole affair.

To add insult to injury Rider & Co. were even attempting to prevent Penrose from using his translation in future public readings of *Le Désir*, but he was asserting his moral rights:

[…] in spite of Rider & Co's threats we shall be reading my translation on February 16th – I enclose an announcement. In this small way I've registered my defiance of these ill-intentioned people, but I am mortified that I can't do anything to prevent the publication of their dishonest edition.[39]

The motive for the cuts was prudery: the editor objected to the 'indecency' of certain passages in Picasso's text.[40]

A few weeks later Penrose had the satisfaction of writing to Picasso to describe the triumphant outcome of his small act of rebellion. The reading of *Desire Caught by the Tail* had taken place, as planned, in the Rudolf Steiner Hall in London in a double programme with William Blake's *An Island in the Moon*, and such was the level of interest that 'we had to turn hundreds of people away at the door'.[41] According to the report in *Picture Post*, the play was read 'with gusto, but without "acting," by an enthusiastic cast'.[42] The Welsh poet Dylan Thomas intoned Picasso's stage directions in

his fruity, rolling, public-performance voice and Valentine Dyall, a popular actor best known at the time for his radio work, recreated the role of Big Foot, which he had taken in the original reading in 1947. There was further cause for pride when the Watergate Theatre applied to Picasso to be allowed to use Penrose's translation for a full-dress production that October.[43] In another letter Penrose thanked Picasso for granting them permission to do so and reported – with no pretence of regret – that the infamous head of Rider & Co. had just committed suicide: 'A coincidence perhaps, but there is no more talk of the mangled edition – nor, sadly, of an honest edition as far as I know.' In the same letter Penrose explained that there would be no holiday in the south of France for Lee or for himself that summer because they were leaving their London house and setting up home in Farley Farm, 'where we hope to find more peace'.[44]

A spread from Picture Post, 4 March 1950, showing members of the cast and audience at the first London reading of Picasso's play, Desire Caught by the Tail

Picasso visits England, November 1950

The other significant event of 1950 brought Picasso to England for the first time since 1919. The occasion was the Second World Peace Conference held in Sheffield. The conference, backed by the Soviet Union, was supposed to last seven days (13–19 November). Picasso had designed the poster depicting a white 'dove of peace' flying over the land.[45] Panicking at the prospect of a Communist 'invasion', at the last minute the Labour Government authorised a massive security clamp-down by immigration officials at all sea- and air-ports. Of the sixty or so French delegates who arrived in Dover on 11 November, only Picasso and one or two others were allowed to land. The whole fiasco was extensively reported in the British press, since many distinguished intellectuals in the PCF, including Frédéric Joliot-Curie, the Nobel Prize-winning atom scientist and president of the Congress, were summarily denied visas and forced to turn back, and Winston Churchill, while endorsing the Government's basic position, used Parliamentary question-time to criticise the Home Secretary's inept handling of the affair.[46] Penrose was able to report events from first hand in *Picasso: His Life and Work*:

It so happened that at the same time [as the Peace Conference] an exhibition of recent paintings and ceramics by Picasso, organised by the Arts Council, was being held in London, and either for this or for some other reason never yet divulged, Picasso was allowed into the country. Having been warned that he was on his way, but not yet knowing what had happened to his companions, I hurried to Victoria Station to meet him. The night-ferry was unaccountably late and to my surprise, when I finally caught sight of the small figure of Picasso dressed in a grey suit and a black beret carrying his suitcase, he was alone. As soon as we met he explained that his friends, almost without exception, had been turned back from Dover as dangerous revolutionaries, 'and I,' he said with anxiety, 'what can I have done that they should allow me through?'[47]

Capitalising on the situation, Penrose immediately invited Picasso to come for the night to Farley Farm, which he did. The next morning Picasso took the train to Sheffield, where he received an ovation for a short speech in which, instead of speaking directly about politics, he explained how he had learned to paint doves from his father and finished by declaring: 'I stand with life against death; I stand for peace against war.'[48]

Because of the government ban the Sheffield Conference was closed after only a day. Picasso did not follow the other delegates to Warsaw, where it reconvened, but returned to London. He was greeted as a hero at St Pancras Station by the painter Rodrigo Moynihan and fifty of his students from the Royal College of Art, who swarmed around his carriage door, cheering, shaking his hand and pushing forward their autograph books.[49] As a way of registering his anger at the treatment of fellow delegates to the Congress, Picasso refused to attend the Arts Council exhibition, but in other respects he entered into the spirit of the various entertainments put on for him. A party was held at the London house of John Desmond Bernal, the renowned scientist, ardent Marxist and founder-member of the World Peace Council, and in front of the assembled guests Picasso made an elegant drawing of the heads of an angelic, garlanded couple on a specially prepared wall – a virtuoso display greeted with delighted applause.[50]

For Penrose there was a solid silver lining to the embarrassing flop of the Sheffield Peace Conference. Picasso returned to Farley Farm before going back to France and, to judge by a series of relaxed and charming photographs taken by both Lee and Roland, he greatly enjoyed himself meeting the animals with three-year-old Tony and looking at Roland's work in his studio (see pp. 66–67). Lee described his visit in a spirited article published in *Vogue*:

In London, our Edwardian bay window looks down the length of Pitt Street. The street-name sign reminded Picasso that when he first left Spain for France he had been longing and intending to come to England, but was side-tracked in Paris. The English, to him, were most extraordinary and admirable, principally because they had produced William Pitt's niece, Lady Hester Stanhope. He had been enthralled by books of her adventures and life with the Bedouin, but instead of wanting to follow her footsteps into the desert, he dreamed of meeting in England someone like her.[51]

Perhaps Picasso also remarked on the striking similarities between Lady Stanhope and his equally intrepid and unconventional hostess who, wearing Arab costume, had gone on long and hazardous photographic expeditions in the Egyptian desert before the war.

Miller went on to describe Picasso's stay at Farley Farm:

At our farm in Sussex, Picasso found the world was very English; the landscape of downs with Constable clouds, the prudish Long Man of Wilmington, left-handed driving, red and white Ayrshires, open log fires, whisky and soda night cap, hot-water bottles, cooked breakfast and tea. A tinned plum pudding, holly-wreathed and flaming, was indeed English, very English, superb and quite unimaginable.

Our three-year-old son Tony was in ecstasy. Picasso and he became great friends, telling secrets, finding treasures of spider webs and seed pods, rough-housing, and looking at pictures. In Tony's early vocabulary the words picture and Picasso were synonymous, I suppose because Roland and I referred to the same painting as 'picture' and 'Picasso' interchangeably and the words started the same. [...]

You can't have a rough-house in secret. Picasso and Tony pummelled each other amid squeals and roars. Each meeting, here and in France, added to the repertoire: giggling, ambushes from behind sofas, bellowing bulls, the olé, olé of approval. The crescendo of violence rose through ear-twisting and kicking to biting. Picasso bit back sharply [...] 'the biter bitten,' and in the astounded silence which followed said, 'Pensez! C'est le premier Anglais que j'ai jamais mordu!'[52]

She adds that among the many trophies Picasso took back to France were postcards of Brighton Pavilion, peaked school caps for himself and Claude, a photograph of Roland's great-aunt Priscilla Hannah at the Bath Peace Congress in 1875 and a toy red London bus.[53]

In return, Picasso left behind two bold watercolours. In Hornton Street he embellished Penrose's copy of *Vingt Poèmes de Góngora*, which is illustrated with a suite of his etchings, with a dazzling watercolour depicting a satyr-like figure brandishing a sword and mounted on a horse.[54] On the same day, apparently using the same inks and watercolours but at Farley Farm, Picasso inaugurated the Visitors' Book of the ICA with a flamboyant design of four blazing yellow suns and three winged bulls mounted like grasshoppers on leafy stems. The same eye-catching design was later adapted for a silk scarf sold in aid of the ICA, for ingenious money-raising schemes of one kind or another were constantly needed to generate income.[55] Over the years Penrose succeeded in extracting many other valuable gifts from Picasso, who became in effect the ICA's version of a patron saint.

The days Picasso spent *en famille* with Penrose brought a significant change in their relationship: for the first time they began to *tutoie* each other. It had taken them fourteen years to move from the formal to the informal mode of address and the general tone of Penrose's subsequent letters to Picasso is much more relaxed and affectionate, as if at last he felt that it was unnecessary to be quite so respectful. His first letter after the momentous visit registers this shift, although he still addresses the artist by his surname – colleague to colleague, as it were. It is worth quoting in full, not because it contains any significant comments or news, but because it marks a new stage:

Dear Picasso

I ought to have sent you this receipt before, but anyway here it is.
We are still basking in marvellous memories of your visit but regret that it

was so short. Your exhibition here is a great success and there's always a crowd of people looking at it. Everyone who sees it admires the coloured drawing[s] you made in the Visitors' Book of the Institute of Contemporary Arts and in the Góngora.

Lee joins me in sending our warmest good wishes to Françoise and she sends you her very best love.

Yours very affectionately
Roland[56]

Picasso at Chiddingly signpost, East Sussex, November 1950. Photo Lee Miller

Roland Penrose and Picasso in Penrose's studio at Farley Farm, East Sussex, November 1950. Photo Lee Miller

For most English speakers the shift from 'vous' to 'tu' is a little worrying as well as pleasing. Should one ever make the first move? Should one respond instantly in kind, or wait to make sure there hasn't been some slip of the tongue? And so on. But for Penrose it had a special emotional resonance. In *Scrap Book* he fondly recalled the 'theeing' and 'thouing' of his Quaker aunts and great-aunts during family holidays in Peckover House when he was a child. He had missed it when he grew up, he says, but 'this loss of intimacy was restored for me by the second personal singular of the French language'.[57]

Meanwhile, in 1950, the London Gallery – a commercial failure since it had reopened in 1946 – closed down, thus bringing to an end Penrose's long partnership with Mesens. The two had not been on good terms for several years, largely because they took opposite sides in the ideological breach between Breton and Eluard – a breach which widened after Breton returned to Paris from America at the end of the war and became more vociferous in his denunciation of the Communist Party. Whereas Penrose remained, of course, utterly devoted to Eluard, Mesens took Breton's part – the only choice for a true Surrealist in his view.[58]

Another distinguished friend and visitor to Sussex was Alfred Barr, Director of the Museum of Modern Art in New York, here posing as the Long Man of Wilmington with Margaret Scolari Barr and their daughter Victoria, *c.* 1952. Photo Lee Miller

The demise of the London Gallery more or less coincided with the re-naissance of the ICA, which finally moved into its own premises in Dover Street, Mayfair, in the spring of 1950. The following autumn Picasso's seventieth birthday was celebrated with a 'homage'-style retrospective exhibition of his drawings and watercolours in the new gallery.[59] The show was organised by Penrose and many of the works were loaned by the artist himself. Perhaps they had discussed the show during Picasso's visit to England. No doubt they discussed it in mid-February 1951 when Penrose visited Picasso in Paris: Picasso commemorated their meeting with a decorative crayon drawing of a grinning, bearded head in Penrose's copy of Reverdy's *Le Chant des Morts*.[60] At any rate, there were many chances to mull over the selection with Picasso during the summer. Roland, Lee and Tony all spent a week in St Tropez in the middle of June and were present at Eluard's marriage to Dominique Laure on 15 June. (Nusch had died prematurely in 1946, having never fully recovered from the privations endured during the Occupation.) Picasso and Françoise were the witnesses and after the ceremony in the *mairie* Picasso invited them all to a 'sumptuous meal' in the town.[61] Lee commemorated the occasion in a sequence of photographs (see p. 70). From Penrose's diary we also know that he had a series of meetings with Picasso in Paris a few weeks later, when plans for the exhibition were presumably more or less finalised.[62] Back in Sussex, Penrose wrote to inform Picasso that everything was going well and to remind him to supply four recent drawings 'to complete the story to 1951'. The letter ends with the usual invitation to come to London to see the show and with a wry joke: 'if you're afraid of too much publicity' – clearly a reference to the dramatic events of the previous year – 'come disguised as your brother, who is so extraordinarily like you'.[63]

Picasso was evidently gratified by Penrose's efforts to make an exhibition which would throw light on the crucial role of drawing in his creative process.[64] This was something that also fascinated him, leading him to preserve and date meticulously all his drawings, however slight or scrappy in appearance. He not only lent generously, but even put pen to paper when sending Penrose a caricatural drawing of an English critic he had made in 1919 in London while working on the designs for *Le Tricorne* for Diaghilev's Ballets Russes:

My dear Roland
    I don't know if you know this Monsieur EVANS (a critic). I've just turned him up while moving house. Greetings to Lee and to you,
        Yours Picasso PARIS, 23 August 1951[65]

The exhibition opened on 11 October but the handsomely produced accompanying book, with an introduction by Penrose and the Visitors' Book watercolour reproduced on the cover, was timed to come out on the artist's actual birthday, 25 October.[66] There was, however, an embarrassing incident to cloud Penrose's pleasurable sense of achievement. One of the drawings turned out to be a fake, as Picasso immediately realised when he saw the reproduction in the catalogue. But since he believed that the faker was none other than Jean Cocteau, he refused to permit any discussion of the matter, let alone any legal action. The lender of the fake was Sybil Mesens and, given the tension between her husband and Penrose at this time, one has to wonder whether the duping of Penrose was not a malicious plot to humiliate him before Picasso and Picasso's friends. At all events, Picasso himself never seems to have held this lapse of connoisseurship against Penrose and their friendship suffered no ill effects.[67]

To make up for Picasso's non-attendance at the ICA exhibition, Eluard came to London and delivered a lecture entitled 'Aujourd'hui, Pablo Picasso, le plus jeune artiste du monde, a 70 ans' (Today, Picasso, the youngest artist in the world, is 70 years old). He and Dominique stayed for a week with the Penroses. All seemed set for a prolongation of the friendship that had united Penrose, Picasso and Eluard since 1936, but little more than a year later Eluard was dead, victim of an angina attack on 18 November 1952. Penrose was devastated. For the rest of his life he venerated Eluard's memory and

Paul Eluard and
Françoise Gilot on the
occasion of Eluard's
marriage to Dominique
Laure, St Tropez, June
1951. Photo Lee Miller

everything Eluard had written about Picasso became in his eyes uniquely perceptive. His acute sense of loss was accompanied by longing for the compensation of closer friendship with Picasso but also by feelings of inadequacy. The friendship between Picasso and Eluard had been a friendship based on a sense of sympathy and also of equality. But Penrose did not consider himself the equal of Picasso and in a spur-of-the-moment visit to Vallauris a month to the day after Eluard's death he was inhibited by an overwhelming sense of diffidence.[68] After procrastinating for weeks, on 4 February 1953 he eventually summoned up the courage to write to Picasso to try to explain why he had felt impelled to make the impromptu journey south. Characteristically, the letter stops short of describing his emotions and launches instead into a hymn of praise to Picasso:

My dear Picasso,

Since that luminous day in December I've often meant to write to you to tell you once again what a joy it was to see you and to thank you for the unforgettable welcome that you gave me – above all at the station in the middle of the night. And those great paintings were a revelation – a new world to which I return in my thoughts and thus find refreshment.

I wasn't able to explain to you why I wanted to see you so urgently at that moment. It was something very personal for which only you have the magic cure. It was Paul's death – and the worst of it is that I couldn't even say a word to you about it.

But seeing you did me so much good – that glimpse of your latest works and the atmosphere of sunshine in which Françoise's beauty presides over the landscape and everywhere else recharged me with vigour and courage.

Our immediate plan is to organise an evening in honour of Paul at our Institute on February 25th – he gave such a beautiful lecture there at the time of the exhibition of your drawings. We'll read his poems and talk about him and I hope we'll have recordings of him speaking. It's nothing much but I think we'll get a small crowd of his admirers.

At the moment I'm working hard on the exhibition 'Wonders and Horrors of the Human Head'.[69] Among the wonders I've been lucky enough to be able to borrow is your portrait of Nusch as 'The Woman of Arles'.[70] I'll send you the catalogue as soon as it's ready.

Lee and I send you and Françoise our warmest love.

Much love to you both from us both.

Roland.

I'm trying to fix my next journey to the Golfe for June – aside from anything else it will be a splendid way of escaping the craziness of the Coronation[71] – but above all I'm thinking that perhaps your chapel will be finished and we can make a joyful pilgrimage.[72]

The episode as a whole is an insight into Penrose's tendency to hero-worship. His devotion to Eluard was blended with veneration and his immediate reaction to the tragedy was to organise an *hommage* at the ICA, which sounds from his description as if it were modelled on a Quaker memorial 'meeting'. With Picasso the instinct to venerate was much more highly developed: Penrose could not love him or his work without worshipping him and it utterly. The death of Eluard also left a void in Picasso's life, but a void that could not be filled by someone who idealised him and hung on his every word. Probably Penrose could never have been that person, if only because he lived too far away. But one cannot help suspecting that this was an opportunity he missed to move his relationship with Picasso onto a rather more equal footing.

Visiting Paris, St Tropez and Vallauris, Summer 1953

The trip to the south of France to which Penrose alluded in the postscript to his letter took place as planned. One motive was to visit Vallauris and see Picasso's latest work; another was to stay in St Tropez with Eluard's widow Dominique so that Penrose could work on a translation of Eluard's last completed poem *Le Château des pauvres*.[73] The intention was to publish the translation in an edition with illustrations by Picasso, but in the end the project came to nothing.[74] It was during this holiday that Penrose started to keep rough but vividly evocative notes of the main events of the day, anticipating the practice he adopted systematically when, a year later, he started work on his biography of Picasso.

Before journeying south, Roland and Lee spent a few intensely active days in Paris, seeing their friends and visiting exhibitions. They made a point of going to the show of Picasso's recent work at the Galerie Leiris,[75] and were accompanied by their great friend Peggy (or Rosamond) Bernier, who with her husband Georges edited *L'Œil*, one of the best respected art journals of the period. In his notebook Penrose swiftly jotted down his reactions to the show:

[…] Can't understand why Herbert Read & other critics have found it disappointing. Although somewhat uneven, and much of best recent work sent to big show in Rome,[76] it included some wonderful landscapes of Vallauris by night (those [that] Paul Eluard spoke of with enthusiasm as being a new version never before attempted of the Midi landscape). Some very lovely doves in pottery and bronzes of owls and a stork made up of scrap material – screws and nails become bristling plumage. Bronze painted in black & white.[77] [1]

A couple of days later, on 19 June, the Penroses dined with the Berniers and Max and Dorothea Ernst and the conversation turned to the hopeless last-ditch efforts to save Julius and Ethel Rosenberg from execution as Soviet spies.[78] Like Picasso, who was a member of the French committee formed to defend the Rosenbergs,[79] Lee and Roland had protested and petitioned on the couple's behalf, and Roland's despair and outrage at the dénouement is expressed in his description of the party:

[…] The whole evening was under a cloud owing to the news on the radio that the last appeal for the Rosenbergs had failed. Paris is taking this case very much to heart. All parties are in agreement. The 'Figaro' has just published their Death House letters. All regard it as a shocking blunder on Eisenhower's part not to have called off the Death Sentence, which he could so easily have done when he came into power. It is now a triumph for McCarthy and all his forces of reaction and gives the Soviets new martyrs. It is reason and human rights that [are] again seriously in danger. It seems more & more clear that opinion of Europe is of no importance to U.S. […] [1]

As we shall see, the subject returned when Penrose saw Picasso a week later.

The holiday in St Tropez proved delightful in the way the holidays in Mougins before the war had been,[80] and Penrose was charmed by Dominique Eluard's flat despite what he describes as 'the continual yearn for Paul':

[…] Our stay at St. T. memorable for completely uneventful laze, except for visit to Picasso, and delightful company. Weather absurdly varied, about three days so perfect that nothing more in the way of sun, temperature & gentle breezes could be hoped for. Bathing good on the whole. Dominique's flat overlooking the fort with its fresh white walls, cool tiled floors, bathrooms and all in good taste was perfect place to stay except for the powerful memories of two years ago and the presence of Paul in every detail of all our thoughts. I work on my translation of 'Le Château des Pauvres' in his little study looking out over the pink roofs encircled by the shrieking swifts, dominated by the church tower, its crumbling plaster, its bells and white-faced clock. Spikes of insulators carrying wires in every direction to feed light into the agglomeration of old houses that hang together in an inseparable, friendly mass. Detachment from the gay holiday life of the fort was complete. [...] [1]

Penrose's notes include a brief description of the day spent in Vallauris with Picasso, his son Paulo and Jean Cocteau, where talk turned once again to the Rosenbergs and the Communist Party. Penrose remarked with interest Picasso's estrangement from his old comrade Aragon – an estrangement contingent on the scandal that had erupted within the Party over the publication of Picasso's posthumous portrait of Stalin in *Les Lettres françaises* in March 1953:[81]

Arriving at Golfe Juan, Lee, Diane and me, we found P. with Paulo at the station, who took us up to V[allauris] to see Françoise. We all met at the studios. [Edouard] Pignon & wife [Hélène Parmelin] joined the party and we returned to G[olfe] J[uan] for a sumptuous lunch at a beach restaurant. Lobsters, la rouille,[82] a Muscadet produced by Cocteau and a procession of good things to eat & drink.

We continued to talk, eat and drink round the table and later at Juan-les-Pins until about 7.30. Main topics were painting and Cocteau's anger at a misrepresentation by Aragon in 'Les Lettres françaises' of his sympathy for the Rosenbergs, who had just be[en] executed. He feared that this would bar America to him for visits and sales. Picasso sympathised and showed no liking for A. There seems to be an increasing split among C.P. intellectuals, A. attempting to be more orthodox than Moscow.

P. then took us to a hotel where we were to spend the night and then back to dinner at V., Cocteau having left us. The evening was spent in talk, singing of innumerable French songs in which Diane & Paulo excel, and Paulo's girlfriend added a large repertoire of music hall & apache songs. P[icasso] had recently bought a piano mécanique from a local brothel. It played with frantic vigour and we danced to it until the children went to sleep. [1]

The Diane mentioned here is Diane Deriaz. Having heard about her colourful life as a trapeze artist from Eluard, who might have married her after Nusch's death had the PCF not regarded her as a politically suspect and wholly unsuitable spouse,[83] Penrose was primed to fall under her sway himself. The free-and-easy beach life of St Tropez and the dining and dancing in

the evenings enhanced Diane's natural charisma and in his notebook he
charted his growing enchantment, although at this point he seems to have
had no premonition of the strength of her impact on his life:

[…] The looks of our six girls on the beach did a lot of good to Man and
myself. His humour, which was brittle and quarrelsome as we left Paris,
changed so completely that we were all delighted, he was as youthful and
happy as in our prewar days. The girls were wonderfully relaxed, their bare
breasts in the sun were an intoxication. Diane's fair hair, strength and grace,
joined with the extraordinary tough circus life and intuition of a poet, give
her a unique charm. Fortunately Lee liked her too and was very tolerant of
my infatuation, the long walks we went together and wild dancing at [the]
Palmyre.[84] The fact that both of us had such a great love for Paul formed an
immediate link. [1]

On 30 June the idyll came to an end and the notes describing the rest of
the trip are correspondingly much more matter-of-fact. On the way back to

Paris the Penroses stopped in Lyons to see the Picasso exhibition in the Musée des Beaux-Arts to which they had lent a number of works,[85] and once in Paris Roland called on Louise Leiris 'and discussed Picasso, exhibition & prices'. On 5 July, after yet more museum visits and socialising, the Penroses returned to Sussex. From there Roland sent Picasso a postcard describing his impressions of the exhibition in Lyons. His trenchant criticisms of the selection and the catalogue are those of the experienced curator and suggest that he nursed ambitions to put on a Picasso retrospective himself – something altogether larger and grander than the show of drawings he had organised at the ICA in 1951:

Pablo Picasso, Paulo Picasso, Diane Deriaz, Lee Miller, Françoise Gilot and Edouard Pignon, Golfe Juan, summer 1953. Photo Roland Penrose

Dear Picasso,

We have come home to rain but with very good memories of our visit to Vallauris. We stopped in Lyons and spent several hours in the exhibition, which is splendid and full of things from all periods that I didn't know. The one thing missing, I felt, was large paintings – still lifes from 1925–30, big canvases of around 1935, 'Night fishing at Antibes',[86] etc., etc. It didn't need many, but two or three would have given more variety in size. The catalogue had various errors and omissions but they promise me they will be corrected. Despite these small blemishes, the impression of the ensemble is overwhelming and the recent canvases show such vigour that the end of the gallery is filled with light and colour. Lee joins me in sending our very best wishes.

Yours affectionately Roland
Send our love to the beautiful Françoise and to your children.[87]

If Penrose realised that Picasso's relationship with Gilot was in its death throes that summer, he gave no sign of it. Perhaps this was simply discretion – tactfully pretending not to notice the domestic dramas of his friends. At all events, he must have heard about Françoise's brusque return to Paris in September, since gossip about the collapse of her liaison with Picasso was rife at the time. In a curious parallel, Penrose's own marriage was running into serious trouble at exactly the same moment, as his infatuation with Diane Deriaz developed into a more urgent and profound feeling. Initially, Lee, who for reasons of her own condoned and even encouraged Roland's passing infidelities, smiled on this new affair, but as it became plain that her prime position in his life was under threat, so her tolerance gave way to anger and unhappiness.[88] The change seems to have crystallized that Christmas when a large house party that included Valentine, Dominique Eluard and Diane foregathered at Farley Farm. According to Tony Penrose, the whole occasion was 'fraught' – something of an understatement given his description of the hysterical scenes that ensued.[89] Indeed, had Diane shown any inclination to sacrifice her treasured independence or to break up the family at Farley Farm, the marriage between Roland and Lee might well have ended the following year. As it was, Diane refused Roland's offers of marriage, although she continued to meet him in Paris. Did Picasso have any inkling of these dramas? Maybe. Certainly, none of Penrose's letters to him at this or any other time gave the slightest hint of his secret dilemmas. Instead, he continued to pass on Lee's affectionate messages and her news, just as if their marriage were as stable as a rock. English reserve worked with Quaker reticence against self-revelation or attempts to breach the privacy of others.

In Vallauris with Georges Braque, June 1954

Accompanied by Lee, Roland paid his next visit to Vallauris in February 1954, no doubt in order to see the newly installed *War and Peace* murals

Picasso had painted for the deconsecrated medieval chapel in the town square.[90] They found Picasso 'lonely, profoundly troubled but living in the same banal little villa where before we had known him surrounded and animated by a youthful family which included the amiable Paulo, and his bullfighter friends from Spain. A blight had fallen on the place.'[91] And in the draft of a text found among his papers he evoked the dreariness of La Galloise and the desolation of the Midi landscape during that bleak winter visit:

Vallauris visit Feb. 1954
The snow was just clearing from the vineyards, leaving pools of icy water against which the twisted unpruned vine stems protruded from solid black stumps, standing like figures with their heads in the mud and their limbs sticking up into the air, or transformed by their reflection so that they appeared to be black stars poised in a patch of brilliant blue sky, which was now appearing as the ice-cold morning mist dragged itself out of the pine-covered valleys. As usual the iron gate was locked and the wire fencing looked discouraging enough to send the unknowing visitor back on his tracks. But to friends it was recognisable as a first line of defence, easily penetrable by going round to a side gate. The steep path leads straight up between terraces of vines and peaches. The reservoir on a level with the house, in summer teeming [with] green croaking frogs and fiercely beautiful dragonflies, was now dead and half frozen. The bare branches of the two mulberry trees fail to screen the childish geometry of the formal gable front of the stucco villa. No detail suggests any exception from the common run of thousands of unimaginative little houses which grew up all over the Côte d'Azur in the first decades of this century. [...][92] [3]

In fact, Picasso's 'loneliness' was short-lived: Jacqueline Roque was poised to take up the position left vacant by Françoise.[93] But perhaps the Penroses were unaware of this development.

When they next visited Vallauris in June 1954, Picasso's mood was very different and an air of bonhomie reigned at La Galloise. This time Tony and Patsy Murray, their housekeeper, accompanied them and there was a series of relaxed and enjoyable meetings.[94] Thus on 4 June they went to see the *War and Peace* murals again and had lunch with Picasso and Totote Hugué, widow of the Catalan sculptor Manolo, and her adopted daughter Rosita. To judge by the clothes both Picasso and Tony were wearing, it was on that same day that Lee photographed her son and his favourite playmate standing beside the outlandish sculpture nicknamed *The Madame*,[95] which Picasso had constructed entirely from fireclay elements used in potters' kilns and then equipped with a real key (see p. 78). The sculpture had only just been cast in bronze and, to amuse Tony, Picasso thrust a pottery dish on the woman's head to suggest a curly wig. On a later visit Picasso embellished Penrose's copy of Eluard's *Picasso Dessins* with two drawings, thus continuing the tradition established in such spectacular fashion when he visited London in 1950.[96]

But the most memorable meeting took place on 22 June. The Penroses arrived at the disused scent factory in rue du Fournas where Picasso had set up sculpture studios and storage for his thousands of ceramics, to find Georges Braque and his wife Marcelle. Picasso was in a particularly cheerful mood and there was much teasing and banter. Tony's presence encouraged this playfulness: Picasso was relishing the role of libertarian 'uncle'.

On our return to the scent factory Picasso brought out large sculptures he was working on. Shards and pot-handles put together by him became a baby in a push-cart [*see pp. 80–81*].[97] Playing with all manner of solutions, each position he tried brought a surprise, sometimes so outrageous that only a polite grin came from Braque, but even so that communication between the two inventors of cubism who had understood each other so thoroughly some half century before was still present. The mystery of the meaning of form, the uncertainty of our interpretations and the metamorphoses that take place were forever of vital importance to them both, but for Braque it seemed that the refinement of form in the ceramic doves that Picasso showed him was of greater importance than his friend's more outrageous and sometimes bawdy jokes. In Pablo there was more vitality whereas in Braque there was a sensation of the great wise old man now beyond frivolity.[98]

Alive to the historic nature of this reunion, Lee took shot after shot, perfectly capturing this distinction in the two artists' characters. Picasso beams with pleasure, radiating a benevolence quite different from the transfixing, daunting intensity of his gaze in many of her other photographs; Braque

smiles indulgently, while holding himself slightly aloof from all the antics, but, irresistibly attracted by the naturalism of the doves, reaches out to caress their pottery feathers. On this occasion, Lee's photographs tell us much more than Roland's very scanty notes:

Picasso and Georges Braque, Vallauris, June 1954. Photo Lee Miller

Picasso–Braque June 1954
P. showing portraits of girl with horsetail,[99] realist nude, etc., 'I do those to start with [and] after I do what I want with it.'

Showing unfinished assembly of pot handles, broken pieces of jars amidst general laughter, 'Yes, one must laugh, but it is not in mockery, it is in sympathy.' [7]

From London, Penrose wrote to Picasso on 5 July to report on the end of their French holiday. In Paris he had been 'several times to gorge myself on

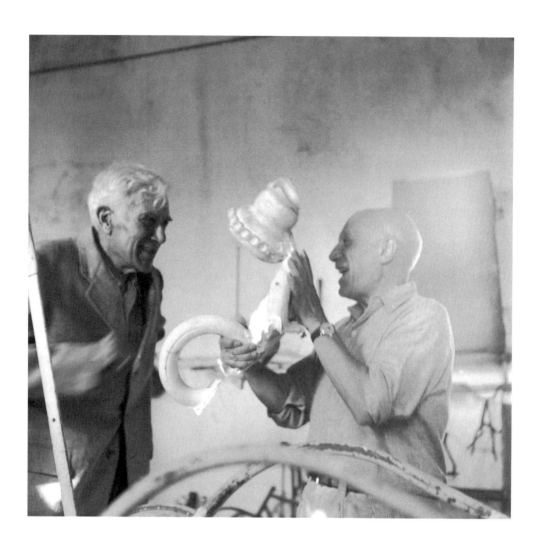

your exhibition at the Maison de la Pensée'. 'I was astonished,' he said, 'by the brilliant colours of those canvases that I had only known in black and white. They're in excellent condition too and look deliciously fresh. It was really extremely moving to see them: I do so much hope that it will be possible to show them here in London.'[100] The exhibition in question was such a revelation because it included thirty-seven canvases loaned by the Hermitage and Pushkin museums, and for Penrose and most other visitors represented a unique opportunity to see paintings which had been more or less inaccessible in the Soviet Union since the outbreak of the First World War.[101] As it turned out, Penrose was very lucky indeed to catch the exhibition at all: Irina Shchukin, daughter of the great Russian collector Sergei Shchukin, had stated her right to retrieve the pictures, which had been requisitioned at the time of the Revolution. In panic, the Soviet Embassy closed the show down suddenly – a move neither Picasso himself nor the Communist-run Maison de la Pensée Française were in a position to oppose, much as they might lament it.[102] The press buzzed with news of these events and Penrose followed the story with the keenest interest, for he had been busy negotiating with the Arts Council to bring the Russian pictures to London – to no avail, however, for within a few weeks the Soviet authorities had shipped the pictures back to Russia, out of reach of Madame Shchukin and her lawyers. It was frustrating to be thwarted in this way, but Penrose's disappointment quickly faded when another entirely different project was suddenly presented to him.

Picasso with his assemblage-sculpture *Woman with a Pushchair,* and (opposite) with Georges Braque, Vallauris, June 1954. Photos Lee Miller

Chapter 3

Into the Vast Territories: The Novice Biographer, 1954–1955

A publishing offer accepted

Towards the end of July 1954 Lee set off for America to see her parents in Poughkeepsie, New York State. It was their fiftieth wedding anniversary but, with cruel irony, her mother was diagnosed with cancer and Lee passed much of her time by the sickbed. Roland remained in England with Tony. At some point just after Lee's departure, Victor Gollancz made his life-changing offer. Exactly when this happened is unclear but it may have been on 30 July 1954 during Penrose's lunch engagement with Hilary Rubinstein, Gollancz's nephew and a recent recruit into the family firm, for most of the correspondence about the book came through him.[1] Rubinstein remembers meeting Penrose for the first time in 1953 at a party held at the ICA to launch Alain Gheerbrant's *The Impossible Adventure*, and it was apparently Gheerbrant who suggested Penrose as a suitable author for the Picasso biography.[2] In his memoirs Penrose claims that the commission came as a complete shock and that it was only much later that he learned of Gheerbrant's role.[3]

With Lee absent in America, Penrose turned to Alfred Barr for advice. Barr's opinion mattered so much to him because his *Picasso: Fifty Years of his Art* was by far the best English-language survey available.[4] Penrose's letter reveals his sense of the frightening enormity of the task, but also how strongly tempted he was by Gollancz's proposal:

There is a problem on which I would very much like a word of advice from you. I have been asked by a big London publisher to write a 100,000 word life of Picasso, illustrated. The idea seems to me absurd unless I can spend some five years with that as my major preoccupation, and even then there are so many books on Picasso already published and so many more in preparation – who can say how many? – that I'm surprised that the publisher wants another. Also I have not much confidence in my own ability as a literary genius. Never have I fancied myself as an author & particularly not on such a scale. If you with your immense ability and experience could give me an idea as to whether or not you think it worthwhile – I mean, if there would be any interest in such a book or if it would be submerged in an ocean of much more competent works. It would mean, should I accept, cutting down on the time

I spend working for the ICA, which is a serious matter but a choice that *I* shall have to make. Maybe if Lee can get away from her mother's sickbed she could meet you in N.Y. and you could have a talk with her about it. Naturally her cooperation would be essential in every way and so far I think she is doubtful about it herself, but the idea only cropped up after she had left and we only discussed it by letter.[5]

As the days passed and no reply came from Barr, Penrose grew impatient. Perhaps Hilary Rubinstein was putting him under pressure to give an answer – they met again on 1 September in London.[6] The death of Penrose's mother-in-law on 11 September put paid to any hope that Lee would return home soon and, unable to settle to anything while the great question remained unresolved, Roland decided to visit Picasso in Perpignan, where he was staying with the art-loving Comte and Comtesse de Lazerme in their grand country mansion. Picasso had met the de Lazermes the previous year through Totote Hugué, and was so obviously fascinated by Paule de Lazerme's girlish charm that there was even talk of an affair. At all events he took up their offer to spend the whole of the summer of 1954 with them and set up a studio in their house. A powerful incentive was the proximity to the border: Picasso always said that being in Perpignan was like being in Spain and he loved the casual contact with his compatriots.[7] A frequent visitor was Jacqueline Roque, a young divorcee with a daughter called Catherine. Picasso had met her at the Madoura factory in 1952 and it was clear to everyone that she was intent on replacing Françoise Gilot as Picasso's acknowledged mistress.[8]

The story of what happened during Penrose's visit to Perpignan is told in blow-by-blow detail in the notes he wrote up rapidly in his spare moments in this, his first true 'Picasso notebook'. And one learns a great deal from it: about Penrose's eagerness to write the biography (the euphoria following Picasso's go-ahead made him eager to record as much as he possibly could, for all was potentially grist to the mill); about Picasso's nostalgia for Spain and dreams of a 'Temple of Peace' to rival Matisse's Chapel at Vence; above all, about the seigneurial manner in which Picasso conducted his life while a guest of the de Lazermes, surrounded by a harem of women, by his children, by friends and hangers-on, all of whom watched and waited for him to take the lead, just as if he were the sun and they the orbiting planets. Fascinated by the spectacle, relishing the intrigues and content to be a minor planet, Penrose makes the perfect observer – a Samuel Pepys at the court of King Pablo:

Thurs. 16 Sept. '54, Perpignan
By chance the hotel the taxi-driver recommended was 100 yds from the rue de l'Ange, the address Françoise [Gilot] had given me. No. 16 was [a] large house with courtyard and wide staircases. After a discreet wait until past 11.0, penetrated to upper floor and found first, to my delight, Totote (Mme.

Manolo). P. was there but not up. Every morning they [went] to Collioure where the children were staying with a girl who looked after them. P. arrived looking well, sunburnt and beaming friendship. He took me round the solemn bourgeois drawing rooms where sunlight falling through chinks in the shutters on immaculate polished floors lit up family portraits, swords, cockades. All that amused us greatly. It was very remote from any Communist atmosphere but P. was equally, perhaps slightly more, at home

Claude and Paloma Picasso, Vallauris, summer 1953. Photo Lee Miller than when I have seen him surrounded by comrades. Jacques de L[azerme] arrived. Very warm welcome, said he knew my painting, produced Eluard book with reproduction.[9]

We then left for C[ollioure], the Manolo ladies, our hostess Paule, P. and self with Jacqueline [Roque] driving. C. is a little fortified fishing village near the S[panish] frontier. In the centre is a fortress, part of which was built by the Templars. P. pointed out the chapel of which he had been given the key in the hope that he would decide to use it as a studio. The idea amused him greatly but there was little likelihood of it being realised. Claude & Paloma looked wonderfully brown and healthy on the beach. We played with them and bathed. As we were leaving the beach I told P. that I wanted to write a book about him. His reaction was more encouraging than I had dared to hope. He seized me with both hands and his black eyes looked deep into me as he said, 'C'est vrai? C'est bien.'[10] I told him I had had an offer from a publisher, that I had considered all the obstacles – own inability, heavy competition, vastness of subject, etc. He said – hit by some doubt – 'but is this an idea you have just had now or have you already written something?' I told him the idea had always been there and that I had written prefaces and lectures but that it now took on new and greater proportions. It might take me five years to do, which surprised him, so I said, 'Well, maybe three.' He told me D[ouglas] Cooper was writing something about portraits by him, which I agreed was a good idea. In a field so vast it is better to pick some aspect and treat it thoroughly than get lost in generalisations. But there does not appear to be a book in English of the type I was proposing and so far as P. knew none in preparation. I told him I would have to come to France to write it and see as much as I could of him without getting in his way. In general I think he likes the idea and certainly has nothing against it. [*Inserted addition*] He said, 'Even if there are other books each person has his own views, sees the question differently and that's what makes a book worthwhile.'[11] [*Main text continues*] At lunch I asked him about Aragon's preface to the present Paris show of the portraits of Sylvette [David] in which [he] makes a bloomer by describing a picture which is obviously a portrait of J. not S., as S. in a grown-up mood. He laughed and said, 'What do you think? Don't you think A. did it on purpose?'[12]

(Incident with Belgian painter.) We left for Perp. and the de Ls. asked me to dinner – I had already become part of the family and wandered in and out as I liked. After dinner J. proposed a visit to the big café on the Place where they dance the Sardana. We all went and sat just under the orchestra getting drunk with the noise but not the Eau de Boulon. As we left P. and J. started to dance [the] Sardana in the entrance, in which we all joined. P. was as light on his feet as the best of them. All were delighted to see him in such good humour. He insisted on going on to another more distinguished café w[h]ere we had a last tilleul and discussed the Maillol bronze, which although without a good background, dominates the Place.

[Scored lightly through in pencil] *Fenosa 28 S[eptember] '54*
P. talks of God with Cocteau. C. is silent in presence of such spontaneous wit. 'God creates things – he takes some earth, rolls it in his hands – it is a turnip. He adds a tail – it is a fish. He adds wings – it is a swallow.'

Derain to Picasso – 'The higher he goes the more mistakes he makes – and this applies to everyone.'

P. has over 100 of Fenosa's bronzes.[13]

Collioure
A young Belgian painter ask[ed] P. to look at 2 paintings of his at café. Paintings show very little talent and strong influences of Chagall, Surrealism. P. embarrassed. Points out influences, says they are weak. Then after pause – 'But what does it matter what I say? The essential thing in all this is inside you, it's for you to decide and make your choice.' Kindly but firmly said goodbye & left.

Picasso's father used collage. Painted pigeons, etc. on cut-out piece of canvas, which he pinned onto picture in various positions to help [him] compose.

Showed him Rousseau 'Marianne'. Said, 'I wouldn't buy it for myself. That's the test I always give to see if a picture is authentic.' I pointed out that background was better painted than figure. 'That's just the part that's so much easier.'

Study of hens painted on small wooden panel at age of 11 (col[lection] Jacques de Lazerme). […]

2nd day, Friday 17 Sept. '54
The day started at 11.0. Called at the palatial and ancient house of the de Lazermes. Met by Totote there alone, all others not yet up or out. (Had long conversation about Barcelona with her.) The latest news. Paulo, Françoise and Pierre [Baudouin] had arrived during the night from Paris [in] Vallauris. F. had come to fetch the children back to Paris for school. This likely to cause some tension as children, devoted to both parents, had spent 6 weeks on a beach nearby P. while F. [was] in Paris, and were now to change parent. Then they begin to arrive, Françoise with the two [Muñoz] boys telling their story of breakdowns on road and sleepless night, Picasso and Jacqueline. Picasso in red shirt, fresh and vigorous. After much light talk we all take off in two cars for the beach, Collioure, to find the children. Jacqueline is discreetly out of sight when P. & F. appear on the beach and Claude comes racing across the pebbles with Paloma near behind. All bathe. Anyone looking for awkward situation or jealous looks throughout the day could not have found one. But to judge from glances and gestures P. is still in love with F. but also very happy with the more placid J. F. and J. each have roughly what they want and show no signs of anything but close friendship. In the middle of a sumptuous lunch at the little hotel café restaurant in the

main street, where they have been lunching every day, arrive the Muñoz brothers and their sister, whom they had just collected at the S[panish] frontier. They are Republicans & cannot go to Franco S[pain]. Their sister was arriving for the christening of first son at Arles to coincide with big Corrida. They are the impresarios who arranged the great 2-day Corrida at Vallauris in which P. was the leading spirit and made posters, led orchestra and presided over the fight. When F., mounted on a fine horse and looking most impressive, entered the ring to ask for the keys, it was to P. that all the high stepping & bowing was addressed and it was F. who received from him the 'key' of the arena and the accolade.[14] The two days of feasting were a family affair. Although the ring held 3000 and was full it never lost its intimate character of an improvised Baccanale.

The Muñoz had now stopped in to persuade P. to come to the christening and stay the next day for the bullfight. They were unfortunate because P. had just decided to go with all present company to [the] fight at Céret and at first refused flatly, but the Muñoz could be very persuasive and sat down to show photos of the Vallauris Corrida and talk at great length of their plans for this next feast, also bring[ing] in their ideas for a greater and more lively Vallauris C[orrida] next summer. The afternoon passed without anyone knowing what was to happen next. The small cafés and narrow streets of C[ollioure] added to the mystery, as at every moment one or more of the party would have disappeared on some errand.

Everyone was waiting but without the least impatience for a decision to come from P. So finally the children's luggage was collected from their hotel and decision to move was evidently in the air. However instead of moving back to Perpignan (it was now about 6 o'clock) we set off in the other direction. I was in Jacqueline's car. In front were J. & F. and children, behind Paule de Lazerme, P. & self. At the edge of Col[lioure] J. suggested that we should stop at the espadrille shop and buy a pair for F. The whole procession drew up in front of the little shop. 3 cars, the last being an enormous old Delage owned by the bullfighters. The sandals were bought, including a pair for Lee, and all paid for, in spite of protests, by P. Outside the usual small crowd of holiday makers were pointing and whispering, 'Picasso!' The party continued to Banyuls. P. very enthusiastic about the landscape and comparing it very favourably with Golfe Juan, which is vulgar, pretty and overrun in comparison. Here there is a treeless austerity. The mountains are a subtle green grey. The beaches are grey and the sea has been of a blue in the mornings which outdoes the other coast. The mountains and lower hills are topped by castles and watchtowers which have very precise shapes, like small sculptures well set against the sky. One overlooking both Port Vendres & Collioure is for sale and P. has said more than once looking up at it, 'I could buy that and move there tomorrow.' But we are not going to look for castles at Banyuls. It is the newish hotel that dominates the scene to which we mount. At once, well received by the host, the party straggle onto the terrace overlooking the little town with its pebble beach and fishing boats. The evening light is very lovely, subtle greys and greens dominate and the architect[ure] of the town below is unmistakably cubist. Spain is only 20 kms. and the atmosphere is already completely Spanish. P. makes frequent reference to it, his nostalgia is unmistakable. P. examines the rooms of the hotel with an eye to a future visit. His impression is favourable and as it is getting dark the party splits up again into its various cars and returns to Collioure. Here indecision still reigns – but the children must be fed. P. wanders around talking with one or other, male or female, friend or stranger indiscriminately. The Muñoz watch every chance of pushing their plea for tomorrow. P. sunburnt with his fringe of white hair round the back of his head, his never tiring black eyes, his red shirt, is always the centre of everyone's thoughts, especially as everyone else's movements depend on his and no one, not even he, knows what it will be. As the children finish eating a move is made to the cars. The Muñoz say goodbye, still uncertain if they have won and with the odds slightly against them. We return to Perpignan and after a last tilleul with Toto[te] & Rosita at a café, P. reappears in Jac.'s car with P[aule], having finally bedded down F. & children, and left Paulo and Pierre to go out on the town.

Sat. [18 September]
The day passed without much interest. Lunch again at Collioure with the same company less the Muñoz. Slight peevishness on part of Jacqueline when she had to leave us to fetch her daughter from Font Romeu and had to leave P. with F. & children. Rosita & her mother went with her. The rest of us returned via Argelès. We stopped to look at one of the farms belonging to our host where they were making wine, a simple unpretentious piece of real countryside. P. with burst of enthusiasm was saying that that was w[h]ere he would like to live and work, undisturbed, far from the town. Returned [to] Perpignan and with F. & hostess visited remote parts of the big family house full of relics of Don Carlos, who stayed there, and fascinating prints and bibelots. P. had been given very nice rooms and studio. But production had been small and frequently interrupted. There was a gouache portrait of Paule unfinished, about which P. was very shy. He wanted to hide it or destroy it but met with protests from F. and self. It was a beautiful portrait with a delicacy in treatment of features and a cold diffused light but without the finality one usually expects from P.[15] He showed us [a] drawing for a proposed temple of peace to be built on top of a mountain overlooking Spain and the sea. Sketches had not gone far but showed general idea of heavy irregular marble columns holding a heavy flat roof on which would stand a large dove-like creature. Showed some studies of dove-woman figures to fit in somewhere. Idea was still nebulous but an ambition which is close to his heart. He has never yet had a serious architectural project. He would like to make a non-Christian temple and is always talking of the mystery of the Matisse chapel,[16] the Braque windows at Varengeville,[17] etc. 'L'art religieux' is to him an absurdity, as he says how can you make

a religious art one day and another kind of art the next? Then the site of this temple pleases him greatly, on top of a mountain with marble quarries nearby and a great view [of] two countries and the sea. The temple will be seen from miles away in Spain. We talked about this again later in the evening, his enthusiasm not lacking – who knows?

Meeting Paulo & Pierre in the street, they took me on a tour of two brothels they had discovered. One particularly, in a very narrow street, was the classical small family brothel. Waiting room which was also kitchen. Three girls, all pretty and respectable to all appearances. Old white-haired dame and helper cooking supper in background. As we left Paulo was speculating on getting his father there one evening – not inconceivable and probably a great success. On return to house – all still awaiting return of J. & R. from Font Romeu. Hostess has two 'livres d'or', very good paper and good simple bindings, one for a picture, other for a nice complimentary poem or what you like. Both have pieces by Picasso. The drawing is particularly lovely – winged bulls in a tree (the only other drawing of this subject, he says, is the one in the ICA 'livre d'or'). P. was very insistent that F., Pierre and I should add our contributions, which we did. This pleased him immensely. He kept looking over shoulders, apologising for doing so, joking and making charming and amusing compliments when finished. J. & R. returned very tired, particularly J. who was still a bit sulky. Her daughter, about Claude's age, started at once in wild games with C. & Paloma while we dined. During dinner their shouts became so wild from the other room that T. went to the rescue – they had finished nearly all the chocolates and drunk a lot of muscatel; as it was by then past 10.30 they were taken off to bed.

P. brought out the copy of Reverdy's 'Chants des Morts' decorated by him that he had just given to host & hostess.[18] We went through it on the floor, page by page, reading most of the poems. 'Ca, quand même vous rends plus heureux et vous fait plus de bien que de lire les journaux,'[19] said P. and went on to praise the powers of poetry. He said also that Eluard had greatly admired this book, which he himself liked better than any other of his illustrated books, but it had not sold well. The public were not satisfied, they felt cheated because there were no faces or human forms, but what else could you do with a poem of such high philosophic tone? He had meant the decorations as an accompaniment, like a musical theme. P. then produced proofs of the forthcoming number of 'Verve', which we looked at and discussed at length on the dining room table. Many of them in coloured chalk had originated in drawings for the children in Paris. Knights in armour, clowns, horses, painters & models, etc.[20] He always asking and always interested in our reactions, so much so that one began to feel a participation in their creation – remote but real. Paule's last words were, 'Come early tomorrow because we must lunch at 12.30 before starting for the Corrida.'

Well, the Corrida – it was like this. The weather was impeccable. The walk I went to the Citadel to see the Palace of the Kings of Majorca and to think over all that was happening was the perfect Sunday morning walk in a strange Mediterranean town. I enjoyed the severe outlines and the arches that jump higher into the air than you would ever expect. It all had a very appetising visual smell of Spain, reminding me of Manzanilla and green olives. The great plain with the Pyrenees at its end was powdered with heat and very Spanish in its contrast, new white buildings, very green fruit trees and vines and bare treeless mountains in silhouette. I arrived at the de

Roland Penrose, Paulo Picasso, Pablo Picasso and others at Restaurant Le Vallauris, Vallauris, *c.* 1954. Photo Lee Miller

Lazerme house on time to find lunch still in preparation and some tension showing in the faces of R. & J., who were helping arrange the flowers. Some guests arrived, F. & children, Picasso and all the others. J. de L. appeared look[ing] ill and telling us all about it. The famous Paella lunch began, very well cooked by Spanish painter friend, but no great animation. Bursts of conversation, sudden animation [from] P. who told a couple of funny stories – one about an old lady who at the fête at Corunna swallow[ed] a rocket as it came down. Lunch finished rather abruptly to leave time to get to Céret for the Corrida. At the arena we arrived just in time and packed into the two front rows – three children and all. The Corrida was not a good one – so they said – but the 6 bulls were bursting with brutish life until they were dead and the Matadors were handsome, agile, and with one exception very brave. I was just behind P., next to him was Claude, who started yawning after the 3rd bull and took it all with complete indifference, then J. and her daughter and F. & Paloma. It seemed to have no effect on the children. The blood streamed down and all I heard was from Claude, 'Il a le garet tout rouge.'[21] P. was very attentive and critical. Fortunately I had R. beside me, who could tell me what was wrong with the fight and the only person that P. had any remarks for was her – always in Spanish, technical and with humour noir. There was a young undersized Matador with gipsy blood who[m] I thought tremendously brave – he did passes on his knees and turned his back when he shouldn't. But R. & P. were absolutely in agreement that he was a 'Burro'[22] playing [to] the gallery and a bad joke. There was a fat Picador that they knew and who shook hands across the barrier. He wasn't too good but he was Spanish and a friend – we never saw him again. P. was Spanish, just like an Englishman at a cup tie, but with no cheering – he never applauded but it wasn't a good Corrida for them. Afterwards I said I had enjoyed it – I was no judge and he replied, 'Oui c'est comme les tableaux, il n'y a pas de bons tableaux, il y a seulement ce qui vous disent quelque chose.'[23]

We returned to Perp. in various cars, very thirsty in spite of a quick drink of Perrier at the café, and arriving back in the rue de l'Ange the atmosphere began to thicken into wisps of drama and indecision. Françoise was due to leave shortly with the children on the night train for Paris. Paulo was in his most efficient mood, all ready to load up for the station about an hour too soon. I then realised, as we stood talking with Jacques de L. in the cobbled courtyard of his home, that J. had decided to leave too – by car with daughter for Cagnes. Why – no one knew. So we stood around as it grew dark, F. and children with R., who has been everybody's personal friend all the time, packed into the Hispano, causing [a] traffic jam in the limited space of the rue de l'Ange, and with P. we waved goodbye as Paulo drove them off. This made a considerable vacuum but Jacques & Paule were even more distressed at the thought that soon J. would be gone too and a very lonely and sad P. left for them to cheer. J.'s car was parked some thirty yards down the narrow street and P. went with her to it. The rest of us stood

talking about the first thing that came into our heads, thinking he would
return. He was only too visible in front of a lighted shop but his conversation
was endless and we moved upstairs – and here we come to an end because
my train was due to leave and Jacques had promised to take me to the
station. As we came out in his car, P. broke off to say an affectionate goodbye
and I kissed a wet and quivering cheek of J. at her steering wheel.

Sequel from Pierre Baudouin
J. left soon after I had gone. With Jacques back from the station, those left
behind went upstairs with a certain feeling of relief that P. was now free of
drama and could get on with his work. But only a[n] hour or two passed
before knocking on the door announced the unexpected arrival of a girl
P. had known at Vichy with her husband. In the next few days they were
with some difficulty kept out. The big carriage doors had to be kept locked
as she was so insistent. Also next morning a phone call from J. announced
that she had only gone 50 kms. and was staying with friends. She was told
to stay on if she liked and wait for a phone call. The call came 3 days later
and she returned. [4]

Penrose arrived home on 22 September and it may have been that
October that he saw Luciano Emmer's film about Picasso for the first time.[24]
His notes, split between two different files, reveal that, although he was captivated by the scenes of Picasso at work, he disapproved of the simplistic
Communist interpretation of the paintings provided in the voice-over commentary by the Italian painter and prominent Party member Renato
Guttuso. Although he never criticised Picasso for his politics, Penrose was
always sceptical about Marxist interpretations of his work and took the view
that Picasso was essentially apolitical – in no sense a doctrinaire Party man
in the manner of, say, Aragon:

Emmer
P. is a mixture of the dove and the owl – his great tragedy is to be exiled
from Spain – Franco would do anything to get him back – 'Ma Jolie' was
a dedication to his girl (Eva?).[25]
Social realist angle of film – Guttuso commentary.
Frequent returns to 'Reason'.
The gypsy murder, 1934, brought in to justify realism. [7]

Emmer film
Two beautiful sequences of P. drawing early in film – a landscape of
Vallauris in charcoal, cubist construction of composition. Determined line.
Later – drawing of mythical creatures on wall of chapel – sensation that
they existed there before. Variation of 'War & Peace'. Girls dancing together
oblivious of menacing bird-man who wishes to capture them. Bird monster
defeated. Chronological sequence of work in remarkably successful colour

(taken all from originals at Milan show except 'Demoiselles d'Avignon').[26]
Commentary (Guttuso & [*left blank*]) tendentious.[27] Social realism lurks
in background & at every moment we return to a[n] easily understood
representation – the gipsy murder 1935? etc. to excuse.

Extravagance of other work.

Cubist period slighted and no mention of its place in later work
('Guernica', etc.).

Continual use of such phrases as 'but he was soon to return to reason'
or something like this wording.

Sequence of making figure & modelling of dove in Vallauris studio very
good but too solemn – this true of whole film – never a touch of humour
of any sort.

Great emphasis on the family and love of children, the dove & the
madonna (non-Christian).

Tendency to excuse the extravagances of P. and to explain them as
temporary experiments, dangerous adventures.

French commentary by Claude Roy not much better but some of the more
blatant 'excuses' left out.

Mutilation of pictures to fit cinema screen. [8]

**Within a week or so of Penrose's return to England, Alfred Barr's reply
to his request for advice arrived – too late, of course, to affect his decision.
It is a candid and shrewd assessment of the central problem faced by anyone who writes about a living person, especially when that person is
a friend. 'Of course, I'd be very much interested in reading whatever you
have to write about Picasso. I hope you will go ahead and soon, so that I can
plagiarize,' joked Barr, before getting to the point:**

My only misgivings about your book have to do with your possibly uncritical admiration for Picasso. As his devoted friend, you may find it difficult to
write critically of him, even should you feel certain doubts. My only major
questions about Picasso concern what I feel to be his own highly uncritical
attitude towards his own work which permits him to send out into the world
a good deal of what appear to me to be repetitious exercises, in some cases
pretty inferior in quality; and secondly his bland indifference to what seems
to me the frightfully serious predicament of the artist under the Communist
tyranny. I think that I understand his mind and perhaps can even guess what
you might say about both questions, and yet I cannot bring myself to approve
his attitude at all, or even sincerely to excuse him – not that he cares a fig for
my opinion.

Anyway, by all means go ahead and strength to your pen![28]

**Barr's second 'misgiving' cannot have come as a surprise to Penrose, for
although Barr was an outspoken opponent of both Congressman George**

Dondero and Senator Joseph McCarthy, he was an equally outspoken opponent of Stalinism. During the winter of 1952–53 Penrose had invited Barr to give a lecture at the ICA and Barr had suggested the title 'Is Modern Art Communistic?' In his reply Penrose asked him to consider substituting the inoffensively philosophical 'Is Art political?'[29] Barr's response was characteristically blunt: he would not give the lecture at all, because 'I doubt the propriety of my talking on a subject which will seem to a lot of our English friends more American anti-Communist propaganda'.[30]

When Lee returned from the United States at the beginning of December 1954, Penrose replied to Barr's letter. Thanking him for his 'very helpful' comments, Penrose continued:

The political question with Picasso is one which will not be easy, especially since so many people would take the view that he must be condemned in advance for his Communism and that naturally I refuse to do. However I do not despair of being able to treat the whole question with fairness. It goes of course much further than him, the influence of many others such as Eluard, Aragon, Cocteau, etc. must be taken into account. He is certainly less politically minded at moments when he is left alone with his work.

And in a postscript, he added:

I agree with you thoroughly about the major difficulty in producing my Picasso book. It will be difficult to be sufficiently objective and it is in any case difficult to write a biography of a man who is still alive. These two points made me hesitate for some while but I finally accepted the task because the subject interests me so intensely and I hope that, being conscious of the pitfalls, I may be able to avoid them. You certainly did not upset me by your remarks.[31]

In fact, Penrose had committed himself to writing the book and had made a first research trip to Paris even before Lee got home. The draft contract with Gollancz is dated 5 November 1954 and stipulates that the manuscript of between 100,000 and 150,000 words should be delivered by 1 May 1957 – barely half the amount of time Penrose had originally predicted he would need. There were to be no more than sixteen pages of illustrations, although each page could have 'as many separate illustrations as the Author desires'. Penrose was held responsible for the photographic costs, including 'all copyright fees', and the total advance was set at £1,000.[32] As we shall see, things did not go entirely to plan and there were several minor skirmishes with Gollancz before *Picasso: His Life and Work* reached the printing press. Indeed, trouble started almost immediately, for on 29 November 1954 Rubinstein wrote to give Penrose the unwelcome news that a rival book by the well-respected French biographer Antonina Vallentin had just been announced and to urge him to try to complete his book in two, not three years. And, predictably, the American publisher, Harper and Brothers, was already fretting about whether Penrose would 'take a sufficiently critical attitude' to 'the curious political aspects of Picasso's life'.[33] Undeterred by these rain clouds, Penrose signed the contract and on 23 December received the first installment of his advance.

Penrose launches his research campaign

Between receiving the draft contract and signing it, Penrose went to Paris and started asking questions. His notes are not as copiously descriptive as those he took in Perpignan and there is more quotation and reported speech. His research campaign proper dates from this moment, and from the first he mixed visits to Picasso with informal interviews with mutual friends:

Visit to Léger exhibition at la Maison de la Pensée Française, [Paris,] Nov. 1954[34]
[Picasso:] 'Léger ne se tempe jamais. Comme peinture c'est mieux que Michel Ange mais j'aime mieux M.A. comme peintre.'
    'C'est les hommes qui sont plus important que la peinture. Qu'est ce que tu preferera une femme ou Venus?[35]
    Of Emmer's film of which he [Picasso] had only seen the English version: 'Le film est affreux.'[36]

He has a large rough amethyst weighing some 10 lbs. with a pocket of water inside it which trickles about as you move the stone – how did it get there? – the water is as old as the stone – how old? – what would it taste like? Gave him my crystal ball – very excited to receive it – talked of Bernal's opinion that it was a very rare piece – told Kahnweiler how he had seen stones and metals living and changing in B.'s lab.

Talked of G. Stein – has very low opinion of her and her 'talents'.

Looking at medals of P. and Le Corb[usier] made by French Gov[ernment]. Very bad likenesses of both. On reverse of P. medal a dove and skull of bull. P. pointed out that the bull was given long upper front teeth like a horse or dog, which is wrong – talk about observation. 'Il faut apprendre à voir. J'ai regardé des fourmis toute ma vie mais je ne comprends rien d'eux. Quelqu'un qui a suivi leur habitudes pour longtemps saura voir les fourmis. Ca ne suffit pas de voir, il faut connaître, savoir ce qui est la aussi.'[37]
P. [5]

Paris, Nov. '54
Françoise Gilot
Tells story of how at the time of the Bateau Lavoir Picasso, as always, was very keen that his friends should be happily married. He found a bride for

Braque, she was the daughter of the patron of the Cabaret du Néant. It was decided that all the friends, Max Jacob, etc., should accompany Braque on his visit to propose the fiançailles. They all hired the best clothes, top hats, canes, etc. and set out. The patron was delighted and thought them very entertaining [and] intelligent and Mons. Braque just the boy for a fiancé. But the atmosphere degenerated and on the way out they had no means of recognising their hired coats, hats & sticks, so they helped themselves freely to the ones they found most elegant.

Marcelle, who became permanently Mme. Braque, was Picasso's find, so was Alice Derain.[38] [6]

21 Nov. 1954, Paris

Called on P. before leaving for London at 12.30. He was in bed. Inès [Sassier] downstairs was cooking a most wonderfully fragrant pot au [feu]. Jacqueline welcomed me and took me up to his bedside. He was sad, looked smaller, more wrinkled and paler than a week ago. Not forthcoming in conversation so I talked about anything to get started. Paulo arrived and the question of putting Boisgeloup in order was raised. It is in very bad condition – evacuated of all things of interest – pictures, sculptures, hippopotamus skull, negro masks, etc., it has been abandoned for years. P. put most of the important treasures in a bank in Paris in 1939 against the advice of his best friends, who said that Paris would be destroyed and that they would be better in the country – on the contrary Boisgeloup was plundered, he says by the French, but the bank remained intact. He got up and we lunched together with Jacqueline. Talked of Matisse whose death he certainly feels heavily.[39] He denied that Matisse was deeply Catholic, as the press tries to make out. The chapel became possible through his friend and nurse who is an ardent Catholic.[40] Matisse thought of the project as a means to make more paintings, etc. P. said he had often reproached M. for his religious tendencies but […] apart from that he said, 'Il a fait des Matisses et ça c'est important.'[41] P. is obviously in fear of death since this year so many of his generation have died: Derain, Matisse, Maurice Raynal, Sabartès's wife. He asked me about Churchill à propos of nothing – unless perhaps at the back of his mind an admiration for his long life and continued vigour. I told him of [Graham] Sutherland's portrait. Talked about the Bateau Lavoir, which I had visited two days before. Still just as it was in 1905. Its construction is peculiar as it is built on the side of the hill and you enter by the top floor. P.'s studio was directly opposite the entrance on the same floor. In spite of being high up it had only a view of other houses and roofs but there was a precipice below into which P. said he remembered seeing a man, who was sweeping snow of[f] a roof, fall to his death. He said it had not changed at all, the studios of Gris, Max Jacob and the others were just the same. He had returned to visit them not long ago. We talked of the revolver that he had been given by Alfred Jarry, which he carried with him for a long time and fired it as a means of expressing high spirits or frightening people.[42] Talked of Valentine – I said it was a very difficult thing to be [a] poet and nothing else. He said that it was impossible because when one wrote poetry, and he had done so, it was 'toujours la même chose', meaning, I think, that with painting there was always a diversity because of the contact with objects in all their variety.

Fin [Vilató][43] talking of the end of the Spanish War when he and [Javier] Vilató arrived in France without a nationality. P. said he would design a new flag for depatriated people which would be a piece of gruyère cheese with holes for the countries that have disappeared.

The friends of Picasso tolerate his behaviour when the same act in another would be condemned. When a friend calls it is not uncommon for him to say, 'Why do you want to go away? You are not in a hurry, wait a little until I have had a word with so and so, I will come back.' But he fails to come back. There has been a rush of people who own an example of his work taking it to him for verification and signature. He is very tired of this procedure which often is simply founded on a desire to increase the value of the work. Recently a dealer from [the] U.S. brought in two or three drawing[s], one of which was recognised by Kahnweiler as one he remembered, but P. took them all and wrote 'reproduction' on the back in ink. The dealer was followed by a Catalan sculptor with a pink period drawing that had formerly belonged to me. P. did the same to it. But later when I called again with the drawing and left it with Sabartès explaining that it was impossible that it could be a reproduction, and that my reputation also was involved, he returned it to me next time I called, signed and with 'reproduction' crossed out. [6]

Whenever he was in Paris, Penrose made a point of seeing Frank McEwen, then the Fine Arts Officer of the British Council. The following undated notes may record a conversation that took place at this time:

Frank McEwen[44]
Paul Eluard had told him that P. had said, 'Braque c'est la femme qui m'aimé le plus.'[45]
    Braque said that in early cubist time P. would call on him, look at everything, then hurry back to develop B.'s new ideas.
    B. said that after 1916 P. became very mondain[46] and loved to dress up for society, take most conspicuous box at the theatre, etc.
    B. cannot stop talking about P. [7]

This first research trip to Paris had been useful, but to make significant headway Penrose had first to overcome his own doubts about his capacities as a scholar. He had gone up to Cambridge in 1919 with the intention of reading for an Honours degree in History and only switched to a B.A. in

Architectural Studies after getting a rather humiliating Third in the Tripos exams in May 1920. His record in Architecture was much more distinguished and he graduated with a First in June 1922.[47] But he was probably aware of the fact that although his university friends thought him excellent company and gifted artistically, they rated him less brilliant or promising than his older brother Lionel, who went up to Cambridge at exactly the same time and was therefore compared directly with him.[48]

As we have seen, Penrose was not inexperienced as a writer when he accepted Gollancz's offer. But catalogue introductions and short magazine articles are of a different order from a substantial book, and in his mid-fifties he had to reinvent himself as a biographer-cum-art historian. He did, of course, have the inestimable advantage of an intimate knowledge of a wide range of Picasso's works – several major masterpieces were hanging on his walls at home – and he capitalised on this and on his acute sensitivity to all things visual by spending a lot of time looking at paintings in public collections, temporary exhibitions, dealers' galleries, and above all chez Picasso. This was the part of the work that Penrose enjoyed and that gave him the energy to carry on with the less congenial business of assembling and sifting the mass of historical information. He took no short cuts with the latter task, however, and buckled down to a steady campaign of reading. His notebooks frequently break into lists of books and articles, with ticks and crossings as he gradually ploughed through them. Like any research student in the pre-computer era, he accumulated sheaves of handwritten notes and they are models of their kind in their conscientiousness. Consequently, *Picasso: His Life and Work* came out with footnotes and a bibliography. If this seems only normal, we do well to remember that there was not a single footnote in Antonina Vallentin's rival one-volume biography of Picasso. Nor are there bibliographies or footnotes in the biographies by Pierre Cabanne and Patrick O'Brian, which came out in the wake of Picasso's death and were intended to supplant Penrose's book. In other words, although he was writing for the general reader, not the clique of Picasso scholars, Penrose was determined to produce a biography that could justly claim to be authoritative and well-founded.

Unfortunately, it is not always possible to reconstruct the precise chronology of Penrose's interview campaign: his diaries reveal that he saw some of his sources repeatedly and he sometimes failed to date his notes of their conversations; at a later stage he would often dismember his pocket notebooks to order information under thematic headings. Nevertheless, it seems likely that two of his earliest interviews, after his return from the first research trip to Paris, were with the writer Clive Bell and Lydia Keynes, wife of the economist Maynard Keynes. As Lydia Lopokova she had been one of the stars of Diaghilev's Ballets Russes and, like Bell, had got to know Picasso well when he was designing for Diaghilev during the early years of his marriage to Olga Khokhlova. Both were old friends of Penrose's and he gleaned some piquant scraps of information.

On 19 December 1954 Penrose had the first of probably three meetings with Lydia Keynes. The following notes may have been taken then or on one of their meetings the following year:[49]

To ask Lydia Keynes
Q. How & when did P. meet Olga Khokhlova?
1917 Rome. She was Russian general's daughter. Very pretty. Had no boyfriend but [a] nice girl. She wanted P. to adopt her kind of bourgeois life. As P. said when we met in 1950, reason why they separated was that she asked too much. Olga only danced small parts. She left the Ballet when it went to S. America to go with P. to Barcelona. She dance[d] one of the 4 girls in 'Good Humoured Ladies'[50] and continued to take daily lessons after she was married. She kept the flat [in] rue La Boétie very tidy and furnished in bourgeois style. Extraordinary chairs.

Q. Who was P.'s most intimate friend in Rome? in London?
None. Polunin to some extent as he was [an] excellent craftsman.[51]

Q. What was P.'s attitude to Cocteau?
'Le coq et L'Arlequin'. 'Parade'.[52]

Q. Had P. any political opinions round about 1920?
No, nor had any of the ballet folk.
   In London they stayed at Savoy as Diaghilev's guests. Some of the portrait drawings were done there.[53] Lydia danced in 'Parade'. [7]

Penrose filed the following notes in a different folder and they probably derive from a different conversation:

The Russian Ballet
Lydia says Derain & P. were great friends. Diaghilev was looking for a painter to do [the] décor for 'La Boutique'.[54] P. produced Derain, everyone very pleased. (Later P. & D. had very little in common and never met, particularly unfriendly after D.'s collaboration in war.) [...]
   'Parade' & 'Mercure'[55] [were his] most important ballets. [2]

Penrose met Clive Bell in January 1955 and then again that August.[56] The following undated notes were evidently written on two different occasions:

Clive Bell
Says that the admiration for the mathematics of [Maurice] Princet was purely aesthetic. P., B[raque], etc. did not understand mathematics but enjoyed his pretty equations, beautifully written out and generally admired at the café. [...]

Clive Bell, 1919

P. in London. Stayed at Savoy with Olga, dressed up in dinner jacket for all evening shows. Derain on the contrary refused to dress even when taking a curtain [call] and lived in cheap Bloomsbury hotel with girls he picked up.

Bloomsbury party for Picasso at Clive's. [Ernest] Ansermet and Lytton [Strachey] at heads of table. Diaghilev not asked.

At Boeuf sur le Toit in 1920's Cocteau, always to be found there, ask[ed] P. if it can be done to put a miracle on the stage, thinking of 'Orphée' that he was then writing.[57] P. says, 'But of course, miracles happen all the time. It is a miracle each day that I do not dissolve in my bath.' Later Clive tells story to Derain who remarks, 'A few years ago the miracle would have been for him to have a bath at all.'

Olga insisted on Pablo taking a country house near Fontainebleau.[58] P. ordered a pissotière and a bec de gaz[59] to be sent down from Paris and installed on the lawn. [2]

Penrose and Lee Miller in collaboration: visiting France and Spain, February–March 1955

On Lee's return from America, Roland was able to plan a more ambitious foreign trip. As he had told Barr when writing to give him news of the commission, he considered Lee an essential ally. He had great respect for her gifts as a photographer, knowing that he could rely on her not just to record accurately but to analyse with shrewdness and wit. And she could be a great asset socially, with her vivacity, worldliness and earthy sense of humour. There was undeniably a 'drink problem' but the bad scenes generally took place at home. As for Lee, visiting all Picasso's haunts in France and Spain hardly required the fortitude, courage and daring she had shown on her photographic missions before and during the war, but in its own way it was challenging and stimulating and she entered energetically into this new assignment. Both, it seems, were glad to have a common project to help them patch up the rift produced by Roland's love affair with Diane Deriaz.

Nervous but also excited, Penrose wrote to Barr on 17 January 1955 a few weeks before they set off:

I am entering more and more deeply into the vast territories of my book and alarmed at each new vista that opens before me. Thank Alfred, I say each moment when I feel really lost and can refer once more to your books. Without them the wood would be invisible and the first tree too wide and too tall. As our plans go we are off, Lee & I, into the heart of it next month – Paris and probably Barcelona for some weeks. Picasso is still in Paris and I gather is recovering from a period of unparalleled gloom after the final rupture with Françoise and the death of Matisse. As usual it is impossible to know how or when it will be possible to make the prolonged contact with him which is essential – we shall see.[60]

Penrose had been reading Barr's magisterial *Matisse: His Art and His Public,* as we know from his surviving notes.[61] That he had decided to use it as a model when structuring his own text into a sequence of lucidly sub-divided chapters is clear from the chapter plans he had already started to draw up. Barr's *Matisse* was also his model when it came to attempting to balance the detailed, factual story of Picasso's life with probing analysis of the art, for he was determined not to allow pure biography to gain the upper hand. It was a comfort to the unself-confident author to have Barr as mentor as well as friend.

On 10 February 1955 the Penroses set off for Paris on the first stage of their trip, paying several visits to Picasso in his studio at rue des Grands-Augustins before heading for Spain.[62] It may have been during one of those visits that Roland got answers to a couple of the questions he had prepared in advance. Oddly enough, although Kahnweiler himself is on record expressing certain reservations about *Les Demoiselles d'Avignon,* Picasso told Penrose that Kahnweiler was the one person who understood the painting at the time.[63]

Reasons for being a Communist in France
C.P.F. is large, well organised, long record of struggle including resistance years.

Gives him a feeling of contact with the common people, a sort of freemasonry. They recognise him and whisper in his ear that they are party members, his friends – like the car park man at Eden Rock. This means they like him, admire him for his attitude, though they may not appreciate his work.

Questions to ask of Picasso
Q. Did you ever paint or draw as a child in your earliest youth? If so are any of these drawings in existence?
A. Non, je n'ai jamais designé comme un enfant.[64] […]

Q. Did anyone (a) like (b) understand 'Les Demoiselles' the first time they saw it?
A. D-H. Kahnweiler. [7]

In Picasso's studio Penrose enjoyed a privileged early viewing of the suite of variations inspired by Delacroix's *The Women of Algiers*[65] and his impressions and his recollection of what Picasso told him make these notes particularly valuable. They were the basis of a celebrated passage in *Picasso: His Life and Work* but, as is so often the case, the informal version is both fuller and more nuanced.[66] The final canvas in the Delacroix series, known as 'Version O', is dated 14 February 1955, just two days before Penrose's first visit. But Picasso went on making drawings for several more weeks,[67] and Penrose's notes reveal not only that the artist continued to work on some of

the larger canvases after mid-February, but also that he had no sense at the time that 'Version O' was his final statement on this theme. Thus the notebook confirms that the precisely dated inscriptions on the backs of Picasso's paintings should not be taken too literally: changes were often made, sometimes over a prolonged period of time, yet inscriptions only occasionally register the time lapse. But Penrose was not only interested in Picasso's latest work: he was equally alert to Picasso's fluctuating moods and recorded some of his more personal, and unpublishable, utterances – a brief but fascinating exchange about suicide and a callous response to recent photographs of his sister Lola.

Visit 16 Feb. '55, Paris
P. showed me about 6 large canvases and 12 small. The theme taken from Delacroix['s] 'Demoiselle[s] d'Alger' which he has not seen for years and refuses to look at while he is still at work [on] this series. He is working very hard, has not be[en] out for three weeks and is well and happy in spite of

Visitors to the exhibition of Picasso's suite of variations inspired by Delacroix's *The Women of Algiers*, Musée des Arts décoratifs, Paris, summer 1955. Photo Robert Doisneau

Olga's death last week.[68] The paintings range from the earlier ones, which are to some degree representational, with large white fleshed nude legs in the air and a hieratic veiled seated figure in the foreground, a negress bringing coffee and a seated odalisque further back, to more abstract, cubist, versions of the same composition. Of these K[ahnweiler] remarked that they are the logical development of cubism, in spite of the 1914–1918 break in its development. The colour has an oriental taste – 'my idea of the orient in spite of never having been there' – a Moorish atmosphere of cool rooms sheltered from the outside heat. There is no direct movement from representational in the early ones to abstraction later, only a tendency – he agreed that he never knew what was coming next, just as when discussing a large aquatint figure composition a little later he said, 'Tell me what it means, you should know – I don't, I never do. If I did I should be finished.'

At lunch with Sabartès & Jacqueline we talked about [Antoni] Gaudí. P. had never known him personally but had great respect for his work both as a maker of ornaments-sculptor and as [an] engineer. S. had met him and also admired him greatly but said he was a bigot and highly conventional in his religion. His reputation in Barcelona was at its height about 1900–1910 but it became a snob affair since his prices were very high – he was the most expensive architect in Spain. P. agreed that it was curious that his influence had died so soon – it was Cubism that killed it.

After departure of Sabartès we discussed his greatly improved health. P. said he had expected him to kill himself last autumn after the death of his wife, but 'it is very difficult to kill yourself'. I asked, 'Have you ever tried?' 'No,' says P., 'but it is, and once you have decided it's too difficult. You find new reasons to want to live.'

A youth, son of [Fernand] Crommelynck, the playwright, came from Lacourière with a copper plate for P. and was sent out again to get 'blanc d'espagne', 'miror',[69] etc. to clean it. He had the seriousness and knowledge of an excellent craftsman.[70] P. set to work with him in the kitchen to prepare his plates for the afternoon's work. He works also a great deal by night just now.

Of the 'Femmes d'Alger' pictures he said, 'Matisse has left me his Odalisques as a legacy.' He certainly thinks a lot about Matisse, especially since his death, but the pictures show no obvious influence and in a curious way the nudes are more erotic and more vicious than the hotel orientalism of M. The colour contains a slight reminiscence of M. In some cases he has drawn the nudes in black or blue line on plain white canvas, which becomes illuminated with tender subtle pinks and flesh tones. With this he is very pleased. Some of the big pictures are almost without colour. [9]

On Penrose's second visit, the poet and ex-Dadaist Tristan Tzara and the painter Balthus were both present:

Visit 24 Feb. 1955
Tzara with proofs of etchings by P. for a poem of his, 'La flamme haute',

asking for P.'s approval.[71] Several proofs of each, some more inked than others. P. inclined to like those that had been wiped most but said, 'It doesn't matter, they both have their interest. Why not vary them in each book?' Balthus arrived and we went upstairs to see the paintings again. One large one had undergone several changes. He spoke of them all as sketches and said he was working toward a solution which he wants to paint very big. All these studies are necessary so as 'to get behind the canvas'. Some large canvases (4ft. x 6ft. approx.) had been painted in a few hours. Balthus was envious of such speed, saying it took him months to come to a final result. P. said his method was the same: in the end it took him 100 studies [and] pictures instead of a hundred days. Pictures were never finished in the sense that they were put in a frame, signed, and done with. They [were] usually finished because one went away or some change took place to b[r]eak the continuity of thought – more possible to come back to sculpture after a break – 'On ne peint pas avec la pensée mais avec les mains.'[72]

One large picture almost in monochrome is very impressive and seems to contain more colour than those with bright pinks, red, yellows and green, more cubist in style and wonderfully three-dimensional. It seemed the most resolved of any and was the nearest to the great final picture that P. had in mind.[73] 'Je continuerai d'ouvrir des fenêtres là dedans et peut être ça viendra.'[74] He talked of his admiration for Delacroix, how he had foreseen how to treat figures – some of the studies show memories of other pictures, particularly a more representational earlier one in which there is a nude very like the 'Death of Sardanapalus'[75] where both front and back of the figure are seen simultaneously – exaggerated in P.'s study. These pictures are Matisse's legacy of odalisques and also of colour & pattern, but are more profound and escape any reference to the decorative. It is a kind of marriage between Matisse and P. in which M. appears as feminine charm. P. is thinking of other collaborations: talking of certain similarities in composition with these studies and the 'Bain Turc' of Ingres,[76] he said he wanted some day to do a version of the Odalisque of Ingres[77] à la Van Gogh.

Saw some new aquatints he is working on – one very fine large plate – artist and model subject with several figures.[78] He brought out some pictures to look at together – first a 1939 Balthus large painting which he likes very much,[79] the Cézanne L'Estaque landscape,[80] early Bonnard,[81] 2 Matisse[s]. Asked about the Matisse portrait of Marguerite that he chose according to G. Stein so as to mock at Matisse, he said he still had it and that the story was sheer nonsense.[82]

Studio more crowded with things than ever, the hippo skull from Boisgeloup, a crucifix in the corner, of which only one great arm could be seen raised above a mass of unpacked parcels of proofs or books, innumerable bronzes, some lying on the floor, canvases piled against each other. In some of the lower strata I could see canvases that I had been shown in 1946 – the whole effect fascinating and tantalising as it is most unlikely that anyone will ever get to the bottom of it so long as P. is alive.

Visit 2nd March, 1955

P. suffering from pains in the back, had been in bed for two days and was seeing no one. Had a long talk with S[abartès] about my trip to Spain which was to start next day – very helpful about Málaga & Madrid. P. appeared unexpectedly in white bathrobe and soon after his arrival Peggy Bernier was announced and allowed in as she had come with photos of the Vilató family taken on her recent visit to Barcelona, and P., always intrigued by pictures especially when related to himself or his family, welcomed Peggy and soon began to forget his pains under the combined influence of her charm and memories of the paintings and his sister and family. The flat in Barcelona is fairly spacious but overcrowded with pictures, mostly painted by P. during his visit in 1917 when the Ballet went to Barcelona for a season and P. with Olga stayed on in a friend's flat on the Ramblas – there is a view of the Columbus monument on the quai painted by him from the window.[83] The other pictures are all of a group, their colour is unlike any other period, violet and yellowish green predominate. They vary from flat surface cubism, with a sign language of a rather hasty nature, to a very careful lifelike portrait of a girl in a mantilla in pointillist technique and extreme realism.[84] Photos of the family showed P.'s sister sitting up in a chair clothed in a white shawl. She is unable to move about and sits like a monument presiding over the conversation, singing and entertainment produced by her sons and daughter. In true Spanish style they live by night but even so the lighting in the flat is always insufficient as bulbs are continually breaking. Peggy's account of her visit amused P. greatly, especially the lack of light for nocturnal habits. He looked at his sister's photo and remembering how beautiful she had been and how often he had made her portrait he said, 'C'est affreux, on devrait la tuer, n'est-ce pas? Ma mère disait dans le temps qu'il n'y a rien de plus affreux pour une femme que devenir vieille, car ça veux dire devenir laide.'[85] I remarked that his sister's expression was very lively and showed great charm and that her eyes were as dark and sparkling as ever, but he could only see the swollen formless chin, the flabby cheeks and tousled grey hair, which surmounted the pyramid of white in which she was swathed. Other details that interested him greatly were some works of his father's mixed in among the medical plaster casts in cases that one of his nephews, a foot doctor, keeps about the flat. A landscape with trees of northern type and a Virgin placed on a table received much attention. The Virgin was placed on a small 18th-cent. table which had been painted black in Ripolin by his father and later white all over, both of which attempts to improve it were 'bien laid',[86] and the Virgin herself had been made from a plaster cast of the head of a Greek goddess that his father had painted over with the utmost realism, giving it eyelashes and a look of sorrow with golden tears stuck to her cheeks. The conventional scarf draping the Virgin's head was made of cloth dipped in plaster and painted over so as to harmonise with the painted bust. The whole effect was convincing and troubling, the Greek features adapted to the Spanish drama of sorrow, the cloth and paint made a form of 'collage' of borrowed elements.

P. was delighted at this forerunner of 'collage' and admired the way two round lamps had been placed where breasts might be, giving the Virgin a new form of illumination. [9]

In one of Penrose's files there is a summary of an undated conversation with Sabartès. Since it is concerned exclusively with Picasso's earliest years in Spain and now and then glosses Sabartès's own book about Picasso, it almost certainly records the 'helpful' conversation of 2 March 1955:

Sabartès
[…] The picture of the pigeon cote painted by Don José is still stored away in Málaga high up in a loft, but on examination S. found that instead of thousands of pigeons there were only seven.[87] In his pictures Don J. always combined some moral or amorous significance – two happy birds cooing before the entrance to their nest with a sullen third party sitting below.

S. insists that the pigeon is supposed to bring bad luck.

The broadsheets of 19th-cent. woodcuts with moral stories in pictures are called 'Ancas' meaning 'Hallelujahs'. They all finish in tragedy with skulls, coffins, etc. Spanish stories do not have happy endings. Death is there always at the end.

S. has revised his refusal to believe in Italian origin of Picasso family. He now has seen proof that the grandfather of P.'s mother came from a village near Genoa within a few miles of Recco where Mateo Picasso was born. But he still insists that an Arab origin to the family is highly probable.

The story of numbers in the exam in Málaga was written by S. on good authority but he made up the numbers as he went along.[88] When P. read it he said, 'Oui c'est ça et je crois même que c'était bien ça les chiffres.'[89] Numbers have always been an obsession. They reoccur in poems much later as personalities in themselves.

[Manuel] Pallarès was a painter but without any understanding of P. He was a friend and therefore remained [a] friend. He has long ago ceased to paint and now works for his son, a dentist in Barcelona, as assistant. Has a great fear of becoming involved in things he does not understand.

Horta de San Juan was called Horta de Ebro by P. It is near the river in a fertile plain. […]

Merli is very inaccurate for early period – no visit to Majorca, no ceramics – but can be relied on for Cubist period.[90] He is very 'mal vu'[91] because he stole the drawings belonging to P. from Lola. [10]

Penrose kept notes of other conversations held in Paris. One informant was the banker and collector André Lefèvre:

Conversation with André Lefèvre, 23 Feb. '55
The portraits of Vollard and Uhde[92] are amazing likenesses but at the time they were painted A.L. did not realise it. The newness of the style blinded him, he admired them as pictures but not as portraits. It takes time for a new style to become familiar but it does so by infiltrating into all forms of life and taste and the young, to whom it does not come as a shock, take less time to appreciate it. [...] [2]

A fascinating conversation with Dora Maar may date from the same time:[93]

Dora
P. worked in a studio belonging to Vollard at [Le] Tremblay-sur-Mauldre from about 1935 to Vollard's death in 1939.
     One should follow ideas to their ultimate end with the greatest tenacity. Like a dog who picks up a scent and does not leave it until he has found his quarry and who is also always on the lookout for new tracks. One fails in life through lack of curiosity and lack of concentration.
     P. tried to divorce Olga when Maya was born in order to marry Marie-Thérèse. He failed owing to legal complications and finally Franco abolished divorce. Dora met P. in 1936 and Olga's jealousy was directed entirely against her. She had a genius for making scenes and would turn up out of the blue to embarrass him & D. all she could. But in some wa[y]s P. seemed to enjoy her violence. Once they escaped from Paris without a word to anyone and sought refuge with Braque but O. arrived in the middle of lunch having by instinct guessed where they were. In her scenes she usually complained of being left without money, which was untrue. Her anger later was directed against Françoise. She walked deliberately on her hands as she lay on the beach, would suggest to P. that Paulo was not his son, never appeared without making trouble. Never attacked Marie-Thérèse.
     Greatest influences in his life since 1920 were Cocteau, Eluard. Only came to know P.E. in 1935. P.E. believed firmly in 1944–5 that the Communists would gain the power in France. His reasons for joining party were humanitarian, love of poor people and belief [/] in party line which he managed to swallow whole. He was used by them as their cultural ambassador. Very much due to his influence that P. became Communist. He was used much in same way. Sent to Peace Congress, London – Warsaw 1950, posters, demonstrations.
     On the walls of Dora's apartment there are insects very realistically painted by P. during the war. They began by splashes of paint on the white wall to which he added, making them into fantastic bugs. D. keeps them from being covered from successive coats of distemper. [2; 9]

Penrose also spoke to his friend, Michel de Brunhoff:[94]

Michel de Brunhoff. 1917. At the front there was one night a particularly bloody local attack and hand to hand fighting in which Sgt. de Brunhoff was involved. Next morning the post brought him a letter from his mother enclosing the catalogue of 'Parade' with P.'s Chinaman on the cover. She said she had not wanted to go to such a splendid and mondain event, thinking of him, but had been persuaded to attend the first night.[95] The idea of these two worlds, so different and yet so near together, filled Michel with disgust for his own lot and envy for the life of those in Paris who could spend their time so much more profitably. [9]

On 3 March 1955 the Penroses left Paris and, with stops at Burgos, Madrid and Granada, arrived in Málaga on 9 March. They remained there for five days, visiting and photographing all the places Picasso had known like the back of his hand, including his birthplace in Plaza de la Merced and the 'half-abandoned art school', where his father had taught drawing, with its 'rows of dust-covered plaster casts, stuffed birds, easels and drawing boards'.[96] At some point they must also have visited Toledo because Roland made a few very brief notes about the great El Greco altarpiece, *The Disrobing of Christ*, in the Sacristy of the Cathedral, seeing a curious pre-monition of Cubism in the underlying geometry of the composition. On 14 March they headed back to Madrid and three days later returned to Paris. The all-important trip to Barcelona was deferred until the middle of June, when it was combined with a visit to Picasso's new villa in Cannes.[97]

Strikingly different in style from those recording his latest visits to Picasso's studio, some of Penrose's notes relating to this first trip to Spain read like a first draft for the opening, scene-setting chapter of the biography. Maybe he experimented with writing up his findings during the long after-noon siestas when nothing was open and interviews could not be arranged. This descriptive passage is typical:

Bare mountains, vines and sea. White villages spread across their flanks look out across rich plains covered with crops of sugar cane, oranges and all kinds of fruit and vegetables. Palm trees and eucalyptus alternate their accents, either dark and explosive or tall and almost transparent. Above the limits of irrigation, olive groves and almond trees cover the slopes with regular spotted pattern and the soil usually scorched by the sun changes from greenish grey or buff to bluish with terracotta and the pink of a bullfinch's breast. The dazzling crown of snow forever caps the highest peaks of the Sierra Nevada but can also be seen on clear days across the narrowing strait of blue sea that swells into the bay of Málaga. […] [11]

Evidently, Picasso's cousin Ricardo Huelin y Ruiz Blasco (to give him his full name) was the source of a good deal of the detailed information about the Ruiz family which Penrose incorporated into the draft because a list of the principal characters appears under his name. He also told Penrose that 'P. [was] very fond of Conchita, a cousin', and then went on to describe how one of Picasso's most accomplished and penetrating early portraits came to be painted:

The family thought it would be a fine thing if Pablo could paint the portrait of Tia P. but both Pablo & Tia Pepa refused. It was only after long persuasion of Pablo's mother that finally she appeared for a sitting with her ornate gold chain and frills, but in the portrait none of these adornments appear[s].[98] [11]

Another source of information, recommended either by Picasso or Sabartès, was Juan Temboury, whose name appears on the front of the notebook Penrose was using in Spain. On a loose sheet of paper, Penrose rapidly summarised the salient points he had made:

Temboury sees in Málaga the origins of all P.'s tendencies. Born in a house built on the foundations of an old convent de la Paz next door to headquarters of the liberal movement of Tonija[99], who as a child he would have seen sallying forth to the barricades. His father renowned [for] his paintings of doves. The Málaga temperament seen particularly among the people. Unsurpassable gaiety and quick wit. Antiquity. Greek origins. [2]

The day after Roland and Lee got back to Paris they went to see Picasso to give him their presents and news of their trip. They found him surrounded by visitors and Penrose was obliged to wait a few days before he got the chance to have a proper conversation. On that occasion Edouard Pignon was also there and in the presence of two fellow painters Picasso expatiated enthusiastically on the superior qualities of household paint over conventional artists' colours, demonstrating his argument with reference to his own pictures. One is reminded of the earlier conversation in which he reminisced about his father's occasional use of Ripolin and collage: ironically, it may have been from his ostensibly conservative father that Picasso first learned the value of experimenting with novel materials and techniques.

Visit 18th March '55, Paris
On return from Spain with various presents, chorizo, Málaga wine, custard apples, photos, etc. from Juan Temboury, Ricardo Huelin and us. P. opened the parcels with eagerness; his enthusiasm for Spanish tastes and smells full of memories was delightful. He was glad to hear of our visit. He talked of the plasterwork in the Victorias church with astonishment, saying that it was a unique piece, laughed about the bad academic painters who are the glory of Málaga. But he was very preoccupied with business matters and too many visitors.

Visit 21 March

Explaining to Pignon sugar process for engraving and later had a long discussion of paints. Explaining that nothing was a better basis than Ripolin Mat, which he used mixed with ordinary oil colour. [It] dried fast and became very hard. He produced pictures thickly painted in 1934 to prove his point: they were as fresh as ever and no signs of a crack. He said that this had given new possibilities to painting; the limits of oil paint from tubes had been reached. This gave new possibilities in speed and texture. Produced several pictures of great variety, some very rich in colour, particularly a portrait of Françoise in which he had played on contrasts of surface, some areas painted thinly and with very simple pattern and colour, such as the chequered blouse, and some very heavily. The hair filled with subtle shades of olive and spinach green, a play on the richness of dull greens with their acid flavour contrasting with yellow and pink. Another portrait of a flamboyant blonde, who[m] he called the blackmarketeer, was a gorgeous caricature which he chuckled over as he brought it out, golden hair in whirlwinds, plump pink cheeks and lecherous mouth combined with a sober grey dress on which a sphinx-head brooch sat between her breasts.[100] The next to appear was confined in colour to Goyaesque silver greys, a most moving portrait in its quiet refinement. There was also a taller picture of a woman in black in which the only bright colour was a passage from pale pink to a Venetian red, very like the graduation in earth in a Spanish field, a patch of light which welcomed attention and revealed at the same time the gentle contours of a cheek.[101] The big canvases of the 'Femmes d'Alger' had not progressed since my last visit except for [the] one with much bright colour mostly applied in flat surfaces.[102] Some passages were very exciting in their complex movement but seemed not entirely resolved. P. remarked that it was unfinished, he was amusing himself or rather not amusing himself at all. A few days ago he had said to a journalist that he intend[ed] to carry the idea much further and that he must get angry before the solution would appear. [9]

Penrose also recorded a conversation with Pignon's journalist wife, Hélène Parmelin, who was an influential figure in the intelligentsia of the PCF and had been an intimate friend of Picasso's since the Liberation. No doubt she too was present in the studio on 21 March:[103]

Hélène Parmelin

[The] Pignons possess a picture painted by P. in Vallauris. Pignon was working in [a] studio lent by P. and had left an unfinished study for a Mother & Child on the easel when he went out. Meanwhile P. came in, saw the study and proceeded to paint a picture from it on a similar canvas. When Pignon returned with friends they at once took an interest in the new picture and asked Pignon about it. He had not yet seen what had happened and replied that it was just a small unfinished study of his of no consequence, but the truth very soon became apparent. [9]

Penrose also met up with Paulo's friend, Pierre Baudouin:[104]

Pierre Baudouin
Vallauris. There is an American couple called Batigne.[105] He is professor in
some U.S. university. They spend half the year at Vallauris living in a very
modest way and have been very helpful in organising things for P. They also
have given Victor Brauner a studio. It was thanks to them that the studio in
which 'War and Peace' was painted was fixed up with movable scaffolding
on which P. could stand and the panels prepared and placed ready for him.
('Guernica' had been painted in much less favourable conditions, the space
in the Gds. Augustins studio did not allow enough room for it to be stretched
vertically. The lower part was near, but for the upper part a long brush was
necessary and the only ladder was a light rickety pair of steps that had to be
constantly moved.) 'War and Peace' took 2 months to paint. P. locked himself
in and told Paulo, the only person who had a key, never to allow anyone in
until it was finished. Even if P. himself invited friends to see it Paulo, like the
crew of Ulysses, was to turn a deaf ear and refuse admittance. P. worked on
the panels every day and often late into the night. He would begin by going
to the pottery in the morning, perhaps making a pot or two and talking to
those at work until he felt in the mood to retire into his solitude. Finally in
October, the day that Françoise had said she was leaving, on the pretext of
sending Pierre to fetch some cigarettes the first visitors were allowed in,
including Françoise and P[ierre] B[audouin]. The panels were in fact
finished. By the door there stood on a table an alarm clock and a calendar
on which the date of beginning was marked and two months mapped out.
He had kept to his programme to a day and in addition to the two great
panels there were some six or seven portraits and more landscapes and still
lifes. The drawings for the panels were done mostly before painting began
but there were a great many more round the studio. [9]

Elsewhere Penrose jotted down this scrap of gossip about Françoise Gilot:

Pierre Baudouin was present when some friends were trying gently to
persuade P. that Françoise was not such a wonderful character. P. opened
a portfolio of drawings which he had hidden away and took out two very
beautiful and finished drawings of F. into which much more time and labour
had been put than usual. They all remarked on this and P. said, 'Oui on ne
peut faire ça seulement si on aime quelqu'on et l'aime beaucoup.'[106] [7]

**Like everybody else Penrose was fascinated by the saga of Françoise's rela-
tionship with Picasso, which was entering a more bitter, recriminatory phase
as her marriage to the painter Luc Simon approached and lawyers became
involved in arrangements for the custody of Claude and Paloma. Penrose
had just learned from Paulo Picasso of a row that had blown up over owner-
ship of La Galloise and this painful topic surfaced during his final visit to**

Picasso's studio. A chance meeting with Françoise on the eve of his departure for England resulted in an intriguing verbatim report of her side of the story, which, needless to say, never found its way into *Picasso: His Life and Work*. Penrose was still close to Françoise at this stage, but eventually he would be obliged to shun her and range himself unequivocally in Picasso's camp:[107]

Visit 23 March
Called at 12.45 with Miró and his wife. Had heard evening before from Paulo that Françoise had brought about a crisis which upset P. very much. She had without warning announced her intention of taking La Galloise for herself and fiancé, plus the children and offering to sell P. his studios at Vallauris. All the property there had been placed in Françoise's name and legally she had every right to do this, but this abrupt and unjustified act from every other angle outraged P. and all his friends. This explained his preoccupied looks and lack of vivacity on my previous visit. Today however he was again himself, delighted to see Miró, with whom he talked Catalan, and eagerly producing his latest engravings, drawings, etc. In a leather-bound sketch book he had in the last few days made some very comic drawings, some of Cocteau, mocking his election to the Académie Française, and a series of line drawings of Sabartès in various circumstances – seated in a chair with an old cap & reading the paper, eating spaghetti or examining the results of his latest contribution to the w.c. before pulling the plug.[108] He also produced some songs he had written in short rhymed verses for Sabartès that were Rabelaisian in style and a delight to all who were shown them. Geneviève Laporte had brought the announcement of her new book of poems illustrated by Cocteau.[109] P. joked affectionately about girls becoming poets nowadays and wearing trousers. Stayed on to lunch with Maya and S[abartès] and talked about Málaga & Spain in general. He was very interested to hear that Valentine was doing a new horoscope with the correct hour for his birth given in Sabartès's book and asked to see it.[110] Before leaving I told him how sorry I was to hear of his new worries and without bitterness he explained how extremely awkward the position was. He had bought back the studios but would have nowhere to live in Vallauris. He was leaving on the night train to see what he could do. As I left his gaiety left him and the look of preoccupation came over him again like a heavy veil. He looked old and sad. [9]

24 March
Met Françoise in the street by chance and got drawn into a conversation about the row with P. She denied having done anything out of spite or even without the suggestion coming from him. Some days before she had told him that she was going to marry Luc Simon and it seemed that that had roused his anger again. Last October he had already threatened to fight her in every way he could. It was on the recommendation of P.'s lawyer that she had made an arrangement for him to have the studios and as a proof that she was

not grasping she said that she had never taken advice or asked for legal help independently. She knew & liked the lawyer and was prepared to do anything he suggested. He himself had blamed P. for not making provision for the children and it now seemed that P. was scared that Luc and F. would legitimise the children. F. had no intention of doing this but it was impossible to allay his fears, and he refused to acknowledge them himself. F. had proposed a 'conseil de famille'[111] at which the lawyer, P.'s bank manager and the two of them should be present as the best way of settling all these matters, but nothing had been done. She pointed out that she was not asking for any support on her own. She had said that she wanted to go to Vallauris to fetch some of her belongings and since the children liked going there she would take them too, but she had absolutely no intention of installing herself there with Luc. Now, since so many people were discussing it and blaming her, she would give up the idea of going to V. to fetch her things and get the Ramiés to send them. She was very upset by the whole business and angry at having been misrepresented. She blamed certain friends of P.'s who had always criticised her behind her back, while protesting that they were friends so long as she was with P. That was one of the reasons why she had left him – because the gossip and backbiting were so sordid. These were the same friends who turned against Dora when P. broke with her. Now they were turning against her and P. could not forgive her for leaving him. He had loved her and she had loved him very much. It was the first time a girl had ever left him and nothing could make up for that. She hoped it would all be forgotten soon and longed for a happier and calmer state of affairs.[112] [9]

Visiting Paris, Barcelona and Cannes, June–July 1955

The Penroses returned to Paris on 2 June 1955 just before the opening of the retrospective of Picasso's paintings in the Musée des Arts décoratifs.[113] Many of the pictures came from Picasso's collection and the exhibition culminated with all fifteen variations after *The Women of Algiers* (see p. 103). A companion retrospective of Picasso's prints was mounted at the Bibliothèque Nationale.[114] Both exhibitions could hardly have been more timely for Penrose, who paid many visits with his pocket notebook at the ready. Looking, for example, at *Guernica*, he noticed that scale was irrational and used to generate drama, and he realised that the drawing of the bull's third eye 'helps to give movement to eyes and shifty look'.[115]

From his diary, we know that Penrose met Rosita Hugué on 9 June and it was probably then that she told him the following stories about her adoptive father, the notorious prankster Manolo, and about the art critic Maurice Raynal, whom Picasso had first met in 1905:

Manolo. 10 yrs. older than P. At 14 [Manolo] used to introduce him [Picasso] as his daughter Paula. P. would explode with indignation.

When M. Raynal died autumn 1954, P. said to Rosita, 'This morning I forgot to name him. I always go through all my friends dead and alive but today I forgot M.R.' Rosita said, 'But you did not kill him all the same.' But P. repeated, 'No, but I forgot him and now he's dead.' [12]

Penrose also had several rendezvous with Dora Maar,[116] and at one point they talked of Picasso's relationship with Max Jacob, his oldest French friend, who had converted to Catholicism and in 1921 withdrawn to a Benedictine monastery at St Benoît-sur-Loire. Deported to the concentration camp at Drancy, he died there on 5 March 1944:

P. visit. 1937 1 Jan. to Max J. 'pour faire la famille', M.J.[117]

Rosary left to P., trousers to Bérard.[118]

Return journey. P. talks about M.J.'s poverty with admiration for his disinterested way of living.[119]
    Said to Dora, 'Regarder quelle puissance il y a la dedans.'[120]

Sausage which was full of air and bust when both P. & M.J. had bought it with last sou.[121] P. retells story as a joke, M.J. with sentiment.

P. in Bateau Lavoir days never talked. In any case he is worried in company because he has no conversation. His conversation is 'par boutarde'.[122]

P. is not an atheist – preoccupation with death.

Dora Maar
When P. sold very early pictures for what seemed a lot of money he spent it nearly all buying a great stock of colours & brushes thinking that he might not be able to do so for a long time. He couldn't believe in his good fortune.

Dora
P. and nails razors
pour décourager des amateurs[123] [12]

From Paris the Penroses travelled to Barcelona on 16 June 1955. A postcard they sent Picasso mentions their visit to a bullfight – Lee's first corrida – and an evening spent singing flamenco songs with Lola Vilató and her family:[124] understanding Picasso meant absorbing the full Spanish experience. The main purpose of the trip was for Penrose to immerse himself in the world Picasso knew before he settled in Paris in 1904, and to his great relief he found that the artist's Catalan friends and the local historians preferred to speak French, for by his own admission, his Spanish was 'thoroughly inadequate'.[125] He cheerfully abandoned himself to an intensive, guided tour of the ancient heart of the city and to numerous visits to public and private collections containing works by the young Picasso and the bohemian set he had frequented at the café-cabaret 'Els Quatre Gats' (The Four Cats) – artists like Isidre Nonell, Ricard Canals and Ramon Casas. He also reimmersed himself in Catalan Romanesque art, first encountered on his trip to Barcelona with Valentine and the Zervoses in 1936. He knew it was the great passion of the entire 'Quatre Gats' group but he was also convinced that it was a crucial source for Picasso's Cubism and for his later mythologising work. The following typical extracts give a flavour of Penrose's observations:

Catalan art, Barcelona
[…] Byzantine symbolism and its formal arrangements find their echoes throughout the work of Picasso. The dominating oval that frames the image of the deity or the Virgin & Child reminds one of that predilection found in cubist painting for an oval composition with a solid mass often evolved/deduced from a woman with a guitar. The open book exposing in bold letters short simple words, such as EGO SUM LUX MDI, is akin to the lettering in the synthetic cubist period.

The drawing of faces with a black line or a flat background often suggest[s] the beginning of the combined profile and full face […]. The restraint in colour evokes the early cubist landscapes of the Horta [period]. Earth colours are sometimes used to the exclusion of all others, terre verte, ochre, venetian red and grey.

Mythology often with pagan origins abounds. The apostles have heads of bulls & eagles: archangels have wings covered with eyes. Animals play their part in the human family. The Lamb of God has seven eyes. The signs of human suffering are apparent in the innumerable scenes of martyrdom. The corrugated ribs of Christ and saints in agony, the skull drawn with stark simplicity and the torments of hell. Picasso's feeling for myths became fully manifest in the 'Minotaure' period having lain dormant for some twenty-five years.[126] […]

Picasso's painting, Barcelona
Early work in subject and sentiment very like many of the '4 Gats' group, particularly Casas and Canals in their Toulouse-Lautrec style – young women in hats, blouses and long skirts. Pastels. Others in same style [by] Joaquim Sunyer, [Ricardo] Opisso, Nonell. But in every case the work of P. is stronger in execution and meaning, satirical, pathetic, inventive, when the others are never untouched by commonplace, sentimental or fashionable considerations.

Very early 1900 pastel signed Ruiz Picasso in Museum is masterly in impressionist use of colour. Colour as light. Girl with large hat looks into mirror placed on a blue table. The glow of colour from the girl's blouse, the table legs and curtain illuminates the whole picture. Full of dark warm glow.[127] Another pastel of a couple embracing in a vacant lot has similar

qualities, red blouse & green skirt. The arms wrap the couple like girths.[128]
[…]

Paintings belonging to Señora Lola Vilató
'First Communion'. Girl in white kneeling at altar. Very conventional and
not in good preservation.[129]
    'Science & Charity'. Very impressive in size and masterly technique.
Painting throughout is consistently good and strong.[130]

Various cubist pictures. 1917. None of these are of great significance. He was
probably preoccupied with the Ballet and Olga – felt out of tune with his
surroundings. One small still life, a compotier with fruit, is outstanding
for its precision of design and pale subtle colour.[131] There is a lovely small
landscape of the Colon monument seen through open shutters with Spanish
flag among the trees.[132] According to Miró, during this [visit] he did not stay
as usual with his mother in the Calle de Merced but at the Ritz with Olga.
Probably the Ballet were staying there too. P.'s mother was very fond of Olga.
    The Ballet season in Barcelona (date). 'Parade' was performed and watched
by Miró & Prats from the gallery. They were both greatly impressed.[133] […]

Disease. This was the age of the poète maudit.[134] Disease was thought of as
a necessary asset. Nonell died of syphilis according to Sucre. Everyone had
their own private disease which allowed/gave them the cachet necessary for
an artist. He says P. had syphilis too.
    Anyhow there is a remarkable difference between the self-portraits of
the Blue Period and before in which he has a lean, romantic look and the
portrait after cubist period in which he becomes very robust, boxer type. [8]

**The poet and critic Josep Maria de Sucre was evidently a great source of
information. Either Picasso or Sabartès must have given Penrose his address
and there is a quite extended summary of their conversation:**[135]

Sucre
An important early influence was Burne-Jones, known to P. through
reproductions. He admired the easy curves of drapery and ripples in water.
Picture of maidens standing round a pool was favourite.[136] He would show
how he could do better himself and same curves occur in several early
pictures. Tradition of B.-J., Walter Crane & William Morris appreciated.
Main streams of influence came from (1) England. Carlyle, English liberals
& social reformers. Ruskin. Wilde. (2) France Symbolists. Impressionists
(never really understood in Spain. School of [Joaquín] Sorolla [and
Hermengild] Anglada [Camarasa], etc., luminists. [They] did not
understand French sensibility and search to analyse light. Their effects
were direct and dramatic – colours pretty pallid). (3) German, Nietzsche,
Böcklin & Ibsen. Expressionist feeling in all Spanish painting.

The interest in England came from a desire for more and better organised industry. Catalan workers went to England to work in dock – learnt textile trades and came back to set up Catalan textile industry with workers' dwellings. Realised importance of industrial revolution and need for liberalism. Liberalism took form of anarchism, influenced by Bakunin and Tolstoy. Anarchism main doctrine of intellectuals.

P.'s father, followed by little P., used to go round colombophile meetings and ask to be commissioned to paint winning birds [in] early days in Barcelona. Plaza [de] Cataluña was fairground. Soler paid for P.'s trip to Madrid when 'Art Joven' was founded by becoming pedlar for a new invention of electric belts made to rejuvenate.

Costumes at 'Quatre Gats' period based on Anarchist agitation. See Casas drawing. It was fashionable to have a secret disease (syph[ilis]) and most took a touch of cocaine. The poet damné[137] atmosphere reigned.

Illustrated magazines such as 'Studio', 'Gil Blas', 'Simplicissmus' (later) were received with avidity. Gavarni was favourite for a time, also Steinlen & Lautrec.

'4 Gats' was not a new building – already 10 yrs. old, but in neo-gothic style with elaborate gargoyles and carving. Owing to Gaudí's influence the landlord forbade entrance to all women except mère[s] de famille[138] for the puppet shows. After evenings of long discussion P. would go with Junyer & others armed with big sticks to fight the pim[p]s for their girls in the Barrio Chino.[139] P. would sing sometimes. He could talk Catalan but was often silent.

The dwarf dancer is taken from Velázquez.[140] Shows mostly in form & angle of skirt. The two pictures, notice shape of skirt, in reproduction [*thumbnail drawing*], were hung opposite each other.

Gaudí hated '4 Gats' group. He was a religious fanatic. They were anarchists and did not care for religion or ever go to church. Founded Circulo San Luc[141] which was to outlive '4 Gats', [but] it had a religious background and none of the freedom of rival. Took over old premises. Miró & Prats went to art school there because it was better than its only rival, the official Bellas Artes.

'Abstract art is a purification of representational art. Like Arab art, it presents itself in geometric form. Seeks the likeness of god in pure form rather than give it human shape.' 'P. has Jewish blood coming through Arabs on Ruiz side and is of Italian [descent] on Picasso side.' [2]

In amongst the jottings in his pocket notebook there are also a few scraps of family lore passed on by Picasso's sister, Lola Vilató:

First word P. ever tried to say was 'lapiz',[142] which got reduced to 'piz, piz'. He drew spirals saying they were a kind of sugar cake called pistol de capaillart[143] (same sort of cake in Perpignan), which means to get someone in a mess.

He drew long before he could speak. [...]

Lola remarked that the photo (Sabartès Doc.)[144] of her & Pablo together very young is exactly like Claude & Paloma. [12]

Penrose arrived in Cannes shortly after Picasso and Jacqueline moved into La Californie, a large Belle Epoque villa built on the hillside above the town.[145] On this leg of the trip he was entirely dependent on notetaking because Lee had returned to England. He was particularly fascinated by the preparations for Henri Clouzot's film *Le Mystère Picasso*, which was made from start to finish in close collaboration with Picasso. Unlike Emmer's documentary, this film had no political agenda and focused instead on the artist in the heat of spontaneous, exploratory creativity. The mystery – and drama – of the creative process were naturally of the deepest concern to Penrose, as an artist and a Surrealist, and the Clouzot film occupied a good deal of space in his subsequent notebooks and was treated at some length in *Picasso: His Life and Work*.[146] Penrose's notes start in staccato style with disparate topics before becoming more leisurely and descriptive:

Period of Marie-Thérèse big heads [and] sleeping blond paintings is lunar. P. says she has always done just what she wanted – strayed, wandered, changed her way of living. Massive heads made up of simple fruit-like forms. Joke of covering part of head so that hair looks like buttocks, head detached from earth. Long neck carries it like the moon racing through clouds, eye scratch[ed] on surface or added like a ball, a satellite. Of these heads P. said he was sorry he had spoilt them. Originally he had built up a very complicated construction of wire, which looked like nothing except when a light projected its shadow on the wall. Then the shadow became the truthful profile of Marie-Thérèse. He was delighted in this projection from a mass otherwise undecipherable. But he went on, added plaster and gave it its present form.[147] […]

'La réalité est ce qu'on crée et c'est tout.'[148]

'Quand on travaille on ne sait pas ce qui va sortir. Ce n'est pas l'indécision, c'est que ça change en travaillant.'[149]

Dislike of people who fawn on him at Eden Rock. Said it made him feel ill.

Unable with Clouzot to give any verbal indication of what he was going to do next. Complete spontaneity essential, anything that interferes breaks the spell. C. wanted him to say 'Stop' – even that [was] impossible. […]

I say, 'It is strange that your friends have usually been poets.' 'Yes, but the painters are too stupid and their conversation is boring.'

From the pile of Negro sculpture on the settee table P. takes out a Balumbo [mask] [*marginal note*: French Equatorial Africa] with smooth gentle

features whitened with lime. 'This is the first mask I ever bought,' he says.[150] Many of the pieces were of only moderate quality.

Arrived Cannes 5 July with Jacques & Paule de Lazerme, Totote & Rosita.[151] Found P. at home at La Californie. He showed us round the garden, obviously happy at our surprise at its extent and the size of [the] eucalyptus & palm trees. The house is hideous in the style of a Crédit Lyonnais banque stuck in a largish park of its own, but it is solidly built [and has] large rooms, parquet floors, high ceilings, windows and doors, which open wide and give feeling of light, coolness and space. Into these palatial surroundings has been moved the vast mixture, the unexplainable hazards and encounters of Picasso's possessions. Released from concentration camps in and around Paris they have now arrived in the promised land where there is room for all, where they can at last thrive in their own surroundings cared for by their master. Some have at once profited of the new situation. 'L'homme au mouton' stands alone on a piece of newly broken soil, his feet in the earth and his struggling charge lit by the full glare of the July sun.[152] A dense background of jungle foliage suggest[s] the presence of Rousseau, whose portrait with that of his wife, each beside their oil lamps,[153] have already been installed in a glass case upstairs. Other bronzes form a magic circle on the newly dug flower beds in front of the marble steps. Forming a chorus of small earthlike creatures, the cat,[154] the monkey carrying its young,[155] the clown,[156] surround a more solemn hieratic group huddled in conversation together. The great bronze heads of Marie-Thérèse[157] with small nude figures exchange glances while in their midst has fallen a dead man's head.[158] The

central room opens up to right and left while an inner hall connects with
the gravel of the entrance. Grouped in corners a party of guitars still in their
wrappings are huddled together. Canvases are piled together, cases half open
disclose an infinite variety of chattels, books and works of art of all ages and
from all parts of the world. On a table lie together the masks and statues from
Africa, on the walls hang dark and forbidding masks. One harmony unites this
chaos, a harmony due to the love that has brought them together. But many
more await repatriation and as they arrive the basic pattern behind this strange
reunion and the spirit which has chosen them becomes more apparent.

   Among this apparently disordered company P. moves and works. His eyes
wide open, receptive and restless, P. sets up an easel in the centre of the great

Picasso with recent
paintings in his studio
at La Californie, Cannes,
June 1956. Photo Lee
Miller

room. He is working on a new idea, a film to be made with Clouzot, whose technical skill and understanding of the painter's problems, together with his love of P. himself, make him a unique collaborator.[159] Their idea is to make the drawings appear on the screen by absorption onto the back of their paper. The artist will be hidden but each stroke of the brush will appear like magic as it is made. But the difficulties begin to be felt as P. makes various trials. (Course de taureaux.)[160] Each drawing grows from his brush with unexpected lines and patches. As though in a trance he makes an image hitherto invisible become real. Starting with a few rapid structural lines the subject appears in spontaneous realisation, the authors being himself and his material. Braque, he says, once said that to see him drawing was like a hand removing the dust from a hidden image. But there are moments when dramatic changes take place. The position of an eye already placed in a head which is taking shape fails to satisfy him and is blacked out, whereupon without hesitation it reappears in the only place left, a patch of white that remains, and there with the aid of this luminous highlight it takes its final inevitable position, as though it had always meant to be there, and triumphantly looks out from the drawing, the solution perfect and final. These drawings start from a stark white sheet and, in the space of five minutes, this arid reflector of light which blinds has been transformed into a face, a landscape, a jug holding flowers, in which the light emanates from the objects and lives within them. These drawings were in black and white with modulations of grey. The black, used sometimes as a heavy patch, could come forward or retreat into the distance but never did – it became a hole breaking through the surface of the canvas. All the play of depth appears to be between you and the canvas, although in reality the canvas has disappeared and become the image. This preoccupation dates from cubist times, although the modulations then were much more gentle and a jump from white to black inconceivable. The patient subtlety of changes from light to dark has given way to more rapid violent treatment, but the same principle is preserved, and the same three-dimensional play gives depth to the image. The further the drawing is carried with detail and half tones the more akin it is to analytical cubism. One finished only 3 days ago combines the most tender modulations with a very well determined design. It is a coloured drawing of bathers in the cool shadows of a pool, which resembles in colour the green light that filters through the palm and eucalyptus trees of La Californie. The nude women carry on the whiteness of their flesh heavy, b[l]ack patches which could so easily destroy the fulness of their bodies, but on the contrary the patches, as well as forming a rhythmic pattern throughout the picture, seem to accentuate their fulness and culminate their contours. Clouzot had called in one of his technicians to give advice and his immediate and enthusiastic cooperation brought a long afternoon's work to an end.

After they had gone I told P. that I was sure the project would be a brilliant success. He agreed that the chances were good but said, 'But supposing I fall on a bad day. That could happen and all would be wasted. It is like a bullfight

– the Torero must be [o]n his best form.' At which Jacqueline remarked that with such a Torero all would be well. But says P., 'There is the bull to be accounted for – the canvas.' However it is no question of one bad day spoiling the film. Clouzot is allowing three weeks for it and as always there is bound to be a crescendo of enthusiasm as the work progresses. If not P. will abandon all at a moment's notice. But in this case it seems most unlikely. The experiment of entering into the process of creation by showing how a drawing comes into being fascinates P. It would be impossible in poetry or music to demonstrate it in the same way and, what is more, this demonstration can become a work of art in itself. The scale alone, Clouzot is thinking in terms of eventually using cinescope, should give it great dramatic possibilities. It is a combination of research into the complicated, spontaneous appearances from the artist's mind and hand and the art of animated drawing on the screen. [12]

This long description of the aims and methods of *Le Mystère Picasso* is complemented by a succinct, quasi-filmic summary of the actions performed by Picasso:

Cannes July 1955, Picasso & Clouzot
I watched P. do a series of drawings trying out the technique that they were going to use in the film. From notes taken at time:

Certainty of touch – rapid, convincing. Stands back periodically to look at drawing but not for long. Returns with brush ready for its task laden with paint and stroke about to appear hidden within it – feeling that at that moment he knew already just what he was going to do. Stroke made firmly, deliberately, exactly w[h]ere wanted with measured determination. No hurry or impatience. If the paint runs – an exclamation, pause to see what may happen or immediate action to stop damage. Afterwards long contemplation of/communion with finished work while seated on couch. [2]

It was probably during this visit to the Midi, rather than in September 1954, that Penrose talked to Totote Hugué, who always enjoyed gossiping about the early days and especially about Picasso's love life:

Totote Manolo
Fernande was very beautiful (Alice Toklas said the same): mouth of great perfection, eyes and general bearing of rare distinction. Though she had flat feet she walked like a queen. She was a real woman and T. has always regretted the break. P. has sent her money ever since without her knowing from whom it came. She had a low forehead and wore her hair so as to cover it.

Céret discovered by Manolo in [1910]. P. came soon after, first stayed in hotel then took rooms in the Maison [Delcros-Paraye] which had fine park. Braque came and stayed at hotel, later Gris. Matisse was at times at Collioure. Derain ? Maillol at Banyuls.

Two intermediary stages and the finished canvas which was to
appear in the background of the film.

Preceding pages
Spread from the
maquette of *Picasso at
Work* (1965), showing
Picasso with his
daughter Maya during
the filming of *Le Mystère
Picasso* in Nice in 1955.
Photos Edward Quinn

1910 period. Fernande was with P.

P. was the only one of the group to have money.

1953, after departure of Françoise, during autumn a girl (Italian) called at Vallauris sent by friends. He kept her a week or two, did many very fine drawings, detailed finished nudes, then told her to go. She hesitated and was shown the door. Just after this he began the 'Verve' series.[161]

T. perpetually teased by P. Calls her la petite du Pape.[162] Says he has had a phone call from Rome asking if la petite is there, etc.

At Céret there was a very good looking girl who often passed in front of the café where P. & the Manolos were sitting. One day, to explain to Manolo who was passing without him having to turn round, P. drew the girl in profile upside down on the table. The likeness was unmistakable.

In Paris there was a German poet who bored everyone by reciting his poems. One night P., Manolo and he were riding home in a fiacre and as usual he was boring them stiff, so P. takes out his revolver and shoots through the roof.[163] In the confusion P. & M. slip out on opposite sides of the fiacre leaving the bewildered German to cope with the driver and later be taken for the night to the Poste de Police. [2]

One day while Picasso himself was taken up with a fashion-shoot – this kind of interruption became quite common during the 1950s – Penrose resumed his inventory of the unique, heterogeneous clutter of objects in La Californie, before breaking off to reflect upon Picasso's ambivalent attitude towards his children:

[…] Shelf with objects on it: violin, lamp, foot, crane, bottle … great head of Dora[164] … vase with dead flowers. Why don't writers take a shelf like this for their cast, animating each object with its correct personality? Tolstoy used so much material in 'War & Peace' but the same thing could happen on a shelf.

Next to a thermometer
A chain belt for penance hangs on the wall of the salon near the table, piled up like a heap of corpses stricken with the plague, with negro sculpture, on top of which floats a rigid male figure long and thin, the group suggesting the 'Charnel house'.[165] The proximity of death never is allowed to disappear. While posing for a series of fashion photos with this and layer upon layer of pictures in the background, Picasso adds to the drama of the elegant fashion model standing beside the old and wrinkled master by placing at their feet the bronze death's head,[166] saying 'Alas, poor Yorick!' The girl reacts and becomes even more youthful and lovable. The[y] move to another part

of the studio. P. finds his Lock bowler[167] and the two take poses as though dancing a ballet. The presence of death, disorder and anguish serves only to heighten the drama. The brilliant colour of the girl's clothes, her lithe movements and poses, the sunshine on the green jungle through the window, contain all the more meaning and enchantment. The cry of horror becomes a cry of joy.

[*Annotation in pencil identifying the model*] This was Bettina [Graziani] before she met Aly Khan.

The initial structure becomes obscured as work progresses. It becomes integrated into the forms that grow around it, but each drawing begins with a few rapid straight lines intersecting each other.

violin & bow
three-branch brass lamp fitted with electric bulbs
tin of furniture polish with rag
wire basket for eggs in form of cock with scarlet crest
a bottle
a brass foot
the 'Crane' painted bronze[168]
two glass vases
table lamp with silk shade, soiled
brass object use unknown
large Marquesas statue in wood[169]
pile of books and cardboard boxes
great bronze head of Dora
ashtray with half-smoked cigarette
electric light plug
sea-worn tile ashtray
perfume bottle
china vase
bronze owl
Indian fetish
lamp stand, big, fitted with shade
large bird vase with withered lily
dismantled table lamp
pot containing paint brushes
'Le fou' bronze head of 1904?[170]
pile of photos
tracing paper pinned to wall with written message, 'Penrose arrive par le train 10 Hs lundi'.[171] […]

Whatever humour may dominate there is always instability in P.'s mood. While in the happiest of moods, for some imperceptible reason a shadow falls across his face. It becomes pale, ridden with care and his eyes blacken like two nails driven deep into anguishing sensibility on which his face seems to hang. There is no doubt that he loves his children and he is generous towards them, but once they are grown up he has no interest in playing with them or understanding their problems. He knows them too well. Usually there is a tacit agreement not to have a row and hostility rises on the side of the children, balanced by attempted indifference on the other. Maya asks if she may go out with a boyfriend who will bring her back to the house before 11. The refusal is complete and instantaneous. 'Tu feras ce que tu veut quand tu n'est pas ici mais je ne veut pas que tes amis vienent à la maison et je ne veut pas que tu sort. Je n'ai jamais été fils et je ne veut pas être père.'[172] Maya retires violently into herself, thinking of her·pile of love letters from five different countries. But there is another side to the picture. They can enjoy each other's jokes and admire each other's qualities. Maya starts singing some popular air and her father joins in with grimaces, marking time with his feet and inventing absurdities so that one wonders which is the younger. There are moments of complete union on a basis of wholehearted enjoyment of their pleasure of being together. [13]

To put this remarkably intimate passage in context, the Edinburgh Archive contains a letter from Maya in which, having thanked Penrose for the photographs he had sent to La Californie, she announced her intention to study theatre and film in Paris:

Daddy hasn't really cottoned on yet. You know him, one has to repeat the same thing ten times over even though he has understood everything from the start.… Everyone is very well here, even though they pretend the opposite.[173]

Penrose's notes continue with a rapt description of the quasi-miraculous creation of a new painting during a rare hour of freedom from the continuous flow of visitors to La Californie:

After a bathe and late lunch we return to La Californie where Clouzot & Claude Renoir are waiting with their technical advisor to plan the film. Two hours are spent in watching P. draw with the materials required and discussing the technical means of this scheme, which involves entirely new problems. As soon as they have left P. moves round the big room quietly setting up a new canvas on which he settles down to work in a chair. I see him trace rapidly a few straight lines meeting near the centre of the canvas and then leave. About an hour later I return to find him asleep on the couch. Later, when he has woken, I ask to see what he has done and he produces a finished picture of magical strength, a new vision of the head of a shepherd king, a wise man of the East, seen against a night sky with large stars, some like starfish, others like micro pictures of blood corpuscles. In the distance, seated on a wall, a creature half-faun, half-leopard, pipes to the stars or maybe examines them through his telescope. There is an archaic feeling in the wise bucolic face with its beard like seaweed full of phosphorescent sea life and the heavy triangular nose of one who has lived well and unwisely to become wise. The face contains two profiles arguing with each other but they unite to form a strong and harmonious moon-shaped head crowned with dark emblems against the night sky. The luminous heavy blue becomes lighter where it lies against the black edge on the summit of the crown. Light and dark showing off against each other. In less than an hour a completed masterpiece has appeared. P. said, 'It is strange, in Paris I never draw fauns, centaurs and suchlike creatures but they seem to live in these parts,' and 'Magi were not kings, they were wise men, alchemists, but because they brought gold people made them into kings. Actually it was they who made the kings, like in Spain at the coronation of a king the formula was, "We kings who are more powerful than you, we kings make you king."' This noble head is admirable in its weakness. The black triangle that forms the end of the nose and the plumpness of the unshaven cheek spotted with freckles or the stubble of a rebellious beard have a touch of absurdly human weakness, a caricature of the archaic. The horns that surmount the crown suggest a dangerous challenge to its dignity. The dual role of wise man and initiator into the troubled realms of unbridled instinct. The horns are decorated with patterns which imply a status superior to the faun who announces the presence of the god, chief sinner and heart of wisdom.[174]

A round wooden slab with a handle carved on one side with a half-finished design of three figures was lying among all the rest.[175] P. brought it to me, saying he had had the intention of making it the back of a hand mirror. Near it stood a head carved from a straight section of a branch in low relief.[176] Both were typical of the Negro period and neither has been reproduced. (Size of head approx. 12" high x 5" diam.) The head is on the outer surface of the branch, which has been split.

Straw cap or Tyrolean hat covers his bald head, showing a fringe of short white hair. His slightly flattened nose suggests the strong archaic curve of the profile of a goat, the heavy creases that arch over a wide stretched mouth, which when silent is tough and severe but which gives way, as the lips open, with trumpet-like curves to the baroque curves of the orifice of a shell. The cheeks are strained, pale and inclined to be hollow, the colouring loses in Paris its healthy bronze, which gives his whole body a flush of vigour in summer, but the parchment colour of his face only serves to draw more attention [*text ends here*] [13]

In Paris, Penrose had meetings with Sabartés and the musician Guy Bernard and kept brief notes of what they told him.[177] Both mentioned Picasso's painful moments of anxiety and self-doubt – a side to the artist which was rarely acknowledged but which Penrose witnessed on several occasions:

Sabartès
[…] Olga never forgot the ballet, talked about it endlessly and dress[ed]
in extravagant ballet style. Georges Salles owns portrait [of] about 1930
in which she appears as a monster, not unlike in my self-portrait, very lifelike in every way.[178]

Doubts about La Californie. Sabartès tries to reassure him. He asks everyone
if it's not a folly.

Guy Bernard
'Le culte de l'inquietude, inquiet a propos de l'opinion de ses amis.'[179]
    First time he [Bernard] saw the first ceramics he wept but said nothing.
Later P. questioned him, very worried because he had said nothing.

Guy quarrelled with C[ommunist] P[arty] over their attitude to music and
criticism of modern music, left them for that. Eluard told him he was right to
do so.

Treasurer & wife of C.P. lunching with P. – Guy sent for, P. explains that they
do not like his drawings. Laughs at them, saying that his doves are admired
all over [the] world, they should have more confidence.[180] [13]

The next day, 16 July, Penrose saw Tristan Tzara. It was probably then that
they had the following conversation about Picasso's brief participation in
Dada activities in Paris:

Tzara (in conversation). P. associated very little with Dadaists & Surrealists,
though he knew most of them. He was present at riotous evening [*blank
space left*] at Théâtre St. Michel in a box and was inadvertently cause of final
rupture between T. & Breton. At height of row he stood up & raising his arm
shouted, 'Tzara, pas de police ici!'[181] which made Breton think that T. had
already called the police, who arrived just then – it was a journalist who had
called them. [2]

It may have been on the same occasion that Tzara spoke disparagingly of
the Punu mask to which Picasso was particularly attached:

Tzara
Early negro purchase very banal.[182] [12]

As a famously discriminating and knowledgeable collector of African sculpture, Tzara could afford to be dismissive about the generally mediocre, if not
downright bad, quality of Picasso's sprawling collection.

Keeping up the momentum of his visits and interviews, Penrose returned to France in the autumn.[183] He saw Dora Maar both before and after his trip to Cannes, and at least one of the following conversations took place at this time.[184] Maar was prepared to speak so candidly about Picasso's attitude to love and family life only because she knew she could trust Penrose not to betray her. And her trust was not misplaced, for he kept all the most intimate revelations to himself:

D.M.
P. always wanted a mixture of bourgeois and bohemian in his girls. Olga, Colonel's daughter, became [a] dancer. Diaghilev told P. not to marry her, there were so many better – more beautiful, talented, etc., better wait for another to come along. But P. [was] attracted by [the] required mixture.

Marie-Thérèse – strange product of an unsuitable marriage. P. met her when she was 14 – chance encounter – she was two years younger than Dora – came as a relief to conventional life into which he was being forced by Olga 4 years after marriage – first appears in painting about 1926.[185] Maya born as a mistake. M.T. & P. both admitted it. P. always anxious to prove fertility by put[ting] a girl in child but told D. that once a girl had had a baby she became his enemy (?). She had proved to have too much power. Complicated story of M.T.'s mother & sister, optician, who were all supported by P. in flat [on] Ile St. Louis. P.'s desire to found family broken into by arrival of Dora. Two cases where he really set out to found family – Olga & Françoise. P. wanted to divorce Olga because of M.T. & Maya, but jealous anger of Olga fell on Dora. M.T. [was] ignored. M.T. v. jealous of Dora, once came and made a terrible scene ending in a fight. M.T. frustrated by arrival of Dora when she hoped to be winning everything. In '37 when D. was staying with Lise Deharme at St. Tropez, he came over there in a party with Eluard and Lee & self and taking her aside on the beach he announced that he had a daughter. They went back to Mougins that evening together. Dora met P. in 1936.

After death of Eva in 1915 several short-lived affairs: Pâquerette, Fernande Barrey (later mistress of Foujita), Irène Lagut who comes in[to] 'La femme Assise'. Picasso annoyed with Apollinaire for that and for being called 'l'oiseau de Benin. L'Uccello noir'.[186]

Affair with M.T. was reaction from snob world of Rosenbergs, de Beaumonts, Mme. Errazuriz at St. Jean de Luz, Chanel, etc., which Olga loved and which sprang from the Russian ballet.

Dora says that P. told her that when drawing a bull he often had in mind his Airedale dog. The tufts of hair on the head confirm this.

Story of his love of heavy breasts. 'Those I love best are those that have most milk.' Françoise had to suckle both children.

Dora

The pattern of each period is a man, a woman, a dog and the influence of a 'museum period'.

MEN		WOM[E]N	[DOG]
M[ax] J[acob], Apollinaire, Jarry, Moréas, Salmon		Fernande	
" "	Braque	Eva, Irène Lagut	
Diaghilev	Cocteau	Olga	St. Bernard
		Marie-Thérèse	Airedale
Eluard		Dora	Kasbec
"		Françoise	Yong
Prévert		Jacqueline	

P. broke with Fernande on finding a note from … cinema actor.[187] 'Il a le gout d'un fin precipité.'[188]

At once took up [with] Eva, who[m] he already knew. Eva died of cancer – a gentle unintellectual girl of great charm.

P. caught syphilis when he was 19, i.e. first or second visit to Paris – about time of Casagemas suicide.

P. introduced Braque to Marcelle, who[m] he had known for some while, and Alice to Derain.

P. gave Dora all the pictures she now has without her ever asking [for] any.

P. not spontaneous. Moments of great enthusiasm [for] a girl carry him away and for a moment he is capable of anything, [but] die down quickly if not shared by them.

P. said he had never really been in love.

Sentimental at times. Never abandons himself completely.

Passionate but calculating.

Loves children as he loves animals – without feeling of responsibility or desire to educate or change them. His behaviour to child could only be put to the test if he were alone to look after it.

Marie-Thérèse kept at Vollard's house [*blank space left*] in country.[189] P. would go on a Saturday & return Sunday during 'Guernica' summer. Painted many landscapes – portraits of Maya & M.T., etc. and returned to work on 'Guernica'. Said, 'You see I am not only occupied with gloom.' Dora with him in Paris all the time. Paul [Eluard] very largely responsible for 'Guernica' – and attitude to political situation.

P. saw a great deal of Braque in early years.

Vollard had built studio for Rouault, who did not like it and never used it, but P. took it over and when Dora was living with him, M.T. was kept away in the country.

Dora, Paris, 27 O[ctober], '55

Monkeys. A theme that has been permanent. Distortions of Blue Period are like monkeys, crouching in fear, arms crossed, elongated limbs and fingers – first noticed by Dora in Jardin des Plantes, she remarked on it to P., who said, 'Ah, oui, tu as remarqué ça.'[190] He frequently uses as a phrase, 'Nous voilà dans la cage des singes.'[191] Sometimes when the first amiabilities of a visit to friends or a party have been got through out comes this phrase half-joking, half-meant.

The monkey they had in Mougins, 1937, which was always with them, on the beach – everywhere – became so much of a preoccupation that D. became 'jealous' of it and it was got rid of because she insisted.

Egyptian influence in Blue Period – never leaves him – remark of Rousseau.[192]

Three times he has tried to found a home. With Olga it failed and she became 'le monstre', but not Paulo. With Marie-Thérèse – beautiful then at 17 but always 'lunatic', it failed again – eau forte of this family with entrance of 'le monstre'.[193] Third time with Françoise – fille de bonne famille,[194] talented – in pictures of children they are more dismembered and harshly treated than before, though process had begun with Maya. On joining C.P. [he] said, 'I have found my family.'

'P. great invention is the dismembering of the human face.' Sometimes results in great beauty – early portrait of D.[195] – but as age sets in & doubt it becomes more vicious. Said to D. who ('37) brought him breakfast on a tray – 'Comme j'aimerai avoir de vielles femmes m'apporter mes repas comme ça.'[196] In later years she was treated with utmost violence in pictures. 'Femme couchée' (postcard).[197] But being so feminine himself, this vengeance on old age and ugliness was at bottom a vengeance on himself. Since he destroys always – destroyed his families.

Never was pederaste – not even with Max Jacob. Once told D. that Jarry had kissed him on the mouth but she is convinced that if more had occurred, during the 9 years she lived with him he would have told her.[198] That he is a 'homosexuel refoulé'[199] she has no doubt – it is one of the factors that contribute to creative work.

Picasso artist & mystic – a religious side which makes him want to blaspheme as well as adore.

Mother's death did not touch him – D. was there when news came – he made no show of emotion – said he had not seen her for so long that she was already dead to him[200] – compare reaction to death of Olga and remarks on seeing photos of Lola from Barcelona.

Not schizophrenic – no sign of the detail so typical of their work – Klee more likely was.

Dora
[…] When D. went to Barcelona, before she knew P., she was very struck by the great quantity of blind beggars. She took photos and later showed them to P., who was very impressed.

The poems of P. are very personal and hermetic. D. can understand meaning and see origins only of those parts inspired by her and their life together. In the 'Desire caught by the tail' the descriptions of her with fingers smelling of turpentine, etc. are clear – also the electric stove, which was one of her gadgets, always given credit for any successful cooking. Other passages – 'the man hanging in the curtains, etc.' are very obscure, but all belong to distant memories and haunting events.

Dora
P. continued to live [in] rue La Boétie until transport during the war became too difficult. He then began sleeping [in] rue des Gds. Augustins. Rue La Boétie was a very pleasant apartment looking on a garden to the south. Two floors. Drawing room on street, dining room – same space upstairs where he had studios and bedroom. Bedroom was in superb state of disorder. Two brass single bedsteads, but when Olga's became unused it was piled up with papers. The trunk from the Hispano placed on the bed was used as a desk because it locked up easily. In dining room hung a very fine Renoir of bacchanalian scene and 'Le Château noir' of Cézanne.[201]
    When Dora arrived P. asked her to supervise complete cleaning of the flat by old dishonest femme de ménage,[202] who spied on them for Olga until she got the sack – that was the only systematic cleaning that she [Dora] ever saw.
    Dora found the Gds. Augustins for P. She had been to Geo[rges] Bataille's 'Contre Attaque' meetings on the top floor. On the floor below was a workshop full of looms. [2]

Since Penrose's previous visit to Cannes in July 1955 *Le Mystère Picasso* had been completed, leaving Picasso exhausted by the experience of being filmed day after day in a stuffy studio at the height of a Mediterranean summer.

The after-effects of this gruelling work are one topic of Penrose's notes, another Picasso's sceptical attitude to the French Communist Party. The remainder of Penrose's notes record miscellaneous pieces of information and his first impressions of a brand-new series of pictures inspired by the spacious studios in La Californie. At one point, Picasso issued a crucial and provocative warning: 'You mustn't always believe what I say. Questions tempt one to tell lies because there is no answer.' Penrose did not forget these words and in his memoirs records another, similar caution. Jacqueline had suggested he 'bombard' Picasso with questions, but,

I was enjoying quietly and intensely our intimacy and all I could say was that I found it extremely difficult to know how and when to ask the right question. 'Yes,' said Pablo decisively, 'if you ask me the wrong questions I shall give you the wrong answers.'[203]

Visit Cannes, 6 Nov. 1955
P. has been very tired and worried about his health. The film made with Clouzot was a tax on his resources. Every day for weeks together he went to the studios at Nice and worked under the heat of arc lamps which made the sun outside seem cold 'like Siberia'. For [the] last month he has been refusing to see everyone and only going out once a week to see his doctor – who says tension,[204] so complete rest. No smoking. Saltless diet. No drink. Jacqueline, more beautiful than before and with greater assurance, has been nursing him very well and he seems tired but nothing otherwise wrong. Visit from [Laurent] Casanova, who had come to talk C.P. business.[205] Recently P. had refused to see Aragon. Casanova arrived unannounced and was made welcome. During lunch conversation turned on Cocteau – P. described the swords he had designed, including one not reproduced in press – 'épé de cabinet'.[206] Then said that to him Cocteau & Aragon were the same thing – they had been all along from days of Surrealism.

P.'s telephone had been out of order. J. said she thought they had fitted up a 'table d'ecoute',[207] which was the cause. Discussed likelihood of this. C[asanova] & P. in agreement that his conversations were recorded. P. had been told by a Préfet how to prevent it from working.

C. talked a lot about politics and spoke with reverence of the cleverness of professional politicians of the right in keeping going a government which was only held together by intrigue. P. afterwards said he admired C. as a talented politician but, 'What a métier!' P. did not seem overjoyed by the visit but there was no sign of his wavering in his loyalty to the C.P.

Told me that the Hotel Madrilène, where I am staying, was taken by him in 1928 for the summer. In those days it was a villa with a large studio occupying whole of top floor. Unusual for him to take a studio, he had always worked in hotel rooms. Result was that he hardly worked at all all summer – just a few drawings.

'Demoiselles d'Avignon'. Braque's first comment, 'It is [as if] one were expected to exchange one's usual diet for one of tow & paraffin.' [Leo] Stein & Matisse were overheard by P. discussing the picture in his studio. Stein said, 'He is trying to make the 4th dimension.' Both roared with laughter. [*Inserted addition*] 4th dimension was later to interest many cubists. Metzinger, Duchamp, Braque (a little). See Barr 259.[208] [*Main text continues*] Braque, 'étoupe et petrole'.[209]

Leo Stein & Matisse laugh. '4th dimension, rendre des formes à plat sans faire des trous dans la toile et peindre une oeil comme une oeil et pas autre chose.'[210] The title [of *Les Demoiselles d'Avignon*], partly 'à cause de la calle de Avignon',[211] partly because mother was born in Avignon. Painted in Paris [so] no one understood.

Reproductions – non-existent – first sight of Impressionists was at Durand-Ruel, rue Laffitte. Before that [Miquel] Utrillo had talked about what he had seen. Painting at that time was appallingly bad and was seen everywhere. In Spain painters of '80s & '90s constructed the scenes they wanted to paint like cinema sets in their studios or, if they were more ambitious, outdoors, like one in Málaga who painted an enormous canvas in the bullring, with complete set of horses, bulls, toreadors, etc. Don José used to go and watch him at work. Another, José Maria Garnelo,[212] in Barcelona *c.* 1895 reconstructed Lourdes with stretchers, shrine, sick, priests, tru[c]s[213] and all. Even those who painted peasant interiors and still lifes had décor built up as their model.

Don José in Málaga would replenish his stock of stuffed birds from the seminary and sell them later.

Rousseau thought 'Demoiselle[s]' fine – he was uncritical – liked painting. Picasso or Bouguereau, all the same [to him].

Talking of Bernal & visit to London 1950. P. said he had seen crystals forming under microscope. B. could give a formula for making crystals – could he deduce a formula from a painting by P.? – relate it to an element? (compare crystallisation of cubist style, 1909) (Barr, p. 66).[214]

'L'homme a l'agneau'. Stands well on the soil of the garden. He half stumbles, half walks with his restive burden, in difficulty but still in control. The irregularity of the lumpy modelling becomes increasing[ly] convincing as one contemplates it. It is not merely there to catch the light, it is full of the strain necessary for the man's poise. Twisted hand, popping eyes, contorted face, straight peg legs & flat feet.

Swiss mathematician came to P. and asked him to collaborate in solving painting by mathematics. P. replied, 'It can no more be done than a mathematical problem can be solved by painting. They are two different things.' Theories that he makes calculations to help him paint are absurd since he hardly knows how to calculate his change in a shop. Breton's theory absurd (Barr 260).[215] He has sometimes said as a joke when people asked, 'What does that represent?' 'To you that represents 500,000 francs.'

Eluard's understanding of him and his work was more complete than Max Jacob or Apollinaire. They were younger then.

8 Nov.

All afternoon he worked on further drawings of his interior with coloured crayons while he had sent me to Vallauris in his car. When I returned he showed me four drawings, all of the same subject but each one different. A Baroque vigour had possessed him that made the windows and the mirror sway in [a] rhythmic dance behind the static poise of the chair and plaster head on its stand.[216]

I then settled down to read his play written in Aug. '48, 'Les Quatre Jeune Filles',[217] while he went back to work by the dining table and made two more drawings. The great rooms are more bleak than ever when lit by a powerful bulb in the centre of each. No part is reserved exclusively for any one purpose. The dining table becomes his drawing desk or is used for reading his mail. Disorder spreads everywhere over and under the furniture. There is nowhere any attempt at decorative effects or tidiness. There are no curtains. If pictures are hung they are placed anywhere and yet the objects scattered everywhere are all of interest. Even the vulgarity of a brass bull made in Vallauris and given by some admirer, or the naïve plaster dove on a silver painted pedestal made specially for him by a local tradesman for his birthday, will very likely take their place in some future composition inspired by the architecture of spontaneous disorder and there become entirely in their place.

Meals round the oval dining table are of the simplest kind. Jacqueline cooks plain wholesome food with no salt to comply with his diet. He drinks no wine or alcohol of any sort but when Casanova was there at lunch he started praising drink and even opium for its great value as a stimulant, admitting that it was dangerous as a habit. He tries not to smoke and succeeds partially.

Matisse 'La Joie de Vivre'[218] was finished before 'Demoiselles'. Gauguin influence.

9.11.55

'Customs of Aragon' won some sort of medal in Madrid and was painted over many times. P. used same canvas again often, not only because of being hard up, but simply that it was easier than going out to buy another.

Gaudí. P. knew of the Güell palace. It was finished ten years before he came to Barcelona, but Gaudí's problems were not the painter's problems. He [Picasso] was not interested. (In fact he is not interested in architecture at all.)

The paintings on walls of Angel de Soto's studio, Riera de San Juan, were a joke among friends. Everything was there to make it look rich, pieces of money left on the dressing table – the housemaid and the groom.

Don José, red-haired, very tall, English tastes, chairs, Chippendale and Hepplewhite bought in Málaga – filtered through from Gib[raltar]. He had no real interest in religion or politics, thoroughly conventional. P. painted portrait of Republican minister in Corunna simply because he lived across the street.[219] No liberal tradition in family.

Politics of '4 Gats' mainly came from rich dilettante separatists such as Rusiñol. They risked nothing by their wild talk.

Explanation of Breton's statement quoted by Barr p. 260.[220] P. was making a tracing of a cubist picture to remember and analyse his original intentions – the main outlines of construction. He made no measurements and no calculations, purely a visual, painter's exercise.

Saint Lazare was a hospital for venereal diseases. P. happened to know one of the doctors, who allowed him to visit when he liked. He did many drawings of the inmates. Those who were in for treatment wore a special 'Phrygian' cap. The moment most interesting to P. was as they left and settled in the nearest bistro for a drink. He came & went as one of the staff, washing his hands in disinfectant as he left.

[Gustave] Coquiot was a writer of some distinction. The dancers in [the] background of his portrait are pure fantasy – as though reflected in a mirror. Originally in the portrait he had a great stand with which he was playing. P. thinks he wrote a book called 'La terre frotté d'ail'.[221]

P. met Matisse about 1905 and Braque not till 1907, when 'Les Demoiselles' was already finished.
    Les Fauves did not interest him (more to say later).

[Henri] Bloch is a violinist. Still comes to call.[222]

Eva remains mysterious, only one photo in Japanese costume bought in Marseille. She was very sweet and charming.

Numbers. Though no mathematician, numbers have always fascinated him. Often he has filled sheets with them but he has never added them up or made calculations – if an answer is given it is invented. His love of figures is purely platonic.

Asking questions. Answers cannot be expected easily. Some questions can imply a falsehood and therefore can only merit a lie or a paradox as an answer. There are no definite answers. Is that blue? No, it is red. There is no such thing as blue by itself. It is a balance between intuition and intelligence. Science tries to force us into precise answers, black or white, but theory of relativity should admit that there are no precise answers where art is concerned – only appreciation and paradox. Without appreciation no explanation is possible. P. said, 'Il ne faut pas croire toujours ce que je dis, les questions vous tentent à dire des mensonges parcequ'il n'y a pas de reponse.'[223]

The cup in form of a breast [was] made this summer.[224] He added the fly as [the] finishing touch to break the too perfect, too sublime. Hates and fears the sublime and the finished. The only finished work that is tolerable is one that leads to further creation, a sort of manure to new ideas. Death becomes life, for the finish[ed] work is otherwise dead. The fly on the breast, which is already in reverse relief, makes it more difficult to situate. Concave in reality, the breast by illusion become[s] convex, nipple and fly are suspended on an imaginary surface. The fly is comic, bathos, absurd in situation and significance. It is the essential poetic touch.

Film, 'Les Grandes Manoeuvres' (René Clair), 9 Nov. '55, was heartily disliked by P., Jacqueline and myself. Reasons given by P. were that he was not fond of the past – had no nostalgia for that period, which he remembered in principle as snobbish and absurd in its customs. He disliked military life above all and a film based on that was bound to be stupid – army life was even more imbecile than shown in the film. Situations were all dominated by just those conventions that we detest and try to upset. Even accepting the falseness, artificiality of situation, not well played, not dramatic. (P. does not accept a conventional atmosphere even if story is good – would never say this is an absurd situation but good theatre.)

The C.P. line put out in a glowing review by Aragon is that the film is excellent – like Watteau – a piece of French genius. Casanova had repeated this faithfully at lunch on Sunday, saying that it was most moving and a splendid piece. P. found this incomprehensible. Neither was it well played – Gérard Philipe and Michèle Morgan both disappointing – nor could it have any significance as far as love or behaviour were concerned. Customs have changed for the better – less hypocrisy – people live their own lives less terrorised by convention. P. had no sympathy with party line – said that when Casanova came for long discussions he had great difficulty in refraining himself from saying disagreeable things.

'Les quatre petites filles'. A play in six acts of poetic soliloquies varying in duration. 4 little girls, delightfully skittish and usually nude, display their innocence mixed with evil instincts. Like in 'Desire caught by the tail', stage directions play an important part with parades and dumbshow. Certain passages are very robust in their visual poetry – a wonderful piece on the yellow of blue, the blue of blue, the blue of red, etc. and this

'Petite fille II		Seule l'oeil du taureau qui meurt dans l'arêne voit
"	I	Il se voit
"	IV	La glace deformante voit
"	II	La mort cette eau claire
"	I	Et très lourde.'[225]

Lights at night. The Croisette was wet after a shower. Street lamps and neon signs made brilliant streaks of colour. P. says he has often wanted to paint night lighting – impossible to get enough intensity. If it could be done people would say it was false – exaggerated.

Jacqueline says he sings to her comic songs from operettas and dances. I remarked that Salmon says that in Bateau Lavoir days he never sang but enjoyed Max J[acob]'s singing. J. said, 'Mais maintenant c'est lui qui chante et il faut le mettre dans le livre.'[226] She is so devoted that it is at times embarrassing, but he now seems to enjoy such attention and she is nursing him with the greatest love and not without intelligence. She understands his moods and divines his humour very well.

Charlie Chaplin talks too much when he comes to call – it all has to be translated and is too full of bright ideas – everything he says is a bright idea. Once he came in a car with his wife to say he couldn't come. They arrived all dressed up in splendid furs in spite of the weather [and] delivered the letter saying they couldn't come in person and left. [14]

These notes were written up on large sheets of paper at Penrose's leisure, with the pocket notebook he carried with him to La Californie functioning as his *aide-mémoire*. Among the disparate, hasty jottings in that notebook are these few snatches of Picasso's conversation:

Italian origin certainly possible, but P. likes idea of Arab blood at earlier period to account for taste for bullfight, gitanos, etc. […]
Showing drawings: 'Enfin c'est tout ce que je sais faire.'[227]

'I don't know how to sharpen a burin if it's blunt. I go on working, hacking it out just the same. I don't know the names of colours in tubes.' […]
Row about ballet Miró-Ernst from Surrealists. Tried to exclude them but dare[d] not touch P. He got jobs in Ballet for other Surrealists and then they were implicated.[228]

Promises de Rothschild to go over to Bordeaux and make him a sculpture (a sheep) with no intention of doing it. […] [15]

Although tired, following a strict diet on doctor's orders and attempting to give up smoking, Picasso was evidently in a benign and cooperative mood throughout Penrose's visit. As a sign of friendship, on 8 November he presented Penrose with a manuscript copy of a poem entitled 'Ojo' (eye) written for Sabartès.[229] On the same day he wrote a dedication on a photograph Dora Maar had taken of him in 1937 as a bronzed demi-god or pagan priest, holding a bull's skull in one hand and a forked stick in the other (see p. 142). Since Dora Maar also wrote a dedication on the same photograph Penrose must have shown it to her when they met in Paris after his return from Cannes.[230] The photograph had been taken on the beach at Golfe-Juan when Roland and Lee, as well as Paul and Nusch Eluard, were present, so it was a precious memento of a golden moment in all their lives, and in obtaining both Picasso's and Dora's signatures Roland effected a symbolic momentary reunion of the former lovers.

Penrose stayed on in Paris for several days and one of the friends he met was Man Ray.[231] Inevitably, the conversation turned to Picasso:

Man Ray says when Picasso went to see Mme. Errazuriz at Biarritz he was given a small whitewashed room. He had no paints with him but without her knowing [he] covered her walls with paintings done with a rag and ink. She had complete confidence in anything he did and accepted it at once. [2]

As we shall see, the story of these murals, painted in 1918 when Picasso was on his honeymoon with Olga, has a surprising twist that reflects badly on the character of the colourful art-lover and society hostess Eugenia Errazuriz.

Penrose returned to England bearing another gift from Picasso – a drawing of a bullfight for the ICA's forthcoming fundraising sale. His thank-you letter gushes delight and gratitude for this welcome injection of aid: 'Yet again you have spread happiness and joy amongst all of us and we thank you from the bottom of our hearts.' It was all sincerely meant, and no doubt the 'commercial artist' who was lucky enough to acquire the drawing in the sale did feel 'boundless joy' when he discovered he had scooped the biggest prize.[232] But Penrose's bedazzled reaction to everything Picasso did eventually became oppressive to the recipient of all these fulsome encomia. Striking a balance between welcome and unwelcome levels of flattery is always a delicate matter, but with someone of Picasso's mercurial character there was no predicting his response. There was no backlash from him at this stage, but the quicksands became more treacherous for Penrose a few years further down the line.

At the end of his thank-you letter Penrose broached a new project that would occupy much of his time over the coming months: a documentary

Pour mon cher Roland
son ami Picasso
Cannes le 8.11.55.

Pour Roland
Affectueusement
Dora.

exhibition to celebrate Picasso's seventy-fifth birthday on 25 October 1956. 'With the cooperation of Sabartès, Kahnweiler and Man Ray,' he explained,

I hope to be able to gather a great quantity of documents about you, the places where you have worked, etc. and your friends such as Apollinaire, Max Jacob, Eluard, Cocteau, etc., etc. I believe that this will be of great interest to us and to the general public.[233]

It turned out to be a very good idea indeed. 'Picasso Himself', as the exhibition was called, was not only a popular success but also speeded up Penrose's progress on the biography, for which, in effect, it functioned as a blueprint as well as an excellent advertisement. 'The Vallentin woman', as she was resentfully referred to in Hilary Rubinstein's letters, might – and in fact did – beat Penrose in the race to publish, but at least 'Picasso Himself' would establish Penrose's total independence and moral priority.

Opposite
Photograph by Dora Maar of Picasso holding a bull's skull and forked stick, summer 1937, dedicated to Penrose by Picasso and Maar in November 1955

Chapter 4

The Biography Completed, 1956–1958

Visiting Paris and Cannes, February–March 1956

Penrose's next trip to France lasted for almost seven weeks. He arrived in Paris on 4 February 1956.[1] Between then and his departure for Cannes two weeks later he was busy assembling material for his documentary exhibition at the ICA and also asking questions. Judging by his notes, he gleaned only small scraps of information and the occasional anecdote. Guy Weelen, for example, repeated a typically pithy comparison Picasso had drawn between himself and his old partner Braque:

P., looking at a cubist Braque of great charm, said, 'Avec Braque toujours la crème – moi jamais.'[2] [16]

Penrose lunched a couple of times with Max Ernst, who told him that 'in 1922 or thereabouts' he had found in a Montmartre junk shop several early drawings by Picasso, one depicting Sarah Bernhardt and the others prostitutes. Ernst paid '3 to 5 frs. apiece' – an astonishing coup given that Picasso was already famous at the time.[3] During one of his regular visits to the Galerie Leiris, Kahnweiler passed on the story that 'Max Jacob was model for lower part of face' of the 1905 sculpture *The Jester*, and that Picasso 'set to work [on it] on coming home late at night after an orgy'.[4] In *Picasso: His Life and Work* Penrose gave a suitably toned-down version: 'It was begun late one evening after returning home from the circus with Max Jacob.'[5]

Penrose also met Georges Salles, sometime Directeur des Musées de France, and heard his account of the famous occasion in the spring of 1947 when the twelve paintings Picasso had just donated to the Musée National d'Art Moderne were taken into the galleries of the Louvre and placed alongside Picasso's favourite Spanish and French pictures so that he could compare the effect:[6]

Georges Salles
When P. gave his pictures to the Mus[ée] d'Art Moderne, Salles had them in the Louvre for formalities. He invited P. to come round and see them saying, 'Il tiens bien parmi les maîtres.'[7] P. arrived as usual in company with friends with an anxious look on his face. Pictures were in a room of Davids, etc. 'grand

machine'[8] and held their own well. Salles then suggested they should be tried out in Spanish room. P. looking even more 'inquiet'[9] agreed. Again they held their own and P. becoming happier said, 'Vous voyez c'est la même chose.'

'Il n'y a pas de génie méconnu.'[10] […] [17]

Over a year had passed since the signing of the contract and, in an effort to consolidate his research, Penrose drew up a list of strictly factual questions to be fired at Kahnweiler, Sabartès and Picasso himself.[11] Most apparently remained unanswered, but one question, 'Has P. ever asked for French nationality or wanted it?', elicited the intriguing answer from Sabartès, 'At time of divorce?' – a reference to Picasso's abortive attempt to get a divorce from Olga in order to marry Marie-Thérèse Walter and legitimise their daughter, Maya. The full facts surrounding his unsuccessful application for French citizenship, made early in 1940, have only just become public knowledge and give the lie to the widely held belief that Picasso never considered relinquishing his Spanish nationality.[12]

Lee did not accompany Roland to Cannes but she was not forgotten, and Picasso, Jacqueline and Sabartès, who was on one of his periodic visits to the Midi, joined him in sending her a postcard of a bathing beauty wittily adapted by Picasso with caricatures of the myopic, bespectacled Sabartès.[13] Penrose took extensive notes during his stay, writing them up on loose sheets of paper back at his hotel. The following hasty and fragmentary summaries of Picasso's conversation were, however, made on the spot in a pocket notebook:

[…] 'On ne fait jamais ce qu'on veut. On commence en voulant faire quelque chose et il vous fait faire d'autre chose.'[14]

When he [Picasso] went out to see the floods [in] Paris 1955, March, photographers tried to take pictures of him. He got angry and never went into [the] street again. At Cannes [he] goes out v. little. […]

'I love candles and a simple life but one has to give in to invention. The Bateau Lavoir had no gas or electricity and the other day when it gave out here it was pretty enough, but we turned it on as soon as it came back. It's like my car – I have always refused to know anything about it but I use it all the same.

'Cubism is me. It is not another "ism". We wanted to go deep into things. What was wrong with [the] Surrealists was that they did not go inside, they took the surface effects of the subconscious. They did not understand the inside of the object or themselves.'

Following this last quotation, Penrose added a few remarks of his own:

Many reasons for loving P. but one of his most seductive characteristics is his refusal to admit finality or any absolute in anything, least of all in his work.

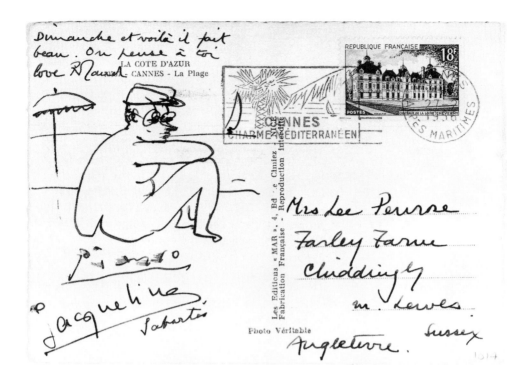

Why does he like London? Because of an old romantic dream of an atmosphere, the contrary to Spain, & 'les mendiants en chapeaux d'haute forme'.[15]

The same notebook also records an observation made by Suzanne Ramié, who with her husband ran the Madoura factory in Vallauris where Picasso made most of his ceramics:

Mme Ramié[16]
He does everything he shouldn't. When we do it, it ends in disaster. I try to warn him but he goes straight on using things the wrong way and it succeeds every time. [15]

In his more formal notes Penrose not only recounted events and recorded his immediate impressions of the latest work in the studio, but also reflected on Picasso's personality and state of mind, which he discussed frankly with Sabartès. He was, of course, obliged to be more circumspect in the biography itself, but it was essential for him to try to comprehend the whole person, with his faults, before he began the process of constructing a portrait that corresponded with his overarching, idealised vision of Picasso. In these pages Penrose struggled to penetrate his subject more deeply, without sacrificing

Postcard to Lee Miller from Roland Penrose, Picasso, Jacqueline Roque and Jaime Sabartès, with a Picasso drawing of Sabartès, February 1956 the feeling of ardent admiration that fuelled the whole endeavour: finding the feet of clay was never his goal. In effect, he was starting to draft his text, and leitmotifs that would run through the finished book – notably the conflict between surface sociability and inner solitude, and the obsession with death – are sketched here in their concrete actuality. In *Picasso: His Life and Work* these traits are treated in a more abstract, mythologising manner:

Cannes, 21 Feb. '56
P. says he never writes and paints at same time, only writes when he can't paint. One exception [was] during stay at Royan when everything was so horrible that he kept himself busy in every way he could.[17] Rousseau [was a] little simple man, everyone laughed at him. Painted a portrait of Jarry but Jarry cut out the face because he didn't like the background. P. owns also the crowned heads paying homage to the republic, portrait of Yadwiga and portraits of Rousseau & wife.[18] P. & [Robert] Delaunay [were] the first to take R. seriously. Jarry & Rousseau were both natives of Laval. Jarry went to Closerie [des Lilas] a lot. […]
  'Le mal que vous avez fait à la peinture est incalculable.'[19] Letter from unknown writer, Algiers, Feb '56.

23rd Feb. At lunch P. began talking about leaving things to children – 'No,' he said, 'it is mad to do so because they have no idea of values – leave them money, that's all right, they can understand that, but not objects.' – Talked to Sabartès about this after[wards]. Not very helpful but implied that P. might be thinking of a dispersal of his belongings to no one knows who[m]. S. talked at length of difficulties of life with P., always afraid of being in the way and of a scene should he try to leave. As soon as he has what he wants, he wants it no longer. Paradox at every moment.

A printer,[20] who is printing recent linocuts, brought in some proofs. P. very pleased with result – explained that in Paris he made engravings & lithos because specialists were at hand to help him. Here he had begun ceramics for same reason, now linocuts. Took the printer down to workshop in cellar where he has installed etching press and other facilities for engraving, asked if his son would like to come and learn so as to be of help. Printer, caught by enthusiasm, promised to see what could be done. This may be another case where P. sets others to work and inspires them with his knowledge and vigour.

25 Feb. It is at times obvious that P. is very fond of his friends and looks forward to seeing them. If they manage not to impose on him, or force their ideas on him, or keep him from his work, he is sorry to see them go.
  Sabartès knows when he receives an invitation that P. really wants him to come but realises that as soon as he arrives P. may find him a burden. At the same time it is not easy to get away, even for a walk, without long explanations.

P. clutches at friendship, perhaps all the more since so many former friends have died. His friends still are not usually painters or intellectuals. Of these only a few remain close for any length of time. He likes people who have genuine affection for him, even if they understand little of his work. They give him a feeling of the family – of not being alone in life. In his work he has lost all fear of being alone, he is too used to and too proud of his isolation. The stimulus he needs is always present in the people & objects around him and in the great panorama of his imagination.

After a heavy lunch of paella at the Ramiés, without the accompaniment of stimulating talk which could have made the food less of an imposition, he came [home] bad-tempered, saying that sort of thing was not for him, why did people expect that of him? He never looks for distractions, anything that takes him away from his work is suspect. His motto could be that of Don Quixote, 'My work is my repose.' […]

His attitude towards criticism is increasingly one of detachment. Having been so often attacked, so often misunderstood for so many reasons, great and small, he takes an olympian disregard to work of critics – saying, 'That is what they have thought – others will think differently – each person has his own point of view.' At the same time he watches keenly to see the effect of a recent painting on a newcomer and shows immediate pleasure in a remark that shows that the emotion he wants to convey has made itself felt.

The strength of his personality lies in the accord between his impulses and his actions. He never looks vague or at a loss. Doubt and conflict are always present at the back of his mind but there is always a clear determined decision, which at the last moment seems to triumph. Everything with him is a paradox. The final decisive control is all the more astonishing owing to the diversity and richness of the impulses which demand attention. He is the great performer who masters the perilous accidents that lay in his path, placed there often by his own invention. His hand never trembles but his inner spirit is in turmoil.

'When you look at the Last Judgement of Michelangelo,' he said, 'you don't think of the subject, you think of it as painting.'[21] When people look at devils in Medieval sculpture they are no longer frightened.' The aesthetic pleasures of civilised man have weakened the intensity with which he feels works of art. P. has spent a lifetime getting behind aesthetic emotion to the cruder, more violent emotions. As a child he was fascinated and horrified by the elephantine legs of his grandmother and would creep round to peep under her skirts. The medieval dragon has become nursery fare, new adult monsters are necessary as companions to the innocent, the adorable, the beautiful.

Wed. 29th Feb.
When I rang yesterday morning, having been visiting Dubuffet in Cannes the day before,[22] Jacqueline told me that Picasso was in bed and could see no one that day. The doctor had been and found nothing seriously wrong –

would I ring the following morning? I did so to find that Paulo and Christine [Pauplin] had arrived and that I was expected for lunch. The meal was uneventful but P. seemed tired. He had worked some more on the big upright composition of two nudes, which was looking very fine.[23] I commented on the increased volume of one of the figures and he said, 'It's probably no better but it's different, it goes on changing, that's all.' After lunch we left him with Jacqueline and I walked into Cannes with Sabartès, but when I rang up at 8 o'clock Jacqueline told me that she had had to call the doctor again, who again found nothing wrong physically, but said that he was suffering from cerebral fatigue and must remain in bed or undisturbed for a fortnight – would I come round for supper with the others all the same? The trouble seems chiefly that in order to be happy he must work and working brings on undue nervous fatigue, he gets a resounding noise in his head and feels ill at ease. When he rests he is haunted by his reoccurring fear of death and knows that the only way to forget it is to work. He suffers greatly from this insoluble dilemma. Fear of death is like a plaything to him when he feels well. The first evening of my visit the snow had cut off the electricity and he amused us by putting a skull on the dining table lit by candles and admiring the mysterious romantic effect.

At lunch Paulo talked about Boisgeloup, which he is now cleaning up. P. suggested that I should go over from Paris and help Paulo sort out the innumerable photos, etc. that lay about – I accepted eagerly, we shall see what comes of it. It is a great shock to see that his condition is after all very precarious – he has much that he wants to do – finish the Vallauris chapel – do the mural for UNESCO – continue his immediate work on the large nude compositions and the tiles that he sends every few days to Vallauris to be baked, but a conflict within him seems to bring about this state of fatigue which alarms him and makes work impossible. He also is very anxious to see the finished version of the film, which it is announced will be shown at the Cannes film festival in April – can he surmount the anguish and fear that make activity too much of a burden at the moment? We shall see. Unfortunately, unknown to him, his horoscope is not encouraging.[24]

On the day of my arrival (19 Feb.) P. gave us (Jacqueline, Sabartès and myself) a show of all the pictures he had painted since my last visit. There was a series of paintings of Jacqueline dressed in a Turkish jacket and hat, some admirable likenesses, others fantastic.[25] Some in brilliant flat colours reminiscent of Matisse, rapidly painted, powerful designs. There were two with flesh jet black and gay colour and patterning.[26] Several large canvases of nudes based on Jacqueline, one so realistic and voluminous that you could almost smell the flesh – eyes very disproportionate in size, one great black round eye much bigger than the other and partly overlapping it.[27] He had also worked on tiles. Some portraits of Jacqueline – face in profile, the usual mastery of line and a precision in the line, especially round the eye, that was most exciting. No distortion, no sense of caricature – a great love and respect of his model's beauty. Other tiles were mostly grotesque faces – the sun – the moon or clowns with enormous noses. One of the most finished canvases was a horizontal version of the interior of the house – a symposium of all the smaller previous studies. Very moving in its cathedral-like effect, scale of objects giving it a great sense of space. Cubism had evolved into a superb architectural effect in which each object played its essential role in the composition. Very beautiful all-pervading light and happy green-yellow on palm trees seen through the windows. Grey tracery of the window frames gave a feeling of the ribs of a whale seen from within.[28]

There are two paintings, unfinished, each a composition of two nudes, one of them very big.[29] The other, an upright picture of two standing figures, one combing her hair, is near completion but he may work on it a lot more – he has altered one of the figures several times in the last few days, sometimes returning to nearly what was there before, but the picture at no time appears hesitant [*see p. 163*].[30] The nudes are opened out so as to present front and back at the same time. They are like great buildings constructed with all the parts of a female body – breasts – belly – buttocks – arms – legs, and the heads themselves are split open and put together in the same way. One of the nude figures in the large unfinished picture crouches over herself giving a cavernous feeling. It could be constructed as a great sculpture beneath which one could shelter. Both pictures are almost in monochrome, chiefly burnt sienna darkened into black.

Today's[31] collapse is very worrying chiefly because the cause is unknown and the only cure suggested is rest, which gives him all the more opportunity for his hypochondriac tendencies and his morbid thoughts. He has not been overworking, he is cared for with minute attention by Jacqueline, he has been following the doctor's instructions for the last four months and, as he said at lunch, he wonders if he would have felt any worse if he hadn't. He has been seeing very few people and goes out very little. If the reasons are physical the doctor is unable to discover them – cerebral fatigue, which is his diagnosis, should have a predictable cause. If it is purely psychological it can only be that his means of surmounting his innate morbid tendencies are giving out. It would seem that some inhibition is attacking the very roots of the mechanism that keeps him alive, upsetting the balance between this will to live, that is to work, and his knowledge that one day he will die. Let's hope once more his vitality, of which there is still a tremendous reserve, will triumph.

Thurs. 1st March
I went alone to Antibes and made two rounds of the Palais Grimaldi looking with undisturbed attention at every exhibit. Delighted with the arcadian frivolity which takes its place with such ease in paintings that are purged of every sign of sentimentality or classical platitudes & unbearably sad to think that Picasso might now be in his decline; that the Picasso of today might no

longer be the Picasso who will be remembered, that this man already immortal was still in the throes of mortality, sinking into an intolerable decrescendo which would slowly gain on him and leave him impotent. On my return to Cannes by luck I found some exotic flowers which I sent to him [*sketch of Bird of Paradise flower*], together with a pink cyclamen with blooms frizzled like a parrot tulip for Jacqueline, adding a note 'Drole de Fleurs, Portent Bonheur'.[32] Later I climbed up to La Californie to learn the latest news. To my joy everything was more hopeful. I sat beside his bed and gossiped for half an hour with Sabartès and Picasso [who was] looking more like a boy who has been kept in bed for a bilious attack than a sick man. Jacqueline says the doctor has ordered him doses of ambergris, an extraordinary remedy in keeping with his character. Without knowing its medical significance as a cure it will certainly work on his imagination. She adds that his trouble is that he cannot admit old age, the threshold of death his relentless nightmare. Only a week or two ago he painted an enormous canvas, the two seated nudes,[33] in three hours. When he feels strong his energy is disconcerting to all around him, but suddenly, as happened yesterday, doubt sets in and robs him of all his vigour; he listens to the noises resounding in his head and he feels his own decomposition taking place. But today there are signs that powerful reactions are still in store, the battle and enjoyment of life are not over. He was delighted with the flowers – he said, 'I told Jacqueline not to give them water. They live longer without.' He's right. There are some downstairs parched and still proud among the monumental disorder of cherished objects.

2 March. Today he is better. After lunch I talked to him in bed for a while. He was annoyed about the way people sponge on him. There is no end to it. He told me how he gave the proceeds of two pictures to someone, who immediately thought he should have given them more. He is annoyed at having to give money when he has spent all his life giving his lifeblood in his work. When I returned in the evening he was at work and came upstairs in good form – told two comic stories and went to bed. Jacqueline says the doctor, since the ambergris, has ordered platinum and now phosphorus for him. He takes all his pills with meticulous care – or rather Jacqueline sees that he does, and he asks her later if he has taken them to make sure. Sabartès says he never talks about death but J. says he is obsessed by it. [16]

The fluctuation between acute anxiety and delighted relief expressed in the second half of these notes is moving testimony to Penrose's love. But alone in his hotel he also felt impelled to write a poem for Picasso, which he composed in English and dated 'Feb 21.22.23.29':[34]

It was a little before dawn when the white dolphin spoke this to the owl light house keeper.
Bathed flesh backed by the night blue shell
I am woman – a dwelling house of many parts

I am built of wind polished stones gathered from the desert
The thousand fragments of Osiris cemented with sand and tears
I am built of your loves and of your cares
Each morsel can speak is cherished
Envied crushed by violent desires
Squeezed bitten gnawed digested
Yet remains immutable.

You who overpowered me broke me as you were broken
Who pierced me entered me as I lay open to the dew
The salt sea filling my caverns you dismembered me
Flung my arms into the trees
My legs across a mule
My hair to the snorting bull
My breasts as bells to your horse
My belly placed upright in a temple
Hands joined across in prayer
Hands that weave two hands
That knit that twist an endless cord
The spiral path of history two eyes
Two eyes that fertilise each other
One sharp edged laughing the other
Open like a well whose spring
Lies too deep to quench your thirst.

I have given you my mouths
You have sheltered in the warm perfume of my valleys
You have been out over the windswept screes of my shoulders
And you have never ceased to marvel at the audacity of my fearless breasts
Heavy like the full moon they spread a festive awning that rolls across the
fields for your head.

I am your music my long white neck your strings
Your trumpet mouth erect blown full with sound
The cry of life the ejaculation of the hanged
Your finger nor my throat knowing the meaning as suddenly
A door opens flooding me inside with light
The ruined tower is rebuilt
My womb talks to itself sings quietly into itself
There was water now there is rock
There was rock now tender as a living thing
Before my eyes as I open the curtains of my hair
My hands stitch a new horizon
A new wedding of earth and sky.

My arena is this earth this labyrinth around which in sun and shadow
Sit your future sons. You have painted on its soil a face washed over
By the sea by waves that leap into the air rather than die on a shallow beach.
Life alone can kill death. You have killed it and death shamefaced
lies dead stuck to its phosphorescent hide, more blind than
darkness and more deaf than silence. Your work is life. [16]

Penrose translated his poem into French and wrote it out neatly in black ink on two large sheets of Ingres paper, folded in half to form a booklet. This he then decorated with schematic designs in red and blue crayon, inscribing it on the front cover, 'A Pablo Picasso après d'avoir vu ses tableaux recents' (To Pablo Picasso, after seeing his recent paintings).[35] In his notes Penrose had remarked on the fact that Jacqueline was the inspiration of many of Picasso's recent paintings and in the poem he adopts the voice, as it were, of the beloved, voluptuous, ever-responsive, ever-nurturing, but dominated and plundered female body. However, the use of the first person cannot but make one aware of a fantasised identification with the mythic female principle. Just as Jacqueline's life revolved around Picasso's, so in a real sense did Penrose's, and one cannot but wonder whether there was a sublimated sexual dimension to his love. Does the expression 'in love' properly define the nature of his devotion to Picasso – as Dorothy Morland believed?[36] Did he cultivate close ties with Dora Maar and Françoise Gilot not just because he appreciated both these intelligent, gifted and beautiful women and benefited greatly from his conversations with them, but because they had been Picasso's lovers? Perhaps. At all events, the poem is a document of great psychological interest, telling us far more about its author than about Picasso's paintings of the winter of 1955–56.

While in Cannes Penrose also composed a surrealist prose-poem entitled 'New devils for old'. This was not offered to Picasso, but it too must have been composed under his powerful influence, so that the apostrophised 'You' is in some sense Picasso. Significantly, the same strain of masochism runs through it, notably in the line 'Destroy me I need to be destroyed':

New devils for old
Stand at the street corner pitch your voice so high as to break every window pane so that they leave their tinned hams and ten valve sets and ask who it is that breaks the lovely double feature wide screen dish master, who slights the princess who claws at the horse faced glory of the front page.

You have spoken to us with both hands you have caressed the naked tenderness of her body and lead us in and out of its delight, you have not hidden her companion.

Does the bloom covering the fruit mean to be its protection? Or does it speak in provocation asking for its own destruction and the mangling tearing pulverising action which it needs. Destroy me I need to be destroyed.

You have heard you have found the weak joints you have dismembered the flaying limbs you have lifted the pudic veil of virgins & of reason pierced the hardened protective scales of the dreadnought, loosened the rusted clutching anchors that tied the old hull to its rocky bed. You have poked into the shocking slime that repelled with its stench the sacrifice of heroes and you have laughed as you drew out of it the precious child of eternal hope.[37] [15]

Penrose got back to Paris on 4 March 1956 and immediately resumed his campaign of interviewing. Picasso had given him an introduction to the banker and collector Max Pellequer and Penrose's diary reveals that they met twice.[38] He was able to study Pellequer's collection at his leisure and noted down the following anecdote, which is of interest because it reflects the deep suspicion with which Picasso viewed any overtures from Spaniards whom he did not personally know, for there was always the possibility that his enemies in Franco's Spain would try to damage his work as well as his reputation:

2 Spaniards of doubtful appearance came with a letter from P. to ask Max Pellequer to lend pictures to an exhibition in Spain. He refused and afterwards told P., who said, 'Yes you were right. I was on the point of phoning you to say don't have anything to do with them.' [15]

Penrose also visited Alice B. Toklas, Gertrude Stein's partner, and as he so often did when he spoke to women, he learned intriguing details about Picasso's love affairs:

Alice B. T.[39]
Eva was with Marcoussis. Friend of Fernande. Came all four to see G[ertrude] Stein. [Eva was] very bourgeoise – and tidy. Small hips. Contrary in every way to F[ernande]. Died after short and terrible illness.
    P. wrote letter to G.S. saying she had been v. good to him & he would miss her. No serious & lasting attachment until Olga.
    Irène Lagut only passing affair. (Also see Apollinaire.)[40]
    Olga from provincial aristocracy. Father objected to her being ballet girl. He disappeared in war. Mother found in Crimea by American relief but then lost again.
    A.B.T. saw Olga in hospital near end. Said to A., with great emotion, that P. & Paulo had been so good to her – P. exchanged her heavy bracelet watch for small light one when she was so thin that she had no strength.
    A.B.T. thinks P. has helped Fernande anonymously. She had slight reddish tinge in brown hair – a v. beautiful voice in which she read La Fontaine during painting of Gertrude's portrait.
    Braque [had] cowboy walk – father peintre de batiment.[41] [15]

Penrose also spoke to the journalist André Salmon, one of Picasso's closest friends before his marriage to Olga. The most surprising piece of information Salmon provided was that *Les Demoiselles d'Avignon* was painted 'very fast'. Although Picasso certainly spent months planning the composition and reworked substantial sections of the canvas at a late stage, Salmon's testimony is not incompatible with the very broadly painted unaltered passages, notably the two central nude figures. If the 'very fast' is taken to refer to the first state of the painting, then it may be accurate:[42]

André Salmon[43]
'P. commencait de voir rouge quand on parlait du cubism ou de l'art negre.'[44]
   'Demoiselles' painted very fast. 48 hrs.
   Princet, the actuary for a large insurance co., was v. poor. Did not live in Bateau L[avoir]. Made his theories after seeing pictures. Followed by [Albert] Gleizes, [Jean] Metzinger, etc.
   Braque never went to Closerie [des Lilas]. No good in literary circles. P. no conversation either, but would listen and say a few extraordinary things.
   The important thing was the mixture of great seriousness and boisterous humour.

Cubism influenced literature in its form. Multiple image and clear classical structure, more than in experiments such as Caligrammes.

G[uillaume] A[pollinaire], Max [Jacob] & S. would play joke visits to P. as Degas, Baudelaire, etc. and give him a vicious mock criticism of his latest work.

No question of disease with production of 'Demoiselles'.

Jarry understood v. little of painting. Cut up Rousseau portrait of him to roll it.

No one at Closerie understood much about painting except P. & 3 friends. Charles Guérin [was] about [the] only painter who attended.

Fernande reliable except when [it is a] question of women. Book first publish[ed] in 'Paris Soir' or something, title 'Jours chez Picasso'.[45] P. objected to a lot that was in it. It was cut when published.

Apollinaire
Apollinaire important as an animator. Everything that could be part of 'l'Effort moderne' was good. Perhaps too eclectic and indiscriminate. People said all he did was go to Bib[liothèque] Nat[ionale] and come out every day with a new story. K[ahnweiler] reproaches his praise of futurists. [15]

   The Surrealist painter Roberto Matta talked to Penrose principally about the theatricality of Picasso's work:

Matta[46]

'Picasso aime le spectacle.'[47]

Story of seeing Matadors carried shoulder high as a child and saying, 'I would like that to happen to me.'

Surrealism never touched P. deeply, all his ideas came from the object – material. Did not need to explore madness.

The great juggler – throws forms into the air and keeps them in a perpetual dance.

All his ideas spring from objects and can be understood as objects. Matta tries to paint sensations that are unexplainable in other terms than painting.

The sense of the 'parade' in P. reveals itself in his love of theatre & ballet. The blind man is a theatrical idea to him. [15]

Penrose also saw Kahnweiler at least once:[48]

Kahnweiler

Derain said of P., 'Nous le trouverons pendu derrière sa grande toile.'[49] (Demoiselles).

Eva was pretty and charming [but] too much of a slave. [...]

Matisse a wonderful talker. Must have had fascinating conversations with P. – none recorded. [...]

Mallarmé et la peinture.[50] Kahnweiler [says] Gris & Picasso knew [the work of] Mallarmé & Rimbaud. [15]

The following note, filed elsewhere, may derive from the same conversation:

1912–1914. Cubism. (Synthetic). Collage.

Note. Certain paintings belonging to this period have Russian words or lettering. Kahnweiler says these [were] derived from Russian newspapers found in a parcel of canvases returned to him from Russia. P. liked the look of the lettering – no idea of it being a compliment to Shchukin, nor a sign that pictures in question were bought by him. One which was included in claim by the daughter of Shchukin in summer '54 belonged to Gertrude Stein & was lent by A[lice] B. T[oklas].[51] [2]

While in Paris, Penrose had inaugurated a new pocket notebook. Among its contents is the following summary of an amusing and definitely off-the-record conversation with the art critic and collector, Georges Besson. The complex, fifty-year relationship of Matisse and Picasso fascinated their friends and there were many anecdotes about their supposedly bitter rivalry

– anecdotes which infuriated Picasso because they tended to mask the real admiration each felt for the other's work:

Besson[52]
An old friend of Matisse, owns 3 portraits of himself by M. and other pictures.

Describing difference between Matisse & P.
   M. was madly jealous of P. P. is generous but M. very mean. He ordered a glass of port and then said, 'I can't drink this, it is costing me too much.'

Besson asked him, 'What do you think of love making?' He answered, 'Every time I make love I always think that it will mean two pictures less during the next few days.' [17]

The longest interview recorded in this notebook was with Pierre Baudouin, who, like Sabartès, was prepared to talk candidly. It is especially interesting on the subject of Picasso's relationship with his son Paulo, suggesting a greater degree of paternal tenderness than is commonly attributed to him. Indeed, taken together, Penrose's notebooks present a more sympathetic and nuanced picture of Paulo, who is usually represented as weak, shiftless and unintelligent, bullied, dominated and mistreated by his father:

Baudouin[53]
B. was the only friend who had the courage to tell P. that Paulo was seriously ill.[54] P. at once took up [the] phone and rang the surgeon saying, 'You probably know more about painting than I do about medicine, but if in painting I was in serious difficulties I would consult a friend whose advice I respected. I want you to do the same for my son and realise that it is his life that is in question. You may ring me at any time and you know now what you have to do.' Then to the assembled company he said, 'B. is the only one who has had the courage to tell me about Paulo. The fact is he and I are the only ones that love him.' Look of sheepish silence on all faces.

To Pierre Matisse he said, 'I will go and see your father if he needs me and stay as long as he likes, but only if he needs me. Otherwise I should be disturbing him in his work and work is the only thing worth doing for him and me.'

Conversation between Aragon, Casanova & P. after appearance in '[L'] Humanité' of A.'s articles on Social Realism [in] about '54. P. asked what A. would think if he started telling young writers how they should write and told A. he never had understood anything about painting, that he should leave that to the painters, that if they wanted a policy for painters he would give it them, but there must be no disputing him. Casanova took P.'s side. Aragon was crushed and humiliated.[55]

'La chèvre, vous sentez bien qu'il a été modelé par le bon dieux. Toute la crâne la mâchoire, là sur le pupille des yeux il a hesité mais autour c'est tout modelé par ses mains. On sens ses doigts comme s'il avait modelé dans la terre. Mais Karl Marx n'aura pas su le modeler. Ce qui est beau avec Marx c'est qui a voulu modeler la societé mais il n'est pas le bon dieu, le preuve – qu'il est mort.'[56]

One evening at Vallauris P. was tired out after a long day with some Italian visitors. B., looking for Paulo, found him [Picasso] resting in a chair on the terrace. P. told him to sit down and keep him company. After a long pause B. asked if he did not want to go to Paris and see the pictures from Russia on show at the Maison de la Pensée.[57] 'No,' said P. 'You must understand that I don't like to see exhibitions of my pictures. In the past I refused for many years to exhibit or even have pictures photographed. But I realised finally that one had to exhibit – to strip oneself naked like a whore. That takes courage and the whore who does it has courage. But people don't realise what they have when they own a picture by me, each picture is a "fiole"[58] filled with my blood. That is what has gone into it.'

At the restaurant at Golfe-Juan there was one evening a gay party: Françoise, B., the German nurse who looked after Claude and who, having started with skirts to her ankles, came in such scanty shorts that P. said, 'Ah! that's wonderful. Soon a watch glass will be sufficient,' and there were others too. P. wanting everyone to enjoy themselves started making masks with the tablecloths and most of the guests put them on, but some began to smuggle them under the table as valuable souvenirs. P., seeing this, look[ed] around with an angry face and, collecting all the masks, crumpled them up and threw them into the sea.

P. one morning told a dream he had just had. La Pasionaria had been arrested by Franco and they came to ask him if he knew her and wanted to take her side.[59] 'No,' said P., 'I was much too frightened to intervene.'

P. is often very frightened, like the toreador before he enters the arena shaking with fear. P. places himself in a position that frightens him. He finds himself compelled to seek this position and, although profoundly scared, he then faces up to it.

He always asks his friends when he meets them if they are working – to him work is the only lasting happiness.

He has given to each of his 4 children the portraits he has made of them and there are 4 copies of 'La chèvre' for them.[60]

On return to Paris from Céret, it sometimes took [him] 2 days from Quai d'Orsay to rue Ravignan, stopping at all the bistrots with friends.[61]

Extraordinary memory for exact proportions. Clouzot told how during film he matched up figure drawn on piece of paper to fit in with big Garoupe picture, without any reference. He added that he had done same thing with large two-sheet drawings of 'Homme à [l'agneau]', adding legs to torso and always finding he could do so without measuring up between them.[62] [17]

Penrose returned to England on 20 March. During his absence a letter had come from Alfred Barr asking for his help. The Museum of Modern Art was planning its own celebration of Picasso's seventy-fifth birthday and Barr wanted to know when the artist was 'likely to be least preoccupied and most able to give some sympathetic attention to the problem'.[63] On 28 March Penrose replied, as one hardened campaigner to another, and also gave an account of Picasso's new work which amplifies his commentary in the Cannes notebooks. In particular, he reveals an astute understanding of the connection between the series of pictures representing the studio at La Californie and the death of Matisse – that these haunting and haunted pictures, with their thin washes of paint and subtle monochrome hues, were an act of profound homage. As Penrose realised, Picasso was still in mourning:

My dear Alfred,

I am ashamed that I have not found time to answer your letters and Marga's very nice letter to Lee that she sent on [to] me in France.

I have just got back from six weeks over there, two of which were spent close to Picasso in Cannes. I made some useful progress with my book but every now and then became appalled at the task before me. Sabartès was there too and very helpful.

You ask when would be the best time to see P. That's an impossible question to answer but the months when everyone is there in summer are certainly the least propitious. After July 15th he is usually besieged and difficult to see for any length of time until October. There is to be a first showing of the film – Picasso-Clouzot – at the Cannes Festival about May 1st. Again there will be a crowd around him then. I intend to go for my own pleasure and information but don't expect to see much of him. [...]

Picasso has been working – as always – a series of interiors and some colossal nudes – tiles, lino-cuts and vast quantities of drawings. The series of interiors is, I think, very important. He has allowed influences from Matisse to filter in, and mixed with cubist traditions they make a synthesis which is perhaps less violent but more complete than the 'Femmes d'Alger'. He goes through periods of fatigue and depression which are sad to see – when he feels age creeping over him he becomes frightened of death and terribly diminished in his melancholy; fortunately that does not last long. His new girl Jacqueline is completely devoted and very tactful. She is the perfect beautiful slave and that is exactly what he needs at the present time. He is soon on his feet again, thanks to her care and his own immense resources of energy, and back to work with his old vigour. His life has only two alternatives, bed or work. That of course is during the season when visitors are few and can be easily kept at bay by Jacqueline. […]

In the same letter Penrose also responded to Barr's latest attempt to persuade him to sell *Girl with a Mandolin*:

Oddly enough, I had another offer that same morning that your letter arrived for $5000 more, but I turned it down. I still want to keep the picture and so long as I can I shall refuse to be tempted. I'm sorry not to be more helpful. […][64]

But, motivated by the desire to buy land at Burgh Hill that adjoined Farley Farm, he did succumb to temptation before the end of the year, agreeing to sell the painting to Nelson A. Rockefeller on the understanding that it would eventually go into the Museum of Modern Art collection. So, Barr's patience and persistence were eventually rewarded and on 16 December 1956 Penrose wrote to reassure him that 'she' was in the hands of the shippers.[65]

Le Mystère Picasso at the Cannes Film Festival, May 1956

On 1 May Lee and Roland arrived in Cannes to attend the gala screening of *Le Mystère Picasso* at the Film Festival. They found Picasso sick with dread and threatening to stay at home. There was an unpleasant undercurrent to the somewhat farcical preliminaries because when they arrived in the film theatre they found Picasso had been mischief-making and put them in the same box as Douglas Cooper, a man Roland could not abide and whom he correctly identified as a scheming rival. Not that Penrose dwelt on his chagrin in his notes: such incidents were etched all too permanently onto his consciousness for the need of an *aide-mémoire*:

Clouzot – Film 1st Night
Cannes
Visit May 1st to 5th '56
Day of arrival telephoned and found Jacqueline, who said P. was working but would be glad to see us next morning.
  2 May. Went to La Californie about noon. Found P. in bed looking pale. Welcome[d] Lee & self warmly – Jacqueline looking beautiful and happy. Main topic the film. Clouzot arrives with tickets – P. announces that he is not going to be there – looks worried – explains he is ill, that even visits disturb him, exhaust him and interfere with his work – the only thing he finds worthwhile. Clouzot tries to argue. Says it will be interpreted as a disapproval of the film or a quarrel between them. P. will not listen to persuasion. Says it will make no difference and in any case it must not be mentioned that he is ill

(the only excuse that would relieve the film of suspicion). Clouzot leaves very unhappy. Paulo, Christine, Baudouin & Muñoz arrive. P. chats in more relaxed mood. We all leave with regrets that we shall not see him that evening, but none of us sure what will happen. Jacqueline obviously had not lost hope. During Clouzot's visit he went out and reappeared in a red Indian headdress, a white jumper and a beard saying if he did come that is what he would wear.

When we arrived at the Festival Hall we found we had been given seats in same box as D. Cooper & Richardson – a joke that greatly amused P. Box was next to central box where P., Auric[66] & Clouzot were expected. A short Hungarian film of wild animal life was in progress and soon after our arrival in came P. with all those expected, much to everyone's delight. Up till an hour before he had stayed in bed – Clouzot had phoned through a report that the afternoon session had not gone well – whistling and some walk out – that had not changed his decision – but just after nine Jacqueline with the Ramiés, who had just come in on their way to the film, suddenly managed to persuade him. He was up and dressed in his 1929 English dinner jacket in no time – with bowler hat. He arrived to a tremendous welcome. Shouts of 'Vive Pablo!' and batteries of flash. Film was very well received – as he left he was nearly mobbed but got away to a party with all his friends at the Casino nightclub. Sitting between Clouzot & Auric he seemed very happy – on leaving he danced with Jacqueline for the photographers and invited Lee & me to lunch next day.

3 May. Very delightful lunch en famille with Paulo, etc. present. Clouzot and friends came in before for a while. P. seemed better, more alive and genuinely happy. Saw his recent work – more interiors, with seated figure, pictures, etc. Use of white patches, often untouched canvas, in wonderfully subtle, luminous effects – I suggested they could be called 'l'epoque blanche'.[67] He agreed. The two great nudes, one combing hair are finished. (?)[68] A friend pointed out that if one looks at picture from bottom to top or the reverse, figures appear to move. There has been great activity since beginning of March and splendid vigour – there still seem to be traces of Matisse – as though he had taken over Matisse and strengthened his style without losing his masterly sense of design. One large canvas recently begun was an abstract composition in monochrome more reminiscent of Léger.[69] We all left in [the] afternoon and paid a visit to Vallauris – dined together in Antibes.

4 May. P. asked us to come again at lunch time. Found Auric, [Georges] Sadoul and some eight more. Auric admitted that the music had been difficult. P. had said to us before he was not too happy about it – too loud and obtrusive but with excellent passages – specially drums & flamenco. But all agreed that since the public demand music with film, it was as good as could be.

Stayed on to lunch alone. Warm welcome from Jacqueline – excellent lunch. Talked about Avignon 1914. He had found Les Clochettes by chance, nowhere else to let. Stayed with Braque during both visits, second time in Avignon itself.

Paulo, expected early, turned up with his friends after lunch. Lee took photos of P. I got information for exhibition. Left about 4 and met again at Festival Hall to see Russian film. 'Othello'. P. introduced to blonde Russian Desdemona.[70] Tried to pay her compliments in Russian [but] found it difficult to remember any words. Sudden arrival in cinema of Aga Khan. P. leapt up and went over to talk to him, full of enthusiasm to find his old friend. A.K. asked after his work and said he always liked it. Film was v. bad. Heavy melodramatic historical setting [and] as we went out [it was] difficult to find any comment that was not rude. We said goodbye in the street surrounded by autograph hunters. I rang later and we joked about [the]

Picasso at La Californie, Cannes, May 1956. In the background are *Women at their Toilette* (left) and contemporary paintings of his studio. Photo Lee Miller

film. I thanked him warmly for everything and said I would like to return in June. 'As soon as you like,' he said. [18]

In telegraphic style, Penrose took detailed notes about *Le Mystère Picasso*:

Starts with noise of pencil on paper – like a surgeon's knife cuts an image out of blank space.

Music very dramatic – announces like circus or bullfight – orchestra. Drum sequence for two faces built up fast and taken to bits. Guitars for arena drawing – speed that figures appear – a squiggle and it's a toreador. Speed of his imagination can be felt. Backgrounds with trees, clouds, ships, slip into place.

Drawing – line placed always right – spat out of little man's mouth. Figures first – three-dimensional – space between lines becomes pregnant. Background blocked out and decorated – alterations. Never afraid to change anything. Sequence of great nude with face that changes twenty times, each time more lovely. A painting must reach a state where nothing can be added or taken away – this happens and then, to astonish all, it changes. Great picture at end goes through a hundred changes – no knowing where next change will appear or how drastic. Scale, colour, shapes all change.

Winged face like a dove.

First drawings.

Guiding lines dividing space, establishing construction. Nude seated. No guidelines. Profile trickles down screen like water down an uneven surface shaping a form that appears by magic – a form that [it] seems was already there. Grotesque head of old man leering at nude. Body grows completer.

Painter begin[s] work on his canvas. Canvas in profile, subject lying nude appears in front of and around him, envelops him. Set of squares appear, storks, flowers, encircled by a line becomes fish, becomes cock, becomes head of faun.

Drawings grow, heavier lines appear, emphasis, shaded areas fill in like blood. Enlargement of line gives intimate view of actually how it forms on paper. Series of small parallel lines shoot across screen filling in to one solid line as ink soaks through immediately. Ink drying takes on more permanent, flatter look.

Large purple shape, like boomerang standing on one point, appears. Vertical & horizontal. Two closed eyelids, head of sleeping girl – balance between filled-in shape and line. Form of face there with so little to suggest it. Colour sober, liquid, flows onto screen like blood – green, brown, orange, pinks.

P. 'Ça c'est bien – mais si on allé au fond des choses – comme je fais dans l'atelier. Voir un tableau comme il est fait avec cent tableau l'un sur l'autre.'
C. 'Ça va être dangereux – très dangereux.'
P. 'Je sais. C'est ça que j'ai toujours voulu. Donnez moi une grande toile.'

P. 'Ça va mal – et encore plus mal avant que ça soit finit.'
C. 'C'est mauvais.'
P. 'C'est mauvais pour qui?'
C. 'Pour le public.'
P. 'Ça m'est egale. Je n'ai jamais pensé au public.'[71] [19]

Le Mystère Picasso was a critical success and won the Prix spécial du Jury. As Penrose's notes reveal, he found the film so riveting because it captured simultaneously the movement of the artist's creative imagination and the movement of his hand, as images metamorphosed before the spectator's eyes in an almost magical fashion. The film trapped and also accentuated something Penrose had often felt when watching Picasso at work – that each line he drew looked so right and inevitable that it seemed as if it had always been there, invisible to all except the artist himself. 'With Clouzot's ability to hold his audience in suspense added to Picasso's brilliant display, the film becomes a rare and valuable account of the workings of genius,' was his verdict in *Picasso: His Life and Work.*[72]

Celebrating Picasso's seventy-fifth birthday, October 1956

Since the beginning of the year much of Penrose's time had been devoted to assembling the drawings, photographs and other documents for 'Picasso Himself' and *Portrait of Picasso*, as the accompanying book was called, and on 14 June he was back in Paris again. He made numerous appointments with people on whose help he counted, including Kahnweiler, Zervos, Sabartès and the photographer Brassaï, and the little pocket notebook he carried around with him is stuffed with jottings about the content and organisation of the exhibition (omitted here), as well as the usual mixture of reported speech and description of events witnessed. On the eve of his departure for the Midi, Penrose saw Sabartès, who was in the mood to complain of Picasso's maddeningly paradoxical character:[73]

Sabartès believes that P. can be deliberately mean. Recently S.'s doctor, who is also doctor of Jacques Villon and a great admirer of P., decided to go and call on him with J.V. at Cannes. S. encouraged them and was deeply wounded when P. refused to see them. S. feels he can never again show his face at his doctor's in spite of his need for treatment. He also feels sure that P. did this deliberately to hurt them all. He has seen the same happen to others who often manage to squeeze something out of P. when his mood changes and he feels repentant. S. is too proud to think of this.
   On the other hand P. is often generous. Gives S. all his lithos. as they come out. Unreasonably generous & unreasonably mean. Exaggerated in both cases. […] [21]

The account of the days Roland and Lee spent in Cannes gives a vivid impression of the anarchic régime of clowning and gossiping, trips to Vallauris and favourite restaurants, and – the climax of a successful visit – quick-change displays of the brand-new work, which characterised life at La Californie at this period, when Picasso was just as famous as the Hollywood movie stars who sought him out:

Stories, 23 June–6 July
At Vallauris P. had a sudden call to empty his bowels. Had to ask garage man outside chapel where to go. All he could do was take P. into the old château where he knew of a closet. No sooner had P. installed himself than [the] door was opened by an angry old woman with spectacles who said, 'Que ce que vous faite là.' P. 'Mais vous voyez bien ce que je fait.' 'Mais quell droit avez vous de venir ici.' P. 'Ce n'est pas un droit c'est un besoin.'[74] She continued to argue with P. firmly seated and continuing his need. He came out in a jubilant state telling story to admiring friends. All the town knows him except the old woman, who was sure to be informed later.

Gary Cooper, wife & daughter called and we spent day together with P. & the Barrs. Late lunch at Félix on the Croisette. Then to Vallauris where the master potter Agard showed his skill. Cooper family duly impressed. Visited chapel and then back to La Californie where to Alfred Barr's delight he showed us a great quantity of pictures. Nudes, J. in Turkish costume, portraits of J., including one very realistic and many very like her. Tall canvases in very fine cubist-Matisse style, two of them painted in same day, very impressive and very new.[75] Brilliance of colour, subtle use of plain white canvas. Interiors in great quantity, some very Spanish in feel. P. joking that they were just like Velázquez. Strong contrasts in light. Whites very luminous. Variations on theme [of] architecture and objects. Art nouveau, furniture & sculpture all taken from actual objects.
   The later interiors have evolved towards greater simplicity in colour and selection among objects. Theme the same, variations infinite. Reoccurring picture within the picture. Black & white in strong contrast. Dramatic. Feel of illuminated space. Tranquil. The crowded studio becomes the well-ordered, cool anterooms of a palace. Theme of seated figure, pictures within picture, orientalisms – brasero,[76] coffee pot, etc [*see p. 163*]. Recent pictures tend to be more horizontal.[77] 'Le Printemps', large with bright greens and trees, painted [with] heavy paint with palette knife.[78] [Dated] 20.3.56. P. remarked it was last day of spring without him knowing. Goat and faun in landscape. Unlike all others. Interiors in simple flat colours and lines. Rapid, brilliant. Charm pictures. Bullfight sketches. Drowsy nude (J.).
   Cinemascope pictures shown, including nude cut from film, with two faces look[ing] lecherously through window.[79] P. described difficulty of having to stop so often for filming. Painted by daylight, filming done with projectors, made process even longer. La Garoupe sequence took 8 days.[80]

As he watches film again P. says his thought runs ahead – 'That's where I would make a line or put a dot' – and it happens just as he would have done it again. Line or dot appear just where he wants them.

When Coopers arrived P. repeated same opening gambit as he had done with Barrs. Going to sideboard with mirror picks up comic disguises, glasses and black beard, put them on with nautical cap, cowboy hat, bowler, etc., and with comic gestures makes all laugh. Easy way of making contact with foreigners who don't talk French and means of overcoming his own shyness. Brandishes cutlass, brings out elaborate knives, gadgets, music box lighter, presents of all sorts given by all sorts. Barr gave him 2 pairs of comic spectacles, which caused great mirth, especially when he and Cooper did duet together. Very interested to hear from Barr of his Moscow visit and how his pictures were being shown again (not cubist).[81] Talked of change of attitude to Stalin and laughed at politicians, saying that nothing had ever been more uncertain than at present time.[82] I asked what he thought Eluard would have said. He said, 'On a vu venir ça depuis longtemps.'[83] Laughed off situation but said it was astonishing that they should have concealed such lies for so long.

Coopers anxious to buy three pictures but he would not listen to offers. Referred them to K[ahnweiler], but finally said he was willing to let K. know which they wanted and so they may get them. However, he is very reluctant to let anything out of his hands – says they are not finished, that he is still

Picasso with Gary Cooper and Cooper's daughter at the Madoura Pottery, Vallauris, June 1956. Photo Lee Miller wanting to refer to them, that they are personal documents (portraits of Jacqueline). Cooper showed in quiet way great interest and respect. They made strange contrast. He tall, nordic, blue-eyed, reserved. P. susceptible to his charm. Signed cards for him and gave him special demonstrations of making pots [*see p. 167*]. Joked about being cinema star also.

Picasso's story
Windy afternoon Nov. 1918. After working on self-portrait he went walking in arcades of rue de Rivoli. As he passed a widow her veil blew round him and entangled him. He returned home and they rang up to tell him that Apollinaire was dead.[84] […]

Before leaving early on 6 July I asked night before for catalogue of Arts Council's show sent by P[hilip] James for him to autograph.[85] After a long search it had to be given up as lost. We said goodbye and left. On returning about 11.30 from dinner at Antibes with the Barrs, the night porter said a little man had come to enquire for us and leave a small parcel. The night porter wanted to fold it up and put it in our mail shelf. The little man had objected strongly, seized the package & run off. Since then he had telephoned several times, the porter had refused to help. No clue as to who little man could be. A few minutes later I heard from top of stairs porter answering phone, rudely saying M. Penrose was in bed and had given orders not to be woken. I rushed down and found it was Jacqueline saying the catalogue had been found and they had tried to deliver it. At once we went up to La Californie to collect it. As we turned the corner by the house the headlights lit up the red shirt of Picasso who was waiting for us outside in the road. [*Inserted addition*] Both were in very good humour. P. had been cooking for Jacqueline an omelette made of the green part of the leaf of blate.[86] He said he did this contrary to everyone else who thought the only good part was the white. [*Main text continues*] We went in and enjoyed an hour with them listening to record of Prévert poem and having hilarious time looking at ourselves in a distorting mirror in Jacqueline's room. Finally left affectionately and very late. […]

He sees a great many people and complains about not working. He says, 'It is my business to paint, not to be the showman or salesman.' Yet when people come he can never send them away and often takes them out to lunch, so that the whole day goes by with talking and showing them his work. He brings out canvases from the back room which he keeps locked. Moves them around himself and steps back with a serious and bored look among the spectators, often watching the effect on them, but more often engrossed in looking again at his own work. When an intelligent remark is made he brightens up and adds eagerly, 'C'est ça.'[87] He is always wary of questions, appears at first not to understand, then gives a simple answer to a simple question, and to an awkward or stupid question answers anything that comes into his head.

He has a new cage of fantail pigeons in the middle of the room and talks of making a great aviary just outside.

He complains of too many visits and the work it gives him to show his pictures. He must have painted some 80 in the last year, not counting the film, many of them six foot long. His relationship with J. seems very happy. She has found her way of making him happy and has a strength of character which develops as she gains confidence. He is completely occupied with her physique. Her eyes, profile shape of head, wide hips, small waist and well-developed breasts reoccur in so many works. She follows every movement of his, is a model of devotion. Never sleeps while he is at work, which may be nearly all night, and sits whenever wanted as his model. But her health is not good, she has violent nervous heart troubles, very painful and frightening.

P. said, 'Nowadays they teach children to paint like children which is absurd. I never drew like a child. I learned to draw very young. If they had tried to teach me the way they do now it would only have been a setback.' [21]

In Vallauris, Penrose made contact with René Batigne, the driving force behind the conversion of the ancient, deconsecrated chapel into a museum and behind the preparation of the flexible panels on which Picasso painted the *War and Peace* murals to cover the vault:[88]

Lunch with Batigne. Vallauris, 28 June, 1956
P. has worked with dentist of Vallauris.[89] Fascinated by minute work in gold and tools, he made jewelry with him and gave [it] to dentist's wife. Also made de Lazerme necklace in gold.

Batigne told story of how 'Homme au mouton' [*see p. 219*] came to be given to Vallauris. It had been offered to Antibes but difficulties arose and he withdrew offer. One day in street [Picasso] said to B. spontaneously, 'What would you say if I gave it to V.?' B. took proposal before Municipal Council who debated whether they should accept. Suspicious at first of offer. Asked was he really so famous an artist? What did it look like? When told it looked like a man with a sheep, blacksmith said, 'That is a pity, if it looks like any other statue.' Only when told of value in francs of statue and its attraction to tourists did they accept, at which B. scolded them for haggling over such a generous offer, saying that P. was thinking of their good and his friendship for them. Statue was fetched from Paris and set up temporarily in apse of chapel with old olive mill as base. Look[ed] very well in this setting. Lighting and 12th-cent. architectural background suited it. Casanova and Eluard were worried that it might become confused with religious ideas and insisted on its being moved to the square. (Originally the Mun[icipal] Cou[ncil] wanted to put it in the big Place des Ecoles, where it would have been hopelessly dwarfed. Idea that P. wanted it accessible to all 'pourque les enfant jouent avec et les chiens pissent dessus'[90] had made the Mun. Cou. doubt its value.) However, finally it was moved to new site and inaugurated.

Banquet given by potters of Vallauris to P. on 70th birthday in nave of chapel. At that moment P. said he must do something to decorate it. Armature made by local carpenter v. skilfully. Panels flexible so as to bend to shape of vault. B. set up studio with strip lighting, same as would be used [in the chapel] and mobile scaffolding to paint from. P. locked himself in for long hours. Only Paulo allowed in. Disappointing in Rome & Milan exhibitions because [the two murals were] separated and in wrong setting.[91] Conception of walls completely covered and scale of great towering figures could only be realised when they were brought together in vault. He wanted you to enter into the picture. Once set up he immediately saw that end door to street must be closed with a painting to cover whole wall. Problems of lighting and crowds solved as they arise.[92] [2]

On his return to Paris Penrose kept up his campaign of interviewing. He saw Dora Maar twice but left only a minimal record of their conversations:[93]

Dora
Rue la B[oétie]. Dora was once allowed to clean out flat with maid. After a week of cleaning and putting everything back in its place, her [the maid's] only remark was, 'Eh bien, on aura tout vu.'[94] She was mad and used to spy for Olga, watching them from behind tree trunks.

P. the dragon: conscious of his own monstrous character, trying to make up for it. [21]

Usually Dora Maar stressed the symbiotic relationship between Picasso's work and his private life when she talked to Penrose, thus fostering his propensity to read Picasso's imagery and style in biographical terms. But on one occasion at least, when speaking to Alfred Barr, she took a significantly different line. Barr summarised what she had said in a letter to Penrose in which he questioned the latter's interpretation of the extreme distortions of the female form in his text for *Portrait of Picasso*:[95]

[…] I was particularly interested in your explanation, or at least association, of the extremely distorted images of women with Picasso's difficulties with his various ladies. Are you really convinced that these horrific metamorphoses are expressions of sexual anger? In this connection, I asked Dora Maar whether she could associate any specific emotion on Picasso's part with the distorted images which he painted with her. When I asked the question, we were standing in front of the rather realistic and elegant portrait reproduced in *Picasso: 50* [*Years of his Art*], page 232.[96] She said, no, she didn't think so. She couldn't remember any recognizable differences, mood or emotion, which she could attach to either this realistic image of herself or to the distorted images. We then walked into the next room where one of the really bizarre portraits was hanging on the wall. She pointed to it and said that the canvas had originally been just as realistic as the previous picture but that Picasso had then little by little changed it into a grotesque metamorphosis.

Although I think we did not use the word 'form', I had the impression, rather to my surprise, that she felt that a good deal of the transformation was a kind of expression of formal invention rather than an expression of love or hate.

This is a very important point and I am sure that you must have a good deal of evidence. Also, it may be that Dora Maar was being discreet.[97]

Committed to his view, Penrose did not debate the matter with Barr; nor did he alter his text.

While in Paris Penrose met Georges and Marcelle Braque and asked them about the Cubist years:

Braque, 14 July 1956
Marcelle B. said that P. & B. never really suffered from poverty. Since she knew them they always sold their work. They argued violently but were never mean and never out for money – never gave serious thought to money. Montmartre life very complete & happy – everything accessible and wants easily satisfied.

Long months spent at Sorgues – after 8 or 9 months work returned to Paris and sold plenty.

P. found Sorgues – B. suggested Avignon, [which was] full up so took train to terminus which happened to be S. – rented Villa des Clochettes. B. followed and rented Villa Bel Air – went about on bicycles – went to bullfights, met at café every evening. In 1914 Derain also nearby. 14 rue St Bernard, Avignon, taken by P. was next door to morgue – between morgue and hospital – rue Schoelcher also looked onto cemetery. [2]

In his pocket notebook Penrose also jotted down Braque's verdict on the role of Apollinaire:

Both he & P. agree that Jacob & Apollinaire understood nothing of their research.

But A. showed their influence clearly in [his] calligrammes.

Value was extension of boundaries of painting & poetry and lively interchange of ideas. [21]

In pursuit of more first-hand recollections about the pre-First World War period, Penrose visited Alice Toklas again:

Toklas says
Fernande v. placid. Cultivated. Read beautifully but v. boring.

P. gave G[ertrude] S[tein] her portrait.[98] Said years later, 'Well, between giving it you and you paying for it, there was not much difference in those days.'

In [Picasso's] move to Montrouge all cubist constructions destroyed. G.S. saved one small one.[99]

Penrose must have questioned Picasso later about his constructions because he annotated this passage:

Not exact. Some were damaged but P. thinks that several are stored away somewhere still intact. [21]

In the same pocket notebook Penrose drew together a few shrewd observations about Picasso's need to dominate:

Power is an important factor in his character. Pleasure in having it, fear of losing it. Fear of others having power over him – portrait of Jacqueline sitting, one of first. P. said, 'Celui là est raté – parcequ'elle m'a dominé.'[100]

Key 'fetish' and insistence on locking everything up – again sense of power in doing so. (Remember series of bathing house women with key holes.)[101] [21]

Picasso himself evidently liked the idea of Penrose's documentary exhibition and was very cooperative. Thus Jacqueline supplied new photographs and Picasso lent others from his huge stock, and when, thanks to the extraordinary coincidence of having the same barber as the owner's husband, Penrose discovered a self-portrait drawing of 1901, Picasso was so delighted to see it again for the first time in decades that he annotated the photograph Penrose had sent him with detailed information – a testimony to his legendary memory:

Cannes, 19.9.56
2nd arrival in Paris.
The lady is not Suzanne Valadon.
The small bearded man is Monsieur Jaume Andreu Bonshons or Bonsons, a friend of mine at the time, who came to Paris with me that year.
Note that at the ticket office of the Moulin Rouge one can see the entrance price, 3 francs.
The signature on the drawing is a fake.
I'd really appreciate it if you sent me another photo of the drawing.
Your friend Picasso[102]

Picasso also penned in Spanish a friendly salutation to the ICA, thus giving the exhibition his seal of approval: it was reproduced in the invitation to the private view, in the catalogue and in Portrait of Picasso.[103]

Paulo Picasso, who appreciated the fact that Penrose – unlike some of his

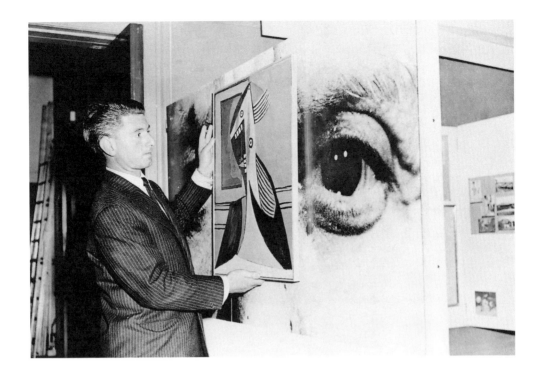

Paulo Picasso at the opening of 'Picasso Himself', Institute of Contemporary Arts, London, October 1956

father's friends – always treated him with respect, also took a keen interest in the exhibition. He had invited Penrose to Boisgeloup in the spring and dug out various rare documents,[104] and he came to the opening at the ICA on 25 October as his father's representative. He was photographed for the press holding up *Woman's Head and Self-Portrait* in front of an enormous blow-up of Picasso's eyes – a poignant juxtaposition, for the screaming harpy in the painting is usually interpreted as a symbolic representation of Olga in a jealous rage. Thus their hapless son is, as it were, trapped between his father's hypnotising, all-conquering gaze and his mother's impotent but vicious fury.[105] Paulo was accompanied by Christine Pauplin and the couple stayed *en famille* with the Penroses. On the day after the opening Penrose had time to jot down what he had learnt about the latest, curious turn in Picasso's experiments with decorating ceramics:

26 Oct '56. Christine said P. is now painting dinner plates with new varnishes which fuse and take on startling colours when fired. Last year, when vast piles of a dinner service bought by Olga in the twenties arrived, he wanted to throw them all out. Jacqueline wanted to keep them – now he has taken so many for his new process that J. has hardly enough. [2]

Fin Vilató also came to London for the opening, reinforcing the sense of an event blessed by the Master himself. All went well on the night, as Penrose enthusiastically reported in a letter he sent Picasso a few days later. Indeed, the gallery was so crowded that some people had to be turned away:

Of course, your presence dominated everything, Nearly four hundred pictures of you at every age looked out at us from the walls and the vital power surging even from these images filled everyone present with joy. Once again the Picasso magic worked.[106]

The English press was generally extremely favourable and the exhibition attracted a large attendance in London. Gratifyingly, the French were keen to take it and, in a modified form, it opened at Galerie La Hune in Paris on 5 March 1957, several weeks before Antonina Vallentin's book came out. Later the Arts Council toured a reduced version to various cities in Britain, which was, of course, the best possible publicity for the forthcoming Gollancz biography.

The companion book, *Portrait of Picasso*, proved lastingly successful. In effect, Penrose had created a subtly effective hybrid genre in which biography and autobiography could barely be distinguished from one another, for the life-story he was telling was being told largely through images Picasso had either created himself or in which he had had a hand by causing them, or allowing them, to be created. Penrose had, furthermore, found a medium ideally suited to his subject because it operated primarily through images not text. More clearly than anyone at the time, except perhaps Sabartès,[107] he had understood that one of Picasso's many achievements was the construction of a potent and convincing persona for himself, partly through making dramatised self-portrait drawings and the occasional painting – few could be described as straightforwardly objective – but largely through letting others portray him in innumerable intimate and informal photographs taken in his studios and residences. Realising that fundamentally Picasso was a shy man, who used masks and theatrical disguises to conceal his shyness, Penrose also understood that this carefully stage-managed construction provided Picasso with a protective screen, for while apparently allowing the world at large unprecedented freedom of access to him, the 'photobiography' actually gave him the privacy to go on working as he wished without having to explain his 'intentions' verbally. In other words, Penrose grasped that the type of 'biographical' photography which flourished around Picasso was an important expressive medium for the artist himself: all those photographs, like the films of Emmer and Clouzot, stood in for the memoir-cum-manifesto Picasso never dreamed of writing.[108]

Penrose's confidence in his ability to interpret the trajectory of Picasso's career was greatly boosted by the positive response to 'Picasso Himself' and, in conjunction with *Portrait of Picasso*, the exhibition was of inestimable value as a blueprint for his book as he drew the threads of his research together in preparation for the toughest task of all – writing everything up. By dint of arranging the hundreds of images chronologically and in coherent thematic sequences of his own devising, Penrose was able to sum-marise his knowledge and map out *in visual form* the essential structure for his narrative. That, for him, was far more congenial and natural than working exclusively with text. An album of photographs records the entire exhibition,[109] and one can imagine him often referring back to it as he wrote and rewrote the thirteen chapters of *Picasso: His Life and Work* over the course of the following year.

To mark the artist's seventy-fifth birthday in a more personal way, Penrose had a plaster cast of a rare Polynesian statue in the British Museum made for him.[110] (The cast Penrose owned himself can be seen in the back-ground of the photograph of Picasso with him in his studio at Farley Farm, p. 67.) Picasso was thrilled and immediately conceived the plan of having it cast in bronze – which he did once he had obtained the Museum's go-ahead.[111] It was an inspired choice of gift, honouring both Picasso's long-standing love of 'primitive' sculpture and his surreal imagination. The 'bonhomme', as Picasso affectionately called it, can be glimpsed in many subsequent photo-graphs taken at La Californie. Penrose's second twelve-month period of work on his *magnum opus* thus ended on the most harmonious note.

Picasso and politics, Autumn 1956

On 17 November 1956 Penrose arrived in Paris to take up a three-year, part-time post as Fine Arts Officer for the British Council. He had been a member of the Council's Fine Arts Committee since December 1953 and had served on the selection panel for the 1956 Venice Biennale, so, with his immense experience of the art world in Paris, he was the obvious choice to replace the previous incumbent Frank McEwen. Inevitably, his workload increased substantially and he had less time than before to devote exclusively to the biography, but he consoled himself with the thought that he would have readier access to the people closest to Picasso – Sabartés, Kahnweiler, and Michel and Zette Leiris – and that contact with Picasso himself would also be facilitated. From a succession of rented flats in the heart of the city, Roland and Lee proceeded to immerse themselves in an incessant social round of café rendezvous, private views and parties, and the pages of Roland's diaries at this period are even more jammed than usual with appointments. Yet although he periodically complained of never having the time or the peace to concentrate on *Picasso: His Life and Work,* in reality Penrose seems to have thrived on what appears from the outside to have been a stressful and exhausting way of life.

Soon after settling in Paris, Penrose sought out Sabartés and it was prob-ably then that the following stories were told:[112]

Don José became almost blind before he died. When shown a blank sheet of paper at art school he said to the pupil, 'You should make your drawing stronger.' He retired from post at school because of blindness. […]

Sabartès tells a story of one of the moves during the war when, after leaving Royan finally for Paris, an important series of drawings could not be found. A thorough search was made and all the bundles and parcels checked but still they were missing. Picasso, very annoyed, said they had been stolen. Sabartès, thoroughly upset, some weeks later had a dream in which he saw P. in his studio moving cautiously around as though he were a thief. S. watched carefully and saw him go to one of the parcels from Royan that contained lithographs. At that moment he woke. Next morning they went together and opened the parcel in which they found, as well as the lithographs, the missing drawings. Sabartès, greatly relieved, asked Picasso why he said they were stolen and the answer was, 'I said they were stolen not because I believed they were but so that I could at last forget them.' [2]

He also had one of his typically intimate, off-the-record conversations with Dora Maar. Although he attributed it to October 1956, it must in fact have taken place in November or December:[113]

Oct. 1956
Dora met P. [on] 21 Jan. 1936 through P[aul] E[luard] in connection with a Surrealist manifestation against the anniversary of Louis XVI. Maya born in '35. P. went with M[arie]-T[hérèse] to Juan-les-Pins in Spring, did series of Minotaur with girls. D.M. begins to appear in drawings. (D.M. says earliest portraits of his girls creep into paintings, hardly visibly.) In '37 picture of Minotaur carrying M.T. unconscious into boat, D.M. [appears] as a mermaid watching.[114] D.M. says he painted M.T. after he had left her, in one case dressed in clothes given by P. to D.M. He thinks [in] terms of woman, not of one individual. P. met M.T. in '27.

At the time of the crisis with Françoise, when P. was in Paris and ready to break with Geneviève Laporte, he sent word just before leaving for Vallauris to Dora to come round to la rue des Gds. Augustins. When she arrived he said, 'Well shall we go?' Dora, taken aback by such an unexpected and abrupt proposal, refused. He left for Vallauris alone. [2]

Meanwhile for Picasso the autumn of 1956 turned out to be traumatic, despite all the flattering celebrations that surrounded his seventy-fifth birthday. On 23 October a popular anti-Communist uprising broke out in Hungary. It was brutally suppressed by Soviet military forces in early November – thousands were slaughtered – and a massive exodus of refugees began. While huge crowds demonstrated in support of the Hungarians in the Champs-Elysées, and Jean-Paul Sartre, Simone de Beauvoir and prominent left-wing French intellectuals close to Picasso, including Michel Leiris and Jacques Prévert, publicly denounced Soviet aggression, Picasso himself remained silent – to the intense relief of Communist Party officials. Of course, the silence of the painter of *Guernica* did not pass unnoticed and

Picasso came under sustained pressure to distance himself publicly from the Party line. The climax to this campaign took the form of an impassioned letter from James Lord, a close friend of Dora Maar's, which, as a further provocation, Lord published in *Combat* on 17 November.[115] John Richardson recalls that Picasso, who objected strongly to this friendship between his former lover and a man he dismissed as a publicity-craving opportunist, was 'in a black rage' about the letter.[116] To aggravate his plight, Picasso was also being harried by his Communist friends, who offered him conflicting advice about what he should do.[117] In the end he joined Pignon, Parmelin and seven other Communist intellectuals in signing a letter criticising the obfuscation in *L'Humanité*'s reporting of events and requesting the convocation of a special session, but neither explicitly denouncing the Soviet action nor renouncing the Party. The letter was published in *Le Monde* on 22 November and the signatories were ritually reprimanded for their disloyalty in *L'Humanité* on 30 November.[118]

Penrose watched this drama unfold, first from London, then from Paris. That he was fully informed is obvious from the numerous press cuttings he collected.[119] Although he did not enter the lists on one side or the other, or presume to cross-question the artist directly, he was keen to hear first-hand accounts of Picasso's reactions, noted down anything to the point that he heard Picasso say and touched on the issue in his contemporary correspondence with Barr. He noted, for example, that Picasso was glad that the Poles had displayed a reproduction of his painting *Massacre at Korea*[120] on the

Roland Penrose and Picasso, La Californie, Cannes, December 1956. In the background, on its side, is Picasso's *Massacre at Korea*. Photo Lee Miller

streets of Warsaw as a form of protest against the massacres in Budapest – a significant observation since the French Communist Party had disapproved of the picture when it was first exhibited at the Salon de Mai in 1951 and was angry that it had been used against the Soviets in this way during the current crisis. As we shall see, Penrose made use of Picasso's comment to promote his own view of the artist as an idealist and a humanitarian, the very opposite of a hardline Party man, and also to express obliquely his own revulsion at the Soviet action.[121] The Hungary crisis thus forms an undercurrent in the notes Penrose kept of his and Lee's brief visit to Cannes in December 1956:

10.12 '56, Cannes
'Massacre de Corée' was his title. He was very pleased it should have been used in Warsaw streets.

He painted a portrait of Pallarès in 1909 which has disappeared. No landscapes of cave.[122]

He [h]as painted a great many tiles, some on old floor tiles, some on new. One of the best series is of heads of bearded men & fauns. The surprises of his use [of] glazes are wonderful. He has let them run and the outer halo of a dried blot becomes the most exquisite line, drawing an eye or a mouth. The material has obeyed him miraculously. He said they were a bunch that had been spoiled in the kiln by being put upright and the glaze running. He worked on them again and from failures made the most exciting series of the lot.

He has worked a great deal in the last six months, mostly on small rapidly done things. Tiles, figures made out of 3 ply and painted,[123] which he places in front of large canvases, seats them in chairs, holds them like children. He said he had been working too much because he has so little time. 'If I had more time I should work less, or rather, slower. It is because I have so little that I am always doing small things fast.'

He gave me a paper with [a] cutting about himself lined round in coloured chalk. He said, 'Keep it, [it] is of no value.' I said joking, 'It is, now that you have lined it round.' To which he said, 'It's miserable, I can do nothing without it becoming worth something. A terrible state of affairs.' He looked really worried and then laughed.

He has made large figures fitted together with square pieces [of] ceramic which stand [in] the garden – 10ft. tall.[124] He is also making figures out of scrap pieces of wood, mostly from old packing cases, and including a long curved thin piece I had found on the beach last summer.[125] He was laughing about making things out of worthless material and having them cast at great cost in bronze.

Politics

Sabartès says recent letter signed by him and ten others has eased his mind.[126] Before he had been very worried and could not work. The open letter from James Lord was made into a poster and plastered on the walls leading up to La Californie. Since then he is again himself, working vigorously and joking. He said, 'That period is now passed,' meaning, I think, his Communist period. 'It is now a new period that begins.' He had seen it coming.

Photo drawings. He has worked [on] negatives, sometimes leaving details, such as a faun, and making new figures and backgrounds with chalk and strange chance effects, which look most mysterious when printed.[127]

Rousseau portrait.[128] Soulié knew it was a Rousseau. He told P., 'This canvas is good, you can paint it over.' Sold it for 5 frs. P. had only seen the head and was surprised to find a large full-length portrait. It is an early Rousseau and P. says [he] likes it 'pardessus tout'.[129] Dress is black. Collar and belt blue like a packet of Gitanes. R. told him it was a Polish governess he had known. The curtain was put in to 'faire orientale', the landscape was 'les fortifs'.[130] She holds a branch upside down.

Paulo[131]

'After separation from Olga my father had a period when he was perpetually in cafés. We went together from the Flore to Lipp to 2 Magots to Flore, and so on. Then he saw I was bored and gave me money to go where I like[d], or home. He loves cafés but now he can't go to them because at once he is set on by autograph hunters. That is terrible but maybe he asks for it and likes it.

'When I come home late or spend nights out he says, "I'm lucky to have a son who is so reasonable. In my time the things we did put all that in the shade."

'He once said to me, talking about beautiful women, "I have never noticed that in the cemeteries there is ever a corner marked reserved for beautiful women."' [22]

No doubt it was while Penrose was in Cannes that Picasso gave him a drawing for the annual Christmas sale in aid of the ICA.[132] It was not, of course, the first time Picasso had donated something to the ICA auction, but on this occasion the gift was also a way of silently thanking Penrose, not just for putting on the birthday exhibition, but for his rectitude and unquestioning loyalty. Such loyalty was more than welcome at the end of an inglorious and controversial episode in his career, which had caused him a great deal of private anguish even though he tried to brush it off as insignificant and belonging to the past.

Portrait of Picasso had sold well during the ICA exhibition and an expanded version was commissioned by the Museum of Modern Art for sale during their touring Picasso show.[133] While he was in France, Penrose assembled the additional material and wrote to Barr to explain how he intended to handle the contentious issue of Picasso's politics. Predictably, Barr was much less inclined to exonerate Picasso for his ambiguous response to the Hungary crisis:

[...] Of course I am pleased that he signed the open letter to 'L'Humanité', but can't help feeling a certain sense of disgust that it should have taken him so long to declare what has been so painfully obvious to the rest of the world, namely that the Communist press everywhere is a great deal more corrupt than the non-Communist press.[134]

On this particular question, Penrose and Barr tacitly agreed to differ and the relevant passage in the American edition of *Portrait of Picasso* is, in effect, a defence of the artist. Thus Penrose emphasised Picasso's detachment from the 'real' world – 'he is not interested in politics, regarding them as a crafty game outside his sphere' – and sought to dissociate him from the strict Party line by insinuating that he had been more outspoken in denouncing the Soviet invasion of Hungary than was actually the case. Thus he noted that Picasso had 'welcomed the purpose to which his painting [*Massacre in Korea*] had been put by the Poles' because 'the picture had been painted as an outcry against war and military violence, and its appeal was intended by him to be universal'. Penrose also made a point of mentioning the open letter Picasso had signed, implying that it was strongly denunciatory in tone. Two photographs of *Massacre in Korea*, framed in a black shroud and set up on an easel in the centre of Warsaw, complemented his account.[135] This moulding of the evidence for the American audience was expedient, especially in light of the anti-American, pro-Soviet sentiments that had motivated the allegorical imagery of the painting itself.[136] But Penrose evidently felt it was justified because he believed that Picasso's 'Communist period' was to all intents and purposes over. He was probably thinking not only of what Picasso had said in his hearing during his visit to Cannes – 'That period is now passed' – but of what Kahnweiler had said in his lecture at the ICA on 1 November 1956 at the height of the crisis and during the run of 'Picasso Himself':

You must understand that [Picasso's] Communism is quite unpolitical. He has never read a line of Karl Marx, nor of Engels of course. His Communism is sentimental. [...] [H]e once said to me, 'Pour moi, le Parti Communiste est le parti des pauvres.'[137]

In response to the question from the floor, 'Is Picasso a Roman Catholic?', Kahnweiler had replied:

Well, I shall answer you with something Picasso has said to me last Friday. He discussed what happens to Communism just now and he said, 'Well, after all, my family has always been – they have always been Catholics. They didn't like the priests and they didn't go to mass, but they were Catholics. Well I am a Communist and I …'[138]

American attitudes to Picasso at this acutely troubled period are thrown into relief by the manoeuvres of another habitué of La Californie, the swash-buckling American photojournalist David Douglas Duncan. During the summer of 1957 Duncan, who must often have heard Picasso express sharp dissent from the Party line, nursed delusions about co-opting him into the war against Communism by luring him to the Wild West and fêting him as a hero of democracy. In a letter to Richard Nixon, then Vice-President of the United States, Duncan laid out his fantastic scheme:

[…] Look, amigo, I really know this man very, very well. He's pure Spaniard. He's as proud as any man on earth. If officially invited to visit the United States his pride would overflow. I feel certain he'd come. […] Later, if I know the man at all, I'll bet right now that he would come out with a pro-West statement that would be a cultural body-blow to the Communists. It could be as great a victory for us as was the Commies' use of his famous dove poster, which wasn't intended for that use at all. How about getting someone high up to shepherd him as a crash project for this autumn? He'll come! We've spent so much of our free time talking about California, Arizona, cowboys – our West. I've told him as much as I can remember. It excites him. It sounds like his homeland. Let's let him see it all for himself. You can swing it.[139]

Nixon took this seriously enough to reply: the artist could have a visa imme-diately, but 'time was too short and the question too complex for Picasso to be invited as the official guest of the government'.[140] This astonishing exchange provides the context for the problems Penrose regularly encoun-tered when he acted as ambassador for Picasso's work in the United States.

Completing the biography

On 3 January 1957 Penrose returned to Paris. There were many distractions from his writing as he settled into his job for the British Council, including, for instance, catalogue essays for exhibitions of works by Francis Bacon and Henry Moore.[141] For these he wrote short, poetic texts in the French belles lettres style that are entirely different from those intended for Anglo-Saxon consumption. And there was much partying in the rented apartment: the only two references to the Penroses in Michel Leiris's diary mention bouts of heavy drinking in the spring of 1957.[142] Penrose coped remarkably well with the bibulous socialising because he was so disciplined and orderly in other respects. His friend John Thompson saw this in terms of the 'fascinating mixture' within him of the strictly brought-up Quaker gentleman and the bohemian, observing: 'No matter how heavy the night before had been he was meticulous first thing in the morning, well-groomed and at his desk going through his papers.' Patsy Murray, the Penroses' housekeeper in Sussex, agreed, recalling that when he was working on a text Roland was always up early and always wrote methodically, whatever had happened the night before.[143]

In Paris, Penrose continued to interview mutual friends when the opportunity arose:

Conversation with Dora & Balthus, 12 Jan. '57
Balthus. L'angoisse[144] is not a motive of interest in art. There is already too much of it in German expressionism.
R.P.   What about 'Guernica'?
B.   Picasso is not moved by a woman weeping when he paints. He is a detached observer. It is his sense of humour and vitality that allow him to be detached.
D.M.   He has often said, 'Plus il y a de l'ame plus c'est mauvais.'[145] When he paints he is cold and unemotional – that allows him to be truthful.
R.P.   But surely he is sensitive to tragedy?
B.   Yes, but he leads beyond tragedy to something more durable and universal. L'angoisse is the fashion among all the young school of moderns. Picasso cannot interest himself in an incomplete, partial emotion. To create it is essential to be detached. [23]

One of Penrose's informants told him an anecdote about Mary (aka Meric) Callery, the American sculptor and collector who became a friend of Picasso's during the 1930s. Because the story revealed Picasso in his most attractive political guise as the devoted friend of democracy and the generous supporter of the innocent victims of war, it had particular resonance for Penrose in the aftermath of the Hungary *débâcle*:

1936–1939
Kosnitzky[146] – Mary Callery was presented with several large paintings by her Italian friend, [*name missing*], rich industrialist who was selling arms to Franco.[147] They called on P. with the intention of buying a painting direct from him. Having chosen an important canvas, he asked the price.[148]
P. named a figure nearly twice the sum he would have had to pay if he had bought a similar painting from a dealer. The Italian, who was well informed, expressed his surprise but P. said, 'Yes, I know it is a higher price than usual. You would have to pay less if you bought it from Rosenberg, but if you want to buy it from me that's the price.' However, because they wanted to buy direct from the master the Italian took out his cheque book and wrote out a cheque for the full price asked and gave it to P. P. thanked him, and said, 'But that's not all, wait a moment.' Taking a pen he endorsed

the cheque and wrote on the back, 'Pay to the Relief Fund for the children of the Spanish Republic'. Handing it back he said, 'Would you please pay that in for me?' [2]

Major or minor, there were too many diversions in Paris and, as the deadline for the submission of his manuscript loomed, Penrose found that he could only make headway with his book when he was somewhere else. In order to move things along more rapidly he decided to take the whole family to Cannes for a couple of weeks during the Easter holidays – Lee, Tony and Patsy Murray. They borrowed a flat on La Croisette and visited La Californie as often as possible, although to Penrose's chagrin at first they found many rivals for Picasso's attention, including the dreaded Douglas Cooper. While Lee took rolls of photographs documenting daily life chez Picasso, Roland dashed off notes containing the usual mix of detailed observations of the artist's latest work, gossip about events he had witnessed and disparate pieces of essential information. Some of Picasso's anecdotes are startling, especially his account of the faking, at Madame Errazuriz's instigation, of the murals he had painted for her in 1918. Prompted by the diverting spectacle on their last visit of Picasso insouciantly decorating ceramics with fishbones left over from his lunch, Penrose strove to sum up his thoughts about the role of play in Picasso's work – a snapshot of the biographer formulating his ideas to parallel the snapshot of the artist in mid-creation.

Visit to Cannes, 1st–15 Ap. 1957. (Lee, Tony, Patsy & self) 81 La Croisette.
We found ourselves on the same plane as Sabartès. Arrived at Nice after dark in pouring rain. P., Jacqueline & the Leirises were at the airport to meet Sabartès. We all exchanged greetings and left for Cannes.

In some ways it was not a good moment to arrive. P. had had a great many people round. Zette Leiris planning exhibition for Barr in NY. Cooper working on ceramic ex[hibition] for London.[149] P. also was working hard on ceramics. Did not see him for three days. Thursday evening 4 Ap. Jacqueline called asking us to join them at a display given by the dancers of the Marquis de Cuevas Ballet, who were at Cannes rehearsing. [Hjahnaar] Boyesen had improvised with them a ballet in honour of Picasso, representing in mime the various periods of his work. It was performed in a bare hall in the Hôtel Martinez to a small audience of some 40 friends. The dancers were pretty, agile and devoted in their attempt to give pleasure to a man they admired. Their improvisation was charming but not always very inspired. All went well and P. was in a happy mood. A party was given after at Boyesen's studio and later we had supper together with Ramiés, Coopers and Sabartès at Félix.
    5 Ap. Visited Vallauris Friday morning and saw all the ceramics chosen for exhibition with Arts Council in London. All recent pieces were still in his studio and not available for the exhibition. He never lets things go until he

feels sufficiently detached from them. We lunched at Antibes and after visiting the Grimaldi museum,[150] which I wanted Tony to see, we met him with the de Lazermes, [Frank] Haviland, who has recently been made director of the Céret Museum, and others.

7 Ap. On Sunday we went to La Californie for lunch. Since all the canvases painted in the last two years have gone to Paris I was expecting the rooms to be relatively empty. This was not the case. The floor was almost entirely covered with tiles and bricks painted by him in a variety of different styles. Many were owls or faces that profited of the shape of the brick for their

Picasso's studio at La Californie, Cannes, April 1957. Photo Lee Miller outline. There was a series of large plates with owls and some large vases inspired by Greek themes. Quantities of bulls, fish, etc. modelled in clay were drying precariously, set out on cases. It was difficult to move without knocking something over. [*Sketches to show the shape of the tiles and how they fitted together.*] He told me he had made a plate the day before on which he had placed some clay fish with a knife and fork – a few minutes later he found it covered with flies. It is true, the realism of these plates was very striking; one he had made for his amusement had a half-eaten cutlet and other debris, including cigarette stubs. Among the litter of ceramics spread everywhere were bird cages on the floor, and a twitter of love birds would rise from unexpected places. Picasso has a young goat which is tethered in the garden but when it rains, as it did during lunch, it is taken upstairs and lives in a box on the first-floor landing.[151] We talked about Holland during lunch and [he] remembered the solitude of the place he had stayed in on a canal.[152] Later, talking about language and how you could get on without understanding a word, he remembered rolling down the dunes in a delightful silent embrace with a Dutch girl. Lee had brought a Dutch smoked eel, which he ate with great pleasure and later placed what remained of the head and tail on an easel to remind him to make some eels in ceramic. He seemed very happy and vigorous and was anxious to hear about the exhibition at La Hune and Kahnweiler's opening.[153] When we left we brought Sabartès home with us and later Jacqueline arrived with Tony, who had stayed behind to play with Cathy, Jacqueline's daughter.

8 Ap. On Monday, P., Jacqueline and Sabartès came to our flat to lunch. Tony had considerable success with the monsters he has been making from driftwood. Lunch was quiet and they were very appreciative of Lee's cooking. Talking about the rue Schoelcher, I asked why he had gone to Montrouge. He said, simply because he wanted a change. There was a garden there, it was a house instead of a flat, but that didn't matter much because he was never there. He went to Paris almost every morning and came back late at night. As it was wartime trains were scarce and he usually walked, often with Satie, who lived in Arcueil even further [out]. Looking at a small bronze repro. of the Discobolus on the mantlepiece, he said from a distance he had thought the disc held up in the air was a head and the head an arm – 'Not so bad,' he thought, better than its appearance from near to, which looked like a 'crotte de chien'.[154]

During lunch P. asked me how I managed to keep a farm going. He has always shown great interest in my farm and still speaks of his visit there as a memorable event. He said he had often thought of doing the same, except that it would have taken up too much time and the idea of finding a man who could run it and was honest was too difficult. But perhaps a bull ranch on the Camargue was still possible. He would think about it when he goes to the Easter bullfight at Nîmes in a fortnight's time. He gave me a reproduction of a drawing he had made for the birthday of the son of his friend Paco Muñoz with an inscription which runs – 'Here I send you, Dear

Paco, a good dish of little fried bulls for Currito to eat on his birthday with a glass of Valdepeñas and a porron of Priorat. You see that I remember Your Picasso Cannes 6/2/57.' The little fried bulls lie like sardines on a plate, complete with their horns, tails and hoofs.[155]

He has several ceramic vases made by Paco Durio – very Gauguinesque in design mixed with Art Nouveau. They are not very good but he keeps them as a souvenir.

10 Ap. I called at La Californie to take to P. the album of photos that I had made up of the London exhibition – each screen photographed so that each detail was visible. He was very pleased and commented on the great amount of work involved. Going through each page carefully he looked at each photo. (P. was wearing trousers with a horizontal stripe. He said he had always wanted a pair like these – the same that Courbet is wearing in his picture of 'L'Atelier'.[156]) When I arrived [Pierre] Seghers the editor was there with his wife, but soon left, but Duncan the photographer stayed on, taking innumerable photos of Jacqueline, P. and myself as we went through the book. I then started asking him a mixed lot of questions for my book, which he answered very readily.

Jacqueline, who had been out of the room, came back to say that the pigeons had been in their bedroom and messed everywhere, so we went up to the top floor to see them. On a terrace outside an empty bedroom P. has built a cage for some dozen pigeons of a variety of breeds – fantails, and others, some with very handsome plumage. The nesting boxes, which covered the back wall to a height of some six feet, had been made by him in a rough style out of old boxes; something in their proportions made me think of a cubist painting. He said laughing, 'That's my Corbusier – "la cité radieuse".'[157] The pigeons are now allowed their liberty. They were flying round and perching on the dead branches of a tree that had been set up on a cement base. In a separate cage was a young pigeon that had nearly been pecked to death, like its brother, by a particularly vicious white hen pigeon, who[m] he called the assassin. We watched the birds, all very tame, flying in and out, courting and eating. P. took the greatest pleasure in following their movements, their ways of stalking proudly on each other, shivering, pouting, ruffling their feathers, quarrelling and stretching their wings. He seemed to be watching each antic for the first time with the delight of a child, so that one felt oneself that never before had one been so close to understanding the soft, timid and acutely alive creatures. We looked down on the garden and talked about the beauty of the palms and the great eucalyptus tree while Duncan never stopped taking pictures. Having got down to the studio again Duncan left us and, realising that he probably wanted to work, I began to make my way out. He was most affectionate and asked several times about my work. He showed me the great picture of two nudes which is one of the few important recent pictures left and which is also leaving for Paris for the Salon de Mai [*see p. 163*].[158] It is a painting that I have watched going through many changes since he started it in the autumn of '55. In its final state it is one of the most monumental and most moving of recent works. I said goodbye but once outside the gate I found I had forgotten a book. When I got back he was sitting at the table absorbed in my album. I watched him address an envelope to Pignon in which he was sending a photo of the 'two nudes'. He got out a box of coloured chalks and selecting a different colour for each word he wrote the address in a grand and gay style. Each word seemed to him a delight as he formed the letter in orange, blue, green or red. I left with this rich letter, which was to astonish the woman in the post office where it was handed in. She blinked and smiled as she stuck on the stamps.

Answers to questions. The Italian futurists had been in Paris as early as 1909. Marinetti knew P. then. They watched every development in Cubism and borrowed all they could. The only one he considered to have real talent was Boccioni, who was killed in [the] 14–18 war. They were all on friendly terms with him [Picasso], specially Severini, who was gentle and attentive. They were mixed up with what became fascism. Mussolini wrote in their reviews.

Don José's eyesight was bad only in his last years and even then not unusually bad for his age.

Letter to Braque, Mon Cher Wilbur: He confirmed that they were very interested in flying machines. The letter seems to have been written just before Wilbur Wright died. (Find date.)

Fanny Tellier was a very pretty model sent to him by a painter friend. When she came in and took off her clothes P. was at a loss to know what to do. He had not used a model since the days when his father at the Beaux-Arts in Barcelona insisted on him doing so. She was too pretty for his taste in any case and [he] seemed surprised when I insisted that he had somehow managed to convey this in the picture [*see p. 49*].[159] He never liked models. Once in Barcelona they had been asked to do a portrait of a lady in a fine dress. He couldn't get on with her there, so dressed Pallarès with his big black moustache up in her clothes.

The great heads made at Boisgeloup were in plaster but the 'Homme au mouton' was first made in clay, then cast in plaster and finally bronze.

Rue la Boétie was becoming a dealer's street. He moved there so as to be next door to Paul Rosenberg. For Rosenberg P. was an innovation.

The Apollinaire Monument: many sketches in 1927–28 (Barr 150, 153) turned down. P. has now offered the bronze head of Dora and even that they cannot agree to accept.[160] He said, 'I can't after all give them a muse holding a torch.'

Life at Dinard was very unlike life on the coast. He was there alone with Olga & Paulo. In 1922 Olga fell very ill and had to be brought back to Paris with ice on her belly to be operated. Paulo was sick all the way in the car. Paulo was born in the apartment [at] rue La Boétie. They went to Fontainebleau after[wards] to escape the heat.

Visit to Klee in 1936, mentioned by Grohmann, happened when he had gone to Switzerland for some affair to do with Paulo. He called on Klee who, he says, was an 'homme magnifique',[161] very dignified and demanding respect for his attitude and his work. He was already rather ill but greeted P. with great friendliness. Frau Klee was there also and P. seems to remember that she played to them. The studio was pleasant and well arranged but more like a laboratory than a studio. P. denies that he ever said the remark quoted by Grohmann – 'You are the master of le petit format, I am master of the large.'[162] At the same time he admires greatly his work.

Epoque Dora Maar should also be called époque Kasbec.[163] He says there were two dominating themes in his portraits then, Dora & Kasbec, they alternated.

Monday 15 Ap. Went at 3.0 with Lee to La Calif[ornie]. Found him at work in the dining room on one of the large plates he is decorating with birds. Duncan was hovering round ticking off his cameras in his usual unobtrusive style. P. stopped and welcomed us. Very soon he asked Lee if she was taking pictures, which gave the clue for her to say that she had come armed to take his picture for my book. He at once accepted and asked where he should pose. In spite of the fact that Duncan had sent 2000 shots to be developed yesterday he welcomed the idea of a posed portrait and cooperated all the time. He has recently had given him an African xylophone made of split wood and gourds. It is a modern piece strongly made in traditional style and with very sweet tone. Picasso enjoys playing it. He improvises with an excellent sense of rhythm and enjoys the most unexpected sequences of notes. He played to us while the photographers on all sides, Jacqueline joining in, clicked away at him [*see p. 190*].

Rosenbergs. Léonce not so clever a dealer as Paul but first to take interest in cubists. After Kahnweiler's departure he took them all. Paul, well established, took P. later as an innovation, not the others. Paul had sent his family to Biarritz when Paris was menaced.

Mme. Errazuriz, a rich Chilean, had also retreated to Biarritz. P. & O[lga] went to visit her Sept. '18. She wanted later to remove the frescoes he painted on her walls to sell them, but it was not possible.[164] In consequence she had them copied and sold them to Pierre Loeb as originals. P. found them there and so as to avoid a scandal and save Pierre from embarrassment he bought them from him.

Erik Satie wrote many letters to Valentine Hugo (G[ross]) about the time of 'Parade'. Many of them say very bitter things about Cocteau but nice things about P. P. advised me to see Matarasso, who has a large collection of these letters.

Dada & Surrealism interested P. from their birth. First Dada review had his drawings. 'C'etait ce qu'il avait de mieux,'[165] he said of both movements. He knew Breton & Aragon when they were still in uniform and Eluard about the same time. He does not consider that they ran after him or tried to use his reputation. They were his friends, he enjoyed their activities, was present when there were manifestations, which sometimes ended in a bagarre.[166]

Drawing of Dining room Montrouge.[167] Seated at table are himself and Olga (he seemed not very sure about it being Olga). The maid stands behind. Two dogs. On the wall a negro mask – a very fine one, he says, which he still has.

The eyes are protruding cylinders.[168] A small round table with black fringe, which was there beside him at La Californie. In spite of his apparent disregard for furniture he has still got many of his old pieces around him in daily use. I found I was sitting in what he called the musicians' chair – a light armchair with reed seat – in which he had made drawings of Satie, Stravinsky & de Falla in 1920.[169] At the other side of the table was the chair on which Apollinaire sat for his portrait in 1916.[170] He showed me a portrait drawn in Feb. last of Poulenc seated in the same musicians' chair.[171]

Beach scene 1918.[172] I was in doubt about the date. P. confirmed it and said the lighthouse & beach [were] Biarritz.

Two peasants 1919 was drawn from a photo, also Diaghilev & Selisburg, Three Ballet Dancers, Renoir.[173]

'Massacre of Korea' shown in streets of Warsaw. I asked if he had seen my mention of this event in autumn 1956 in American edition of 'Portrait of Picasso'. He said, 'Yes,' and approved the way it had been done thoroughly.

Antonina Vallentin's book had just been sent to him. I asked if he had read it. 'No,' he said, 'I don't intend to. If it is true what she says I know it already, if not, it will upset me and I do not want to be upset by her. In any case it will teach me nothing.'

16 Ap. Lee & I went after lunch to say goodbye. He had just finished lunch and welcomed us to coffee. He said they had had sole for lunch and would I come to see what he had done with them. On a flat slab of damp clay he had made an impression of the backbone, beautifully sharp. He had placed paper over the bones and rolled it in with a milk bottle. Three skeletons were imprinted. The first, he pointed out, had some flesh and blood sticking to it, which would disappear in the kiln. Later he fetched one of the big new plates made on the Spanish model with a domed centre saying he would put the fish on it. Placing the plate upside down on his brass turntable he first scratched radiating lines with a serrated bread knife and then with a sharp pointed tool drew four frames in which he drew very simple faces, an oval with eyes, nose and mouth, in each. 'So easy,' he said. Then cutting round the backbone the shape of a fish, he applied it to the other side of the plate. Should he put one or all three? No, one was enough, the others could have plates for themselves, he would make a black ground for them. While working, his hands functioned with tenderness and precision. His left hand held the plate firmly, as though holding the hands of a friend, his right attacked slowly and firmly the line he had determined. Though thoroughly concentrated, he laughed and talked with us while he worked.

He told me 'The Crucifixion' 1930[174] was still in U.S., where it had been since 1939. It was a small picture with violent colour. I said it was important because it was prophetic of 'Guernica', etc. He said, 'Naturally, it is always me.' He agreed that it was unique.

Duncan, who was there as usual, said he was astonished at the variety of things that happened all the time.

We said goodbye and he regretted that we would not be going with him to the Corrida at Nîmes next Monday (Easter). A great many people, Cocteau & others were going. Jacqueline was very affectionate and they both saw us off from the doorstep.

The plates and tiles he has been doing recently are all decorated front and back. A portrait of Cathy had a series of faces, each with extraordinary personality, on the back. Old men, peasant women, a series of profiles, each like a portrait of some definite character.

Under a table, surrounded by a diversity of objects, I noticed for the first time a very large skull of a giraffe.

Play: P. varies his occupations and the intensity with which he works. Work is an intensive, concentrated form of play. P. has never played a game in the conventional sense but is all the time inventing games for himself. Duncan saw him sit down to his elegant brass turntable on which he decorates his plates. It turns very smoothly and, having cleared its to[p], he set it up near the dining-room table and made a black mark on the edge of each. He then started spinning the turntable, starting again and again until the black spot stopped exactly opposite the spot on the big table. No near misses were of any account, but as soon as he got a stop perfectly in position, with a sigh of satisfaction he stopped playing. One day he picked up a narrow piece of red cellophane ruban[175] and amused himself by decorating my button hole with it as though it were a 'legion d'honneur'. His masks and disguises, kept always at hand, are a continual source of fun. He has a new disguise which consist[s] of a bald pate with black side hair and the twisted syphilitic nose of an Italian grocer; completed by a bowler hat, he walks round making noises and nudging people in the inane fashion of [a] small self-confident Neapolitan tout. He loves making noises that resemble languages he is unable to speak. Often over the phone he insists on making English noises to me which mean nothing but which have a friendly ring. He plays for hours to himself on his Negro xylophone, improvising rhythms and melodies.

A mountain landscape painted in the first years in Barcelona had turned up. He had painted it from sketches made on the spot.[176] Long desolate ridges of rock ran parallel into a misty distance; on the top of the nearest ridge among the boulders was a smouldering fire with a long cloud of smoke blowing from it. A mournful scene – nothing in it to give a clue that it was a Picasso. [24]

After a brief interlude for Easter in England, Penrose was back in Paris again by 1 May. He intended to spend the summer in England completing the biography and so he crammed in as many interviews as possible, conscious that they would be the last.[177]

Conversation 13 May '57 with Castro. Mme. Goldscheider. Peissi[178]
Castro. At the time of Góngora, when the weather became dark and threatening [and] black storm clouds approached, the peasants would call this menacing unexpected change of atmosphere a 'Góngora'.[179] In the same way the name of Picasso has come to signify the incomprehensible, the

Picasso in hat and mask, La Californie, Cannes, April 1957. Photo Lee Miller

outrageous, the mad. In a crowded street a man tried to pass in front of his taxi and nearly got knock[ed] down. 'Espece de Picasso,'[180] shouted the driver.

Peissi. The name Picasso has become a generic term for all modern art, including Negro. His maid broke a Negro mask and said, 'Je ne toucherai plus à vos Picassos.' Usually it is the grotesque which provokes, 'On dirai un Picasso.'[181] [2]

[…] H[enri]-P[ierre] Roché.[182] P. used to try & sell drawings for 200 frs. Suddenly he brought [the] price down to 5 frs. All his painter friends were outraged, but he sold many.

At first sight 'Les Demoiselles' did not strike him as being an epoch-making picture. It did appear strange and highly original. H.P.R. saw it first when shown at a gallery next door to Poiret about 1910.[183] Doucet bought it blind – it had been rolled up on the floor for many yrs. when he found it about 1923. He put it in a place of honour in his collection. [7]

For Penrose the most exciting interviews conducted at this time must have been those with Fernande Olivier, who was delighted to be asked and glad of the chance to reminisce.[184] Her own first book of memoirs, *Picasso et ses amis*, had been published in France in 1933 but still awaited translation into English:

Fernande Olivier, 23 May '57
F. is six months younger than P. Married a mad sculptor so as to escape from her aunt at age 17. He died about 1905 but she did not know until about 1908. She came to live in a room on the square at Bateau Lavoir about the same time as P. Would sit out with a girl friend in the square in the summer. One day a storm made them run in for shelter, it was then she met P. with the kitten and went into his studio for the first time. At once impressed by the Blue period pictures she saw all around and by him but she held him off for some six to eight months in spite of his advances. He wanted her to marry him; she refused because already married and not daring to let him know. During courting he made a drawing of her which was afterwards stolen, mounted it on a blue chemise he asked her to give him, and framed it under glass. With this he made the shrine, as a teasing homage to her. Her parents were makers of plumes and hat ornaments. When they [Olivier and Picasso] went to Barcelona they did not stay with [his] parents but Don José liked her and urged P. to marry.[185] Could not believe him when he said he had asked and it was F. who refused. Even after she knew her husband was dead she still refused. She was proud and independent. She left him because of Eva, all of a sudden with only ten francs. When he asked her through friends to come back she said, 'Let him come and fetch me.'
He painted many portraits of her and she comes into many pictures (Girl holding mirror.[186] Gósol). She loved the country, specially Gósol, got on well

with peasant smugglers. At Horta she hardly saw him during the day; always hidden in a studio.[187] His cubism came from the angular shapes and subdued colour of Spanish landscape – from what he saw. Departure for Gósol made possible by Vollard buying the whole studio for 2000 frs. A sculptor, Casanovas, told them about Gósol. It was typhoid that made them leave in a hurry. Place very remote and P. panicked at thought of being ill there.

He was a jealous and generous lover, would buy her scent even when they had hardly a sou. Her best friend was Max [Jacob]. G[uillaume] A[pollinaire] & Marie L[aurencin] ignored her after break. P. has recently given her a large sum of money, thanks largely to Marcelle Braque's persuasion, but she lives in poverty, one room, and suffers much from rheumatism. Has still a lively personality and in spite of ravages her profile is distinguished and her eyes keen. She is convinced she is the only one he really loved. [2]

20 June '57. Fernande Olivier. During all the years spent at the B[ateau] L[avoir] F. scarcely ever had a meal alone with P. The usual routine was the arrival of G.A., M.J., Salmon & Manolo about midday. F. always did marketing and cook[ed] well. Guests paid her compliments. She had nothing more than a paraffin stove. Every now and then she got fed up with cooking and they would go out to Azon opposite or other restaurants nearby. The studio was large. P. worked at night seated on the floor with a lampe Matador[188] hanging over his head, often till 6 in morning. That's why he hated early callers. Olivier Sainsère, Conseiller d'Etat,[189] dressed with top hat, was tolerated. Concierge would knock saying, 'Il faut ouvrir, c'est serieux.'[190] F. would hide and P. open in his nightshirt. Sainsère would say, 'Please put on a pair of trousers, you will catch cold.' He bought paintings, drawings and engravings for his own satisfaction. It was so cold in winter that ice formed in the tea cups and in summer the heat was appalling. The coal merchant, who loved F.'s eyes, gave them coal and sometimes would announce that he had cabbage soup at home if they cared to come. You should have heard G.A.'s grateful laugh as they trooped off. The disorder was always terrible. When Poiret came to call shortly before they moved, Mme. Poiret had to lift her skirts to her knees to climb over paints and canvases. The Poirets asked them to dine quite often. He understood little about painting but spotted genius. F. remembers a dinner party about 1911 to which all the band had been invited. G.A. had annoyed Poiret by saying that while la couture was an art, it was only a minor one. He left early and as soon as he was gone all his friends started running him down, particular[ly] M.J. P. managed to seem detached but F. suddenly stood up and told them all they were cowards to talk in such terms behind his back. After F. left P. she worked for Poiret for several years. She had left with eleven francs, nothing more. P.'s friends, with the exception of the gossip-lover M.J., all cut her. G.A. & M.L. even crossed to the other side of the street not to meet her. They were so anxious not to anger P.

P. was never jealous of other artists, he had confidence in his own talent. Matisse's jealousy took the form of violent anger against P. He was angry that

P. should take such liberties with form. F. heard him say, 'Je coulerai P. Ça ne doit pas exister comme ça.'[191] P. is a 'refoulé',[192] he could have been a successful classical painter but something inside him would not allow it and he was too honest with himself and too careless of success to mind. He threw away success. At a glance he took in what he saw. He could very quickly analyse and remember the work of other painters and afterwards, if he wanted, to copy it in all its essentials.

When Vollard bought up his studio he paid 2000 frs for it – 15 to 20 canvases. P. knew it was cheap but wanted to go to Spain. They left at once for Barcelona & Gósol. Kahnweiler was a hard bargainer, would argue for hours until P. would say aside to F., 'You take him over. I've had enough.' F. was firmer about prices than P. [2]

In June Penrose conducted several other interviews before returning to England for the summer. In the first, with the sculptor Nadine Effront,[193] he learned a few details about the ignominious end of Fernande Olivier's affair with Picasso, which Fernande had chosen to keep to herself:

12 June. Story told by Nadine Effront, quoting Marcelle Braque.
Fernande received a message from a friend, a good-looking painter,[194] that he would kill himself if she did not come to see him. Meeting M[arcelle] and the wife of a painter (name not told) she asked them what she should do. They said, 'Go to see him, we will keep the secret from Pablo.' But Mme. X did not. Going straight to P. she told him what was happening and when F. returned P. asked where she had been. On receiving the reply, 'With Marcelle,' he became very angry, smacked her and told her to leave, saying, 'I don't love you any more.' F. went towards the door and turned back, looked at him and said, 'If you say that once more I shan't come back.' Picasso repeated, 'I don't love you any more.' F. went out with nothing but what she was carrying. (F. had told me that some days later he asked her through friends to come back, to which she answered, 'Let him come and fetch me.' He never did.) (Dora's story, quoting P., says that P. had foun[d] traces in his own apartment of visits from F.'s lover – F.'s story was that he was already running after Eva – in any case the break seems to have been inevitable and may have come from both sides.)

Nadine, talking of Braque, said how shocked and sad he is when he hears news of the boyish, show-off antic[s] of P. He has reached a stage when wisdom and a quiet gentle retirement from life [are] what he hopes for. The large white birds flying across an empty sky are pictures of himself departing.[195] He told N. he had seen a large bird in his studio that flew away and identified himself with it. The contrast between the quiet resignation of Braque and the angry refusal to admit old age by P. form a complete contrast. [2]

Penrose also spoke to his old friend, the Surrealist poet and collagist Georges Hugnet, and to Matisse's daughter Marguerite Duthuit:

13 June. Georges Hugnet spent his summer at Dinard in 1928 and saw P. almost every day. P. had taken a large, ugly, art nouveau villa with a garden near the spot where the ferry from St. Malo came in. He often hailed Georges from the window as he arrived and would leave Olga for long expeditions on the crowded beaches with him. He saw very few people. The rooms of the villa were desolate except those in which he worked, where the usual creative disorder prevailed. He was often glad to escape from Olga and would do so saying simply, 'Je m'en vais avec Georges.'[196] [2]

June '57. Marguerite Duthuit. Talking about P. during 14–18 war said that, unlike artists who refuse to have anything to do with official regulations, P. was, like all Spaniards, scared of the police and very anxious to have his papers in order. He even spent hours when necessary waiting in offices to get them straight. Matisse, who was still living at Quai St. Michel, saw P. fairly often.

I asked about P.'s visits to Nice to see Matisse, conversations unfortunately unrecorded – she said they mostly talked about banalities, not wanting to give away 'le fond de leur pensée.'[197] [2]

As his research neared its conclusion, Penrose came under increased pressure from Gollancz to hand in his manuscript before the renegotiated deadline of 1 October,[198] and at the end of June he wrote to Picasso outlining his plans for a summer of monastic seclusion:

We are on the point of departure, abandoning our lovely apartment in the centre of Paris for our farm, where I'm going to shut myself away and set to work quietly on my book, so as to finish it before the end of the year if possible. […] Everyone is speaking about the corrida in Arles in honour of your exhibition of drawings.[199] It maddens me that I can't be present at such a thrilling event, but there's nothing to be done. Until October, my book about you must take precedence above everything else, and then I intend to come to see you in reality after having lived with you in my thoughts for so many weeks.[200]

In a differently styled letter to Alfred Barr written a fortnight later Penrose described his state of mind and his impressions of the entertaining and garrulous, but not very reliable, Fernande Olivier:

My dear Alfred,

I too am damn glad to have got back to the country and to my book. Paris was all very well but it was nearly impossible to get any of my own work done. Now I have got to catch up. The Vallentin book is out in Paris and Gollancz want me to finish mine so that it can appear before her American edition, but that's highly improbable as I refuse to be stampeded. It was very kind of you to include me in your gift to Fernande O. She is still quite a remarkable character, though terribly crippled with arthritis and only one tooth. She loves talking but is often obviously inaccurate in her assertions. Incidentally she is much happier since P. gave her a million francs recently but she wants to give lessons in French. She is particularly good at correcting bad accents in French. Her English doesn't go far. I keep on getting news of your Picasso show – great enthusiasm everywhere. I still keep alive a hope that I shall manage to see it, but when and where I am unable to decide. Paris starts again in November and I want to spend a month in Cannes, which is even more important to me at the present time, in October. [...] [201]

The trip to Cannes had to be delayed and curtailed as the October deadline slipped: completing the manuscript proved harder and slower than Penrose had bargained for and it seemed to him, as he told Picasso, that his closeted summer of 'unremitting work' had 'flown by with unimaginable speed'.[202] Before he left for France,[203] Penrose received another firmly worded letter from his impatient publisher: the manuscript must be delivered 'not later than December 1st'; the budget did not permit any extra illustrations; he must keep the text as far below 150,000 words as possible.[204] All this browbeating was disagreeable, but now that he had got so far Penrose was disposed to be mulishly obstinate. He refused to trim his text and exceeded the word-limit by a significant margin, and once he was sure that Gollancz liked the manuscript he cajoled and nagged until he was allowed a few extra pages of plates at the back of the book and a few documentary photographs to break up the text. As the famously domineering Gollancz grudgingly made these concessions at the end of March 1958, he reminded Penrose that he had systematically broken all their basic agreements, thus jeopardising realistic hopes of a reasonable profit: 'this really must be the end: I will not even listen to any further demands!', he exclaimed as he wound up his letter.[205]

Penrose had not yet fought these battles when he arrived in Cannes in October 1957 intent on tying up the loose ends in his manuscript. It was only then that he hit upon the perfect subject for the concluding pages – the suite of variations after Velázquez's *Las Meninas*, on which Picasso had worked intensively throughout the latter part of the summer, save for an interlude in September when he painted several pictures of his flock of pigeons in their aviary on the terrace outside the studio window. The first of the *Meninas* variations is dated 17 August 1957 and when Penrose visited La Californie in mid-October Picasso was still absorbed by this great new project and full of ideas for its development. Penrose had already decided to close his narrative with an account of work that was still in progress because he wanted to give the sense of Picasso as an active creative force, not an artist at the end of his career, and it dawned on him that ending with a *series*, rather than a single, unfinished masterpiece, was ideal since a series implies both evolution and continuation, not finality. The description of the *Meninas* variations, which comes midway through the notebook he used in Cannes, is not the usual rapid record of initial impressions, but a first draft for the corresponding passage in the book, which Penrose pointedly entitled 'Work in Progress: *Las Meninas*'.[206] By contrast, the first and last pages of the notebook were used for more informal or hasty jottings, such as reminders to himself of points he must make, citations of scraps of Picasso's conversation, information about the UNESCO commission and a startlingly vivid evocation of Picasso's physical presence.

This was Penrose's final visit to Picasso before he completed his book and the notes are heavily marked with red crayon: a comparison between them and the final pages of the 1958 edition of *Picasso: His Life and Work* reveals an exceptional degree of similitude. Nowhere else perhaps, amongst all the preparatory material that has survived, does one come closer than here to the process of composition and this lends these notes a special charm and personality:

Cannes 15 Oct. 1957
P. has a little owl brought to him recently. It is in a cage in the studio. He watches it closely as it looks gravely at him and feeds it balls of raw meat. He said, 'It is strange that I have always liked owls. In the first etching I ever did – the one of the Picador – there is an owl.[207] They haunt me. The other night when I was at work a very large owl flew in at the window and crashed against the glass as it tried to get out. I thought I could catch it there but it flew off and alighted at the top of the canvas I was painting. Stayed there for a while and then flew away.

Duncan has made a very fine photo of his eyes. Their round black mirrors, in which there is no difference between iris and pupil, reflect clearly the windows of the studio.

Taking an enlargement he drew an owl's face in line on white paper with which he covered the photo, making holes like a mask to fit his own eyes. He placed it in the centre of a white canvas with astonishing effect – the bird with his eyes. […]

'Demoiselles d'Avignon'
Canvas made specially. Cheap smooth canvas mounted on stayone.[208]
[Félix] Fénéon, on seeing picture, said P. should make caricatures. […]
Of Salmon
'All my friends go wrong.' M[ax] J[acob] signed letter supporting Franco.[209] […]

Voice. Short sentences clipped by 'N'est pas?'[210] Gesture of a touch on the shoulder. Voice modulated between grave, low tones and high, excited pitch, which breaks into higher pitched laugh. Diabolical stare softening to passionate look of affection. Obstinate look. 'Je ne peut pas le faire.'[211] Implacable. […]

UNESCO.[212]
Misery at realising that space allotted was too big for him to cover.
'I [am] no longer 25.'

Could be done by enlargement of a sketch by decorator – and touched up by him, but he did not want that solution. Wanted to *live* [the] picture himself, otherwise it became la décoration. 'There is a solution but I must find it myself.' No final defeat but a problem still to solve.

Difference between Mich[el]An[gelo] & modern methods – they could paint small detail each day knowing what was coming round it. P. had to be able to cover whole surface at any time.

The victory is ours. The arts are freed. No modern technique, tachisme, etc. does not owe its debt to P. Now what? The gate is open. The wide open spaces of the future may be disconcerting. Not only the achievements but the character of P., his life, is a guide. Study his resolution, his persistence, his disregard for success, his love of success. [...]

'Les sujets n'existent plus.'[213]

'These things happen as provocations to the imagination.' He is more permanently interested in the problem as painting. (Conversation with Pignon.)

At this point Penrose turned the notebook on its side to make shorter but wider pages and embarked on the draft of the peroration of his book:

The ground floor has already been cleared of the more cumbersome objects and refilled again several times during the last two years. When one batch of canvases, ceramics, prints and sculptures leaves, new white canvases larger than ever take their place ready for a new period of activity, while the old landmarks such as the sideboard covered with hats and masks, the projectors hung with toys, the portraits of Jacqueline and the tattered furniture submerged in books, letters and other objects remain. The entrance hall is still blocked with bronzes and large cases of unpacked treasures. But for work Picasso has left this Ali Baba's scrap yard, which is too crowded with objects and too accessible to visitors to give him the seclusion he needs for work, and moved his studio to the top of the house.

There, on the floor above the bedrooms and the corridors inhabited by his goat, are more well-lit rooms, which have become a rambling suite of studios. At any time Picasso can disappear into this region and continue his painting with nothing more to distract him than his pigeons in the cage he has built for them on the terrace, and the view across palms and eucalyptus trees to the Lerins Islands lying below the horizon. Neither of these things of charm can disturb him greatly in his work, which according [to his tradition] he does mostly at night. Nothing but the stark, poverty-stricken pattern of the faded yellow wallpaper, the small marble mantlepiece (relics of former owners) and the high power electric bulb in the middle of the ceiling. There is no furniture except two small tattered armchairs and a packing case, the bottom of which he uses as a work table and around which are gathered an attroupement[214] of tins of paint. Palette and brushes are equally primitive.

Any scrap of board or tin is suitable for him to mix his colours and no brush resists for long the violent scrubbing, scraping and the great distances that its bristles are made to travel at high speed. Though they are nearly all worn to their last hair, he still finds no difficulty in getting from them to do just what he wants, he still extracts from them the effects he wants. Surrounded by the night, with Jacqueline watching attentively, ready to give whatever help is wanted, he covers canvases with tremendous, control[led] speed. Two themes develop concurrently. One is a series of paintings of the view from where he stands, where by day the pigeons fly from the shelter of their improvised dovecote in the corner of the terrace into the blue sunlit space with the sea in the distance.[215] Everything is eligible to find its place in the paintings but never do they take rigid motionless positions as they would in a photo. On the contrary, the movement of the pigeons and his movement as he shifts from one place to another is contained in the limits of the canvas, bring the sense of life, of shifting light, of movement to animate the painting as it animates the subject itself. In the other theme the model is not present. Once more Picasso has taken a subject from the great fraternity of his peers who live permanently in his thought. After Poussin, Le Nain, Cranach, Courbet, El Greco and Delacroix, he has turned to 'La[s] Meninas' of Velázquez as the painting which is to feed him with ideas and immediate variations on the work of another Spaniard.

'Las Meninas' is a painting that Picasso admires for the many obvious virtues that it possesses. There are many other paintings, however, which also contain similar qualities in their composition, colour, drawing, lighting, etc. These in fact are the things which interest him least and which he is ready to sacrifice first in the transformations that he is about to make. The picture in addition contains some very strange relationships between the painter, the model and the spectator. 'Look at the picture,' says Picasso, 'and try to find where these are situated.' Velázquez appears in the picture. His canvas turns its back to us while he turns his back on the Infanta, who is presumably his model and faces the spectators, who are the king and queen. They in fact are not in the picture at all because all we can see of them is their reflection in the mirror, which means that they must be able to see us in the same mirror and not the canvas that is being painted at all. Velázquez, we deduce, must be painting the king and queen with us standing beside them and not, [as] most people suppose, Las Meninas. Such confusion between the reality implied inside the picture communicating with the outside reality raises a most enjoyable problem for Picasso, who has always wanted to involve the spectator in the web of his picture, like a spider enticing a fly.

In silence and solitude, the glare of the electric light bulb shining on his paintings and the black curtainless windows, Picasso works on, deeply absorbed, calm and with new ideas coming to life as he proceeds. His mood is one of detachment, he has freed himself of the turmoil of emotion. 'Plus il y a de l'ame plus c'est mauvais,'[216] he likes to explain. Even when he painted

the agonising women of 'Guernica' he did so as a detached observer, as one who knows the passion that such things evoke and who knows also that to realise such emotion in a work of art, vitality, which can lift above it, and a sense of humour are necessary.[217]

Picasso's inspiration is nourished continually by his sense of humour. As part of the game that he plays with reality he is always ready to imagine anything, preferably the most solemn and respected things, from a ridiculous angle. Obsessed by his new preoccupation with 'Las Meninas', he takes a delight in seeing every object in the composition in a new, extravagantly

Picasso's studio at La Californie, Cannes, April 1957, with his collage *Portrait of Jacqueline* in the left foreground. Photo Lee Miller absurd light, the ingenuity of which is too diverse to describe. To give one example, he emphasises the hooks in the ceiling from which lamps should be hung and tells his friends that he is going to hang from them hams and sausages in the royal apartment.[218]

'Laughter is satanic,' said Baudelaire. 'It is thus profoundly human and … essentially contradictory.' He adds, 'The Spaniards are very well endowed in this matter. They are quick to arrive at the cruel stage, and their most grotesque fantasies often contain a dark element.'[219] With Picasso this observation agrees strikingly. The little Italian clown, who waves his hands as though he is playing an invisible piano, is given a piano to play by Picasso and the vertical line in the panelling which springs from the back of his neck becomes a cord by which he is hung – a helpless tinkling marionette.[220]

An accompaniment of jokes, in which Velázquez's characters suffer grotesque changes, accompanies other less obvious developments based on the original theme.

The airy light of the room in the original is rendered by a subtle but conventional perspective; its great depth is made all the more dramatic by […] the open door at its extreme end through which the 'aposentador'[221] lets in a stream of light. Picasso here brings to bear the long experience he has gained in using cubist methods to establish space. Without repetition he develops in a score of different ways a new sense of depth made from facets, like the lenses in the eye of a bee greatly magnified, which all lead the eye far away in the centre of the picture to the aposentador silhouetted against the light, so far away that you would have to shout.[222]

When Picasso has been launch[ed] by his daemon on a new experience he sees no end to the developments which may mark out the road. In this case, as when he started the series of 'Les femmes d'Alger', the first canvas, though different in dimensions, bore a closer resemblance to the original than those that followed.[223] As he continues making quantities of studies of details – the Infanta reappears in many small canvases with enchanting variety in the yellows & whites of her dress – he works towards a grand final solution, which may or may not be achieved but which is always in mind. With 'Les femmes d'Alger' family affairs distracted him when it might have happened, but in this case there is a new object in view. The wall that he has been asked to decorate in the new UNESCO building in Paris is by far the greatest surface that he has ever been asked to cover with a painting that is not like the drop curtain for 'Parade', a temporary amusement. The dimensions that he has been given, 9 metres by 10, make it a physical ordeal for a man of his age, which must be carefully planned so that it can be achieved without the fatigue of the work destroying spontaneity.

Picasso sees the culmination of the 'Las Meninas' series as a great picture which can incorporate the traditions of Spanish painting. The 'Burial of the Duke of Orgaz' of El Greco & Goya's self-portrait he talks of incorporating in his own way, as well as the masterpiece of Velázquez. At the moment of writing it is too soon to know with what originality he will find the solution, and whatever may happen it is the excitement of new discoveries that keeps him alive, the challenge of unsolved problems that disquiets him and the elusive solution which runs before him, just as it did fifty years ago, that keeps his inspiration aglow and his vitality unimpaired, rather than the final perfection which, like death, he shrinks from facing. Picasso has presented us with a vision of life, within a realisation of liberty, which presents new vital problems by his achievements and his understanding of the nature of life. He speaks to us but even more he speaks to future generations. In his generosity of spirit he is the source which can grow endlessly and whose influences can know no limit.

Bat perches on his shoulder the evening he saw Sputnik.[224]

Looking at green patch painted lightly, showing brush strokes, hair of a Meninas, 'See all the quality in it. Just one touch and it's finished. That's the "modelé"[225] of Velázquez in modern terms. Take this small area and it is an abstract painting, but that's not all, it's a detail. It's good in itself but it's not enough. You need literature as well – de la bonne literature.'
   The subjects are only a pretext – necessary, but they are not all.
   Three figures on grey ground. Each complete, the background working as well. Each a flat colour making each figure a unity. Very little drawing, no outline. [*rough pencil sketch*][226] […]
   'Le clarté viens pas d'intelligence.'[227] […] [25]

The notebook also contains Penrose's stuttering attempts to draft the last, rounding-up sentences of the book. His definitive version runs:

Meanwhile Picasso's disarming passionate vision and ceaseless energy have continued to widen our horizons. Today his art enriches us and its prodigious variety will provide future generations with a profound joy and an understanding of our human condition.[228]

Before he left the south of France, Penrose went to Nîmes with Picasso, Jacqueline, Edouard Pignon and Hélène Parmelin, and they all signed a postcard to Lee. Picasso added a tiny drawing of a bullfight – the object of the trip.[229] Maybe it was this episode that Parmelin had in mind when she characterised a boisterous, uninhibited Penrose in her book of memoirs, *Picasso Plain*: 'There was Penrose, who was an English writer, and who sang Russian songs in Spanish in the backs of cars when he had drunk Bandol wine and it was pouring cats and dogs after corridas.'[230] Penrose was also present at Picasso's birthday lunch on 25 October 1957 at the Auberge Josse, near Mougins, and he marked the occasion with one of his most exuberant handmade birthday cards, addressing it to 'Pablo Picasso, still the youngest artist in the world'.[231] Presumably, it was also while he was still in the south of France that he succeeded in obtaining another gift from Picasso for the ICA's annual fundraising 'Picture Fair'. This time it was a drawing of a monkey-painter well suited to the 'Institut de Singes', Picasso's nickname for the ICA.[232]

The 'final' final deadline set by Gollancz came and went. But at last, in the first weeks of the new year, Penrose completed his overdue manuscript, with the indispensable aid of his secretary Joyce Reeves, who acted unofficially as an editor as well as a typist, untangling his sometimes tangled syntax and silently correcting his faulty spelling. As the moment to despatch the text drew near, Penrose was subject to all the feelings of dread and doubt that torment the unself-confident author who has no more excuse to procrastinate. He did not burden Picasso with his fears – he had his pride after all, and, anyway, Picasso was not one to sympathise with abjection – but he did draft a 'Foreword' into which he poured some of his anguish:

I must warn readers who may expect from this book more than it can give. A biography of a living man is by its nature presumptuous, since his future acts can reverse the truth of any conclusions that the author may be foolish enough to make. No final justification can be found for such a book. It is no more than a trace of a story which must be so condensed that seventy-seven years of the life of a man can be read from birth to old age in a few hours. It can be written with no better appreciation than that of a fly walking over the eye of the sphinx, when distance which only the flight of time can provide is essential for it to be seen in true perspective. In these respects this book, I tell you, must be a failure, I can recommend it to none, but let me say that, knowing this, I have written it, and hope that it will be read with appreciation of its inevitable limitations, because I have wanted to share with others an experience. It is an experience which has had great importance in my life, enchanting and torturing me because it comes from a source which is in itself a contradiction – a man, alive amid death, loving cruelly and speaking in silence. Between the mountain and the ocean there are streams. As one among many, my task has been to bring from these incomprehensible heights of genius a few samples, limited by my own choice, for the sea to taste, enjoy and absorb. This book attempts to form a bridge between the public and that which is sometimes believed to be inaccessible. [10]

Penrose's sense of incapacity comes over with painful clarity, not only in the words he uses about himself (presumptuous, foolish, failure), but in the gulf he sets between himself – a mere 'fly', or at best a 'stream' – and his subject – the 'mountain', with its 'incomprehensible heights of genius'. And, one might add, his sense of panic is communicated unintentionally in the tortuous peroration. Psychologically, the text offers further precious insights into the dark emotional drama at the core of his relationship with Picasso – enchantment, but also torture at the hands of one who loves 'cruelly' and, like the dreaded sphinx, is 'alive amid death'. One is reminded of the long poem Penrose dedicated to Picasso in February 1956 on another occasion when he felt enslaved and overwhelmed by the artist's genius.

Did Penrose send this 'Foreword' to Gollancz? The carbon copy of the typescript is corrected by hand, so it went through at least two drafts. Did Lee, or Joyce Reeves, or another well-wisher tactfully suggest that it was not perhaps a good idea to lay himself bare in this manner? At all events the 'Foreword' was dropped. In its place Penrose chose two brief quotations for the title page which succinctly but obliquely summarise its key messages. The first, *Je parle de ce qui m'aide à vivre*, 'I speak of that which helps me to live', quotes Paul Eluard and thus honours the only other person who could match Picasso in his estimation, while at the same time stating a literal truth for the 'enchanted' Penrose. The second, *Rien de ce qu'on peut dire de Picasso n'est exact…*, 'Nothing that can be said of Picasso is exact', quotes the ex-Dada writer Georges Ribemont-Dessaignes, and aptly expresses Penrose's sense of the fundamental impossibility of attempting to come to general conclusions about work as multiform and multitudinous as Picasso's. It thus hints at the torture experienced by one who attempts the crazy task.[233]

On 15 February 1958 Penrose was at last able to write to Picasso to announce that the book was in the hands of his publisher. A faint echo of the heartfelt, abandoned Foreword can be heard behind his words:

Finally, after continual demands from my publisher, I sent him the manuscript several days ago, having worked on it day and night during the final fortnight. There are still lots of corrections to be made to the proofs and the illustrations to choose, but the bulk of the work is done and now I wait to hear what others will think of it. For me this has been more than three years of unremitting work but I realise more and more that it is nothing beside the marvellous subject which I have tried to make a little more accessible to the Anglo-Saxons.

I shall give a copy of the manuscript to Kahnweiler this week in order to have his opinion and if you want to see it in its present state, before it is printed, I shall send it to you with the greatest pleasure. But it is all in English and I doubt that it will interest you much.[234]

Penrose was right: Picasso was notoriously indifferent to what critics had to say about his work and had expressed that indifference in a crushing negative when Penrose nervously asked him whether he had read Antonina Vallentin's biography. For Penrose, the completion of *Picasso: His Life and Work* was a tremendously important moment and his life would never be quite the same afterwards. But he was under no delusions about its importance for Picasso.

The biography published, October 1958

On Monday 20 October 1958, just five days before Picasso's seventy-seventh birthday, *Picasso: His Life and Work* came out – a chunky, 400-page volume, clad in a bold red dust jacket ornamented only with the title and the author's name in big, white capital letters and with Gollancz's smart black logo on the spine. The choice of red and white was most unusual for Gollancz, who normally insisted that all the books he published have a brilliant yellow wrapper with black and magenta lettering. One can only assume that red was chosen purposefully and provocatively – a red cover for a Red artist. This, the jacket implied, would not be a bland account presenting Picasso as an aloof figure stranded in his ivory tower, but a picture of a passionate, revolutionary artist immersed in the political realities of contemporary life. Founder of the Left Book Club, Gollancz had been an active and forceful socialist during the 1930s and 1940s and, like Penrose, was a committed pacifist. His views had moderated by the late 1950s, but he was still a man 'of the left'. One would love to know who first suggested red – Gollancz or Penrose.[235] At all events, when the book came out in America the following spring, it was packaged quite differently: an inoffensive abstract design of small black smudges on a light terracotta ground and not a touch of red in sight.[236]

Penrose was in the Midi on publication day. The previous day had seen the first reviews in *The Sunday Times* and *The Observer*, and, cheeringly, they were wholly positive about the book, if not about Picasso's work.[237] Repeatedly, as they trickled out during the ensuing weeks, the reviews emphasised the virtues of Penrose as a sober-minded, unpretentious, informative, penetrating and lucid interpreter of the already legendary artist, and predicted that the book would be both a popular success and the foundation for all future studies. Eric Newton may have been partisan but his judgement is typical:

What makes Mr Penrose's book not only important but necessary is that not on a single page is Picasso obliterated by his work, yet the difficulties involved in interpreting or explaining his work are never shirked. What Mr Penrose has done seems simple and obvious once he has done it. He explains and interprets the work in the light of the man who has produced it. At once half the difficulties disappear (one says 'half' advisedly: many mysteries remain unsolved) and one sees that what once seemed perverse and unreasonable is really the direct reaction of a fearlessly creative genius to the situation of the moment. Again and again one of Mr Penrose's sensible, unemphatic sentences clears away a cloud of difficulties.[238]

Particularly gratifying were the excellent reviews of French critics such as the highly respected Guy Habasque, who praised Penrose for his exceptional honesty and modesty and for writing a thoroughly researched study:

[…] the author never tries to arrange the facts to fit a preconceived portrait, a subjective and arbitrary image already formed of the man or artist. […] [H]is work is based on exceptionally solid and extensive foundations […]. This is a book based on first-hand knowledge and, since we are talking of Picasso, a statement of this order is not meagre praise.'[239]

In addition to the published reviews, Penrose was showered with private letters expressing similar sentiments. Henri-Pierre Roché was enthusiastic: having opened the book he had not been able to put it down. 'It is a simple, useful, noble book. The manner in which you mix his life and his painting is so true, direct, clear,' he wrote.[240] Penrose must have been nervously keen to know what Barr thought and at last in January 1959 news came: Barr was still in the middle of reading it but what he had read 'impresses me very much indeed. […] I think all your friends are delighted and your enemies confounded by the quality and character of what you have done.'[241]

Inevitably, the praise was occasionally tempered by criticism of the writer as well as his subject. Thus although David Sylvester saw much to admire in the strictly biographical elements, he found the book as a whole 'too long' and the style 'pedestrian' and 'stiff', and he complained that Penrose was too undiscriminating about Picasso's work: 'Mr. Penrose is a good deal less effective about the work than about the life. […] Too much of the time he seems to be expounding because he feels he should rather than because he has something urgent or fresh to say.'[242] But in Penrose's collection of press cuttings there is only one insultingly dismissive review of the first edition. It was published anonymously three years after the book came out – after, that is, it had already acquired the status of a classic – and the author was Douglas Cooper, as everyone in the art world immediately realised:

Mr. Penrose, having been a friend of Picasso for several years, started off with many advantages over other writers and there was every reason to expect that his book would be revelatory, lively, packed with personal details and especially fascinating on the subject of Picasso's art. Unfortunately it is not that. Mr. Penrose is a dull writer, appears to lack the warmth and imagination necessary to encompass and bring alive the complex personality of Picasso, and above all has failed to write meaningfully about his art, which here occupies a lesser space. None the less he has put a great deal of effort into preparing his biography and it is likely to remain for some while the most useful and informative handbook, despite its shortcomings and surprising inaccuracies.[243]

As we shall see, Cooper's animosity towards Penrose developed apace during the three years that separated this review from the publication of *Picasso: His Life and Work*, and the source of his bitterness was a glittering prize that he too had craved but that Penrose won.

Chapter 5

The Story of an Exhibition, 1958–1960

The commission

No sooner had Penrose despatched the manuscript of the biography to Gollancz than he plunged into a new Picasso project – a major retrospective for the Arts Council of Great Britain. The idea for such an exhibition had been mooted some five years before but had taken firm shape only in 1957.[1] At the beginning of March 1958 Penrose wrote to Picasso to let him know how matters stood:

Dear Pablo

I have just got back from London where I spent a couple of days. During my visit I was asked officially to take charge of the organisation of the great 'Picasso exhibition', which will take place at the Tate Gallery in 1960 under the auspices of the Arts Council.

I spoke to you about this exhibition when I was in Cannes last autumn and at that time you were in favour of the project.[2] I sincerely hope you haven't changed your mind because we want to make a really important show, the first of this scale ever to be held in England. This afternoon I spoke to Kahnweiler, who already knew about it and has promised to cooperate.

Even though there is plenty of time I am going to get started at once. As you can imagine I am enchanted and delighted to have been asked to do something that is so close to my heart. […][3]

This letter gives the impression that the choice of curator had never been in question. In reality, however, things were not so simple and the repercussions of the Arts Council's decision to bestow the coveted task on Penrose reached their melodramatic and farcical climax only during the run of the show itself. His rival was Douglas Cooper and the decision was reached at the meeting of the Art Panel on 27 February 1958. In the laconic prose of the minutes, 'The Panel felt that the appointment of a single organiser was desirable, and by a large majority vote selected Mr Penrose who accepted the Panel's recommendation'.[4] As everyone present was well aware, Penrose and Cooper had been at loggerheads for years and their rivalry was at its most acute where Picasso was concerned: there was no chance of them working together harmoniously on a Picasso exhibition, so it was a case of either one or the other.

On the face of it, the choice was an easy one because Cooper was notoriously arrogant and devious and had a history of bitter enmity with John Rothenstein, the Director of the Tate Gallery, where the exhibition would be held. (Cooper had attempted to get Rothenstein sacked for incompetence during a prolonged, very public campaign in 1952–54.[5]) Moreover, there had been embarrassing difficulties between Cooper and the Arts Council itself: a project in 1956 for an exhibition of Picasso's recent work had collapsed largely because Cooper tried to by-pass Kahnweiler and the Galerie Leiris.[6] On the other hand, Cooper had already curated several successful Arts Council exhibitions and had a greater reputation as a scholar than Penrose.[7] More to the point, he had as much knowledge of Picasso's work and was, arguably, on more intimate terms than Penrose with the artist. This was partly a simple matter of geography: Cooper lived in Provence and was able to visit La Californie regularly and to reciprocate by entertaining Picasso and Jacqueline at lavish dinner parties in the Château de Castille, his theatrical, colonnaded mansion near Arles. But it was also a matter of personalities: Picasso adored gossiping with the malicious, amusing, flamboyant Cooper, while Jacqueline got on famously with John Richardson, Cooper's charming and handsome partner. According to Richardson, Picasso was also highly diverted by his and Cooper's volatile relationship, which he said reminded him of Diaghilev's stormy affairs with Léonide Massine, Serge Lifar and the other male stars in the Ballets Russes company.[8] In comparison, Penrose, with his good manners, decency and unimpeachable fidelity, was less entertaining. Then there was the question of Cooper's splendid art collection, which contained Picassos of the highest quality, and of his large network of rich and influential collector-friends. In passing Cooper over, the Arts Council would incur his wrath, almost certainly sacrifice all hope of borrowing any of his pictures and, furthermore, run the risk of him poisoning Picasso's mind against the whole project. By contrast, if Penrose were passed over he could be counted upon to behave magnanimously in spite of his disappointment.

When the Panel came to its decision there was therefore much foreboding and Penrose was instructed to try to limit the damage by coming to some kind of accommodation with Cooper – if humanly possible. In July 1958, attempting to suppress his mistrust and aversion, Penrose went to the Château de Castille and invited Cooper to collaborate by advising on the selection, lending from his collection and contributing to the catalogue. The meeting was not a success. Cooper twisted what Penrose had said, took an intransigent line on the shortcomings of the Tate's exhibition galleries and, after a flurry of heated epistolary exchanges with Penrose and William Coldstream, the Chairman of the Art Panel, metaphorically slammed the door in Penrose's face. 'I have a principle,' he wrote,

not to associate myself in any way with an exhibition unless I have some measure of control over its organisation. The world of art is nowadays so much in the hands of cretinous busybodies and pretentious bureaucrats that it is the responsibility of those of us who know and can do better to beware. The present potentates can't help making a mess of whatever they take up, and so they like to call in serious people at the last minute to help them disguise it. But their calls for help should remain unanswered, for by their messes will their incompetence be recognised.

It is very kind of you to suggest that I might like to do some unpaid secretarial work on the catalogue of your exhibition. Unfortunately I have no leisure to devote to part-time activities, for I am fully occupied writing books.[9]

In the letter he wrote to Coldstream a few days later, Cooper revealed that he had already started to stir up trouble with Picasso:

Picasso, who has recently discussed his London exhibition with me after seeing Mr. Penrose, is well aware of all this and regrets simply that the collaboration which he hoped for is opposed by the Arts Council and Mr. Penrose, who have apparently made up their minds to disregard his feelings.[10]

Wisely, Penrose had kept Picasso informed of all the attempts at peacemaking and on 25 August wrote with weary resignation to tell him of their failure:

[…] I've recently heard again from our friend Douglas. After my efforts, which you know of, to arrive at an understanding with him about your exhibition in London, I have received a letter from him which I fear must be considered a final defeat. He writes that *as a matter of principle* it is impossible for him to associate himself with an exhibition unless he has a measure of control over its organisation – a very convenient principle when one has no desire to be involved – and that he is too busy with the books he is writing to help me on the catalogue without being paid. Naturally, I didn't begin my negotiations with so great a prince by offering money!

As you know, I had little hope of succeeding with him because he is so profoundly hurt not to have been asked to do the exhibition himself. But, as you and I agreed the other day, his refusal should not diminish in the least the attraction of the exhibition, which I fully intend – even without his pictures – to be a more beautiful and consequently more astonishing selection than has ever been seen so far.

In London I've already had several conversations with the officials for the show and everyone is very enthusiastic and very grateful to you for agreeing to help us by lending pictures. […][11]

In the small black address book in which he kept notes about collectors, their pictures and the state of play with regard to loans, Penrose struck out the list of works beside Cooper's name, as if to draw a line under the whole sorry

affair.[12] He must have known that things would not end cleanly at this point, but if he could retain Picasso's good will and keep Kahnweiler, with whom he was on excellent terms, fully on his side, then the exhibition would be more or less safe from Cooper's machinations. A crucial ally was, of course, Alfred Barr and Penrose wasted no time in writing to ask for his cooperation. Barr replied instantly in the affirmative: 'because you are in charge I will do everything I can to help you.'[13]

While waiting for his book to be published and starting to plan the content of the exhibition, Penrose kept up the momentum of his relationship with Picasso. In early April he went to Cannes and used the opportunity to view the UNESCO mural, on exhibition in Vallauris prior to its installation in the lobby of the new building. He found it moving and haunting and when it was attacked for 'frivolity' he leapt instantly to its defence in a letter to *The Times*.[14] He returned to Cannes in the middle of July, noting what he saw in the studio with an eye to what he might borrow for the Arts Council exhibition:[15]

Visit 19 July '58
Great red nature morte with bull's head in front of window [*see p. 211*] painted on return from Whitsun corrida, which was great success. Dominguin.[16] 'Il a était peint avec des gros mots,'[17] said P.

[*Added later*] He told [me] that he was worried by the political events of 13 mai and avenged himself in painting.[18]

The goat sculpture [*see p. 217*] – the important point is the fullness and fertility of the beast splitting her sides and full of milk. She is bound to give birth at any moment. Her stance, four legs dug into the ground, weighed down with enormous feet, draws attention in her immobility to the inner motion of her womb.[19]

In an hour he filled a complete sketchbook with some two dozen pencil drawings of A[rthur] Rubinstein, the musician.[20]

Fine head of an intelligent old Jew. Each drawing was astonishingly different and yet lifelike. Only one did not please the sitter.

P. said, 'Chaque portrait doit être un nouveaux tableau.'[21] The variety in line – firm and almost mechanical to trembling and sensitive – was extraordinary but the variety in expression even more.

Several new portraits of an Arlésienne rather like Jacqueline. One in particular was painted with no sign of a brush mark nor knife. On enquiry he told me that he had found pigeon feathers lying about and used them. The result is astonishing, great precision in the detail. The paint has taken form without a sign of the means employed. Often run together liquid or brushed with feather tips. Colour – blues and greens chiefly with pinky white & white blue lips.[22]

Very fine, big landscape of La Croisette in blues.[23]

He is using very liquid colour poured onto the canvas, but the process is a mixture of accident and control and the result has the appearance of masterly intention miraculously realised. [26]

According to Pierre Daix, the editor of *Les Lettres françaises* and one of the young Communist intellectuals closest to the artist, Picasso was in a sour mood that summer. Various factors contributed to his bad temper. Although he had at last completed the decoration of the chapel at Vallauris with a semi-circular panel covering the back wall of the vault, plans to inaugurate the 'Temple of Peace' in July 1958 were suddenly abandoned, probably for reasons of political expediency in the wake of de Gaulle's accession to power. Daix also believes that Picasso was 'anxious and undoubtedly displeased with what he had done for UNESCO', as well as annoyed by the awkward, obstructed space allocated to the mural.[24] Another major source of irritation was the fact that La Californie, purchased because it seemed like the ideal refuge, was now threatened by a massive property development in the vicinity. Picasso, who felt that everybody's eyes were upon him whenever he ventured to the beach or to a restaurant with friends, was appalled at the thought that he would be spied upon even when he was at home. Until he found an alternative place to live and work he could not relax, even trying to cajole Cooper into selling him the Château de Castille. It was indeed Cooper and Richardson who alerted him to the fact that the Château de Vauvenargues, situated at the foot of the Montagne Sainte-Victoire, was up for sale.[25] Remote, bleak and forbidding, Vauvenargues has been likened to the Escorial and could hardly have been less like La Californie architecturally. But Picasso was delighted by the thought that he would own a stake in Cézanne's beloved mountain and bought the château on impulse in September 1958 after driving over to see it with the Pignons.[26]

Restless and preoccupied, Picasso was in no mood to celebrate anything and in no mood to receive visits. Penrose was one of those to be turned away when he came to the Midi on the eve of Picasso's birthday and of the publication of the biography – a rejection he must have felt all the more acutely since this should by rights have been a moment when Picasso received him with special warmth. It was also worrying to be denied access so firmly: did it mean that Don Pablo intended to wash his hands of the London exhibition? In the letter he wrote after the brush-off, perched awkwardly on a park bench in Montpellier, Penrose's sense of grievance is palpable, although he tried to make the best of things by expressing ardent admiration for the much criticised UNESCO mural. Merely writing the letter was evidently a relief and one detects an upsurge of the old optimism at the end:

Dear Pablo,

I know you are right to flee the celebrations and cheering but it was a great disappointment for me not to see and embrace you. It's all very well saying 'See you soon', but that means months pass without the joy of seeing you. Well, next time I shall try to pick on a moment when the headlights are not beaming on you and I'll come with Lee to greet you secretly on the ramparts of Vauvenargues.

I'm all the sadder because there were things I wanted to say to you about the great UNESCO painting. Seeing it on the spot, I was very moved and above all amazed at the manner in which you were able to profit from such a bad position. I thought when I saw it in Vallauris that it was the first and the last time that it would be seen to advantage, without being completely obscured by the fabrications of the lordly architects. But no, on the contrary, you obviously realised how to make the most of the situation. The dark figure in the middle of the picture is well hidden when one enters the lobby, but at every step as one moves forward he seems to be falling from a distant sky, until one is so close that one can almost touch him and one can see the entire picture with all these large, overwhelming figures. This gives it a drama it didn't have in Vallauris. It means that the picture is beautiful when you see the whole of it and are crushed by its enormous scale and also when it is half-hidden. Truly, you have triumphed over circumstances in an astonishing way. No doubt others have told you this already, but permit me to repeat it. It was already not bad going to have agreed to do something for such a difficult site, but to turn it to one's advantage, especially without being on the spot, is nothing short of miraculous.

Dear Pablo, I send you my love. I am, at least, delighted that one of your birthdays has been annulled – it's another sign of your fabulous youth. Send Jacqueline my love.

With all my best wishes

Roland.

Please forgive these scrawled pages written on my knees on a bench.[27]

Visiting Cannes and Vauvenargues, April 1959

Months passed before Penrose could spare the time to travel to the south of France again. However, he kept in touch by letter and as usual there were little irritants to spoil the pleasure of contact. His publisher had made an astounding and humiliating gaffe, billing Picasso – twice – for the copies of the biography Penrose had sent him as a present, so profuse apologies were in order.[28] Then he had to ask Picasso to waive his reproduction rights for the French edition, as he had done for the English edition, otherwise the publisher, Bernard Grasset, intended to pull out. Picasso did agree, but begging these sorts of favours was a disagreeable business.[29] Meanwhile, Penrose continued to lay his plans for the great retrospective exhibition, visiting collectors and museums in Brussels, Berne, Zurich and Geneva in order to negotiate loans.[30] He was well liked, well known and well respected, especially since the publication of *Picasso: His Life and Work*, and hardly anyone refused.

At last, in late April 1959 Penrose was able to spend a few days in Picasso's company. Since his previous visit, Picasso had taken to spending time and painting in the Château de Vauvenargues, which he had made somewhat more comfortable by fixing the heating, lighting and plumbing. When he arrived in Cannes Penrose found major changes taking place at La Californie as it was stripped of its sculptures so that Vauvenargues could be made to feel more like home. Picasso had always treated his sculpture differently from his painting: he was a 'professional' painter, who lived by and had grown rich through selling his paintings, but he never thought of himself as a 'professional' sculptor and, except for the early pieces which Vollard had acquired in 1910, very few of his sculptures were cast in editions with an intention to sell. Instead they were treated like members of his family and as part of the furniture of the house and garden. His children rode on the back of the bronze *Goat*, he himself would rest against its bulging flanks, and his pet goat would be tethered to its tail; Jacqueline liked sitting on the stalking, pregnant cat. Moving the sculpture to Vauvenargues was therefore a sign that La Californie was being demoted to the status of 'second home' and might be abandoned altogether. Penrose had always admired Picasso's sculpture but he had two reasons to pay it particular attention at this moment: he had just been commissioned to write a short study for a multilingual series on modern sculptors,[31] and he intended to include sculpture in the forthcoming Arts Council exhibition.[32]

The first notes Penrose made during this visit are devoted to what happened at La Californie where, despite being 'in most endearing form all evening', Picasso did not resist the golden opportunity to tease him with the threat of a lunch the following day with Douglas Cooper, while at the same

Several of Picasso's sculptures, including *The Goat* (right), in the garden at the Château de Vauvenargues, April 1959. Photo Roland Penrose

time assuring him that he was 'entirely in favour of [the] London show and thought it better in my hands'. (This tiny vignette in the midst of Penrose's notes captures Picasso at his most wickedly manipulative.) Cooper had written the catalogue for the exhibition that was about to open at the Musée Cantini in Marseille and Picasso had lent generously to it.[33] For Penrose, bursting with plans for the London exhibition, but as yet with no firm promise of a single loan from Picasso himself, this unforeseen encounter with his enemy could hardly have been less welcome. But refusing the lunch invitation was out of the question – he would be mocked mercilessly and gossiped about behind his back and Picasso might decide to take offence. Penrose's stoical discomfort can be sensed in the absence of any description of the lunch itself, although he evidently found an ally in the photographer David Douglas Duncan, who was an almost permanent member of Picasso's household at this period:

Visit to Picasso 22 Ap. '59
Evening. Went to La Californie. Found P. & Jacqueline in excellent form. Place rather empty and a lot of canvases set aside for the Marseille ex[hibition], which are to leave tomorrow, including one interior of *c*. '57 [I've] never seen before with [an] empty canvas in middle.[34] David Duncan arrived from Rome w. his photos of the Kremlin, which P. enjoyed seeing. Dr. Souriac arrived. Dinner long and excellent. P. after showed us Degas brothel scenes.[35] V. good. Went down to cellar to look at sculptures (bronzes) & engraving workshop. P. in most endearing form all evening. Some awkward talk about Dominique Eluard selling his letters to Paul. P. announced arrival of D[ouglas] C[ooper] for tomorrow and asked me to lunch too. P. entirely in favour of London show and thought it better in my hands.

Sculpture
One of the tall bronzes for the fountain (manikin pis) stood in the studio with a wicker bull's head on top.[36] Fitted perfectly – guying his own work. Said he would like to have it cast like that, but too dear.
    Visited cellar where several bronzes were stored. One a unique cast of female head & torso (cire perdu),[37] very beautiful. Figures made of simple chance pieces of wood, depending on proportions and gestures to become alive.[38] A head made from a wooden box turn[ed] on end, with eyes and nose hanging in front of cavernous empty interior. Use of void and severity.[39] [27]

Cannes 23 Ap. '59[40]
When I arrived at La Calif. about 12.30 a great change had taken place since the night before. A van was being loaded w. paintings to the ex. at Marseille, and just before one had left for V[auvenargues] with a cargo of sculpture, etc., including the 'Man w. the Sheep', the 'Goat' and a dozen others. D[ouglas] D[uncan] was hopping round with camera, told me of how the 'Man w. sheep' had been carried like a corpse by three bearers. P. much

impressed. 'The Goat' went in a wheelbarrow. After lunch chez Félix, D.D. & I went back with P. & J. to empty rooms – only relatively empty – like Paris in August. Still two copies of great head of D[ora] M[aar],[41] two of tall recent bronzes staring at paint-spattered floor. Chippendale chairs and the print cabinet, formerly Matisse's,[42] as well as portraits of Jacqueline on walls and the piles of minor junk, among which a copy of 'Express' with row of photos of Eisenhower, Khrushchev w. P. in the middle – caption 'les trois "cailloux"' (bald heads).

As we sat round the oval dining table, J. going through the mail and P. giving his opinions, all a bit depressed since it was now obvious that overnight the decision had been taken to quit La Calif., or rather at 8.30 that morning, when the camion[43] arrived and extra help to move the statues had to be called at a moment's notice. P. had opened the french windows and little by little an invasion began from outside – pigeons, gold brown, white, grey, from the dovecote upstairs, started adventuring in until the floor was covered with them busily picking crumbs off the floor – the newly made space seemed to attract them. 'What are all these letters?' said P. – 'Today's?' 'No, today's,' said J., 'are in the bathtub. I'll go and fetch them.' 'Don't do that,' said P. 'You are tired enough already and I don't want them now – what I do want is to telephone Kahnweiler – and tell him he can again start selling some pictures' – (for some months he has not been allowed to) – 'I need money! That will make him laugh, no?'

Man With a Sheep and other sculptures by Picasso, Château de Vauvenargues, April 1959. Photo Roland Penrose

A spread from Roland Penrose's notebook, showing a drawing of his bedroom window at Vauvenargues, April 1959

While P. was telephoning I asked D.D. what were his plans. 'Oh – just stick around – I ought to be in Paris by now but this is much better – he talks of going to V. this evening. If so I shall go along too – if not, maybe we'll be off tomorrow morning.' Actually, they were both v. tired. J. up since early morning was resting in a long chair. P. proposed they should rest – then that they should go at seven o'clock – finally they decided to rest. [28]

The following day Penrose followed Picasso and Jacqueline to Vauvenargues – his first visit to the château. The new Marquis – the title went with the property – was in ebullient mood and gave him the full guided tour. He also found a moment to ornament a copy of *Picasso: His Life and Work* with a comical drawing (see p. 348). To his joy Penrose was invited to stay overnight – an unusual privilege because when he visited Picasso he normally stayed in a hotel. When the intimate evening party broke up, he retired to his room and, intoxicated by the warmth and harmony of the visit and the austere beauty of the place, quietly sketched the window opening out to the night sky.

[…] *Friday [24 April]. Vauvenargues*

I took a taxi from Aix to V. in the afternoon. With the Montagne St. Victoire towering above the forest, to the right one suddenly came in sight of the great ochre-coloured château admirably placed so as to crown a small hill in the centre of the valley. On all sides the ground falls away to green valleys from which rise the sound of water – delicious and rare in the dry limestone rocks of the forest.

The château is well guarded by its ramparts and the great ironwork gate, which is kept permanently locked & only opened by the gardener. In front of the great stone stairs leading up to a front door, said to be designed by Portuguese masons in the 16th cent., is a terrace with two grotesque heads gushing water into ornamental stone troughs. In the formal garden laid out with box hedges the drive was lined with spectators, who appeared to be awaiting the arrival of some notable but who were in fact bronzes from Cannes, who had been dumped there that morning and who are likely to stand in line, the 'Man with the Sheep' at their head, for many weeks before P. decides to place them [*see pp. 217, 219*].

Paulo, who had just arrived from Paris, was the first to welcome me and after a moment at the central window high above the door the small white head of P. appeared, smiling and asking me to come up. Enormous stone vaults, stone floors and a great staircase in a square lead [from] the centre of the château to the upper floors. The rooms on the first floor have mostly been taken over as studios and sleeping quarters for himself and J. Lofty whitewashed walls with splendid fireplaces displaying portraits of the Vauvencey[44] and heroic figures adorn these apartments. Their proportions are noble and the light that invades every corner gives a spaciousness that surpasses the studios of the rue des Gds. Augustins. But already they are not empty. Propped against the walls and sparse pieces of furniture are recent paintings – portraits of J. P. delights in writing on the canvas Jacqueline de Vauvenargues[45] – still lifes and a riotous parody of Velázquez urchins eating cherries.[46]

The first thing that is strikingly new is the colour. Dominated by strong reds and greens these paintings have an atmosphere which belongs mysteriously to V. and nowhere else. The most unadulterated vermilion borders on green equally strong and somehow, perhaps because of the areas of black and the skilful dosing, they do not fight. 'On les voir n'est-ce pas,'[47] says P. Particularly in the portraits, there is a rigour and simplicity in the colour, which can only succeed due to an extraordinary control of the right amount of colour in the right place. The still lifes in which jars with ornamental heads are placed next to guitars, whose contortions remind one of lobsters:[48] here the colour is less contrasted; there are delicate pinks and pale yellowish greens like young leaves – the colours of the rocks and the plants that grow between them, not the lush greens of spring but the more tentative greens of the arid mountain vegetation.

D.D. was there shooting everything and getting P. to pose holding canvases or seated on chairs painted by him with suns and stripes of red, yellow or green. P. sat looking straight at the sun – when J. asked how he could do so he said 'I've looked at the sun as a child. I could stare at it for a long time.'

P. took me round – showed me his bedroom and the enormous bathroom next to it. He was obviously proud of his new house and conscious of its noble build. As a joke he showed me the lavish quantity of lavatories, wc[s], showers, etc. which had been installed during its occupation by the military. There is a smaller room on the ground floor still with red wallpaper and a monstrous portrait of a Cardinal [de Vauvenargues]. In a small room leading off it is the private chapel of Saint (St …) with an altar & relics. P. accepted this with a doubtful smile and no comment. In the room were stacked a collection of paintings just arrived from Paris. The one given a place of honour on an easel was the Cézanne landscape, 'L'Estaque'.[49] Beside it were several Matisse[s],[50] the Courbet chamois's head with its two delicate curve[d] horns,[51] which he said was the origin of the antlers on the Rocking Chair picture of *c.* 1941,[52] small Corots,[53] a Braque of 1923, which he said he had never before unpacked and which he rather despised.[54] He had a Gauguin landscape of Pont Aven period, in bad condition but that didn't worry him. He saw in it colours & forms prophetic of Tahiti.[55] In another room nearby he had already hung a great painting by Le Nain of a procession of men with garlands leading bulls.[56]

The tour of the kitchen, well fitted with modern stoves, etc., and the great vaulted hall at the back finished, we settled down round a roaring fire in the dining room. A simple fruitwood table with benches fitted the surroundings admirably, but he had added a heavily carved buffet with caryatids and bas reliefs in false perspective.[57] Its pompous incongruity and bourgeois bad taste amused him greatly. In front of the fire, looking very lifelike, was one of his bronze cats.[58]

As the daylight faded and firelight took its place, J. remarked that only the serenade from a few troubadours was missing. P. got up and took from the sideboard a Spanish mandolin with only two remaining strings, which he had recently bought. The serenade he gave us lasted some five minutes. It was fierce, wailing, and lively in turns. With an enormous grin he finally put down the instrument. It was a splendid piece of clowning and much delighted us.

When night came, after an excellent dinner at the long bare table in the dining room, D.D. took leave of us and we went upstairs to find our beds. P. proudly showed the second-floor rooms, still waiting to be redecorated but warm and clean. He was delighted at the space, the sanitary arrangements and the remnants of former plasterwork of 18th cent. My room had an oval window looking out onto the forest – like a cubist picture. The room & the nightingales were intoxicating.[59]

The notes about the visit to Vauvenargues end abruptly at this point. Probably Penrose fully intended to write more but just never got around to it. But he must have been taken on a tour of the area near the château by Picasso, Jacqueline and Paulo because on 25 April they sent cheerful post-cards from the village to Lee at Farley Farm.[60] And according to his diary, he went to the corrida at Arles on Sunday the 26th, to lunch at Vauvenargues on Monday the 27th, and the following day set off for Paris from Avignon.[61]

Picasso's love affair with Vauvenargues was short-lived. When he bought the château, Kahnweiler had warned him that he would become deeply melancholy in so isolated a place and that the savage weather would often make it unbearably cold, in spite of the new central heating. Picasso had replied that, as a Spaniard, he was not afraid of harshness.[62] In fact, however, after an initial, exalted period when he found the aristocratic grandeur of the great house and its dramatic landscape inspiring, he hardly worked there at all, and in 1961 the more congenial and convenient Mas Notre-Dame-de-Vie in Mougins became his principal home and place of work. In the inter-vening period, La Californie was reinstated. Now and then he would visit Vauvenargues en route to a corrida or to show the work gathered there to friends, but Jacqueline found the place profoundly depressing and these brief sojourns became increasingly rare as Picasso grew older.[63]

Final preparations for the Picasso exhibition

Meanwhile the exhibition was taking shape on the ambitious scale Penrose had envisaged from the start and in early July he went with Lee to visit Picasso at La Californie. If Penrose kept notes of this visit they are now missing, but in *Scrap Book* he recounted what happened. His secretary Joyce Reeves had presented him with a specially bound copy of the biography and suggested that he ask Picasso to sign it. Picasso had still not read the book at this point but he responded with a handsome coloured chalk drawing of a mask-like face that decorates the entire half-title.[64] On the same occasion he dedicated a copy of the Musée Cantini exhibition to Lee, with a comical face in profile which is surely intended as an affectionate caricature of her.[65] In light of the rivalry between Penrose and Cooper, the author of the Musée Cantini catalogue, one is bound to question Picasso's motives for choosing this particular item to decorate for Lee. Was he perhaps in some kind of play-ful conspiracy with her? Or did it amuse him to present the couple with a gift they would be bound to value but which was cruelly barbed? Whatever lay behind this gesture, it cannot have been entirely innocent.

During the autumn Penrose travelled to the United States, partly on British Council, partly on Arts Council business. The first stop was Brazil, where he was the British Council's representative on the committee for the

São Paulo Bienal. By a happy chance, he found himself on the same flight as Jean Leymarie, who, like him, was due to attend the congress of the International Association of Art Critics in Brasilia. Leymarie was a good deal younger than Penrose but he too was an aficionado of Picasso's work and a friend of the artist. The two men hit it off immediately and in *Scrap Book* Penrose recalled that during their time together in Brazil Leymarie gave him much useful information about sources of Picasso's work in the United States.[66] It must have been either on the transatlantic flight or in Brazil that they gossiped companionably about the dramatic time when Françoise Gilot finally walked out on Picasso. The following note is a brief summary of Leymarie's vivid story:

Leymarie 1959
With P. a day or two before separation [from Françoise Gilot]. Toreadors around. L. went to [see] Françoise's paintings. On coming out P. shot at him w. a toy revolver. Later at lunch L. sat next [to] F. P. looked at him with angry jealous eyes. In came a conjuror. P. disappeared with him. Returned [an] hour later having learnt all the tricks and did them to astonishment of the large lunch party. Later took Paloma on his knees and kissed tenderly her feet. [29]

Picasso's animosity towards Françoise Gilot had increased rather than diminished with the passage of time and, although in 1959 it was still possible to have contact with her without sacrificing his good will, the time was fast approaching when the Penroses would be obliged to shun her as a pariah.

From Brazil and Mexico, Roland flew to Chicago and then New York, where he met up with Lee and embarked on a frenetic round of loan-gathering visits to museum directors, dealers and collectors in the major American 'art cities'.[67] On 24 November he wrote triumphantly to Picasso on a postcard of Manet's *Incident in a Bullfight* in the Frick Collection:

The American corrida – mine – is almost over and the prospects for the London exhibition are really rather brilliant. About thirty sublime Picassos will embark for England in June to bring us joy. I am longing to see you and to tell you everything. We both send you our love
Roland.[68]

Back at home, Penrose plunged into the final preparations for the exhibition. His three-year British Council post in Paris came to an end that autumn and he could devote himself to it more or less full-time. The Arts Council exhibition officer in charge of all the paperwork was Joanna Drew, with whom Penrose had already worked on several smaller exhibitions (see p. 211). She matched him in energy and determination, and every means possible was used to attempt to secure the crucial, outstanding loans – from the simple expedient of including a copy of *Picasso: His Life and Work* with the request to persuading highly influential people to exert their influence at the highest levels. Studying the many hundreds of documents generated in the quest to assemble the best possible selection of pictures is, indeed, an object-lesson in how to mount a major exhibition. The single longest running, most time-consuming campaign revolved around the Russian pictures, and the overflowing Arts Council files show that there is nothing new about the naked forms of bribery commonly employed by institutions nowadays. Thus the huge loan exhibition of 'British Painting (1720–1960)' due to open in Moscow in May 1960 was used as a lever, the Tate Gallery promising a string of extra pictures if the Hermitage and the Pushkin agreed to release some of their Picassos. As we shall see, the issue of the Russian Picassos remained a cliffhanger even at the thirteenth hour.

A still unresolved question at the dawn of the new year was what Picasso himself would lend and in early February 1960 Penrose went to Cannes to try to sort this out.[69] From Cannes, he wrote to Gabriel White, Director of Art at the Arts Council, to update him on their discussions. The news was good except that Picasso was stubbornly opposed to the inclusion of sculpture in the exhibition:

My dear Gabriel,
I have seen Picasso and will be seeing him again tomorrow and probably the day after. I have found him very cooperative and have had only one rebuff – sculpture.
I have asked him for all the paintings I have on my list and he is willing to lend some 32 paintings dating from 1895 to 1955. In addition to this he will select some 10–12 paintings from 1956 onwards. [...]
'Sculpture.' He has again told me he does not want to lend any sculpture. I think the real reason behind this is that he wants someday to have a show of his sculpture alone – at least he does not want it mixed with painting in this particular show and would rather keep something in reserve. I told him we could, at great expense, get large bronzes from the U.S. and that we already had many small pieces promised, but he was still against it. I am rather at a loss as to what I should do and intend to discuss it with Kahnweiler on my return to Paris, but my feeling is that it might be better to drop the sculpture altogether. We shall certainly be more popular with him if we do. What is your reaction to this? Please let me know.
On the other hand he is willing to lend the entire series of 'Las Meninas', which has only been seen once at the Galerie Louise Leiris last summer.[70] The condition is that the whole series amounting to some 50 to 60 paintings be shown together. [...][71]

Eventually Picasso loaned just under one hundred paintings, including the full set of variations after *Las Meninas* and the nine paintings of pigeons, which he considered inseparable from the Velázquez series. The ban on including sculpture was a grave disappointment to Penrose but, latching onto a hint dropped by the artist, he began to dream of a follow-up exhibition devoted entirely to Picasso's sculpture. Within a year this had become an obsession.

Picasso's resistance to the inclusion of his sculpture was counterbalanced by his positive promotion of his large-scale decorative paintings. Early in January 1960 Penrose wrote to tell him that Jean Cassou of the Musée National d'Art Moderne in Paris had agreed to lend the vast drop-curtain depicting a motley band of circus performers and *commedia dell'arte* characters relaxing amid theatre scenery which Picasso had created for *Parade*, his first ballet for Diaghilev.[72] Cassou was an old friend of Picasso's and it is likely that the artist not only suggested the curtain be included but also intervened to sanction the loan. To complement and contrast with it, Penrose borrowed a three-metre-high, ultra-schematic décor designed in 1923 for one of Count Etienne de Beaumont's famously extravagant masked balls.[73] To underline the continuity within his decorative work, after his association with Diaghilev and de Beaumont had ceased, Picasso lent the tapestry cartoon *Women at their Toilette* – an enormous collage of garish contemporary wallpapers made in 1938 – and two woven tapestries reproducing designs of the early 1930s.[74] Together, these pieces were evidently intended to provide the context for the *Meninas* variations and the companion series of pigeons.[75] The cycle of paintings in Antibes, the *War and Peace* murals in Vallauris and the UNESCO decoration are further evidence of a concerted effort on his part, pursued ever since the end of the war, to produce a major decorative oeuvre and thus emulate the achievement of the great masters of the past, who increasingly obsessed him. In short, Picasso took advantage of the London exhibition to press his claim to be taken seriously as a decorative artist as well as an easel painter. That Penrose believed this claim was fully justified and was eager to promote it emerges from his notebooks, with all their references to special visits to Antibes, Vallauris and the UNESCO building.

When planning exhibitions, Penrose had his own method of calculating how much wall-space he would need and where pictures should hang. Each work was represented by a rectangle meticulously cut to scale on graph paper and, using scaled plans of the galleries, he would experiment with various layouts, room by room. But he was never bound by these 'draft' hangs and made final decisions only when the works were physically present and he could assess the visual effect of the groupings he had envisaged.[76] Of course, he did not need his scissors, scale rule and graph paper to tell him that the five huge decorations and the set of *Meninas* variations meant that he needed far more space than had originally been allocated, and he set about convincing Rothenstein, the Director of the Tate Gallery, to allow the show to double its floor space and to expand into the North and South Duveen Sculpture Galleries, which run like a nave through the centre of the Millbank building. On 25 February he wrote jubilantly to Picasso to report on his success and to announce that the Duke of Edinburgh would attend the gala opening – a major publicity boost for the ICA, as well as the exhibition itself.[77] In spite of his Surrealist past, his left-wing sympathies and his friendship with card-carrying Communists, Penrose could not conceal his pride at this accolade from the Royal Family and the Duke's visit popped up repeatedly in his subsequent letters to Picasso:

Dear Pablo,

Here we are at home again and I'm happy to report that preparations for the exhibition are going well. The director of the Tate Gallery has assured me that there will be plenty of space and has put two large galleries at our disposal. This means that your exhibition will occupy twice as much space as any exhibition devoted to a single artist thus far. It's going to be sensational. [...]

We were delighted to find you so well and so active. It was a really good week that we spent in Cannes and I'm extremely grateful for all the help you are giving me over the exhibition. It's going to be an unprecedented event in London. The Duke of Edinburgh has said that he will attend the reception given by our Institute of Contemporary Arts on the evening of the opening. It's the first time he has done such a thing. [...][78]

Towards the end of April Penrose paid another rapid visit to Cannes to check information on the pictures Picasso was lending so that he could complete his catalogue notes.[79] Was it perhaps on this occasion that Picasso at last passed comment on the great biography? The story appears nowhere in Penrose's notebooks but is recounted in his memoirs:

[T]he following summer, when I was again visiting La Californie, Picasso surprised me by announcing suddenly that he had read my book, adding, 'C'est très bien.' In fact a Spanish publisher in Madrid had had it translated and had sent Picasso an advance copy, a gesture that annoyed me because at least thirty pages, bearing references to communism, Guernica and the Spanish Civil War, had been censored. But Picasso's approval of the book even in its mutilated condition was encouraging. As usual at midday Picasso took his visitors [...] to lunch by the sea. On our return to La Californie after an exceedingly gay interlude I was surprised to see Don Pablo come over alone to me in a corner of the great room where everything happened, painting, meals, visits, tomfoolery with comic masks as well as long hours of concentration on his work. 'Yes,' he said, 'I read your book. It's good, in fact so good that often it seemed to me that we were sitting at the same table and writing it together.' The direct simplicity with which this was said made it more than a compliment.[80]

One can imagine Penrose repeating those delicious words to himself many times in the glowing aftermath of the moment – surely one of the supreme moments of his life. To be told that he and his god had been partners, mentally and spiritually, during the three years he had devoted to the book, was like being showered with gold. Unfortunately he is vague about the date of this great event. All he tells us is that it took place at La Californie 'in the summer', after the Spanish translation was published in the autumn of 1959.[81] Since he did not visit Cannes during the summer of 1960, it must have happened either during this spring visit or his next visit in the autumn. It would be nice to think that it happened in the spring and that he returned to England for the final, frantic push to get the exhibition up and running uplifted by the intoxicating joy of Picasso's praise.[82]

The final weeks before the private view on 5 July were packed with incident and Penrose's regular bulletins to Picasso allow us to observe everything through his eyes. Three weeks before the exhibition was due to open, Sam White's regular 'Letter from Paris' in the *Evening Standard* carried the story of Penrose's row with Cooper, but in Cooper's mendacious version:

RIVALRY

A long-standing rivalry between two Englishmen, who have long been the foremost interpreters of Picasso's work, now threatens to mar the quality of the forthcoming Tate Gallery show of Picasso's paintings.

The two men are Mr Roland Penrose and art historian Mr Douglas Cooper.

Mr Cooper told me when I saw him in his South of France home this week that Mr Penrose had not asked to borrow a single picture from his collection of Picassos, which some people consider to be the best Picasso collection in English hands.

Mr Cooper also said that he had offered to collaborate with Mr Penrose in organising the exhibition; but that his offer had been refused.

BOTH RICH

Both Penrose and Cooper are rich; both enjoy Picasso's close friendship. There the resemblances end. For whereas Cooper is ebullient and brilliant, Penrose is a much more self-effacing character.

Every now and again Picasso, who appears to enjoy the situation, tries to bring his two English champions together.

It is a touching sight, often repeated, when he makes them shake hands and, like two errant schoolboys, promise not to quarrel again.

Invariably, of course, it is not a handshake after a disagreement, but a prelude to a new round of hostilities.

Cooper is a man who has aroused violent enmities in English art circles. And he is convinced that he is being deliberately cold-shouldered over the Picasso show. […]

He claims that Picasso himself is disappointed at the scope of the Tate show.

He quotes Picasso as saying that 'only pictures that have already been reproduced or published will be shown. There will be no novelties.' […][83]

Penrose was furious but he did not panic and he acted decisively. It was important to forestall inaccurate gossip in France and so he wrote to Picasso enclosing the offending article:

My dear Pablo,

I'm sending you this simply in order to inform you that this article appeared last Friday in a major London evening newspaper.

You'll see that Cooper has told his friend the journalist Sam White that I neither asked him to lend his pictures to your exhibition nor to collaborate on the catalogue.

Such a colossal lie wouldn't bother me, even though Sam White, whom I know well, was fully informed about the steps I took two years ago when Douglas refused his pictures and his help, but you are said to be unhappy about the choice I've made. As the article is full of lies and frankly written against me, I am not too anxious, but I do hope it's not the case! Yes, indeed!

Here preparations for the exhibition are going satisfactorily. 'Les Demoiselles' and many other paintings from America have already arrived and we're expecting your pictures and the others from Paris this week. I'll keep you informed. As for Russia we still don't know the result of our latest efforts.

Lee joins me in sending you and dearest Jacqueline lots of love
Roland.[84]

He also wrote to the Editor of the *Evening Standard* demanding the newspaper publish a refutation of the 'lie' in White's article, pointing out that he had letters from Cooper 'to prove my case'. And he wrote sharply to Sam White:

Dear Sam,

re. your article 10 June 1960.

If you didn't know that this is an absolute lie you are very badly lacking in memory and gullible.

If you did, you are a dishonest journalist.

Remembering our conversation after my return from the Château de Castille in the summer of 1958, when Cooper had refused my requests for loans of his pictures and collaboration in the catalogue, I would like to know which of the above you claim to be.

Yours,[85]

These sallies had an effect. On 14 June the *Evening Standard* hastened to meet Penrose's demands by printing a short piece predicting that the exhibition would be a major event in the art calendar and quoting him: 'He [Cooper] flatly refused to give any further help.'

The problem with the Russian pictures was more substantial and, since it had become obvious that if they did ever reach London, it would be after the opening, the pragmatic decision was taken to set aside a gallery for them, rather than to attempt to integrate them with the rest of the paintings. Negotiations continued up to the last minute and the breakthrough came only when the Soviet writer Ilya Ehrenburg, a close friend of Picasso's, met Penrose in London on 26 June and saw the exhibition being installed.[86] Greatly impressed by the display, he intervened personally with the Soviet officials and on 24 July 1960 wrote to Penrose from Moscow assuring him that the pictures were on their way to London.[87]

When Penrose wrote to Picasso on 23 June there was still no sign of a resolution. But he was in the midst of installing the exhibition and in the state of euphoria that comes from contact with works of art with which one has been obsessed for months, and he no longer minded so much:

My dear Pablo,

I pass my days surrounded by what I love. The great galleries of the Tate are full of your canvases and I cannot get over the richness and variety of this marvellous panorama. The exhibition is going to be dazzling and with the help of a dedicated team I'm striving to ensure that the presentation, the catalogue, etc., etc., are of the highest standard. Almost all the pictures have arrived except those from Russia, and despite all our efforts we still don't know whether we will get them. Who knows? Perhaps. Perhaps not.

Crowds of Londoners and foreigners want to invade us, on top of the visits of friends. Today, John Richardson (without Douglas) came and was very complimentary about the whole ensemble.[88] The catalogue is almost ready and will, I hope, be to your taste. For the cover we've taken the motif of 'La cuisine', which is also reproduced, like all the other pictures, inside.[89] I hope you have already received the invitation card and the poster is being printed by [Fernand] Mourlot, so I'm sure it will be good. The gala evening reception organised by our Institute is becoming an event of great significance. Prince Philip will come in full evening dress with all his decorations [*various hiero-glyphs*], and you, I explain ten times a day that you prefer to stay quietly at home – but what a presence you have established without being present! And how grateful we are!

So, very moved, I send you and sweet Jacqueline my love. I'll write again soon.

Yours ever
Roland[90]

Penrose must have known that Picasso would not make the journey to London, but he could not resist trying to persuade him to change his mind and reverted to the subject in several of his letters. He even laid on accommodation in the house of a friend where, he assured Picasso, there would be total privacy.[91] Picasso remained unpersuadable, and when Brassaï asked him whether he intended to go to London his response was characteristically dismissive:

Why should I waste my time going to see my paintings again? I have a good memory, and I remember all of them. I loaned a great many of my own canvases to the exhibition, and that gave me quite enough trouble. [...] Exhibitions don't mean a great deal to me anymore. My old paintings no longer interest me. I'm much more curious about those I haven't yet done.[92]

This had been his invariable attitude to major retrospectives ever since settling in Cannes. No matter how hard anyone laboured to create a fitting memorial to his work, he held himself aloof, claiming to care exclusively about the work he was making at the moment. It was only the prospect of a corrida in Nîmes or Arles that could tempt him to stay away from home, for he no longer even made the trip to Paris. Some consolation for Penrose on this occasion came in the form of a 'reconnaissance' visit from Paulo Picasso, as his father's representative.[93]

'Picassomania'

The gala reception to which Penrose often referred in his letters to Picasso had preoccupied him for months and a special 'ladies' committee' was set up to organise it and plan the menu – champagne and paella – and the music – flamenco. Holding it under the auspices of the ICA was an ingenious idea, both a highly effective form of advertisement for the Institute and a way of raising much-needed funds, and 2,000 tickets at five guineas each were sold. The gala generated a good deal of press interest – getting the Duke of Edinburgh was a great coup and there were plenty of other celebrities as well, including a contingent of Hollywood movie stars. A typical piece published in the *Daily Mail* gushed about the special guests and continued: 'In present-day, art-mad Britain, it is not only an event. It is the Biggest Event. Tourists are already flocking to London hoping to see the grand old man.'[94] So, when

PAGE 10

IN ART CRAZY LONDON I GET A PREVIEW OF THE BIGGEST COLLECTION EVER

They've even insured Pablo for ten million

● Imagine the Duke of Edinburgh, Helena Rubinstein, Baron Rothschild, Mr. Kingsley Martin, poetess Kathleen Raine, Mr. Digby Morton and the Princesse de Broglie at a party . . .
They're shouting 'ole' while they eat 'amor frio' which means cold love. It's really fruit salad with cinnamon. Someone is singing a flamenco song, Ole !

The sitter . . . Mrs Penrose.

And the portrait . . . by Picasso, of course

GET that picture of the party in your mind's eye. It explains why I'm studying the difficult art of Pablo Picasso. The party for the exhibition of his works will be the high spot of the London season.

When the doors of the Tate Gallery open next week to show 270 of his paintings, in the greatest exhibition of Picasso ever seen, police will have to keep back the crowds.

And the C.I.D. will have

by OLGA FRANKLIN

Spanish Rioja wine in his

in the cold at a do like this, which is all for art, except for the funds which are for the Institute of Contemporary Art and the new big art centre Mr. Felix Fenston plans to build ?

I went along to the Tate Gallery to talk to the close friend and biographer of

No, he didn't think Picasso would come to the party. He was at present working in his 16th century Chateau de Vauvenargues near Aix-en-Provence, his hideout, as he calls it.

Pablo didn't like crowds, said Mr. Penrose, and would be bored to death by the party in spite of the paellas for dinner. They

you never really know what you will find.'

Two of Picasso's painter nephews, Monsieur Fin and Javier Vilato (sons of Pablo's late sister Lola), will be at the party, but Jacqueline could not possibly leave his side. " She is a wonderful, devoted person who looks after him in such an

wonderful experience. Among a party of admirers he met, the New York blonde girl photographer Lee Miller and married her.

At Mougins in 1937, Picasso did a portrait of Mrs. Penrose. So I went along to see her.

She was with her son An-

Penrose wrote to Picasso just after the opening he already knew he had created a 'blockbuster'. This and his subsequent letters not only express his elation and pride but also give a vivid picture of the unfolding drama as the phenomenon of 'Picassomania' gripped the country. Assured of resounding success, he was able to dismiss as pure farce Cooper's various hysterical interventions:

My dear Pablo

In haste I am writing to give you the first impressions of the Picasso explosion in London. It's overwhelming. Never before has there been so appreciative or copious a response from the press or indeed the general public. Already over 10,000 people have visited the show. There are queues the entire day until eight o'clock in the evening when the gallery closes. The enthusiasm, especially among the English, is phenomenal. You have conquered London – people are enchanted and dazzled by your presence on the walls.

The great gala reception for our Institute was wonderful – never has there been a more elegant, cosmopolitan and delighted crowd. But neither the satins, nor the diamonds, nor the decorations, nor the beautiful eyes of the women could rival the splendour of your pictures. The Duke of Edinburgh did a tour of the exhibition guided by me. He was very impressed and I think he'll come back to see it again in peace. I'll tell you more about that later. It was an enormous and informal gathering in which the power of your spirit enchanted everyone. Everyone was happy, everyone left rejoicing and with the sense that you had filled us with life and comprehension, and we all shared this experience.

I do hope you have now received the catalogue and the poster. Soon I'll send you the enormous and ever-increasing pile of press cuttings.

As for Cooper, he diverts the people in the galleries by proclaiming at the top of his voice that he is the special and personal envoy of Pablo Picasso, sent by you to supervise the way we treat your pictures, and that he was never officially asked to lend his canvases. We all know him and no one pays much attention to all this.

My dear Pablo, thank you, thank you, thank you for everything and above all for the generosity of spirit that this vast crowd of Londoners is beginning to appreciate in your work. We send you our deepest love.

Your friend

Roland

Tell Jacqueline that her portrait has made a great impression on people, especially with the inscription,[95] and send her Lee's and my warmest love. I'm also sending you the brochure that we distributed on the evening of the opening.[96]

Penrose was not exaggerating. Originally, around 150,000 visitors had been anticipated during the 77-day run, but by the time of the opening this had been revised to a quarter of a million and the opening hours extended with this in mind.[97] In the end, the show attracted over 460,000 visitors and

Opposite
Roland Penrose (far right) with the Duke of Edinburgh (centre) at the gala opening of the 'Picasso' exhibition, Tate Gallery, London, 1960. John Rothenstein is visible just behind Penrose

sometimes the galleries were so full they had to be closed. When Penrose told Picasso that there was an average of 5,000 visitors a day, he was significantly underestimating the number.[98] In fact, during the first week there were sometimes as many as 10,000 in a single day, and even after the figure had levelled out to around 6,000 by the end of July, 'the viewing of the pictures is no easy matter,' as a report in *The Times* grimly noted.[99] Such was the pressure on the warders that several suffered a nervous collapse and battalions of extra staff had to be drafted in. Merely keeping the gallery floors swept and clean became a matter of grave directorial concern.[100]

The press loved all this, of course, and there were regular stories of people fainting under the August sun as they stood in the queues that snaked down Millbank, of the motley nature of the crowds, and of the bewilderment of 'Mr and Mrs Average' when finally they confronted the pictures they had waited so patiently to see. Speaking for them, the self-confessed 'layman' S. A. Tuck described his experience in a local newspaper:

Pressing through a seething mass of people, I at last reached the pay-desk, coughed up my 3s 6d and came face to face with Picasso. Well, not exactly with Picasso himself, but with his work, which is probably much the same thing. Taking stock of the spectators that hectic hour in the Tate was in itself an experience. Some were obviously suffering, some looked anxious, some startled, a few enthralled, and quite a number carried a blank expression. I fervently hope I belonged to the last group.[101]

So, not exactly the universal, unadulterated enthusiasm that Penrose conveyed in his letters to Picasso, but certainly the most extraordinary manifestation of curiosity about a living artist's work ever seen in London up to that time.

Penrose was quite justified in telling Picasso that the reviews of the exhibition were glowing. Lawrence Gowing was overwhelmed:

The glory of the exhibition is to show Picasso the painter at full-length in broad daylight for the first time. The effect is stunning; it is as if we had never seen him at all. Suddenly one is aware of something which even the best of earlier exhibitions left half invisible. Firstly and finally Picasso's paintings are marvellously sensuous physical things. At the Tate all their other qualities come second to this. [...] If Mr Penrose's exhibition is not the exhibition of the century it will be surprising.[102]

The probing intelligence of other serious reviews vindicated Penrose's choice of works, in particular the inclusion of the entire *Las Meninas* suite, even when the writer, as in the case of David Sylvester, was sceptical about the ultimate greatness of Picasso's post-Cubist work.[103] John Golding's review particularly pleased Penrose, not just because Golding praised the selection for including only 'intensely serious' work – 'Despite the large number of brilliantly coloured canvases the total impression is one of severity and restraint' – but also because he stressed the 'revolutionary' character of all Picasso's work, 'even when he is at his most classical'. Of the recent 'copies' of works by Courbet, Delacroix and Velázquez, Golding said:

his gesture is not primarily a reversion to traditional themes and forms, or a turning back to the past for inspiration. Rather he is looking back from the point which he has reached, and, so to speak, pulling the past up through time towards him.[104]

For Penrose, too, Picasso was always a revolutionary, never simply a brilliant pasticheur, and he and Golding became friends at this time as they ran into one another in frequent out-of-hours visits to the exhibition.[105] It was a friendship that later bore fruit in a book of essays about Picasso which they edited together in 1973 and in the final Picasso exhibition of Penrose's career, 'Picasso's Picassos' at the Hayward Gallery in 1981.[106]

There were a few hostile reviews, notably from the redoubtable Professor Thomas Bodkin, who could be relied upon to be outraged by the 'excesses' of the avant-garde. But although he deplored Picasso's 'perversity' and 'his horrible distortions of humanity', damning the *Meninas* series as a vicious 'travesty', even Bodkin had to admit to being 'fascinated' by the exhibition.[107] And, of course, Cooper did not remain silent, using the Letters page of *The Listener* to compare the exhibition very unfavourably with previous retrospectives and to insist that the Tate show 'lacks masterpieces […] and is far from representing Picasso's pictorial achievements at their best'.[108] Penrose replied with a hot defence of the selection and bitter references to Cooper's habit of refusing to lend his pictures.[109] Thus their feud rumbled on in public, with no sign of a gentlemanly truce.

Nothing succeeds like success and to Penrose's delight the Queen expressed her desire to see the exhibition. His breathless description of this extraordinary event is the comic gem of his entire correspondence with Picasso:

My dear Pablo,
Honestly, London has never seen anything like this. The crowds in your exhibition augment daily and interest in it penetrates into every imaginable sphere – now they're even selling PIC*ESSO* to make cars go faster! And then on Thursday a friend of the Duke[110] informed me – in the greatest secrecy so as to avoid a stampede to the Tate of all the journalists in the world – that the Queen wanted to come in the evening with a dozen friends to see the show. I wasn't to say a word to anyone and no official was to be present to show them the pictures, only me. And that's exactly what happened. The Queen and the Duke arrived first and later the Queen Mother joined us.
Intimidated as I was to find myself in this situation, which as you know is not what I'm used to, I started giving some explanations of the Blue period

pictures that surrounded us in the first room. And yet again I must thank you – your superb presence surrounding us everywhere gave me confidence, and the eyes of the Queens lit up with enthusiasm – with genuine interest and admiration. We moved to your portrait, to 'La Vie', to 'The Soler Family', and suddenly the Queen let out a little shriek of terror when she saw the sightless head in 'The Blindman's Meal'. We moved on to 'Les Demoiselles d'Avignon' and she still showed interest and made some really quite intelligent remarks, although they wouldn't add anything much to the history of art.

I'd been advised not to insist on the difficult pictures and to avoid going into the cubist room[111] – but I wasn't happy about that and to my delight she went in with an enthusiasm that increased with each step – stopping in front of each picture – 'Portrait of Uhde', which she thought magnificent, 'Girl with a Mandolin', 'Still Life with Chair Caning', which she really liked, the collages, the little construction with gruyère and sausage in front of which she stopped and said, 'Oh how lovely that is! How I should like to make something like that myself!'

We carried on slowly, often turning back to look at something again. Of course she went straight to pictures which are easy to understand, the 'Portrait of Paulo', the 'Women Running on the Beach', but in front of 'Three Musicians' she stopped for a long time and asked me questions. I'm telling you all this because you asked me to write to you and also because this Royal Family has never shone in their appreciation of the arts, and your work really did seem to touch them, perhaps for the first time at the depths of their being. And so it went on – very enthusiastic about the great still life of 1931 and very disquieted in front of the paintings of the 'Guernica' period and the war. At last we reached the 'Bay of Cannes', which the Queen Mother found superb, when someone else joined us – and turning to me the Queen said, 'May I introduce my sister Margaret?' And there was the beautiful princess of our dreams with her photographer husband. Finally, having seen everything and talked at length surrounded by the 'Meninas', the Queen, saying that she would soon have to go, asked me to show the entire exhibition all over again to Margaret. Which I did, and when she asked me whether you were going to come I said that I thought that, even though you had expressed no desire to come, you would be sad not to have been there to meet her this evening. And she smiled enchantingly and I think I glimpsed a blush spreading beneath her tan.

And so, after two hours, they all left and as soon as I got home the Duke's friend telephoned me to tell me that the Queen had declared that she hadn't spent such a pleasant evening for a long time. And as for me, I was very relieved after a far from ordinary day, because in the afternoon I had had to give my lecture about you, and I fell asleep only to wake to new excitement the next day about the Russians. We have suddenly learned, just at the moment when we had given up all hope, that ten paintings will leave for London by plane at the beginning of next week. This is the list: 'The Embrace'

1900, 'The Old Jew' 1903, 'Acrobat on a Ball' 1905, 'Nude with Drapery' 1907, 'Still Life with a Skull' 1907, 'Two Nudes (Friendship)' 1908, 'Carafe and Three Bowls' 1908, 'The Farmer's Wife' 1908, 'The Dryad' 1908, 'Factory at Horta' 1909. So everything will begin all over again – a new opening – ever vaster crowds – and, who knows, another visit from the Queen?

In the midst of all this, what a joy it would be if you took the plane and came to see us! We would keep the secret just as closely for you as for the Queen – no one would know, except your friends. I won't say any more, and I send you all my love as usual. Lee also sends much love to you and Jacqueline

Roland[112]

The Edinburgh Archive contains five pages of notes of who said what during that memorable visit. Whereas Penrose's letter is a set-piece, pandering to Picasso's lurid erotic fantasies about the Queen and especially about Princess Margaret,[113] the notes report actual fragments of conversation and must have been written immediately after the Royal party had left the Tate Gallery. The following is a short selection:

Visit to Picasso exhibition at Tate
Queen, Prince Philip, Queen Mother, Margaret & Tony, June 1960
[…] Demoiselles – no comment.
Cubist room
Great interest in Uhde. Q.
'I can see character in it.' Q.
'I like letting my eyes wander from surface to surface without worrying about what it means.' M.
'What fun it must be to make collage.' M.
Construction – real enjoyment, 'Oh, how delightful. I wish I could make things like that myself.' Q.
P. [Philip] coming in: 'DO realise, Darling, there are 270 pictures to see and we have hardly begun.'
'Why does he use so many different styles?' Q.
Horror at story of razor blades. Q.[114] […]
'These are the ones that make me feel a bit drunk, I'm afraid.' P. La Muse, etc.[115]
'Why does he want to put 2 eyes on same side of face?' Q.
'Did he love her v. much?' M. (Portrait of Dora)[116] […]
Liked the Kitchen & thought it v. good at end of gallery. QM.[117]
Bay at Cannes greatly appreciated by QM & Q.
Meninas subtlety of colour, restraint and feeling of texture noticed & enjoyed by QM.
Pigeons much admired.
Portrait of Jacqueline noticed [by] M.
'What a tremendous output! He is the greatest of our time.' QM.[118]

The newspapers were full of the Royal visits and for some of his Surrealist friends the spectacle of Penrose in evening dress guiding the Windsors round the exhibition was the last straw – an inexcusable betrayal of all his and their fundamental principles. George Melly, the protégé of Mesens and former secretary at the London Gallery, wrote him a furious letter, signing off 'Yours disgustedly':

I know you admire Jarry but this is a little far out. What are you up to? I hope you will enjoy the little jokes HRH will presumably make in front of the pictures. Perhaps he will suggest that Prince Charles could do better. Honestly, I find the whole concept an insult to a great painter. What are you after? A title? An invitation to lunch at the palace? A ticket for the Royal Enclosure?

I wish to put it on record now that I shall lend no picture to an exhibition in the future under the aegis of yourself or the ICA.[119]

An equally scornful letter came from Mesens, attacking Penrose for a string of supposed crimes against himself and against Surrealism, and concluding:

Me, I remain, in 1960, proudly SURREALIST.
You, you busy yourself with the great Picasso, on the banks of the Thames and under the high patronage of His Royal Highness The Duke of Edinburgh,
E. L. T. Mesens[120]

Melly and Mesens knew the Establishment side to Penrose's character of old – the side that had drawn him irresistibly to the purchase of Farley Farm and to his ambassadorial post at the British Council in Paris – and they had always been suspicious of it. His weakness for the Royal Family was, in their eyes, merely a more inexcusable form of the same intrinsic 'flaw'.

Meanwhile, as Penrose had foreseen, the late arrival of the ten Russian paintings kept the exhibition in the public eye. This palpable sign of cooperation between the British Government and the Soviet Union at the height of the Cold War fascinated the media and in a letter to Picasso of 6 August Penrose reported that two days earlier, the first day that the Russian pictures had gone on display, 8,000 visitors pressed through the doors. 'As there is such congestion in the galleries,' he joked, 'I'm proposing that everyone does a kilometre on their knees before they are allowed in.' 'Now,' he added proudly, 'one can perhaps say without fear of contradiction that this is the most beautiful and complete exhibition of your work that has ever been seen.'[121] Joanna Drew remembered the whole episode as intensely exciting but also nerve-wracking:

This was the first time that the Arts Council had ever requested loans to an exhibition from the Soviet Union and it's difficult now to recall the extraordinary and nightmarish atmosphere surrounding any attempted dealings with this unknown and unpredictable state.

The Arts Council had been told there would be a courier and that on no account must the crates be opened unless that person was present. But the crates arrived, without escort or explanation, and it was only after hours of suspense and a frantic exchange of telegrams via the Embassy that Drew received confirmation that the technicians could get on with unpacking and hanging the pictures.[122] No wonder Penrose felt triumphant when at last the special gallery set aside for the Russian pictures opened to the public.

On 18 September 1960 the exhibition closed: 6,175 people had been through the doors on that day alone – a Sunday, when it was open for only six hours instead of the usual ten. As we have seen, getting on for half a million people in total had seen it – more than double the number who went to the retrospective in Paris in 1955. Breaking all existing records for a monographic show, around half a million postcards and 92,000 catalogues were sold.[123] The term 'Picassomania' was banded about in the press as reporters strove to understand the phenomenon of vast crowds queuing for hours and paying money to see an exhibition of paintings that, as one journalist put it, 'are not for the home'. 'What man or woman, coming home after a busy and exhausting day, would take a chair and spend half an hour refreshing the soul before a Picasso?' he asked rhetorically, with an approving nod in the direction of the more harmonious and sensuous paintings of Matisse and his much-quoted 'dream' of creating through his art 'a soothing, calming influence on the mind, something like a good armchair which provides relaxation from physical fatigue'.[124]

Another person might have wanted to relax after the unremitting intensity of the exhibition, especially since there was no break between beginning work on it and completing the Gollancz biography, but Penrose's way of coping with the combined sense of loss and anti-climax was to immerse himself immediately in another major Picasso project. The prospect of having no reason to visit Picasso regularly must have been simply too bleak to contemplate.

Chapter 6

Three New Projects, 1960–1965

A new campaign: *The Three Dancers*

On the day after the Picasso retrospective closed, *The Times* reported that: 'The trustees of the Tate hope to retain one of the paintings on loan permanently for the gallery if there is sufficient public support.'[1] It was not in fact a question of a loan but of the purchase of *The Three Dancers*, the great canvas painted in 1925 that Penrose and Picasso himself regarded as a masterpiece on a par with *Les Demoiselles d'Avignon*. Penrose had been appointed a Trustee of the Tate in the summer of 1959 and he was now given the delicate task of persuading Picasso to sell the picture, if possible at a *prix d'ami*. Knowing this would be no easy matter, he wasted no time in opening his campaign. Accordingly, on 25 September 1960 he wrote from Paris announcing his imminent arrival in Cannes and we know from his diary that he stayed there for four days.[2] His follow-up letter to Picasso makes it clear that the purchase of *The Three Dancers* had featured in their conversations:

My dear Pablo,

From Paris I came here [Huismes] to spend a few days with Max Ernst. I'm working with him on his exhibition for the Museum of Modern Art in New York. As you can see, I've already plunged back into writing and paintings. It's the best way because I left Cannes the other day with a heavy heart thinking that your exhibition – that marvel – was really over and still feeling that I hadn't been able to communicate to you just how important this event had been in London. For a very long time people will remember this exhibition as 'the most astonishing of the century'.

Anyway, when you have had time to reflect about 'The Three Dancers' of 1925 perhaps we shall be able to rejoice in the thought of having this picture in London as a permanent reminder of the exhibition and as a major representation of your work. I know your generosity would be appreciated in the highest degree if you felt you could let us have a work of this importance.

In any case I want to thank you for everything you have already done for the exhibition – above all for having painted the pictures! – and, speaking personally, for the immense joy you give me. Thank you also for the drawing for the ICA.

I will be back in London in ten days' time and shall telephone you from there.

Opposite
Charles Murphy, Norman Schlossman, William Hartmann, Picasso and Roland Penrose, with the model of the Chicago Civic Center, at Notre-Dame-de-Vie, Mougins, May 1963. Photo Lee Miller

Please give sweet Jacqueline my love. I often think of you both and of the beautiful house on the hillside.

Yours ever

Roland.[3]

Simultaneously, Lee sent gifts to La Californie. This latest parcel elicited a grateful card from Jacqueline ending, 'Long live Picasso and the organiser of exhibition no. 1! Kisses to you.'[4] Having Jacqueline on his side was crucial to the success of this new endeavour, so Penrose must have been glad to see her friendly note when he got home. The Penroses' annual telegram to Picasso on his birthday was even more effusive than usual: 'NOUS TEM-BRASSONS CHER PABLO WE LOVE YOU TU NOUS DONNES LA VIE ET LA JEUNESSE TOUJOURS = ROLAND LEE TONY.'[5] And to judge from the letter Penrose wrote after another visit to Cannes in mid-November, the artist was feeling particularly well disposed towards him at the time, for Penrose came home with a drawing for the ICA auction, an amusing felt-tip pen drawing for Lee depicting a fashion show – Picasso had jokingly signed it 'TABLEAU de Roque (PAUL)' – and a drawing for Tony.[6] Evidently, they had discussed the purchase of *The Three Dancers* again and although Picasso was very hesitant he had not refused outright. Knowing it would amuse him, Penrose closed his letter by reporting an exchange during a lecture he had just given: 'At the end an old woman asked if I thought your pictures were good for pregnant women! "There's nothing better," I replied.'[7] It was by gossamer threads of affectionate humour like this that Penrose hoped eventually to wear down Picasso's resistance.

The astounding success of the exhibition at the Tate Gallery continued to reverberate for months after it closed and, in fulfilment of George Melly's sarcastic predictions, Penrose was made a Commander of the British Empire in the New Year's Honours list. He did not think of declining, although when writing to tell Picasso what had happened he pretended to find the whole thing absurd and embarrassing, despite being, as he put it, 'proud to be the "Picasso Man"'. The postscript to his letter – 'I do hope that your decision in favour of the Tate Gallery will be taken in this lovely January sunshine' – was no doubt intended to look like a spontaneous afterthought, but Picasso cannot have been fooled.[8] He knew the courteous but stubborn Englishman well enough to know that he would never abandon this latest quest while there was any hope of succeeding. Indeed, whether they had any inkling of it or not, they were about to embark on a new phase in their relationship characterised less by cooperation than by tussling, as Penrose set himself to overcome Picasso's opposition to not just one, but three major projects.

The first ominous signs of change occurred in March 1961 when Picasso broke an appointment to see Penrose in Cannes: he always cancelled appointments when he did not want to be pestered to make troublesome decisions. Nevertheless, Penrose decided to press on boldly when next writing to the artist:

Dear Picasso,

After having spoken to you I learned from Zette that you are busy on Sunday and I shall therefore put off my visit. I am sad about this change because I have so much to tell you and it would have been such a pleasure to see you again. Also there are things I need to tell you about the Tate Gallery, which still hopes that you will give it the opportunity to press the government to acquire one of your important canvases.

The Trustees of the Gallery are all agreed and the public is enthusiastic, as you have seen from the success of your exhibition. There is only the government, which holds the purse strings, to be convinced and I and some friends will make the necessary effort in order to succeed. Obviously, the more indulgent you can be over the price, the more grateful we will be. And if 'The Three Dancers', the canvas we most covet, really is not available, the 'Two Women at their Toilette', the great canvas of 1954 (I think), would be a marvellous acquisition.[9]

This afternoon I spoke to Kahnweiler about this project, which for me and for the whole population of England is vitally important. He understands the situation perfectly, but perhaps I can come and see you another day and explain everything in detail.

Forgive me for boring you with these matters. In truth, it was to see you and embrace you without any other consideration that I wanted to come. […][10]

When he wrote this letter Penrose was still ignorant of the fact that on 2 March 1961 Picasso and Jacqueline had married in the strictest secrecy in the town hall at Vallauris. The story broke only on 14 March. Even then, according to Penrose, most of the couple's friends 'believed it to be no more than a rumour'.[11] The news must have pleased and also comforted him: Picasso was, in effect, on his honeymoon when he cancelled their meeting – a legitimate reason by any standards – and now there could be no doubt that Jacqueline, with whom he had developed a good relationship and who had already proved an effective ally, was a permanent fixture.

At the end of June 1961 Roland and Lee spent a few days in Antibes. One motive was to show Picasso the maquette of the French edition of *Picasso: His Life and Work,* and if Penrose secretly hoped that Picasso would design a cover for it there and then he was not disappointed. On the day of their visit to La Californie, Picasso quickly mapped out an abstracted design in coloured chalks on the bare cover of the maquette, emblazoning the front with his signature in red.[12] Back in London a few weeks later Penrose thanked him effusively: 'the magical cover you made for my book is a huge success. Everyone thinks it admirable and my editor was in ecstasies. It was really marvellous to see it emerge so quickly from your hand.' Far from becoming more measured with the passage of time, Penrose's veneration for Picasso's genius continued to grow: the sheer confidence, fluency and abundance of Picasso's creative imagination always dazzled him and as he grew older the spectacle of a design taking form struck him as more, not less, magical. The rest of the letter is largely taken up with Penrose's plans for a small documentary exhibition at the ICA to celebrate Picasso's eightieth birthday, but at the end he reported that he had just seen Françoise Gilot and Claude in London.[13] This continued intimacy with Gilot and the children, far from serving his cause, got Penrose into trouble later.

The celebrations mounted in honour of Picasso's eightieth birthday in Nice, Vallauris and Cannes were on the most lavish scale and ran over two entire days: a festival of music, song and dance in Nice on the first day; on the second, a guard of helmeted motorcycle police and a clutch of flamenco guitarists to serenade Picasso and Jacqueline during their 'walkabout' in the main square of Vallauris, then a lunch with speeches and gift-giving, followed by a full Spanish bullfight in the Place des Ecoles, and finally a grand firework display in Cannes. The whole extravaganza was watched by huge crowds and, instead of feigning sickness or refusing to participate, Picasso entered wholeheartedly into the festivities, apparently relishing his coronation as Roi Soleil.[14] Penrose could not be there to watch it all but, alongside the usual enthusiastic and affectionate telegram, sent a handsome gift, which he knew would appeal to both the printmaker and the *animalier* in Picasso – George Stubbs's famous *The Anatomy of a Horse*, 1766.[15] It is noticeable that the letters he sent around this time were filled with news of all his efforts to disseminate his knowledge and appreciation of Picasso's work – the ICA exhibition, various popularising books and a series of radio broadcasts – but remain silent on the subject of *The Three Dancers*. Clearly, the broken appointment in March had alarmed him and brought a change of tactics: he would back off until the signs were propitious.

In Paris that December Penrose met Pierre Baudouin, whose astute observations of Picasso's fluctuating moods he always found interesting. On a page in his pocket notebook he scrawled the following summary:

Paris 16.12.61
Baudouin
Discussing the paintings P. had kept, among which there are a majority of portraits. P. said [of] late Cézanne, the first paintings of his to be accepted by the public were the still lifes, next the landscapes and last the portraits. B. thought that this showed a special uncertainty in P. about his portraits, esp[ecially] those with violent distortions – doubt as to how true they were when considered as portraits – also an outrage to the human head. [30]

Reading between the lines, it seems that Baudouin believed Picasso was not only troubled by the traditional issue of 'truth' to a sitter's likeness, but also felt qualms when the 'outrageous' distortions to which he subjected the human head were confused with portraiture proper. The presence of this 'special uncertainty' gives the lie to the tendency to regard Picasso as a ruthless, indeed monstrous egotist, who cared nothing for the identity of those – his lovers in particular – who inspired his most aggressively distorted pictures. Penrose himself regarded love as the supreme goal in life and in his notes he often remarked upon the tender, voluptuous and idealising character of the paintings inspired by Jacqueline. Although he recorded Baudouin's words without comment, they surely struck him because they chimed with the less reductive, more humane and sympathetic image of Picasso to which he personally was committed.

Lee and Roland put off their trip to the Midi until the New Year (on this occasion Tony accompanied them and took the role of photographer). It was their first visit to Mas Notre-Dame-de-Vie, the isolated but easily accessible farmhouse set on a hillside just outside Mougins that Picasso had bought soon after his marriage to Jacqueline. The visit went well and Penrose bore home with him a copy of the French edition of his book ornamented with a colourful dedication on the title-page, 'Pour Roland Penrose son ami Picasso le 9.1.62'.[16] At one point Penrose showed Picasso a mathematical puzzle devised by his older brother Lionel and the following conversation took place:[17]

9 Jan. '61 [error: 9 Jan. '62]. [Added later] *Notre-Dame-de-Vie*
Showed P. the impossible triangle. He looked at it, puzzled for some minutes, then started making other versions of it. 'Your brother should have been a cubist,' he said. 'It's an attempt to catch the 4th dimension. They always say

A collection of Picasso's sculptures at Notre-Dame-de-Vie, Mougins, January 1962. Photo Antony Penrose

the cubists were trying to catch the truth – they were really trying to make a deception – just like this – cubism was full of deception. Your brother should have worked with us; we would have found a lot in common.'

He then broke off from these geometric trompe l'oeils and we went next door into his studio. He pointed at some new canvases – heads in which the same movement from front to behind was done with his means. 'One travels round the head seeing it from different angles,' he said.

There was a superb head of a woman – lit on one side and dark turbulent red on the other, a brilliant green stripe ran down the centre.[18] 'It is the colour that solidifies it – unites it.'[19] [30]

Apparently, Picasso considered his latest work in essence Cubist – a perception justified not only by the complex interlocking of different viewpoints in his paintings but by the recent explosion of sculptures copied in cut and bent sheet-metal from cardboard and paper maquettes that are the direct descendants of his original Cubist constructions. This new development was of particular interest to Penrose because it was further proof of the centrality of sculpture to Picasso's creativity.

A second project: exhibiting Picasso's sculpture

When Penrose next visited Notre-Dame-de-Vie in June 1962 he kept fuller notes of what he had observed. The impression given is of excessive fertility, a fertility Picasso did not seek to control and barely to direct – of suites of drawings that came, as it were, unbidden, and of a spate of paintings, linocuts, ceramics and sculptures. And although immersed in his own work, the eighty-year-old artist was still open to the work of younger artists like Francis Bacon and prepared to stay up half the night reading Valentine Penrose's latest book.

23 June '62 N.-D.-de-Vie
P. tells story of Leo Stein who used to say he was frightened of showing rare prints to P. because he devoured them with his eyes till nothing was left on the paper.

Looking at lino prints, P. was pointing out the miraculous way in which colours changed, black became grey when black was printed on it.

Brought out two recent canvases, one of which was a copy (though dimensions of canvas not the same) by J. Very good too. P. told her to try one day when she was bored; gave her the colours. She enjoyed it and results good. [*Added later*] Could be mistaken for P. – but, says J., 'It's all right, I'm not doing any more.'

P. no philanthrope – talking of Africa – said it was risky to lend – better not. If the Africans thought we laugh at their art, perhaps they are right.

One great new canvas with seated woman and Afghan dog. Head of woman great complex of heads within heads, eyes and ears joined together as a garland across face.[20] Several other highly analytical constructions in near monochrome – large painting of trussed cock on chair.[21] Large quantities of tiles, each with a face, usually a girl.[22] J. very tender and beautiful, also very lovely head of J. in greens and greys and a brilliant linocut retouched in radiant colour. At the present time, for one cruel dissection of female there are twenty tender, exquisite versions.

The 'Déjeuner sur l'herbe' drawings continue in great quantities. 'Je continue toujours des "déjeuners" (surtout des dessins en quantité) – pour ceux qui sont en retard.'[23] Also a new series begun a few days ago in pencil – a Dickensian family – old seated couple, faces drawn with incredible freedom – & young couple. Girl of great beauty, absurd, serious young man. In one drawing Cocteau in profile.[24] 'Je ne sais pas ce qu'il fait la. Je ne le voulait pas, il est venu tout seule.' – 'Et qui son ces gens! Ils sont tous venu ici je ne sait pas d'où – mais ils ne sont pas n'importe qui. [*Inserted later*] De Dickens, de Balzac? qui sait? Ils sont arrivés l'autre jour et je ne sais pas qui ils sont.'[25] Each has a personality so definite that their presence is very surprising.

Model of the Museum in Barcelona.[26] P. is making linocut reliefs to be cast in bronze in Spain for a great entrance door.

Sculpture: several painted heads in bent sheet iron with drawing in solder on surface – very subtle & strong. The figure pushing pram, begun 5½ years ago, nearing completion [*see pp. 80, 81*].[27]

Great Greek vase with baked oil on surface.

Small animal figures: monkeys made of cut-out sheet copper – painted.[28]

Anonymity: artist god – artisan (Duchamp).
    Arnera – linocut printer. Vallauris.

28 Juin [Added later] *Visit to Picasso 1962 Notre-Dame-de-Vie*
Found P. and J. seated together at a small table doing business letters. P. in very good mood. Said he had looked at Bacon catalogue and liked it – some of it very much – please tell B. Liked ideas and technique – sometimes v. good.[29] Had been reading Valentine's book up to 5 in morning – 'magnifique – surtout le style et facon de comprendre'.[30]
    Agreed to sculpture exhibition in principle. First.
    Said he had done a drawing – dove above broken swords for Moscow Peace Congress.[31] I said I was at work on UNESCO, 'Art accuse la guerre'. He said, 'Oui, nous travaillons pour la paix, les autres pour d'autre chose – chaque un son metier.'[32]
    He did a drawing of a head with colour for the ICA with readiness.

New book – Carmen – edited by Marcel Duhamel coming out soon.[33]

Showed him my ideas for fountains – they seemed to amuse him greatly – liked particularly spray of water for hair – promised to send him maquette.[34] [31]

In the midst of all these disparate notations it is easy to overlook the laconic statement: 'Agreed to sculpture exhibition in principle. First.' Yet for Penrose this must have been the climactic moment, if not the principal objective, of his visit to Mougins, for he had longed to curate an exhibition of Picasso's sculpture since 1959, if not before. The thought that it would be a truly pioneering show, the revelation of an oeuvre that was barely known outside Picasso's immediate circle, lent it special significance, and in expectation of the stir it would cause, the decision was taken to make it the inaugural exhibition of the new Arts Council gallery then under construction on London's South Bank. Perhaps the brevity of Penrose's passing allusion was simply a reflection of his realism: he knew that an agreement 'in principle' guaranteed nothing and that overcoming Picasso's reluctance to let his sculpture out of his sight would require great patience and cunning. Still, this was a start and he now had a major Picasso project on which to focus, equivalent in importance to the 1960 retrospective. If Penrose dared to mention *The Three Dancers* during this visit to Mougins, there is no sign of it in his notes.

A third project: a monument for Chicago

As if these two precious schemes were not a sufficient diplomatic challenge, in the spring of 1963 Penrose agreed to take on a third. Like the other two, this also developed into a protracted struggle which he almost lost. The affair began early in April with a letter from William Hartmann, of the high-profile Chicago architectural practice of Skidmore, Owings and Merrill, asking for Penrose's help and guidance in obtaining a design from Picasso for a monument to stand on the piazza in front of the new Civic Center building in Chicago. The proposal came with the full endorsement of Alfred Barr and the Art Institute of Chicago.[35] In his reply Penrose offered to accompany Hartmann when he went to see Picasso and suggested that the best solution might be to commission the Norwegian sculptor Carl Nesjar to make a monumental concrete enlargement of one of Picasso's cardboard maquettes, since Picasso evidently approved of Nesjar's work.[36] A few days later Penrose wrote to Alfred Barr and, friend to friend, expressed his misgivings about this latest venture:

I have had a letter and a call from Allan McNab & Hartmann from Chicago about a project which they say you know all about – once more it's the old story of introductions to Picasso – I dream of the days when I went to see him for no other reason than because I loved him – but this does seem a really important proposal and might fit in with his work at the present time.[37]

Given his reluctance, one has to ask why Penrose agreed to take this project on at all.

At one level the answer is self-evident: Penrose had become addicted to these elaborate rituals of courtship. There were probably other essentially 'selfish' motives, too: it was flattering to be considered indispensable to this important foreign mission and there was perhaps a financial incentive – the 'generous gift' which Penrose split between his own and the ICA's accounts.[38] Moreover, conscious of how much he owed him, Penrose did not like letting Alfred Barr down.[39] His other motives had, however, everything to do with Picasso's stature.

During his most recent visit to Mougins, Penrose had realised that monumental projects were much on Picasso's mind. He knew, for instance, that the indefatigable Nesjar had just completed a giant concrete version of the sheet-metal *Woman with Outstretched Arms* for Kahnweiler's garden at Chalo-Saint-Mars and was about to embark on a series of wall-engravings, based on Picasso's drawings, for Cooper's Château de Castille.[40] The Chicago project was in line with this trajectory. From Penrose's perspective, this embrace of monumental scale and public commissions, such as the UNESCO mural, was also entirely fitting, indeed necessary, now that Picasso was in his eighties and had only limited time left: as the colossus of the twentieth century, the modern Michelangelo, he *ought* to work on this scale and do so worldwide. The 1950s and 1960s saw a vast boom in monumental public sculpture and Penrose may well have thought that Picasso was not dominating the field in the way he ought to. If he, Penrose, could facilitate the creation of this new sculpture for Chicago, he would be acting as midwife to Picasso's genius and glory, and thereby making the world a more thrilling and beautiful place. It was his *duty* as Picasso's Knight to take this on. It is perhaps in these terms that one should understand Penrose's tightrope-walking at this period. The Tate purchase of *The Three Dancers*, the Arts Council exhibition of Picasso's sculpture, the Chicago monument, were all part of the same grand purpose to reveal, memorialise and *extend* Picasso's genius.

On 9 May Penrose made his first move, sending a carefully worded letter to Picasso outlining the Chicago project and proposing a meeting:

[…] Lee and I plan to come to Antibes for a week starting 20 May and if you're not too absorbed by your work it would be a great pleasure for us to visit you. Apart from the joy of seeing you and Jacqueline, there is an ambitious project to speak to you about. Some American friends from Chicago have written and telephoned me twice to ask if you might be tempted to design the maquette for a monumental sculpture to be erected in the principal square in the centre of Chicago. I believe they've already written to you announcing the project.

Thinking that perhaps an idea of this importance might interest you, I have encouraged them to submit their proposal to you. It seemed to me that perhaps a sculpture of the type that Kahnweiler owns might be exactly what they want, but of course I have no idea how you will react.

Mr. Hartmann, a highly qualified architect and a friend of Alfred Barr's, is coming to Cannes especially to show you the plans for the skyscraper, which will be Chicago's new town hall. There will be gardens at the front where he wants to place a monumental sculpture by you. If you would like to see him, I could come with him so that he can explain everything to you.[…][41]

Picasso did not attempt to put him off and the first of three meetings was arranged for the afternoon of 20 May.

Conscious of the need to be able to provide an accurate progress report, Penrose kept vivid and detailed notes of these visits, in which he also broached the topic of the sculpture exhibition and yet another sensitive issue, the loan of Picasso's two paintings by Miró to the retrospective he was organising for the Arts Council.[42] But although burdened by this nagging agenda, he was also fascinated by the mass of new work he saw in the Notre-Dame-de-Vie studios, for he never lost sight of what ultimately mattered most about Picasso. Picasso knew and appreciated this, seeking and valuing Penrose's opinion because he had a fellow artist's eye and was quick to catch on to the changes he saw. From the notes it also emerges that Picasso was prone to petulant outbursts if pressed too hard: he longed to be left in peace to get on with his own work and all these outside demands were, he grumbled, irritating, above all time-consuming distractions. To get what he wanted, Penrose had to close his ears to this perpetual refrain:

Visit to Picasso. Monday 20 May '63
There were three reasons for this visit which once more made it a visit with a purpose rather than just a friendly call. (1) To prepare the ground for Wm. Hartmann of S[kidmore], O[wings] & M[errill] and his two associates, who want P. to make a monumental sculpture for the open space in front of the new skyscraper Town Hall that is being built by them in Chicago. (2) To ask him if he would be willing to let me organise an exhibition of his sculpture for the opening of the new Arts Council Gallery on the S[outh] Bank. (3) To ask if he will lend his two Mirós to the exhibition at the Tate in 1965 [*sic*]. P. and Jacqueline welcomed us with their usual affection and we stayed a good three hours looking at the vast production of painting and sculpture, all new since my visit last June. He was in excellent form asking after mutual friends, showing great interest in our activities and progress of Tony, our visit to Africa, etc.[43] I showed him transparencies of the fountain at the farm, which Jacqueline then showed with her projector, followed by a long series of photos she had taken of paintings in P.'s studio. P. seemed really to like the fountain from what could be seen. We then were shown round the sculpture hall and the 2 new studios he has added to the house, as well as the two existing ones. The paintings, of great vigour and undiminished inventiveness, were of the painter and his model, self-portrait of the painter – two of the painter, a fiercely bearded man, painting his self-portrait, that is, seen painting with his left hand, a canvas seen from the back. i.e. it is a portrait

of the person looking at the canvas – the canvas itself is a mirror reflecting an imaginary painter.[44]

There is a new 'discord' in the colour in some of these paintings which is disturbing at first sight, pinky purple–yellow green arrangements, which give a new 'harmony' – a new taste, rather bittersweet and disquieting. The series of painter & model is vast, some big canvases very gay in colour, others small, rapid, liquid. There were many very fine heads mostly based on Jacqueline – very sculptural, sombre in colour, monumental. The eyes, sometimes two in one almond, sometimes like a cave within a hairpin bend on a mountainside, vary astonishingly in their expression.[45] One or two among the dozens he showed seemed repetitious and weak, but in general the effect of being shown so many so fast was overwhelming. He said after showing some 60 or 70, 'Je te fatigue, n'est pas?'[46] I had to admit I could not take in enough

Picasso with one of his painted sheet-metal portraits of Jacqueline, Notre-Dame-de-Vie, Mougins, May 1963. Photo Lee Miller

at such high speed. There were several large canvases of the Rape of the Sabines – very grand compositions – absurd warriors intent on braining each other, women rolled on the ground and the only survivor and figure that commands respect – the child rising from its mother's arms yelling, indignant;[47] also several great pictures of a woman with a dog – the new Afghan.[48] Among the many sculptures – heads of women mostly, made out of bent metal and painted, recent work [*see p. 251*] – was a head in bronze made some 5 to 10 years ago. P. showed me this with special lighting. He said he had worked a great deal on it and was obviously very fond of it. It is very noble and serene and has great stature though not big.[49]

The girl skipping has been cast at last. After about ten years he finally found the solution he wanted for the face, which until then had remained a blank circle.[50] The little girl flying over her rope, her clumsy boots dangling like the clappers of a bell, now looks down, her eyes half closed in concentration and a look of profound seriousness in her play. P. showed us several cubist sculptures mostly in tin, painted, which had been discovered in some hideout in Paris – rust and dust but with all their original strength intact. Lee took a lot of pictures.

We talked about the Chicago project, in which he seemed really interested, and [he] ask[ed] me to bring the architects round next afternoon. I asked about the London show – he was not keen but did not say no. When I pressed him, in a sudden outburst he said, 'Des expositions, les projets pour Chicago, Marseille ou n'importe où *ne m'interesse pas*. C'est seulement le travail, mon travail, que m'interesse et je n'ai jamais assez de temps.' I said the show would not be before more than a year and would be the first in the new gallery, etc. He said, 'Eh bien, on verra.'[51]

While looking at the bronze goat[52] we noticed a v. small lizard on its nose – frightened it fell off and lay upside down like dead on the floor. J. went to pick it up – 'Dead,' she said, 'how sad.' – 'No,' said P., 'just pretending.' This soon could be seen to be true. 'Comment as-tu su?' said J. 'Comment tu comprends les bêtes si bien?' 'C'est comme ça,' said P.[53]

Tues. 21 May '63
At 2.30, as arranged, Lee & I arrived with Wm. Hartmann, [Charles] Murphy & [Norman] Schlossman. They had with them a model of the centre of Chicago and a number of large photos of the site and general atmosphere. P. met us outside as we drove up. First sign of interest, which helped to encourage the architects, who were very nervous about the reception they might get. Only Hartmann spoke a few words of French but all three were madly hoping that he would accept their proposal. P. was at once impressed by the model, a very well constructed job [*see p. 241*], and sat down to study it. Very quickly he summed up the situation and became astonished at the immense scale of the buildings. 'Il faut quelque chose d'énorme,' he said, 'quelque chose grand comme ça,' placing his cigarette lighter in the open space where the sculpture is to go. 'Oui, comme ça peutêtre, un briquet qui donnera du feu à tous les gens de Chicago.'[54] Hartmann then showed him

the photos including eminent men born in Chicago. P. recognised them all with delight, especially [Ernest] Hemingway. Very quickly he entered into the idea, began discussing scale, materials, colour, lighting, durability, etc. Should it be in concrete like the figure at St. Hilaire, or a steel construction like those of 1929?[55] All sorts of possibilities were discussed as he warmed to the idea. The architects were shown all the sculptures new and old and various materials – sandblasted concrete, bronze, painted iron, etc. and the little cardboard maquettes from which the metal sculptures had been made up before being painted by him. Hartmann asked if he wanted a really big model – 12ft. high to work with. He refused at once; already he had got the

Picasso with the unfinished *Little Girl Skipping*, photographed in his sculpture studio at Vallauris in June 1954. Photo Lee Miller sense of scale, as we looked down on a match box on the floor realising that his monumental piece would be seen often from above and would look very small from the top of the building. Finally Hartmann, seeing that he was accepting the idea, proposed that he should think it over until October, at which time he would call again. Then with embarrassment he asked what arrangements P. would like to make about payment. 'Ne me parlez pas d'argent,' said P. 'Ça m'embarasse. Maintenant le tout c'est de se mettre au travail. Peut être quand tout est finit vous me donnerez quelque chose, mais surtout ne me parlez pas de ça maintenant. L'idee de la sculpture en fer me semble bonne, mais ça c'est mon idée aujourd'hui. Demain ça sera peut être d'autre chose. Il faut voir.'[56] We left in high spirits, all delighted at the receptive way in which he had entered into the project.

The architects left in high spirits – celebration dinner at Beaulieu – Hartmann said he was too elated to sleep that night. We met him next morning having already paid an early visit to the Palais Grimaldi.

At one moment we looked at some samples of new plastic materials given to P. by someone – very flashy with inset colour and metal substances – 'Ça m'effraye un peu,'[57] said P.

Sat. 25 May. On arrival immediate reference to the American architects, who had made a good impression. 'Peut être je ferai quelque chose,' he repeated.[58] In fact it looks likely. Through the glass doors looking into the studio I saw several large new paintings. Two heads of J. on white ground, one with red vertical lines in a long neck, like blood and wine running, was particularly vital though J. has no long neck.[59] In fact they are not portraits at all. Behind them was a large reclining nude in thin sepia and blue. Hands, raised above her head framing it and joined by fingers touching, were in strong relief making contrast with much flatter, more summary treatment of body. Breast, navel and sex seem draped together like a necklace, all adding to the landscape effect of head. Dark night blue filters from patch in background into forehead and eyes giving mysterious depth set off by architectural terrace; wall-like feeling of legs. P. said he had painted it in a quarter of an hour.[60] These three & several more smaller were all dated 24.5.63 or 23 – a great flush of energy, typical of present activities. Lionel Prejger was only other present and our enthusiasm warmed P. He brought out several large canvases of painter & model. Some v. gay colour, pink, green, yellow on white grounds. The pink-green contrasts very brilliant and fresh – new harmony. Stacks of painting surrounded us [as] we sat with J. and P. and chatted in sun-filled room.

P. talked at length of Argentinian who had a collection of doors by famous painters in his palatial Av[enue] de Saxe apartment.[61] During war he gave luxury parties with masses of food. His two great heroes – photos everywhere – were P. & Hitler. This changed overnight at Liberation – but admiration for P. remains. P's stories v. funny, full of mocking humour. P. & J. came outside house to say goodbye. J. again chided him for not going out more. Ten years since he has been to Paris – but feels no urge to travel. In fact idea of changes he would find depresses him. Happy where he is because he can work as much as he wants and when he wants. Said he would let me know about Chicago and in any case expected us back in Oct. [32]

On his return to England Penrose had other pressing work to attend to, notably the Miró retrospective exhibition for the Arts Council. But he wrote every month to Picasso throughout that summer to ensure that the Chicago project was not forgotten, and each time he tried to find a new way of describing it that would be peculiarly seductive. Thus in his letter of 19 June it was the unique glamour and magic of downtown Chicago that Penrose emphasised, whereas in his next letter on 10 July he sought to appeal to the darker, surreal side of Picasso's imagination. On 14 August he tried a quite different tack by emphasising the huge numbers that visited the Art Institute annually and the enthusiasm of the people of Chicago for Picasso's earlier work.[62]

But although he gave the monument the first place in all these letters, Penrose was canny enough not to make it his sole topic. Thus in the first of the letters he told Picasso about a linocut of a woman in a red beret he had just bought: 'Her beautiful eyes are more and more seductive the closer one looks at them. I am hypnotised by her.'[63] This was tactful not just because Picasso liked to hear of friends buying his work instead of always expecting gifts, but because for several years he had been engrossed in the linocut process. And in the third letter Penrose explained that he had agreed to write a text to accompany Edward Quinn's book of photographs of Picasso at home and at work, guessing that Jacqueline would particularly favour this project because the photographs enshrined her as Picasso's indispensable and beloved muse and companion. '[T]he subject thrills me,' he wrote,

and I've decided, if Quinn agrees, to get to work on it, and I very much hope we'll be able to produce something that will not displease you. In any case it's a pleasure to have images of you, Jacqueline, your work and your love for one another once again before my eyes.[64]

Penrose did not (of course) reveal that the commission had come to him by way of Herbert Read, who had flatly turned it down on the grounds that it was too trivial a publication for a philosopher like himself. 'They need only 14–18 pages of typescript, which I should have thought you could do while milking the cows!' Read added, by way of backhanded recommendation.[65]

There was no reply from Mougins to any of these letters and the Americans started to get restless. Prompted by Hartmann, Penrose wrote again to Picasso in September and in October, at which point he learned what he had suspected all along, that Picasso had done nothing and would have nothing to show them in November when they were all supposed to meet again.[66] Nevertheless, Picasso did agree to see Penrose, as arranged, and both the monument and the sculpture exhibition were on the agenda.[67]

Mougins Nov. 1963 [added later]
Picasso tells me: 'Cassou m'a ecrit qu'il fait un exposition de ce peintre "naif" Rousseau. Enfin, c'est lui le naif s'il croit que je vais preter mes toiles de cette façon.'[68] […]

Picasso
Sculpture, London '66. 'Eh bien peut être oui. Enfin j'aurais des sculptures en '66.'[69] I then explained at length the importance of this idea. […]

P. 'C'est vrai je donne du travail aux autres. Il y a des quantités de gens qui sont content de travail à cause de moi et ça c'est magnifique. Je suis content de ça mais c'est seulement parceque je continue de travailler.'[70]
    He was speaking of Arnera, Crommelynck, Quinn, etc., who had just left, and thinking of many others.

The process he had invented for making line prints from linocuts pleased him greatly and we spent hours in a bathroom painting over the white ink prints with chinese ink and then washing it off in the tub. [33]

Penrose described this episode in detail in the second edition of *Picasso: His Life and Work*:

On one occasion I found him with some large white sheets of paper which had just been returned by the printer. Impressions in white printer's ink which were almost invisible had been taken on them from the block of a large lino-cut. This had not penetrated into the lines of a drawing incised in the lino which could still be seen faintly. Picasso, armed with a large pot of indian ink and a brush, asked me to accompany him and Jacqueline to an upstairs bathroom. With sweeping gestures he covered entirely each sheet of paper with the ink, and then handed them one by one to Jacqueline and myself to wash off under the shower. The result was astonishing. The black ink was almost entirely washed away from the surfaces protected by the white printer's ink, leaving only a grey uneven ground over the whole print, but it remained and stood out boldly where the indian ink had entered into the lines engraved in the linoleum. The process Picasso had invented was as simple as Columbus and the egg once you had seen it done and gave a unique and lively quality to the print. We now had before us a splendid image, a line drawing of a satyr struggling with a naked nymph.[71]

But although Picasso had evidently enjoyed the hours spent working alongside Penrose in the bathroom and was generally in a sanguine and cooperative mood, there were ominous outbursts of complaining about the

intolerable pressure he was always under:

Picasso
In an outburst to Mme. Crémieux[72] & Crommelynck & self after an afternoon's work: 'Et c'est toujours comme ça. Je ne m'arrete jamais et encore c'est toute la nuit et si ce que je faisait etait moins bien ça sera la même chose. C'est epouvantable.'[73]

Looks at us for approval, his eyes fixing us in turn with a look of being possessed – in the clutches of his daemon – appealing to us to understand his inexorable plight.

Has a drawing & an etching by Gauguin of Mallarmé, a portrait of Satie by Zuloaga.
   Some 1914 cubist objects – a round painted wood bas relief, very good, a cardboard guitar.[74]
   Asked me to go and have a look at the 'Woman w. a pram' being cast at Valsuani.[75]

Hartmann
He intends to do the sculpture. J. confirms this.
   Just has not got round to it – 'Tu vois, j'ai trop à faire. Quand voudras-tu que je m'en occupe de ça et de mille autres choses qu'on me demande?'
   I explained at length Hartmann's difficulties and time factor.
   'J'en penserai, j'en pense toujours et maintenant que tu en parle je penserai d'avantage. Tu sais c'est drole – je n'accepte jamais des commissions mais voilà que j'ai ces deux que je veux faire – tous les deux seul pour les ville de gangsters. Marseille[76] et Chicago. Peut être nous allons voir une bataille entre eux pour en être la première.'
   All this was confirmed again during my last visit. He said to J., 'Fait moi penser à Chicago tous les jours.'[77]
   We also talked about the sculpture show. He even seemed keen at the idea. J. was delighted and said they must visit London.
   P. started talking about the absurd dreams he has – in bed with Queen Elizabeth and Margaret. Remembers noticing the colour of their poils.[78] Often dreams of celebrities – de Gaulle, etc., even Franco.
   I asked if he had ever done a portrait of Shakespeare.
   'Non, mais je pourrais peut être le faire. Envoie moi des portraits, des gravures de lui. Peut être j'en ferai quelque chose. Dernierement j'ai fait Rimbaud et il y a aussi Balzac, Gongora et bien d'autres.'[79] [...] [33]

   Encouraged, Penrose wrote a cheerful and affectionate letter to Picasso on his return to England, from which we learn that the enjoyable printmaking experiments had resulted in the gift of an erotic linocut for Lee[80] and a drawing for the annual ICA auction. Aware that nagging would be counter-productive,

Penrose did not mention his two great projects again but described instead his visit to the Valsuani foundry to see the cast of *Woman with a Pushchair*:

[…] Thank you so much for suggesting I go because, despite the poor light, I was able to see a tall, mysterious, hieratic personage, who with her fine hands and from a great distance manipulated the little carriage in which the child twists about like macaroni. The woman's flower-like breasts, placed so high up, and her small head and long hair, seemed so far away in the dusty fog at Valsuani's. It is very beautiful and very moving and it will be even better when seen in sunlight. […][81]

As he examined the sculpture, which he had seen in its still incomplete, uncast state during the memorable visit to the studios in Vallauris when Braque also happened to be present (see pp. 80, 81),[82] Penrose must have tried to visualise it on display in London among its peers. But although he was destined to be thwarted in his ambition to be the first to mount an exhibition devoted to Picasso's sculpture, the honour of being the first to *think* of doing so must go to him.

Visiting Mougins, March–June 1964

1964 proved to be one of the most demanding in all Penrose's years of dealing with Picasso as he tried to ease the reluctant artist towards two vital decisions – the sale of *The Three Dancers* to the Tate Gallery and the design of the Chicago monument. In the midst of the agonisingly protracted negotiations came the publication of Françoise Gilot's memoirs, *Life with Picasso*. For Penrose this was terrible news, not because he was forced to make up his mind about which side to take – despite their formerly close friendship, he denounced Françoise without hesitation or remorse – but because Picasso's anger and suspicion were aroused and obtaining his agreement to anything became correspondingly more difficult.

Although Penrose's visit to Mougins in November 1963 had given some cause for optimism, when he discussed the Chicago monument with Kahnweiler in the new year the latter 'was unable to give me any encouragement', as he duly reported to Hartmann.[83] Driven to use more imaginative methods of persuasion, Penrose's next letter to Picasso took the form of a fictitious, disarmingly self-mocking *récit de rêve*, ornamented at the end with abstract designs in coloured crayons. (Such decorations often appeared on especially important letters to Picasso.)

Dear Pablo,

I had the great good fortune of seeing you last night and I'm eager to tell you, for what it's worth, what happened. I began by dreaming that I wasn't asleep and then … 3.30 … we were late – and I was running with an Englishman through the countryside somewhere – we had to run because there was very little time before the departure of my train. Suddenly I found myself at your house, towards the end of a visit which seemed already to have lasted quite a time, and we were about to leave, again in a hurry because of the train. Lee was there and several other men and beautiful ladies, including a beautiful Belgian lady whom I didn't know. The others were preparing to leave by passing down a narrow corridor and you, still sitting down, said to me, with a mysterious smile and a look betokening something out of the ordinary, 'Well, have you come again about the project, or not?' Actually, to tell the truth, I was so happy to be there that I had forgotten to speak about it, and I told you that I was happy to have come, for once, without having a favour to ask. With an incredulous and again mysterious smile, you said to me, 'Well, I've made them something *very* modern. I don't know what they'll say but I can promise you it's modern.' At that moment you got up and we followed the others. Towards the exit we became embroiled with them and although I was very keen for you to show me what you had done, in the confusion all I could say was, 'What should I tell Hartmann?'! 'The same thing as always,' you replied, and then you refused to follow the route to the door, which passed through some bailiff's office, and, still in the best of moods, you hid in a great fireplace behind a fire that had gone out and then you reemerged laughing … I find myself in the garden talking to the Belgian beauty, knowing that I have missed the train, that I don't give a damn and that Lee won't be angry. Amongst the vines I speak of some acquaintances in Brussels. You join us and, telling me to follow you into your studio, you say, 'Very modern' – and I wake up.

Having written this down I flung myself back into bed to find out what happened next, with the intention of sending you a sketch of what you had shown me. But thanks to an absurd misunderstanding I couldn't get in contact and your ideas for Chicago remain a mystery.

Lee and I send you and the very beautiful Jacqueline all our love.

Roland[84]

Perhaps Picasso was charmed. At any rate, he did not attempt to forestall Penrose's next visit to Mougins. Roland went without Lee and his notebook tells an absorbing narrative of the emotional vicissitudes he stoically endured:

Visit of 2–7 March 1964
Tues. [3 March]. On arriving in Cannes from Venice I rang up Picasso at about 3.0 p.m. and was asked to go up to see him at once. I found there the Zervos[es] and a couple from Cavalaire who make bad tapestries of his paintings.[85] They had brought one round for him to see. Rather better than earlier attempts. He showed us some recent paintings mostly in blues and greens – large seated woman, reclining nude.[86] We then went down to the sculpture hall, which is being enlarged and in which some hundreds of sculptures, big and small, of all periods, are strewn about. Among them in places of honour are the girl skipping and the girl with the child in a pram.[87]

Both superb pieces. Former in a very baroque, clumsy style – very robust. Other perhaps the finest ever, with bold, completely convincing incongruities.

P. talked about Chicago. Brought out two 1930 wire sculptures, said probably they would suit better than anything.[88]

Everyone in very good humour. Jacqueline gay and affectionate. The Zervos[es] both full of old friendship. P. in excellent form. We began looking at bronzes in detail. X. (tapestry man) took great pleasure in lifting them one by one onto a turntable, well lit, and we examined them in detail. P. sat or mysteriously went around bringing out small pieces, cutouts, and talked about how little sculpture was understood. How difficult it was. How surfaces had to join – a glass of water poured over the top should wet the sculpture all over as it runs down – proof of related surfaces. X. began to show off his knowledge of sculpture, criticising in an academic way, saying boring and critical things with no regard for P.'s feelings. P. wonderfully tolerant, agreeing with stupid remarks against his early work. As X. heaved new heavy pieces onto the stand P.'s only remark was, 'Don't let it fall, it will crush your foot.' No sign of annoyance, only enjoyment at seeing pieces which had been hidden on the floor in dark corners, well lit and at leisure. We looked at about 20 to 30 pieces. Many of them large bronzes of early thirties. Finally the small crouching figure of a woman, P.'s earliest sculpture, came in for X.'s criticism: 'Joie evidement mais plein de faiblesse, seulement interessant parce-que c'est l'oeuvre d'un très jeune homme.'[89] By this time all except P. were exasperated with X. He was still patient. 'Vous etes bien sensible a la sculpture.' 'Je suis sculpteur,' says X.[90]

X., Mme. X. & baby (with which P. had been attentive & kind in spite of inherited banality & ugliness) left. The Z.s went off to work on the reproductions of 3 to 4000 drawings P. had produced for them from the depths of his stores, all black with the soot of Paris and very exciting – so many unexpected things from such widely different periods.

I found myself at last alone with P. and three things I wanted to put to him. (1) Chicago. He took me into the studio next door and showed me a new project for a great head made in metal with a strange connection in rods between the large sheets that suggested hair, or la coiffe Niçoise,[91] and the profile.[92] [It] suggested to me the face of a mandril, but with great force and subtle appreciation of a woman's head. I saw in this a new start for the Chicago project, great and quite astonishingly new. The connection between the profile and the hair with rods gave a transparency to the head, a balance between solidity and void, which I think can be very happy in skyscraper surroundings.

I tried to tell him how right I thought it would be. He said Hartmann had not liked the 1930 wire sculpture last June. I said H. had not disliked it but would rather have something new. [*Inserted addition*] End of conversation (1) 'Oui la tête pourrait peutêtre être bien, pas comme ça. Il faut le monter plus haut. Et qui sais peutêtre ça ne sera pas du tout comme ça. Je pense à ça.'[93]

[*Main text continues*] (2) Tate purchase of 'Three Dancers'. I told him Tate at last has money. First picture they want is '3 D.'. No knowledge of what that might cost, incalculable. But they want it. I started on this just after he had told me how much he admired Britain. His reply, 'Vraiment. Ils se rappelent toujours de ce tableau? C'est bien.' I insisted that it was in no way forgotten – 'Le President lui même avait parlé le premier.'[94] We then tried to calculate what £80,000 meant in New Francs – a mess. We had to wait till Jacqueline arrived and then she did the sum the wrong way round. Finally it seemed to be more than 1,000,000 NF, which seemed good enough for the moment because, in any case, I had to explain that Parliament had not yet voted it, although we could consider it as good as voted. P. said, 'Enfin ce n'est pas l'argent qui compte. Je vais reflechir.'[95]

(3) Showed him the Cézanne Murder picture in photo – very interested – could not take eyes off photo – left it with him.[96] Joked, laughed. Gave him my presents. Said goodbye. He said, 'Je suis toujours ici. Telephone moi quand tu veux et reviens.'[97] [34]

In another notebook Penrose recorded the following fragments of Picasso's conversation and their various fumbling attempts to convert the Tate's offer into *nouveaux francs*. The sum 1,096,000 NF is underlined twice:

Picasso [added later]
Mougins. 3 March '64
P. 'C'est des ratages qu'on arrive à quelque chose. Ce n'ai pas en faisant Raphael, mais en ratant Raphael, qu'on arrive. C'est un double ratage.'

'En faisant une sculpture il faudra verser doucement un vers d'eau sur le sommet et en coulant sur la surface ça doit le mouiller toute entierement. Chaque surface communique avec son voisin.'

'Tete 1909 – j'ai pensé que les courbes qu'on voit doivent continuer à l'interieur. J'avais l'idée de le faire en fil de fer. Mais c'est très intellectuel comme idée. C'est trop de la peinture, mais c'est ça qui a permit d'autre chose plus tard.'[98]

1932? reclining nude was made originally in separate pieces which could be moved around – arms & breasts – head and body – leg – leg. But when cast in bronze they were fixed together.[99] [35]

This first visit had gone well, despite the tiresome interventions of the pretentious 'X.'. There had been much discussion of sculpture which, optimistically, could be interpreted to mean that Picasso was now reconciled to exhibiting his sculpture en masse in London. A more tangible sign of progress was the strange, half-human, half-animal, sheet-metal head Picasso had shown Penrose. With his customary visual acuteness and sense of architectural scale, Penrose had understood immediately that it would suit the Chicago site perfectly. If only he could persuade Picasso to believe this, the deadlock would be broken and a new masterpiece would be born. One can imagine his happy reverie in the hotel bar that evening as he ruminated on the auspicious signs.

The next day, however, brought a sudden and crushing change and one of the humiliating freeze-outs that all Picasso's friends suffered now and again:

Wed. I phone about 3.0 p.m. 'Mons. et Mme. ne sont pas là.'[100] I try later, same reply.

Thurs. I phone about 11.0 am. 'Mons. et Mme. vous font dire qu'ils ne peuvent pas vous recevoir aujourd'hui.'[101]

I ring the Z.s who are staying in same hotel. They tell me that there has been a great crisis at [Notre-Dame-de-Vie].

P. has been in a terrible state of nerves. Old friend Yvonne Z. has been the only person allowed into his intimacy. Z. said he had paid for it too. He was sent a message that there were no more drawings, when he was sure there [were] still a great many to catalogue. Two days later four more portfolios were brought to him with no comment. I said, 'How long can this go on?' Z., 'Only two days at the most and when it's over it won't happen again for a while because it's so intense and so disturbing to him, as well as everyone else, he has to calm down.' He was right.

We meet for dinner, she [Yvonne Zervos] tells me of passionate scene. P.'s confidence broken, saying, 'Oui tout le monde dit: "Oui c'est merveilleux" et je reconnaisse très bien les faiblesse. C'est [cette] affaire Chicago. Je veux bien en faire, mais comment? Et ce pauvre Penrose que j'ai refusé voir aujourd'hui?'[102] And according to Y. he was so violently involved he wept. [34]

In *Scrap Book*, in which this visit to Mougins is recalled in some detail, Penrose gave a different version of Yvonne Zervos's story. No doubt both are true: in the notebook he recorded only what was relevant to the 'business' that then preoccupied him, whereas in his memoirs he recorded the humanly touching aspects of the drama:

She [Yvonne Zervos] told me that on the day after our visit she had managed to penetrate into a room where she found an extraordinary sight. Don Pablo was seated alone with the traditional red student's cap that I had brought back from Venice for him on his head. He had hoped to amuse Jacqueline's daughter and her young friend who lived with them, but having failed he sat with tears rolling down his cheeks claiming to be in everything a miserable failure.[103]

Penrose heeded the Zervoses' wise counsel and decided to ride out the storm. As he hung around in his hotel waiting for a return of the cheerful mood of the first day, he derived some small solace from versifying, in French, his feelings of impotence and his compassion for Picasso in such episodes of self-lacerating despair. But realising his verses amounted to therapy not poetry, Penrose did not present them to Picasso.[104] In his notebook he took up the narrative again:

Fri. [6 March]. I decide to postpone my departure for a day. I phone again at 12.10 p.m. and get Jacqueline at once. 'Viens à 3.30.'[105] I find as I expected the Z.s and Frua de Angeli with his wife.[106] Same visit with important variations: paintings, garden, sculpture. Much softer atmosphere, no awkward comments. Frua leaves early and Z.s, full of cooperation, leave me alone with P. I again insist on value of new head for Chicago. It's not right, we all know, but the idea is there and splendid. J. puts on a show of her photos to try to give me a good run alone. He insists on seeing photos too. Finally we sit down together – long and relaxed talk.

(1) Approves my telegram to H[artmann]. Says he wants to do Chicago Sculpture – must have time.

(2) Says he must ask friends if they think he is doing an idiocy or not. Wants letter when money is granted and proposal definite. I say: 'Oui, il faut reflechir. C'est le prix le plus fort que le Tate a jamais offert.' – P. 'Oui, mais jusqu'ici il n'ont pas eu l'argent.' – 'Mais si tu trouve que ce n'est pas assez dit nous toute de suite.'[107] He smiled.

(3) Cézanne – 'Pourquoi l'acheter? Je pourrai en faire quand je veux.'[108]

Then *Playboy*. He was never consulted about 'Wisdom of Picasso'. Received it as a fait accompli. I volunteer to write in protest – Yes, he will be very glad.[109]

This meeting was as friendly, amusing and marvellous as ever. He had apologised when I arrived, saying, 'Tu comprends, ça a été difficile.'[110]

Then it was forgotten. Said I would be back in May. [34]

Back in England Penrose tried to keep things simmering by sending friendly, newsy letters. But his tact did not have the desired effect. When he and Lee next met up with Hartmann and his associates in Antibes at the end of April, Picasso saw to it that the gates of Notre-Dame-de-Vie remained firmly shut against them and gave out that he had gone away.[111] But although Penrose was obliged to submit on this occasion, the letter, tinged with irony, that he sent Picasso on 5 May makes it clear that he was not defeated:

Dear Pablo,

It seems that bad luck reigned over my visit to Cannes these past days and that if I had consulted the stars I would have known it was not a propitious moment. Without knowing the reasons for your absence, I imagine that a multitude of things assailed you. Lee and I hope above all that it was not that you were unwell and that, in this beautiful weather, both you and Jacqueline are in good health. [...]

Before leaving Cannes we said our goodbyes to the skyscrapists of Chicago, who left resigned to the thought that they would have to wait. Their admiration for you and their good faith are, it must be said, limitless.

Lee and I will leave Palma next Sunday and, as it's on our way to Paris, we will spend Monday 11 May in Cannes. Perhaps you will be there and we shall have the joy of embracing you. [...][112]

His persistence was rewarded, but only at the very last minute:

Picasso. 12 May '64
After a heartbreaking silence when we arrived in Cannes on 29th April we were invited to call at 3.30 this afternoon. It was an eleventh-hour attempt to see him. Our bags were packed and we were about to leave for Paris on the 2.30 plane. The main purpose of our visit was the Chicago monument. Hartmann and five other architects had come over in the hope of seeing a maquette. It turned out that he [Picasso] had got no further than when I was there in early March. He had done a great deal of painting but no sculpture. In consequence he did not want to [see] the architects and his way of saying so was to have phone calls answered by saying he was out or had gone away. On our return from Palma – the architects all gone – we got to N.-D.-de-Vie at last and found Hélène P[armelin] there. He was nervously dispatching forty small terracottas, made some ten years before, to be cast. His temper was not easy but the good humour of Lee & Hélène and the firmness of Jacqueline, who called his bluff, made him break down and laugh at his own bad mood. He then showed us some 20 to 30 large paintings, all since Feb., all nudes, mostly of a girl playing with a black kitten. Great variety but all limited in colour. Some black & white, some white, blue, grey, with v. subtle pinks, whites and yellows. Reclining nudes like vast landscapes. Marvellous antics of kitten and play between it and woman. Great inventions of human architecture.[113] Interesting scraps of conversation.

'Ce qui est bête c'est que ça finesse, un tableau doit continuer à l'infinit.' Going to a canvas he traced over a line with his finger saying: 'Pourquoi ça s'arret la? Ça doit continuer dehors, loin comme un Sputnik. Et voilà ça finit et on perde l'interêt. On ne sait pas ce qu'on fait jusqu'on l'a fait et ce n'est plus interesant. Et si on savait d'avance ce qu'on allait faire, ça sera déjà le passé et sans interêt.'[114]

We talked later about several things. 'Chicago.' He still seems to intend to do something, but when? I assured him that architects had great patience, would go to any expense in making models and preferred bronze to other metals.

'3 Dancers for Tate.' Seems to intend to let us have it for 1 million new francs. Said, 'C'est mieux que ça va quelque part ou on l'apprecie. Ça sera le premier oeuvre acheté par un gouverment – mais non – L'Espagne, chose extraordinaire, vient d'acheter trois Peintre et son modele pour le pavillon Espagnol dans le World Fair.'[115] I think we shall get it.

'Miró portraits.'[116] Will I think lend them for Tate Show.

On arrival he gave me three drawings he had made of Shakespeare.[117]

Before leaving we watched all-in wrestling on T.V. He makes a point of watching this programme twice a week. J. cannot stand it. So he usually watches alone. Affectionate goodbyes and enquiries about our next visit.

When looking at a picture, one should say that makes me think of … more associations it can open up the better. [37]

It was no doubt with this episode in mind that Penrose wrote ruefully in *Scrap Book* of the tribulations he endured during the years Picasso dwelt at Notre-Dame-de-Vie:

Although always animated with the same excitement and expectation, each visit to the great man was different and there were days when I drew a blank. I always rang up beforehand, often the reply would be 'Come at once,' but it was equally possible that it would be an unequivocal 'No' which went out that day to all would-be visitors. Picasso was working and seeing no-one. I found I had to cultivate a patience sometimes approaching that of an Armenian refugee squatting on his baggage waiting for that rare and wonderful thing, a train. From no one else in the world would I have accepted or probably received such treatment, and yet like so many others I found that the rewards on seeing him again handsomely outweighed any resentment.[118]

Penrose's 'Armenian' endurance began to pay dividends in the middle of June when Picasso at last consented to see Hartmann and they inched forward in the direction of a deal over the Chicago monument:

Picasso. 17–19 June '64
Wed. 17th
The rebuff the American architects had met with made me very pessimistic about our last attempt to visit P. with Bill Hartmann, who had been in Europe waiting this chance for more than a month.

Formerly I had warned him [Picasso] always by phone or letter of my intended visit, but this time we decided to say nothing – arrive in Cannes en route for Venice – Bill for Chicago, and trust to luck, leaving only one afternoon and one whole day to see him.

First phone call at 1.0 p.m. was the usual answer, 'Ils ne sont pas là – mais vous pouver essayer plus tard.' Second call was – 'Oui vous pouvez venir toute de suite.'[119] We found P. & J. outside sitting in the sun. Their welcome to us, all three, was warm and led on to a relaxed and charming afternoon, joined by Geiser, who has been very ill, his daughter & their Swiss Dr. Fanti. We did a tour of the sculpture gallery and finally got round to the Chicago monument. Bill was immediately enthusiastic when shown the head I had been shown in March. P. complained he had not had time to develop it further but assured us he was still interested. Bill showed him photos of the site and P. seemed to take an increasing liking for him. Dr. F. tried to draw him out about his methods. 'Do you sometimes paint when you are very tired and find it brings new ideas?' P. looked at him astonished – 'Mais je ne suis jamais fatigué quand je peins; au contraire quand je me couche après d'avoir travailler je ne peux pas dormir pendant longtemps je suis remplit d'idées.'[120]

J. hinted that I should suggest going out to dinner together and he agreed. We were all delighted until he found that the chauffeur had gone and, in a sudden angry outburst, he ranted at him and said we could go out, but without him. Finally he was won back when it appeared there was ample room in the two cars we had for all, and a delightful dinner at Mougins (La Maussade) followed. We returned home late, all three very pleased and intending to ring next morning. J. had confided in Lee that she felt sure he wanted to go out more, as did she, and welcomed our intrusion. Before dinner I had given P. Colin Anderson's letter asking officially for purchase of '3 Dancers'. He took it saying, 'Merci, je le lirerai et te donner une reponse toute de suite.' – Laughter from all especially J. – 'Eh bien je reflechirai toute de suite et longement.'[121] He gave me a copy of 'Les Lettres Françaises' in which some more Shakespeare drawings were reproduced – Hamlet at the grave with a great head of S. – monumental in size, watching. On the wrapper he had made a quick drawing in red ink of S., which he also gave me, saying 'Tout ça c'est grace a toi.'[122]

Thurs. 18th
I phoned at 1.0: 'Venez quand vous voulez.'[123] We decided to go at once, were let in with the usual caution and ushered into the sitting room. Offered drinks by Marcelline while we waited for them. After some minutes she returned looking v. embarrassed. 'Monsieur qui avait dit oui d'abord maintenant ne voulait pas descendre et était remonté se coucher. Madame ne descendera non plus.'[124] We wrote a note and, very sad, left – Marcelline hinted we might phone again about 4.0 – Geiser was coming then. After lunch at Juan-les-Pins I phoned again – 'Venez toute de suite.'[125] We arrive to find him charming, reproaching us for having disappeared. G. was there looking through vast quantities of prints – etchings, aquatints, vernis mou[126] and many inventions – use of crayon lithographique, etc. Prints of all periods collected together by J. G. was making plans to start a long study of undocumented prints for a third volume of his book.

P. was eager to talk about Chicago. 'Maintenant que vous êtes ici je pense tout le temps.'[127] We went back to look at the head. He was worried about wind pressure and asked if the large surfaces of sheet metal should have holes made in them. Bill agreed that this was possible, but that they should be thought of rather as hollow constructions, like the wings of a plane – the whole being cast in bronze. A very useful conversation followed in which Bill got on very well in his indifferent French and P. opened up towards him.

I then chose a moment when he was out of the room to ask J. about the loan of the 2 early Mirós for the London exhibition. He came in just then and asked suspiciously what I wanted. 'C'est les deux Miró que tu as si gentilment dit que tu preteras pour Londres.' – 'Tu veux dire ces Mirós que je ne prête pas à Londres.' – 'Tu ne les prêtes pas! Quel désastre pour nous tous.' 'Eh bien c'est comme ça. J'en ai assez qu'on me demande des choses – toujours on me demande. Je les ai achetés. Ils sont a moi. Je les garde ici.' – 'Oui je sais qu'on te demande des choses – et tous le temps et c'est encore moi qui t'emmerde le plus dans ce sense.' I continued to exaggerate and just as suddenly as his anger had risen it suddenly disappeared and in a voice of resignation, 'Eh bien, si tu veux – je les prêtes.'[128]

We then went into the garden and sat for a long time discussing vaguely anything that came. I said we were going on to Venice – Bill to Chicago. P. said, 'Moi j'aimerai mieux aller à Chicago – la il y a l'avenir et la vie.'[129]

We discussed the Maeght Foundation. P. said he realised the architecture must be good, Miró ceramics also, but he couldn't understand the reason for it all. Why so much effort in such a remote place? Who is it for? Its perfection, tranquillity, etc. were the contrary to his idea of an active centre. Perfection and good taste always dangerous.

An hour or two passed very pleasantly and we offered to leave – 'Pourquoi? – on va aller diner à Nice si vous voulez.'[130] General delight at this suggestion. Some time before J. had been talking to Lee in the house. 'I bet,' she said, 'that he will suggest that we go out to dinner – he will want to make amends for his peevishness about the Mirós.'

We got into the cars and arriving late in a restaurant [on] the coast beyond Nice where we ate a lavish meal of lobsters, all in very good spirits and said an affectionate goodbye before starting for Cannes.

Next morning we sent flowers to J. and she phoned just before we left, very affectionate. My last words were about the '3 Dancers' for the Tate – she promised to insist that he gives an early reply and seemed hopeful.

P.S. In the garden Geiser reminded P. of his visit to Berne and their call on Klee. 'De tout les peintres c'était le plus beau,' said P. 'Quelle tête magnifique et quel distinction.'[131] [38]

Françoise Gilot versus Picasso

From London Penrose tried to get Picasso to commit himself finally to the sale of *The Three Dancers* so that the good news could be announced at the next meeting of the Tate Trustees. He telephoned and sent letters, but to no avail.[132] Then, suddenly, a new crisis that threatened to derail everything he had worked for so patiently blew up in his face: he was accused of socialising with Françoise Gilot when he was in St-Paul-de-Vence in August for the inauguration of the Maeght Foundation – an accusation that was plausible because he had remained in touch with her after her separation from Picasso. Within Picasso's circle, news of the imminent publication of her memoirs in the United States, where she had made her home, was creating an atmosphere of paranoia, and any contact with her was regarded as an unforgivable act of betrayal. Knowing how harmful this rumour would be, Penrose hastened to defend himself:

Dear Pablo,

I was in the Midi briefly the other day for the opening of the Maeght Foundation and guessing that I would not find you in that galley, I telephoned on my arrival in Cannes just to say hello. Unfortunately, you were not there that day.

I wanted to talk to Miró about his exhibition in London and in fact I did see him, along with two thousand others, on the terraces of St. Paul. The next day at dawn I looked down at you from the clouds on my way to Paris. Then, a few days after this flying visit, I had a phone call from a friend which greatly surprised me and left me wondering. She asked me if it was true that I had left the party at Maeght's early in order to go and spend the evening with Françoise Gilot. Of course I replied with a categorical no, but I do wonder who could have been the perpetrator of so colossal a lie. Above all, I realised you might take it very badly at this particular time, because I've recently learned something from my old editor in London, Victor Gollancz, that you must already know. He says that he was offered from America the manuscript of a book dictated by Françoise and written by a journalist called Carlton Lake. He added that he wouldn't publish it for all the world. Françoise has seen fit to describe her life with you by inventing, from her supposedly 'total' recall, long conversations with you and her version of events. Gollancz considers that the motives that presumably lie behind this book, along with all the unpardonable indiscretions, render it completely untouchable as far as he is concerned, but of course he can't prevent others from publishing it, and that I fear is what is happening.[133]

Fortunately, your Olympian habit of ignoring this sort of publicity, even when it comes from so poisoned a source, will enable you to surmount this attack, but I am terribly sorry that anyone should attempt to torment you in this way. Gollancz tells me that there are passages in the book that take the form of conversations with you about art, which some may feel alleviate the monotonous complaints of a vindictive woman, but that the style in English is so vulgar that in places it is virtually unreadable.

As you can imagine, Lee and I are disgusted by this whole affair. We just hope that you will find a way of ignoring it completely and that neither you nor Jacqueline will be hurt by it.

As always, we send you our fondest love, dear Pablo. Please give our love to the adorable Jacqueline.

With love[134]

The 'colossal' liar was none other than Penrose's *bête noire*, Douglas Cooper. Penrose knew this, but was too canny to call Picasso's bluff. Confirmation comes from an entirely trustworthy witness, Joanna Drew, whom Penrose had taken to the Maeght Foundation opening. Cooper crossed paths with Drew there but pretended not to recognize her. He then put it about that the woman he had seen with Penrose was Gilot. Chivalrously, Penrose did not tell Drew that she was the innocent source of the damaging gossip and she only learned the truth later.[135] The whole episode – comical in its pettiness in retrospect, but potentially disastrous at the time – proved that where Françoise Gilot was concerned Penrose could not be too careful. The pictures by her that hung in Farley Farm were removed from the walls and henceforth both Roland and Lee spoke of her as an unpardonable traitor.[136] As for Cooper, this was just another reason for Penrose to detest him. Only a few months before the Maeght Foundation affair, he had angrily threatened to pull out of his collaboration on Edward Quinn's book of photographs because Cooper was given too much prominence in the layout of the chapter entitled 'Visitors'.[137] But this latest piece of mischief-making was a more serious matter.

Picasso, meanwhile, kept up his régime of punishment, and when Penrose and Hartmann next attempted to visit Notre-Dame-de-Vie at the end of September they found the gates shut against them. Having tried and failed to gain admittance, Penrose sent a plaintive letter from his hotel explaining that he could defer his return to London no longer and that he would leave his and Hartmann's gifts in the lobby. Repeating his denial of Cooper's story, he insisted that he had not even spoken to Françoise for several years:

It troubles me deeply that you seem to be reproaching me for this ignoble book, when in fact I am as indignant about it as you. As soon as I was able secretly to obtain a copy of the proofs, I read it and I immediately sent the letter that you must have received. [...] This wretched book will soon be forgotten, I am sure, and I am convinced that neither you nor Jacqueline will be damaged by her darts, which are poisoned, but too insignificant to trouble you. I am terribly sorry that all this has happened but I am sure you must know the unshakeable integrity of my feelings towards you and Jacqueline, and I hope that this viper will never have the satisfaction of imagining that she can drive a wedge between you and your friends. [...][138]

Penrose's predictions about the fate of *Life with Picasso* could not have been more wrong: the book was an immediate hit with the public and has remained in print ever since. Nevertheless, his pathetic letter did the trick. Jacqueline telephoned the hotel and Penrose and Hartmann were allowed to visit on the afternoon of 2 October.[139] Maybe Picasso decided he had tortured Penrose enough; maybe he could not resist the temptation to look at Hartmann's new projections showing how the metal head, enlarged to the right scale, would look in front of the Chicago skyscraper. No significant progress was made during the reunion, but at least friendly communications had been restored.

Less than two months later Penrose paid the first of two critically important visits to Notre-Dame-de-Vie. The first page of his notebook indicates that Françoise Gilot's book was still a source of anxiety because it contains the draft of a short and brutal note to her, evidently written with the intention of putting paid once and for all to the rumours of his 'infidelity':

Dear F.

I feel obliged to tell you how much I despise you for the way you are exploiting your 'Life' with Picasso. I should not have thought you capable of such flagrant lies.

R.P.[140] [39]

Elsewhere there is the following record of a conversation with Leiris:

Michel Leiris[141]
Françoise's stories nearly all very untrue. Eluard-Fougeron story happened in Eluard's apartment with Dora [and] Michel present. Paul, after a v. amicable meal using V[ictor] Hugo's glasses for first time, suddenly became v. angry and nearly hit Dora on head with chair – v. ashamed and apologetic after, but for 2 months there was a break between him & Picasso.[142]
   No need to moralise – tackle the book. […]

Book falsifies conversations and gives inaccurate accounts of events. Story about Michel riding a bicycle & insulting police pure fabrication.[143] Others unscrupulous distortions.

Michel present at meeting between P. & Matisse, rue des Gds. Augustins and again in the chapel at Vence – in both cases an extraordinary quiet politeness & respect between them – more remarkable for what was not said, but understood, than that which was said. Physically so different – M. older, bearded, glasses. P. small athlete.

Their [Gilot's detractors'] loyalty to P. may have exaggerated the high moral tone of their statements, but it is the authenticity of the statements attributed to P. that is important, and here there is overwhelming evidence that the truth is so often pitiably distorted that no confidence can be given to the conversations of which she was the sole witness. [40]

During the winter of 1964–65 Picasso's entourage was in the grip of collective hysteria as the shock waves caused by Gilot's intimate revelations gathered momentum in the aftermath of the publication of the American edition. Stirred up by Hélène Parmelin, the artist's supporters hastened to rally round him publicly, signing open letters denouncing the book as a pack of lies and petitions to have the French translation banned.[144] Needless to say, these panic measures merely served to inflame press and public curiosity and boost sales in the bookshops. Inevitably, Penrose was pestered for his opinion by British journalists and when he did attack the book in a radio interview he followed Leiris's advice quite closely.[145] Later, when he came to write about the episode in the revised edition of *Picasso: His Life and Work*, he made it plain that he regarded the book as both disloyal and in the worst possible taste, but again focused mainly on Gilot's lack of credibility.[146] For her part, Françoise was lastingly grieved by Penrose's hostility: singling him out among the crowd who shunned her, she noted sadly that he had been 'a very dear friend of mine too'.[147]

Although Penrose's visit to Notre-Dame-de-Vie in November 1964 took place in the dark shadow cast by the Gilot affair, his main preoccupations lay elsewhere and his notes candidly record the often rather hollow arguments he used as he tried to persuade Picasso to give in on first one, then the next, and finally the third of the three outstanding issues that had bedevilled their relationship for so long. His back against the wall, Picasso stubbornly restated his right to be left alone to get on with the work he wanted to do in the short time he had left. The simple justice of this claim, expressed with great dignity, was unanswerable and a less determined negotiator than Penrose would have given up and left 'the old devil' alone. But, sustained by a quasi-religious conviction in the rightness of his mission, Penrose could be quite as intractable as Picasso – soaking up the punishment with a martyr's fortitude and sticking resolutely to his agenda. As he noted in a rueful aside, it was a psychological battle and in the end he proved the stronger of the two because he was, in these particular matters, the more single-minded. Picasso was strongly tempted to say no to all three proposals, but he was also strongly tempted to say yes. Being in two minds, he was defeatable, and on the second day of this latest visit to Mougins Penrose made his breakthrough. He deserved his victory, but one must feel some sympathy for Picasso, under constant siege from his dozens of suitors. On this occasion, for example, Pierre Daix was also present and he too had an 'axe to grind':

Mougins Sat 28 Nov. '64
Pierre Daix had brought his new book on P.[148]

R[oland]. 'Je suis venu malgré l'avis de Kahnweiler parce que je sais que tu changes d'avis même rapidement.'
   P. 'Ah non, j'ai un grand plan très determiné dans l'indecision.'[149]
   On the three questions, Chicago, Tate and Sculpture Ex[hibition], I got no encouragement.
   Chicago – he has made no progress but is still interested – so he says.
   Tate – said he had thought of giving it but now thinks that would be wrong. I said we would pay and needed it v. much – all the more so since Cézanne, since [the] purchase of '[Les] Grandes Baigneuses', is now well represented.[150] Talked for some time about its [*The Three Dancers*'] merits – he said some people had told him they preferred it to 'Les Demoiselles' – in fact, it is more complete in composition and conception. We looked at a bad colour repro[duction] together. I said it would really bring great pleasure to many in London. He said, 'Ça, quand même est bien, si ça les fera plaisir.'[151] He said he didn't know where it was. I said I had seen it stacked at La Calif[ornie] with all the others after [the] London show. He, 'It must then still be there.'

Ex[hibition]. 'Ça m'interesse pas. Ce qui m'interesse c'est de faire les sculptures – les exposer m'interesse pas. Que vous faites ce que vous voulez, avec Barr ou sans lui, je ne veux pas qu'on me dérange. Je veux travailler et qu'on me laisse tranquille.'[152]

I told him I would, but that we all wanted an exhibition – since I was not capable of making his sculpture, I felt the need to work on an exhibition.

[Picasso] 'Oui, tu as raison de travailler à ça – tu aime travailler a ça parce que c'est difficile – très difficile.'

[Penrose] 'C'est vrai, mais je ne suis pas un masochiste – si je n'ai pas de cooperation je l'abandonne.'[153]

Ask. 'Prête nous "3 danseuses" – "Guernica" prêté. Pourquoi favoriser U.S.?
Tu m'as aider avec les dessins et des toiles – pourquoi pas la sculpture?
Dessins, il fallait chercher toiles. Tres compliqué. "Meninas", etc.'[154]

[Picasso] 'Dans le temps à Mougins il y avait Eluard & N[usch], Dora, toi et ta femme. On avait le temps, on se baignait, on mangeait, on visité les boite de nuit, on parlé, on se promenait et on travaillait et il y avait le temps. Maintenant c'est tout different. On a le temps pour rien. Tout est pressé.'[155]

'Nous sommes tous pressés aujourdhui. Moi je n'ai plus la patience,' – looking at a repro. of etching Blind man & woman. 'Je me mettrerai à faire ça aujourdhui et je m'ennouierai vite. Il faut que je travaille rapidment.'[156]

[Penrose] 'But it can always be said that you have spent all your life doing it, even if it took only 5 minutes.'

'Oui, mais ce n'est pas la même chose maintenent. On est pressé. On vie son travail. Dans le temps on l'executé. Les peintres executé un travail. Les choses vont de plus en plu vite et on a de moins en moin de temps. Ça finira par un explosion.'[157]

Pierre Daix asked him to do something for 100 years of [Miguel de] Unamuno. He took idea seriously then said, 'U. est un homme qui a fait beaucoup de bien – a dit des choses bien et des choses mal. Je ne voudrais pas m'associer avec lui parce que je ne sais pas si je pense du bien ou du mal de lui.'[158]

It was a bad day for both of us in spite of the fact that we had both been welcomed without hesitation. I could feel his (P.D.)'s resentment for my presence and I expect he felt the same for me.

J. was charming and more non-commital than ever. Lee's presence would have helped. The difference is that before I had no axe to grind and now I've got a hundredweight of axes and no idea how to grind them. The battle is so deeply psychological. The old devil cannot give in – he must torment both friends and enemies – perhaps friends most. His parting words, after having asked for my address, were, 'Alors c'est bien, on peut se telephoner demain.'[159]

Let's see.

29 Nov.
Things started better – the rain had cleared & a light mistral was clearing the sky – P. & J. were there alone – the dog did not try to bite my bottom as it had yesterday. P. began – saying if we were keen on '3 D[ancer]s' he would sell it us for the £80,000 offered.

P.D. arrives and I have a long look on my own at the small bronzes & Chicago head. In v. good humour we talk about C[hicago] project & sculpture. I say I have noticed he loves his sculpture more than his painting – won't part with it. P., 'Oui c'est vrai – les autres n'aiment pas, mais moi, oui.'[160] I protest it's because they are not known that they are not appreciated. But – one success at a time – I let the ex. drop for the present and, with some encouraging remarks about the C. head, that also.

We go upstairs to see his latest paintings. Theme Painter & Model, much simplified – very new in style & colour.[161] Faces [with an] X., pinks pale & sensitive, pale greens & some ochre, blacks. Many v. slight & lovely. Two much worked on, large upright canvases, v. grand.[162] Artist & Model closely united on a level.

Went down to big new studio – several earlier versions in pinks & greens – one very comic – irate model w. head of frightened painter.[163] Several heads of p[ainter] much worked on set against lightly painted model – mysterious balance between solid architecture of head and vaporous tender description of model. Brilliant use of signs to indicate key parts of human form – female sex – eyes – breasts – hands – faces. Both sign painting and realist.

After sitting quietly surrounded by some 30 or more paintings of all sizes – immersed – exchanging a few words here and there – P. says, 'Leve-toi, il y a une autre peinture dehors,' giving me a hand.[164] I get up and look out at a sunset in pink and green – like the pictures.

I'm alarmed at the crossed-out faces [*sketch of face crossed through with X*]. It looks like a negation of the face – perhaps himself – or, better, it looks like the eternal mark, the affirmation, signature of even the illiterate, X.[165]

We go downstairs to find J. and sit round the table talking. P.D. has a lot to say about Aragon, whom he dislikes. He [Daix] is editor of 'Lettres Françaises' and knows a lot. P. signs copies of his new book – all v. friendly and warm.

I leave happy. [39]

That 'I leave happy' is typically understated. But Penrose's description of the quiet afternoon spent looking at Picasso's latest pictures and then at the sunset painting the sky with the same pinks and greens is one of the most moving passages in all his notebooks. One senses that for him it must have been a moment of profound peace and resolution – perhaps even a moment of Quaker 'inner light'.

That evening Penrose relayed the wonderful news about *The Three Dancers* to Colin Anderson, the Chairman of the Tate Trustees, who had shared all the emotional highs and lows of the long adventure and was able to sympathise fully with his elation. Apart from any other consideration, the picture had been acquired for a bargain price – perhaps a third of its current market value. In an enthusiastic letter of thanks and congratulations, Anderson joked, 'I am thinking of calling it the Penrose Dancers – on the analogy of the Rokeby Venus & the Elgin Marbles. Do you mind!?'[166] It would, of course, have been most imprudent to relax or procrastinate: Picasso was quite capable of a sudden volte-face and both men went into action immediately on Penrose's return to England. Anderson sent an official letter to Picasso confirming the deal and a cheque for half the total amount of £80,000 followed in the new year. Meanwhile, as he had promised, Penrose sent off photographs of all the Picassos the Tate Gallery owned already or had on long-term loan, remarking in his accompanying letter that the deficiencies of the collection were all too obvious but that *The Three Dancers* would go a great way to remedying the situation.[167]

The priority was to transport the painting to London with the minimum delay and on 29 January 1965 Penrose arrived in Mougins to finalise arrangements. Lee accompanied him on this triumphant visit and in one of her photographs Picasso, looking extraordinarily youthful and energetic, stands beside Roland, headmasterish in his horn-rimmed spectacles, tweed jacket and grey flannel bags. The two wives, screened from their husbands by the painting, giggle girlishly over a secret joke. This was Lee's way of subverting the solemnity of the occasion, which for Roland had the profound significance of a treaty negotiated between two world powers, and for her – and no doubt also for Jacqueline – spelled the end of a debilitating trial of strength.

During their visit Penrose discussed the great picture at length with Picasso and the original notebook report proves to be fuller, as well as more vivid, than the well-known published version. Part of that compelling sense of immediacy comes from Picasso's stray, mostly complimentary comments about Winston Churchill, whose state funeral he had been avidly watching on the television.[168] The funeral awakened potent memories of the war and hence a reflective state of mind, which is perhaps why he was more forthcoming than usual about the origins of his painting and the anguished feelings expressed in *The Three Dancers*. Penrose also looked closely at Picasso's most recent paintings with Kahnweiler and the Leirises and his perceptive remarks reveal that he not only admired their shockingly brutal, hasty style and child-like, raw technique but was also sensitive to the surprising beauty and delicacy of their colour harmonies. Without this ready understanding of the subtler qualities of the late work, he would not have

succeeded in persuading Picasso to sell *The Three Dancers*, nor would he have retained his place within the shrinking circle of Picasso's intimates:

29 Jan. '65 Mougins[169]

P. said he had received cheque for 1½ dancers but had not cashed it. I saw the envelope in which it must have come lying on the floor of his studio – perhaps with cheque still inside. He said he had no desire for the price to be known to the public and would keep it secret. He was very interested in imagining the reactions of the British public and how it would be hung. He did not want it framed with anything more than the baguette it has now. I assured him it would be given a place of honour on a plain background and well lit.

Lee Miller, Jacqueline Picasso, Roland Penrose and Pablo Picasso beside *The Three Dancers* at Notre-Dame-de-Vie, Mougins, January 1965. Photo Lee Miller

29 Jan. '65–31 Jan.
'Pendant que je peignais ce tableau un ami est mort, Ramon Pichot, et je pense plutôt que ça doit s'appeler "La Mort de Pichot" que "Les Trois Danseuses".'[170]
(Pichot was a Spanish painter who lived in Paris.)

Talking of Churchill's funeral:
'Après tout c'est une drôle de chose la chair – d'être construit en chair – imagine une maison fait de chair – ça ne durera pas longtemps.'[171]

He showed us a great many early paintings and a whole stack of splendid pictures including Cézanne – 'Château Noir'. (He said this was to him the most wonderful of all.) Cézanne 'L'Estaque', Matisse 'Still life' of Algeria period (he said Matisse wept he was so pleased when he heard P. had bought it), Matisse 'Portrait of Marguerite', early flower piece, Modigliani portrait, Braque 1910 still life, Le Nain group of peasants.[172]

3 Dancers
I said I had been looking for other pictures like it and had found only the 'Crucifixion'.[173]
P. said, 'Non, il n'y a pas d'autres qui le resemble – aucun. "La Crucifixion", oui, il y a quelque chose, mais c'est le seul et c'est très différent.'[174]
J. thought she had seen some drawings – he said no.
Probably painted after visit to Monte Carlo but nothing to do with ballet.[175]

Talking of Churchill, I said:
'Quand même nous l'aimons bien parce qu'il a sauvé l'Angleterre.'
P. 'L'Angleterre et bien plus – c'est il a sauvé nous tous.'[176]

Next day – he had been listening to the funeral, etc. and continued to admire – 'Malgré il a dit qu'il voudrait me donner un coup de pied dans le cul je l'admire. J'aurais du lui jeter mon gant pour faire un duel mais non – Il aura pu gagner sa vie comme peintre malgré que c'était banal ce qu'il faisait.'[177]
In fact P. was much more gracious and appreciative of C. than C. had been of him.

I said, 'One can see the beginnings of "Guernica" in "3 Dancers".'
P. 'Peut-être mais des deux tableaux je prefère de beaucoup les "3 D". C'est peint comme un tableau sans arrière-pensée.'[178]

I asked how it was he had not sold it until now.
P. 'Parce que je ne voulais pas. On m'a demandé cent fois le vendre – des Américains, Kahnweiler et bien d'autres mais j'ai toujours refusé. […] D'ailleurs c'est la *première fois* que je vends un tableau à un Musée directement.'[179]

Sunday

Kahnweiler, Jardot, Michel & Zette [Leiris]. Showed us more than 100 paintings of all sizes, all painted within last year, mostly since my last visit in Nov.

'Ce que je fais maintenant c'est détruire la peinture moderne – on a déjà détruit la peinture ancienne et maintenant il faut détruire la moderne.'[180]

In fact it's very difficult to describe what he has done. As K. said: 'Voici la peinture naive – la vrai,' while he was repeating: 'Ça c'est le réalisme espagnol, c'est moi qui le fait parce que j'ai toujours mon passeport espagnol et il n'y a que les Espagnols qui ont su faire du réalisme. Les Français, les Italiens, les Allemands ils on fait d'autre chose mais le réalisme est aux Espagnols.'[181]

Roland Penrose, Michel Leiris, Maurice Jardot, Daniel-Henry Kahnweiler and Picasso at Notre-Dame-de-Vie, Mougins, 1965 or 1966. Photo Lee Miller

Total mastery

There is no formula, no rule, no trick that counts any longer. He has arrived at such complete mastery of his material that it behaves miraculously, as he wants, in a thousand different ways – brush, knife, drip, smear, lines broad, thin, untouched areas of canvas, dripping wet paint, dots – all with no apparent effort play their part in the picture. Never before has he used such freedom and achieved such freshness. There is always a subject – Painter and model,[182] Nude,[183] Heads (male and female),[184] Nude girl with cat,[185] Cat and lobster,[186] Kings and Queens of La Fête des Rois.[187] One very small landscape of the view from his windows by night, painted with several others, of Xmas eve.[188]

He has invented a new way of making a face. Earlier versions were based on a double nose, line drawn with a broad brush, like two intertwining ribands of different colours, like the snakes of Mercury's wand, with sometimes a narrow central line. Later this became a broad St. Andrew's cross, with central nose line and dots for eyes drawn on top. This strange negation or affirmation of a face becomes remarkably 3-dimensional.[189] Colour is often extremely subtle: pale pink, ochre, olive green, pale blue, pink like the floor tiles, ochre like the outside walls; the gentleness of these colours is balanced by strong accents of black and grey. There are other nudes in strong colours, rich reds and yellows dominate. Instead of the nude giving feeling of a landscape it is more like a gorgeous cornucopia with strong circular rhythms.

A large canvas of man playing trombone or trumpet to sleeping nude. Strong yellow and red background. Nude like vaporous winter sky – pale blue and transparent white clouds. Heads of intense realism by new methods – you feel sure you know each person, their characters are strong and candid – rugged, healthy.[190] Sometimes the means are so slight that one marvels at the completeness of the painting – a few pink circles, a profile, black eye and hair and it is a nude, as luscious as any Renoir.

Female sex appears often like a tree growing from a black hole – the earth – a symbol and realism together.[191]

He said to K., 'You have written often about my painting – to describe those you will be obliged to find new words.'

Many artists use all sorts of means to arrive at a charming sensation of abstract colour, etc., but with P. the result is the startling presence of human beings – faces alive with expression and deep feeling.

'Et ce n'est jamais de la caricature,'[192] Michel.

P. & Freud & Leonardo

'Freud n'aurait pas de mal a trouver des symboles dans ces tableaux – comme il a trouvé le vautour dans Léonard – [ici] (montrant une grande tache griffonné dans une toile à l'envers) il y en a partout.'[193] [...]

Penrose's notes of their conversation about *The Three Dancers* continue:

P. 'Enfin si je le vends aux anglais c'est à cause de toi – et s'ils désirent l'avoir, c'est toi qui l'a fait.'
R. 'Non, ça c'est impossible, c'est *toi* qui l'a fait.'[194]

R. 'When looking at the great picture "Les Baigneuses" in the P[eggy] Gug[genheim] collection,[195] I wondered why the two women should be concentrating so intensely on a toy boat, and then remembered the slice of melon at the feet of the "Demoiselles d'A[vignon]". Delighted at this parallel between the two.'

P. looked at me surprised and as though I was reproaching him, 'Mais oui, mais on se repète des fois malgré tout.'[196]

I hurried to assure him that I was delighted to find this reference to a symbol which could be Harlequin's hat, the crescent moon at the feet of the Virgin and also the Egyptian ship, symbol of the voyage to other worlds.

P. 'Oui, si tu veux c'est tout ça mais tu feras l'interprétation que tu veux, tu diras ce que tu veux, ça m'est égal.'[197]

I was surprised to see so clearly in his reaction how little he is conscious of the symbols, archetypes, that are so clearly present in his work. They arrive spontaneously, he is never consciously creating symbols. Free of this calculation, which debases the work of so many, he uses archetypes just as primitive people do – with unconscious conviction, and it is for this reason that they are so right and profound. Once the symbol is used consciously it is impoverished in its impact, the hard intellectual crust that we allow to form stifles the direct instinctive use of forms and shapes of archetypal significance. P. has remained an innocent miraculously in spite of his great knowledge and understanding. Never has he painted anything for its symbolic value. He has painted to give us an image of reality.

From Brassaï: 'L'art est le langage des signes.' 'Mais on n'invente pas un signe. Il faut fortement viser à la ressemblance pour aboutir au signe.'[198]

What attracted P. to surrealism was the idea of a reality beyond form and colour, in which things present themselves. Nothing is calculated, nothing is gratuitous in his present work.

R.P. Notes on visit to Picasso 29–31 Jan. 1965 [41]

In February Penrose sent Colin Anderson a tidied-up, English-language version of his notes for publication in the next *Tate Gallery Report*.[199] The following passages amplify the original notebook version:

[…] I asked if it [*The Three Dancers*] were connected with his visit to Monte

Carlo the same year when he had done so many drawings of the ballet.

Picasso: 'No, that has nothing to do with it.'

He was not certain but it seems likely that it was painted in Paris after his return from Monte Carlo. [...]

I said the central window with blue sky or sea beyond and the red patch which suggests a mountainous coastline, such as the Esterel, reminded me of the still life compositions of St. Raphaël, 1919.[200] Picasso reminded me that there were several others of the same kind painted in Paris.[201]

I examined closely the cracks in the paint on the left side, specially round the head of the dancer. Noticing my interest Picasso said, 'The paint is solid enough and will not flake off. Some people might want to touch them out but I think they add to the painting. On the face you see how they reveal the eye that was painted underneath.' I said I thought it much better to leave them as they are, and he agreed emphatically. We agreed that the painting was in splendid condition, it was only his signature that was lacking. He said he would sign it but had not yet decided just where or how it should be done, but historically it was necessary it should be signed.[202]

Such was Penrose's enthusiasm for Picasso's late work that he wondered if it was not the artist's supreme accomplishment – a 'late style' on a par with that of such great geniuses as Michelangelo, Titian and Rembrandt. This emerges from a letter he wrote to Herbert Read just after getting back to England. Read had asked him to vet an encyclopaedia entry on Picasso he had just drafted, and the only thing Penrose found fault with was the treatment of the recent work:

It is impossible to make a clear assessment of the importance of this mass of work at the present time, but what I regret in your piece is the feeling that the late years are a diminuendo. It is too soon to say, but I have a feeling that they are the great achievement of his life, and that they tackle with extraordinary freshness the problems of *painting*.[203]

And in his follow-up letter to Picasso, Penrose reiterated his admiration for this latest 'fantastic flowering':

I am full of wonder at the absence now of any barrier between you and your work. It seems to be an immediate expression that has lost nothing by way of significance or freshness in the process of creation.

His main purpose in writing was, however, to announce that the Tate was ready to receive *The Three Dancers* and that every precaution was being taken to insure its safety in the wake of the ink-bombing of the Leonardo Cartoon, purchased for the National Gallery in 1962 for £800,000.[204] Possibly Penrose really did fear vandalism for he cannot have believed his own stories about the British public's ardent desire to own the painting. Possibly he simply wanted to flatter Picasso by the comparison with Leonardo and the titillating prospect of a public scandal, for Picasso did not relish his status as an institution no longer capable of surprising or shocking. In any case, for Penrose the buzz created by the arrival of *The Three Dancers* in London brought back delightful memories of the furore surrounding the opening of the 1960 retrospective and he revelled in the drama, writing ebulliently to Mougins a week later to describe the wild speculation in the press about the price the Tate had paid.[205]

On 9 March there was something more substantial to pass on – the attack, launched in Parliament, by Lady Summerskill:

Dear Pablo,

As I promised to keep you informed of the British reaction to 'The Three Dancers' I must tell you of the attack made on it last week by a female Lord. (You see how democracy and feminism attack us and even the sacred realms of male aristocracy are now invaded by petticoats.) At least it was an ennobled petticoat, Lady Summerskill, who fulminated furiously against your picture in the House of Lords, demanding to know why the Government had allowed one or two 'idiosyncratic' persons to waste public money on such monstrosities, when hospitals were in dire need of operating theatres.

I was asked, without prior warning, to confront this lady on the television and we spent five minutes in aggressive altercation, listened to by an enormous audience because it was at six o'clock in the evening. Since then I've been inundated with letters that remind me of the good old days when retired colonels came to brandish their umbrellas and spit on modern art. All this was more than counterbalanced by a crowd of very enthusiastic friends. It's wonderful that your work leaves no one indifferent. Even English phlegm dissipates before your miraculous, southern assault.

Any minute now I shall be sending you a photo of the installation in the gallery, and I assure you that the attacks of ignoramuses like this poor lady are in no way representative of the general reception of your picture.[206]

The spat with Lady Summerskill was profoundly satisfying to Penrose. It proved that *The Three Dancers* was as disturbing and provocative in 1965 as it had been in 1925 – that it was an authentically revolutionary painting. The outrage articulated by the philistine establishment proved that Britain needed this challenge as much as it had needed the Surrealist exhibition in 1936. An impassioned response, albeit a hostile one, was as stimulating as an electric charge, providing Penrose with the impetus to push on with his two other, still outstanding Picasso projects.

Chapter 7

Picasso Sculptor, 1965–1967

The Chicago monument: second phase

With his reputation as 'The Picasso Man' Penrose was often solicited for contributions to the growing stream of publications on Picasso, just as he was often in demand as a lecturer, and before turning his attention to his two great, unfinished sculptural projects he despatched a couple of much lighter tasks. The first involved writing the introduction for the English translation of Brassaï's *Conversations avec Picasso*.[1] Penrose had known the photographer for many years but because he had been doing something similar himself was especially keen to learn about Brassaï's method for recording his conversations with Picasso. The two men met in Paris early in 1965:

Brassaï
Book began as a box. Made notes on scraps of paper and threw them in – sometimes entry was insufficient to recall whole conversation in early days – but technique improved – listened to other people's conversations in a café where he could write unseen – useless to write daily journal without becoming self-conscious.

Wrote as he takes photos. 'You don't invent in a photo – you must observe, remain objective and select.'

Knew P. since '32 – did not take notes then.[2]

The content of Brassaï's diary of his meetings with Picasso must have enthralled Penrose since the period covered in most depth – 1943–1947 – predated the years of his greatest intimacy with the artist, and part of that time coincided with the very period when he was forcibly cut off from contact with Paris. Penrose's introduction was generous and sympathetic and the qualities he singled out in the book were those that he himself aspired to both as witness and biographer. Thus he praised Brassaï for his self-effacing determination to transmit truthfully what he had seen and heard:

Brassaï knows from his own experience that in photography you don't invent. You observe, select, and above all remain objective, and for this we are

particularly indebted to him. […] Thanks to Brassaï we live in the anteroom of inspiration and are given a taste of the stimulants needed for the fecundation of Picasso's genius.[3]

It did not, I am sure, ever occur to Penrose that one day his own bundles of Picasso notebooks would be valued for their candour and ransacked for their revelations.

The second commission for a short essay on Picasso's sculpture fitted perfectly with his main preoccupations.[4] Penrose was able to draw on the experience of looking closely at the huge army of works massed in the vaulted downstairs rooms at Notre-Dame-de-Vie, and composing the essay allowed him to formulate certain ideas about the place of sculpture in Picasso's life and oeuvre and thus prepare himself for the more demanding job of selecting the Arts Council exhibition and, eventually, writing the catalogue. It was a happy coincidence that Brassaï's memoirs should come out at precisely this moment since Brassaï had specialised in photographing Picasso's sculpture, first in Boisgeloup in December 1932, then in the rue des Grands-Augustins studio during the Occupation. Moreover, many of his most revealing conversations with Picasso had revolved around sculpture – both Picasso's own and also the prehistoric and tribal sculpture which was often its inspiration. His book was therefore an invaluable adjunct to Penrose's own first-hand observations.

Having completed these two short essays in March 1965, Penrose pressed on with the Chicago project. This time Picasso raised no objection to his and Hartmann's request for a meeting:

Cannes. 23 Ap. '65
Called at Mougins with Lee, Hartmann. Found P. & J. alone and v. warm welcome. Lee had brought shells as present and he showed his usual excitement at the astonishing perfection and invention of nature.

'C'est à vous faire desesperer de la peint[u]re. Personne ne peut faire mieux que ça – et lui non plus il n'aura pas pu faire mieux et il n'aura pas pu faire la sourire de la Gioconde non plus – ça nous console un peut.'[5]
He enjoyed the shells as a child who had never seen such things before.

Pierre Gaut, the collector, was there when we arrived and left soon after. He had brought a still life of '41 to be signed. (It was he who exchanged the house at Mougins for a painting.)[6] P. went off to sign and came back with the painting, saying he had looked for the right place to sign and found he had signed it already. By a curious trick in colour contrast it was hardly visible. He was intrigued by finding he wanted to sign just where he had decided to sign it 24 years ago – about halfway up the right-hand side.[7]

We did not stay long. He had some business that bored him to do. He asked us to come back for lunch next day.

There was some talk about Françoise [Gilot]'s book but neither P. [n]or J. seemed worried.[8]

Asked P. about my interpretation of the Minotaur as Sculptor in him.[9] He approved and said, 'Yes it might be interesting to follow through those characters in my work.'

Sat. 24 Ap.
Went up to N. de V. with H[artmann]. Found Mme. Gris there.[10] Nesjar arrived soon after. Went down to lunch at La Voile au Vent in the port. Nothing had been said so far about the major subject on our minds – the Chicago Monument. The presence of Nesjar was ambiguous. H. was not keen on having another of his concrete figures, made from his version of a small paper figure, but he [Nesjar] seemed to be in full agreement with P. and had at once shown him photos of large figures for Amsterdam and Stockholm. It turned out he had no idea he was going to find us there and H. decided to bring him in if necessary on the Chicago figure, but insisted it must be in bronze. [42]

On 30 April they called again at Notre-Dame-de-Vie and this time real progress was made:

Cannes 30 April '65 [Added later] *Chicago Monument with Hartmann*
'Would you like it to be put outdoors?' Jacqueline asked, while P. was still engrossed with Charles Feld looking at the first copy of H[élène] P[armelin]'s second volume.[11] Cars were moved and a space prepared outside the front door, where the table with four cross-legs could be placed on the level to receive the newly made cylinder, some four foot high, and on top was placed the head which had been conceived more than a year before, making in three pieces a monument about ten foot high. B[ill] H[artmann] calculated the orientation so that the sun lighted it as it would at midday in its intended site in Chicago, but instead of skyscrapers its setting was olive trees and the low stone wall of P.'s studio.

The head now looked dignified and imposing on the bare iron cylinder that supported it, but, in spite of our enthusiasm at seeing it set up high and in full sunlight, there was a bleakness and a monumental detachment about the head.

P. arrived asking us at once what we thought and making enquiries about the scale in comparison to its final background.[12] Fortunately, the model was found and he at once noticed that a square patch of water coincided with the site for the sculpture. We looked up at the figure from all angles as it rocked gently in the breeze. Marius & Jean[13] stood by watching. Taking a chip of wood cut to the scale of the model, P. placed it in the patch of water saying, 'That's where it should go,' and from that moment things began to happen. 'It needs arms,' said P., applying a small piece of wood to the cylinder, 'go and get some pieces of wood.' Jean & Marius disappeared in different directions, and return[ed] each with a long shaft of scrap wood – as though by premeditation, the pieces turn out to be very much alike in measurements.

P. has them held against [the] cylinder. They tuck under the neck of the head and protrude against the bare table-top at the sides. The effect is obviously an improvement. The cylinder is no longer a rather clumsy base to a head, with no real connection, it has become a body. And the table, which before was not part of the scheme, now became crossed legs or a transparent support – an aerial female sex for the body – the metamorphosis had happened. It was no longer a monumental head placed out of reach on a giant column, but a whole body rising from the water.

All illuminated with this new idea, went to lunch at the Voile au Vent. As we got into the car saying we were hungry P. picks up dog's old bone, pretends to gnaw, and then holds it as a continuation of his nose. J. protests.

We pointed to the new lamps some 8 m. high round the port and told P. the finished sculpture would be taller. On the way he said, 'On va travailler toute à l'heure – travailler c'est ça que je peut toujours faire et c'est ça qui me plaît.'[14] A communion of thought enveloped us and throughout lunch we continually returned to the height of skyscrapers, comparative sizes, etc. (One tired remark only escaped from him – talking of wigs, 'Les femmes mettent des perruques pour que les autres les voir changer moi je voudrais en mettre pas pour les autres mais me voir moi même.')[15]

Back at N.D. the pieces had been taken in. We proceeded to set them up by the parrot cage, surrounded by books, chairs, tables, papers on [the] floor – an [in]describable mixture. Cross-legged table, cylinder, head – the arms had to be supported on piles of books from below – and surface of water indicated by sheets of crinkly paper halfway up legs. P. disappears and comes back with a hand drawn on a piece of white paper, which he cuts out and pins to bottom of right arm so that fingertips come down to level of water. We discuss how to fix them. 'On doit les fixer du haut et les laisser balancer dans le vent si c'est possible mais probablement que non.'[16] He asks B.H. often about structure, and as soon as he is sure it is reasonably possible he says, 'Eh bien ça c'est l'affaire de vous ingénieurs – si ils peuvent faire des gratteciels ils peuvent faire ceci.' And, 'Il sera possible maintenant de faire ce sculpture par telephone, je pourrais le telephoner à Chicago avec tous les dimensions exactes – n'est-ce pas?'[17]

We examine it again from all angles – try out the sister version on a shorter cylinder, look at it in the mirror, photograph it – discuss effect on Chicago government. B.H. says it will now be harder to get [it] accepted, but it's worth it – it's now more alive, more of a great presence. Water round it [an] excellent idea, isolates, frames, reflects.

Mons[ieur] Thiola the metalworker has been summoned.[18] He arrives and P. explains how he wants arms and table made up, tells him size of finished figure. Mons. Thiola lights up with joy, talks about techniques, bronze, copper, steel with copper covering, thinks it feasible, takes measures – shown model – goes away delighted, saying he'll have it all ready tomorrow. P. has inspired and transformed him by getting him to work for him – skilled craftsman, now P.'s associate – refuses to be paid. He takes away arms, hand

and drawings of table. We leave soon after – I cancel my reservation for next morning, prepared to stay a day or two longer.

Talking about commissions, P. said he had never accepted one, but this was not first time he had started on a project for Chicago. Once, about 1911, a rich man from Chicago had asked him to do mural paintings for his library. P. had done quite a lot of work and then abandoned it all – the preliminary paintings must be somewhere among his things, but more likely lost.[19] [43]

The following day they all foregathered once again at Notre-Dame-de-Vie:

Sat. 1st May 1.0 N. D. de V.
Ch[arles] & J. Feld & Jacqueline sit round waiting for P., who was asleep till 2.30. Talked about Françoise.
3.15 lunch in kitchen.
Presents of tiles given to each.
Long talk round table in Salon – cows, etc.[20] V. good humour.
P. signs lithos for Feld.
6.30 Felds – Jacqueline – Hartmann & me go to see Thiola at Vallauris.
Find he has finished arms and would have all ready tomorrow [at] noon.
Got back to N.D. de V. Set up arms.
P. asks nervously our opinions.
Leave 8.0. [44]

Intoxicating though it had been to play with alterations to the Chicago sculpture, photographs taken of the head mounted on its abstract torso and with its hanging arms show an outlandish contraption, in comparison to which the original maquette looks irrefutable in its iconic but mysterious simplicity. Picasso had enjoyed the game as much as anyone but by the time Penrose and Hartmann left Mougins the maquette had quietly been restored to its original state and the decision taken to place it directly on the ground, supported only by a low plinth, where 'it would be more accessible, more in touch with the people who were to live with it and its sheer height rising from the pavement of the piazza itself would become all the more impressive'.[21] The final visit Penrose and Hartmann paid to Notre-Dame-de-Vie was uneventful. The notes record snippets of conversation and describe the drawings of fantasy-buildings Picasso had brought out to show them:

P. architect. 2 May '65
Produced a sketchbook, May 1958, of drawings for large apartment houses, 12 storeys & more. Like monument sculptures, with curved surfaces, terraces, etc. on stilts.[22]
    'Why shouldn't we use curved surfaces for walls.'
    'I should like to make houses from inside – like a human body, not just walls with no thought of what they enclose.' 'There was an architect here who

built a big house and forgot the doors – he had only thought of the outside appearance.'

'Although Einstein enjoyed painting, he did not understand what I am doing any more than I can understand his mathematics. There are only chance encounters where we meet and understand that "au fond c'est la même chose".'[23]

'People don't understand what a line means – when you start drawing a line you don't know where it's going to go – it starts and goes on until something stops it or makes it turn. It is wonderful, the growth of a line, as you trace it, but people don't think of it like that. They say, "Oh, I like that", or "Isn't it pretty?" but never follow it with the excitement it can give. "Isn't that pretty?" is everybody's own personal opinion. It's too easy.'

Life is not so much in matter itself as in the form it gives to it. [45]

On his return to England Penrose composed a four-page text describing the history of the project and sent it off to Chicago, giving Hartmann a free hand to 'cut it, alter it, tear it up, just as you think fit'.[24] There was little further he could usefully do: he had brought the two parties together and succeeded, at long last, in overcoming Picasso's resistance; the maquette for the monument had been chosen and a replica despatched to Chicago.[25] It was now up to the Chicagoans to find a means of enlarging it that Picasso would find acceptable. The moment had come for Penrose to focus his energies on the last of his grand Picasso schemes – the one that meant most to him personally.

The sculpture exhibition: obstacles and setbacks

Hitherto Picasso had remained impervious to all attempts to win his approval of a comprehensive retrospective of his sculpture and now, just when Penrose was preparing to reopen the campaign on behalf both of the Arts Council and the Museum of Modern Art, an unexpected development threatened to dash his hopes. Kahnweiler, who had promised Penrose and Barr his full support, wrote to warn them that it had been decided to include sculpture in the vast retrospective being planned by the French State to honour Picasso on his eighty-fifth birthday. Barr immediately communicated his fears to Penrose: they had had the idea years before the French, but would this carry any weight with Picasso, and would he lend his sculpture to London and New York as well?[26] Penrose's response was characteristically pragmatic: rather than repine about being upstaged, he attempted to make the new situation work to their advantage. Together they quickly reached the conclusion that they must, in Barr's words, 'try and hitch our exhibition on to this Paris show',[27] and when they learned that Jean Leymarie had been appointed curator of the French exhibition they both felt much more optimistic.[28] Leymarie was a good friend and, unlike some fellow professionals, could be counted on to help rather than hinder them. The great difficulty would be convincing Picasso to allow his beloved sculptures out of his sight for so long and finding the right moment to press him would be crucial.

The next obstacle was of a different order and potentially posed a greater threat. Penrose had intended to visit Mougins with Hartmann in the autumn, but on 6 October 1965 he received a telegram to say that 'les Picasso' could not see them because they were 'fleeing Cannes'.[29] No reason was given but the motive was in fact illness brought on by the stress occasioned by the humiliating revelations in Gilot's book, the fiasco of the failed court case and the ceaseless press speculation and criticism. Tainted by association with their mother, Claude and Paloma, who had seen very little of their father for several years, were now effectively banned from Notre-Dame-de-Vie – a source of additional trauma, even though Picasso put on a good show of remorseless obduracy.[30] Not resilient at the best of times, Jacqueline suffered a nervous breakdown and the ulcers that had troubled Picasso for some time flared up so violently that an operation was deemed necessary.[31] Gaining admittance to Notre-Dame-de-Vie at this, one of the darkest periods of Picasso's life, became virtually impossible for all but his most intimate friends.

To judge by a letter he wrote to Hartmann in December, Penrose had no idea what was wrong with Picasso.[32] Total secrecy surrounded both his illness and his operation: in mid-November he travelled incognito to Paris, was registered at the American Hospital in Neuilly as Diego Ruiz and refused to allow Jacqueline to tell anyone what was happening.[33] When the news did leak out, Picasso hastened to squash rumours of a life-threatening illness and up-beat reports of his rapid recovery appeared in the French press at the end of the year.[34] In fact, however, he was exhausted and initially was obliged to give up painting altogether and concentrate solely on drawing and printmaking.

Defending Picasso during this troubling period when it was impossible to see him was a sacred duty to Penrose and he took it upon himself to denounce John Berger's *Success and Failure of Picasso* in a review published that November.[35] A Marxist cautionary tale written with verve and passion, the book presented the aging Picasso as an isolated and pathetic figure, corrupted by fame, wealth and his court of sycophants, vacillating and directionless and destined to produce ever more trivial work. It would have outraged the artist and his devotees at any time, but in the wake of Gilot's scarring portrait of life in his entourage it was particularly damaging. The fact that the assault came from an English writer only increased Penrose's sense of obligation as he waited impatiently for a sign that he would be welcome at Notre-Dame-de-Vie.

Fundraising and petitioning

On 1 January 1966 Penrose's name appeared once again in the Honours list. He was sixty-five years old and as full of ambitious projects as ever, and the public recognition symbolised by a knighthood gave him real satisfaction. When friends teased or upbraided him for substituting Establishment for Surrealist values, he tried to make a joke of it: 'I am now a Sir-Realist,' he quipped to one.[36] But he had to put up with heckling at some of his public lectures and with the contempt of some of his colleagues. Odd as it may seem, Lee was not averse to being Lady Penrose: perhaps it tickled her to be the modern incarnation of aristocrat-adventuresses like Picasso's heroine, Lady Hester Stanhope. So, although the way Roland and Lee had conducted their lives, and particularly their marriage, was anything but conventional, both used their titles without any pretence of reluctance.[37] By contrast, Picasso, who had accepted the Lenin Peace Prize in 1962, turned down the Légion d'honneur in 1967.

Penrose was impatient to visit Notre-Dame-de-Vie again. Out of simple affection, he was anxious to see for himself whether Picasso really had recovered from his operation. But, as usual, his motivation was embarrassingly complex. The Chicago monument was still unfinished business and the Arts Council urgently needed confirmation of Picasso's agreement to the sculpture exhibition. And now Penrose had a third objective linked with the future of his cherished ICA. The lease on the Institute's old Dover Street premises had run out and new, much larger premises had been found in one of John Nash's fine Regency houses in Carlton House Terrace. The move to this location so close to London's smartest clubs, not to mention Buckingham Palace, polarised opinion among the founder-members, particularly because it involved joining a 'consortium' of societies, comprised mainly of industrial designers and landscape architects, and thus compromising the ICA's independence. But the Carlton House Terrace project was the brainchild of Lord Goodman, head of the Arts Council, and had the full support of Jenny Lee, Minister for the Arts in the Labour Government, and Penrose, eager to see the ICA at last mature into an internationally renowned centre for the arts, threw himself behind it: the promise of substantial Arts Council grants seemed to offer the best hope for a secure future.[38] Ever since the ICA's foundation, Penrose had given unstintingly of his time, energy and money, but, ironically, this apparently highly desirable solution – in hindsight Penrose called it 'dangerously ambitious' – would demand far greater sacrifices from him and eventually bring him much misery.[39]

Setting aside whatever nagging reservations he may have had, Penrose flung himself wholeheartedly into fundraising. Getting Picasso on board became an *idée fixe* once he had succeeded in enrolling his other artist- and collector-friends, and, even though he knew this was a bad moment to be asking for additional favours, in the middle of January 1966 he telephoned Picasso to try to fix a meeting.[40] But Picasso was seeing no one and there was nothing for it but to compose as persuasive a letter as possible instead:

Hearing your voice on the telephone the other day gave me the greatest pleasure. It was a voice that reassured me and made me dream of the possibility of seeing you and your beautiful Jacqueline, but I will call you again before making any plan to fly to the Midi. I won't think of doing so until you truly feel the genuine desire to see your old friends again. In the meantime, there is something I want to speak to you about, even at the risk of annoying you. But I've asked myself, how can one embark on a project as important as this without letting you know about it? – a project concerning the future of our Institute – and I say 'our' because you have been with us since the very beginning through your thinking and your work and not least through your generosity.

Let me begin by explaining why I'm sending you the photo of this very beautiful drawing, which I'm sure you will remember is the very one you made, to great applause, in London at Desmond Bernal's house in 1950. Bernal is in poor health at the moment and he has called me to say that the house where we all met is in even worse shape than he is. In fact, it will be demolished in six months' time and he tells me that if I can find the right place to house your mural drawing, where it will be really appreciated, he will give it to that organisation, provided that experts come to remove and reinstall it. This offer comes like a gift from heaven, just at the moment when I can offer the ideal solution, because for several months now I've been working with friends on a wonderful scheme to rehouse our Institute in a magnificent building. The exterior is classified as a 'historic monument' but we can modernise the interior just as we like – which will allow us to create a large and very beautiful gallery for exhibitions, a small theatre with a foyer and bar, and also a club that will be a centre for the arts better than any London has ever yet had. The street is called Carlton House Terrace, and it's two steps from Trafalgar Square, in St. James's Park, which is full of birds – pigeons, ducks, pelicans and so on. I'm also enclosing a photograph of it with details on the back. This will enable us to place your drawing in a position where people will see it in the best conditions. Bernal agrees and we very much hope that you will have no objection to having the place of honour in an atmosphere which you have done so much already to create. For us it will be a symbol of the highest importance representing the things we hold most dear, you and peace.

To help us succeed in this project, which demands enormous sums of money, the great Peter Wilson of Sotheby's has offered to hold a commission-free auction in June. We are hoping that it will bring in 1,370,000 nouveaux francs.[41] We already have the promise of works from about twenty painters and sculptors, including Henry Moore, Bacon, Sutherland, Max Ernst, Miró, etc., etc., etc. But everyone is asking whether there will also be a Picasso. I have said there definitely will be because if by chance our great friend decides that he has been generous enough already to the ICA, I will donate one of his works myself. This time I really am pulling out all the stops to ensure we succeed. I've already spoken to Kahnweiler about our project and he has promised to donate a beautiful picture on his own account, and so the moment has come when I must ask you the same question.

I loathe myself for doing this. You have helped us so much and so constantly with gifts of drawings and everything else, but this is a project of such magnitude. If only you would donate a beautiful canvas, it would not only bring in a sum of money that would help us enormously, but it would also make a great impression throughout the world. If this idea appeals to you, you could simply say a word to Kahnweiler and everything would run as easily as water through a tap.[42]

The sheer length of this letter, the rhetorical style of the flattery, the laborious manner in which Penrose inched his way to the point, all suggest fundamental discomfort. One can sense Penrose gritting his teeth at the beginning and the 'Je me déteste d'avoir à faire une chose pareille' (I loathe myself for doing this) does not have a hollow ring. However one may judge it – as a masterly or demeaning exercise in arm-twisting – one must acknowledge the steely courage behind the velvet tones.

Penrose would need more steel before he achieved his end. Not only did the letter go unanswered but his next attempt to see Picasso also met with total failure, even though he had been told he would be welcome. He arrived in Cannes on 26 March and went through the usual routine of telephoning at regular intervals, only to be informed that 'Monsieur et Madame' were not at home.[43] After hanging around for several days, he admitted defeat and wrote resignedly from Antibes on the eve of his departure for London:

Dear Don Pablo,

Of course it is painful for me to leave without seeing you and without knowing for sure what the reasons are. In the first place and above all, I hope that it has nothing to do with your health – I hope that you will regain your habitual strength without delay. But I fear that in your eyes I must now have the reputation of someone who only comes to see you when he wants something. And even though it is not for my personal profit, I have to admit there is some foundation for this supposition, given the projects which I have had to initiate on behalf of others – encouraged, it must be said, by the extraordinary generosity you have shown me for many years.

As for these projects – Chicago, the painting for the ICA auction, the exhibition of your sculpture that London and New York long to put on following your great exhibition in Paris – I won't insist upon them any more, in spite of the loss this will mean, because it all infuriates you. In the end, these aren't the things that matter to me and I want to dissociate myself from these requests – even though they are so important for others and for the public who love you, and even though nothing can happen without your permission.

For me, it is you and your well-being that are essential and I beg your pardon if, against my will, I have come to epitomise the big pain in the ass.

The proposal that has come to me from UNESCO, which I mentioned in my last letter, is another matter.[44] It's simply a small book they want me to write on some aspect of your work, and I've chosen a theme that has interested me for a long time – the astonishing and diverse ways in which the eye is represented in your paintings and drawings. In this case, obviously, you have done everything already, and it merely remains for me to give an impression, as faithfully as I can, of the richness of the eye's appearances and metamorphoses as revealed in thousands of examples.

So, my dear Pablo, I hope you will not take a dim view of this exercise and that one of these days you will see with your own eyes what I plan to say about your eyes.

I'm writing this before catching the plane this evening, sitting on Guy Bernard's terrace. He wants to join me in expressing his affection for you – you, who are always splendid and beyond the law.

Once again, I send you all my love, dear Don Pablo.

Please give my love to dearest Jacqueline.[45]

The ambivalence at the core of this letter is psychologically fascinating. Penrose loved Picasso deeply and in a sense it was true that what he really wanted was to be Picasso's beloved friend. Yet he was incapable of being 'simply' a friend. The 'pain-in-the-ass' projects were what bound the two together and anchored – and motivated – their relationship. Furthermore, writing about Picasso's work had become an addiction, and even in this letter of apology and renunciation Penrose did not offer to withdraw from his latest commission for a text. He had experienced rejection in the past and it had never been final, so once again, as he signed off, there was an upsurge of the old optimism. At bottom, he was convinced Picasso would not refuse him in the long run. But this certitude did not protect Penrose from anguish and a faint echo of his suffering on this occasion at the hands of 'Don Diabolus' is audible in the letter he received from Guy Bernard a couple of weeks later. Likening the locked gates of Notre-Dame-de-Vie to the locked bronze doors of Death in a Symbolist play by Maeterlinck, Bernard wrote: 'I too enjoyed the salutary hours spent with you in the shadow of your disappointment. I admired your angelic strength of character and patience.'[46]

More weeks passed with no sign from Mougins. Then, in the middle of June, Penrose managed to get through by telephone and, although he was driven almost to distraction by the crackling line, he gathered that Picasso was prepared to donate a painting to the ICA auction after all. He wrote jubilantly to express his gratitude and to explain that, since they already had more than enough works for the first sale on 23 June, Picasso's gift would be the centrepiece of a second sale at a later date.[47] Then at last, at the end of July, Roland and Lee were readmitted to Notre-Dame-de-Vie and although they came away empty-handed – Penrose was obliged to swallow his pride and write yet another begging letter the following day[48] – on his next visit in September he was rewarded with an oil painting from a series inspired by Jacqueline.[49] It was rather perfunctory in execution but at least it corresponded to the popular notion of a Picasso – a distorted female head combining several viewpoints and communicating emotional tension – but without doing so in a manner likely to put off more squeamish bidders. And it played a useful part in financing the ICA's move to Carlton House Terrace when it was auctioned at the second sale in December 1967.

Visiting Mougins: Autumn 1966, Spring 1967

Meanwhile the news from Chicago was excellent. On the inspired advice of Penrose, the architects had decided to use Cor-ten steel for the monument instead of bronze, partly because it was much cheaper, partly because it had the right structural and aesthetic properties.[50] However, Picasso's Communism was generating a lot of negative criticism within a vocal and influential sector of Chicago society and Penrose was roped in to write a soothing explanation to defuse this latest crisis. The result was a skilful text in which Penrose argued that in his Communism, as in every other aspect of his life, Picasso was a law unto himself, not a Party man, and that to him Communism meant quite simply the Brotherhood of Man, 'very like the fundamental conceptions of Christianity, Liberté Egalité Fraternité and the Declaration of Independence'.[51] From beginning to end of the whole Chicago saga – and the word is surely deserved – Penrose had been the wily, tireless, indispensable enabler. Hartmann knew it, and when in September 1966 he wrote exultantly to Penrose to announce that 'all is in perfect shape', he had the good grace to add: 'I can't express my gratitude for your important, essential, part in all of this!'[52]

To his intense relief, Penrose found the atmosphere in Notre-Dame-de-Vie greatly lightened when he arrived there in mid-September. He made four visits and found Picasso 'wonderfully kind and affectionate'. Picasso was still unable to paint and was 'unhappy on this account', but he had been 'drawing a great deal and making ceramics & linocuts', and in general he seemed to be 'in excellent health and good humour'. Jacqueline's health was also much improved. The furore over Gilot's book had subsided, and helping Jean Leymarie to select works for the huge Paris retrospective was having a healing and energising effect on both of them. Jacqueline had always favoured the idea of a truly comprehensive exhibition and, from being at best indifferent, Picasso had, Penrose noted, 'become reconciled, even enthusiastic and co-operative'.[53] In the letter he wrote on his return to London to Monroe Wheeler of the Museum of Modern Art, Penrose explained that 'Picasso had completely come round to the idea of the sculptures going to Paris and kept on producing new pieces from dark corners'. Indeed, Picasso was even repairing his Cubist reliefs, 'which he had formerly discarded as hopelessly damaged'. As he observed all this cheerful activity, Penrose itched to exploit the propitious situation, but, as he told Wheeler, he was obliged to restrain himself:

I asked Zette [Leiris] and Jacqueline whether they thought it the right moment to make a definite claim for London and New York and both with one accord said: 'For heaven's sake wait until everything is out of the house – at that moment it should be easy.' But knowing the sudden changes in his humour they thought it most unwise to risk anything at a moment when everything was going so well. I had no choice, and following their advice I put off saying anything until my next visit, which will be during the autumn.[54]

Any frustration he felt must, however, have been more than mitigated by Picasso's generosity, for he not only obtained the coveted gift for the ICA but also a painting for his and Lee's collection.[55]

On 19 November Penrose attended the *vernissage* of 'Hommage à Pablo Picasso' in Paris. Both the Grand Palais and the Petit Palais were used, the former taking the paintings, the latter the drawings, sculptures and ceramics. Whatever one may think of separating Picasso's work in this manner, for Penrose it was extremely useful since he intended to include ceramics in the Arts Council exhibition and also to throw light on Picasso's working processes through a selection of drawings. As was his wont Picasso refused to attend the show but he was avid for news, and Roland and Lee were welcome guests when they arrived in Cannes to relay their impressions. Roland's notes give a flavour of the good humour reigning in Notre-Dame-de-Vie, where Picasso was engrossed in experiments with etching and aquatint and enjoying all the press attention, despite fretting about the 'danger' of such crowds of people being exposed to the full range of his work – dangerous for them but also dangerous for his art:

Mougins. Nov. '66 after opening of Paris exhibitions
'Peutêtre on ne dois pas permettre au gens de voir ce que j'ai fait. C'est peut-être dangereux que tous le monde le voit.'

'Les arabes a un [*illegible word*] donné interdit qu'on fasse des representations des choses.'

'Tout est dans l'aquatint. C'est plus rich que la peinture.'

'Je voudrais faire des choses que les gens ne comprennent pas – que je ne comprens pas moi même. En faisant des lignes qui ne veut rien dire on trouve tout et c'est comme ça que j'aime travailler! Si on fait un nez ou un oreille, ça reste nez ou oreille et c'est tout.'[56]

New invention is working on copper plate with litho[graphic] pencil. Plate has resin coat. Very difficult because it is like working in negative, black for white.[57]

Acid applied with brush on copper plate. Impossible to see effect while working, and no 'repentis'[58] possible. Darkest points are where acid is applied first. So he often draws [a] figure by, say, black hair and black toes, knowing what comes in between and joining it all together later.

He judges instinctively how long he should leave acid and, without seeing what he has done, removes acid or adds more, obtaining miraculous effects.

Sunday morning: in comes Pablo marching, chest stuck out and making great gestures, saying 'Salutations au genie!' and then laughing, 'Enfin c'est ça qu'on a trouvé! Je ne sais pas pourquoi!'[59]

Having shown us a great number of recent engravings, many of which were on a black ground, he said, 'Ça rappelle la manière noir à laquelle les anglais était le plus expert – surtout celui que tu m'as montré en angleterre' – this was Martin's engravings for 'Paradise Lost'.[60]

'Los Ojos de Picasso' Alberti.[61]

Todos es Nada[62]
He wanted us to see a present he had received from an admirer in Japan. Beautifully packed in a cedar box a yard long and say 4" square, rolled in fine tissue paper, was a scroll. Very beautifully mounted on purple silk was a grey panel with the words 'Todos es Nada' written in bold script across it. P. was pleased and astonished at such an attention and in full agreement with the statement. He wanted to hang it on the wall but no place could be found, so it was carefully rolled up and put back in its box.

When I said casually, 'Et l'exposition de Sculpture à Londres?' he turned to me with a twinkle and a charming smile – 'Eh bien. Je ne peux pas te refuser maintenant.'[63] So it's now up to me to arrange it. I said later, 'Do you want ceramics too?' – 'Je ne sais pas,' he said, 'ça c'est pour toi à choisir. Tu me diriras ce que tu veux.'[64]

A year ago when the surgeon M. [Hepp] operated on him P. said, 'It's impossible for me to choose a good surgeon because I don't know the difference between them. But if I were to choose one, as I would choose among painters I have known, I would say you are Matisse.'

Talking to P. about the book I was writing, 'The Eyes of P.', he told me that Eugenio d'Ors had written a book on the Eyes of Goya, and did [a] drawing.[65] […] [47]

Given the amount of energy and time Penrose had expended on manoeuvering to bring Picasso's sculpture to London, the undemonstrative manner in which he noted his triumph seems paradoxical, to say the least. In the midst of all the jotted quotations and disparate scraps of information, it would be easy to overlook the announcement altogether and to miss the drama in Penrose's all-too brief résumé of that defining moment – the seemingly casual question, 'Et l'exposition de Sculpture à Londres?', the artist's impish response, the deal clinched in the twinkling of an eye after seven years of waiting and plotting. But it was not a case of English reserve: Penrose was stunned and he still sounds stunned – and weary – in the slightly wooden letter he sent Picasso on his return to England:

The news that you have agreed to the sculpture exhibition coming to London after it closes in Paris was greeted with enormous satisfaction, and you will soon receive an official letter thanking you warmly for your immense generosity in granting us so rare and sensational an event. We intend to hold your exhibition in the Tate Gallery, as we did in 1960, because the Arts Council gallery, which is under construction at the moment, won't be ready. And I must say that the staff at the Tate are thrilled to take it. The entire organisation, insurance, packing, transport, etc. will be handled with the same efficiency as for the exhibition of your paintings. Indeed, here in London I shall be working with the same team of experts, so I very much hope that you won't feel the least anxiety.

I've explained to colleagues in the Museum of Modern Art in New York that you are still undecided as to whether the exhibition should go to them, after it closes in London. Obviously, if you feel that since it is on the road anyway it could make a final stop in New York, they would be absolutely delighted, and Alfred Barr, who, I'm told, is soon to retire, will feel sixty years younger if ever he should get this news.

Anyway, it is entirely your decision and I simply want to thank you again from the bottom of my heart for this great privilege. London will be ennobled by your presence yet again. [...][66]

Penrose's below-par reaction derived from the suspicion that it was all too good to be true. In writing to Barr, he candidly articulated his fears:

I am afraid it is still very tricky. In general he is in excellent form and enjoyed from a distance the success of the Paris shows, but we know how quickly his humour can change and although he has been so generous this autumn in lending, who knows when the reaction may set in? It is again purely a matter of trying to judge his psychological state from a distance. [...]

I am of course very anxious that the New York show shall take place, though I feel sure we must guard against any idea of it travelling further, but I am equally anxious that his good intentions towards London shall not be jeopardized, and I will try to find out how the land lies before writing to him to suggest a visit from us. [...][67]

Initially, everything continued to go surprisingly well and when Barr went alone to Mougins in the new year Picasso agreed to let the sculptures travel to New York.[68] In the new year Penrose wrote to Picasso to inform him that he and the Arts Council team were paying a special visit to the Petit Palais to study the sculptures again and work on their installation plan.[69] He would like, he continued, to pay a flying visit to Mougins and, remembering the long discussions of printmaking techniques they had had in November, he promised to bring some English mezzotints as a gift.[70] This was a typically tactful move: present-giving was an important ritual *chez les Picasso* and mezzotints would make a refreshing change from the funny hats, flamboyant shirts and ridiculous gadgets.

There was no attempt to put obstacles in the way of Penrose's visit and he arrived, as planned, on 29 January. All was harmonious while they looked at the latest drawings but when Penrose brought up the subject of the exhibition Picasso threw a violent tantrum:

Visit 29–30 Jan. 1967
'Ce n'est pas le tableau qui est nouveau c'est l'artist. Le tableau n'est qu'un temoinage passagère du peintre.'[71]

Showed wonderful set of new drawings.
Joueur de flute.
Boy eating pasteque.
Old shepherd.
Nude girl.
New 3-figure composition.
A strong vigorous line no mistakes.
Head of flute player detached from body, sitting on flute 'like an owl'.[72]

Very difficult about drawings with sculptures, ceramics, etc.

Had told Kahnweiler & Zette that London show was off. Ehrenburg['s] presence seemed to incite him to be more difficult. Jacqueline very nervous – Heine [Kahnweiler] tactless – a lot of shouting. Finally agreed again to let us have show, but without drawings – then said we could have four for 'Man with sheep' – one for cubist head – one for Negro period wood figure.[73] [48]

Penrose was used to Picasso's sudden *voltes-face* and waiting stoically for the fit to pass was the only sensible response. In this case, with the sculptures safely in Paris, he had much less to fear than on earlier occasions. His next letter to Picasso gives no hint of further unpleasant scenes and describes instead the busy preparations for the exhibition:

My dear Pablo,

For several days I have been tormented by the overriding desire to write to you. At last I've found a peaceful moment to do so.

First of all, as you can imagine, I am preoccupied by you and as always that makes me happy. Your sculptures have arrived at the Tate Gallery. The transport was handled with the greatest care and they are in perfect condition. But what work! Those men were like spiders, wrapping their flies so carefully that they remain perfectly preserved throughout the winter. Now it's the turn of the photographers and we have a whole team working on the installation. My main task is the catalogue and the introduction, and they're making me spill ink like a tanker on the rocks, mainly because New York wants everything to be very thorough and their catalogue to be like a copiously illustrated book, with a wide distribution. I am aware of the great inadequacy of my talents for so important a task and one that means so very much to me.

On top of this, we – our Institute – are organising a dinner in your honour at the Tate the evening before the official private view, that is on Thursday 8 June, and we have invited the girlfriend of your dreams, her Royal Highness the Princess Margaret, to preside, and she has graciously agreed, and tra la la! Now all that is missing to make the most marvellous Tate ball ever is you and your beautiful Marquise. So, formally, with all due protocol, starched collar, etc., etc., I invite you both, and what a joyous miracle it would be to see you both arrive!

If I can get far enough ahead with my work I should like to make a quick trip to Amsterdam to see the great collection once again before it is dispersed,[74] and perhaps I'll take advantage of the opportunity to jump on a plane to the Midi in the hope that you will be at home and prepared to spare me five minutes. I've masses more things to tell you but for me it is so much more agreeable to be able to see you in person and embrace you and darling Jacqueline.

I shall write to you again soon.

In the meantime Lee and I send you our best love

with love.[75]

Something else that preoccupied Penrose at this moment was the sale of *Portrait of Wilhelm Uhde*, the only one of Picasso's Cubist portraits of his dealers still in private hands. He began by offering it to the Tate Gallery but the Tate was unable to raise the money and when he approached the Museum of Modern Art the story was the same. At that point the great collector from St Louis, Joseph Pulitzer, stepped in and by the beginning of April Penrose knew he had clinched the sale.[76] *Portrait of Uhde* thus became the next in the steady trickle of works originally bought from René Gaffé in 1937 to leave the Penrose collection. In this case the motive was the purchase of Burgh Hill Farm, which adjoined Farley Farm.[77] Not for the only time, the landowner had won out over the art lover: almost exactly a decade before, *Girl with a Mandolin* had been translated into fertile acres.[78]

It may seem odd that Penrose was prepared to sell any of his Picassos, given his fixation on the artist. But because he had never thought of himself as a collector, he was prepared to use the works of art he owned to support himself and his family, to purchase land or to plough into good causes – the ICA, first and foremost. He enjoyed buying art, particularly if he had worked closely with the artist on an exhibition or if the artist were young and in need of help and encouragement. His attitude was, indeed, rather similar to that of Eluard and Breton, and like their collections his moved and changed a good deal. Like them, he was susceptible to the *coup de foudre* and bought when lightning struck. Rehanging his pictures and rearranging the mass of heteroclite objects he owned was one of his great pleasures in life: a static collection had no appeal for him.

The block purchase of the Gaffé pictures was, as we saw, originally undertaken with a commercial end in view shortly before Penrose set up the London Gallery with Mesens, and although he must have felt regret at parting with a painting of the quality of the Uhde portrait he appears to have suffered no moral qualms. Whenever he needed money the Gaffé pictures were his stand-by, and the amount of money he needed conditioned the choice of picture to be sold. It was a different matter when it came to the Picassos he had acquired from Eluard. True, they were much less valuable, but for Penrose they had a unique sentimental importance and the only one he had parted with at this stage, 1967, was *The Pencil that Talks* – his gift to the first ICA auction. Nor did he dream of profiting from the pictures he had bought directly from Picasso at a very advantageous price, let alone from Picasso's gifts to him.[79] This said, according to Joanna Drew, *Woman Lying in the Sun on the Beach* narrowly missed going the way of *The Pencil that Talks*. Although it was like a talisman to him, Penrose had decided to sacrifice it on the altar of the ICA by donating it to the second auction. Drew remembered going to collect it from Hornton Street but having her way barred by a furious Lee: 'She asked me what I was doing so I told her. She said "If that goes, I go!" I just put it down and fled!'[80] The picture was still in the Penrose collection at the time of Roland's death.

Penrose mentioned the sale of *Portrait of Uhde* when he next visited Picasso and was relieved to find him quite unmoved by the news. The artist had resumed painting and was working with astonishing speed, as if to make up for lost time. As ever, Penrose was fascinated by the new pictures, many of which were like the freest of free variations on themes drawn from the work of Rembrandt, one of Picasso's favourite Old Masters. Among other subjects, they spoke of Picasso's forced eviction from the great studios at rue des Grands-Augustins on the grounds that he had not lived or worked there since 1955 and the space was needed for municipal offices. Ironically, this affair blew up during the 'Hommage' exhibition in Paris and, despite having made vague promises to safeguard Picasso's interests, André Malraux did not intervene to overrule the eviction order. As De Gaulle's Minister of Cultural Affairs, Malraux was at the other end of the French political spectrum to Picasso and his attitude was fundamentally ambivalent. To Picasso, the eviction was not only outrageous, but another inopportune distraction just at the moment when he needed to devote himself utterly to his painting.[81]

22 Ap. '67
Went with Lee at 5.0.

Spaceman
Illusion of space in painting very old. Perspective linear or atmospheric.

P. now organises space in an entirely new way. A face is made up of detached, flat areas of colour with blank space in between them, surrounded by [...]. Features sometimes drawn on top, floating in space. Head takes shape out of void.

Wigs like grey storm clouds – features like wheeling birds in clear patch of sky. No apparent system runs through, but effect of transparent space taking form of men happens each time.[82]

Series of imaginary gents from 17th-cent. Rembrandt ancestors – said he had thought of putting ea[ch] in heavy gold frame.[83]

Talking about making copies from Old Masters, he said it would be much more difficult – impossible – to copy one of his because of chance

A corner of Picasso's studio at Notre-Dame-de-Vie, Mougins, in January 1968, showing paintings executed between April and October 1967. Photo Lee Miller

happenings in the paint [that were] unrepeatable.

With Lee – [Jacqueline] said, 'Oui, ça allait mal pendant des semaines – mais maintenant je vais bien parcequ'il va bien et il peint de nouveau.'[84] He talked of Breton with great affection and was sad at his death.[85]

We gave him [a] Narwhal tusk, which pleased him.

23 Ap.
Went to see him again at 5.0. No one there except Crommelynck. Signed prints.

Said he had liked what I had said day before about space in paintings. Said two visitors expected soon – Negus[86] & Sophia Loren.

Asked about sculpture. Iron figures thrown out of window at Boisgeloup by retreating French.[87] He has found concrete sculptures from Spanish pavilion – damaged, now being repaired at Mougins.[88]

Gds. Augustin[s] has been evacuated and offices [are] being installed there – what a scandal!

He asked after many friends, Hayter, Mesens. Sabartès is much better, can even see again a little.

'Ce qu'on fait maintenent et plus dangereux – la vie est plus dangereux.'[89]

Talking of sale of Uhde [portrait], I said it was extraordinary the amount of land that could be bought for only half of one of his canvases. He laughed when I pointed at a picture and said – 'Imagine, il nous prendra au moins une journée pour marcher de là à là – et pas beau temps en plus.'[90]

He seemed quite unconcerned that I had sold the portrait.

Signing proofs of eau forte with Crommelynck. He said, 'Pourquoi me donner toute cette paine. J'ai deja dit, ils ont tous ces faussaires en prison, pourquoi ne pas les laisser faire ça pour moi?'[91]

Jacqueline appeared in very good form – looking splendid – got on v. well.

Referring back to his opening comments about the sensations of space in Picasso's latest paintings, Penrose added the following brief commentary:

Spring '67
The story is not unlike my memories of the taunt made at school that I was no more than a hole in the air. The interest lies in the air being considered as comparable to a solid shape. This is precisely what P. has achieved in the C.C.s.[92] The spaces filled with air between, circumscribed by the curves of

solid material, or partially walled in, become saturated with the invisible presence which completes the form in general. [49]

Picasso's sculpture in London

If Penrose expected that the sculpture exhibition would arouse the same degree of interest in the press and the public as the retrospective of Picasso's paintings had done in 1960 he must have been disappointed. The reaction was more muted and the attendance, although high at over 100,000, was not front-page news.[93] He sent Picasso affectionate bulletins in May to keep him informed of progress, but they were shorter and less euphoric than their equivalents seven years earlier.[94] Photographs show him conducting Princess Margaret and the Earl of Snowdon round the exhibition at the evening reception organised on behalf of the ICA on 8 June (see p. 304), but that too was a more select and sophisticated affair than the boisterous party in 1960 – no paella, flamenco music or marquees on the lawn, but a dinner for one hundred in the Tate restaurant.[95] Penrose made a short formal speech, toasting Picasso in his absence – a duty that must have filled him with dread, to judge by the much revised drafts in the Edinburgh Archive.[96] The following day he despatched an enthusiastic telegram to Mougins – 'London vanquished Stop Are completely involved with your sculptures Stop Princess captivated Stop Public filled with wonder. Love Lee Roland'.[97] But there was no need ever to write a breathless account of a late-night secret tour for the Royal Family and this time Penrose could not truthfully claim that London was gripped by 'Picassomania'.

If the 1967 exhibition was not a 'blockbuster', this was partly because sculpture is generally less of a crowd-puller than painting. In Paris, huge crowds had thronged the Grand Palais but many of those visitors never crossed the road to see the sculpture in the Petit Palais. Also, aside from a few early pieces, such as the Cubist *Head of a Woman*,[98] Picasso's sculpture was still hardly known outside a very small circle of experts, and few critics, let alone members of the general public, knew what to make of it or how to place it within the history of modern art. Given the often playful and humorous character of the *objet-trouvé* sculptures and ceramics created in Vallauris after the war, some frankly doubted that it should be taken seriously at all.[99] In London there were fewer ceramics and the installation was more spacious, thoughtful and handsome than in Paris, but the problems of ignorance and perception were the same. Furthermore, whereas in 1960 the British press machine could proudly trumpet the uniqueness of the exhibition, in 1967 it looked as if London were merely borrowing a ready-made French show and only part of it at that.

In Britain, critical reaction to the sculpture itself was mixed even though the exhibition *qua* exhibition was very widely praised. Bryan Robertson was one of the few to write a rave review of 'this devastating exhibition', which to his mind was final proof that 'Picasso is the supreme animator of our

Lord Snowdon and
Princess Margaret with the
maquette for the Chicago
monument at the gala
opening of 'Picasso
Sculpture, Ceramics,
Graphic Art', Tate Gallery,
London, June 1967

century'. 'If you stroll around his sculpture show,' Robertson wrote, 'it is impossible not to see that everything there presages almost everything else in modern sculpture.' All other twentieth-century sculptors seemed to him pitifully one-track in comparison: they 'have done only one kind of thing whereas he has made a universe, a complete mythology'.[100] By contrast, although Robert Hughes described the exhibition as 'exhilarating', he was bemused by Picasso's desire to work within the gap that traditionally separates painting from sculpture, condemning some of the work as redundant and as 'a confusion in three dimensions of what was articulate in two'. 'He seems to have sometimes transferred procedures from his paintings into a medium where they do not work – where they hang like pendants to an already accomplished feat,' Hughes complained.[101] From several of the reviews it also emerges that John Berger's negative assessment of Picasso's post-*Guernica* work was widely shared, although the writers did not hold the political views that underpinned Berger's censure. Thus while John Russell admired the sculpture because it 'has been in process of continuous renewal', he found Picasso's painting 'over the last twenty years' often 'slack and repetitious'.[102]

For Penrose what ultimately counted was the long-term effect of the exhibition – the revaluation of Picasso's entire achievement in light of the recognition that sculpture belonged at the centre, not the periphery of his oeuvre. As he explained in his catalogue introduction:

Throughout the great diversity of his work it is noticeable how closely knit are all forms of expression and in particular the two major arts in question [painting and sculpture]. It is impossible to consider one without the other since there are so many drawings and paintings that are virtually projects for sculpture or in which the form is so emphasised as to appear solid. [...] The application of colour to sculpture is an ancient practice, one that Picasso as a sculptor uses when he puts colour into cubist constructions or, as a painter, when he paints human features on the flat surfaces of his sheet-iron sculptures. The result is a frequent reversal of techniques and his disrespect for conventions is rich in unexpected combinations and both arts become fused in his treatment of ceramics.[103]

This vision of the integrity of Picasso's oeuvre explains why Penrose was so determined to include examples of the ceramics, some obviously sculptural drawings – here Picasso thwarted him by refusing to lend more than a handful – and etchings from 'The Sculptor's Studio' chapter of the *Vollard Suite* that offer a mythologised narrative of the life of the archetypal sculptor.

If his argument seems self-evident now, in 1967 in his typically unpretentious, unostentatious style Penrose was breaking new ground, and his introduction to the Arts Council catalogue has a good claim to be the foundation of all the subsequent, weightier, specialist studies of Picasso's sculpture.[104] His long, bruising fight to convince Picasso to show his sculpture *en masse* had been undertaken with the simple aim of revealing a hidden oeuvre, knowledge of which was essential to a proper appreciation of Picasso's true achievement, and he was convinced that, through exposure to it, people would come to understand that Picasso's sculpture was as revolutionary and expressive in its own way as his painting. That mission, one can safely say, has been accomplished.

A few days after the exhibition opened in London, Penrose flew to Cannes to give Picasso a first-hand account. Sadly for us, his notes of their conversation are cursory. On the other hand, they provide a revealing snapshot of a typical day at Notre-Dame-de-Vie at this period, when Picasso's advanced age was beginning to tell and Jacqueline, more highly strung than ever, was prone to outbursts of exasperation and self-pity:

Visit to Mougins 11 June '67
Arrived for lunch.

Pierre and Françoise Daix there. Jacqueline went out to baptism party. Gave Pablo catalogues of sculpture show. He was very keen to hear how it all went and what [Princess] Margaret thought. Very amiable, asking for news of everyone. Apologised in leaving us for siesta. Told us to go and see his giant oaks and garden.

Came back to find us talking in sitting room about wars, etc.

Told us he was being approached about some decoration – would not accept – why should gov[ernment] take away Gds. Augustins and offer him L[égion] d'honneur instead.

He said, 'What makes it impossible is I never throw anything away. Even a pen like this, I keep, because some day I might want to transform it into a Venus.'

Then Jacqueline was announced by Inès [Sassier]. She was back with all the christening party. Jean Marais was parain,[105] and it was Cocteau's boyfriend – the father.[106] There was a fine party going on, sweets, savouries and very good Blanc de Blanc. The[re] was also a Benedictine priest in plain clothes – a pansy, aggressive and intent on making an impression with Pablo. He asked to see the latest paintings and persisted till Pablo took us up to the studio saying that he was very shy and reluctant ever to show his work. Jean M. – 'Yes, while you are acting it's all right. It's the curtain at the end that is demoralising and obscene.'

The new paintings, four of which – one v. large – had been painted the evening before, were mostly 'Mousquetaire' portraits using blank spaces.[107]

Some very exciting, some rather unfinished, all showing great vitality and mastery of paint. Showed us other studio. The whole house is now studios – three on ground floor, sculptures in basement and two or three on first floor.

There were two paintings of a baptism [painted in] '65 – his gardener's baby – 'Je peint ce qui je vois autour de moi.'[108] A painting dated 25.10.65, [executed on] his birthday & just before his operation.[109]

As they were leaving the priest became even more aggressive and offered his services as aumonier[110] – said he wanted to come again. P. said he would have to come at 9.0 a.m. and bring sandwiches to see all he wanted – and insisted he should call up anytime and fix it. It seemed a doubtful offer.

After they had all gone, I was saying goodbye when a phone call from some dame who had be[en] promised a visit came. He was at once bad-humoured and told the Spanish servant to tell J. to refuse. A row flared up in which J. said she had had enough of doing his dirty work. Why couldn't he tell her? J. became very angry. He turned to the olive tree at the door, saying to Inès, 'Tiens il y a un trou ladedans regardez je peux m'enfoncer la main très loin.'[111] Quite unperturbed. J. really angry. I tried to soothe her, and after a few more explosions about how all the blame fell on her, the storm passed and I kissed them goodbye for the tenth time and got into the car, the engine having been running for a good 10 minutes.

If I had had the wit to say it, this is what I ought to have said – 'Jacqueline n'imagine pas qu'on va te blamer pour ces crises inexplicable à tes amis – tous le monde sait que c'est lui Don Pablo qui a la caractere le plus impossible du monde que personne peut savoir d'un moment à l'autre son humeur – il est comme les vents comme les force de la nature et toi comme nous tous sont en admiration et victime. C'est notre diable de vie et nous l'aimons pour ça.'[112] [50]

Inauguration of the Chicago monument

Meanwhile, in Chicago all was moving rapidly to a conclusion. By the end of May 1967 the ground in front of the Civic Center had been broken in readiness for the 50-foot-high, 162-ton monument, and by the end of July, when Hartmann wrote to Penrose to report on plans for the unveiling ceremony, the sculpture was already in place. Sandblasting turned the Cor-ten steel a rusty brown, in imitation of the sheet-metal maquette.[113] There was additional cause for celebration in Chicago because Picasso had refused the offered fee of $100,000 and had given the sheet-metal maquette to the Art Institute.[114] Penrose was unable to attend the inauguration on 15 August because he was making a film about Picasso's sculpture that had to be shot before the works were packed up for transport to New York.[115] So, he had to make do with Hartmann's enthusiastic account and a small piece of the turquoise veil that had shrouded the monument.[116] Had he been present, the American press might have given a rather more balanced account of the background story. As it was, Hartmann was presented as the hero who, single-handedly, had worn down Picasso's resistance by presenting him with an album of photographs of famous citizens of Chicago, a fire chief's helmet, a White Sox uniform, an Indian headdress and a Chicago Bears uniform – 'homey souvenirs of a lusty American city', as a local journalist put it.[117] If Penrose minded about being written out of the popular record he gave no sign and Hartmann remained a friend. However, he did devote an entire section of his memoirs to the monument because he was proud of his essential role in its creation.[118]

Penrose was able to judge the effect of the monument for himself when he went to the States that autumn. His first stop was New York for the

THE WEATHER

Partly cloudy, low tonight in the lower 60s. Tomorrow chance of showers late in day, high in lower 80s. Precipitation probabilities: 10 per cent tonight, 20 tomorrow. Southerly winds 6 to 12 m. p. h. tonight. Thursday chance of showers. Details on page 3. POLLEN COUNT: 19

Chicago's AMERICAN
Always On Top Of The News

FINAL MARKETS
GREEN STREAK
COMPLETE

7¢

The shroud falls! Arrow locates William Hartmann and Mayor Daley (nearest statue).

[CHICAGO'S AMERICAN Photo]

THIS IS IT!

Picasso Statue Hailed by Daley

See editorial, page 10

BY BOB SMITH

There was a fanfare by the Chicago Symphony orchestra. Mayor Daley tugged on a rope. And a 200-pound blue shroud fell from the new symbol of Chicago—a giant 162-tun, 5-story, rust-colored steel Picasso.

Climaxing a cultural outpouring seldom seen in a civic ceremony here, the mayor today dedicated the towering sculpture, the gift of Pablo Picasso, one of the century's greatest artists.

Daley hailed the sculpture as "a monument that portrays the creative courage of the people of Chicago" and "symbolic of a very exciting era in our city's history."

President Johnson sent a telegram extending his congratulations "on another historic first for the city beautiful," and even Picasso himself, who seldom talks to anyone, announced his "warm friendship and best wishes to Chicago" in a phone call.

An estimated 50,000 persons attended the ceremonies in the Civic center plaza, and thousands more peered from windows of office buildings.

Newsmen from both the east and west coasts covered the unveiling, as did representatives of four national magazines and all major wire services, including Reuters.

The program began with a concert by the orchestra, conducted by Seiji Ozawa, which included "Overture Candide" by Bernstein, Gershwin's "An American in Paris," and excerpts from symphonic themes from "West Side Story," also by Bernstein.

It was the orchestra's first civic appearance and demon-

strated the cultural significance the city attaches to the Picasso.

A Huge Bird?

In his brief address Daley mentioned the controversy the monumental art work has created.

Picasso has declined to reveal his interpretation of the statue's meaning. Other artists and laymen have said the work is the head of a woman or a huge bird.

"The Chicago Picasso, like the creation of any exciting work of art, very naturally develops a dialog and difference of opinion," the mayor said.

"But it seems to me that Picasso gave us the secret clew as to what this sculpture should mean to us. He said he was making a gift in tribute to the vitality of Chicago."

Daley referred to the city as a "laboratory of human experience, a preserver of individuality, the cradle of democracy, and the wellspring of innovation."

"The sculpture has been hailed as a new representation, a new image, a new interpretation of the city's soul," he said.

The real value of the statue now and for all time to come, he said, "is its stimulation of appreciation of all fine arts."

The mayor said, "I think it

[Continued on page 4, col 4]

Full page of pictures on back page; another photo on page 4.

GET OFF THE TRACK TO ENDSVILLE

Dropout? Baby Get Back Where Action Is!

L. F. Palmer Jr., Chicago's American reporter, has been a teacher in Chicago inner city schools and wrote about his experiences in a series of articles published in this newspaper. Today he has advice for dropouts or potential dropouts.

BY L. F. PALMER JR.

IF YOU'VE PULLED OUT of school, or if you've got the urge to merge with the dropout society, you'd better listen. I'm going to tell it like it is.

This world out here's got a one track mind. You get derailed, baby, you're dead. Forget it.

Endsville.

You want to go somewhere, you'd better get on that track and never look back. You got to have some fuel burning in the brain. Without it, man, everything and everybody moves—everybody but you.

That's where school comes in, baby. That's where the fuel is. You ain't never going to win a ball game outside the park.

COURSE EVERY TEAM isn't sitting on top of the heap. And every school's not a champion, either. But like Kansas City and those poor ol' Yankees, at least they're in the majors. And being in the big league starts with that high school diploma.

I heard a University of Chicago prof speaking the other day and he said a high school diploma is just like having a union card. Without a union card, you're frozen out of some good jobs.

Without that high school diploma the man at the hiring desk is almost sure to tell you: "Don't call us. We'll call you." Then he throws the phone number away.

YOU SEE, THAT PIECE of paper tells him you know how to stick it out. You're just a quitter. You can set a goal and reach it.

That's what working is. And who wants a guy on the job if you can't be sure he'll stick with it?

You need that diploma, baby. It's your fare for that rocket named Success. Don't get me wrong; it won't guarantee a ride to the top, but it'll sure get you aboard.

The folks who know say that every year you stay in high school will add $238 to your annual income when you go to work. And when you get that diploma, it'll mean an extra $446 a year.

Figure it out for yourself. Multiply that extra dough times 46 years of working life. That's a lot of bread.

YOU WANT TO START BAKING? Stay in school. You already dropped out? Admit it's rough out on the street. Drop back in school, baby.

The Chicago Urban league's got it all figured out for you. They're pitching a back-to-school campaign like they do every year. Back-to-School week is Aug. 27 to Sept. 2, but the league's battling every day to strike out the dropout.

To get back in, drop by to see your former principal or counselor. School's are open Aug. 31 and Sept. 1 for freshmen orientation. But they'll be glad to talk to you about getting back on the track.

When you go, take your mom or dad or guardian with you. Have your birth certificate and something to prove where you live—a gas bill or electric bill is fine. Take your course grade book and a record of any credits you may have earned in summer or evening school.

IF THE PRINCIPAL doesn't want to take you back, go see the district superintendent and let him know you mean business, that you've grown up a little.

Or check out the Urban Youth program at 64 E. Lake st. They've got a "Decibe E" program which puts education and employment back to back. It might be just what you need.

This world out here ain't playing. It'll give you back what you put in it. But—and this is the truth—it'll also give you a hand if you reach out and grab it.

If you're in school, play it out to the end. If you're not, get back where the action is.

O.K. 2 Billion for Poverty Programs

WASHINGTON (P)—The Senate poverty subcommittee today approved a 2.3-billion dollar extension of the "war on poverty" program and added in a 2 a billion-dollar emergency program to deal with slum jobs.

The combined 5.2 billion-dollar measure was sent to the full labor committee which tentatively scheduled a session on it for Thursday. Sen. Joseph S. Clark (D., Pa.), the subcommittee chairman, said he was hopeful the measure could be passed by the Senate before the Labor day recess.

The subcommittee granted all of the 2.06 billion dollars asked by President Johnson for the anti-poverty program in the current fiscal year and added 148 million dollars to this for a variety of programs.

Art Experts to Look, Tell

Two Chicago art experts will present their impressions of the controversial Picasso in CHICAGO'S AMERICAN tomorrow. They are:

Don J. Anderson, art critic for THE AMERICAN.

Jan van der Marck, director of the Museum of Contemporary Art.

They will view the figure as artists and sculptors and then form their opinions of just what Chicago got from the Spanish artist.

Maybe they'll like it. Maybe they won't. Whatever they decide, they'll tell you the reasoning behind their verdicts in tomorrow's AMERICAN.

Harry D. Bocras, sculptor and former artist in residence at the University of Chicago, also was scheduled to write his impressions of the figure for THE AMERICAN, but was unable to attend the unveiling because of illness.

Bulletins, Late Races

Stocks Close Higher; D-J Up 2.83

NEW YORK [Special]—The stock market closed higher today is active trading, despite late profit-taking which reduced earlier gains. Allis-Chalmers, the most active issue, rose $1.37 to $41.87. The Dow-Jones industrial average closed at $105.15, up 2.883. Details in Financial section.

Plane with 71 in Safe Emergency Landing

COLUMBUS, O. (P)—An American Airlines Boeing 727 jet, carrying 64 passengers and a crew of 7, made a safe emergency landing at Port Columbus today after the plane's hydraulic system operating the landing gear failed to function.

TODAY IN THE AMERICAN

Action Line	4
Amusements	18, 19
Bacharach	18
Classified	24, 25
Crossword	25
Dear Abby	14
Editorial	10
Fashions—Food	13-15
Financial	15-18
Mabley's Report	3

The Ton-Agers Sure Aren't Waisting Away

opening of the sculpture exhibition at the Museum of Modern Art. From there, he went to Chicago to give a lecture on the place of the monument in Picasso's sculpture as a whole. Back in England at the end of the month, he hastened to communicate his delight and awe to Picasso:

I had always known it would be a very important work, but seeing it suddenly like that, enlarged to a gigantic size, and finding myself at its feet in the moonlight in that strange city was very moving.

I studied the reactions both of people passing in the street and lots of others, including [Mayor Daley] himself, and you really have created a focus of interest in the city. Everyone is united in a kind of wonder and pride at having such a fantastic monument in the city centre.

And he took pleasure in reporting that the sculpture exhibition in New York was 'fantastically successful', attracting 'an average of 4000 visitors a day'.[119] The marathon of diplomacy had eventually paid off. Penrose could look back on 1967 as the year in which his two great projects to establish Picasso's reputation as the towering sculptor of his generation had come to fruition.

Chapter 8

Picasso's Last Years, 1968–1973

Visiting Mougins, 1968

Penrose had promised that he would be personally responsible for the well-being of Picasso's sculptures between the closure of the 'Hommage' exhibition in Paris and their return to Notre-Dame-de-Vie from New York.[1] Accordingly, with Joanna Drew, the Arts Council's official courier, and Lee, who photographed proceedings, he went to oversee the unpacking.[2] Drew had not met Picasso before and was struck by the simplicity and informality of the domestic arrangements in Mougins and the easy familiarity of the conversations that sprang up. She was amused by Picasso's addiction to the all-in wrestling on television and his appetite for old Hollywood movies like Henry Hathaway's *The Lives of a Bengal Lancer* (1935), starring his friend Gary Cooper.[3] Fortunately, Penrose recorded a lively exchange between her and Picasso about the monumental wartime sculpture *Man with a Sheep*:

Mougins 21 Jan. '68
[Picasso] 'Dans le temps on a beaucoup parlé de l'Art – que c'est serieux. Mais pour moi ce n'est pas ça – c'est un blague comme font les enfants – et regarde les chose merveilleuses qu'ils font.'[4]

   Joanna: 'Quand l'homme au mouton était à Londres j'ai trouvé des cocons d'insectes dans les fentes du bronze et je les encouragais de rester tranquille jusqu'au moment ils retrouve un climat plus doux.'
   Picasso: 'Ah oui mais vous savez un jour à Vauvenargues l'homme au mouton été dehors et je passais ma main sur le surface quand je sentis quelque chose d'étrange entre ses jambes – En regardant je trouve que c'est un nid de guepe et je le fait partir – sans que ça le fasse du mal.'
   Joanna: 'Sans que ça fasse du mal a ce qui n'est pas là.'
   Picasso (surpris): 'En effet – ce qui n'est pas là – oui en generale je fait beaucoup d'attention aux sexes – peut être trop – mais plus aux femmes que aux hommes mais en effet à l'homme au mouton je n'ai pas fait attention à ça – peut être il n'a pas besoin mais en tout cas je l'ai laissé sans le finir. Après d'avoir fait beaucoup de dessins je l'ai modelé avec de la terre très vite en faisant des boules de terre que j'ai appliqué pour les joues, un oeil – les doits j'ai roulé – allongé et appliqué à la main. C'était fait si vite et l'armature était

mal fait alors le tout commencé de derangoler – le mouton est tombé parterre et il a fallu attacher l'homme par le cou au marches de l'escalier. Mais je l'ai rattrapé et j'ai vite fait venir un homme pour faire un moulage en plâtre.'

R.P. 'En faisant tous ces dessins, as tu pensé à faire une peinture ou un sculpture.'

P. 'Qui peut savoir – quand on travail c'est comme la fumé, on ne sait pas quelle forme ça va prendre.'[5]

It had been announced from New York that one of the bronzes that has a teaspoon for a head and table forks for hands had had the head broken off.[6] Great concern was shown and apologies from all responsible. Referring to this he said, 'On est affollé parceque une cuiller c'est cassé – ce n'est pas grave – j'aurais pu mettre une brosse à dent comme tête toute aussi bien.'[7] This was the only comment about breakages, of which there were three ceramics, which had been broken but so well repaired that it was difficult to find any trace. [51]

Drew herself recalled an amusing episode during the visit:

Picasso asked me if I had anything for him to sign. When I said that I hadn't, he asked Jacqueline to go and get something. She asked what, and he said, 'Oh, n'importe quoi.'[8] So she came back with a book and winked at us. Picasso was just about to inscribe it to me when he exclaimed, 'Mais pas ça!'[9] It was his favourite 'Tintin' book![10]

Picasso had evidently enjoyed the Penroses' visit and they left Mougins bearing two large erotic drawings, one for Lee of a voluptuous reclining nude watched by an old man squatting on a chamber pot, the other of a pasha in his harem for Roland.[11] He also gave Penrose a chart of the industrial paints that he was using at this time – a sign that he appreciated a fellow artist's keen interest in the technicalities of his work.[12] Perhaps it was also at this moment that Picasso gave Penrose three tiny containers encrusted with paint in which he had mixed his colours in Boisgeloup during the early 1930s. Penrose preserved these precious relics religiously but for once failed to record the date of the gift.[13]

Sad news came just three weeks later. On 13 February Sabartès died in Paris, a loss that Picasso felt acutely for he had known Sabartès for seventy years and had relied upon his utter fidelity at critical moments in his own life. Apart from Manuel Pallarès, there was really nobody left with whom Picasso could mull over the whole of his past, and at this twilight period of his life when so much of his work – especially his prints and drawings – reveals an obsessive recapitulation of his youth in Spain, the loss was especially painful. Rather than driving him into depression and inactivity, however, Sabartès's death spurred Picasso to work even more spontaneously

Opposite
Jacqueline Picasso and
Joanna Drew at Notre-
Dame-de-Vie, Mougins,
January 1968. Photo
Lee Miller

and intensively, for it was by refusing to admit any slackening of his energy that he held infirmity and death at bay. Sabartès had been instrumental in setting up the Museu Picasso in Barcelona in 1963 and his personal collection was its nucleus. In honour of him, Picasso now donated to the museum a Blue period portrait and the entire series of *Las Meninas* variations, together with the companion pictures of pigeons. He thus ensured that the decorative ensemble that had formed the climax of the retrospective in London in 1960 be preserved in perpetuity.

On hearing of Sabartès's death, Penrose wrote immediately to commiserate with Picasso. In the same letter he described the hectic last-minute preparations for the relaunch of the ICA in its grand new surroundings in Carlton House Terrace.[14] The theme of the inaugural exhibition, 'The Obsessive Image 1960–1968', was proposed by Julie Lawson, who had worked alongside Penrose at the ICA almost since its foundation and now held the position of Deputy Director.[15] (Penrose himself was Chairman.) As Penrose admitted in his memoirs, in focusing on contemporary representations of mankind the show intentionally offered 'an antidote to the current drift towards "minimal" and "conceptual" art', which he, as did Picasso, regarded as a cul-de-sac.[16] Omitting the Institute's patron saint from this first exhibition on the new premises would have been inconceivable to Penrose and the exhibition included a couple of recent paintings by Picasso, who was thus presented as the godfather of the enduring 'humanist' and 'expressionist' tendency in contemporary art.[17] This undisguised commitment to continuity with the values of the old ICA was one of the factors that led eventually to the complete breakdown of Penrose's relationship with the new administration and to his resignation in November 1976.[18]

Throughout 1968 Penrose was absorbed by the problems of the ICA, which lurched into its first financial crisis within months of the reopening. For the first time in years he had no mission requiring intricate negotiations with Picasso, but if he experienced a sense of disorientation, even of deprivation, for Picasso the cessation of all Penrose's 'pain-in-the-ass' projects must undoubtedly have come as a relief. As one after another of his old and dear companions died, Penrose in his persona as a 'simple' friend became more welcome as a visitor and during the last few years of Picasso's life the gates of Notre-Dame-de-Vie were opened to admit Roland and Lee whereas many others were repeatedly and ignominiously turned away.[19]

The first visit of this final, far more peaceful phase in their relationship took place in July 1968. Penrose's notes portray the aged Picasso at his most good-humoured and exuberantly Spanish:

N.-D.-de-Vie, 21 July '68 [added later]
Picasso presides – seated in Spanish chair – 4 Manitas de Plata gypsies – concentrated enjoyment of whole performance.
    1. Gypsies v. handsome – father eldest one –blondish curly hair – blue eyes – gold teeth – sunburnt – Velázquez – v. slim – green embroidered shirt

– tight fit – rings on fingers – gold bracelets – borrowed P.'s shoes for dancing (flamenco). Went off with them – splendid virtuoso guitarist.

2. Son in bright green shirt – wonderful cante hondo singer – guitarist.

3. Black hair, black eyes – gave everything when he sang – neck swollen like penis – mouth round and wide open – great energy – went out ill for half an hour – came back stronger than ever.

4. Less character – greatly admired by Jacqueline – excellent guitarist.

All related – French, but Spanish-speaking – music a cross between flamenco & Camargue gypsy.

None could read or write – whole life in music.

Surprised at disorder in P.'s room – pile of disguises – hats, masks – 'Vous êtes un de nous'.[20]

4 guitars together – 'very rare, like an orchestra,' says P.

P. signs all four guitars, scratching name & date into varnish with terrific noise.

'Je voudrais entendre les guitars de P.'[21] Cocteau quoted by Lucien Clergue, who was there and had discovered the group.

Splendid entertainment till very late. Food, wine, endless singing & music.

P. disappeared & came back disguised with mask of Spanish girl w. black pigtails and straw hat. Danced like a girl w[ith] v. supple arm gestures.

Next day
Gave him skeleton of bat – very pleased – said his best treasures, like crystal ball, were presents from me.
[Gustavo] Gili & Clergue arrived – saw proofs of Duc de Orgaz book.[22]
Showed small engravings – new techniques.
Crommelyncks there said he had never worked on engraving so hard & so consistently – results staggering. [52]

Another visit followed in early October.[23] No summary has been found but we can be sure that Penrose pored over the mass of prints that came to be known as *Suite 347* – the last few were made only two days before his visit – marvelling at the combination of narrative invention, scabrous humour and technical virtuosity.[24] All 347 prints were executed between 16 March and 5 October 1968 in a rampant display of death-defying creativity and, with their myriad allusions to Spanish art and literature and to Picasso's own youthful Spanish works, they were at one level a memorial to Sabartès, to whom Picasso had given copies of every print he had made. It was probably during this visit that Penrose formed the plan to exhibit the entire suite at the ICA.

Perhaps he also talked to Picasso of his desire to translate *Les quatre petites filles* so that the play could be performed in London in a double bill with *Le Désir attrapé par la queue*. He had first mooted the idea during a visit to Mougins in September 1966 and Picasso had agreed in principle. All his other Picasso missions successfully completed, Penrose now longed to engage in this new task of mediation and thus fill the intolerable vacuum. Translation brings one into a peculiarly intimate creative communion with another's genius and this lent it a unique appeal to Penrose, but the main obstacle to progress was, as usual, Picasso himself. For a long time Michel Leiris had been trying to get his hands on the manuscript so that it could be published by Gallimard, but Picasso had equivocated and procrastinated. When he learned that the French edition was at last in preparation, Penrose was therefore delighted and enlisted Leiris's help in persuading Picasso to agree formally to a translation.[25] He dreaded a repeat of the fiasco over the translation of *Le Désir attrapé par la queue*, but this time there was no unforeseen rival and by the following autumn, after much tinkering and fine-tuning, his version of *Les quatre petites filles* was ready.[26]

The Penrose burglary, Spring 1969

Work on the translation of *Les quatre petites filles* was played out against the backcloth of a major domestic drama. The Penroses were at Farley Farm for Easter 1969 when news came that their London flat had been burgled. Shattered glass on the floors and empty frames left dangling on the walls led to fears that many of the stolen works would be badly damaged, if, indeed, they were ever retrieved. The burglary made front-page news on 8 April and in most of the press reports it was the theft of the Picassos, especially *Weeping Woman*, that was the headline story. It was, as Penrose told Picasso, 'a disaster of the first order. […] Both Lee and I are wretched, desolate – there are no words to describe it.'[27]

The collection was seriously under-insured and at first the reward for information leading to the conviction of the thieves and the recovery of the paintings was set at a mere £7,500. There was no breakthrough and in May, at the urging of the police, Penrose raised the reward to £30,000.[28] It is no coincidence that at precisely this moment he sold the Cubist still-life construction he had bought from Eluard to the Tate Gallery for almost the same sum – a painful sacrifice, but the only way of immediately raising the necessary money.[29] Presumably mistaking the little sculpture for worthless junk, the burglars had left it untouched in the flat. The 'war of nerves', as Penrose described it in a letter to Picasso,[30] continued for weeks before the thieves finally cracked, but the circumstances in which the paintings were recovered were bizarre and farcical. They had been hidden in the basement of a derelict shop and were discovered by two workmen clearing out the building who had not the slightest idea of their value or significance. Having tried to sell them for a few pounds at a nearby factory, the workmen were, apparently, on the point of burning them with all the other rubbish when it dawned on them that it might be sensible to seek advice at the local art shop. There, fortunately, *Weeping Woman* was recognised and the police alerted.[31]

For Penrose the outcome of this excruciating ordeal could hardly have been better: miraculously, no painting was lost and the damage was far less grave than expected, and because the gang had escaped the police net he did not have to pay out the £30,000 reward. A few days later he gave Picasso a colourful account of his joyous reunion with the pictures in Chelsea police station:

The whole Art Squad had come – it was just like one of those pictures of wild game hunters, smiling and proud, almost with a triumphant foot placed on the head of the 'Weeping Woman'. [...] It was marvellous to see them again. It looks to me as if 'Weeping Woman' has not been damaged at all, but there is a little hole in 'Still Life with a Gas Jet', and the bastards have cut off the top right corner of the 'Negro Dancer', where you signed it. The police explained that that was their first move in an orchestrated campaign and I would have received small pieces of the pictures by post every few days. [...][32]

When he next went to Mougins at the beginning of November, Penrose travelled with the mutilated, but already restored *Negro Dancer*, intending to get the lost signature replaced. Picasso's increasing deafness made communication difficult but there was no diminution in his fondness for toying with those who demanded this kind of market-driven favour:

Visit to Picasso 8–10 Nov. '69
Both P. and J. in very good health. P. had worked till 2.30 [a.m.] previous night.
    Conversation gets less easy owing to deafness. He listens and then answers, not having understood, or shows signs of annoyance. Speaking slowly I can get over this but it interrupts what was an easy flow before. Conversation was mostly about the burglary. He at once offered to sign 'La Danseuse Nègre' and complimented John Bull on a very good job.[33]
    I left it with him overnight. Next day he suggested signing with Indian ink, which didn't work, so [he] then took oil paint. I think he was hoping ink would do, all the time knowing better. At one moment he said, 'But I hate spoiling a picture with a signature. Every part of it is my signature.' He was then worried that it would not dry in time and would smudge. I showed him the careful arrangements made by J[ohn] B[ull] for this & he was delighted. [53]

Remembering the episode in *Scrap Book*, Penrose presented it as a sparring match between two canny opponents who knew each other's game inside out.[34]
    The burglary was not the sole topic of conversation and, as ever, Penrose was staggered by the boldness and variety of Picasso's latest rush of paintings:

We sat round the table P., J. & myself talking trivialities and watching Catch on the T.V. Left him with invitation to come next day. We had talked about

E. Fry's book and 'D[emoiselles] de A[vignon]'. At first he would not admit E.F.'s mistake but told me had never repainted 'D. de A.' after showing it in 1907.[35]

Talk about '4 little girls'. Not written in one day. Cannot find drawings he had promised[36] – very pleased we were going to act it in London at time of 347 engravings show.

Last visit very short as I had to catch plane. Showed me about 30 large recent paintings – splendid in strength and invention – some mousquetaires, nudes, kissing heads, flower pieces – superb invention, colour and a variety in construction.

Great portraits of men – boys in hats, crowned with laurels. Poetic pensive boys. Some close-up portraits – la Fornarina & Raphael – some Spanish dwarfs, Velázquez origin – fierce, robust, incredibly inventive. Colour of flowers v. beautiful – acid yellows.[37]

Chicago. Talked at length about how monument came about. Said he had received photo from U.S. newspaper from me with men swarming up to escape from police – a refuge – ([I] believe it wasn't quite so simple but said nothing).[38] His belief is he gave monument to City of Chicago and he can't be bothered about more detail.

Painting now not careful intellectual research of cubism, rather an exuberance and complete liberation of all […] his abilities. Astonishing variety and invention within given range of subjects – subject the peg to hang daring experiments in form & colour – but expression in face & eyes never slighted. [53]

Suite 347 in London

By letter Penrose kept Picasso fully informed about the lead-in to the exhibition of *Suite 347* at the ICA in March 1970.[39] As he explained in a letter sent a month before the exhibition opened, Rebecca West – famous not only as a critic, political commentator, novelist and feminist, but also as the sometime mistress of H. G. Wells – had readily agreed to make a speech at the opening, and there would be lectures, films and, he fondly hoped, a performance of *Les quatre petites filles* in his translation with sets by Lucian Freud.[40] (In fact, the play was not staged until the following year and then without Freud's involvement.) As the opening approached, he passed on news of the 'commotion' building up around the erotic images, especially the notorious sequence of twenty-four etchings depicting Raphael making passionate love to his mistress La Fornarina.[41] Journalists delighted in pointing out that these 'obscene' prints would go on public display in London, whereas in Paris – supposedly a far more permissive city – they had been hung in a private room and shown only to the chosen few, and, furthermore, that all of them would be reproduced in the catalogue, whereas in Paris twenty had been omitted.[42] Anticipating that the police might invoke the obscenity laws and seize the offending prints, Penrose published a couple of preemptive essays in which he vigorously defended Picasso against the charge of pornography by stressing the Rabelaisian humour and naturalism of his representations of genitalia and copulation. His essay for *Art and Artists* concludes:

The figleaf with its fake memory of the Arcadian grove has melted away. The authority that demanded that it should cover our shame and remind us permanently of original sin has been dissolved. Hypocrisy and fear are banished by the innocence and the poetic power of Picasso's vision.[43]

Optimistic though this sweeping statement undoubtedly was, the exhibition was not closed down, although the erotic prints were cited in the obscenity case brought against works by John Lennon that had recently been shown in a Bond Street gallery.[44]

Penrose had both personal and also ideological motives for admiring Picasso's libertine imagination and cherishing the hope that he was witnessing the final defeat of the crippling taboos that had ruled his Quaker family. But in a broader sense the exhibition could hardly have been more timely: this was 'swinging London' and the revolution in sexual mores seemed to be mirrored in the rampant lust celebrated in Picasso's late work. The London critics were divided as to the artistic merits of the prints, for the strong bias towards allusion-laden narrative did not accord with the prevailing avant-garde preference for minimalist abstraction or conceptual art. To some, *Suite 347* was further evidence that Picasso's work since the 1950s was essentially decadent, if not actually senile, and he was castigated for permitting so many ill-considered scrawls 'to leave the studio at all'.[45] That he had done so merely proved that he was 'a victim of his own absurdly-inflated reputation'.[46] While most conceded that, for a man in his late eighties, Picasso's energy was astounding, they also read intimations of impotence into the orgiastic scenes and saw the shadow of death over the suite as a whole. Some of the reviewers were clearly impatient to write his obituary.

For Penrose, a morbid interpretation of Picasso's late work was anathema and he firmly refuted it in the passage about *Suite 347* in the revised edition of *Picasso: His Life and Work*. To him Picasso was the very embodiment of 'the force of nature' and his late work a purer expression of vitality than anything preceding it:

Throughout the sequence of wildly erotic love scenes between Raphael and his model, La Fornarina, there is present in every engraving an old man sometimes crowned as the pope and at others with a dunce's cap. Critics who take the easy line of interpreting this figure as a symbol of the artist's impotence are biased or ignorant. Picasso draws as he thinks and as he lives. The whole drama of love, life and the inevitability of death is present due to his own participation in life, combined with an Olympian detachment. In recent years his imagery has never been richer and more universal nor has his technique ever been more vigorous and inventive. Every line or stroke of the brush is the signature of his inner being revealing the full scope of his emotions, an extended self-portrait surpassing the limits of time.[47]

When the exhibition was up and running, Penrose hastened to Mougins to give Picasso a first-hand account, at the same time presenting him with copies of his translation of *Le Désir attrapé par la queue*. His notes of their meetings, although extremely brief, give an idea of the thrust of the conversation and the direction of Picasso's thoughts. On the first day, in the presence of Piero Crommelynck, printmaking was the main subject – not only Picasso's latest prints but also Degas's brothel monotypes, which Picasso claimed to admire above anything Degas had done. Exactly a year later, the monotypes would inspire another spate of prints in which Degas himself is shown on the threshold of a brothel, an aloof but intent observer:

Visit to Picasso 13.3.70
Rosengart & Angela [Rosengart].
Mme. Piero C[rommelynck] & later C[rommelynck].
Jacqueline.
Showed new engravings, worked on sometimes to 8th version.

La fête de la patronne.[48]

B[r]ought out Degas monotypes of this subject, one retouched by D. with pastel. Admired sensual sensibility.

Signed my trans[lation] of 'Desire Caught by Tail'.[49]

Angela's story of [Serge] Lifar coming to ask P. to do décor for a ballet in Cairo – good for tourism – firmly turned down and out. [54]

In the presence of trusted friends like Penrose and the Swiss father-and-daughter team of dealers, Siegfried and Angela Rosengart, family troubles were also freely aired. Claude, also acting for Paloma, was suing Picasso through the court in Grasse to compel him to recognise his paternity, thus according them the right to a share in his estate. Claude and Paloma lost their case, but the adverse and intrusive publicity before, during and after the trial opened up old wounds at Notre-Dame-de-Vie and further deepened the chasm between the children and their father. To Penrose, it seemed that the relationship was now so 'envenomed' that the breach was irreparable.[50] Another topic during the visit was Picasso's recent gift to the Museu Picasso in Barcelona of all the works he had left in the 'safe-keeping' of his sister and her sons – namely, a great quantity of his earliest surviving works and the majority of the paintings executed during his long stay in Spain in 1917. But this bequest to Barcelona did not signal any change of heart towards Madrid and, as the conversation with Penrose shows, Picasso was always glad to hear denunciations of Franco:

Jean Leymarie. Story of François[e's] attempt to seduce him – three days before she left Picasso.

Process[51] in Grasse, 17 March – children suing for money after writing stupid and insulting letters.

Gift of pictures to Barcelona Museum – all things that belonged to him and were kept in store in his sister's house – mostly v. early work. No change of attitude towards Franco – Zette says in '20s there was a row because P.'s mother sold off a picture or two.[52]

We talked about Gibraltar – P. said, 'Perhaps the English will give it back to Spain one day.' – I said, 'Yes, maybe, but not while Franco is there,' to which he agreed completely. [55]

On the second day, the conversation turned to the subject of fakes and to the production in London of *Les quatre petites filles*. The laconic note, 'Watched Catch', indicates that Penrose submitted graciously to the obligatory diet of televised wrestling:

14 March '70
[…] Talking about fakes. P. said, 'I once made a fake Daumier and while I was away in Holland my friends sold it and gave me 60 frs. from the proceeds – I have no idea where it is now. The signature was very good. I can still see how you made his initials H.D.'

I said, 'We are having trouble finding four little girls who can speak poetry such as you wrote for the 4 little girls. Should they all be of [a] different colour?' He said, 'No, the four little girls should be four tall gawky Englishmen.' [55]

Visiting Mougins, May–June 1970

On 1 May 1970 Penrose wrote to Picasso to announce his and Lee's next trip to the Midi:

We have taken a room for three weeks in the Hôtel de France at Mougins and I'm going to shut myself away there to write the chapter that is intended to bring my book about you up to date.[53]

Another task was to update *Portrait of Picasso* by adding photographs covering the years between 1956, when it was first published, and 1971, when the new edition was to come out in time for Picasso's ninetieth birthday. Penrose planned to visit Notre-Dame-de-Vie whenever possible but he also wanted to spend time in the exhibition at Avignon, which contained virtually every painting Picasso had executed since the beginning of 1969 and therefore offered an unparalleled opportunity to take stock of his most recent work in a more leisurely fashion than was ever possible in studio visits.[54]

Penrose's first visit to Notre-Dame-de-Vie was marked by the ceremony of gift-giving and the gratifying news that his arch-rival, Douglas Cooper, was *persona non grata*. There had been a violent row when, prompted by Claude, Cooper urged Picasso to write a will – something he had never done – and to name his illegitimate children among the beneficiaries. From this moment on, Cooper was banned from Notre-Dame-de-Vie for ever:[55]

Mougins 27 May [Added later] *1970*
Found P. sitting alone at the round table drawing. He stopped and showed me three other drawings he had just done with a fine pencil – nudes drawn in beautiful fine line, wonderfully full in form & alive – just as though they had been before his eyes.

In excellent form and easy to talk to – full of affectionate questions.

Had a green red-crested parrot given yesterday by Mme. Gili.

Talked about Prague – was unhappy about old friends there.[56]

Douglas C[ooper] – 'Il est quand meme fou, mais il n'a pas l'air comme tous le monde est fou. Il n'a pas l'air mais il est fou.'[57]

Gave him a patchwork silk shirt. A few minutes later Norman Granz arrives with two sumptuous ties.[58] Already he had shown me ties given by [Edward] Quinn. Then Sam Kootz arrives with some very expensive sport vests. He accepted all with charm.

N. G[ranz] had come from Avignon with catalogues full of admiration for show. P. said of all shows it was the one he intended least to see.

Sam K. speaks not a word of French. P. says that's why they get on so well together – met in 1946 – S.K. bought 100 pictures [and] gave P. an Oldsmobile. Now has only 5 – no reproaches. Afterwards said he liked Sam and thought of him as Uncle Sam.

Jacqueline did not appear – fatiguée – Catherine helpful and discreet.

The great tapestry is finished at the Gobelins and is coming for him to see – they are making a copy in black & white – I said it must have caused them a lot of trouble – P. said no, it's a routine affair.[59]

P. has large boxes of cigars sent by Castro – but he doesn't know where to find them. He has packets of Dunhill tobacco that were given him twenty years ago by S.K. which he smells but doesn't smoke – they are in his 'museum'.

Return of Harlequin – two figures together.[60] [56]

While in Mougins, Penrose took the opportunity to visit the Madoura factory in Vallauris and talk to Madame Ramié about the general pattern of Picasso's ceramic work over the last twelve years:

Mme. Ramié [Added later] *1970*
Years of great activity in ceramics before 1957. Now variable. [In] 1969 about 50 pieces.
   Les carreaux,[61] in general, are more recent.
   This year about 15 – owls – but who knows what may come?

Wed. doctor's day.
   Tues. dentist. J. encourages him to think his teeth need attention so as to get him out. Difficult even to get him into the garden.

Story of him leaving Mme. R. with a sketchbook to draw in a café, saying, 'On verra ce qui viens.'[62]

It was P.'s discovery of how to use a turned pot that was unique.[63] He always looked for accidents but knew that the technique of the artisan must be respected – unlike Chagall, who made messes on his own.

Owls made recently. [57]

Pleading tiredness, Jacqueline had not put in an appearance during Penrose's first visit on 27 May and from this and other observations scattered in the notes he kept during this three-week stay in Mougins, it emerges that she was temperamental, prone to tirades against Françoise Gilot and nervously protective of Picasso. Claude's court case in March had outraged Picasso, but intense emotion had always powered his work and paintings, drawings and prints continued to flood out of the studio at an exorbitant rate. Jacqueline, by contrast, had no creative outlet for her bitterness and became depressed and querulous. Chivalrously, Penrose did not hint, even in his private notes, at the drinking that exacerbated her condition: he was only too used to searing, alcohol-fuelled rows with Lee at home. But although he continued to treat Jacqueline with his customary gentleness and solicitude, he did allow himself the occasional tart observation privately:

6 June
Went with Lee to N.-D.-de-Vie. Jacqueline welcomed us.

Mme. Gili there – had brought cheap ed[ition] of 'El Entierro del Conde de Orgaz'. [She had] been met day before at airport by P. & J., went on tour of Nice, Antibes, Vallauris – v. rare event. P. did very pretty dedicase[64] for me with architect's pen & colour.

Cicero Dias arrived w. Mme. & daughter.[65]

Quinn arrives. Takes many photos but P. would not allow tape recording. Became quite angry – said, 'Apportez ça dans les cabinets.'[66]

Saw a great pile of new engravings.

P. in talkative mood. J. anxious he would overtire. Asked us to leave. Much talk of past and people who had died recently, which made J. nervous.[67] [57]

While in Mougins, Penrose filled another pocket notebook with a varied mix of questions that needed answering, lists of people, places and events, scraps of factual information, brief summaries of work seen in the studio, verbatim quotations from Picasso, candid observations of day-to-day life in Notre-Dame-de-Vie and records of conversations with others. The mix and the method are familiar from the notebooks he filled on his first research visits to Picasso in the mid-1950s. Naturally, Penrose was eager to discuss the exhibition at the Palais des Papes, and his first question concerned a new painting of Harlequin, which struck him forcibly because it was far more brutal in conception than Picasso's early essays on the same theme:[68]

Picasso, Mougins, June '70[69]
Harlequin? – not the sensitive outcast, rather aggressive type with bludgeon – modern violence? […]

'Ce qui est domage c'est que nous n'avons pas une langage qui nous reunit – les scientistes parle de ce qu'ils connaissent et moi je parle de ce que je connais et c'est deux langage differentes.

Il faut arriver à se comprendre trouver une langage commune.'[70]

'Non, le Harlequin de '69 est plus agressive. Il ne resemble pas à l'Harlequin de l'epoque bleu. Mais il est bassé sur l'Harlequin du Mardi Gras et le baton qu'il tient est traditionale.

Je pensais à Cezanne et la demarche de l'Harlequin de Mardi Gras.'[71]

Les Hidalgos – 'le dessin qu'il a fait dans mon catalogue a une resemblance avec ce portrait avec une perruque de 1898(?).'[72]

Copy of 'El Entierro' illustrated for J. Some thirty full-page drawings and many added in the text on every page.

Drawings made with fine pen. Nudes, faces, landscape backgrounds. Some using fine single line, some heavily worked. Inexhaustible variety, continuous homage to female.[73]

Superb draughtsmanship, page after page of delight. Wants facsimile to be made. Same idea as the Buffon he decorated for Dora, but much more so & very gay, instead of wartime images.[74]

Mézières vitrines never done.
   N.Y. bronzes never done.[75]

Marseille sculpture. Sculptor who proposed it had done War Memorial in Nîmes, was very enthusiastic that P. should do a great carving like him. Could never find money and ask[ed] P. to contribute. Now killed in car accident.[76]

Output greater now than ever. Drawings for J. more in size and number than for Dora, but a gay insouciance rather than tragic. Arcadian. Snarls come from dog & grotesque man.

Line has never been more sure – flood of images, clear, sensual, solid.

More wrapped up in himself and his work – complaining of time wasted with visitors.

J. wants story of children, law suits & all in book.[77] Will read typescript.

F[rançoise] not really expecting to return – had decided to marry & lied about it – wanted to keep her influence – jealous – lying – mad.

No one speaks enough of P.'s generosity – gives all the time to old friends, mistresses, etc.

Asked about still life for Tate. Probably has it – J. will look.

P. had long letter from Nesjar this morning – Sylvette statue in Holland?[78]

Drawing more perfect than painting but less profuse in inventions. Painting gives unlimited scope.

Showed P. photo of early self-portrait in white smock – he described exactly colour of scarf – orange pink.[79]

P. has a new Afghan puppy, rather redder in colour except for head – same aristocratic elegance, charming puppy manners – sharpens teeth on your trousers. This has been favourite type of dog since Kasbec – some link between aristocratic hidalgo & dog – long face seems to have special appeal to P. […] [58]

At some point while he was in the Midi Penrose met up with Jean Leymarie, who had given Picasso the new dog and was now an habitué of Notre-Dame-de-Vie. The two friends gossiped freely as usual:

Jean Leymarie
Contrarity of P.
J[ean] takes him the flyleaf of a book of P.'s belonging to a friend in Geneva for a signature. P. asks, 'Is he a close friend?' – 'Not particularly' – at which P. sets to work and does an elaborate and wonderful drawing.
After hours of running round collecting books for him to sign for Spanish painters, all done with great care at 3 a.m., he signs a small v. ordinary book for Jean with no drawings just – 'à mon cher ami'.[80] [...]
Real portraits in his drawings. For a while after Jean had given him Afghan dog, his face mixed with Marie Paule[81] and dog appeared often.
Pallarès invited every year for 10 days. He was painter, now P.'s oldest friend. Visits with his son. [...] [58]

At this or another meeting Leymarie passed on a few scraps of Picasso's conversation:

[...] J[ean] tells P. that his students want to know the difference between art and eroticism – 'Mais il y a pas de difference,'[82] says P. seriously.

Giacometti refused to see P. at time of opening of Fondation Maeght although he really wanted to very much. P. had disappeared to Toulon.

P. tells J. that he is so tired after a visit from Cooper. [...] [59]

One episode described in detail in the notebook, and recounted in the new edition of *Picasso: His Life and Work*, concerns the delivery of the tapestry reproducing an enormous cartoon created in 1938 entirely from pieces of patterned wallpaper. Commissioned by Marie Cuttoli, it proved too demanding a task for the weavers at that turbulent period and nothing was done until Pierre Baudouin took up the challenge of seeing the production through from start to finish. On 13 June he delivered the tapestry to Notre-Dame-de-Vie, where it had to be rolled out on the gravel drive because there was no wall indoors big enough to take it. Lee took her camera and, sometimes from ground-level, sometimes from the balcony, recorded the large gathering of friends who had come to witness the long-awaited event. Although Picasso was delighted with the superlative craftsmanship, a quarrel flared up later when Baudouin attempted to get him to sign a contract. All too familiar with such passing storms, Penrose watched the drama unfold, doing his best to defuse it at several points:

Mougins, Fri. 13 June

Lee, Tommy[83] & I went at 5.0 p.m. for arrival of the great tapestry. Hartmann & wife there later. Hirshhorns, Dürrbachs, Iliazds, French-American couple w. baby arrived.[84]

Finally Pierre Baudouin [arrived] w. tapestry, which was spread on gravel path beneath balcony. P. looked at it attentively. B. explained he had made yellows rather stronger than in maquette because they would fade slightly. General effect splendid. P. v. pleased.

Went down below to see it closely. Everyone astonished at accuracy of technique.

At one moment P. found himself alone upstairs with 4 girls. Started comedy of striptease to make fun. Hat, German hunter's, had [been] given him recently. In v. good form.

Tapestry made at Gobelins took two years 8 months to weave. Three weavers. Very faithful – all torn edges of paper visible. Maps w. small printing legible.[85]

This copy for P. and another in black & white. 2nd copy for State.[86] […]

16 June

Called with Lee about 5.0 p.m. Found Baudouin & Mme. Ramié with P.

William Hartmann (left) and Pierre Baudouin (right) unrolling the tapestry of *Women at their Toilette*, observed by Joseph Hirshhorn and Picasso (centre), Roland Penrose and Julie Lawson (behind Baudouin) and other friends, Notre-Dame-de-Vie, Mougins, June 1970. Photo Lee Miller

Both look[ed] v. worried. P. passed a typewritten sheet over to me saying, 'Tu es avocat regardes ça et dit moi ce que tu pense.'[87]

It was a formal, official statement saying the tapestry was made for him, one more copy would be made, which would belong to the State. It asked him to sign so as to state he was in agreement. I said it did not seem at all 'mechant'.[88]

'Non c'est moi qui est mechant. Toujours on me demande à signer et une fois fait ils fasse ce qu'ils veulent. Non je ne peux pas signer. Ils feront autant de copies qu'ils veulent et moi ce que j'aurai. J'ai déjà donné beaucoup en les laissant faire la tapisserie.'[89]

B. tried hard to explain that no other copies could be made if he signed, but he would not agree. He suggested asking his lawyer, adding, 'Probably he will tell me to sign and that will be worse.' Like a naught[y] child he refused to see their point.

'Et si je ne signe pas qu'est qu'il se passera.'

B. 'Moi je serai bien embeté – on me demandera qu'est ce que j'ai fait de la tapiserrie. Il peuvent croire que je l'ai gardé pour moi même.'

[Picasso] 'Eh bien on demandera à J.'[90]

When J. came in again with the S. baby[91] she was looking after for the day, she said emphatically – rudely, 'Non je ne dirai pas ce que vous devrez faire. Si je dis signe vous ne signerez pas et le contraire. J'ai assez que vous vous moquez de moi. Je ne dis rien.'[92]

Finally he was persuaded that it was an edition of two that was agreed and no further copies could be made. In fact the State was being generous and would certainly stand by the agreement, but P. was amusing himself at expense of B. & Mme. R. Chuckling at their embarrassment, playing with a piece of blue chalk, saying again and again, 'Eh bien je signe,'[93] and then going off into all sorts of irrelevant talk and not signing.

Finally he gave up & signed. Great relief. Mme. R. had another small problem about a ceramic that had broken in the kiln.

'Je dois vous expliquer comme ça c'est fait mais aujourd'hui vous etes trop mechant et je vous dis rien.'[94]

However she did explain and he finally agreed she was right. They then left and P. turned to me radiant, saying with a chuckle, 'Ils sont trop jeune pour comprendre. Oui je suis mechant ci ça m'amuse.'[95]

He then became serious, we talked about politics & the general confusion today, which is so unlike [19]30s & 40s – Russia & China – Prague.

I asked if all work of '69 was at Avignon but could not get a clear answer. Some had been sold. 'Ask Kahnweiler, he does all these calculations.'

Said [he] was v. annoyed about sale of Gds. Augustins. 'Si ça avait été un usine on n'aura rien fait.'[96]

Equally annoyed because he had been refused permission to build a studio on top of [the] house, for aesthetic reasons. 'Moi je veux travailler je m'en fou des raisons aesthetic.'[97]

Said mayor, who had refused, had died of it recently – now he had had a letter saying, 'Nous avons bien reflechit et peutêtre ça peut se faire.'[98]

J. not in good humour. Agreed he had been playing but said she found his play v. tiring. I said, 'Oui il faut être en bonne santé comme lui pour pouvoir l'apprecier.'[99] He continued to talk with a diabolical twinkle in his eye.

Played with baby, whistling to it.

Has been drawing & engraving. Reminded them of cubist picture for J[ohn] Golding.[100]

B. said Paulo was getting on better. He knew more about his father's work than you would think – had taken Malraux round expo. in '66. Given v. intelligent account.

Agreed F. was a monster. Said Carlton Lake was responsible for Americanisation of book.

Later P. said he had had long letters from Paulo, who was in Alicante. Bullfights. Paulo has son Pablo by first wife and Bernard by Christine.

P. had tried hard to get Miró accepted by Kahnweiler – who refused to take him on, say[ing] to have both would be too much. [...]

Judgement on book given on moral grounds. Accuracy of meaning not considered.[101]

Stress Jacqueline. [...]

[Picasso] 'I live too long.' 'Il veulent que je me depêche.'[102]

Doctor told Zette that if P. was alive it was thanks to J.

Matisse only has conversation w. him. [58]

If Penrose hoped to be able to come and go as freely at Notre-Dame-de-Vie as he had come and gone at La Californie, he must have been disappointed. There is no evidence of frequent visiting during the Penroses' three-week stay and a pleading letter Penrose addressed to Jacqueline a week before they were due to leave begging her to help him, 'without disturbing Pablo and without troubling you too much', to obtain recent photographs for the updated edition of *Portrait of Picasso* tells its own story of foiled attempts to gain admittance.[103] Jacqueline did make some useful suggestions and, as we have seen, the Penroses were welcomed again, but there was no mistaking the signs of Picasso's increasing isolation. The need to placate the now dominant Jacqueline substantially affected Penrose's subsequent actions.

After what he described as 'weeks of relentless struggle' passed in his study at Farley Farm, Penrose was able to write to Picasso early in October to say that he had finished the revisions to the biography: 'As ever, it was fascinating and very difficult, and, as I promised, I should like to show you the manuscript so that you and Jacqueline can tell me what you think,' he added.[104] Jacqueline's approval was in reality far more important than Picasso's, for she was the one who handled permissions and all the other tedious business surrounding rights and reproductions: without her good will, neither books nor exhibitions could happen. It was Jacqueline, further-more, who had insisted that Penrose discuss, rather than pass over in discreet silence, the wrenching family dramas of the past few years, and if he put a foot wrong he, like Douglas Cooper, might never be admitted to Notre-Dame-de-Vie again. Striking a balance between pleasing her and safeguarding the integrity of his book as an independent, reliable source was tricky but Penrose came up with an ingenious solution. Several precious pages were devoted to recounting in detail the outwardly trivial episode of the signing of the con-tract for the tapestries of *Women at their Toilette*.[105] This showed Picasso at his most capricious and childish – just, in fact, as he had appeared in many episodes in Françoise Gilot's book – but in Penrose's published version all turned out well in the end thanks to the exemplary good sense of Jacqueline, who tactfully but firmly – not 'rudely' (as in the notebook account) – called Picasso's bluff, and by dint of her wisdom and love for him succeeded in bringing matters to a satisfactory conclusion. By implication Jacqueline is thus presented as the ideal opposite to the disloyal, unfaithful Françoise, and Penrose used the story as the lead-in to a handsome tribute to her. Stressing the extreme difficulty of her role as intermediary between the mercurial Picasso and his friends, he praised her for her selfless devotion and care, con-cluding: 'She has become not only the great lady of Notre Dame de Vie but the main influence in the continued life and vitality of Picasso himself while at the same time she remains the source of his inspiration.'[106]

As for Cooper, the spectacle of his rival's continued intimacy with the Picassos was too galling to stomach and he mounted a scorching attack on the new editions of *Portrait of Picasso* and *Picasso: His Life and Work* in the in-house magazine of Foyles, then London's most famous bookshop: the first, a 'pathetic scrap album', was 'yet another attempt to make money out of the commotion surrounding Picasso's 90th birthday', and the second not only reproduced all the faults of the original, 'negligent, factually erroneous and often illiterate text', but added insult to injury by including new chap-ters 'spoilt by fawning and effusive flattery'.[107] Thus the Cooper-Penrose feud carried on into both men's old age.

Picasso at ninety

Early in the new year Penrose went to Barcelona to see the greatly enlarged and newly installed collections of the Museu Picasso.[108] On his way home he stopped in Cannes, hoping to get answers to last-minute questions. Publishers everywhere were rushing to get their ninetieth-birthday *hommage* volumes ready for the printers and Penrose had several other texts in preparation on top of the revisions to *Portrait of Picasso* and *Picasso: His Life and Work*. He was also planning a small, celebratory exhibition at the ICA.[109] He kept only the briefest notes of the visit, but Picasso's old Republican friend, the poet Rafael Alberti, was present and Penrose, who had been wrestling with Picasso's eccentric French, was able to discuss the eccentricities of his Spanish and the characteristics of his poetry:

Alberti has written preface to Avignon pictures. The characters are to him the former population of the Palais, not just people sent there by P.

P. liked shell I gave to Cathy. [...]

Alberti, Andalusian born in Cadiz, boisterous, modest, erudite, adores P. Says he has rare knowledge of words, remembers Andalou slang, invents words, puns, always erotic, very difficult to translate, a great poet. [60]

It must have been during this visit that Picasso executed a drawing on the title-page of Penrose's copy of *El entierro del Conde de Orgaz* (see p. 332).[110] Penrose had splashed out on buying this splendidly produced book the previous autumn and must have brought it with him to Mougins in the hope that Picasso would make some sort of embellishment. He was in luck because the drawing spreading across the opening is a wonderfully fluent and assured example of Picasso's late graphic style. A characteristic blend of beauty and grotesquerie, full of witty echoes of Spanish painting of the Golden Age, it contrives to suggest through the three characters depicted an entire narrative of cheerful pagan sensuality, lachrymose Catholic guilt and worldly cynicism – an archetypal scene from the eternal *comédie humaine*. No wonder Lee 'was crazy with admiration when she saw it', as Penrose told Picasso when he wrote to announce that a photograph of the drawing was on its way to Mougins.[111]

On his next visit to Notre-Dame-de-Vie Roland was accompanied by Lee. En route, they stopped off in Arles to see François Hugo.[112] Their conversation is particularly interesting for the references to Olga, who, for once, is not described as a jealous harpy but as docile, dominated and straitlaced. And Hugo's testimony carries some weight because he was an habitué of the Ballets Russes milieu and first met Picasso just after the First World War through Jean Cocteau and his sister-in-law Valentine Gross. He had therefore observed the first Picasso *ménage* at close quarters:

François Hugo[113]
Says Alice Derain has excellent memory of early years. She was P.'s girl until he handed her over to D[erain].

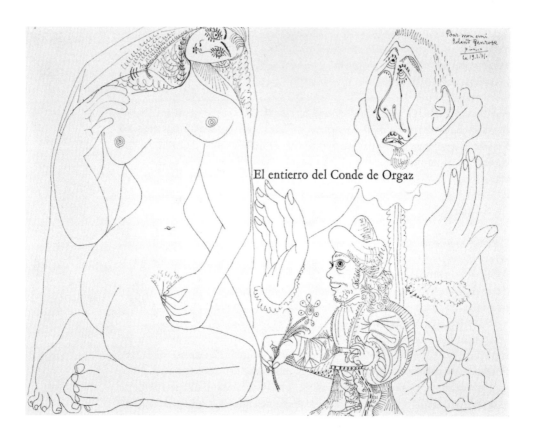

El entierro del Conde de Orgaz

Denies that Olga was main cause of P. becoming mondain in '20s – whole Russian Ballet atmosphere, Misia Sert, Errazuriz and his own taste for society responsible.

Olga not a bully. Very soumise,[114] unsexy.

'Mona Lisa' theft a great joke set up by Apollinaire!![115]

[Picasso] gave F[rançois] drawings for sides of square vase in gold. F. made it and it turned out to be a great mistake. P. sat on it – then hid it away.[116] [61]

In the hurried notes of the Penroses' visit to Notre-Dame-de-Vie on 12 May there is a brief summary of Aldo Crommelynck's insights into the changing patterns of Picasso's creativity at this period, when printmaking was assuming ever greater importance for the artist:[117]

Engravings absorb him entirely.
    Drawings happen more often when he is also painting. [...]

Aldo has noticed that [a] period [of] engravings often precedes a burst of painting – [Picasso] seems to [feel] greater freedom an[d] scope for experiment in graphics – more so than with drawing. Drawings come during painting period. [61]

Picasso himself was, Penrose noted, 'very anxious about J.'s health', and the most intriguing passage in the notebook records a conversation with Inès Sassier in which she complained bitterly of Jacqueline's unwarranted ill-treatment of her. Stories of Jacqueline's neurotic behaviour were rife at this time and Penrose, who was himself beginning to find her tiresome, was evidently not averse to hearing hostile gossip from an insider:

Inès. Full of love and admiration for P. but very upset at being kept out by J. (I don't know what can be the cause.) Has many portraits, drawings, linocuts given by P. usually on 1st Jan. Said she could not understand J.'s animosity and [is] heartbroken at being refused admission after 30 yrs. of devotion & responsibility, particular[ly] 'depuis je n'ai pas couchée avec lui quand il y avait tellement que le faisaient'.[118]

In this bewildering confusion that we call life every one of us finds his own individual conclusion. There are those who hang themselves to be rid of the problem and there are those who wait in expectancy of the Funeral of Achilles. [61]

Signs that things were unravelling at Notre-Dame-de-Vie, as Picasso's ninetieth birthday approached and frenzy overtook the international art establishment as well as the popular press, can also be detected in the correspondence surviving in the Penrose Archive. On 31 August 1971 Picasso's secretary Miguel, who took on more duties as Jacqueline's health began to crack, wrote to Penrose to report an incident in which a journalist turned up at the gates claiming to have come on Penrose's say-so, and proceeded to behave in 'an intolerable fashion'.[119] Miguel's letter was perfectly polite and no accusation was made, so Penrose was able to write back calmly confirming that the journalist had lied.[120] But the incident must have caused him a pang of anxiety since he had suffered from malicious tale-telling in the past. His next surviving letter to Picasso suggests that they had had no direct contact, even by telephone, for several months:

It feels like a long time since I had direct news of you, but even so I am passing whole days entirely surrounded by you, by your presence as it emanates from your work, and in our preparations to celebrate your birthday towards the end of this month. I hope all is well with you, that both you and Jacqueline are in good health and that you are working with your usual energy.

Here, the new editions of my books on you are with the printers so as to be out before the 25th. The BBC has made a film in colour for the television.

It lasts 70 minutes and they are very proud of it. I've seen it and really it isn't bad, despite the fact that I am shown in an interview with an art critic lasting about half an hour. I do hope that I have managed to convey something of the enthusiasm I have felt for you all these years.

At the ICA we are putting on an exhibition of your paintings, drawings and sculptures lent by collectors in London. They have been generous and we shall have more than 40 works, beginning with a very charming little land scape of the port of Málaga done in 1895, and ending with two large canvases loaned by Norman Granz, 'The Rape of the Sabines' and a 'Musketeer' of 1969.[121] On the evening of the 25th we shall celebrate your birthday with a party in the exhibition, and in other galleries the BBC film will be projected for a second time and there will be an excellent Spanish guitarist.

The production of 'The Four Little Girls' which we also want to do has had to be put off until December, in order to get everything properly in order.

So, you can see that we are thinking of you and I do so much hope that your birthday will be a time of rejoicing for you as well as the rest of us. I shall of course send you the books, catalogues and everything else as soon as they are out. Lee and I send you and the beautiful Jacqueline much love and hope to come and salute you in person sometime in November.[122]

The symbolically critical birthday came and went and although Picasso read newspaper accounts and saw television coverage of the numerous events held in his honour he took part in none of them. In Vallauris, a stage was erected in the square in front of *Man with a Sheep* and a programme of folkloric singing and dancing was organised. An enormous photograph of a benignly smiling Picasso hung aloft, printed on transparent plastic sheeting – a cult image curiously reminiscent both of the processional banners of religious orders in the Age of Faith and of propagandist portraits of dictators. Picasso and Jacqueline had promised to attend the celebrations but they never turned up and David Douglas Duncan was obliged to photograph instead all the upturned, gazing faces of Communist Party dignatories, old friends and nameless members of the crowd, as they waited patiently in the autumn sunshine for a glimpse of their idol.[123] At Notre-Dame-de-Vie, where a mountain of gifts, telegrams, cards, appeals for help and offers to buy pictures at any price accumulated, and a horde of journalists with telephoto lenses hung about at the gates, there was no sign of life and the telephone was disconnected.[124]

No doubt the Penroses contributed to the mountain with a gift and an effusive telegram, perhaps with one of Roland's touching, handmade cards: the disappearance of the original letters leaves us in the dark. In any case, Penrose wisely allowed the dust to settle before writing to announce that they were hoping to drop in on their way back from Barcelona.[125] And so they did, on 26 November at 5 p.m., the time usually set for visits at this period, for Picasso now needed a long siesta. On this occasion Notre-Dame-de-Vie was buzzing with visitors and although Penrose was cheered at the beginning of the visit by the sight of the Picassos 'in excellent form', by the end of the evening he was feeling out of sorts, irritated to be just one of a crowd and by the no longer quite so 'adorable' Jacqueline, and depressed by the obstacle of Picasso's increased deafness. His account of the visit suggests that the ritual of showing off all the latest work was much curtailed and this too must have been a disappointment:

26 N[ovember] '71
5.0 N.-D.-de-Vie
P. & J. both in excellent form. J., hair cut short, plump and healthy. Both proud of having fooled public by living in 'maqui'[126] during birthday. Went longish trips in car, once to a restaurant [in] Var.

Skira with wife & brother-in-law there. Rehashed story of P. sounding bugle call to S[kira] whose office was three floors below in the rue de La Boétie. This meant that P. had a plate or drawing ready for the 'Minotaure'.[127]

P. asked about Tony and when told he was in Persia it reminded him of story of … Berwick, R[ussian] Ballet dancer who married Persian prince, who gave a banquet – when 3 guests failed to arrive, dinner began with an enormous dish of rice which was found to contain heads of 3 guests.

P. interested to hear of Barcelona & troubles – 4 aggressions against displays in his honour in a week. 2 of them at Sala Gaspar expo.[128] He seemed unperturbed. Full of anecdotes. Skira left and Arias, the Spanish hairdresser, arrived – finally P., covered with white sheets, had his sparse crop of white hair trimmed skilfully. A[rias] has a special box decorated in pokerwork by P. in which he keeps special set of scissors, etc. only for P.[129] Like everyone at barbers, P.'s expression became entirely passive and innocent. It was artist and model, with P. as model.

P. has been working chiefly on etchings – says more than 347 completed recently. Some large pencil drawings done a few days previous – girls entwined. Gave one to photographer [Ralph] Gatti. After long evening with so many visitors he still seemed full of energy. But he is more deaf and conversation often incoherent because he does not hear, making for disjointed talk and jokes. Jacqueline dominated more than ever and did not make conversation more interesting. Very keen to show off love & power over him. Cathy rather sullen in background. General effect of evening for first time rather depressing.

P. showed me a sheet with a rather misty colour photo of a landing on the moon and written underneath, 'To a great explorer in another realm. With congratulations on his 90th birthday.'
    Signed
    … Shepard.[130]
(words may not be totally correct).
This was the only birthday card I saw. All the rest had been hidden.

Pallarès told me there never was a factory at Horta. Chimney & buildings of 1909 painting invented.[131] [62]

At the end of the year Penrose at last had the satisfaction of seeing his version of *Les quatres petites filles* performed in London at the Open Space Theatre. It was a belated birthday tribute and on 17 December he wrote excitedly to tell Picasso about the appropriately surreal production:

Yesterday evening London became acquainted with your 'Four Little Girls' in a dress rehearsal attended by lots of people. Everyone was stunned by the poetry the girls were able to communicate both through the words and their natural beauty. This morning, in the most serious newspapers, there is talk of all this fantasy, to which the English are, of course, most susceptible.

Well, you never cease to amaze us! Charles Marowitz, who directed the play, did a wonderful job, and in spite of certain modifications forced upon him by the difficulty of finding flying dogs and enough blood to drown the entire audience, he brought off some very successful effects. Chance sometimes intervened to help him in unplanned ways, as when the theatre's black cat suddenly arrived on scene. The wonderful thing was that the extravagance and the nudity of the lovely young people increased rather than diminished the astonishing poetry of the text, and one could understand perfectly every word, even the most unexpected words, because of the clarity of the little girls' diction.

I really think you would have been amused and I can assure you that the audience was extremely enthusiastic. Let me thank you once again from the bottom of my heart for giving us pleasures of this order.

As soon as possible I'll send you the programme, which is a very modest affair, and photographs of the girls and of the set, which was, incidentally, very simple. There were no seats and the entire floor of the theatre was covered with a well-padded pink grass carpet and the audience had to sit on that.

Lee joins me in sending you and the beautiful Jacqueline our best love.[132]

In subsequent letters Penrose gave news of his and Lee's doings and, hoping to please Picasso, continued the story of the London production:

[...] The play was a tremendous success in this tiny, intimate theatre with room for only 150 people seated on the ground for each performance. It played to full houses every evening for almost two months, and the little girls themselves had such a good time that on the last night they all wept at the thought of not being able to go on playing, singing and reciting your unique verses every evening. There is still a chance that some of the invitations coming from abroad, particularly France, will be accepted, but an invitation from Yugoslavia has been turned down on the gounds that it really would be too complicated. [...][133]

Sending these regular letters packed with news and affectionate greetings was a way of maintaining contact but one senses that Penrose knew he was writing into a void.

The last visits to Picasso and Jacqueline

The production of *Four Little Girls* was the last gift of his talents and devotion that Penrose was able to lay at Picasso's feet during the artist's lifetime. On their next visit to Mougins at the end of June 1972, Roland and Lee could not help noticing that he seemed older, deafer and frailer, and Penrose's notes are touched with valedictory mournfulness:

Picasso 30 June '72
Called with Lee and found the Gilis there. P. looked lively and animated when we arrived but seemed thinner and more deaf, making conversation difficult. He asked as usual after old friends – Max Ernst, Man Ray particularly, Mesens – had difficulty in not telling him M[esens] was dead[134] – he had seen Surrealist exhibition catalogue and asked me if I was still painting – no, all old work.[135] Showed him Madame Tussaud photos of wax effigy they had made – Jacqueline violently against it – he rather amused, though all agreed it was not a good likeness – still he asked for the photos to keep. Told me he has been working on drawings, engravings & paintings – large grey landscape was hanging over glass doors at end of room – a very grand and sombre work with great depth – reminded me of Poussin's 'Deluge' in its austere light – said he had made many more since. Conversation slow owing to deafness & lack of initiative on his part. Jacqueline showed us to the gate and he refused to walk down there – J. worried he does not get out enough.
   Talking of the painting, he pointed to an area in the bottom left corner saying, 'It looks just like writing and people will wonder what it means. Of course, it's not writing and in that way it means nothing.' He had made some curious strokes with his brush which entered into the composition of the foregound without signifying anything specific, whereas elsewhere there were palm trees, hillsides and a mysterious distance, like mountains in winter.[136] [63]

There is no mention in the notes of the extraordinary head-and-shoulders self-portrait drawing in coloured crayons that Picasso made on the very same day.[137] Perhaps it was made that night, after everyone had left. In any case, Picasso did show it to Pierre Daix the following day when he came as usual to gather information for his catalogue raisonné of the Cubist years. Daix has described what happened:

As we were crossing the studio beside the sitting room, left as usual in semi-darkness, with the shutters closed, [Picasso] said to me in passing, 'I did a drawing yesterday; and I think maybe I touched on something. It's not like anything I've done before.' When he had unfolded it and opened the shutters, I saw that look emerge which resembled nothing I had ever seen. He held the drawing beside his face to establish that the fear on the portrait's face was an invention. Then he rolled the drawing up again without a word.

Three months later [...] I saw the drawing spread out on one of the sitting-room armchairs. Picasso had deepened the sepia lines and the garnet-mauve hatchings at the top of the green-blue skull. 'You see, I really did catch something with this one.' His voice was easy, neutral, as if we were talking about something impersonal. [...] As we were preparing to say goodbye, he took me back to the self-portrait. I realized that he wanted me to say what I really thought, without any faking. I said that the colors were the same as those he used in his painting after the death of González.[138] He didn't blink; and I suddenly felt that, like a good Spaniard, he was looking his own death in the face.[139]

Had Picasso shown him the same self-portrait, Penrose could not have missed the shadow of death so candidly registered on the grizzled features or the fear and courage in the huge, dilated, but already glazing eyes, and it would surely have been an unbearably poignant moment for him, as he struggled to hang onto the delusion that Picasso was invulnerable. When Penrose did see the drawing and others related to it displayed in the Galerie Leiris during the winter of 1972–73, he was in no doubt of their importance and instantly bought one executed just a couple of days later.[140] In *Scrap Book* he described its impact: 'a monolithic presence, as though the head were a great rock set against the sky, the crowning feature of a mountain range.' Having compared it to Picasso's self-portrait of 1907 in the National Gallery in Prague,[141] he continued:

The indestructible appearance given to this new version, drawn nine months before he died, becomes a symbol of his enduring influence. Shaped like an inverted guitar, it stands defiantly on the mountain crest. The black mesh [of hair] has vanished, leaving a gap of the same shape. The angular nose in the painting has changed into a bulbous clownlike nose such as those of the masks with which he enjoyed entertaining his friends, and the well-shaped mouth of his youth is now a row of angular tombstones. But the strangest transformation has taken place in the two large circles of the eyes, which appear at first sight to be entirely empty. With humour and foresight, however, knowing how time could be made to work for him and with him, he filled them on the white paper with white chalk which will only become visible with age as the paper darkens bringing light back into his eyes, an allegory of his magic power to give sight to the blind, and his ability to enlist the co-operation of time and its alchemical powers over matter.[142]

This was written eight years after Picasso's death, not in the immediate, desolating aftermath. Yet it is entirely characteristic of his romantic vision of

Picasso as a miracle-working seer that Penrose should have interpreted this tragic, scribbled ghost of a skull as an expression of triumph over mortality.

Penrose saw Picasso once more after the visit to Mougins in June 1972. On a beautiful summer's day at Farley Farm, with both his wives, Julie Lawson, Joanna Drew and the indispensable Patsy Murray seated round him, the conversation inevitably turned to Picasso. On an impulse, a bouquet of roses was despatched to Notre-Dame-de-Vie with a loving note, in which Penrose expressed the hope that he would see Picasso in the autumn.[143] We know from his diary that the meeting took place on 16 September, and in the briefest retrospective note, written after Picasso's death, Penrose summarised what happened:

Alone with Miguel – J. did not appear – deafness slowed down conversation – working on engravings. [64]

And that is all.

He did not, of course, know this was to be his last visit and on 14 December he wrote enthusiastically to Notre-Dame-de-Vie to say how excited he had been by the latest exhibition of drawings at the Leiris gallery – the exhibition from which he purchased the skull-head drawing:

Roland Penrose in his study at Farley Farm, East Sussex, c. 1980. In the background are Picasso's late self-portrait drawing and (far right) Roland's portrait of Valentine Penrose with her cat. Photo Edward Quinn

I spoke with Heini and Zette and we all agreed that these are probably the most beautiful drawings you have ever made. I am now longing to see the second exhibition, with your engravings.[144]

Such ample evidence of undiminished fertility encouraged optimism, making Picasso's death seem reassuringly remote, and the rest of Penrose's letter is taken up with an account of the unveiling of his effigy at Madame Tussaud's:

We thought a lot about you in London on December 5th because there was a large reception to mark your entry in waxen form to join the greats of the entire world. The young woman who creates these effigies and who made, if you recall, the effigy of Rembrandt, which you thought wasn't too bad, has succeeded finally in producing not too bad a likeness. Obviously it's not you and in fact it would have been even more disquieting if it had been you – because of the position you've been put in, between the British government and the Royal Family! At the reception there was a whole gathering of your friends and admirers, which created a truly hallucinatory atmosphere because there were so many heads one recognised, both real and fake. I've ordered some photos of you in your new entourage and I think you will get them quite soon. Unfortunately, they are not very good because the lighting is different from how one sees the waxwork in reality. So, don't be horrified – it really isn't as bad as we feared and in any case we are happy to have you here in London.[145]

With hindsight, the completion of the waxwork in December 1972 seems like the worst piece of timing – a macabre anticipation of Picasso's death a few months later – and Penrose's laboured *badinage* seems curiously inept and insensitive. In June he had noted that Jacqueline was appalled by the prospect and appearance of the wax effigy, and one can sympathise fully with her. She knew Picasso was extremely frail and that, however much she tried to prolong his life by watching over him hour after hour, she was losing that desperate battle. Looking at photographs of the waxwork must have seemed to her like looking at an embalmed corpse. Yet that analogy does not seem to have struck Penrose: he continued to block out the truth.

Penrose made one further attempt to see Picasso. A brief note records his failure:

1973
Jan.[146] Stopped at Cannes on way back from Barcelona – spoke to Miguel on the telephone, who apologised for P. saying he was seeing nobody and wanted time for work. [64]

By this stage, this was the answer almost everybody got, for Picasso had been very ill that winter and too weak and tired to receive visitors. Penrose must have sent his and Lee's usual New Year's greetings card and he may well have sent other handwritten notes that have disappeared, but the only known full-dress letter to Picasso written in 1973 was sent in late March, just a couple of weeks before the artist's death:

I've received the enclosed photographs from Madame Tussaud's. You are keeping company with our good Queen and her mama, and also with Henry Moore in person. They apologise for the poor quality of the one with the Royal Family, and will take others, but in any case perhaps these will amuse you.

We thought and spoke of you a lot with friends who came to visit us recently. There has been a French month at the ICA, with a programme full of serious and sometimes amusing events. At least it gave us the chance to see Lucien Clergue, who is having an exhibition of his photographs, and Jean Leymarie. They both came to the farm and we never stopped talking about you. It was all great fun.

Although I haven't had any direct news of you recently, I do hope that all is well and that you are working as usual and producing splendours that we'll get to see eventually. I gather that there will be another exhibition at Avignon this summer organised by Jacqueline. This is really joyful news and Lee and I will definitely come to see it.

In the meantime, Lee and I send you and the beautiful Jacqueline our warmest love.[147]

The letter has a falsely jocular tone – the kind of thing one writes when one knows, rationally, that the recipient is sinking fast, but when one is still hoping against hope for a reprieve. When he wrote it, Penrose cannot have been ignorant that Picasso's health had declined alarmingly but he shut his ears to the rumours of the imminence of his death. With hindsight, the brevity of the retrospective report of his final visit to Mougins in September 1972 can be interpreted in the same terms: it was simply too painful and frightening to document the inescapable signs of further decline. And if it is the case that Penrose wrote no notes at all about this meeting at the time, then we have a situation that is curiously similar to Picasso's own refusal to write a will. Both were fascinated by horoscopes, palmistry and other forms of divination, and both were prey to superstition: keeping silent was a form of magic.

In *Scrap Book*, under the heading 'La Vida es Sueño' (Life is [a] Dream), Penrose movingly described his reactions to the news of Picasso's death – incredulity at first, then acceptance through faith in the immortality of great art:

For years I was obsessed with the idea that so vital a presence could never cease to illuminate my life. The shock of the news that he had died on Sunday, 8th April 1973 at first seemed incredible, just perhaps another of those diabolic jokes he enjoyed inflicting on his friends to torment them. As I came to realise the truth the only consolation I could find was that beyond death his presence would continue in his work and his influence would endure far beyond my own life.[148]

Penrose was in Farley Farm on 8 April and he did not attend the funeral two days later.[149] Hardly anyone did: Jacqueline saw to that. But he collected newspaper reports and obituaries, condoled with mutual friends and, we can be sure, wrote to Jacqueline. He also noted down what he was told two months later by Ana Maria Gili, one of the few to see Picasso not long before he died and to be present at the funeral:

Ana Maria Gili, 4 June '73
Roads blocked with snow. P. buried a few days after arrival at V[auvenargues] in snow & thunder. A[na] M[aria] with J. waited imprisoned in château – reporters all round, planes overhead and pneumatic drills digging grave in front of steps. Place dug for J. to left of P. Cold in château intense.
    Paulo v. friendly to J. – needs her – allies.
    P. already v. weak – needing oxygen at Xmas – did not dress for Xmas dinner but much better for New Year. Realised he would not live much longer – when A.M. left said, 'Je n'ai pas pour longtemps.'[150]
    His doctor in hospital with throat cancer. P. [went] to see him, [he] died a few days after P. J. in first days demolished but capable of decisions – Paulo demolished – furious at Pablito who had broken into N.-D.-de-Vie in August, drugged.[151]
    J. now in deep mourning visits Avignon exhibition incognito.[152]
    Had installed lift for P.
    P. in bed says to A.M., 'Tu as vu la cathedrale?'[153] She thinks he has gone soft but then realises he is talking of lift. [65]

Penrose also shared his grief with Alfred and Margaret Barr:

My trip to France and Spain was punctuated with fascinating but heartbreaking conversations with friends, who knew something one way or the other about the last days of our great Don Pablo. His end was happily very rapid and the elements took part in a surprising way as they took his body to Vauvenargues – terrible storms of thunder and lightning and snow made the progress very difficult.[154]

The weather just after Picasso's death was, indeed, extraordinary for Provence in the spring. David Douglas Duncan, hastening back to Cannes through the night after hearing the news, describes what happened. April 8th began unexceptionally – hazy sunshine, dry and warm – but by dawn the following day a light drizzle had developed, first into a heavy downpour, then into a violent tempest:

Roads flooded, disappeared – it was a cloudburst. Then fog suddenly isolated every creature; visibility dropped to zero. Nice airport closed, the rarest of events in its operations log. The gods hovering over our sunny Riviera – drooped and drear – seemed to be holding a Gargantuan celestial wake. The next morning, April 10th, the day Jacqueline escorted Pablo's body from his studio in Mougins where he had died, to his Château de Vauvenargues where he would rest forever – that spring morning on the Riviera it snowed.[155]

For those, like Penrose, who considered Picasso a god-like force of nature, this operatic ending was only fitting, and in the postscript to the final edition of *Picasso: His Life and Work* he recounted the Shakespearean 'portents' that 'accompanied Picasso on his last journey': Michel Leiris experienced a series of alarming phenomena affecting himself, his dog and his neighbours' children, and Jean Leymarie 'was struck with an agony totally inexplicable to him until he heard the news on the radio'. The legendary cry, 'Pan, the great Pan is dead!' seemed to voice the sense they all had that the world was altered forever.[156]

Epilogue

A month or so after the funeral Penrose went to Avignon to see the exhibition of Picasso's final paintings. He found the total effect 'overwhelming', but even at this poignant moment he was capable of looking analytically, noticing the patterns in the imagery, the bold experiments with colour and the simple but effective methods used to attract and rivet the spectator. The figures, he noted, 'talk to you – turning their heads – profile – full face, changing expression'. He was fascinated by the urgent eroticism of the work, remarking admiringly on how the lovers, 'goggle-eye[d]' with lust, devoured one another with 'sheer delight'. The utter candour of the paintings moved him deeply. So did the austerity of the presentation in the Palais des Papes, where the unframed canvases hung against the bare stone walls and there was nothing to soften the devastating pictorial spectacle or the raw emotions expressed. In a memorable analogy, he likened this final Picasso to a pavement artist.[1]

Penrose's openness to Picasso's late work was in stark contrast to the censorious response of the great majority of critics. Robert Hughes did not mince his words in *Time Magazine*:

These are, after all, the last Picassos. They are also the worst. It seems hardly imaginable that so great a painter could have whipped off, even in old age, such hasty and superficial doodles. One enters in homage and leaves in embarrassment. [...] Picasso's last show is a depressing commentary on the idea that it is better to paint anything than nothing; two years of silence would have rounded off that singular life better than these calamitious daubs. [...] Unlike Titian or Michelangelo, Picasso failed in old age.[2]

Douglas Cooper's verdict was the most brutally insulting. In a letter to the Editor of *Connaissance des Arts* he denounced the paintings as 'incoherent doodles done by a frenetic dotard in the anteroom of death'.[3] Jacqueline never forgave him for this splenetic outburst. For Penrose, championing the late work in the face of such contempt was a sacred duty and he continued to champion it to the end of his life, by which time many others had come round to his opinion.

In the immediate aftermath of Picasso's death Penrose's most substantial contribution to the burgeoning literature took the form of a book of essays, edited with John Golding.[4] His own contribution, developed from a lecture first given in 1970, gave privileged status to Picasso's drawings as the 'direct statements of his inner vision', and was an imaginative investigation of the co-existence of beauty and monstrousness, good and evil, at the core of the artist's work. This 'disconcerting duality', Penrose argued, was not only the mark of a humane realist but also provided the essential continuity within an oeuvre which, on the surface, appeared bewilderingly diverse and punctuated by gratuitous *volte-faces*.[5] In stressing the principle of reconciled opposites, Penrose spoke as an unrepentant Surrealist and voiced his conviction that Picasso too was 'a born Surrealist' and 'a Surrealist until the end'.[6]

Picasso died intestate. He had made certain bequests, notably the gift to the French State of his art collection, and had decreed that *Guernica* and its studies, together with a cast of *Woman with a Vase*,[7] should go to the Prado when democracy was restored in Spain. But otherwise his affairs were in disorder. The bulk of the estate lay in the vast accumulation of his own work and the first task was to draw up a complete inventory so that the total value could be estimated. The statistics are staggering: 1,880 paintings, 1,335 sculptures, 880 ceramics, 7,089 individual drawings, about 200 sketchbooks and almost 20,000 impressions of his prints.[8]

Once their respective claims had been determined, Picasso's heirs were given the right to pay their inheritance tax in works of art and the project to create a State-run Musée Picasso in Paris, mooted years before, crystallised. The initial selection of works for the new museum was entrusted to Jean Leymarie and Dominique Bozo, the Director designate, but an advisory committee was set up to review their decisions and make recommendations. Penrose was the one foreigner invited to join this select band and he soon formed a close friendship with Bozo.[9] The appointment was a lifeline because the previous couple of years had brought him much misery: the deaths of two of his oldest and dearest friends, Max Ernst and Man Ray, and later of Valentine; the catastrophic deterioration of his relationship with the current management of the ICA and his eventual, despairing resignation; worst of all, Lee's cancer and then death in the summer of 1977. Lee's death left him distraught, for although their marriage had never approximated to the bourgeois ideal and had often struck others as essentially unhappy, they had become indispensable to one another, united by a love encompassing the violent dualities which, Penrose believed, lay at the heart of life itself, just as they lay at the heart of Picasso's art. The new Musée Picasso symbolised rebirth and renewal after this period of prolonged mourning and he described as 'enviable' the intense period spent with the committee finalising the selection in 'the sumptuous vaults beneath a mighty Paris bank', where everything was stored.[10] The museum would, Penrose knew, be the point of entry into Picasso's work for innumerable people from all over the world and it was crucial it be, not a mausoleum full of masterpieces, but a demonstration of Picasso's genius in all its vitality and multiplicity. In helping to make the right selection, Penrose was once again acting as Picasso's instrument and mediator.

As the centenary of Picasso's birth approached, Penrose found himself in constant demand. The third revised edition of *Picasso: His Life and Work*, due out in 1981, required a coda to complete the story.[11] He was keen to include a photograph of the grave at Vauvenargues surmounted by *Woman with a Vase* but getting it would, he knew, be no easy matter. Jacqueline had found the despoliation following the settlement of the estate and the *dation* a bitter second bereavement and had sunk deeper into depression and alcoholism. Nevertheless, Penrose took his courage in his hands and wrote to ask for her help, first in January 1980, then again in December. Although affectionate and solicitous in tone, his letters reveal the extent of their estrangement since Picasso's death, for it is obvious that he had not set foot in Vauvenargues and not seen her for years.[12] The Edinburgh Archive does preserve one sad little note from her written on a scrap of white card:

Dear Roland,

I didn't know that Lee had left us. I don't know how to express my sorrow but you know how well I can understand your own.

As for your work, you must know that everything is blocked and there is nothing I can do to help you at the moment.

With love from

Jacqueline[13]

The note is undated and although it may be an answer to his letter of December 1980, the wording suggests that she was responding to another, missing letter in which he told her of Lee's death and begged a different favour, perhaps her help in obtaining the waiver of all reproduction fees for the updated editions of the biography.[14]

The centenary year was the swansong of Penrose's life as 'The Picasso Man'. The final English-language edition of *Picasso: His Life and Work* came out as planned, but without the former chorus of approval: its discretion and steadfastly loyal tone seemed outdated in the post-Gilot, post-Berger era and other biographies published since Picasso's death had caught the new, more critical mood.[15] Penrose derived greater satisfaction from the publication of the new, post-Franco Spanish translation:[16] the censorship of the original Spanish edition had given his book something of the allure of a *cause célèbre* and the new uncut version was reviewed enthusiastically in the Spanish press. The climax of all this activity came with 'Picasso's Picassos' at the Hayward Gallery in London, one of a series of international exhibitions to draw on the riches of the *dation* during the period before the Musée Picasso actually opened in 1985.[17] In this latest Picasso project Penrose collaborated with Dominique Bozo and, once again, John Golding.

Both in 1960 and in 1967 Penrose had been frustrated in his desire to present Picasso's oeuvre in an integrated manner but now, at last, he got his way: although drawings and watercolours were given centre-stage in the Hayward Gallery selection, paintings and sculptures complemented them and each other. Like the earlier exhibitions, 'Picasso's Picassos' proved a revelation – both intimate in its emphasis on the artist's creative process and grand when, for instance, the large-scale sculptures inspired by Marie-Thérèse Walter were treated like monuments, silhouetted against a blue background that stood in for the sky. Many works offered the pure excitement of the unknown and, never one for smooth harmonies and easy transitions, Penrose brought out the drama of Picasso's work through unsettling juxtapositions and sudden shifts in pace and mood. 'Picasso's Picassos' was a fitting climax to his career as a visually daring, imaginative curator, even if it could not induce in him quite the same euphoria as the exhibitions he had created 'with Picasso' when Picasso was alive.[18]

1981 also saw the publication of *Scrap Book*, which came out in time for Penrose's eighty-first birthday on 14 October – almost to the day, the centenary of Picasso's birth. Inspired by the family photograph albums Penrose had pored over as a child, and loosely modelled on the scrap book of Surrealist memorabilia he had created in spare moments during the war, its piecemeal mode allowed him to reminisce in a relaxed, conversational way, rather than lay himself bare in the type of introspective autobiography for which he had no inclination.[19] His long relationship with Picasso runs as a *leitmotif* through its pages and one cannot but notice that in form *Scrap Book* has a distinct family resemblance to *Portrait of Picasso*, although Penrose himself might have attributed this to a common dependence on the genre of the album rather than to any psychological need to identify as closely as possible with Picasso through the medium of the 'photo-(auto)biography'.

Although Valentine and especially Lee are frequently evoked, Penrose dedicated *Scrap Book* to Diane Deriaz. Like so many others remembered fondly in its pages, she was connected in his mind with Picasso, partly through her association with Paul Eluard, partly because his love for her dated from the time he took his first tentative steps as Picasso's biographer. She had come back into his life after Lee's death and it was Diane who persuaded him to start making postcard collages again for the first time in many years.[20] Appropriately, the final image in *Scrap Book* is a collage dedicated to her in memory of a trip they took to Trouville in the spring of 1980.[21] This late renaissance of the creative artist in him gave Penrose great pleasure and resulted in a large body of new work and well-received exhibitions in Paris and London.[22] Picasso would certainly have approved. *Le travail* meant everything to him and he was always urging his writer and painter friends to get back to their desks and their studios. He had continued working almost to the end and so too did Penrose, producing his last postcard collages on his final holiday in the Seychelles with Diane in January 1984.[23] He died at Farley Farm on 23 April – Lee's birthday. But there is another curiously satisfactory symmetry: Penrose was not only born in the same month, but he also died in the same month as Picasso.

Overleaf
'Pour Penrose', 24 April 1959: Picasso's inscription and ink drawing on the inside cover of the first edition of *Picasso: His Life and Work*

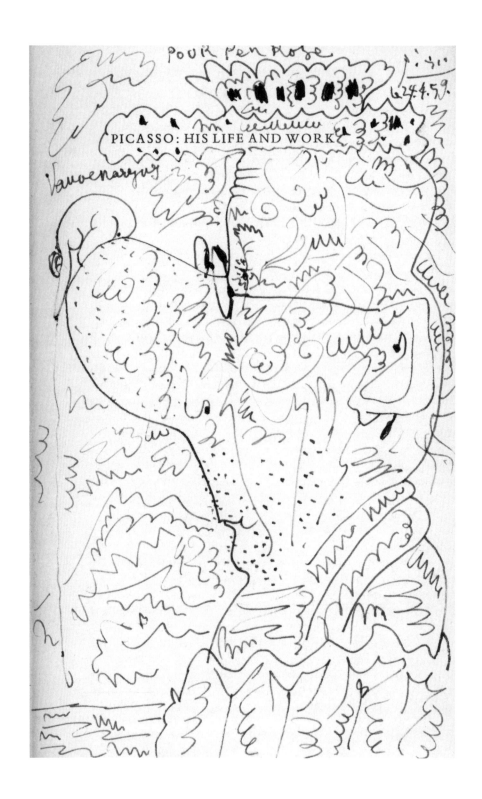

PICASSO: HIS LIFE AND WORK

Notes

Publications cited in abbreviation in the Notes below are fully listed in the Further Reading section (see pp. 400–403).

Other abbreviations used in the Notes are as follows:

ACGB: Arts Council of Great Britain archive, Victoria and Albert Museum, London
AHB, MoMA Archives, NY: Alfred H. Barr, Jr. Papers, The Museum of Modern Art Archives, New York
AP: Archives Picasso, Musée Picasso, Paris
ICA: The Institute of Contemporary Arts, London
LMA: Lee Miller Archives, East Sussex
MoMA: The Museum of Modern Art, New York
MP: Musée Picasso, Paris
MPB: Museu Picasso, Barcelona
RPA: Roland Penrose Archive and Library, Scottish National Gallery of Modern Art Archive, Edinburgh
TGA: Tate Archive, London.

Introduction

1   Picasso's dream is described under the entry for 15 October 1968 in the diary of his confidential secretary Miguel (Montañés, p. 42).
2   RP *SB*, pp. 68, 208, 216, 255.
3   Interview with Dorothy Morland conducted by Michael Sweeney on 5 February 1997 (transcript in RPA).
4   Interview with Terry O'Brien conducted by Michael Sweeney on 21 May 1997 (transcript in RPA).
5   Interview with Joanna Drew conducted by Michael Sweeney on 8 October 1997 (transcript in RPA).
6   Interview with John Golding conducted by Michael Sweeney on 4 June 1997 (transcript in RPA).
7   Interview with Rosamond Russell (aka Rosamond, or Peggy, Bernier) conducted by Michael Sweeney on 2 September 1998 (transcript in RPA).
8   RP *SB*, p. 216. See also below, Chapter 4, p. 165.
9   Penrose preserved every diary from 1934 onwards (RPA 742, 743).
10 Richardson 1991, p. 477.
11 A sense of decorum probably accounts for the absence of probing interviews with family members such as Picasso's son Paulo. Françoise Gilot has recently suggested that Penrose tried to get information from her but that she refused to divulge anything (Gilot 2004, p. 88).
12 Olivier 1933; Sabartès 1946.
13 Gilot 1964.
14 Brassaï 1967.

1   Michael Sweeney, in conversation with the author, 29 May 2004.
2   From the account of Penrose's visit to Picasso in Perpignan, 17 September 1954 [4].

Chapter 1   The Foundation of the Friendship, 1936–1939

1   *Woman Lying in the Sun on the Beach*, 1932 [Z.VII.353].
2   RP *SB*, p. 206. See also *ibid.*, pp. 68–69.
3   According to Penrose's diary, he met Eluard in Paris on 28 October and 2 November 1935 (RPA 742.2).
4   Penrose's diary records a meeting with 'David Gascoigne' on 22 October 1935 (RPA 742.2).
5   See Remy, p. 71. Gascoyne's translation of Breton's text was published by Faber and Faber in 1936 as *What is Surrealism?*
6   The dates for this and the subsequent meetings are recorded in Penrose's diary for April–June 1936 (RPA 742.3).
7   Picasso left Paris on 25 March 1936 and remained in Juan-les-Pins until 14 May (Sabartès 1946, pp. 127–29).
8   On 31 March 1936 Eluard wrote to his former wife Gala (who, in 1934, had married Salvador Dalí), 'Picasso […] est brusquement parti pour longtemps – destination inconnue' ('Picasso has left suddenly for a long time – destination unknown.' Eluard, no. 215).
9   See RP *PLW* 1958, p. 259.
10 *Ibid.*, p. 62, and see below p. 60.
11 RPA 742.3.
12 See *Surrealism*, catalogue of the 'International Surrealist Exhibition', London, New Burlington Galleries, 11 June–4 July 1936, nos. 294–304.
13 In contemporary letters to Gala, Eluard described this break with Breton as 'definitive' – in fact, the definitive break came only in 1938 – and he begged her to ensure Dalí keep his promise to lecture in London. Penrose, he added, 'est vraiment un garçon très gentil, très généreux, très bien' ('is really a very charming, very generous, very decent fellow'. Eluard, nos. 216, 220).
14 '[…] Je veux vous redire quel magnifique souvenir je garde de Londres, avec vous et combien je suis heureux d'avoir trouvé un nouveau, un vrai ami […]' (postcard from Eluard to Penrose dated 15 July 1936; RPA 705).
15 RP *SB*, p. 80.
16 RP *PLW* 1958, pp. 261–62.
17 'un reve inoubliable des merveilles' (undated letter, of mid-October 1936, sent to Picasso from 21 Downshire Hill, London; AP). The only earlier communication from

Penrose in the Archives Picasso is a postcard (postmarked 15 September 1936) sent from Corsica, where Roland and Valentine spent several days in the middle of their holiday in Mougins.

18 In February 2004, however, Nicola Polverino, a local Mougins man who was a boy at the time, told Antony Penrose that it was Picasso who was driving when the accident occurred: irked by the teasing about his inability to drive, Picasso insisted on taking the wheel and crashed into a wall. (There is no support for this colourful story in the Penrose Archive, regrettably.)

19 For Picasso's description of his agonies, see the snatches of his letters cited in Sabartès 1946, pp. 134–35.

20 e.g. Penrose's letter to Picasso of mid-October 1936 (see note 17 above).

21 RP *PLW* 1958, p. 262.

22 See *L'Art de la Catalogne de la seconde moitié du neuvième siècle à la fin du quinzième siècle*, ed. Christian Zervos, Paris, Editions 'Cahiers d'Art', 1937. See below, note 28, for the article defending the Republicans and Anarchists on which Zervos and Penrose collaborated. The exhibition, 'L'Art catalan du Xe au XVe siècle', was mounted at the Musée du Jeu de Paume in March–April 1937, with a catalogue by Joaquim Folch i Torres.

23 Gascoyne, pp. 35–36: entry headed '13.10.36'.

24 Date established by Penrose's diary (RPA 742.3).

25 Open letter from Fenner Brockway, secretary of the Independent Labour Party, preserved with other documents relating to the Penroses' mission to Catalonia (RPA 630).

26 As in note 17 above.

27 RP *SB*, p. 84.

28 Christian Zervos and Roland Penrose, 'Art and the Present Crisis in Catalonia', *Catalan Art from the Ninth to the Fifteenth Centuries*, London and Toronto, William Heinemann, pp. 28–36. (See also above, note 22.)

29 Penrose's diary entry for Tuesday 15 December 1936 notes: '7.00 Eluard' (RPA 742.3).

30 Gascoyne, pp. 49–50.

31 Picasso's *Minotauromachy* [Geiser & Baer 573] was shown for the first time at the Zwemmer Gallery in December 1935 ('For Christmas 1935', 14 December 1935–25 January 1936). It appeared in the catalogue as 'Not Yet Named' and was apparently given its present title by Anton Zwemmer himself (Halliday, p. 132). It was much discussed in reviews of the exhibition and the gallery's sale records (TGA 992.4.3) reveal that a number of impressions, priced at 20 guineas, were sold after the show closed. Penrose bought his impression (no. 2) on 22 February 1936.

32 Picasso, *Head*, 1913, Scottish National Gallery of Modern Art, Edinburgh [DR 595].

33 '[…] je tiens – follement – à garder ce petit tableau que j'ai poursuivi des années avant de pouvoir le contempler à loisir. C'est aussi tout ce qui me reste de Picasso et je crains, ne l'ayant plus, de me sentir plus pauvre encore. Je sais que vous êtes fait pour comprendre admirablement ce sentiment […]' (letter to Penrose from André Breton dated 6 July 1936; RPA 703).

34 Letter to Penrose from Breton dated 20 February 1937 (RPA 703). To judge by an insurance document dated 30 October 1937 (RPA 395), Penrose paid Breton £45.

35 RP *SB*, p. 162. See also Penrose's essay, 'The Pleasures and Miseries of Collecting', *The Magazine of Art*, December 1952, pp. 339–46.

36 On Cooper's collection, see Richardson 1999, especially pp. 19–30, and Dorothy Kosinski's essay in *Cooper* 1988, pp. 13–25. Edward James, whose equally spectacular collection of Surrealist art was also formed during the 1930s, was a collector and patron in the Cooper mould. Penrose's relationship with James was more cordial and less rivalrous than with Cooper, but also not as close.

37 Letter to Picasso dated 11 March 1937, sent from 21 Downshire Hill, London (AP).

38 *Woman Lying in the Sun on the Beach* is reproduced in 'Picasso 1930–1935', special issue of *Cahiers d'Art*, p. 61. The issue is undated but was published in late January or February 1936.

39 RP *SB*, p. 68.

40 *Ibid.* It was not, as we have seen, Penrose's first Picasso, but it was the first work he bought directly from the artist.

41 *Ibid.*, p. 69, fig. 167, where the photograph is misdated 'March 1936'.

42 *Ibid.*, p. 68.

43 Gascoyne, pp. 74–75.

44 It is listed as *La plage* in the insurance document drawn up on 30 October 1937 (RPA 395).

45 '[…] je puis vous dire en toute sincérité que vous avez, du point de vue artistique, fait un coup de maître, mais aussi, du point de vue affaire, une excellente opération. Vous ne tarderez pas à vous en apercevoir. Mais je m'en réjouirai pour vous. Vous avez eu plus de "cran" que les marchands qui auraient dû "sauter" sur une telle affaire […]' (letter to Penrose from René Gaffé dated 30 June 1937; RPA 180).

46 The prices Penrose paid for each work in the Gaffé collection are given in a handwritten list drawn up by Mesens in June–July 1937 (RPA 180). The works are, in order: *Female Nude with Raised Arms*, 1907, Thyssen-Bornemisza Collection, Lugano [DR 54]; *Seated Woman*, 1909–10, Stedelijk van Abbemuseum, Eindhoven [DR 326]; *Portrait of Wilhelm Uhde*, 1910, Emily and Joseph Pulitzer Collection, St Louis [DR 338]; *Girl with a Mandolin (Fanny Tellier)*, 1910, MoMA [DR 346]; *Man with a Violin*, 1912, Gelman Collection, The Metropolitan Museum of Art, New York [DR 535].

47 Moore described the visit in an interview with John and Vera Russell published in *The Sunday Times*, 17 December 1961 (excerpted in Oppler, p. 202). Penrose's diary notes a meeting with Moore in London on 19 May 1937 and various appointments in Paris with Surrealist friends on 22, 23 and 24 May. By the evening of 25 May he was back in London (RPA 742.4). The studio visit must have taken place between 22 and 25 May but is not noted in Penrose's diary.

48 RP *PLW* 1958, p. 275. Moore reminisced with Penrose about this episode when they met on 14 November 1956: a note of their conversation is in RPA 586 [2].

49 Recorded in Penrose's diary (RPA 742.4).

50 A flyer, headed *Spain and Culture*, describes the event thus: 'Grand International Meeting under the auspices of the National Joint Committee for Spanish Relief in aid of the Basque Refugee Children' (RPA 630). A card from E. L. T. Mesens to Picasso, dated 1 July 1937, confirms that Picasso had been expected to attend and notes that the evening raised £15,000 (quoted in Madeline, p. 229).

51 RP *SB*, pp. 104–6.

52 Penrose's diary notes that he and Miller arrived in Mougins on 19 August 1937 and left on 17 September (RPA 742.4).

53 Agar, pp. 132–42.

54 RP *PLW* 1958, pp. 279–80. The portrait of Eluard is Z.VIII.373.

55 Antony Penrose believes the portrait is *The Arlésienne*, dated 11 September 1937 [PP.37.191]. Roland Penrose mentions it in his letter to Lee Miller of 6 October 1937 (LMA), noting that it is about to be shipped to America for inclusion in Picasso's forthcoming retrospective ('Picasso: from 1901 to 1937') at the Valentine Gallery, New York. The Valentine Gallery catalogue gives no dimensions and several pictures fit the brief description given 'L'Arlésienne', 1937.

56 RP *SB*, pp. 108–9. The description is of *Portrait of Lee Miller*, 1937 [PP.37.198 (a)].

57 Agar, pp. 135, 139.

58 Their originality was first celebrated in René Magritte and Paul Nougé, 'Colour-Colours, or an experiment by Roland Penrose', *London Bulletin*, no. 17, 15 June 1939, pp. 9–12.

59 'The Road is Wider Than Long: Sir Roland Penrose at 80', BBC Radio 3. Recorded conversation between Penrose and Edward Lucie-Smith, transmitted on 14 October 1980 (transcript in RPA 390).

60 RPA 742.4.

61 Letter to Lee Miller dated 6 October 1937, sent from the Channel ferry to Alexandria (LMA).

62 Penrose's set of *Dream and Lie of Franco* is numbered 11/150 [Geiser & Baer 615, 616]. In multicoloured crayons, Picasso dedicated each of the plates and wrote at the bottom of his prose poem: 'mon ami Roland/ Penrose/ Picasso/ PARIS le 5 octobre/ MCM.XXXVII'.

63 As in note 61 above.

64 Letter to Lee Miller dated 25–26 October 1937, sent to Cairo from 21 Downshire Hill, London (LMA).

65 *Ibid.*

66 Letter to Lee Miller dated 13 December 1937, sent to Cairo from 21 Downshire Hill, London (LMA).

67 RP *SB*, p. 109.

68 *Weeping Woman*, 1937, Tate, London [Z.IX.73].

69 Letter to Lee Miller dated 18 January 1938, sent to Cairo from Paris (LMA).

70 According to Brigitte Baer, Picasso began work on the copper plate on 1 July 1937 [Geiser & Baer 623]. There were seven states in all. Penrose owned no. 7/15 of the third state and no. 5/15 of the seventh state. Picasso dedicated the prints to Penrose but for once omitted to add the date.

71 RP *SB*, p. 88.

72 *Ibid.*

73 In the memoranda section of his diary for 17–23 January 1938, Penrose wrote: 'Picasso £284   £100 paid £184 paid 4.4.38' (RPA 742.5).

74 For fuller details, see AP 2001, p. 86.

75 'Cher Picasso,
Le moment est enfin arrivé quand je peut payer mes dettes, je vous envoie donc la solde de ce que je vous devais pour votre tableau.
Je suis de plus en plus heureux de posseder cette toile magnifique qui continue à faire un impression enorme sur moi même et des quantités de gens qui l'ont vue. Dans un moment aussi epouvantable quand on vit sur un potage d'evenments l'un plus atroce que l'autre, ce tableau, comme un drug, me donne du courage. Il neglige rien de cet agonie mais il le depasse.
A Londres un evenement d'un autre orde mais qui me touche de près, m'a donné beaucoup de travail dernièrement – c'est l'arrivée de mon ami Mesens qui a prit sur lui le direction d'une petite gallerie de tableau – le London Gallery. Nous avons reussit à grouper autour de cet entreprise plusiers poetes peintres, cineastres, critiques et d'autre enthusiastes et nous esperons commencer, même à cet epoque disastreuse, une activité comme on n'a jamais vu à Londres. Le premier numero du Bulletin de la gallerie, que Mesens propose à editer tous les mois, vous a été expedié – j'éspère que vous ne m'en voudrez pas d'avoir inclus le photo de vous avec Eluard à Mougins. Votre presence dans le premier numero me semblait essentiel et comme nous étions très pressé pour completer tout à temps je n'ai pas eu le temps de vous consulter d'avance. Nous aurons la collaboration dans ce bulletin de Herbert Read, Eluard, Douglas Cooper, Breton [*inserted in margin*: Je cite ces noms seulement pour montrer une certaine diversité], plusieurs Belges et enfin une collection très large de poetes et critiques de tous les pays du monde. En tous cas votre appui est une des choses le plus essentiel pour nous. Vous imaginez quel plaisir une poeme ou un texte de vous pourrait nous faire.
Je n'ai pas fait de projet encore pour mon prochain visite à Paris mais j'espère bien vous revoir pendant le courant de l'été. En attendant je vous envoie mes amitiés sincères.
Très cordialement à vous
Roland Penrose.
– Je ne saurai pas exprimer l'horreur et le degout que les nouvelles de l'Espagne m'inspire. Acceptez je vous prie mes sympathies profondes.'
(Letter to Picasso dated 4 April 1938, sent to 23 rue La Boétie, Paris, from 21 Downshire Hill, London; AP.)

76 Sporting a comic Chamberlain mask and top hat, Penrose participated in the noisy demonstrations in Hyde Park on May Day 1938.

77 I am most grateful to Gijs van Hensbergen for sharing his knowledge of the history of *Guernica* with me and for generously allowing me to read the relevant chapters of his book in draft. Much of the information given below is dependent on his research. (See Hensbergen, especially Chapter 3.)

78 'Aujourd'hui l'affaire se pose comme suit: nous désirons que l'exposition se fasse avec le maximum de relief et de solennité possible, et pour Picasso que plus il sera estimé

plus il pourra être utile à notre cause, et pour notre cause même, car celui-ci est un des rares moyens que nous avons d'atteindre ce secteur de personnes pour lequelles un argument de cette nature peut être convaincant. La question d'en tirer de l'argent ne peut être considérée qu'en deuxième lieu.' (Letter to Penrose from Juan Larrea dated 12 February 1938, sent to 21 Downshire Hill, London, from the Conseil pour l'Expansion de la Culture espagnole à l'Etranger, Paris; RPA 717.)

79 'Notes', *London Bulletin*, nos. 4–5, July 1938, p. 40.

80 Penrose is so described in the illustrated leaflet advertising the 'Exhibition of Picasso's "Guernica"' at the New Burlington Galleries (RPA 535A). The Chairman was Wilfred Roberts, MP.

81 Letter to Lee Miller dated 16 September 1938, sent to Romania from Paris (LMA).

82 'Cher Picasso,
   Les preparations pour l'exposition 'Guernica' continuent toujours et l'interet du public est chaque jour plus grand malgré l'affolement general qu'il y a eu ces jours-ci. A cause de ceci les tableaux n'arriveront qu'aujourd'hui. Mais quand même nous éspérons être pret pour l'ouverture Mardi prochain à 3.30 de l'après-midi.
   Sir Peter Chalmers Mitchell qui doit avec l'ambassadeur de l'Espagne ouvrir l'exposition est un veillard très estimé ici pour son attitude admirable lorsqu'il s'est trouver à Malaga au moment de sa chute. Par ailleurs il était dans le temps le directeur du Jardin Zoologique de Londres. J'espère que vous approuverez notre choix.
   J'ai eu deux demandes déjà pour exposer les tableaux après la fermature ici dans les villes de province. Les cités de Leeds et de Manchester desirent avoir l'exposition dans leurs galeries municipales. Nous pouvons arranger ceci dans les mêmes conditions que nous avons fait ici si vous le desirez, mais ils demandent un reponse assez rapidement.
   Tous les deux de ces cités sont des centres très importants et je crois que l'exposition pourrait y faire grande sensation.
   J'éspère toujours que l'envie vous prendra de venir à Londres avec Dora et les Eluards. Si vous pouvez venir mardi prochain pour l'ouverture tant mieux mais sinon vous serez toujours le bienvenu. Venez quand vous pouvez, ma maison sera à votre disposition Il y a un train de nuit qui va directement par Dunkerque sans changer de compartiment – on dors comme dans un berceau.
   J'étais content d'avoir de vos nouvelles par Larrea.
   Avec mes souvenirs très cordiaux
   Roland Penrose.'
   (Letter to Picasso postmarked 30 September 1938, sent to 23 rue La Boétie, Paris, from 21 Downshire Hill, London; AP.)

83 RP *SB*, p. 87.

84 Letter to Picasso from Paul Eluard, sent from London and dated 8 October 1938 (Madeline, pp. 230–31).

85 Diary entries for October 1938 (RPA 742.5).

86 'L'exposition "Guernica" est terminé à Londres son success moral a été indiscutable mais nous n'avons pas eu la foule de visiteurs que j'éspèrais voir venir. Pour cela je pense que la crise et la demoralisation generale qui l'a suivit est en grand part responsable. […] Deux expositions me semblent maintenant arrangé certainement l'un à Oxford et l'autre dans une quartier populaire de Londres, Whitechapel, où la sympathie pour la cause Espagnole est très grande.' (Letter to Picasso dated 6 November 1938, sent to 23 rue La Boétie, Paris, from 21 Downshire Hill, London; AP.)

87 RPA 742.5.

88 Eric Newton, 'Pictures and Patriotism', *The Sunday Times*, 9 October 1938.

89 Roland Penrose, 'Note', *London Bulletin*, nos. 8–9, January–February 1939, p. 59.

90 '[…] Je voudrai vous donner l'impression profond que vos oeuvres ont provoké parmi ces gens simples et aux reaction relativement pure […]' (letter to Picasso dated 21 January 1939, sent to 23 rue La Boétie, Paris, from 21 Downshire Hill, London; AP).

91 Letter to Lee Miller dated 23 November 1938, sent to Cairo from 21 Downshire Hill, London (LMA).

92 These phrases appear in Penrose's letters to Lee Miller of 19 March and 2 April 1938, describing the purchase and launch of the London Gallery (LMA).

93 RP *SB*, p. 170. A letter Penrose wrote to Lee Miller on 14 June 1938 confirms that Nusch and Paul Eluard were staying with him at that time (LMA). Initial discussions of the sale probably took place then.

94 Handwritten agreement drawn up by Paul Eluard and dated 27 June 1938. In translating part of the document in RP *SB* (p. 170), Penrose mistakenly gave the total amount he paid as £1,500, forgetting that he had made an initial down-payment of £100 on 27 June.

95 Letter to E. L. T. Mesens quoted in Hartley (1), p. 16.

96 Annotation by Penrose to Eluard's original handwritten list (RPA 138).

97 *Still Life*, 1914, Tate, London [DR 746].

98 This list is the only one annotated with individual prices (RPA 138).

99 Letter to Lee Miller dated 27 March 1939, sent to Cairo from 21 Downshire Hill, London (LMA).

100 'mon cher Penrose
   Comme je vous l'ai dit je voudrais que le tableau Guernica et les dessins et autres tableaux qui sont à Londres me soient envoyer le plustôt possible à Paris et n'admets que d'autres que moi ayent la pretention de decider ou ces oeuvres doivent etre envoyer.
   J'ai eté bien content de vous voir l'autre jour et je espere que bientot nous aurons le plaisir de paser un plus long moment ensemble
   Bien à vous
   Picasso'
   (Letter to Penrose from Picasso dated 28 March 1939; RPA 717.) Penrose had seen Picasso in Paris on 23 March 1939, as we know from his letter to Miller of 27 March (see note 99 above).

101 Letter to Picasso dated 15 April 1939, sent to 23 rue La Boétie, Paris, from 21 Downshire Hill, London (AP).

102 Magritte and Nougé praised Penrose for his entrepreneurial skills at the beginning of 'Colour-Colours, or an experiment by Roland Penrose', *London Bulletin*, no. 17, 15 June 1939, p. 9.

103 'give tear out twist and kill …' (translation of 'donne arrache tords et tue', a text by Picasso dated 17 September 1935), *London Bulletin*, nos. 15–16, 15 May 1939, p. 3.

104 *Night Fishing at Antibes*, 1939, MoMA [Z.IX.316].

105 RP *PLW* 1958, pp. 289–90.

106 RP *SB*, p. 124.

107 See Trevelyan, pp. 111–21, for a vivid account of their exploits as *camoufleurs*.

108 The list is headed 'Pictures stored at Bradenham Hall, Thetford, from Penrose collection', and dated September 1939 (RPA 395).

109 *Grand air* [Geiser & Baer 608] was among the illustrations by Picasso in Paul Eluard's *Les Yeux fertiles*, Paris, GLM, 1936 [Goeppert et al 27]. The ten de luxe copies included the original etching.

110 List dated 10 June 1943 drawn up for Duveen & Walker Ltd., Penrose's insurance broker (RPA 385).

111 'Picasso: Forty Years of His Art', MoMA, in collaboration with The Art Institute of Chicago, 1939–40. Penrose lent: *Head (Femme au nez en quart de brie)*, 1907 [DR 35]; *Girl with a Mandolin* [DR 346]; *Man with a Violin* [DR 535]; *Head*, 1913 [DR 595]; *Portrait of Nusch*, 1937 [PP.37.174 (a)]; and *The End of a Monster*, 1937 [PP.37.242].

112 Letter to Penrose from Alfred Barr dated 17 November 1939, sent to 21 Downshire Hill, London, from MoMA (RPA 537).

113 Draft of letter to Barr dated 13 January 1940 (RPA 537). In the same letter Penrose quoted much lower prices for four of the other works he had loaned to the MoMA exhibition.

114 This figure is quoted in the letter Mesens sent Gaffé on 15 August 1939 when Penrose was still in Antibes (copy in RPA 180). The deteriorating political situation brought an abrupt end to these negotiations.

115 Cablegrams sent to Penrose by Barr on 2 April 1940 and 10 April 1942 (RPA 537). On 25 April 1942 Penrose cabled back, refusing Barr's latest offer (AHB [AAA: 2168; 152]. MoMA Archives, NY).

Chapter 2   A Choice of Paths, 1939–1954

1 *London Bulletin*, nos. 18–20, June 1940. The previous issue, no. 17, came out a year earlier on 15 June 1939.

2 A typed list on London Gallery headed paper, captioned by Penrose 'Burnt in warehouse fire 1940', is in RPA 277–278.

3 See Scheler, pp. 101, 148, 168–69, for fuller details and for the relevant letters from Eluard to Parrot and Parrot to Dias in August–October 1942.

4 Paul Eluard, *Poésie et Vérité*, 1942. *Poetry and Truth*. Translated by Roland Penrose and E. L. T. Mesens, London Gallery Editions, 1944. *Poésie et Vérité* was first published in Paris in May 1942 under the imprint of Editions de la Main à Plume. It was republished afterwards in Algiers by Editions de la Revue Fontaine.

5 'Très cher ami,
   Enfin le mur est rompu – on peut rentrer en contact avec vous et nos amis qui nous ont tellement manqué par ce cauchemar interminable. L'interminable est terminé.

Je m'hate de vous ecrire ne sachant pas où et quand ceci peut vous trouver, ni dans quel etat après les privations que vous avez du subir. Il se peut bien que avant que ceci vous trouve vous aurez, si vous êtes à Paris, eu une visite de Lee. Après une guerre de patience et de travail à Londres elle a eu la chance d'aller en France comme War Correspondant attaché à l'armée American et je sais que une de ses buttes sera de vous retrouver le plus vite possible. Moi je n'ai pas eu la même chance, car ayant fait partie de l'armée avec l'idée que ça sera le moyen le plus rapide de rentrer en France je me trouve collé loin dans une ville de province sans le moins d'espoir de voir le continent temps que je reste militaire.

Je voudrai tant avoir de vous nouvelles et des nouvelles de Dora, Paul, Nusch et tant d'autres amis, on n'ose presque pas demander après tant de silence et tant de perils et je ne sais pas où les trouver.

Londres a été d'une sterilité parfaite depuis le contact coupé de Paris. Un seul petit exposition de reproductions de vos recentes peintures à été en vu dernièrement. Reproductions qui m'ont donné fort envie de voir les originaux. Après tous les cris et tous les drapeaux, aussitôt debarassé de khaki de viendrai avec une vitesse incroyable.

Nous avons, Mesens et moi, traduit et publié les poemes de Paul, "Poesie et Verité" 42 qui ont eu un success assez important. Si vous pouvez me donner son adresse je le demanderai la permission un peu en retard pour cette publication.* voir au dos

*J'espère tant que ce geste qui été de tout importance pour nous à Londres ne l'a pas apporté tort. Sachant qu'il fallait éviter à tout prix une publicité qui l'aura livré à l'enemi nous avons hesité jusqu'au moment que ces poemes avait déjà paru dans Fontaine et dans une edition à Algers avant de les editer à Londres. Je serai heureux de savoir que rien ne l'est arrivé à cause de ça.

Il me semble presque incroyable encore de pouvoir vous ecrire – tant la guerre a rendu la mort a tous ce qu'on aimait – La vie prendra du temps a se refaire.

Dites moi ce qui manque à vous et aux amis pour que je peut essayer de vous l'envoyer aussitôt que les communications sera reétablit. A nous il nous manque surtôt la vie, les amis, la poesie.

Cher ami et chers amis je vous voir mon affection profond
   Roland Penrose'
   (Letter to Picasso dated 27 August 1944, sent to 7 rue des Grands-Augustins, Paris, from 21 Downshire Hill, London; AP.)

6 AP 1992, p. 73.

7 'J'ai devant moi un photo de vous avec Lee qui est superbe – Il me fait rager et gemir d'etre aussi à Paris.' (Letter to Picasso dated 16 September 1944, sent to 7 rue des Grands-Augustins, Paris, from 21 Downshire Hill, London; AP.)

8 RP *SB*, p. 136.

9 On a slip of paper in Penrose's diary (RPA 742.11) there is a brief note from Dora Maar sending her love and giving her address (6 rue de Savoie). Penrose used the same slip of paper to jot down details of the wartime atrocities

suffered in Paris (deportations of Jews, executions, etc.) and to list a whole series of 'wants', ranging from cleansing cream to jam.

10 Picasso, 'Why I became a Communist', October 1944, quoted in Utley, p. 43. Penrose preserved the page in the *Daily Worker* for 15 December 1944, which carried Picasso's statement (RPA 529).

11 Philip James, 'Picasso and Matisse', *Exhibition of Paintings by Picasso and Matisse*, Arts Council of Great Britain, 1946, p. 10. The essay was published in the catalogue for the Manchester and Glasgow versions of the exhibition.

12 Eric Newton, 'Storm over Picasso', *The Manchester Guardian*, 22 December 1945, p. 4.

13 Brassaï 1999, p. 293.

14 'Picasso: genius or hoax?', *Evening Standard*, 19 December 1945.

15 Carbon copy of a letter to the Editor of *The Times* dated 31 December 1945 (RPA 538). 'Paul Klee', the exhibition to which Penrose refers, was organised by the Tate Gallery but held at the National Gallery, London, December 1945–February 1946.

16 RP *SB*, p. 138.

17 Interview with John and Cynthia Thompson conducted by Michael Sweeney on 18 November 1997 (transcript in RPA). Thompson later became editor of the *Sunday Telegraph*. His wife worked for *Life Magazine*. They saw a great deal of the Penroses throughout the 1940s.

18 According to Joanna Drew, 'both Lee and Valentine said that they wished Roland would give up working on official committees, exhibitions and so on, and do his own art instead' (interview with Michael Sweeney conducted on 8 October 1997; transcript in RPA).

19 See, for instance, 'Foreword', *40 Years of Modern Art 1907–1947: A Selection from British Collections*, ICA, 10 February–6 March 1948. For a fuller summary of the formation of the ICA, see Hartley (1), pp. 19–22.

20 Eric (aka Peter) Gregory was a prominent figure in the British art world after the war. Among other positions, he was head of the printing and publishing firm of Percy Lund, Humphries and Co. and Honorary Treasurer of the ICA. Peter Watson was a generous patron of the arts and a keen supporter of the journal *Horizon* as well as the ICA. The deaths of Watson in 1956 and Gregory in 1959 were a severe moral and financial blow for the ICA.

21 George Hoellering, the manager of the Academy Cinema, was a founder-member of the ICA.

22 Foreword, *40 Years of Modern Art 1907–1947: A Selection from British Collections*, ICA, 10 February–6 March 1948, n.p.

23 '40,000 Years of Modern Art: A Comparison of Primitive and Modern', ICA, 20 December 1948–29 January 1949.

24 'Cher Picasso

Vous vous rappelerez sans doute de Mlle. Gigi Richter qui vous presentera cette lettre. Comme elle est de passage en France, elle a bien voulu m'aider dans un grand projet pour un exposition cet hiver organisé par notre Institute of Contemporary Arts.

Notre idée est de faire un confrontation de l'Art Primitif et de l'Art Moderne. Du coté primitif nous aurons des pieces prehistoriques, oceaniques, et negres, preté par des Musées d'Oxford, Cambridge Brighton etc ainsi que le Musée de l'Homme. Pour l'art moderne, la pièce de resistance sera "Les Demoiselles d'Avignon" qui nous sera envoyé par le Museum of Modern Art de New York, en plus nous mettrons trois ou quatre toiles importantes de vous et quelques pieces de sculture et des peintures representatif du moment moderne.

Mais ce que nous desirons, pour ajouter un autre element d'importance capitale, c'est de pouvoir exposer trois ou quatre de vos poteries que j'ai vu reproduit dans les Cahiers d'Art.

C'est pour cela, etant dans l'impossibilité d'echapper de Londres moi même que nous vous envoyons la belle Gigi, esperant que vous serez disposé de la confier quelque pieces pour notre exposition.

Je dois ajouter que l'esposition evidement est nullement commerciale – rien ne sera à vendre – mais je me charge de m'occuper personellement de l'assurance et le retour des poteries si vous avez l'aimabilité de nous preter quelques unes.

Il sera pour notre Institute et pour le publique de Londres en general un evenment très important si nous pouvons mettre dans le même exposition "Les Demoiselles" et des exemples de vos derniers oeuvres qui surement d'après les photos sont de toute beauté.

Nous serons donc extremement reconnaissant si vous voyez le possibilité de nous accorder cette demande. Lee se joint à moi en vous envoyant nos amitiés les plus sinceres et nous esperons quand même vous voir quand l'exposition sera terminé.

Bien à vous
Roland Penrose'
(Letter to Picasso dated 11 October 1948, sent from 36 Downshire Hill, London; AP.) Gigi Richter was a German picture restorer attached to the London Gallery.

25 'Poterie et une sculpture de Picasso', Maison de la Pensée Française, Paris, 26 November 1948–5 January 1949.

26 Interview with William Turnbull conducted by Michael Sweeney on 19 September 1998 (transcript in RPA).

27 RP *SB*, p. 180. For fuller details of the purchase of Farley Farm, see AP 2001, pp. 142–43.

28 RPA 742.23.

29 RP *PLW* 1958, p. 62.

30 See below, Chapter 4, p. 186.

31 In Penrose's appointments diary there are notes of meetings with Picasso on 7 February at 6 p.m. and on 16 February at 1 p.m. (RPA 742.13). They must also have met on 12 February 1946 when Picasso dedicated a copy of the 1945 Gallimard edition of his play to Penrose.

32 See Brassaï 1967, pp. 144–45. He misdates the first reading June 1944, however.

33 Penrose's diary notes a meeting with Picasso at noon on 18 January 1947, and readings-cum-rehearsals at the London Gallery on 25 January, 15 February and 19 February 1947 (RPA 742.14).

34 See Anon., 'Picasso's play', *Evening Standard*, 21 February 1947.

35 See Penrose's Foreword to *Desire*, p. 12.

36 RP *SB*, p. 138.

37 'Cher Picasso,
Je vous avais promit de vous donner des nouvelles à propos de la traduction de votre pièce de theatre qu'on propose à publier ici. En rentrant à Londres je suis allé voir l'editeur de la Maison Rider & Co qui m'a montré les épreuves. C'est la même traduction qui à été publi en Amerique intitulé "Desire". Alors l'editeur m'a permit de comparer cette version avec ma traduction et avec l'original et de faire des corrections. En effet il y a avait besoin – il y avait un tas fautes. J'ai tous corrigé et insister que le titre soit remit encore comme l'original – "Desire caught by the tail" – et hier j'ai revue l'editeur qui a accepter toutes mes proposition.

Donc il me reste maintenant à faire la preface et je travaille à ça maintenant ésperant que j'arriverai à faire quelque chose digne d'une pièce si merveilleuse. Je vous enverrai une épreuve aussitôt qu'il sera prêt.

Le midi et son soleil nous manquent beaucoup mais nous avons de si bons souvenirs de nos visites à Valauris. Lee et moi vous envoyons tous les deux nos meilleurs amitiés ainsi qu'à Françoise et Claude.

Bien à vous
Roland Penrose'
(Letter to Picasso dated 16 September 1949, sent to La Galloise, Vallauris, from 36 Downshire Hill, London; AP.) Frechtman's translation was first published as *Desire* by The Philosophical Library, New York, in 1948. It was reprinted with the same short title by Rider & Co. in London and New York in 1950, and again, but as *Desire Caught by the Tail*, by Citadel Press, New York, in 1962.

38 Enclosed with a letter to Picasso dated 28 October 1949; sent to La Galloise, Vallauris, from 36 Downshire Hill, London (AP). Slightly expanded, the 'Foreword' appeared with Penrose's translation when eventually it was published in 1970.

39 '[…] Mais au dernier moment le grand chef de cette maison qui est un enemi mortel de tout art moderne a insisté que beaucoup de passages soient changés ou enlêvé entierement. J'ai protesté vivement mais il, semblait que, selon les termes de leur contact avec le Philosophical Library de New York qui avait acheté les droits d'abord de Gallimard, ils avaient le droit de couper ce qu'ils voulaient. J'ai donc retiré le préface – seule moyen que j'avais à faire sentir mon desapprobation de cet affaire. […] malgré les menaces de la maison Rider nous allons au 16 fevrier lire ma traduction (je vous envoie ci-joint l'annonce). Malgré ce petit defi à ces personnages malententionés je suis navré de voir paraître cet edition malhonnête contre laquelle on ne peut rien faire. […]'
(Letter to Picasso dated 8 February 1950, sent to La Galloise, Vallauris, from 36 Downshire Hill, London; AP.)

40 See the letter Penrose wrote to Picasso on 17 July 1950, quoted in note 44 below.

41 'C'était un grand success et nous avons du refusé l'entrée aux centaines de personnes.' (Letter to Picasso dated 2 March 1950, sent to La Galloise, Vallauris, from 36 Downshire Hill, London; AP.)

42 Anon., 'Pablo Picasso–Playwright', *Picture Post*, 4 March 1950, pp. 20–21.

43 The first performance took place on 9 October 1950.

Directed by William Jay, the play ran for two weeks.

44 '[…] Nous quittons Londres bientôt pour aller vivre à la campagne où nous esperons être plus tranquille. Donc il faut renoncer à ce voyage dans le midi qui pour moi est une des choses la plus merveilleuse de l'année.

Pour la pièce je sais que ces gens du Watergate Theatre feront quelque chose de bien et je suis content que vous etes d'accord qu'ils utilisent ma traduction. En parlant de traduction, savez vous que j'ai voulais publier une edition ici et avec qui je me suis disputé parcequ'il voulait l'estropier en coupant certains passages qu'il croyait indecant, c'est suicidé dernièrement! Coincidence peut-être mais on n'en parle plus de l'edition estropié – ni, malheureusement, d'un edition honnêt, que je sache. […]'
(Letter to Picasso dated 17 July 1950, sent to La Galloise, Vallauris, from 36 Downshire Hill, London; AP.) Change of address cards date the move from 36 Downshire Hill to Farley Farm and 11A Hornton Street to 5 September 1950 (RPA 725).

45 *Dove in Flight*, 9 July 1950, lithograph. Reproduced in *Les Lettres françaises*, 21 September 1950 (Utley, p. 115).

46 Anon., front-page report in the *Evening Standard*, 14 November 1950.

47 RP *PLW* 1958, p. 328. The Arts Council exhibition, 'Picasso in Provence', ended its tour in London at the New Burlington Galleries (15 November–16 December 1950).

48 Quoted in *The Manchester Guardian*, 14 November 1950, p. 7. Penrose did not attend the Sheffield Conference (letter to Lynda Morris dated 30 April 1981; copy in RPA 529).

49 Anon., 'Picasso boycotts exhibition', *Evening Standard*, 14 November 1950, p. 12.

50 Decoration dated 12 November 1950.

51 Miller's article is evidently the source of Penrose's account in RP *PLW* 1958, p. 62.

52 'Just think! That is the first Englishman I've ever bitten!'

53 Lee Miller, 'Picasso Himself', *Vogue*, November 1951, pp. 112–13, 160, 165.

54 Luis de Góngora y Argote, *Vingt poèmes de Góngora*, Paris, Les Grands Peintres modernes et le Livre, 1948 [Goeppert et al 51]. The watercolour is inscribed 'Pour Roland Penrose Picasso à Londres le 15.11.50'.

55 See Jennifer Ramkalawon, 'Roland Penrose and the Visitors' Book of the Institute of Contemporary Arts, London', *The Burlington Magazine*, April 2003, pp. 283–85; also her essay in *Penrose & Miller*, pp. 67–69.

56 'Cher Picasso,
J'aurai à t'envoyer ce reçu avant, mais le voici.

Nous restons toujours dans le souvenir merveilleux de ta visite et le regret que c'etait si courte. Ton exposition ici a beaucoup de success il y a toujours la foule pour le voir et le dessin en couleur dans notre livre d'or de l'Institute of Contemporary Arts excite l'admiration de tous ce qu'il le voir aussi que celui du Gongora.

Lee se joint en envoyant à Françoise nos grandes amitiés et elle t'embrasse de tous coeur
Très affectueusement
Roland'
(Letter to Picasso dated 29 November 1950, sent to 7 rue des Grands-Augustins, Paris, from 11A Hornton Street, London; AP.)

57 RP *SB*, p. 20.

58 See Melly, pp. 17 ff., for a witness-account of the Penrose-Mesens quarrel.

59 'Picasso: Drawings and Watercolours since 1893. An exhibition in honour of the Artist's 70th Birthday', ICA, 11 October–8 December 1951.

60 Pierre Reverdy, *Le Chant des Morts, Poèmes. Lithographies originales de Pablo Picasso*. Paris, Tériade Editeur, 1948 [Goeppert et al 50]. The inscription reads: 'PARIS le 18.2.51. Pour Roland Penrose <u>Picasso</u>'.

61 RP *SB*, p. 210.

62 Penrose's diary notes meetings with Picasso on 30 June and 3, 4 and 5 July 1951 (RPA 742.21).

63 '[…] Les preparations pour exposition vont bien. […] Il nous faudra maintenant les quatre dessins recents que tu avais promit d'ajouter pour completer jusqu'à 1951. […] Nous éspèrons vivement qu'il sera possible pour toi à venir nous voir au moment de l'esposition. Comme tu connais maintenant le chemin et que Paul et Sabartès ont promit de venir aussi le voyage ne doit pas être difficile, et si tu as peur d'avoir trop de publicité viens diguisé comme ton frère qui te resemble una façon si extraordinaire. […]' (Letter to Picasso dated 14 August 1951, sent to 7 rue des Grands-Augustins, Paris, from Farley Farm, Sussex; AP.)

64 The exhibition catalogue (see note 59 above) describes Picasso's drawings as offering 'intimate knowledge of the creative process of his work' and being 'probes with which he has made his discoveries'.

65 'Mon cher Roland
    Je ne sais pas si tu connais ce Monsieur EVANS (critique) je viens de le retrouver à l'instant dans mon demenagement. Bonjour à Lee et à toi
    Votre Picasso PARIS le 23 Août 1951'
    (Letter to Penrose from Picasso dated 23 August 1951, sent to 11A Hornton Street, London, from 7 rue des Grands-Augustins, Paris; RPA 717.) Picasso had been forced to vacate the apartment in rue La Boétie into which he had moved after his marriage to Olga Khokhlova in 1918.

66 *Homage*. Penrose's introduction, 'Drawings of Picasso', is followed by Eluard's 'Picasso Bon Maître de la Liberté', published in the original and in Penrose's translation.

67 The drawing of two ballet dancers was no. 32 in the exhibition catalogue and is there dated 1919. In fact it is a slightly risqué pastiche of a drawing Picasso executed in Monte Carlo in 1925 [Cooper 1968, no. 380]. The reproduction in Penrose's own copy of *Homage* is marked 'faux' (fake), in Picasso's hand. But, to show there was no hard feeling, Picasso also decorated the title-page with a lively drawing of a grasshopper-bull, inscribing it 'POUR Roland Penrose Picasso PARIS le 18 juin 1952'. Into this copy (in LMA) Penrose later slipped various documents about the fake, including two letters from Kahnweiler, and an undated note in his own hand: 'I suspect that the author of the fake drawing was Jean Cocteau R.P.'

68 According to his diary, Penrose arrived in Paris on 14 December 1952 and, having received a telegram from Picasso confirming he would be welcome ('VIENS JEUDI VALLAURIS AMITIES – PICASSO'; RPA 717), he left for

Vallauris on 18 December (RPA 742.22). He returned to Paris on 20 December.

69 'Wonder & Horror of the Human Head: An Anthology', ICA, 6 March–19 April 1953. Penrose was the principal organiser of this highly imaginative, multicultural exhibition and wrote the catalogue essay.

70 *Head of a Woman (Nusch Eluard)*, 1937, Staatliche Museen zu Berlin, Nationalgalerie, Berggruen Collection [PP.37.198 (b)]. The picture was loaned to 'Wonder & Horror of the Human Head' by J. K. Bomford.

71 The coronation of Queen Elizabeth II, 2 June 1953.

72 'Mon cher Picasso,
    Depuis cette journée lumineuse de Decembre j'ai souvent voulu t'écrire pour te dire encore la joie que j'ai eu de te voir et te remercier pour l'acceuile inoubliable que tu m'as fait – surtout à la gare au millieu de la nuit. Et ces grands peintures qui étaient une revelation – un monde nouveau où je retourne dans ma pensée pour me raffaîchir.
    Je n'arrivais pas t'expliquer pourquoi c'était si urgent pour moi de te voir à ce moment là. C'était une chose très personelle delaquelle seule toi tu possedes la magie pour la guerir. C'était la mort de Paul – et le plus fort c'était que je n'ai pas pu t'en dire un mot.
    Mais le fait de te revoir m'a fait un bien si profond – cet apperçu de tes derniers oeuvres et cet atmosphere de soleil où la beauté de Françoise domine dans le paysage et partout m'a rechargé de vie et de courage.
    Nous avons un projet immediate de faire une soirée le 25 fev. de homage à Paul dans notre Institut où au moment de l'exposition de tes dessins il a fait une si belle conference. Nous lirons ses poemes, nous parlerons de lui et nous aurons j'éspère des enregistrements de sa voix. C'est peu de chose mais je crois que nous aurons une petite foule de gens passionés.
    Je travaille beaucoup en ce moment pour arranger cet exposition de Merveilles et Horreurs de la Tête humaine. Sur le côté merveille j'ai eu la chance de pouvoir emprunter ton portrait de Nusch dit "l'Arlesienne". Je t'enverai le catalogue aussitot que c'est pret.
    Lee et moi t'embrasse de tout coeur et Françoise aussi. Much love to you both from us both.
    Roland.
    J'essaye déjà combiner mon prochain voyage au Golfe pour le mois de juin – en dehors de toute autre chose ça sera un moyen magnifique d'echapper aux follies de la couronnement – mais surtout je pense que peutêtre ta chapelle sera finit et nous ferons un joieuse pelerinage.'
    (Letter to Picasso dated 4 February 1953, sent to La Galloise, Vallauris, from 11A Hornton Street, London; AP.) The reference in the postscript is to the *War and Peace* murals, painted in 1952 (see below, p. 76).

73 *Le Château des pauvres* was first published, more or less at the moment of Eluard's death, in *Cahiers du Sud*, no. 314, 1952, pp. 28–42. (For full information, see Paul Eluard, *Oeuvres complètes*, eds. Lucien Scheler and Marcelle Dumas, Bibliothèque de la Pléiade, vol. 2, Paris, Gallimard, 1968, pp. 695–706.)

74 The plan is mentioned in Penrose's letters to Picasso of 24 June, 5 July and 19 July 1954 (AP).

75 'Oeuvres récentes de Picasso', Galerie Louise Leiris, Paris, 19 May–June 1953. In his notebook, Penrose records the date of his visit: Wednesday 17 June.

76 'Picasso', Galleria Nazionale d'Arte Moderna, Rome, 5 May–5 July 1953.

77 *The Crane*, 1951–52 [S.461].

78 The lengthy trial of the Rosenbergs, accused of transmitting classified US military information to the Soviet Union, caused intense controversy worldwide. They were found guilty and condemned to death in 1951. Despite numerous court appeals, pleas for clemency and a coordinated campaign mounted by the Communists and supported by many liberals and religious leaders, they were executed on 19 June 1953 – the first US civilians to suffer the death penalty for espionage.

79 See Utley, pp. 180–81.

80 The Penroses travelled to St Tropez by train with Man Ray and his wife Julie on 21 June 1953. (All dates established by Penrose's diary; RPA 742.23.)

81 See Utley, pp. 182–90. For Picasso's stuttering post-1953 relationship with Aragon, see Daix 1995, pp. 36–38.

82 A spicy Provençal sauce accompanying seafood.

83 Information from Diane Deriaz, 31 March 2004.

84 A chic restaurant with a dance floor (information from Diane Deriaz, 31 March 2004).

85 'Picasso', Musée des Beaux-Arts, Lyons, 1 July–27 September 1953.

86 *Night Fishing at Antibes*, 1939, MoMA [Z.IX.316].

87 'Cher Picasso,
Nous sommes de retour dans la pluie mais avec de très bons souvenirs de notre visite à Vallauris. Nous nous sommes arrêté à Lyon et avons passé plusieurs heures dans l'esposition qui est splendide et pleine des choses inconnus pour moi, de toute les epoques. J'ai trouvé seulement qu'il manquait des toiles de grands dimensions – des natures mortes de '25 à '30, des grandes toiles vers '35 les pêcheurs d'Antibes etc etc. Il n'en fallait pas beaucoup mais deux ou trois aura donné plus de varieté dans le dimensions. Le catalogue avait quelque erreurs et omissions mais on m'a promit de les corriger. Malgré ces details l'impression de l'ensemble est bouleversant et les toiles recentes manifestent un tel vigeur que le fond de la salle est remplit de lumière et de couleur. Avec Lee je t'envoie nos grands amitiés.
Affectueusement Roland
Embrasse la belle Françoise et tes enfants pour nous.'
(Postcard of a detail of Holbein's *French Ambassadors*, dated 13 July 1953, sent to Picasso at La Galloise, Vallauris, from Farley Farm, Sussex; AP.)

88 For her account, see Deriaz, pp. 235 ff. She reports Lee's complaint to Valentine Penrose: 'Diane has not played the game. She has stolen Roland's heart.'

89 AP 2001, p. 148.

90 Penrose's diary notes that they spent 7–8 February in Vallauris and returned to Paris on Tuesday 9 February (RPA 742.24).

91 RP *SB*, p. 212.

92 The literary character of this text, which goes on to describe the appeal of Vallauris for Picasso as an ancient centre of pottery production, suggests that it may have

been a preliminary draft for RP *PLW* 1958 and consequently written during the autumn of 1954 at the earliest. There are certain similarities in observation and phrasing, but the equivalent text in RP *PLW* 1958 (pp. 324–26) is substantially different.

93 See below, Chapter 3, pp. 84 ff.

94 Penrose's diary for June 1954 has the following entries (RPA 742.24):
'Friday 4 June: Vallauris. Saw chapel/called on Picasso/ lunched with him & Mme. Manolo
Friday 11 June: Went to see Picasso with Tony
Saturday 12 June: Picasso & party came to St Tropez/ dined together
Sunday 13 June: lunched at Grimaud with P.
Thursday 17 June: lunch with Picasso at Vallauris
Tuesday 22 June: saw Picasso & Braque at Vallauris'.

95 *Woman with a Key (The Madame)*, 1954 [S.237].

96 Paul Eluard, *Picasso Dessins*, Paris, Editions Braun, 1952. Picasso's inscription reads: 'Pour Roland Penrose. Picasso 13.6.54' (SNGMA Archive).

97 *Woman with a Pushchair*, begun 1950; original assemblage Museum Ludwig, Cologne [S.407].

98 RP *SB*, p. 214.

99 A reference to the stylistically extremely varied portraits of Sylvette David, who modelled for Picasso in Vallauris during the spring of 1954 [Z.XVI.274–315]. Photographs by Lee Miller show Picasso and Braque examining the painted sheet-metal sculptures on the grass in front of the studio.

100 '[…] Paris était une étape court mais très agreeable. Je suis allé plusieurs fois me gaver de ton exposition à la Maison de la Pensée. J'étais etonné de la brilliance de la couleur de ces toiles qu'on a connu seulement en blanc et noir. Il sont aussi en très bonne état et ont une fraicheur delicieuse. C'était vraiment un très grand emotion de les voir: j'éspère tellement qu'on arrivera les montrer ici à Londres. […]' (Letter to Picasso dated 5 July 1954, sent to La Galloise, Vallauris, from 11A Hornton Street, London; AP.) Penrose also speaks of his negotiations to bring the pictures to London in a letter to Picasso dated 19 July 1954 (AP).

101 'Picasso: œuvres des musées de Léningrad et de Moscou, 1900–1914', Maison de la Pensée Française, Paris, June 1954.

102 See Utley, pp. 194, 244 n. 30.

Chapter 3 Into the Vast Territories: The Novice Biographer, 1954–1955

1 The appointment is noted in Penrose's diary for 30 July 1954 (RBA 742.24). The first surviving letter relating to RP *PLW* 1958, from Hilary Rubinstein, is dated 5 November 1954 and accompanied the contract (RPA 589).

2 Information from Hilary Rubinstein, October 2004. Penrose had met 'Geerbrant', the well-known writer and explorer, at Galerie La Hune, Paris, on 2 July 1953 and Gollancz in London on 29 July 1953, and it was presumably then that the launch party for *The Impossible*

Adventure: Journey to the Far Amazon was set up. The launch took place at the ICA on 14 October 1953. (All dates in Penrose's diary; RPA 742.23.)

3   RP *SB*, p. 206.

4   *Picasso: Fifty Years of his Art* (1946) revises and substantially amplifies *Picasso: Forty Years of his Art*, published in 1939 at the time of the retrospective Barr organised for MoMA.

5   Letter to Alfred Barr dated 21 August 1954, sent to MoMA from Farley Farm, Sussex (AHB [AAA: 2180; 1015–1016]. MoMA Archives, NY).

6   Diary entry (RPA 742.24).

7   See Montañés, pp. 104–5.

8   It is usually said that Picasso's liaison with Jacqueline Roque started in 1953, but John Richardson says Picasso introduced her to him and Douglas Cooper 'in the early fall of 1952'. Picasso was embroiled with several other women at this period and Jacqueline was effectively 'on probation' for a couple of years before she moved into rue des Grands-Augustins in the autumn of 1954 (Richardson 1999, pp. 130–31).

9   Paul Eluard, *Voir: poèmes, peintures, dessins*, Paris, Editions des Trois Collines, 1948. This includes reproductions of a drawing by Penrose and the painting, *Faites vos jeux*, 1947, and a poem by Eluard dedicated to Penrose ('La dernière lettre').

10 'Is that so? That's good.'

11 Compare the more burlesque account of Penrose's conversation with Picasso in RP *SB* (p. 207).

12 When the exhibition at the Maison de la Pensée Française of paintings from the Hermitage and Pushkin museums was closed early by the Soviet authorities (see above, Chapter 2, p. 80), Picasso stepped in and, with Kahnweiler's help, put together an exhibition of early and recent paintings. Aragon wrote the preface ('Picasso, Deux périodes: 1900–1914 et 1950–1954', Maison de la Pensée Française, Paris, July 1954).

13 Picasso had known the Catalan sculptor Apel-les Fenosa since the latter's move to France in 1920, and began buying his work a few years later.

14 In hindsight, Françoise Gilot's *paseo*, watched by an admiring Picasso, came to be seen as the symbolic end of their relationship and as her farewell to him. The episode is repeatedly discussed in Gilot 2004.

15 *Portrait of Madame de Lazerme in Catalan Costume*, 1954, Musée Hyacinthe Rigaud, Perpignan.

16 The Dominican Chapel of the Rosary at Vence (1948–51).

17 Braque designed stained-glass windows for the church at Varengeville, near Dieppe, in 1954.

18 Pierre Reverdy, *Le Chant des Morts. Poèmes. Lithographies originales de Pablo Picasso*, Paris, Tériade Editeur, 1948 [Goeppert et al 50]. (See also above, Chapter 2, p. 68.)

19 'When all's said and done, that makes you happier and does you more good than reading newspapers.'

20 'Suite de 180 dessins de Picasso', *Verve*, vol. VIII, nos. 29–30, 15 September 1954. The drawings were executed during the winter of 1953–54.

21 Presuming that Penrose means 'garrot': 'His withers are all red.'

22 'Ass'.

23 'Yes, it's like painting: there are no good paintings, just paintings that mean something to you.'

24 Emmer's *Picasso* was shown at a festival of Italian cinema in London in October 1954, the first chance Penrose would have had to see it. (See *Picasso à l'écran*, p. 52, for a letter from Antonello Trombadori to Picasso mentioning the London screening.) The fact that Penrose discussed the Emmer film with Picasso when he saw him in November 1954 (see below, p. 96) suggests that he saw it at this time, not later.

25 'Ma Jolie' (*Woman with a Zither or Guitar*), 1911–12, MoMA [DR 430], is a 'secret' portrait of Eva Gouel, who supplanted Fernande Olivier and lived with Picasso until her premature death in December 1915.

26 Emmer filmed during the great Picasso retrospective held in Rome, Galleria Nazionale d'Arte Moderna, May–July 1953, and possibly also when the exhibition transferred to the Palazzo Reale, Milan, in the autumn.

27 Apart from Guttuso, the original commentary was supplied by Antonello Trombadori and Antonio del Guercio. Claude Roy provided the commentary in the French version of the film.

28 Letter to Penrose from Alfred Barr dated 24 September 1954, sent to Farley Farm, Sussex, from MoMA (RPA 46).

29 Letter to Barr dated 28 January 1953, sent to MoMA from the ICA (AHB [AAA: 2179; 1126]. MoMA Archives, NY).

30 Letter to Penrose from Barr dated 2 February 1953, sent to the ICA from MoMA (AHB [AAA: 2179; 1122]. MoMA Archives, NY). 'Is Modern Art Communistic?' is the title of an important essay that Barr published in *The New York Times Magazine* on 14 December 1952 (republished in Barr 1986, pp. 214–19). There he demonstrated the fallacy of right-wing claims that avant-garde art was subversive and 'un-American' through a trenchant analysis of the repressive art policies of Nazi Germany and the USSR.

31 Letter to Barr dated 3 December 1954, sent to MoMA from Farley Farm, Sussex. The postscript is dated 4 December 1954 (AHB [AAA: 2179; 661–789]. MoMA Archives, NY).

32 Draft contract between Victor Gollancz and Roland Penrose, dated 5 November 1954 (RPA 589). On 13 December 1954 Hilary Rubinstein acknowledged receipt of the signed contract (RPA 589).

33 Letter to Penrose from Hilary Rubinstein dated 29 November 1954, enclosing a copy of a letter dated 26 November 1954 from Simon Michael Bessie of Harper and Brothers, New York (RPA 589).

34 In the entry in his diary for 12 November 1954 Penrose notes: 'flew to Paris/ saw Picasso lunched with him/ Léger's show/ 5.0 Françoise' (RPA 742.24).

35 'Léger is never wrong. As painting, it's better than Michelangelo, but I prefer Michelangelo as a painter.' 'Men are more important than painting. What would you prefer, a woman or Venus?'

36 'The film is dreadful.' Luciano Emmer's film, *Picasso*, was made in 1953 but distributed in 1954.

37 'One must learn how to see. I've watched ants all my life but I know nothing about them. Someone who has observed their behaviour for a long time would know

how to see them. It's not enough to see, one has to understand, to know what is there too.'

38 Penrose's diary notes meetings with Gilot on 12 and 16 November 1954 (RPA 742.24). Like many other interviews Penrose conducted, this appeared, in an appropriately modified form and without attribution, in RP *PLW* 1958 (pp. 147–48).

39 Matisse died in Nice on 3 November 1954. Picasso did not attend the funeral on 8 November.

40 Sister Jacques-Marie. See Henri Matisse, M.-A. Couturier, L.-B. Rayssiguier, *The Vence Chapel: The Archive of a Creation*, ed. Marcel Billot. Trans. Michael Taylor. Menil Foundation Inc. in association with Skira, Milan, 1999.

41 'He made Matisses and that's the important thing.'

42 In fact, it is unlikely Picasso ever met Jarry. Jarry's revolver probably came to Picasso through Apollinaire, Jacob or another mutual friend, after Jarry's death in 1907. (See Richardson 1991, pp. 362–63.)

43 According to Penrose's diary, he met Fin Vilató, Picasso's nephew, on 21 November 1954 (RPA 742.24).

44 According to Penrose's diary, he met McEwen in Paris on 15 and 20 November 1954 (RPA 742.24).

45 'Braque is the woman who loved me most.'

46 worldly.

47 I am dependent here on Michael Sweeney's research in the Cambridge University archives (transcript in RPA).

48 This opinion is expressed in several interviews with family friends conducted by Michael Sweeney in 1997–98 (transcripts in RPA).

49 RPA 742.24. Penrose's diary entry for 17 January 1955 mentions a tentative appointment, and he met Keynes again on 27 May 1955 (RPA 742.25).

50 *Les femmes de bonne humeur*, first performed in Rome in April 1917; music by Scarlatti, arranged by Tommasini; libretto and choreography by Massine; décor and costumes by Bakst.

51 Vladimir Polunin was the principal scenery painter of the Ballets Russes and with his wife Violette collaborated with Picasso in London in 1919 on the curtain and sets of *Le tricorne*.

52 Cocteau was responsible for the libretto of *Parade* (1917), for which Picasso designed the curtain, décor and costumes. Presumably, Keynes was recommending Penrose to read *Le coq et l'arlequin* (Paris, Editions de la Sirène, 1918), a tract about contemporary music Cocteau wrote in the wake of *Parade*. And Penrose did read it, just as he read Cocteau's *Picasso* (Paris, Stock, 1923): his detailed notes are in RPA 586 [2].

53 Picasso made several portrait drawings of Lydia Lopokova in London in 1919 [Z.III.298, 299, and Z.XXIX.414].

54 *La Boutique fantasque*, first performed London, June 1919; music by Rossini, arranged by Respighi; choreography by Massine; libretto, décor and costumes by Derain.

55 *Mercure*, first performed Paris, June 1924, in Count Etienne de Beaumont's 'Soirée de Paris' programme; music by Satie; libretto and choreography by Massine; curtain, décor and costumes by Picasso.

56 In his diary for 30 January 1955 Penrose notes 'Clive

Bell?'; on 30 August 1955 he notes simply 'Clive' (RPA 742.25).

57 Jean Cocteau, *Orphée: tragédie en un acte et un intervalle*: text dated 14 September 1925; first performed in Paris on 17 June 1926; first published Paris, Librairie Stock, 1927.

58 In 1921, after the birth of their son Paulo.

59 a public urinal and a lamppost.

60 Letter to Alfred Barr dated 17 January 1955, sent to MoMA from Farley Farm, Sussex (AHB [AAA: 2197; 526]. MoMA Archives, NY).

61 Barr 1951. Penrose's 16 pages of notes on this book are in RPA 585 [8].

62 Penrose's appointments diary for 1955 enables us to establish their itinerary (RPA 742.25).

63 In the late 1950s Kahnweiler told John Golding that, despite recognising its crucial historical role, he had never been able to come to terms with *Les Demoiselles*, regarding it as unfinished and unresolved (information from John Golding).

64 'No, I never drew like a child.' See below, Chapter 4, p. 169.

65 Delacroix, *Les Femmes d'Algers*, 1834, Musée du Louvre, Paris. Picasso also knew the much smaller version Delacroix painted in 1849 (Musée Fabre, Montpellier).

66 Compare RP *PLW* 1958, pp. 350–52. Compare also Daniel-Henry Kahnweiler, 'Entretiens avec Picasso au sujet des "Femmes d'Alger"', originally published in *Aujourd'hui, art et architecture*, no. 4, September 1955. Kahnweiler visited Picasso's studio on several occasions between 25 January and 4 March 1955.

67 'Version O' is Z.XVI.360. Picasso began making drawings after Delacroix's *The Women of Algiers* on 5 December 1954 (Léal, cat. 51, 19R–25R). His final drawing, inscribed '7.3.55 VII', is Z.XVI.373.

68 Olga Picasso died in Cannes on 11 February 1955.

69 'Blanc d'espagne' is a white powder used by printmakers for the final polishing of a plate. 'Miror' is the trade-name of a metal polish.

70 Aldo Crommelynck and his brother Piero were apprenticed to the master printmaker Roger Lacourière, with whom Picasso first began working in 1933. The Crommelyncks collaborated particularly closely with Picasso after 1963, when they installed a press in his final home, Notre-Dame-de-Vie.

71 i.e. *A haute flamme*, published privately by Tzara in 1955 [Goeppert et al 72]. Picasso contributed 6 engravings on celluloid.

72 'Paintings aren't done with thoughts but with hands.'

73 The reference is probably to 'Version M' [Z.XVI.357], the largest of the series.

74 'I shall continue to open windows within it and perhaps something will happen.'

75 Delacroix, *The Death of Sardanapalus*, 1827–28, Musée du Louvre, Paris.

76 Ingres, *Turkish Bath*, 1862, Musée d'Orsay, Paris – but in the Louvre in Picasso's day.

77 Ingres, *Grande odalisque*, 1814, Musée du Louvre, Paris.

78 Probably Geiser & Baer 920, which is dated 18 February 1955.

79 Balthus, *The Children, Hubert and Thérèse Blanchard*, 1937, MP.

80 Cézanne, *The Sea at L'Estaque*, 1878–79, MP.

81 Penrose may mean Vuillard's *The Cradle Song*, 1896, MP.

82 Matisse, *Portrait of Marguerite*, 1907, MP. Stein made this claim in her memoirs, *The Autobiography of Alice B. Toklas*, New York, Harcourt, Brace, 1933, p. 64.

83 *Balcony with a View of the Monument to Christopher Columbus*, 1917, MPB [Z.III.47].

84 *Fatma*, 1917, MPB [Z.III.45].

85 'It's awful. She should be killed, shouldn't she? My mother used to say that there's nothing more awful for a woman than getting old, because that means becoming ugly.'

86 'really ugly'. Ripolin is the trade name of a popular household paint.

87 Picasso's gross exaggeration of the number of pigeons in the dovecote painted by his father is mentioned in Sabartès 1946, p. 7.

88 See *ibid.*, pp. 36–39.

89 'Yes, that's it, and I even think those were the very numbers.'

90 Joan Merlí y Pahissa, *Picasso, el artista y la obra de nuestro tiempo*, Buenos Aires, Poseidon, 1942.

91 'disapproved of'. This is presumably a slightly garbled reference to the so-called 'Calvet affair' which hit the headlines in France in 1930. Merlí, a Catalan art dealer, was implicated in it. For a derisory sum of money, Miguel Calvet Martí obtained a mass of early paintings and drawings from Picasso's mother and then started selling them on at a huge profit. Picasso's mother claimed she had merely lent them to him in the belief that they would feature in a projected book on Picasso's early work and Picasso became embroiled in a lengthy court case to retrieve them, which he eventually won in 1938. See Laurence Madeline, 'Picasso and the Calvet affair of 1930', *The Burlington Magazine*, vol. CXLVII, no. 1226, May 2005, pp. 316–23.

92 *Portrait of Ambroise Vollard*, 1910, Pushkin Museum, Moscow [DR 337]; *Portrait of Wilhelm Uhde*, 1910, Pulitzer Collection, St Louis [DR 338].

93 According to Penrose's diary, he met Maar on 19 February 1955 (RPA 742.25). Later, Penrose split these notes and filed them in two different places: the split is registered by a slash mark [/] in the transcription.

94 There is no note of a meeting with Michel de Brunhoff in Penrose's diary. He was the editor of French *Vogue* and an old colleague of Lee Miller's.

95 The première of *Parade* was at the Théâtre du Châtelet, Paris, on 18 May 1917.

96 RP *SB*, p. 215.

97 All these dates are recorded in Penrose's diary for 1955 (RPA 742.25). In RP *SB* (p. 215) Penrose gives the misleading impression that there was only one trip to Spain.

98 *Portrait of Aunt Pepa*, 1896, MPB [Z.XXI.38].

99 Penrose is confused here: by 'Tonija' he must mean General Torrijos, who, having fought against the French during the Napoleonic wars, masterminded various liberal conspiracies intended to overthrow Ferdinand VII after the restoration of the Bourbon monarchy. Torrijos was executed in Málaga in 1831 and is commemorated by an obelisk in Plaza de la Merced (which Penrose mentions in RP *PLW* 1958, p. 28). I am indebted to María Teresa Ocaña for clarifying this passage.

100 *Woman with a Broach*, 1944 [Z.XIII.237].

101 Probably *Portrait of Jacqueline in a Black Scarf*, dated 11 October 1954 [Z.XVI.331].

102 *The Women of Algiers (after Delacroix)*, 'Version O', 1955 [Z.XVI.360].

103 For her first book on Picasso, see Parmelin 1959.

104 According to Penrose's diary, he met Baudouin on 28 February and 22 March 1955 (RPA 742.25).

105 René and Claire Voigt Batigne.

106 'Yes, one can only do that if one loves someone and loves them very much.' One of the drawings Baudouin refers to may be *Portrait of Françoise*, dated 20 May 1946, MP [PP.46.48].

107 Penrose's diary for 1954 notes meetings with Gilot on 27 May, 30 May, 30 June, 12 November and 16 November (RPA 742.24).

108 These drawings have not been identified. Possibly the sketchbook is with the cache of drawings and correspondence that Sabartès left to the MPB, with strict instructions that it should not be opened until fifty years after his death (i.e. 2018). See Otero, p. 182.

109 Geneviève Laporte, *Sous le manteau de feu: poèmes, 12 lithographies originales de Jean Cocteau*, Paris, J. Foret, 1955.

110 Copious, but sometimes indecipherable, notes relating to Valentine Penrose's reading of Picasso's horoscope are gathered in RPA 586 [2]. Penrose's diary records meetings with Valentine on 11 and 14 February and 18 March 1955 (RPA 742.25).

111 'board of guardians'.

112 See Gilot 1964, pp. 342–44, for her own account of the end of her relationship with Picasso.

113 'Picasso', Musée des Arts décoratifs, Paris, June–October 1955.

114 'Picasso: l'œuvre gravé', Bibliothèque Nationale, Paris, 13 June–16 October 1955.

115 These jottings are split between two small pocket notebooks [12; 13].

116 According to Penrose's diary, he met Maar on 5, 10 and 13 June 1955 (RPA 742.25).

117 On 1 January 1937, Picasso, Paulo and Dora Maar visited Max Jacob at St Benoît-sur-Loire. (See Seckel, pp. 240–41.)

118 i.e. in Max Jacob's will. A leading representative of 'Neo-Romanticism' in French painting during the 1930s, Christian Bérard was also famous for his theatre and fashion designs.

119 i.e. on the return from Jacob's funeral (see Seckel, p. 276).

120 'See what power there is in that.'

121 In 1903 a poverty-stricken Picasso shared a room in a cheap hotel in Paris with the equally impoverished Jacob: the much-repeated anecdote about the rotten sausage dates from this period.

122 'in the form of quips'.

123 'to discourage collectors'. This refers to *Guitar*, 1926, a collage created with a dishcloth and large jutting nails, now in the MP [S.65 H]. In RP *PLW* 1958 (p. 232) Penrose says that Picasso told him that he had thought of embedding razor blades around its edges 'so that whoever went to lift it would cut their hands'. Either Dora Maar told him the same story, or she was in fact his informant.

124 Postcard sent from Barcelona to Picasso at La Californie, Cannes, postmarked 21 June 1955; AP.

125 RP *SB*, p. 215.

126 The luxury art review *Minotaure* was published by Albert Skira in Paris in 1933–39. Picasso designed the cover for the first issue.

127 *In the Dressing Room*, 1900, MPB [Z.I.38].

128 *The Embrace in the Street*, 1900, MPB [Z.I.24].

129 *First Communion*, 1895–96, MPB [Z.XXI.49].

130 *Science and Charity*, 1897, MPB [Z.XXI.56].

131 *Compotier with Fruit*, 1917, MPB [Z.III.46].

132 *Balcony with a View of the Monument to Christopher Columbus*, 1917, MPB [Z.III.47].

133 *Parade* was performed in Barcelona in November 1917. According to Penrose's diary, he met Joan Prats, one of Miró's oldest friends, at least three times when he was in Barcelona – on 18, 21 and 24 June 1955 (RPA 742.25).

134 accursed poet.

135 Sucre's address appears in the Memoranda pages of Penrose's diary for 1955 (RPA 742.25).

136 Edward Burne-Jones, *The Mirror of Venus*, 1873–77, Calouste Gulbenkian Museum, Lisbon.

137 damned poet.

138 mothers.

139 Chinese quarter.

140 *Dwarf Dancer*, 1901, MPB [Z.I.66].

141 Circol Artístic de Sant Lluc.

142 Spanish for pencil or crayon.

143 María Teresa Ocaña (personal communication) believes that 'pistol de capaillart' may be a misspelling for 'pistola de capellà', Catalan for 'priest's pistol', but has never heard of a cake with this name. In RP *PLW* 1958 (p. 26) Penrose calls the cake 'torruella'. She suggests that he may mean 'torrija', a popular sugary, fried toast.

144 i.e. Sabartés 1954, pl. 44.

145 According to his diary, Penrose arrived in Cannes on 5 July and returned to Paris on 9 July 1955 (RPA 742.25).

146 RP *PLW* 1958, pp. 360–63.

147 A reference to the modelled heads of 1931 inspired by Marie-Thérèse Walter (particularly S.110, S.131, S.132, S.133).

148 'Reality is what one creates and that's all.'

149 'When one is working, one doesn't know what will come out. It's not indecisiveness, it's that things change as one works.'

150 i.e. the Punu mask (Gabon; now in MP) seen in photographs Picasso took in his Boulevard de Clichy studio in winter 1910–11.

151 Penrose's diary indicates that he joined the de Lazermes and Totote and Rosita Hugué in Perpignan on 4 July 1955 (RPA 742.25).

152 *Man with a Sheep* (also known as *Man with a Lamb*), 1943, bronze [S.280].

153 Henri Rousseau, *Portrait of the Artist with a Lamp*, 1902–3, *Portrait of the Artist's Second Wife*, 1903; both MP.

154 *The Cat*, 1941, bronze [S.195].

155 *Baboon and Young*, 1951, bronze [S.463].

156 *The Jester*, 1905, bronze [S.4].

157 See note 147 above.

158 *Death's Head, c.* 1941, bronze [S.219].

159 According to Penrose's diary, he saw Picasso and Clouzot on both 6 and 7 July 1955 (RPA 742.25).

160 Bullfight.

161 The girl was possibly the model who posed in the nude for drawings dated 6 and 7 December 1953 (e.g. Z.XVI.35) and for *Bust of a Woman and Two Profiles*, dated 11 December 1953 [Z.XVI.53]. These are contemporary with the *Verve* series (see note 20), in which a recurrent theme is the artist working from a posing model (compare, e.g., Z.XVI.77, dated 21 December 1953).

162 The Pope's girlfriend.

163 The revolver had belonged to Alfred Jarry (see note 42 above) and was one of Picasso's most prized possessions.

164 *Head of a Woman (Dora Maar)*, 1941, bronze [S.197].

165 *The Charnel House*, 1945, MoMA [Z.XIV.76].

166 *Death's Head, c.* 1941, bronze [S.219].

167 i.e. a bowler hat from the famous firm of James Lock & Co., St James's Street, London.

168 *The Crane*, 1951–53, painted bronze [S.461].

169 The *Tiki* from the Marquesas Islands, which Picasso acquired in about 1907 (see Seckel-Klein, p. 238).

170 *The Jester*, 1905, bronze [S.4].

171 'Penrose arrives by the 10 a.m. train, Monday.' (See photograph on p. 2.)

172 'You may do what you like when you're not here but I don't want your friends coming to the house and I don't want you going out. I've never been a son and I don't want to be a father.'

173 'Papa n'est pas TRÈS au courant, car vous le connaissez il faut lui répéter les choses 10 fois bien qu'il est compris dès le début … Ici tout le monde va très bien bien qu'ils disent le contraire.' (Letter to Penrose from Maya Picasso, dated 15 September 1955; RPA 563.)

174 *Faun and Starry Night*, 1955, The Metropolitan Museum of Art, New York [Z.XVI.396]. The canvas is dated 9 July 1955.

175 *Three Nudes*, 1907, wood, MP [S.17A].

176 Probably *Head of a Woman*, 1907, wood [S.11].

177 According to Penrose's diary, he met Sabartés at 12.15 and Bernard at 6 p.m. on 15 July 1955 (RPA 742.25). Guy Bernard composed film music, including the music for *Guernica*, a short documentary with a script by Paul Eluard, directed by Alain Resnais and Robert Hessens (Paris, 1949).

178 At the time, Penrose owned *Woman's Head and Self-Portrait*, 1929 [Z.VII.248]. See below, Chapter 4, p. 173.

179 'The cult of anxiety, anxious about his friends' opinions.'

180 A very slightly different version of this conversation, headed 'Conversation with Guy Bernard. July '55', appears in RPA 586 [2].

181 'Tzara, no police here!' The notorious event – in the midst of the 'Soirée du Cœur à Barbe' – took place on 6 July 1922. It is often taken to mark the death of Dada in Paris and the birth of the Surrealist movement under Breton's leadership.

182 See above note 150.

183 According to Penrose's diary, he arrived in Paris on 26 October and was in Cannes on 6–10 November 1955 (RPA 742.25).

184 According to Penrose's diary, he had meetings with Maar on 4 November and 12 November 1955 (RPA 742.25).

The meeting on 27 October 1955 (see below p. 133) is not recorded in his diary.

185 The traditional date of Picasso's first meeting with Marie-Thérèse Walter is January 1927, when she was 17, not 14 years old. The '4 years after marriage' is also inaccurate since Picasso and Olga were married in 1918. (But see also below, p. 133 and Chapter 4, p. 176.) In recent years, scholars have argued that the first meeting took place in 1925 or 1926, but John Richardson (personal communication) is now convinced that the traditional date is correct.

186 Elvire, the heroine of Guillaume Apollinaire's posthumously published roman à clef, *La femme assise* (Paris, NRF, 1920), was modelled on Irène Lagut, with whom Picasso had a tempestuous affair in 1916 (see Richardson 1996, pp. 395–405). Picasso appears there as Pablo Canouris. 'L'Oiseau du Bénin' was Apollinaire's sobriquet for Picasso in another roman à clef, *Le poète assassiné* (Paris, Bibliothèque des Curieux, 1916).

187 Presumably the famous actor and notorious philanderer Roger Karl, whom Fernande met soon after the beginning of her affair with Picasso. He became her long-term lover during the First World War. It is usually said that Picasso used Fernande's affair with the Italian painter Ubaldo Oppi as his excuse to end his liaison with her (see John Richardson, in Olivier 2001, pp. 278–81).

188 'He has a taste for sudden endings.'

189 Le Tremblay-sur-Mauldre.

190 'Ah yes, so you've noticed that.'

191 'Here we are in the monkey cage.'

192 Rousseau is supposed to have said: 'Picasso, you and I are the greatest painters of our time, you in the Egyptian style, I in the Modern' (quoted in RP *PLW* 1958, p. 138).

193 No etching appears to fit this description. Possibly Maar meant the drawings executed in July 1934 which depict a monstrous female stabbing a defenceless Marie-Thérèse- like figure (e.g. *The Murder*, 7 July 1934, MP; Z.VIII.216).

194 girl from a good family.

195 Possibly *Portrait of Dora Maar*, 1936 [Z.VIII.302].

196 'How I should like to have old women bring me my meals like this.'

197 Probably *Reclining Woman with a Book*, 1939 [Z.IX.252].

198 In fact, Picasso almost certainly never met Jarry (see Richardson 1991, p. 362).

199 'repressed homosexual'.

200 Picasso's mother died on 13 January 1939.

201 Renoir, *Bather Seated in Landscape (Eurydice)*, 1895–96, MP; Cézanne, *Château noir*, 1903–4, MP.

202 cleaning lady.

203 RP *SB*, p. 218.

204 high blood pressure.

205 Casanova rose to prominence within the French Communist Party after the Liberation. He was sheltered by the Leirises during the Nazi Occupation and met Picasso at that time.

206 'lavatory sword'. Cocteau was formally elected to the Académie Française on 20 October 1955. On 18 October 1955 Picasso sent him a letter containing five humorous designs for his Academician's ceremonial sword, one of

which is entitled 'épée de cabinet'. The hilt is constructed from a lavatory brush, chain and paper holder. (See *Jean Cocteau, sur le fil du siècle*, Paris, Centre Georges Pompidou, 2003, nos. 134–139.)

207 'bugging device'.

208 Barr 1946, p. 259, discusses the possible influence on Cubism of the mathematical theories of Maurice Princet, noting that Picasso had denied discussing mathematics or the fourth dimension with Princet when both were living in the Bateau Lavoir.

209 'tow and paraffin'.

210 '4th dimension: to flatten forms without making a hole in the canvas and to paint an eye like an eye and not anything else.'

211 'because of Avignon Street [in Barcelona]'.

212 i.e. José Garnelo Alda.

213 waggons.

214 Barr 1946, p. 66, writes under the heading 'Analytical Cubism: 1909–1912': 'At Horta Picasso's style seemed suddenly to crystallize, literally and visually as well as metaphorically.'

215 Barr 1946, p. 260, quotes Breton: 'Recently I saw Picasso studying one of his unfinished works of 1911 or '12. He had already filled several pages with mathematical calculations, and he confided to me that in order to clarify this painting for himself he was obliged to embark on a whole series of measurements.'

216 The four drawings plus two others, numbered I–VI and all dated 8 November 1955, are reproduced in facsimile in *Picasso: carnet de La Californie*, Introduction Georges Boudaille, Paris, Editions Cercle d'Art, 1959.

217 *Les quatre petites filles*, written in French between 24 November 1947 and 13 August 1948. For Penrose's translation, see below Chapter 8, pp. 315–16.

218 Matisse, *Bonheur de vivre*, 1905–6, The Barnes Foundation, Merion, Pennsylvania.

219 *Portrait of Ramón Pérez Costales*, 1895 [Z.XXI.36].

220 See above note 215.

221 *Portrait of Gustave Coquiot*, 1901, Musée National d'Art Moderne, Paris [Z.I.84]. The reference is to: Gustave Coquiot, *La terre frottée d'ail, avec 101 dessins inédits de Raoul Dufy*, Paris, A. Delpech, 1925.

222 Henri Bloch and his sister the opera singer Suzanne made friends with Picasso soon after he settled in Paris. In RP *Portrait* 1956, fig. 53, Penrose reproduced the photograph of Picasso which the artist dedicated to them in 1904.

223 'You mustn't always believe what I say. Questions tempt one to tell lies because there is no answer.'

224 *Le sein*, dated 31 March 1955; two versions, each in an edition of 100 [Ramié, nos. 271, 272]. Penrose acquired copies of these ceramics, presumably during this visit to Cannes.

225 'Little Girl II   Only the eye of the bull that dies in the arena sees.

    Little Girl I   It sees itself.

    Little Girl IV   The deforming mirror sees.

    Little Girl II   Death, that clear water.

    Little Girl I   And is very heavy.'

This is Penrose's translation in RP *PLW* 1958, p. 335, where the same fragment is quoted. (In RP *PLW* 1971,

p. 386, he corrected the slip in the translation of the final line to 'And very heavy'.)

226 'But now it is he who sings and you must put that in the book'.

227 'Well, it's all I know how to do.'

228 A reference to the attack launched by Breton and Aragon on Miró and Ernst for their involvement in the Diaghilev ballet *Romeo and Juliet* in May 1926. By contrast, Picasso was never criticised for his theatre designs.

229 RPA 605. The copy of the poem is inscribed: '(2e copie) et dédié à Roland Penrose ici à Cannes A.M. el 8.11.55.'

230 The photograph is boldly inscribed 'Pour mon cher Roland/ son ami Picasso /Cannes le 8.11.55'. Maar's dedication, 'Pour Roland/ Affectueusement/ Dora', is crammed into a free corner to the left of Picasso's dedication, which suggests that she was filling an available space and therefore that Penrose got the photograph from Picasso and then got her to sign it too, rather than vice versa. (Penrose met Maar in Paris on 12 November 1955; RPA 742.25.)

231 They met on 15 November 1955 (RPA 742.25).

232 The drawing, dated 'le 10.11.55', was won by Gordon Nettleton. Tickets for the Picture Fair draw cost £15 (information in a letter to Julie Lawson from Mrs Nettleton dated 10 July 1977; RPA 502).

233 '[…] Le fait que dès le commencement nous avons pu annoncer qu'il y avait parmi les tableaux exposés un dessin fait express pour cet évènement par toi a assuré toute de suite un success comme nous n'avons jamais connu jusqu'ici.

Ton dessin à été choisit par un artiste commercial qui n'avait pas deviné que tu étais l'auteur, car, comme tu sais, tous les signatures des tableaux été caché. Il l'a choisit d'abord parcequ'il le trouvait un très beau dessin et deuxièmement à cause de son enthusiasm pour les courses de taureaux. Quand il a decouvert que par dessus le maréché c'était toi l'auteur, sa joie était sans bornes.

Une fois de plus tu as repondu le bonheur et la réjouissance pour tout le monde parmi nous et nous te remercions de tout coeur.

Nous avons un projèt nouveau duquel je te parlerai si j'ai la chance de te voir au mois de février. Cet automne nous voulons faire a l'institut une exposition documentaire pour ton 75 anniveraire. J'espère avec le cooperation de Sabartés, Kahnweiler, et Man Ray ramasser une grande quantité de documents sur toi, les endroits où tu as travaillé etc. et tes amis tel qu'Apollinaire, Max Jacob, Eluard, Cocteau etc. etc. Je crois que pour nous et le public en generale ceci aura un très grand interêt. En tout cas nous aurons le temps de parler de ça plus tard. […]'

(Undated letter to Picasso on ICA headed notepaper enclosing the ICA New Year greetings card for 1956, therefore probably sent mid-late December 1955; AP.)

Chapter 4 The Biography Completed, 1956–1958

1 Penrose's itinerary is established by his diary for 1956 (RPA 742.26).

2 'Always cream with Braque – never with me.' Penrose's diary notes a meeting with Weelen on 12 February 1956 (RPA 742.26). Weelen was a prolific writer on art.

3 Penrose's diary notes lunch with 'Max' at the Coupole on 11 February and at Lipp's on 18 February 1956 (RPA 742.26). The brief record of their conversation is filed in RPA 587 [10].

4 RPA 580.11 [16].

5 RP *PLW* 1958, p. 113.

6 Penrose's diary mentions meeting with 'Geo Sales' on 9 and 13 February. For a slightly different version of what happened, see Gilot 1964, pp. 192–93.

7 'He holds up well against the Old Masters.'

8 'History painting'.

9 'anxious'.

10 'You see it's the same thing.' 'There is no misunderstood genius'. In the corresponding passage in RP *PLW* 1958 (p. 350), Penrose quotes only the first of these statements.

11 RPA 588 [B] [15].

12 See Daix & Israël, pp. 105–31. The periods Picasso spent in Paris between October 1939 and May 1940, while Dora Maar remained in Royan, are partly to be explained by this application, which may have been motivated by fears for his personal safety, as a notorious Spanish Republican, as well as by the quest for a divorce. (See Hensbergen, p. 137.)

13 Postcard to Lee Penrose, postmarked 'Cannes 27-2 1956', sent to Farley Farm, Sussex (RPA 717).

14 Picasso's statement, 'One never does what one wants to. One starts out wanting to do something and it [the work] makes you do something else,' is a variant of something he said repeatedly when attempting to characterise the creative process.

15 'beggars in top hats'.

16 There is no note of a rendezvous with Mme Ramié in Penrose's diary. However, his long notes about this trip [16] describe a lunch with the Ramiés on 25 February.

17 Apart from several trips to Paris, Picasso lived in Royan from September 1939 to August 1940.

18 The paintings by Henri Rousseau that Picasso owned (*The Representatives of the Great Powers Arriving to Salute the Republic as a Mark of Peace*, 1907; *Portrait of a Woman*, 1895; *Portrait of the Artist with a Lamp*, 1902–3; and *Portrait of the Artist's Second Wife*, 1903) are now in the MP.

19 'The harm you have done to painting is incalculable.'

20 Hidalgo Arnera.

21 This remark also appears in Penrose's pocket notebook [15] under the date 19 February 1956.

22 Penrose was responsible for an important Dubuffet exhibition at the ICA ('Paintings, Drawings, Sculptures by Jean Dubuffet', 29 March–30 April 1955) and the two were good friends.

23 *Women at their Toilette*, MP [Z.XVII.54]. This is inscribed 4 January 1956, but Penrose's notes of his visits to Cannes reveal that Picasso continued to work on it over an extended period of time.

24 The horoscope cast by Valentine Penrose. See above, Chapter 3, p. 113.

25 e.g. *Jacqueline in Turkish Costume*, 1955 [PP.55.233], and *Jacqueline Nude in a Turkish Hat*, 1955 [Z.XVI.529].

26 *Seated Woman in Turkish Costume*, 1955 [Z.XVI.528] and *Seated Woman in Turkish Costume*, 1955 [Z.XVI.535]. Both paintings are inscribed 22 December 1955.

27 Possibly *Seated Nude Woman (Jacqueline)*, 1956 [Z.XVII.2]. This is dated 31 January 1956. The area around the head has evidently been reworked and may originally have corresponded more closely with Penrose's description. Penrose must also have seen the equally massive *Seated Nude Woman* [Z.XVII.1], which is dated 2 January 1956.

28 Probably *The Studio at La Californie* [Z.XVI.496], which is dated 12 November 1955.

29 *Two Women on the Beach*, 1956, Musée National d'Art Moderne, Paris [Z.XVII.36].

30 See above, note 23.

31 i.e. 29 February 1956. All the notes up to this point were evidently written on that day – hence the lack of strict chronology.

32 'Strange Flowers, Bring Happiness'. The envelope from Floralia, Cannes, and the card survive in the Archives Picasso.

33 *Two Women on the Beach*. See above, note 29.

34 A prose-poem draft, dated 'Feb 21.22.23.', appears in the pocket notebook Penrose used on this trip [15].

35 Archives Picasso.

36 See above, Introduction, p. 12.

37 In a revised form and entitled 'On viewing Picasso', Penrose's poem was published in *Adam. International Review*, nos. 419–421, 1979, pp. 7–8.

38 On 6 and 7 March 1956 (RPA 742.26).

39 From his diary, we know that Penrose met Toklas on 12 March 1956 (RPA 742.26).

40 Apollinaire gave a thinly disguised account of the stormy affair between Irène Lagut (as Elvire) and Picasso (as Pablo Canouris) in *La femme assise* (Paris, NRF, 1920). See above, Chapter 3, p. 131.

41 house decorator.

42 This was confirmed by Michael Duffy, a conservator at MoMA, involved in the latest scientific analysis and conservation of *Les Demoiselles* ('I think he is correct in his assertion that the first stage of *Les Demoiselles* was painted very quickly. [...] I would be hard pressed to say that 48 hours is an accurate assessment of Picasso's time but I do think it is possible'; letter to the author dated 28 October 2004).

43 In the entry in his diary for 12 March 1956 Penrose notes: 'Ring Salmon' (RPA 742.26), but he did not record when they actually met.

44 'Picasso began to see red when people spoke of cubism or Negro art.'

45 Extracts from Fernande Olivier's memoirs were serialised in September 1930 in *Le Soir* under the title 'Quand Picasso était pompier'. Further extracts appeared in *Mercure de France* in May–July 1931. They appeared as a book in 1933 as *Picasso et ses amis*. For full details see Olivier 2001, pp. 10–11.

46 There is no note of a meeting with Matta in Penrose's diary.

47 'Picasso loves spectacle'.

48 According to Penrose's diary, he met Kahnweiler on 15 March 1956 (RPA 742.26).

49 'We shall find him hanged behind his great canvas.'

50 Mallarmé and painting.

51 *Woman with a Guitar*, 1913–14, MoMA [DR 646].

52 Besson's name and address appear in the 'Notes' pages of Penrose's diary for 1956, but there is no record of an appointment.

53 According to Penrose's diary, he met Baudouin on 13, 15 and 18 March (RPA 742.26).

54 Paulo Picasso had an operation in autumn 1954. Picasso's anxiety is also mentioned in Kahnweiler's letter to Penrose dated 6 January 1955 (LMA).

55 For Aragon's leading role in the vexed debate about Socialist Realism in France, see Utley, Chapter 8.

56 'With a goat, you can sense it was modelled by the Good Lord. The whole skull, the jaw, there at the pupil of the eyes he hesitated, but all around it is modelled by his hands. One senses his fingers, as if he were modelling in clay. But Karl Marx couldn't have modelled it. What is beautiful in Marx is that he wanted to model society, but he isn't the Good Lord. The proof – he is dead.' Picasso often drew attention to the sculptural aspects of skulls and bones, of which he had a huge collection.

57 'Picasso: œuvres des musées de Léningrad et de Moscou', Maison de la Pensée Française, Paris, June 1954. See above, Chapter 2, p. 80.

58 'phial'.

59 Dolores Ibárruri, who wrote under the pseudonym 'La Pasionaria', was a founder of the Spanish Communist Party and regarded as a heroine by the Republicans during the Spanish Civil War. She was responsible for the famous slogan 'No pasarán' (They shall not pass).

60 *The Goat*, 1950 [S.409].

61 Picasso visited Céret on several occasions before the First World War, beginning in summer 1911.

62 A reference to the numerous studies for *The Man with the Sheep* (aka *The Man with the Lamb*), 1942–43. One two-sheet drawing is dated 30 March 1943 (MP; Z.XII.241).

63 Letter to Penrose from Alfred Barr dated 2 March 1956, sent from MoMA (carbon copy in AHB 12.V.A.3. MoMA Archives, NY).

64 Letter to Alfred Barr dated 28 March 1956, sent to MoMA from 11A Hornton Street, London (AHB [AAA: 2197; 635–639]. MoMA Archives, NY).

65 Letter to Alfred Barr dated 16 December 1956, sent to MoMA from 29 Place du Marché St Honoré, Paris (AHB 12.II.C. MoMA Archives, NY). The new land, which doubled the existing acreage, made the farm more viable and also protected the views of Penrose's beloved Downs (information from Antony Penrose).

66 Georges Auric composed the incidental music for *Le Mystère Picasso*.

67 'the white period'.

68 *Women at their Toilette*, 1956, MP [Z.XVII.54].

69 Probably the very large *The Studio* [Z.XVII.101], which is dated 29 April 1956.

70 Sergei Yutkevitch won Best Director at the Film Festival for *Othello*. Desdemona was played by Irina Skobtseva.

71 So fascinated was he by this dramatisation of Picasso's creative process that Penrose made two slightly different versions of his summary. In the second version he translated Picasso's exchanges with Clouzot thus:
    P. 'That's all right – but supposing we get to the bottom of things as I do in my studio. See how a picture is made with a hundred pictures on top of each other.'
    C. 'That's going to be dangerous, very dangerous.'
    P. 'I know. That's what I've always wanted. Give me a great canvas.'
    - - - - - -
    P. 'It's going badly – and still worse before it's finished.'
    C. 'That's bad.'
    P. 'That's bad, why?'
    C. 'For the public.'
    P. 'That's all the same to me. I have never worried about the public.' [20]
72 RP *PLW* 1958, p. 363.
73 According to Penrose's diary, he met Sabartès on 23 June 1956 (RPA 742.26).
74 Old Woman: 'What are you doing here?'
    Picasso: 'You can see perfectly well what I'm doing.'
    Old Woman: 'But what right have you to come here?'
    Picasso: 'It's not a right, it's a need.'
75 Possibly the paintings referred to in note 26 above.
76 i.e. the brass charcoal burner shown in many of the studio pictures.
77 See Z.XVII.56–67.
78 *Springtime*, 1956, Musée National d'Art Moderne, Paris [Z.XVII.45].
79 *Large Reclining Nude (The Voyeurs)*, 1955 [PP.55.143].
80 See *Beach at La Garoupe (1)* and *Beach at La Garoupe (2)*, 1955 [PP.55.138, 139].
81 Barr attempted unsuccessfully to borrow some of the Russian pictures for his forthcoming Picasso exhibition at MoMA. (See his letter to Penrose dated 12 May 1956 [AHB 12.V.A.3 MoMA Archives, NY].)
82 A reference to Khrushchev's denunciation of Stalin at the 20th All-Union Party Congress in Moscow in spring 1956.
83 'We've seen it coming for a long time.'
84 Apollinaire died on 9 November 1918, a victim of the devastating Spanish 'flu epidemic. For the identity of the drawing, see Sabartès 1954, no. 122 [Z.III.75].
85 Philip James was Director of Art at the Arts Council of Great Britain. The exhibition, 'Picasso: 50 Years of Graphic Art', ran from 22 June to 5 August 1956. Penrose, elected to the Art Panel in 1956, helped James select the show.
86 Presumably Penrose means 'blette', or more commonly 'bette', French for chard.
87 'That's it.'
88 For a much fuller account, see '*Guerre et Paix*: extrait du journal dactylographié de René Batigne', in *Vallauris*, pp. 121–25.
89 Dr Chataignier.
90 'so that children can play on it and dogs piss on it'.
91 The *War and Peace* murals were exhibited in Picasso's retrospective in Italy in 1953.
92 The notes break off suddenly with the beginning of a new topic: 'Communism of P. not'.

93 His diary notes meetings with Maar on 9 July and 11 July 1956 (RPA 742.26).
94 'Well, now I've seen everything.'
95 Penrose had asked Barr to comment on the draft of his text. In the passage in question Penrose associated the excessive formal distortions with the violent feelings unleashed by the disintegration of Picasso's marriage to Olga (RP *Portrait* 1956, p. 55).
96 *Portrait of Dora Maar*, 1942 [Z.XII.154], reproduced in Barr 1946, p. 232.
97 Copy of a letter to Penrose from Barr dated 28 September 1956, sent to 11A Hornton Street, London (RPA 545).
98 *Portrait of Gertrude Stein*, 1905–6, The Metropolitan Museum of Art, New York [Z.I.352].
99 Picasso moved to 22, rue Victor-Hugo, Montrouge, in the summer of 1916. It remained his studio until he moved to 23, rue La Boétie in autumn 1918. He gave Gertrude Stein the tiny paper construction, *Guitarist with Sheet Music*, 1913 [DR 582].
100 'That one is a failure – because she dominated me.' The two earliest portraits of Jaqueline are said to be Z.XVI.325 (exhibited in 1955 as *Portrait of Mme. Z* and dated 2 June 1954) and *Jacqueline with Arms Crossed*, MP [Z.XVI.324], which is dated 3 June 1954.
101 e.g. *Bather Opening a Beach Hut*, 1928, MP [Z.VII.210].
102 'Cannes le 19.9.56.
    IIe deuxième arrivée à Paris.
    la dame n'est pas Suzanne Valladon
    le petit Monsieur avec une barbe est Monsieur Jaume Andreu Bonshons ou Bonsons ami à cette epoque qui est venu à Paris avec moi cette année
    je te fait remarquer que au guichet du Moulin Rouge on voit le prix d'entrée 3.Francs
    la signature du dessin est fausse.
    Tu serais bien gentil de m'envoyer une autre photo du dessin.
    Ton ami Picasso'
    (Text in pencil in Picasso's hand on the back of a black and white photograph of *Self-Portrait in Front of the Moulin Rouge*, 1901 [Z.XXI.250]; RPA 717.)
103 'Saludos al Instituto de las Artes Contemporaneos de Londres   Picasso   Cannes le 11.8.56'.
104 Confirmed by Penrose's letter to Picasso dated 29 March 1956, sent to La Californie, Cannes, from Farley Farm, Sussex (AP).
105 Penrose owned *Woman's Head and Self-Portrait*, 1929 [Z.VII.248] at the time and although in RP *PLW* 1958 (p. 235) he did not actually state that the woman was Olga, he associated the picture with 'the emotional stress' engendered by the marital crisis. See also above, pp. 170–71, for Barr's response to this interpretation.
106 'Nous sommes arrivés d'ouvrir l'exposition le soir de ton anniversaire et il y avait une foule de gens qui sont venu. On a du renvoyer pas mal du monde car il n'y avait plus de place.
    Bien entendu c'était ta presence qui dominait tout. Près de quatre cents images de toi à tous les ages nous regardaient des murs et la puissance vitale qui surgissait même de ces images a remplit de joie tout le monde qui etait venu. Encore c'était grace à la magie Picasso.'

(Letter to Picasso dated 29 October 1956, sent from Farley Farm, Sussex [AP]. It was delivered to Picasso by Paulo, together with the catalogue, press cuttings, etc.)

107 Sabartès 1954 was the immediate model for RP *Portrait* 1956.

108 Penrose was not, however, aware of the extent of Picasso's own photographic oeuvre: some of the pre-1918 photographs published without attribution in RP *Portrait* 1956 were, as Anne Baldassari has shown, taken by Picasso himself (see *inter alia* Baldassari 1994).

109 RPA 543.

110 The Austral Islands statue depicts the god Tanaroa creating gods and men. Penrose himself owned a plaster cast of the figure, which was made originally for '40,000 Years of Modern Art', ICA, 1948–49 (now on loan to the Scottish National Gallery of Modern Art, Edinburgh).

111 Picasso thanked Penrose enthusiastically for the 'bonhomme en platre' in a letter dated 13 October 1956 (RPA 717). On 22 October 1956, Penrose wrote confirming that the British Museum had no objection to it being cast in bronze (AP).

112 According to Penrose's diary, he met Sabartès on 21 November 1956 (RPA 742.26).

113 According to Penrose's diary, he met Maar on 17 December 1956, but he may have met her on other occasions after his arrival in Paris on 17 November (RPA 742.26).

114 *Bathers, Mermaids, Nude and Minotaur*, March 1937 [Z.IX.97].

115 See Lord, pp. 292–303, for the text of his letter to Picasso and the hostility of Picasso's friends.

116 Richardson 1999, pp. 207–12.

117 Several important letters are published in Madeline, pp. 314–18.

118 See Utley, pp. 197–201, and also Daix 1993, p. 330.

119 Filed in RPA 529.

120 *Massacre at Korea*, 1951, MP [Z.XV.173].

121 See below, p. 181.

122 *Portrait de Manuel Pallarès*, 1909, The Detroit Institute of Arts [DR 274]. In 1898 Picasso and Pallarès had camped out in a cave in the hills outside Horta de Ebro.

123 e.g. *Seated Musician*, 1956 [S.548].

124 e.g. *Standing Flute Player*, 1958, MP. See Quinn, Chapter 3, for photographs of these works in the garden at La Californie.

125 *The Bathers*, 1956, Staatsgalerie Stuttgart [S.503–508].

126 There were, in fact, only nine other signatories.

127 See Baldassari 1997, pp. 222, 228, for a discussion of these experiments.

128 Henri 'le Douanier' Rousseau, *Portrait de femme*, 1895, MP. Picasso bought the painting from the junk dealer 'Père' Soulié in 1908.

129 'more than anything else'.

130 'to give an oriental effect', 'the fortifications' (i.e. the walls of Paris).

131 Paulo Picasso must have been in Cannes at the same time as Penrose. Alternatively, this conversation occurred when Penrose met him in Paris on 24 November 1956 (diary entry; RPA 742.26).

132 Penrose thanked Picasso in a letter dated 30 December 1956, sent to La Californie, Cannes, from Farley Farm, Sussex (AP). On 11 December 1956, Picasso dedicated a copy of André Verdet's *Picasso à son image* (Nice, Galerie H. Matarasso, 1956) to Penrose, with a humorous coloured crayon drawing on the title-page. Verdet's book was mainly about the Clouzot film.

133 'Picasso: 75th Anniversary Exhibition', MoMA, 4 May–8 September 1957 (subsequently at the Art Institute of Chicago and Philadelphia Museum of Art).

134 Letter to Penrose from Barr dated 16 January 1957, sent to 29 Place du Marché St Honoré, Paris, from MoMA (RPA 46). Barr was replying to Penrose's letter of 16 December 1956 describing Picasso's relief after signing the open letter to *L'Humanité* (AHB 12.II.C. MoMA Archives, NY).

135 *Portrait of Picasso*, MoMA, 1957, p. 92.

136 See Utley, pp. 147–52.

137 'For me the Communist Party is the party of the poor.'

138 The text of Kahnweiler's lecture at the ICA on 1 November 1956, and a transcript of the ensuing question-and-answer session, are in RPA 544.

139 Letter to Richard Nixon from David Douglas Duncan dated 23 June 1957 (cited in Duncan 1974, pp. 32–33). On the same day, but in less bullish tones, Duncan wrote to Alfred Barr to make the same proposal (*ibid.*, p. 32).

140 Picasso's request for a visa to enter America in 1950 had been turned down. (See Hensbergen, pp. 196–97.)

141 'Francis Bacon', in *Francis Bacon*, Paris, Galerie Rive Droite, 12 February–10 March 1957; 'A Henry Moore', in *Henry Moore: sculptures et dessins*, Paris, Berggruen et Cie, 1957.

142 Neither entry is dated precisely, but both follow shortly after the entry dated 29–30 May 1957: 'm'étant saoulé chez les Penrose', 'bibition chez les Penrose' (Leiris, pp. 495, 497).

143 Interview with John and Cynthia Thompson conducted by Michael Sweeney on 18 November 1997. I am grateful to Michael Sweeney for passing on Patsy Murray's testimony.

144 anguish.

145 'The more soul there is, the worse it is.' Penrose marked this in red crayon.

146 Kosnitzky has not been identified. According to Penrose's diary, they met on 1 February 1957 (RPA 742.27). The Penroses rented Mary Callery's apartment in Paris (29 Place du Marché St Honoré) during Roland's first six months as Fine Arts Officer of the British Council (from November 1956).

147 Carlo Frua de Angeli, head of a Milanese synthetic textiles empire and a major patron of modern art. He was one of Zervos's principal financial backers and was briefly married to Mary Callery in the mid-1930s. (Information from John Richardson.) He allowed Penrose to reproduce a number of his Picassos in RP *PLW* 1958 and subsequently lent four works to the 1960 Tate exhibition (correspondence regarding these loans in RPA 547).

148 Probably *Woman with Cockerel*, dated 15 February 1938 [Z.IX.109], which Mary Callery lent to Barr's Picasso retrospective in 1939 (Barr 1939, no. 345).

149 'Picasso Ceramics', Arts Council Gallery, London, 18
April–18 May 1957.

150 The Palais Grimaldi, Château d'Antibes, where Picasso
had painted *La joie de vivre* and some twenty other
decorative pictures in autumn 1946.

151 Picasso's inordinate fondness for this goat, a Christmas
gift from Jacqueline, is amusingly described in Parmelin
1959.

152 Picasso stayed in Schoorl, near Alkmaar, during summer
1905.

153 'Picasso Himself' transferred to Galerie La Hune in
March 1957. 'Kahnweiler's opening' refers to: 'Picasso:
Peintures 1955–1956', Galerie Louise Leiris, Paris,
26 March–April 1957.

154 'dog shit'.

155 *Plate of Fried Bulls for Currito*, 1957, Museo Picasso,
Buitrago de Lozoya [Z.XVII.322].

156 Gustave Courbet, *The Studio of the Painter*, 1855, Musée
d'Orsay, Paris.

157 'The Radiant City'.

158 *Women at their Toilette*, 1956, MP [Z.XVII.54].

159 *Girl with a Mandolin (Fanny Tellier)*, 1910, MoMA [DR
346]. Penrose had only just sold the painting to Nelson A.
Rockefeller. See above, p. 161. Penrose told John Golding
that when Picasso discussed the unfinished state of the
painting with him in London in 1950, he remarked 'C'est
mieux comme ça' (It's better like that). (Information from
John Golding.)

160 Picasso was commissioned to make a statue for Apollinaire's
grave in Père Lachaise cemetery, but none of his designs
satisfied the Committee. The bronze *Head of a Woman
(Dora Maar)*, 1941, was eventually accepted, not for the
grave, but for the garden of Square Laurent Prache, near
Apollinaire's flat on Boulevard St Germain. It was
inaugurated on 5 June 1959.

161 'a splendid man'.

162 In Will Grohmann's definitive study of Klee, this
apocryphal remark is not quoted and Picasso's visit to
Berne is correctly attributed to the autumn of 1937 (*Paul
Klee*, London, Lund Humphries, 1954, p. 93). The meeting
was organised by Bernhard Geiser. Paulo Picasso was
being treated in a Swiss clinic at the time.

163 Picasso's Afghan hound.

164 Picasso painted five wall paintings in La Mimoseraie,
Eugenia Errazuriz's villa in Biarritz. They were eventually
removed in 1961.

165 'It was what was best'.

166 fisticuffs.

167 *The Artist's Dining Room at Montrouge*, dated 9 December
1917, MP [Z.III.06].

168 A Grebo mask (Ivory Coast). Reproduced in Seckel-Klein,
p. 247.

169 All three portraits, executed in May–June 1920, are in the
MP [Z.IV.59, 60, 62].

170 *Portrait of Guillaume Apollinaire*, 1916 [Z.XXIX.200].

171 *Portrait of Francis Poulenc*, MP [Z.XVII.327], which is in
fact dated 13 March 1957.

172 *The Bathers*, 1918, MP [Z.III.237].

173 *Italian Peasants*, 1919, The Santa Barbara Museum of
Arts [Z.III.431]; *Portrait of Serge de Diaghilev and Alfred

Seligsberg, 1919, MP [Z.III.301]; *Three Dancers*, 1919,
MP [Z.III.352]; *Portrait of Renoir*, 1919, MP [Z.III.413].

174 *The Crucifixion*, 1930, MP [Z.VII.287].

175 ribbon.

176 Not, in fact, a painting of Barcelona but of Málaga
(*Montes of Málaga*, 1897 [Z.VI.100]).

177 'I have been cramming in all the interviews and visits
which I can while I am still here until the end of this
month' (letter to Alfred Barr dated 16 June 1957, sent
from Paris; AHB [AAA: 2197; 493–536]. MoMA Archives,
NY).

178 The name Sergio de Castro appears in two of Penrose's
address books (RPA 744.1 and 744.2). Conceivably, he
was related to Fabián de Castro, the gipsy guitarist whom
Picasso met at the Bateau Lavoir in 1904 and who, under
Picasso's influence, took up painting (see Richardson
1991, p. 296). Cécile Goldscheider was curator of the
Musée Rodin, Paris. Pierre Peissi wrote widely on
twentieth-century art and especially architecture.

179 Luis de Góngora y Argote (1561–1627) was famed for
the extreme verbal complexity of his poetry and for the
seam of melancholy and irony running through it.

180 'Bloody Picasso!'

181 'I'm never going to touch your Picassos again.' 'One would
think it was a Picasso.'

182 According to Penrose's diary, he met the author Henri-
Pierre Roché on 22 May, 31 May and 11 June 1957 (RPA
742.27). Roché made friends with Picasso soon after the
latter settled in Paris and introduced him to Gertrude and
Leo Stein in autumn 1905. Later he acted as advisor to the
great American collector John Quinn.

183 In fact, *Les Demoiselles d'Avignon* was first exhibited in
1916, not 1910, in premises, known as the Salon d'Antin,
loaned by Paul Poiret.

184 The draft of Penrose's letter to Fernande Olivier, dated
6 May 1957, together with her reply, dated 10 May 1957,
are in RPA 588.

185 Picasso and Olivier went to Barcelona in May 1906, en
route for Gósol.

186 *La toilette*, 1906, Albright-Knox Art Gallery, Buffalo
[Z.I.325].

187 Picasso and Olivier stayed in Horta in summer 1909.

188 A make of oil lamp.

189 A senior member of the French Council of State.

190 'You must open up. It's important.'

191 'I'll sink Picasso. This can't be allowed.'

192 'repressed'.

193 In RP *SB*, pp. 231–32, Penrose describes the social circle
of Nadine Effront and her daughter Ninette Lyon, noting
that their friendship 'widened greatly both public and
private relations for Lee and myself'.

194 Ubaldo Oppi.

195 A reference to Braque's series of eight *Studio* paintings,
1949–56.

196 'I'm going out with Georges.'

197 'their deepest thoughts'. This contrasts strongly with
Françoise Gilot's account of their long discussions about
painting (see Gilot 1964, pp. 243 ff.).

198 Letter to Penrose from Hilary Rubinstein dated 18 June
1957 (RPA 589).

199 'Picasso: dessins, gouaches, aquarelles, 1898–1957', Musée Réattu, Arles, 6 July–2 September 1957.

200 'Nous sommes maintenant au depart, quittant la belle appartement du centre de Paris pour notre ferme où enfermé je vais me mettre tranquillement au travail sur mon livre, de façon de le finir si possible avant le fin de l'année. […] Tout le monde parle de la corrida d'Arles en honneur de ton exposition de dessins. Je rage a mon impuissance de venir pour un evenement aussi passionant mais comment faire, j'ai mon livre sur toi qui prends présidence sur tout jusqu'au mois d'Octobre, quand j'ai l'intention de venir te voir en realité après d'avoir resider avec toi dans ma pensée pour tant de semaines.' (Letter to Picasso dated 26 June 1957, sent to La Californie, Cannes, from Paris; AP.)

201 Letter to Alfred Barr dated 10 July 1957, sent from Farley Farm, Sussex (AHB [AAA: 2197; 559–560]. MoMA Archives, NY). At Penrose's request, Barr had sent Fernande Olivier a copy of Picasso: Fifty Years of His Art, inscribed with their combined best wishes.

202 'L'été s'est passé avec une vitesse inimaginable mais je n'ai pas laché depuis des mois mon travail […]' (letter to Picasso dated 26 September 1957, sent to La Californie, Cannes, from Farley Farm, Sussex; AP).

203 Penrose's diary for 9 October 1957 notes: 'night ferry to Paris' (RPA 742.27).

204 Letter to Penrose from Hilary Rubinstein dated 3 October 1957 (RPA 589).

205 Letter to Penrose from Victor Gollancz dated 28 March 1958 (RPA 589).

206 RP PLW 1958, pp. 370–78.

207 El Zurdo (The Left-Handed Man), 1899 [Geiser & Baer 1].

208 Michael Duffy agreed that the canvas 'may have been specially prepared' but did not believe it was cheap: 'The fine weave of the linen suggests a high-quality material.' Neither he nor his colleagues in the Conservation department at MoMA knew what 'stayone' was, but he is convinced that Picasso did not line the canvas to strengthen it before beginning the painting. (See above note 42, and also M. Duffy, 'Les Demoiselles d'Avignon: Core of Picasso's Laboratory', in Modern Art, New Museums, London, The International Institute for the Conservation of Historic and Artistic Works, p. 133.)

209 Picasso did not forgive André Salmon for accepting the post of war correspondent in 1937 for the pro-Franco Le Petit Parisien, and he was shocked when Max Jacob allowed his photograph and a poem to be published alongside pro-Franco propaganda in L'Occident on 25 December 1937 (Seckel, pp. 249–51).

210 'Isn't that so?'

211 'I can't do it.'

212 The Fall of Icarus, a mural (8 x 10 metres) completed in 1958 for the Hall of the Delegates' Lobby, Maison de l'UNESCO, Paris.

213 'Subjects no longer exist'.

214 gathering.

215 The Pigeons [Z.XVII.394-401]. According to Picasso's inscriptions, all eight canvases were painted between 6 and 12 September 1957.

216 'The more soul there is, the worse it is.'

217 This passage is based closely on Penrose's conversation with Dora Maar and Balthus on 12 January 1957 (see above, p. 183).

218 Picasso never carried out this promise.

219 Charles Baudelaire, 'De l'essence du rire et généralement du comique dans les arts plastiques' (1855), Œuvres complètes, vol. 2, ed. Claude Pichois, Paris, Gallimard, p. 532.

220 The Piano, dated 17 October 1957, MPB [Z.XVII.404].

221 'Chamberlain'.

222 e.g. Las Meninas (after Velázquez), dated 18 September 1957, MPB [Z.XVII.372].

223 Las Meninas (after Velázquez), dated 17 August 1957, MPB [Z.XVII.351].

224 The first artificial satellite, Sputnik I, was launched on 4 October 1957 by the USSR.

225 'modelling'.

226 Penrose's sketch is closest to Las Meninas (after Velázquez). Doña Isabel de Velasco, the Dwarf, the Child and the Dog, dated 24 October 1957, MPB [Z.XVII.384]. The picture was still unfinished when Penrose made his sketch.

227 'Clarity does not come from intelligence.'

228 RP PLW 1958, p. 378.

229 Postcard depicting a bullfight sent to Lee Penrose at 11A Hornton Street, London, from Nîmes, and postmarked 21 October 1957 (RPA 717).

230 Parmelin 1959, p. 72.

231 There is probably an intentional echo of the title of Paul Eluard's lecture at the ICA in 1951, 'Aujourd'hui, Pablo Picasso, le plus jeune artiste du monde, a 70 ans' (see above, Chapter 2, p. 69). The full text on the birthday card reads:
'à Pablo Picasso.
toujours le plus jeune artiste du monde
with love from
Lee & Roland
Penrose
cheval hibou chèvre singe colombe taureau poisson chien chat [these words are inscribed within silhouettes of the creatures concerned]
te saluent
25 Oct. '57'
(AP)

232 Letter thanking Picasso dated 9 January 1958, sent to La Californie, Cannes, from the ICA (AP).

233 The translations given here are those provided by Penrose himself in RP PLW 1971, p. 461.

234 '[…] Finalement après des reclamations continues de mon editeur je lui ai envoyé le manuscrit il y a quelques jours après d'avoir travaillé làdesus jours et nuit pendant les quinze jours finales. Il [y] a encore beaucoup de corrections à faire dans les épreuves et les illustrations à choisir mais le plus gros du travail est terminé et j'attends maintenant à voir ce que les autres vont penser. Pour moi ça a été plus que trois ans de travail assidue mais je me rends compte de plus en plus comme c'est rien à côté du sujet merveilleux que je voudrais essayer de rendre un peu plus accessible aux Anglo-Saxons.

Je vais donner une copie du manuscrit à Kahnweiler cette semaine pour avoir son opinion et si tu as envie de le voir dans cet état avant qu'il soit imprimé je te l'enverrai avec le plus grand plaisir – mais c'est tout en anglais et je ne pense pas que cela va t'intéresser follement. […]'
(Letter to Picasso dated 15 February 1958, sent to La Californie, Cannes, from Paris; AP.)

235 There is no trace of any discussion of the dust jacket in the correspondence in the Edinburgh Archive. Hilary Rubinstein, who did not edit the book, had no recollection of any discussion of the matter, but stressed how unusual it was for Gollancz to depart from the house style of bright yellow (personal communication, October 2004).

236 Published by Harper and Brothers, New York.

237 Raymond Mortimer, 'A Modern Colossus', *The Sunday Times*, 19 October 1958, and Alan Clutton-Brock, 'A Great Barbaric Art', *The Observer*, 19 October 1958.

238 Eric Newton, 'Picasso in Counterpoint', *Time and Tide*, 6 November 1958.

239 Guy Habasque, in *L'Oeil*, no. 50, February 1959: 'l'auteur ne cherche jamais à arranger les faits de manière à les faire coïncider avec un portrait préconçu, une image subjective et arbitraire qu'il se serait formée de l'homme ou du peintre. […] son travail repose sur des bases exceptionnellement solides et étendues […] C'est un ouvrage de première main et lorsqu'il s'agit de Picasso, une constatation de cet ordre n'est pas un mince éloge.' (Translation by Keith Hartley.)

240 'J'ai mis mon nez dans votre "Picasso" sitot reçu, et je ne l'ai pas retiré pendant 4 jours, ne sautant pas un mot, empoigné. C'est un simple, utile, noble livre. La façon dont vous mélangez sa vie et sa peinture est si vraie, directe, évidente. Vous atteignez au lyrique par l'intimité, la franchise et la retenue.' (Letter to Penrose from H.-P. Roché dated 21 October 1958, glued into Penrose's RP *PLW* 1958 scrapbook; RPA 590.)

241 Letter to Penrose from Alfred Barr dated 16 January 1959, sent to 14 Place Dauphine, Paris, from MoMA (RPA 46). Principal among the nameless 'enemies' was Douglas Cooper.

242 David Sylvester, 'Picasso Sits for a Portrait', *Times Literary Supplement*, 2 January 1959.

243 Anon., 'Pablo Picasso: The Artist as Subject', *Times Literary Supplement*, 22 December 1961, pp. 905–8. Cooper was reviewing a series of recent publications on Picasso.

Chapter 5   The Story of an Exhibition, 1958–1960

1 Correspondence in the Arts Council files about a Picasso retrospective dates back to 1953. Penrose's abortive attempt to bring the Russian Picassos to London in 1954 (described in Chapter 2, p. 80) was connected with this project (see ACGB/121/839).

2 On 5 November 1957 Penrose wrote to Philip James at the ACGB to assure him that he had spoken to Picasso about the exhibition 'last week' and that Picasso 'was in full agreement that it should happen' (ACGB/121/839).

3 'Cher Pablo,
Je suis de retour de Londres où je viens de passer deux jours. Pendant ma visite on m'a demandé officiellement de prendre sur moi l'organisation de la grande <u>exposition Picasso</u> qui sera tenu à la Tate Gallery en 1960 sous les auspices du Arts Council.
J'avais déjà parlé à toi de cet exposition quand j'étais à Cannes l'automne dernier et a ce moment là tu étais d'accord sur le projet. J'espère bien que tu n'as pas changé d'avis car nous voudrions faire une exposition vraiment importante, la première sur cet échelle qu'on aura jamais fait en Angleterre. J'ai parlé cet après midi à Kahnweiler qui était déjà aucourant du projèt et il m'a promit sa cooperation.
Malgré qu'on a bien le temps je vais me mettre au travail toute de suite. Comme tu peut imaginer je suis enchanté et heureux qu'on m'a demandé de faire une chose que j'ai tellement au coeur. […]'
(Letter to Picasso dated 1 March 1958, sent to La Californie, Cannes, from 14 Place Dauphine, Paris; AP.)

4 Minutes of the meeting of the Art Panel of the ACGB, London, 27 February 1958 (RPA 547).

5 See Richardson 1999, pp. 158–65.

6 See correspondence between Philip James, Cooper and Penrose in 1955–56 (ACGB/121/839).

7 Apart from the 'Picasso Ceramics' show of 1957, Cooper had curated Arts Council retrospectives of Braque in 1956 and Monet in 1957.

8 Conversation with John Richardson, June 2004.

9 Letter to Penrose from Cooper dated 14 August 1958, sent from Château de Castille and headed 'PRIVATE' (RPA 547).

10 Letter from Cooper to William Coldstream dated 18 August 1958, sent from Château de Castille to ACGB, London (ACGB/121/839).

11 'J'ai eu encore dernièrement des nouvelles de notre Douglas. Après mes efforts d'arriver à une entente avec lui au sujet de ton exposition à Londres des quelles tu es au courant, j'ai reçu une lettre de lui qu'il faut compter je crains comme l'échec final. Il dit qu'il le trouve impossible <u>par principe</u> de s'associer avec une exposition au moins qu'il a une mesure de control sur l'organisation – principe très commode quand on n'a pas envie de s'y mêler – et qu'il est trop occupé avec des livres qu'il est en train d'ecrire pour accepter de m'aider sans être payer, avec le catalogue. Bien entendu je n'ai pas commencé mes pourparlers en offrant de l'argent à un si grand seigneur.
Je n'avais d'ailleurs comme tu sais, pas grand éspoir de reussir avec lui car il est tellement profondement blessé qu'on n'a pas demandé à lui de faire l'exposition, mais comme nous avons dit ensemble l'autre jour son refus ne doit diminuer en rien l'attrait de cet exposition que je compte bien sans ses tableaux faire la plus belle du point de vue de la selection et en consequence le plus étonnant qu'on a jamais vu.
A Londres j'ai déjà eu plusieurs conversations avec les gens responsable officiellement et tous sont très enthousiaste et très reconnaissant que tu es prêt à nous aider en nous prêtant des toiles.'
(Letter to Picasso dated 25 August 1958, sent to La Californie, Cannes, from Farley Farm, Sussex; AP.)

12 RPA 547.

13 Letter to Alfred Barr dated 12 March 1958, sent to MoMA from Paris; reply from Barr dated 18 March 1958 (RPA 547). Richardson says that Cooper was in awe of Barr and did not attempt to play devious games with him (conversation with the author, June 2004).

14 'Picasso Mural', letter to the Editor, *The Times*, 28 June 1958, p. 7.

15 Penrose was still in Cannes on 25 July 1958 when, with Picasso, Jacqueline, John Richardson and others, he signed a postcard addressed to Lee at 11A Hornton Street, London (RPA 717).

16 Luis Miguel Dominguin was a Spanish bullfighter whom Picasso often watched perform in Arles and who became a friend.

17 'It was painted with four-letter words.' The painting is *Still Life with Bull's Head*, 1958, MP [Z.XVIII.237].

18 i.e. the crisis in Algeria in May 1958, which brought General de Gaulle back into power as President of the Republic – interpreted by many on the left in France as a return to fascism.

19 *The Goat*, 1950 [S.409]. A bronze cast was set up in the garden near the entrance to La Californie.

20 The drawings are numbered I–XXI and dated 19 July 1958 [Z.XVIII.275–296].

21 'Every portrait must be a new picture.'

22 *The Arlésienne*, dated 8 July–15 August 1958 [Z.XVIII.299]: Picasso must have continued to work on this picture after Penrose's departure.

23 *The Bay of Cannes*, 1958, MP [Z.XVIII.83].

24 Daix 1993, p. 339. Tabaraud, pp. 116–28, provides the fullest account of the various reasons for the long delay between the completion of the *War and Peace* murals and the opening of the chapel.

25 Richardson 1999, p. 243. The most distinguished former owner was Luc de Clapiers, Marquis de Vauvenargues, a writer and moralist in the circle of Voltaire, famed for his maxims and aphorisms.

26 Parmelin 1959, pp. 244–50.

27 'Cher Pablo,
    Je sais que tu as raison de fuire les fêtes et les acclamations mais c'était une grande deception pour moi de ne pas te revoir et t'embrasser. On a beau dire "à bientôt" mais ça fais toujours des mois qui passent sans avoir la joie de te voir. Enfin le prochain fois je tacherai de choisir un moment quand les phares ne sont pas braqués sur toi et je viendrai avec Lee te saluer en secret dans les ramparts de Vauvenargues.
    Je suis d'autant plus triste parce que j'avais des choses que je voulais te dire sur la grande peinture de l'Unesco. La voyant sur place j'étais très emu et surtout etonné de la façon que tu as pu profiter d'un si mauvais site. Je pensais en le voyant à Vallauris que c'était la première et la dernière fois qu'on la verra convenablement sans qu'elle soit completement cachée par les constructions de ces messieurs les architects – Mais non – au contraire – evidement tu avais bien compris comment tirer partie de cette situation. Le personnage noir au millieu du tableau est bien caché quand on rentre de la salle des pas perdus, mais a chaque pas quand on avance il a l'air de tombé d'un ciel distant jusqu'au moment qu'on est si près qu'on peut presque le toucher et on voit le tableau entier avec tous ces grands personnages qui vous dominent. Ça a un côté dramatique qu'on n'appercevait pas à Vallauris. Ça fait que le tableau est beau qu'on le voir tout entier et qu'elle vous écrase par son echelle enorme et aussi quand c'est moitié caché. Vraiment tu as triomphé des circonstances d'un facon étonnant. Surement d'autres t'ont déjà dit cela mais permets moi de le repeter. C'était déjà pas mal d'accepter de faire quoi que ça soit dans un site si difficile mais de le tourner à ton avantage même sans le voir sur place je trouve vraiment un miracle.
    Cher Pablo, je t'embrasse, au moins je me rejouis que tu as eu un anniversaire annulé, c'est encore signe de ta jeunesse fabuleuse. Embrasse Jacqueline de ma part. De tout coeur
    Roland.
    Excuse, je te prie, ces pages écrit sur mes genous sur un banc.'
    (Letter to Picasso dated 21 October 1958, sent to La Californie, Cannes, from Montpellier; AP.)

28 Letter to Picasso dated 15 February 1959, sent to La Californie, Cannes, from 14 Place Dauphine, Paris (AP).

29 Letters from Penrose to Picasso dated 15 March and 24 March 1959, sent to La Californie, Cannes, from 14 Place Dauphine, Paris (AP).

30 A small blue notebook, inscribed on the front cover 'Brussels, Zurich, Cannes. Spring 1959', is full of notes about the Swiss collections, often with thumbnail sketches of the paintings that most interested Penrose (RPA 547).

31 RP *Picasso*. A. P. J. Kroonenburg of De Lange, Amsterdam, commissioned the text from Penrose in March 1959. Penrose started writing it that summer and finished it the following spring. The correspondence with Kroonenburg – increasingly recriminatory on Penrose's side as one thing after another went wrong – continued sporadically until December 1961 (RPA 583).

32 This emerges from Penrose's correspondence with the ACGB, e.g. his letter to Gabriel White, dated 10 February 1960, quoted below, p. 225.

33 'Picasso', Musée Cantini, Marseille, 11 May–31 July 1959.

34 *The Studio at La Californie*, dated 30 March 1956, MP [Z.XVII.56]. (Cat. 55 in Musée Cantini exhibition.)

35 i.e. the monotypes of brothels by Degas which Picasso acquired in 1958. Douglas Cooper negotiated their purchase, from the collection of Maurice Exsteens, on Picasso's behalf. (See Seckel-Klein, pp. 111–21.)

36 *Fountain-Man*, 1956 [S.505]. This figure is from *The Bathers* group, originally made in wood. In calling it 'manikin pis', Penrose likens it to the famous fountain in Brussels.

37 'lost wax' – a traditional bronze-casting process. Penrose may be referring to *Bust of a Woman*, 1931, bronze, MP (S.131).

38 e.g. *Young Man*, 1958, wood [S.509].

39 *Head*, 1958, wood, plaster and buttons, MoMA [S.539].

40 23 April was Lee's birthday. That day Picasso, Jacqueline, her daughter Cathy, Duncan and Penrose all signed a postcard wishing her 'bonne fête' (RPA 717).

41 *Head of a Woman (Dora Maar)*, 1941, bronze [S.197]. Four casts were made. On 5 June 1959, it was one of these that was set up in Square Laurent Prache, St-Germain-des-Prés, as a monument to Apollinaire.

42 Matisse bequeathed various items to Picasso, including a custom-made cabinet for storing prints and drawings.

43 Truck.

44 A slip of the pen for Vauvenargues. For the contemporary *Guide Bleu* description of the château and its interior, see Georges Monmarché, *Provence, Côte d'Azur*, Paris, Librairie Hachette, 1958, p. 214.

45 *Jacqueline de Vauvenargues*, dated 20 April 1959 [Z.XVII.452].

46 *El Bobo (after Velázquez and Murillo)*, dated 14–15 April 1959 [Z.XVIII.484].

47 'One can see them, can't one?'

48 e.g. *Mandolin, Pitcher and Glass*, dated 13–14 April 1959 [Z.XVIII.440].

49 Cézanne, *The Sea at L'Estaque*, 1878–79, MP.

50 The following works by Matisse can be seen in the photographs taken at the time by Duncan: *Bouquet of Flowers in a Chocolate Pot*, 1902; *Portrait of Marguerite*, 1906; *Still Life with Basket of Oranges*, 1912; *Tulips and Oysters on a Black Ground*, 1943; all MP.

51 *Head of a Chamois Goat*, c. 1875, MP. The painting is now thought to be only partially the work of Courbet.

52 *Woman in a Rocking Chair*, 1943, Musée National d'Art Moderne, Paris [Z.XIII.74].

53 Probably Corot, *La petite Jeannette*, 1848; *The Italian Girl, Maria di Sorre*, 1826–27; both MP.

54 Probably a reference to Braque, *Teapot and Apples*, 1942, MP (which can be seen in Duncan's photographs).

55 The attribution of *Landscape*, MP, to Gauguin is now considered doubtful (see Seckel-Klein, p. 136).

56 *The Procession of the Fatted Ox (The Wine Feast)*, mid-17th century, MP, was acquired by Picasso in 1957 as by Le Nain, but is now attributed to the so-called Master of the Processions.

57 This sideboard, in the style of Henry II, inspired a number of paintings, including the immense *The Vauvenargues Sideboard*, 1959–60, MP [Z.XVIII.395].

58 *The Cat*, 1941 [S.195].

59 Some of Duncan's photographs chronicling the move from La Californie to Vauvenargues and the dinner Penrose describes are reproduced in Duncan 1974, pp. 77–99.

60 The first postcard is from Picasso (ornamented with a little drawing), the second from Jacqueline, Paulo Picasso and Roland himself. Both show the Château de Vauvenargues (RPA 717).

61 RPA 742.29.

62 RP *PLW* 1971, p. 441.

63 See Cabanne (4), p. 105. When it became clear that Vauvenargues did not suit him or Jacqueline, Picasso asked Lionel Prejger, whose brother was an estate agent in Cannes, to find a property for him. When the Prejger brothers proposed Notre-Dame-de-Vie, Picasso instantly agreed to buy it: he already knew the house from his pre-war visits to Mougins. (Personal communication from Lionel Prejger, March 1994.)

64 Reproduced, RP *SB*, p. 222. The inscription reads: 'POUR Roland Penrose son ami Picasso 10.7.59.'

65 Reproduced, RP *SB*, p. 219. The inscription reads: 'POUR Lee Picasso 10.7.59.'

66 RP *SB*, pp. 268–69.

67 Penrose's diary (RPA 742.29) indicates that he was constantly on the move from the time he arrived in Chicago on 15 October 1959 to 3 December, when he and Lee set sail for Southampton.

68 'La Corrida Americana – la mienne – est presque terminé et les projets pour l'exposition de Londres sont vraiment assez brilliants. Une trentaine de Picassos sublimes vont s'embarquer pour l'Angleterre au mois de juin pour faire notre joie. J'ai très envie de te voir bientôt pour te raconter tout ça. Nous t'embrassons Roland.' (Postcard to Picasso dated 24 November 1959, sent to La Californie, Cannes, from New York; AP.)

69 Penrose's diary notes meetings with Picasso in Cannes on 7, 8, 9, 12, 13 and 14 February 1960 (RPA 743.1). On the second day, 8 February, he notes that he 'saw new paintings'.

70 'Picasso: "Les Ménines", 1957', Galerie Louise Leiris, Paris, 22 May–27 June 1959.

71 Letter to Gabriel White dated 10 February 1960, sent to the ACGB, London, from Cannes (ACGB/121/839).

72 *Parade*, 1917, drop curtain, Musée National d'Art Moderne, Paris. Letter to Picasso dated 7 January 1960, sent to La Californie, Cannes, from Farley Farm, Sussex (AP).

73 *Composition for a 'Mardi-Gras' Ball*, 1923, Chrysler Art Museum, Provincetown, Massachusetts.

74 *Women at their Toilette*, 1938, MP [Z.IX.176]; *The Farmer's Wife*, woven tapestry copied from a pastel of 1930 [PP.30.22]; *Two Women*, woven tapestry copied from a collage of 1934 [Z.VIII.268]. The two tapestries were woven in the workshops directed by Marie Cuttoli, who also commissioned the *Women at their Toilette* cartoon. See below, Chapter 8, pp. 326–28, for the tapestry later copied from *Women at their Toilette*.

75 In effect, the climax of the Tate exhibition recapitulated the climax of the retrospective organised by Maurice Jardot at the Musée des Arts Décoratifs in 1955 ('Picasso: Peintures 1900–1955'). Jardot had borrowed the de Beaumont décor, the *Two Women* and *Farmer's Wife* tapestries, and the *Women at their Toilette* cartoon, and instead of the *Parade* curtain, the curtain for *Mercure* (1924). Furthermore, Jardot's exhibition had culminated with Picasso's first series of Old Master variations (*The Women of Algiers*, after Delacroix).

76 Letter to the author from Joanna Drew, dated 21 January 2003.

77 Among the other documents concerning the Duke of Edinburgh's visit is the draft of Penrose's fulsome personal letter of thanks, which ends hopefully: 'If at any time you intend to visit the exhibition again I shall be greatly honoured to offer my services should they be required' (RPA 547).

78 'Cher Pablo,
Nous voici de retour et je suis heureux de constater que les preparatifs pour l'exposition progressent bien. Le

directeur de la Tate Gallery m'assure qu'on ne manquera pas de place. Il a mit encore deux grands salles à notre disposition, ce qui fait que ton exposition occupera plus que le double de l'espace qu'on a donné jusqu'ici pour l'exposition d'un seule artiste. Cela fera quelque chose de sensationelle. [...]

Nous étions très heureux de t'avoir trouvé si bien et si actif. C'etait vraiment une bonne semaine que nous avons passé à Cannes et je suis très reconnaissant pour l'aide que tu me donnes en preparant l'exposition. A Londres ça sera un evenment sans precedent. Il y a le Duke of Edinburgh qui a dit qu'il viendra à la reception qui sera donné par notre Institute of Contemporary Arts le soir de ouverture. C'est le premier fois qu'il fait une chose pareille. [...]

(Letter to Picasso dated 25 February 1960, sent to La Californie, Cannes, from 11A Hornton Street, London; AP.)

79 In a letter to Picasso, dated 16 April 1960 and sent from Farley Farm, Penrose announced his arrival in Cannes on 24 April (AP).

80 RP *SB*, pp. 222–23.

81 The 'mutilated' Spanish edition (*Picasso: vida y obra*, trans. Concha G. de Marco, Madrid, Edíciones Cid, 1959) came out when Penrose was in the United States. En route for England on board the *Queen Elizabeth* he wrote hastily to Picasso to warn him about the crude act of censorship (letter to Picasso dated 7 December 1959; AP).

82 Picasso had certainly been reading the Spanish reviews of the book because he sent a clipping to Penrose in early April 1960. Penrose thanked him in his letter of 16 April 1960 (see note 79 above).

83 *Evening Standard*, Friday 10 June 1960, p. 8.

84 'Mon cher Pablo
Je t'envoie ceci tout simplement pour t'informer de cet article qui a paru vendredi dernier dans un grand journal de soir à Londres.

Tu verras que Cooper a affirmé à son ami le journaliste Sam White que je n'ai jamais demandé à lui de prêter ses tableaux pour ton exposition ni demandé son colaboration dans le catalogue.

Un mensonge tellement colossale n'aura pas d'importance pour moi, malgré que Sam White que je connais bien était aussi completement au courant de mes demarches il y a deux ans quand Douglas m'a refusé carrément ses toiles et son aide, mais on suggere aussi que tu es mécontent du choix que j'ai pu faire. Comme l'article est si plein de mensonges et nettement orienté contre moi je ne suis pas trop inquiet mais j'éspère vivement que ce n'est pas le cas! – ah oui!

Ici les preparatifs de l'exposition font du progress d'un façon satisfaisant. "Les Demoiselles" et bien d'autres toiles de l'Amerique sont déjà arrivees et nous éspèrons recevoir tes toiles avec les autres de Paris cette semaine. Je te tiendrai au courant. De la Russie nous ne savons pas encore le resultat de nos demarches finales.

Lee se joint à moi pour t'embrasser très fort ainsi que la très chère Jacqueline
Roland.'
(Letter to Picasso dated 12 June 1960, sent to La Californie, Cannes, from Farley Farm, Sussex; AP.)

85 Carbon copies of the letters from Penrose to the Editor of the *Evening Standard* and to Sam White, both dated 11 June 1960, are in RPA 547.

86 Penrose mentions Ehrenburg's visit in a letter to Picasso dated 27 June 1960 (AP).

87 Letter to Penrose from Ilya Ehrenburg, dated 24 July 1960 and sent from Moscow to London (ACGB/121/839). Later editions of the exhibition catalogue carried a special note, signed by Gabriel White, thanking the numerous persons involved in the long transactions over the Russian loans, Ehrenburg in particular.

88 The long relationship between Cooper and Richardson was unravelling at this time (see Richardson 1999, p. 276).

89 *The Kitchen*, 1948, MoMA [Z.XV.106].

90 'Mon cher Pablo,
Je passe mes journées entouré de ce que j'aime. Les grandes salles de la Tate Gallery sont remplit de tes toiles et je ne m'habitue pas à la richesse et la varieté de ce panorama merveilleux. L'exposition sera eblouissante et je m'applique avec un equipe devoué d'assurer que la presentation, le catalogue etc etc seront à la hauteur necessaire. Les toiles sont presque tout arrivées sauf celles de la Russie et la malgré tous nos efforts nous ne savons pas encore si nous les aurons. Qui sait? peutêtre – peutêtre pas.

Il y a déjà une foule de Londiniens et des étrangers qui voudraient nous envahir tous les jours en plus des visites des amis. Aujourd'hui John Richardson (sans Douglas) est venu et nous a fait un tas de compliments sur l'ensemble. Le catalogue est presque terminé et sera j'éspère selon tes gouts. Pour la couverture on a pris le motif de "La cuisine" qui aussi est reproduit comme tous les autres toiles à l'interieur. Tu auras déjà reçu la carte d'invitation j'éspère et l'affiche se fait chez Mourlot, donc j'ai confiance que ca sera bien. La grande soirée de gala organisé par notre Institut deviens un evenment de grand importance. Le Prince Philip doit venir en grand tenu avec tous ces decorations et toi, j'explique dix fois par jour que tu aimes mieux rester tranquille chez toi – mais quelle presence tu etablis sans y être! Et comme nous sommes reconnaissant!

Enfin très emu je t'embrasse ainsi que la douce Jacqueline et je t'écrirai de nouveaux bientôt.
A toi toujours
Roland.'
(Letter to Picasso dated 23 June 1960, sent to La Californie, Cannes, from 11A Hornton Street, London; AP.)

91 Letter to Picasso dated 27 June 1960, sent to La Californie, Cannes, from 11A Hornton Street, London (AP).

92 Brassaï 1967, p. 244, reporting a conversation with Picasso in Cannes on 18 May 1960.

93 Reported by Tudor Jenkins in 'Has Picasso bluffed the experts?', *Evening Standard*, 9 September 1960.

94 Olga Franklin, 'They've even insured Pablo for ten million', *Daily Mail*, 1 July 1960, p. 10.

95 *Jacqueline with a Black Scarf*, 1954 [Z.XVI.331]. This is inscribed at the top left corner, 'Pour Jacqueline aimée Picasso'.

96 'Mon cher Pablo
    Je t'écris rapidement pout te signaler les premiers impressions de l'explosion Picasso à Londres. C'est boulversant, jamais on n'a vu une presse aussi appreciative et aussi vaste et on peut dire la même chose pour le public. Déjà plus que 10,000 personnes ont visité l'exposition, on fait la queue toute la journée jusqu'à huit heures le soir quand la gallerie se ferme. L'enthousiasme surtout parmi les anglais est phenomenale. Tu as fait la conquête de Londres – on est émerveillé, eblouit par ta presence sur ses murs.
    La grande soirée de gala pour notre Institut etait formidable – jamais on n'a vu une foule aussi elegante, cosmopolite et gaie. Mais ni les satins, ni les diamants, ni les decorations, ni les beaux yeux des femmes ont rivalisé le splendeur de tes toiles. Le Duc d'Edimborg a fait la tour de l'exposition guidé par moi. Il était très impressioné et je crois qu'il va revenir le revoir tranquillement, je t'en parlerai de ça plus tard. C'était en tout un reunion immense sans formalité et dans lequel la puissance de ton esprit emerveillait tout le monde. On était heureux, on sortait avec rejouissance et la sens que tu nous avait injecté la vie et la comprehension et ceci est une experience partagé par nous tous.
    J'éspère que tu as maintenant reçu le catalogue et l'affiche; je vais t'envoyer plus tard ce collection enorme de coupures de presses qui grandit tous les jours.
    Quand à Cooper il divertit les gens dans les salles en proclamant à haute voix qu'il est l'envoyé special et personel de Pablo Picasso envoyé par toi pour surveiller la manière que nous traitons tes toiles et en plus declarant qu'on n'a jamais lui demander officielment de prêter ses toiles. On le connais et on ne fait pas beaucoup d'attention à tout ça.
    Mon cher Pablo merci, merci, merci pour tout et surtout la generosité de ton ésprit que ce public vaste de Londres commence à gouter dans ton oeuvre. Nous t'embrassons du fond du coeur.
    Ton ami
    Roland.
    Dis à Jacqueline que son portrait fait un grande impression sur les gens surtout avec l'inscription et embrasse la très fort de la part de Lee et de moi. Je t'envoie aussi une brochure que nous avons distribué le soir du vernissage.'
    (Letter to Picasso dated 8 July 1960, sent to La Californie, Cannes, from 11A Hornton Street, London; AP.) The 'brochure' included a text by Lee Miller Penrose entitled 'Picasso Himself' (reprinted in AP 1985, pp. 202–3).
97 John Rothenstein, reported in the 'William Hickey' column, *Daily Express*, 5 July 1960, p. 3. The exhibition was open from 10 a.m. to 8 p.m. on weekdays, and from 2 p.m. to 8 p.m. on Sundays.
98 Letter to Picasso dated 19 July 1960, sent to La Californie, Cannes, from 11A Hornton Street, London (AP). The attendance figures, catalogue sales, etc. quoted here are all derived from Arts Council records (ACGB/121/839).
99 Anon., *The Times*, 2 August 1960.
100 Letter from Norman Reid to Gabriel White dated 28 July

1960 (ACGB/121/839).
101 S. A. Tuck, 'A Layman looks at Picasso', *Eastern Daily Press*, 16 July 1960.
102 Lawrence Gowing, 'Light, Love and Picasso', *The Observer*, 10 July 1960.
103 David Sylvester, 'Picasso at the Tate II', *New Statesman*, 16 July 1960, p. 82.
104 John Golding, 'Picasso and the Image', *The Listener*, 14 July 1960, pp. 52–54.
105 Information from John Golding (May 2004).
106 See below, Epilogue, pp. 346–47.
107 Thomas Bodkin, 'Le Mystère Picasso: the exhibition at the Tate Gallery', *The Birmingham Post*, 8 July 1960.
108 Douglas Cooper, Letter to the Editor, *The Listener*, 28 July 1960, p. 157.
109 Roland Penrose, Letter to the Editor, *The Listener*, 11 August 1960, p. 228.
110 Commander Michael Parker, the Duke of Edinburgh's former private secretary.
111 The advice came from Anthony Blunt, then Surveyor of the Queen's Pictures. See RP *SB*, p. 248.
112 'Mon cher Pablo,
    Evidement Londres n'a jamais vu un evenement pareil, La foule autour de ton exposition augment tous les jours et l'interêt penetre dans tous les sphères imaginable – même pour les voitures on vend le PICESSO pour les faire marcher plus vite. Et voilà jeudi un ami du Duc m'a informé dans le plus grand secret pour eviter la ruée à la Tate de tous les journalistes du monde que la Reine desirais venir le soir avec une douzaine d'amis voir l'exposition – je devais le dire à personne et on voulait qu'aucune personnage officiel soit present seulement moi pour montrer les tableaux – et c'est bien passé comme ça. La Reine et le Duc sont arrivés les premiers et ensuite la Reine-mère nous a rejoint.
    Intimidé comme j'étais de me trouver dans cette situation de laquelle, comme tu sais je n'ai pas l'habitude je commencais faire quelqu'explications des toiles de l'epoque bleu qui nous entouré dans la première salle – et encore j'avais à te remercier – ta presence superbe qui nous entouré partout ma donné confiance et les yeux des Reines s'eclairaient avec enthousiasme – et un interet et admiration veritable. On passe à ton portrait, à La Vie, à la Famille Soler – tout d'un coup la Reine fait un petit crie d'effroi quand elle apperçoit la tête sans yeux dans le repas de l'aveugle. On passe aux Demoiselle d'Avignon et encore elle s'interesse et fait des observations pas bête dutout malgré qu'elles n'ajoute pas grand chose a l'histoire de l'art.
    On m'avait conseillé de ne pas insister sur les toiles difficiles et d'eviter d'entrer dans la salle cubiste – je n'étais pas d'accord et à mon grand plaisir elle est rentrer avec un enthusiasm augmentant à chaque pas – s'arretant devant chaque toile – portrait de Uhde, qu'elle trouvait magnifique, jeune fille à la mandoline, Nature morte à la chaise canée, qui la beau[coup] plut, les collages la petite construction avec le gruyère et le saucisson devant laquelle elle s'est arretée pour dire 'Ah comme c'est jolie! Comme j'aimerai faire quelque chose comme ça moi même!'

On continue lentement et en retournant souvent
pour revoir quelque chose – evidement elle va droit
aux tableaux facile à comprendre, le portrait de Paulo,
les femmes courant sur la plage mais devant les Trois
Musiciens, elle s'est arreté longuement et m'a demandé
des questions. Je te dis tout ceci parce que tu m'as
demandé de t'ecrire et aussi parceque cette famille Royale
n'a jamais brillée dans leur appreciation des arts et ton
oeuvre semblait vraiment les toucher peutêtre pour le
premier fois dans les fonds de leurs natures – et ça
continuait – très enthousiaste de la grande Nature morte
de 1931 et très inquiet devant les toiles de l'epoque
Guernica et de la guerre. Enfin nous étions devant la baie
de Cannes que la Reine Mère trouvait superb quand une
autre nous rejoint – en tournant à moi la Reine dit "Puis-
je vous presenter ma soeur Margaret." Et la voilà la belle
princesse de nos rêves avec son mari photographe.
Finalement ayant tout vu et parlé longtemps entouré des
Meninas la Reine en disant qu'elle doit bientôt partir me
charge de montrer de nouveau tout l'exposition à
Margaret – ce que j'ai fait et même quand elle m'a
demandé si tu allais venir j'ai dis que je pensais que
malgré que tu n'avais pas exprimé le desire de venir tu
sera triste de ne pas avoir été la pour faire sa connaissance
ce soir – elle a fait un sourire exquis et je pensais le voir
rougir sous sa teinte brunit par le soleil.

Et voilà après deux heures ils sont tous partit et aussitôt
rentré à la maison l'ami du Duc me telephone pour me
dire que la Reine à déclaré que depuis longtemps et [elle]
n'avais pas passé une soirée aussi agreeable. Et moi très
soulagé à la fin d'une journée peut ordinaire, car
l'aprèsmidi j'avais ma conference sur toi à donner, je
m'endors pour trouver des nouvelles emotions le
lendemain – les Russes – nous apprenons subitement
au moment que nous avions abandonné tout éspoir,
que dix toiles doivent partir par avion dans les premiers
jours de la semaine prochaine pour Londres. Voilà la liste:
L'Etreinte 1900, Le Vieux Juif 1903, Acrobat sur une boule
1905, Nu à la Draperie 1907, Nature Morte à la Tête de
Mort 1907, Deux Nus (L'Amitié) 1908, Carafon et trois
Bols 1908, La Fermière 1908, La Dryade 1908, L'Usine à
Horta 1909. Donc tout va recommencer – nouveaux
vernissage – foules encore plus vastes – et, qui sait, de
nouveaus une visite de la Reine?

Dans tous ça quelle joie ça sera si tu decidé de prendre
l'avion et venir nous voir. On gardera le même secret pour
toi que nous avons fait pour la reine – personne sauf tes
amis le saurait. Je ne dis plus rien et je t'embrasse comme
toujours de tous coeur – lee fait autant à toi et à
Jacqueline
Roland.'
(Letter to Picasso dated 23 July 1960, sent to La
Californie, Cannes, from 11A Hornton Street, London;
AP. First published in Madeline, pp. 192–93.) The
paintings Penrose mentions are, in order: Self-Portrait,
1901, MP [Z.I.91]; La Vie, 1903, Cleveland Museum of Art
[Z.I.179]; The Soler Family, 1903, Musée des Beaux-Arts,
Liège [Z.I.203, 204]; The Blindman's Meal, 1903, The
Metropolitan Museum of Art, New York [Z.I.168]; Les
Demoiselles d'Avignon, 1907, MoMA [DR 47]; Portrait of

Wilhelm Uhde, 1910, Pulitzer Collection, St Louis [DR
338]; Girl with a Mandolin (Fanny Tellier), 1910, MoMA
[DR 346]; Still Life with Chair Caning, 1912, MP [DR
466]; Still Life, 1914, construction, Tate, London [DR
746]; Portrait of Paul as Harlequin, 1924, MP [Z.V.178];
Women Running on the Beach (The Race), 1922, MP
[Z.IV.380]; Three Musicians, 1921, MoMA [Z.IV.331];
Pitcher and Bowl of Fruit, 1931, MoMA [Z.VII.322]; The
Bay at Cannes, 1958, MP [Z.XVIII.83]; The Embrace, 1900
[Z.I.26], The Old Jew, 1903 [Z.I.175], and Acrobat on a
Ball, 1905 [Z.I.290], all Pushkin Museum, Moscow; Nude
with Drapery, 1907 [DR 95], Still Life with a Skull, 1907
[DR 172], Two Nudes (Friendship), 1908 [DR 104], Carafe
and Three Bowls, 1908 [DR 176], The Farmer's Wife, 1908
[DR 193], The Dryad, 1908 [DR 133], and Factory at
Horta, 1909 [DR 279], all The Hermitage, St Petersburg.

113   See AP 2001, p. 153: 'He [Picasso] had often told Roland
about the extraordinarily erotic dreams he had about the
Queen and Princess Margaret: "If they knew what I had
done in my dreams with your royal ladies, they would
take me to the Tower of London and chop off my head!"
he said with pride.' For Picasso's elaborate spoof about
seeking Princess Margaret's hand in marriage and
bringing her as his consort to La Californie, see
Richardson 1999, p. 176. See also below, Chapter 6, p. 257.

114   Guitar, 1926, MP [S.65H]. See also above, Chapter 3, note
123.

115   The Muse (Young Woman Drawing), 1935, Musée
National d'Art Moderne, Paris [Z.VIII.256].

116   Portrait of Dora Maar, 1941 [Z.XI.145].

117   The Kitchen, 1948, MoMA [Z.XV.106].

118   Notes written in pencil on 5 loose sheets of notebook
paper (RPA 547).

119   Letter to Penrose from George Melly dated 23 June 1960
(RPA 310). Melly told Michael Sweeney that Penrose
never replied to this letter and that he kept his word
about not lending any of his pictures (interview
conducted on 14 August 1997; transcript in RPA).
However, Melly and Penrose were reconciled after
Mesens's death (Melly, p. 182).

120   'Moi, je reste, en 1960, fièrement SURRÉALISTE.
      Toi, tu t'occupes du grand Picasso, sur les bords de la
Tamise et sous le haut patronnage de Son Altesse Royale
le duc d'Edimbourg.
      E. L. T. Mesens'
      (Letter to Penrose from E. L. T. Mesens dated 27 July
1960; RPA 708.)

121   'Très cher Pablo Picasso [the name is written in Russian
characters]
      Ils sont là, enfin, dix très beaux tableaux de Moscou et
Leningrad – et nous sommes heureux. […]
      Maintenant on peut dire peutêtre sans erreur que c'est
le plus belle exposition et le plus complète de ta peinture
qu'on n'a jamais fait. L'enthousiasme augmente à Londres
tous le temps. Avant hier, le premier jour des tableaux
Russes, il y avait 8,000 visteurs! […] Comme il y a une
telle congestion dans la galerie je propose qu'ils fassent un
kilometre à genoux avant d'arriver.'
      (Letter to Picasso dated 6 August 1960, sent to La
Californie, Cannes, from Farley Farm, Sussex; AP.)

122 Letter to the author from Joanna Drew, dated 21 January 2003.

123 Statistics in Arts Council files (ACGB/121/8390).

124 Tudor Jenkins, 'Has Picasso bluffed the experts?', *Evening Standard*, 9 September 1960. The allusion is to Matisse's famous definition of his aims in 'Notes of a Painter', 1908 (in Jack D. Flam, *Matisse on Art*, Oxford, Phaidon, 1978, p. 38).

Chapter 6 Three New Projects, 1960–1965

1 Anon., *The Times*, 19 September 1960.

2 Postcard to Picasso dated 25 September 1960, sent to La Californie, Cannes, from Paris (AP). Penrose's diary notes his arrival in Cannes on 27 September, and on 30 September he left (RPA 743.1). On 29 September Picasso inscribed a copy of the Tate catalogue for him, adding a quick drawing of a head.

3 'Mon cher Pablo,
De Paris je suis venu ici où je passe quelques jours avec Max Ernst. Je travail avec lui à preparer son exposition au Musée d'Art Moderne de New York; alors tu vois je suis de nouveau plongé dans les écrits et les tableaux – ça vaut mieux car j'ai quitté Cannes l'autre jour avec le coeur bien lourd en pensant que ton exposition, cette merveille, était bien finie et encore je n'avais pas la sensation d'avoir pu te dire à quel point on avait apprécié à Londres l'importance de cet evenment. Pendant très longtemps on se rappellera de cet exposition, 'la plus etonnante du siècle'.
Enfin quand tu auras eu le temps de reflechir au sujet des Trois Danseurs de 1925 peutêtre nous pouvons nous rejouir de l'idée d'avoir ce tableau à Londres comme souvenir permanent de l'exposition et manifestation capitale de ton oeuvre. Je sais à quel point on apprecira ta generosité si tu penses que tu peut nous céder une toile d'un tel importance.
En tous cas je te remercie pour tout ce que tu as déjà fait pour l'exposition – en plus d'avoir peint les tableaux !– et aussi, pour moi, la joie enorme que tu me donnes. Merci en plus du dessin pour l'I.C.A.
Je serai rentrer à Londres dans 10 jours et je te telephonerai de là bas.
Embrasse la sweet Jacqueline je te prie. Je pense très souvent à vous et à la belle maison sur la colline.
A toi toujours
Roland.'
(Letter to Picasso dated 4 October 1960, sent to La Californie, Cannes, from Huismes; AP.)

4 'Indeed! Lee tu as le génie des cadeaux. […] Vivent Picasso et l'organisateur de l'exposition no. 1. Baisers à toi. Jacqueline'. (Card to Lee Penrose from Jacqueline Roque dated 5 October 1960, sent to 11A Hornton Street, London, from La Californie, Cannes; RPA 717.)

5 'We embrace you, dear Pablo. We love you. You always give us life and youth. Roland, Lee, Tony.'
(Telegram to Picasso dated 25 October 1960, sent to La Californie, Cannes, from Farley Farm, Sussex; AP.)

6 The 'Tableau de Roque (Paul)', dated 14 November 1960, is reproduced in RP *SB*, p. 221. The joke alludes to the fact that it was made on the back of an invitation to a fashion show addressed to 'Monsieur et Madame Roque'.

7 'Mon cher Pablo,
Le dessin de Roque (Paul) a eu un très grand succès; Lee est littéralement enchantée du talent de cet artiste jusqu'ici inconnu mais qui va trouver sa place parmi les plus grands et qui est sans doute rivale de Picasso même, et Toni est ravi du sien. Il raconte aux amis qu'il a un dessin de toi d'un taureau, une faune et un senator!
Je suis arrivé à Londres juste au temps pour la réunion des Trustees de la Tate Gallery et on m'a demandé tout de suite le résultat de nos conversations au sujet des Trois Danseurs. J'ai expliqué que tu étais encore hésitant mais que tu n'as pas dit "non" et qu'il y avait encore de l'espoir. […]
A la conférence sur toi que j'ai donnée vendredi tout marchait bien – grande assistance enthousiaste. A la fin une vieille qui me demandait si je considérais que tes tableaux etaient recommandables pour les femmes enceintes! "Il n'y a rien de meilleur" j'ai répondu.' […]
(Letter to Picasso dated 21 November 1960, sent from 11A Hornton Street, London; AP.)

8 '[…] Chaque fois qu'on me cite dans un journal c'est en compagnie de toi et j'en suis profondement heureux de cette situation. Je suis fière d'être le "Picasso Man". […] J'éspère que ta decision en faveur de la Tate Gallery va se faire par ce beau soleil de janvier.' (Letter to Picasso dated 14 January 1961, sent to La Californie, Cannes, from 11A Hornton Street, London; AP.) With the letter Penrose sent press cuttings about his CBE.

9 *Women at their Toilette*, 1956, MP [Z.XVII.54]. Penrose had included this picture in the 1960 retrospective exhibition (visible in the photograph on p. 163).

10 'Cher Picasso,
Après de t'avoir parlé j'ai apprit de Zette que tu es occupé dimanche prochain et je vais donc remettre mon voyage. J'en suis triste de ce changement parceque j'avais bien des choses à te dire et cela m'aurait fait une très grande plaisir de te revoir. En plus j'avais des choses à dire su sujet de la Tate Gallery qui éspère toujours que tu la donneras l'occaison de faire un effort envers le government pour acquerir une de tes toiles importantes.
Les Trustees de la Gallery sont tous d'accord et le public, comme tu as vu par le success de ton exposition, enthusiast. Il n'y a que le government sous qui nous sous a convaincre et je m'en charge de faire un effort avec des amis qui pourrait reussir. Evidement plus tu pourras être endulgent pour le prix, plus nous serons reconnaissant. Et si les Trois Danseurs la toile que nous convoitons le plus n'est vraiment pas disponible, il y a les deux femmes à leur toilette, la grand toile de 1954 (je crois) qui sera vraiment une acquisition merveilleuse.
Cette après-midi j'ai parlé a Kahnweiler de ce projet qui est pour moi et pour toute la population de l'Angleterre une chose si importante et il comprends bien la situation mais peutêtre je pourrais venir te voir un autre jour et t'expliquer tout en detail.
Excuse moi de t'embêter toujours avec ces affaires. En somme c'etait pour te voir et t'embrasser sans autres complications que je voudrais venir. […]'
(Letter to Picasso dated 7 March 1961, sent to La Californie, Cannes, from 14 Place Dauphine, Paris; AP.)

11 RP *PLW* 1971, p. 447.

12 Reproduced in RP *SB*, p. 222. *La vie et l'œuvre de Picasso* (trans. Célia Bertin; Paris, Bernard Grasset) was published in October 1961. It was more generously illustrated (even a few colour plates) and more handsomely designed than the original, parsimonious Gollancz edition.

13 '[…] cette couverture magique que tu m'as fait pour mon livre est un très grand success, tout le monde la trouve admirable et mon editeur était en extase. C'était vraiment une merveille de la voir paraître de ta main si vite et je te remercie de nouveau enormement. […] Je vais monter à notre Institut une petite ensemble de photos et documents pour montré ce qui se passe autour de ton anniversaire dans le monde. […] L'autre jour j'ai vu Claude ici à Londres avec Françoise. […]' (Letter to Picasso dated 20 July 1961, sent to La Californie, Cannes, from 11A Hornton Street, London; AP.)

14 See Penrose's account in RP *PLW* 1971, pp. 447–49; see also Tabaraud's eye-witness account, pp. 189–96.

15 Penrose mentions the gift of Stubbs's 'cheval strip-tease' in a letter to Picasso dated 20 October 1961 (AP). The birthday telegram was sent to Cannes on 25 October 1961 (AP).

16 Reproduced in RP *SB*, p. 223.

17 Lionel Penrose, who became a prominent physician, had been fascinated by mathematics since his schooldays.

18 Possibly *Woman with Big Hat*, 1962 [Z.XX.185]. Picasso's inscription suggests that it was painted in two campaigns, on 3 January 1962 and 27 July 1962.

19 On a single sheet of plain writing paper, 25.3 x 20.2, with a diagram of a pyramid with a smaller pyramid inside it, Penrose has written the following, slightly different version of Picasso's words: 'P. & Trompe l'oeil. They always say the cubists were trying to catch the truth – they were really trying to create deception – cubism was full of deception. One travels round a head seeing it from front and back, from all different angles.' [30]

20 Probably *Jacqueline Seated with Kabul*, 1962 [Z.XX.244]. This is inscribed 31 May 1962 and 7 June 1962.

21 *Cock with Tied Feet*, 1962 [Z.XX.222]. This is inscribed 24–27 April 1962.

22 A series of these tiles or plaques is illustrated in Parmelin 1964.

23 'I'm still continuing with the "déjeuners" (above all quantities of drawings) – for the late-comers.' Picasso made numerous drawings on this theme in June 1962 [Z.XX.259 ff.]. We know from his letter to Picasso dated 15 June 1962 (AP) that Penrose attended the vernissage of the exhibition devoted to Picasso's variations after Manet's *Déjeuner sur l'herbe* ('Picasso: Le Déjeuner sur l'herbe, 1960–1961', Galerie Louise Leiris, Paris, 6 June– 13 July 1962).

24 The series of six was begun on 19 June 1962. A figure on the left of *Family Portrait*, 1962, lithograph with coloured crayon, MP [Z.XXIII.4], has been scratched out: this was probably the Cocteau figure Picasso refers to, since there is no 'portrait' of Cocteau in the other members of the series.

25 'I don't know what he [Cocteau] is doing there. I didn't want him, he came all by himself. And who are these people? They just arrived, I don't know where from – but they're not just anyone. From Dickens or Balzac? Who knows? They arrived the other day and I don't know who they are.'

26 The Museu Picasso was inaugurated in the Palau Aguilar in 1963 with the donation of Sabartès's personal collection. The project was energetically promoted by the Mayor of Barcelona, José María de Porcioles, and secretly supported by Picasso himself, who for political reasons had to keep his distance publicly. (See Hensbergen, pp. 229 ff.)

27 *Woman with a Pushchair*, 1950 [S.382]. The very complex construction of this sculpture led to an exceptionally long delay before it was cast.

28 e.g. *Seated Monkey*, 1961 [S.578].

29 'Francis Bacon', Tate, London, 24 May–1 July 1962.

30 'magnificent – above all the style and the comprehension.' A reference to Valentine Penrose, *Erzsébet Báthory, la Comtesse sanglante*, Paris, Mercure de France, 1962.

31 The lithograph for this poster is dated 10 May 1962. See Utley p. 127, fig. 102.

32 'Yes, we are working for peace, others for other things. Each to his own.'

33 Perhaps a reference to *Le Picasso de poche: carnet de croquis de Picasso*, Introduction de Marcel Duhamel, Paris (privately printed), 1964: a facsimile of a small sketchbook of caricatures in a specially decorated envelope which Picasso had given Duhamel on 24 December 1957.

34 For a photograph of the fountain – a cubistic standing female nude slightly reminiscent of Picasso's contemporary sheet-metal sculptures – see RP *SB*, p. 193. Tony Penrose helped his father make it.

35 Letter to Penrose from William Hartmann dated 2 April 1963, enclosing photographs of the plans and site and a supporting letter from Allan McNab, Director of the Art Institute of Chicago (RPA 500).

36 Copy of a letter to William Hartmann dated 11 April 1963 (RPA 500).

37 Letter to Alfred Barr dated 14 April 1963, sent to MoMA from Farley Farm, Sussex (AHB 12.III.A.9. MoMA Archives, NY).

38 The 'generous gift' is mentioned in Penrose's letter to William Hartmann dated 10 July 1963 (copy in RPA 500).

39 Barr's support for the Chicago project was mentioned in the first letters to Penrose from McNab and Hartmann. Penrose expressed his sense of devotion and obligation to Barr in a letter to René d'Harnoncourt included among the *homages* offered to Barr on his 60th birthday (letter dated 23 January 1962; copy in RPA 46).

40 See Fairweather, pp. 49–61. Nesjar was also responsible for the concrete wall engravings at the Colegio Oficial de Arquitectos in Barcelona (1960–61), photographs of which Penrose included in the documentary exhibition he mounted at the ICA at the time of Picasso's eightieth birthday.

41 '[…] Lee et moi ont l'intention de venir à Antibes pour une semaine à partir du 20 mai et si tu n'est pas trop absorbé dans ton travail nous aurons un très grand plaisir de venir te rendre visite. En plus la joie de te revoir, toi et

Jacqueline, il y a un projêt de grande envergure duquel on voudrait te parler. Des amis americains de Chicago m'ont écrit et telephoné à deux reprises pour savoir si tu seras tenté de faire la maquette pour une sculpture monumentale qui sera installée dans la Place principale au centre de Chicago. Je crois qu'ils t'ont déjà ecrit annonçant leur projêt.

Croyant que peutêtre une idée de cet importance pourait te dire quelque chose je les ai encouragé de soumettre leur proposition à toi. J'ai pensé que c'était possible qu'une sculpture dans le même ordre que celui chez Kahnweiler serait exactement ce qu'ils desirent mais evidement je ne sais pas du tout quelles seront tes reactions. Monsieur Hartmann, architect très qualifié et ami d'Alfred Barr, viendra à Cannes exprès pour te presenter les plans du gratte-ciel qui va être la nouvelle Hotel de Ville de Chicago avec des jardins devant sa façade où il voudrait placer une sculpture monumentale de toi. Si tu as envie le voir je pourrais venir avec lui pour qu'il t'explique tout. [...]'

(Letter to Picasso dated 9 May 1963, sent to Notre-Dame-de-Vie, Mougins, from 11A Hornton Street, London; AP.)

42 'Joan Miró', Tate, London, 27 August–11 October 1964. The two pictures were: *Self-Portrait*, 1919, and *Portrait of a Spanish Dancer*, 1921 (both now in MP).

43 In the summer of 1962 Roland, Lee and Tony went to Southern Rhodesia (now Zimbabwe) for the First Biennial Congress of African Culture in Salisbury (now Harare), organised by Frank McEwen, who had been appointed Director of the Rhodes National Gallery in 1956. Penrose delivered a lecture ('African Influences on Picasso and Contemporary Art') at the Congress on 7 August 1962.

44 Picasso embarked on the long series of 'The Artist and Model' in February 1963 [Z.XXIII.154 ff.].

45 e.g. *Large Profile (Jacqueline)*, Kunstsammlung Nordrhein-Westfalen, Düsseldorf [Z.XXIII.117], which is dated 7 January 1963.

46 'I'm tiring you, aren't I?'

47 Probably *The Rape of the Sabines, after Poussin* [Z.XXIII.121], which is dated 9 January 1963 and 7 February 1963.

48 e.g. *Woman with Dog (Jacqueline with Kabul)*, 1962 [Z.XXIII.87].

49 The photographs taken during this visit (LMA) confirm that Penrose is referring to *Head of a Woman*, 1951 [S.412].

50 *Little Girl Skipping*, begun 1950 [S.408]. Penrose is mistaken: the face had acquired facial features by 1951 (as we know from the many studio photographs in the AP). The delay in casting was due to technical problems: the intrinsic fragility and complexity of the piece and Picasso's refusal to allow it to be broken into manageable sections.

51 'Exhibitions, projects for Chicago, Marseille or anywhere else, they do not interest me. It's only work, my work, that interests me and I never have enough time.' 'Well, we'll see.' See also note 76 below.

52 *The Goat*, 1950 [S.409].

53 Jacqueline: 'How did you know? How is it you understand animals so well?' Picasso: 'That's just the way it is.'

54 'It'll need something enormous, something as big as that.... Yes, like that perhaps, a cigarette lighter to set the people of Chicago alight.'

55 'The figure at St. Hilaire' is a reference to Kahnweiler's concrete *Woman with Outstretched Arms*. By 'steel construction like those of 1929', Penrose must be referring to the enlargements in steel of the *Wire Constructions* of 1928 [e.g. S.68].

56 'Don't speak to me about money. That embarrasses me. The point is to get to work now. Perhaps when everything is finished you'll give me something, but above all don't mention it now. The idea of a sculpture in iron seems good to me, but that's just what I think today. Tomorrow I may think differently. We'll have to see.'

57 'That rather horrifies me.'

58 'Perhaps I will do something.'

59 *Head of a Woman*, dated 24 May 1963 (I) [Z.XXIII.279], and *Head of a Woman*, dated 24 May 1963 (II) [Z.XXIII.282].

60 *Reclining Nude* [Z.XXIII.278], which is dated 22 May 1963.

61 Marcelo Fernandez Enchorena.

62 Carbon copies of letters to Picasso dated 19 June 1963 and 14 August 1963 (RPA 717); letter to Picasso dated 10 July 1963, sent to Notre-Dame-de-Vie, Mougins, from 11A Hornton Street, London (AP).

63 *Woman with a Hat*, 1963 [Bloch 1145]. 'Je viens de recevoir ton lino de la belle dame avec béret rouge et fraise que j'avais acheté dernièrement. Ces beaux yeux sont de plus en plus séducteurs le plus on les regarde de près. Je suis hypnotisé par elle' (letter to Picasso dated 19 June 1963; RPA 717).

64 'Enfin, le sujet me passionne tellement que je me suis décidé, si Quinn le veut bien, de m'y mettre au travail, et j'espère vivement qu'on arrivera faire quelquechose qui ne vas pas te déplaire. En tout cas, ça me plaît d'avoir de nouveau des images de toi, Jacqueline, tes oeuvres et tes amours encore sous mes yeux' (letter to Picasso dated 14 August 1963; RPA 717). (See Quinn.)

65 Letter to Penrose from Herbert Read dated 29 July 1963 (RPA 584).

66 Letter to Penrose from William Hartmann dated 6 September 1963; copy of a letter from Penrose to Hartmann, dated 8 October 1963 (both RPA 500); letters from Penrose to Picasso dated 18 September (RPA 717) and 8 October 1963 (AP).

67 The notes are not dated precisely but imply that Penrose went to Notre-Dame-de-Vie at least twice. According to his diary, one of the visits took place on Monday 4 November 1963 at 1 p.m. (RPA 743.4).

68 'Cassou has written to say that he's putting on an exhibition of the "naïve" painter Rousseau. He's the naïve one if he thinks I'm lending my pictures under those circumstances.'

69 'Well, perhaps yes. At least I shall have some sculptures in '66.'

70 'It's true that I give work to others. There are lots of people who are happy to get work because of me, and that's splendid. I'm pleased about that, but it's only because I continue to work.'

71 RP *PLW* 1971, p. 464.

72 Janine, wife of the *L'Humanité* journalist Francis Crémieux.

73 'It's always like that. I never stop and I go on all through the night, and if what I did was less good it would be just the same. It's appalling.'

74 *Glass, Pipe and Playing Card*, 1914, MP [S.45], and probably *Guitar*, 1912, MoMA [S.27A].

75 *Woman with a Pushchair*, 1950, bronze, MP [S.407].

76 Picasso had been commissioned to design a monument for the old port in Marseille, but Greek marble was stipulated – a material Picasso had never used and did not like. The scheme was therefore dropped (RP *PLW* 1971, pp. 458–59).

77 'You see, I've got too much to do. When do you expect me to deal with that and the thousand other things people ask me to do?' 'I'll think about it. I'm always thinking about it and now that you have mentioned it I'll think about it more. You know it's funny, I never accept commissions, but now I have these two which I want to do – both for gangster cities. Marseille and Chicago. Perhaps we shall see them fight it out to be the first.' 'Remind me to think about Chicago every day.'

78 Pubic hair.

79 'No, but I might be able to do one. Send me some portraits, some engravings of him. Perhaps I'll do something with them. Recently I've done Rimbaud and I've also done Balzac, Góngora and many others.' The 400th anniversary of Shakespeare's birth fell in 1964. Picasso's lithographic *Portrait of Rimbaud* is dated 13 December 1960 [Mourlot 270]. In November 1952 he made a series of 12 lithographic portraits of Balzac [Mourlot 216–27]. In February 1947 he made an aquatint portrait of Góngora, based on the portrait by Velázquez [Geiser & Baer 739] for *Góngora: vingt poèmes*, 1948.

80 *L'étreinte II*, 1963, linocut [Bloch 1151].

81 '[…] Je te remercie beaucoup d'avoir suggéré cette visite car malgré la lumière indifférente j'ai pu m'apercevoir d'une personnage haute, mystérieuse et hieratique, qui manipulait avec des mains fines et à grande distance cette petite voiture dans laquelle l'enfant se tordait comme des macaronis. Les seins de la femme posés si haut comme des fleurs et sa petite tête et sa longue chevelure semblaient si loin dans les brumes poussiereuses de Valsuani. C'était très beau et très émouvant, et il sera encore plus beau de le voir au soleil. […]' (Carbon copy of a letter to Picasso dated 15 November 1963; RPA 717.)

82 See above, Chapter 2, p. 79–81.

83 Copy of a letter to William Hartmann dated 15 January 1964 (RPA 500).

84 'Cher Pablo,
J'ai eu la grande chance de te voir cette nuit et je tiens le dire, pour ce que ça vaut, ce qui s'est passé. J'ai commencé en rêvant que je ne dormais pas et puis …..
3.30 … on était en retard – et je courrais avec un anglais à travers une campagne – on courrait parce qu'il y avait très peu de temps avant le départ de mon train. Subitement j'étais chez toi, vers la fin d'une visite qui semblait avoir déjà duré quelque temps et on partait, encore pressé à cause du train. Lee était là et plusieurs autres hommes et des belles dames y compris une belle dame belge que je connaissais pas. Les autres préparaient s'en aller en passant le long d'un corridor étroit et toi toujours assis tu m'as dit avec un grand sourire mystérieux et un regard qui m'a signalé quelquechose de rare, "eh bien, le projet, est-ce que tu es venu pour ça encore ou non?" En effet, heureux d'être là j'avais oublié, à vrai dire, de t'en parler, je te disais que j'étais heureux de venir une fois sans avoir quelquechose de demander. Avec un sourire incrédule et encore mystérieux tu m'as dit, "eh bien, je les ai fait quelquechose de <u>bien</u> moderne je ne sais pas ce qu'ils vont dire mais je t'assure que c'est moderne." En ce moment tu t'es levé et on suit les autres. Vers la sortie il y a un peu de confusion avec les autres et j'avais très envie que tu me montres ce que tu avais fait, mais dans la confusion tout ce que je peux dire c'est "Qu'est ce qu'il faut dire à Hartmann"! "Toujours la même chose" tu me dis et après tu refuses à suivre le chemin vers la porte qui devrait passer par le bureau d'un huissier quelconque et toujours de très bonne humeur tu te caches dans le fond d'une grande cheminée derrière un feu éteint et resort en riant - - Je suis dans le jardin maintenant parlant avec la belle belge et sachant que j'ai manqué le train et que je m'en fous, et Lee ne sera pas fachée. Dans les vignes je parle de quelques connaissances de Bruxelles. Tu nous rejoins et me dis de te suivre vers ton atelier en disant, "très moderne" – je me réveille.
Après avoir écrit ceci je me suis précipité de nouveau dans mon lit pour connaître la suite, avec l'intention de t'envoyer un croquis de ce que tu m'avais montré, mais par un malentendu absurde je n'ai pas eu la communication et tes idées pour Chicago restent dans le mystère.
Lee et moi nous t'embrassons très affectueusement ainsi que la très belle Jacqueline.
Roland'
(Letter to Picasso dated 30 January 1964, sent to Notre-Dame-de-Vie, Mougins, from 11A Hornton Street, London; AP.)

85 Jacqueline de la Baume-Dürrbach and René Dürrbach.

86 Possibly *Jacqueline Seated with her Black Cat* [Z.XXIV.101], which is dated 26 February–3 March 1964, and *Reclining Nude*, Rosengart Collection [Z.XXIV.25], which is dated 9 and 18 January 1964.

87 *Little Girl Skipping* [S.408] and *Woman with a Pushchair* [S.407].

88 i.e. two of the *Wire Constructions* of 1928 [S.68–71], made originally in connection with the commission for a monument for Apollinaire's grave in Père Lachaise cemetery. In *c.* 1962 Picasso had one of them copied in steel and enlarged to 2 metres high, later presenting it to MoMA.

89 'Of course, it's a pleasure [to see it] but it's full of weaknesses, interesting only because it's the work of a very young man.' The sculpture in question is *Seated Woman*, 1902 [S.1].

90 'You're very sensitive to sculpture.' 'I am a sculptor.'

91 The traditional headdress of the women of Nice.

92 *Head*, 1962–64 [S.643 2a].

93 'Yes, the head could perhaps work well, but not like that. It needs mounting higher. And who knows, perhaps it won't be like that at all. I'm thinking about it.'

94 Picasso: 'Really. So they still remember the picture? That's good.' Penrose: 'The president himself spoke first.'
95 'Well, it's not the money that matters. I'll think about it.'
96 Cézanne, *The Murder, c.* 1867–68. This picture was loaned by Wildenstein and Co. to 'Study for an Exhibition of Violence in Contemporary Art', an exhibition mainly of reproductions organised by Penrose at the ICA (20 February–26 March 1964). After the exhibition it was purchased by the Walker Art Gallery, Liverpool.
97 'I'm always here. Telephone me when you like and come back.'
98 'It's by failing that one makes headway. It's not by doing Raphael but by failing to do Raphael that one succeeds. It's a double failure.' 'When making sculpture one ought to pour a glass of water gently over the top and as it runs down it ought to moisten the whole surface completely. Every surface should communicate with its neighbours.' 'Head 1909 [i.e. S.24] – I thought that the curves you see [on the surface] should continue into the interior. I had the idea of doing them in wire. But it was too intellectual, too much like painting. But it's that which led to other things later.' (Penrose cited the final comment in *Picasso* 1967, p. 10.)
99 *Reclining Woman*, 1931, bronze, MP [S.109].
100 'Monsieur and Madame are not at home.'
101 'Monsieur and Madame cannot see you today.'
102 'Yes, everyone says, "Yes, it's marvellous," and I recognise only too well the weaknesses. It's this Chicago business. I'd like to do it, but how? And poor Penrose, whom I refused to see today?'
103 RP *SB*, p. 246.
104 'Dernier Nouvelles – Premiere Legende ou Incertitude concrete'. Penrose dated the poem 5 March 1964 and wrote underneath: 'extraordinarily sensitive to criticism. A few remarks mixed into obvious admiration and he tears himself to pieces.' [36]
105 'Come at 3.30.'
106 For Frua de Angeli, see above Chapter 4, note 147.
107 Penrose: 'Yes, it needs thinking about. It's the largest amount the Tate has ever offered.' Picasso: 'Yes, but they haven't yet got the money.' Penrose: 'If you don't think it's enough, say so at once.'
108 'Why buy it? I can do one when I like.'
109 In January 1964 *Playboy* republished as genuine the fictitious 'interview' with Picasso originally published by Giovanni Papini in 1952, in which Picasso is represented as saying that his art is a *blague* designed to con a gullible public. Papini himself made it clear that the 'interview' was fictitious, but it was repeatedly republished as genuine from the mid-1950s onwards, apparently at the instigation, first of Franco's secret police, later of the Kremlin. At Picasso's request, on 17 March 1964 Penrose wrote to the Editor of *Playboy* demanding a retraction (RPA 601) and in October 1964 published a summary of the affair in the *ICA Bulletin* (no. 140). Picasso also used Pierre Daix to denounce the lie in *Les Lettres françaises* (Daix 1993, p. 354).
110 'You see, it has been difficult.'
111 Miguel, Picasso's confidential secretary from 1968 onwards, frankly admits that this excuse was used

constantly to deflect the endless stream of would-be visitors and petitioners (Montañés, e.g. p. 70).
112 'Cher Pablo,
    C'est evident que la mauvaise chance reignait sur ma visite à Cannes ces jours-ci et que si j'avais étudié les étoiles j'aurais su que le moment n'était pas propice. Sans savoir les motifs de ton absence j'imagine qu'il y avait une multitude de choses qui est tombé sur toi. Nous éspèrons, Lee et moi, surtout que ce n'était pas pour des raisons de santé et qu'avec ce beau temps toi et Jacqueline vous allez bien tous les deux. […]
    Avant de quitter Cannes nous avons fait nos adieux aux grattecielists de Chicago qui sont tous partit résignés à l'idée qu'il fallait attendre. Leur admiration pour toi et leur bonne volonté sont on dirait sans limites.
    Nous quitterons Palma, Lee et moi, dimanche prochain et puisque c'est sur notre chemin à Paris nous allons passer la journée de lundi le 11 mai à Cannes. Peutêtre tu y sera et nous aurons la joie de t'embrasser. […]
    (Letter to Picasso dated 5 May 1964, sent to Notre-Dame-de-Vie, Mougins, from Barcelona; AP.) Penrose had gone to Barcelona to see Miró and finalise arrangements for his forthcoming exhibition at the Tate Gallery.
113 e.g. *Reclining Nude Playing with a Cat*, Von der Heydt-Museum, Wuppertal [Z.XXIV.133], which is dated 7 and 23 March 1964.
114 'What is stupid is that it comes to an end, a picture ought to continue for ever.' 'Why does it [the line] end there? It ought to continue beyond [the edge], far away like a Sputnik. And yet it ends and one loses interest. One doesn't know what one is doing until one has done it and then it's no longer interesting. And if one knew in advance what one was going to do, it would already be the past and without interest.'
115 'It's better for it to go where it's appreciated. It will be the first of my works bought by a government – no – Spain, amazingly, has just bought three "Painter and his Model" pictures for the Spanish pavilion of the Worlds Fair.' The versions of *The Painter and his Model* acquired by the Spanish State are Z.XXIII.196, Z.XXIII.197 and Z.XXIII.202 (now Museo Nacional Centro de Arte Reina Sofía, Madrid). All three pictures were exhibited in 'Picasso: Peintures 1962–1963', Galerie Louise Leiris, Paris, 15 January–15 February 1964.
116 See note 42 above.
117 Of the three drawings of Shakespeare Picasso gave Penrose, two were intended for sale on behalf of the ICA, and the third was a gift to Penrose himself (Penrose reported in the *Daily Express*, 4 October 1965 [RPA 513]). All were done on the same day, 18 April 1964.
118 RP *SB*, p. 246.
119 'They are not at home now but you can try later.' 'Yes, you can come immediately.'
120 'But I am never tired when I'm painting; on the contrary, when I go to bed after having worked I can't get to sleep for ages I am so full of ideas.'
121 'Thank you, I shall read it and give you an answer at once.' 'Well, I will think about it at once and at length.'
122 'All this is thanks to you.' Nine drawings of Shakespeare and Hamlet with the gravediggers, numbered I to IX and

all dated 17 April 1964, were illustrated in *Les Lettres françaises*, no. 1031, 28 May–2 June 1964 (e.g. PP.64.128). The whole issue was devoted to celebrating Shakespeare's quatercentenary.

123 'Come when you like.'

124 'Monsieur, who said yes at first, now doesn't want to come downstairs and has gone back to bed. Madame will not come down either.'

125 'Come at once.'

126 i.e. the varnish used in soft-ground etching.

127 'Now that you are here I'm thinking about it all the time.'

128 Penrose: 'It's about the two Mirós which you so kindly said you would lend to London.' Picasso: 'You mean those Mirós which I shall not lend to London.' Penrose: 'You won't lend them! What a disaster for us!' Picasso: 'Well, that's the way it is. I'm fed up with being asked for things – I'm always being asked for things. I bought them. They are mine. I'm keeping them here.' Penrose: 'Yes, I know you are asked for things – all the time – and it's I who am the greatest nuisance of all in this way.' Picasso: 'Well, if you like I will lend them.'

129 'I should prefer to go to Chicago – that's where the future and life are.'

130 'Why? We could go and dine in Nice if you like.'

131 'He was the best looking of all the painters. What a magnificent head and what distinction!' Picasso visited Klee in October 1937.

132 Penrose wrote to Picasso, from London, on 3 July 1964 (RPA 717) and 10 July 1964 (AP).

133 The first American edition of *Life with Picasso* was published by McGraw-Hill Inc. in 1964, and the first English edition by Thomas Nelson and Sons in 1965.

134 'Cher Pablo,

Je suis venu dans le midi l'autre jour en voyage éclair pour l'ouverture de la Fondation Maeght et divinant que je ne te trouverai pas dans cette galère, j'ai téléphoné à mon arrivée à Cannes pour te saluer. Malheureusement ce jour-là tu n'y étais pas.

Je voudrais voir Miró au sujet de son exposition à Londres et en effet je l'ai vu avec deux mille autres sur les terrasses de St. Paul. Le lendemain à l'aube je te regardais des nuages en route pour Paris. En suite, quelques jours après cette visite si brève, j'ai eu un appel téléphonique d'une amie qui m'a beaucoup surpris et m'a laissé rêveur. Elle m'a demandé si c'était vrai que j'avais quitté la fête chez Maeght de bonne heure pour aller passer la soirée chez Françoise Gilot. Evidemment ma reponse était un non catégorique, mais je me demandais qui avait été à l'origine d'un mensonge si colossale. Surtout je me rendais compte que ça aurait pu être interpreté si mal par toi en ce moment, car j'ai appris dernièrement de mon vieux éditeur à Londres, Victor Gollancz, ce que tu as du savoir déjà. Il m'a dit qu'on lui a offert de l'Amérique le manuscrit d'un livre dicté par Françoise et écrit par un journaliste, Carlton Lake. Il m'a ajouté qu'il ne le publiérait à aucun prix. Françoise a trouvé bon de raconter sa vie avec toi en inventant d'après sa mémoire, soi-disant "total", de longues conversations et des évènements selon sa version. Gollancz trouvait que les motives qu'on peut diviner derrière ce livre, et les

indiscretions impardonables, rendaient ceci absolument intouchable pour lui, mais évidement il ne peut pas empêcher d'autres de le faire et c'est cela je crains qui se fait.

Heureusement ton habitude olympienne d'ignorer ce genre de publicité même quand il vient d'une source aussi empoisonnée te permettras de passer au dessus de cette attaque, mais je suis navré qu'on puisse essayer de te tourmenter ainsi. Gollancz me raconte qu'il y a des passages dans le livre où il s'agit de conversations avec toi sur l'art que pourraient pour certaines personnes attenuer les plaintes monotones d'une femme vindictive mais que le style en anglais est d'un tel vulgarité qu'il y a des passages presque illisibles.

Lee et moi, comme tu peut t'imaginer, sont écoeurés de cette affaire. Nous souhaitons seulement que tu trouveras moyen de l'ignorer complètement et que ni toi ni Jacqueline s'en souffrira.

Nous t'embrassons, cher Pablo, avec toute la grande affection que tu nous inspires. Embrasse pour nous l'adorable Jacqueline,

With love,'

(Copy of a letter to Picasso dated 18 August 1964; RPA 717.) The word 'galère' in the opening sentence is not a misspelling for 'galerie', but an allusion to 'Que diable allait-il faire dans cette galère?' from Molière's *Fourberies de Scapin*.

135 Interview with Joanna Drew conducted by Michael Sweeney, 8 October 1997 (transcript in RPA). Almost exactly a year later a similar rumour, this time involving Alfred Barr, threatened to cause more trouble. Barr was accused of socialising with Gilot and attending a party to promote her book in New York. Penrose wrote to him, urging him to write immediately to Picasso refuting the story, which Barr did (copy of a letter to Barr dated 10 May 1965, and letter to Penrose from Barr dated 13 May 1965; both RPA 46).

136 AP 2001, p. 156.

137 Copy of a letter to A. E. Herzer at Manesse Verlag, Zurich, dated 28 May 1964 (RPA 584). Although the offending photograph of Picasso walking companionably with Cooper in the garden at La Californie was retained, modifications to the layout were made, and *Picasso at Work* came out with Penrose's preface.

138 '[…] Enfin ce qui m'ennui profondement c'est que tu as l'air de me repprocher pour ce livre ignoble et de lequel je suis aussi indigné que toi. Aussitot que j'ai pu procurer candestinement une exemplaire des épreuves je l'ai lu et immédiatement j'ai ecrit la lettre que tu as du recevoir. Ayant entendu que quelque mauvais esprit avais inventé le mensonge que j'étais allez voir Françoise quand au fait je ne l'ai pas parlé ni vu depuis deux ans ou trois ans je voulais t'expliquer rapidement mon indignation à ce qu'elle a trouvé bon à faire et de cette histoire grotesque. Ce livre ignoble sera vite oublié j'en suis sure et je suis convaincu que ni toi ni Jacqueline seront atteint par ses flèches empoisonnés mais trop insignifiantes pour vous troubler. Je suis navré que ceci a pu arriver et je crois que tu sais bien l'integrité inebranlable de mes sentiments envers toi et Jacqueline et j'espère que cette vipère n'aura

jamais la satisfaction d'imaginer qu'elle a pu jeter du trouble entre toi et tes amis. […]' (Draft of a letter to Picasso dated 1 October 1964, sent to Notre-Dame-de-Vie, Mougins, from the Palma Hotel, Cannes; RPA 717.)

139 A handwritten letter to Picasso dated 2 October 1964 survives in the Penrose Archive (RPA 717). Penrose annotated it: '2 Oct. not sent because J. telephoned and asked us to call that afternoon.'

140 'Cher F.
Je tiens vous dire à quel point je vous meprise pour l'exploitation que vous faite de votre 'Vie' avec Picasso. Je n'aurais pas cru que vous étiez capable des mensonges aussi flagrants.
R.P.'

141 Penrose had an appointment at the Musée de l'Homme, where Leiris worked, on 1 December 1964 (RPA 743.5). This conversation may have taken place then.

142 For the related passage in *Life with Picasso*, see Gilot 1964, pp. 299–301.

143 For the related passage in *Life with Picasso*, see Gilot 1964, p. 191.

144 With a host of others, Penrose signed a document entitled 'Solidaires de Picasso' accompanying Pierre Daix's article attacking Gilot's book, 'Picasso et la morale', *Les Lettres françaises*, no. 1085, 17–23 June 1965.

145 'This Time of Day: *My Life with Picasso*', BBC radio. Programme transmitted 4 March 1965.

146 RP *PLW* 1971, pp. 467–68.

147 Gilot 2004, p. 88.

148 Pierre Daix, *Picasso*, Paris, Somogy, 1964.

149 Penrose: 'I came despite Kahnweiler's counsel not to because I know that you change your mind, and sometimes quickly.' Picasso: 'Oh no, I have a very firm grand plan in my indecisiveness.'

150 Cézanne's *Grandes baigneuses* was purchased for the National Gallery, London, in 1964.

151 'If it gave them pleasure that would be good.'

152 'That doesn't interest me. What does interest me is making sculptures. Exhibiting them doesn't interest me. Whether you do what you want with Barr or without him, I don't want to be disturbed. I want to work and to be left in peace.' MoMA was keen to take the sculpture exhibition after it had closed in London.

153 Picasso: 'Yes, you are right to work on that – you like working on that because it's difficult – very difficult.' Penrose: 'It's true, but I'm not a masochist – and if I don't have your cooperation I shall drop it.'

154 'Lend us *The Three Dancers* – *Guernica* is lent. Why favour the United States? You helped me over the drawings and the paintings – why not the sculpture? Drawings, we had to find the paintings. Very complicated. *Meninas*, etc.'

155 'In the past at Mougins there was Eluard and Nusch, Dora, you and your wife. We had the time, we swam, we ate, we went to nightclubs, we talked, we walked and we worked and we had the time. Now it's completely different. We have time for nothing. Everything is rushed.'

156 'We're all in a hurry these days. I no longer have the patience [to execute the etching *The Frugal Repast*, 1904 (Geiser & Baer 2)]. If I started doing that today I would soon get bored. I have to work quickly.'

157 'Yes, but it's not the same now. One is in a hurry. One lives one's work. In the past one executed it. Painters executed their work. Things are going faster and faster and one has less and less time. In the end there'll be an explosion.'

158 'U[namuno] is a man who did much good – he said good things and bad things. I don't want to associate myself with him because I don't know whether I think well or badly of him.'

159 'So, that's fine, we can speak by telephone tomorrow.'

160 'Yes, it's true. Others don't like them but I do.'

161 See Z.XXIV.245 ff.

162 The richly patterned *The Artist and his Model*, dated 16 November and 9 December 1964, Museum Ludwig, Cologne [Z.XXIV.312], is probably one of these.

163 Possibly *The Artist and his Model*, dated 25 October 1964 [Z.XXIV.245].

164 'Get up, there is another painting outside.'

165 e.g. Z.XXIV.259, which is dated 4 November 1964.

166 Undated letter to Penrose from Colin Anderson, written in December 1964 (RPA 517).

167 Copy of a letter to Picasso dated 16 December 1964 (RPA 717).

168 Churchill died on 24 January 1965 and after lying in state was buried amid much pomp on 30 January. In RP *SB*, p. 247, Penrose reminisced about Picasso's fascination with the funeral.

169 Penrose first recorded the conversation in a pocket notebook (RPA 581/3/2). On his return to London, his secretary typed up a slightly shortened version, correcting most of the errors in the French. The transcription given here follows the typescript [41].

170 'While I was painting this picture a friend died, Ramon Pichot, and I think it should be called "The Death of Pichot" rather than "The Three Dancers".' Pichot died on 1 March 1925. A fellow painter, he first met Picasso at 'Els Quatre Gats' in the late 1890s and, like him, settled in Montmartre a few years later.

171 'You know, flesh is a bizarre substance – being constructed of flesh – imagine a house made of flesh – it wouldn't last long.'

172 All these paintings are now in the MP, Paris (see Seckel-Klein). The Matisse 'still life of the Algeria period' is *Still Life with Basket of Oranges*, 1912.

173 *The Crucifixion*, 1930, MP [Z.VII.287].

174 'No, there are no others like it – not one. "The Crucifixion", yes, there is something there, but it's the only one and it's very different.'

175 Picasso and Olga spent several weeks in Monte Carlo with the Ballets Russes company in March–April 1925. While there, Picasso made numerous drawings of male and female dancers, but they do not resemble *The Three Dancers* itself.

176 Penrose: 'Even so, we do like him because he saved England.' Picasso: 'England, and much more besides – he saved us all.'

177 'Despite the fact that he said he wanted to give me a kick up the ass, I admire him. I ought to have thrown down my gauntlet and duelled with him, but no. He could have made a living as a painter, even though what he did was banal.'

178 'Perhaps, but of the two pictures I far prefer "The Three Dancers". It is painted to be a painting, without ulterior motive.'

179 'Because I didn't want to. I've been asked a hundred times to sell it – by the Americans, Kahnweiler and many others, but I have always refused. In fact, it's the <u>first time</u> I've sold a painting directly to a museum.'

180 'What I am doing now is destroying modern painting. The painting of the past has already been destroyed and now one must destroy modern painting.'

181 Kahnweiler: 'This is naïve painting – truly naïve.' Picasso: 'That's Spanish realism. I'm doing it because I still have my Spanish passport and only the Spanish have known how to be realists. The French, the Italians, the Germans have done other things, but realism belongs to the Spanish.'

182 e.g. *The Artist and his Model*, dated 14 and 15 November 1964 [Z.XXIV.269].

183 e.g. *Seated Nude*, dated 7 January 1965 [Z.XXV.7].

184 e.g. the series of *Head of a Man* painted in early December 1964 [Z.XXIV.295, etc.].

185 e.g. *Reclining Nude Playing with a Cat*, dated 10 and 11 May 1964, Beyeler Foundation, Basel [Z.XXIV.145].

186 *Cat and Lobster*, dated 13, 14 January 1965 [Z.XXV.13].

187 e.g. *Seated Woman with Twelfth Night Cake*, dated 11 and 24 January 1965 [Z.XXV.11].

188 *Landscape*, dated 24 December 1964 [Z.XXIV.344].

189 See note 165 above.

190 *The Serenade*, dated 19 and 20 January 1965, Musée du Petit Palais, Geneva [Z.XXV.19].

191 e.g. *Seated Nude*, dated 30 December 1964 [Z.XXIV.357].

192 'And it is never caricature.'

193 'Freud wouldn't have difficulty finding symbols in these paintings – as he found the vulture in Leonardo. Here (pointing to a great mark scribbled on a painting standing upside down) they're everywhere.' (A reference to: Sigmund Freud, *Leonardo da Vinci and a Memory of his Childhood*, first published as *Eine Kindheitserinnerung des Leonardo da Vinci*, Leipzig, Deuticke, 1910.)

194 Picasso: 'Well, if I'm selling it to the English it's because of you – and if they want to have it, it's you who did it.' Penrose: 'No, that's impossible. It's <u>you</u> who did it.' With typical modesty, Penrose edited out this fragment of the conversation when reporting to the Tate everything Picasso had told him about *The Three Dancers*.

195 *Bathing*, 1937, Peggy Guggenheim Collection, Venice, Solomon R. Guggenheim Foundation, New York [Z.VIII.344].

196 'Yes, but one does sometimes repeat oneself, after all.'

197 'Yes, if you like, it's all those things. But you can interpret it how you like, you can say what you like, it's all the same to me.'

198 'Art is the language of signs.' 'But one does not invent a sign. One must aim hard at achieving resemblance to arrive at the sign.' The reference is to Brassaï's *Conversations avec Picasso*, Paris, Gallimard, 1964.

199 The text is dated 9 February 1965. A carbon copy, with Penrose's handwritten corrections, is in RPA 517. With minor modifications it was published in *The Tate Gallery Report 1964–65*, London, 1966, pp. 49–50, and reprinted in Alley, p. 605.

200 e.g. *Still Life in Front of a Window at Saint-Raphaël*, 1919, Berggruen Collection, Berlin [Z.III.396].

201 e.g. *Still Life on a Table Before an Open Window*, 1919, MP [PP.19.293].

202 Picasso signed *The Three Dancers* at the bottom left-hand corner.

203 Letter to Herbert Read dated 9 February 1965 (RPA 718).

204 '[…] Je suis tellement émerveillé qu'il n'y a plus de barrière entre toi et tes oeuvres. Ça semble être une expression immédiate n'ayant rien perdu de sa signifiance et de sa fraîcheur dans le procédé de la création. Je suis parti avec une vision tellement vive et ça reste toujours avec moi, même dans les brumes de Hornton Street.

J'ai fait toutes les démarches nécessaires pour l'envoi du grand tableau. Lefebvre Foinet se met en motion et la Tate Gallery fait des préparations pour sa reception et pour le protéger dans la galerie si nécessaire contre l'attaque des vandales. Quand même l'autre jour un fou a jeté une bouteille d'encre au Léonard qu'on avait acheté pour la National Gallery et malgré qu'on espère témoigner des démonstrations de joie et d'émerveillement plutôt que de rage, nous voulons ne rien risquer. […]'
(Copy of a letter to Picasso dated 10 February 1965; RPA 717.) Ink was flung at the Leonardo Cartoon in May 1962 while it was on display in the National Gallery during the campaign to raise money to 'save it for the nation'.

205 Copy of a letter to Picasso dated 16 February 1965 (RPA 717).

206 'Cher Pablo,
Comme j'ai voué de te tenir au courant des réactions britanniques aux "Trois Danseuses" je dois te raconter l'attaque faite la semaine dernière par une femme Lord. (Tu vois comme la democratie et le féminisme nous attaquent et même les lieux sacrés de l'aristocratie mâle sont maintenant envahis par les jupons.) Enfin c'était un jupon ennobli, Lady Summerskill, qui fulminait de rage en attaquant ton tableau dans la House of Lords et a demandé au Gouvernement pourquoi ils permettaient à une ou deux personnes "idiosyncratiques" de gaspiller l'argent de l'état sur des monstuosités pareils quand on avait besoin des salles d'opérations dans les hopitaux.

On m'a demandé sans avertissement de confronter cette dame à la télévision et nous avons passé cinq minutes de conversation aggressive écoutée par un grand public car c'était six heures du soir. Depuis ça, j'ai eu des lettres de partout qui me rappellent les beaux jours dans le temps que les vieux colonels venaient secouer leurs parapluies et cracher contre l'art moderne. Ceci a été plus qu'équilibré par une foule d'amis très enthousiastes. C'est merveilleux comme on n'arrive pas à traiter ton oeuvre avec indifférence. Même la phlegme anglaise s'évapore avant ton assaut méridional et miraculeux.

Je dois t'envoyer ces jours-ci la photo de l'accrochage qu'on a fait à la galerie, et je t'assure que les attaques des ignares comme cette pauvre dame ne representent pas du tout l'accueil que ton tableau reçoit en général.'
(Copy of a letter to Picasso dated 9 March 1965; RPA 717.)

1 Correspondence about this dates back to 12 November 1964 when Walter Neurath, head of Thames & Hudson, asked Penrose to read and comment on the original French edition. Penrose wrote back on 9 December 1964 urging Neurath to publish a translation and agreeing to write a preface. On 17 March 1965 he sent typescripts of his essay to Neurath and Brassaï. The American edition, published by Doubleday, came out in 1966, and the English edition, published by Thames & Hudson, in 1967. (All documents in RPA 59.)

2 Text written in pencil on a page torn from a pocket notebook (RPA 59).

3 Brassaï 1967, pp. xii, xiv.

4 See RP *Sculptures*. Penrose returned the corrected proofs on 8 May 1965. (Correspondence, etc. in RPA 583.)

5 'It's enough to make you despair of painting. No one can do better than that – and he [God] wouldn't have been able to do better either. But nor could he have done the smile of the Mona Lisa, which is some consolation.'

6 Penrose has made a slip of the pen here: the house which Pierre Gaut exchanged for a painting was in Ménerbes, not Mougins. (I am grateful to John Richardson for alerting me to Penrose's error.) The negotiations were witnessed by Brassaï (who does not name Gaut, but correctly identifies him as a colour merchant). Gaut proposed the exchange of his house 'for the still life he has wanted for so long' on 9 April 1944; on 14 June the deal was concluded (Brassaï 1967, pp. 86–87, 118, 137). Picasso gave the house to Dora Maar (see also Lord, pp. 162–63).

7 Possibly *Vase de fleurs et compotier*, dated 14 September 1943 [Z.XIII.132]. Donated by Pierre Gaut to the Musée National d'Art Moderne, Paris, in memory of Mme Marguerite Savary in 1969. However, the signature is at bottom left, not centre right.

8 The French translation of Gilot's memoirs (*Vivre avec Picasso*, Paris, Calman-Levy) was published early in 1965, despite Picasso's campaign to have it banned.

9 In RP *Sculptures* Penrose described the Minotaur as 'this mythical overlord of Picasso's sculpture'. By contrast, he considered Picasso's Harlequin an essentially pictorial character. (Typescript; RPA 583.)

10 Josette Gris, widow of the Cubist painter Juan Gris. Picasso aided her financially.

11 Hélène Parmelin, *Picasso: le peintre et son modèle*, Paris, Editions Cercle d'Art, 1965 (vol. 2 in the series of three entitled *Secrets d'un alcôve d'atelier*). Feld was Director of Editions du Cercle d'Art.

12 Picasso used two toy models of Don Quixote and Sancho Panza to establish the scale (RP *PLW* 1971, pp. 456–57).

13 Marius and Jean have not been identified and are not mentioned elsewhere in Penrose's notebooks.

14 'We'll get to work later. I'm always ready for work and that's what gives me pleasure.'

15 'Women wear wigs so that others can see changes in them. As for me, I'd like to wear them, not for the sake of others, but in order to see myself.'

16 'They should be fixed at the top and, if possible, left to swing in the wind. But probably that won't work.'

17 'Well, that's the business of you engineers. If they can erect skyscrapers, they can manage that.' 'It must be possible nowadays to make sculpture by telephone. I could telephone Chicago with all the precise dimensions, couldn't I?'

18 Thiola (or Tiola) had a workshop in Vallauris and was responsible for making all the sheet-metal copies of Picasso's cardboard maquettes from 1954 onwards. (See 'Picasso's Sheet-Metal Sculptures: The Story of a Collaboration. Lionel Prejger Interviewed by Elizabeth Cowling and Christine Piot', in Cowling & Golding, pp. 241–53.)

19 i.e. Hamilton Easter Field's commission for paintings to decorate his library. Field was a Brooklyn – not Chicago – painter, critic and patron of American artists. (See Rubin 1989, pp. 63–69.)

20 On this occasion, Picasso gave Penrose an article torn out of a recent issue of *Paris Match* (Jean Marquet, 'Pourquoi le monde va manquer de bifteck'). He had marked it 'Roland Penrose' and 'ojo' (eye – standing for 'look at'). Penrose preserved it religiously (RPA 717).

21 RP *PLW* 1971, p. 457.

22 Pencil drawings dated 8 May 1958 [Z.XVIII.118–134].

23 'at bottom it's the same thing'.

24 Copy of a letter to William Hartmann dated 25 May 1965, plus corrected carbon-copy of a typescript entitled 'Picasso and Chicago' (RPA 500).

25 On 25 May 1965 Hartmann cabled Penrose: 'MOUGINS DAME HAS ARRIVED CHAMPAGNE FOR ALL' (RPA 500).

26 Letter to Penrose from Alfred Barr dated 12 July 1965 (RPA 570).

27 Letter to Gabriel White from Alfred Barr dated 8 November 1965 (ACGB/121/847).

28 In a letter dated 7 April 1966, Penrose warmly congratulated Leymarie on his appointment and described his and Barr's plans (copy in ACGB/121/847).

29 Telegram to Penrose from Picasso dated 6 October 1965, sent to 11A Hornton Street, London (RPA 717). The text reads: 'REGRETTONS ENORMEMENT NE POUVOIR VOUS VOIR MAINTENANT STOP FUYONS CANNES AMITIES = LES PICASSO'.

30 For further details of this unhappy period, see Cabanne (4), pp. 151–58.

31 For Picasso's medical condition, see the account by his surgeon (Jacques Gilbert Hepp, *Pablo Picasso: un mystère dévoilé*, Nanterre, Académie européenne du livre, 1988, pp. 16–18, 69). Picasso had been treated successfully for many years for a duodenal ulcer. It was a large stomach ulcer which, threatening to turn cancerous, necessitated the operation in November 1965.

32 Copy of a letter to Hartmann dated 14 December 1965 (RPA 500).

33 RP *PLW* 1971, p. 267.

34 e.g. report in *France-Soir*, 24 December 1965.

35 'Chopping Picasso down to size', *New Society*, 11 November 1965, p. 31.

36 AP 2001, p. 153.

37 Diane Deriaz (p. 241) describes Penrose's initial qualms about accepting the knighthood but believes he really

'adored' being Sir Roland.

38 A pamphlet dated January 1966 and entitled 'Carlton House Terrace Project' lists the societies in the consortium and explains: 'In these premises, the five societies will be able to mount individually or in collaboration with each other, a programme of exhibitions to demonstrate important trends in national and international art and design.' The Arts Council had promised not only funds towards the conversion of the building, but also an annual grant of £25,000 towards running expenses. (Papers, plans, etc. in RPA 213.)

39 For Penrose's guarded account of the financial and managerial problems at the ICA following the move to Carlton House Terrace, see RP *SB*, pp. 258–66.

40 As he informed Alfred Barr in a letter dated 21 January 1966 (RPA 570).

41 i.e. £100,000 (exchange rate in January 1966).

42 'D'entendre ta voix au téléphone l'autre jour m'a donné la plus grande joie. C'était une voix qui m'a rassuré et qui me faisait rêver de la possibilité de te revoir ainsi que ta belle Jacqueline, mais je te téléphonerai de nouveau avant de me mettre le pied en l'air pour retourner dans le Midi. Il faut surtout que tu te sens bien solidement l'envie de voir tes vieux amis avant que je le fasse. En attendant, je voulais te parler d'une chose au risque de t'embêter, mais je me suis dis comment pourra-t-on embarquer sur un projet aussi important sans te le faire savoir – un projet qui concerne l'avenir de notre Institut – je dis 'notre' parce que toi tu as été avec nous dans ta pensée et ton oeuvre et par ta générosité depuis le commencement.

Je commencerai en t'expliquant pourquoi je t'envoie la photo de ce très beau dessin que tu reconnaîtras sûrement comme celui que tu as fait au milieu des applaudissements londiniens chez Desmond Bernal en 1950. Bernal ne va pas très bien en ce moment et il m'a téléphoné que cette maison où il nous a reçu va encore plus mal que lui. En effet en six mois on doit la démolir et il m'a dit que si je pourrais trouver un endroit pour placer ton dessin mural où il serait vraiment apprécié, il l'offrirait à l'organisation choisie, pourvu qu'on s'occupe de le faire enlever et réinstaller par les experts. Cet offre vraiment tombe du ciel exactement quand je pourrais offrir la solution parfaite parce que depuis plusieurs mois je travaille avec des amis sur un projet formidable pour l'installation de notre Institut dans un bâtiment magnifique qui en dehors est monument historique et au dedans peut être modernisé exactement comme nous voulons – nous donnant la possibilité d'une grande et très belle galerie pour les expositions, petit théâtre avec foyer et bar et en plus un club qui fera un centre pour les arts comme on n'a jamais vu à Londres. Cet endroit s'appelle Carlton House Terrace, c'est à deux pas de Trafalgar Square dans St. James's Park, qui est plein d'oiseaux – pigeons, canards, pélicans etc. Je t'envoie aussi une photo de cela avec une explication au dos. Ceci nous donnera la possibilité de placer ton dessin dans un endroit où les gens peuvent le voir dans les meilleurs conditions. Bernal est d'accord et nous espérons vivement que toi tu n'auras pas d'objection qu'on le donne le place d'honneur dans un atmosphère que tu as déjà fait beaucoup à créer. Ça

sera pour nous un symbole de première importance de ce qui est du plus précieux, toi et la paix.

Pour nous aider à réussir dans ce projet qui demande des fonds très considérables, il y a le grand Peter Wilson de la maison Sotheby qui nous a offert une vente aux enchères sans aucun frais pour nous au mois de juin prochain. Nous comptons que ceci pourrait nous rapporter la somme de N.F. 1,370,000. Nous avons déjà des promesses d'une vingtaine de peintres et sculpteurs y compris Henry Moore, Bacon, Sutherland, Max Ernst, Miró etc. etc. etc. et tout le monde demande s'il y aura aussi un Picasso. Je lui ai dit oui sans faute parce que si par hazard notre grand ami trouve qu'il a déjà été assez généreux pour l'I.C.A. j'en donnerai une toile moi-même, car cette fois-ci c'est vraiment le maximum d'effort que je fais pour que cette idée réussisse. J'ai déjà parlé à Kahnweiler du projet et il m'a dit qu'il donnera une belle toile de son propre compte et le moment est maintenant arrivé que je dois poser à toi cette même question.

Je me déteste d'avoir à faire une chose pareille. Tu nous a tellement aidé d'une façon si constante avec les dessins et tout que tu nous as donné, mais cette fois-ci c'est une opération de telle importance. Si seulement nous pourrons avoir une belle toile donnée par toi ça ferait pas seulement une somme qui nous aiderait énormément mais une impression capitale sur le monde entier. Si cette idée te plaît par hazard tu pourrais peut-être dire un mot à Kahnweiler et tout se passerait comme de l'eau dans le robinet.'

(Copy of a letter to Picasso dated 27 January 1966; RPA 717.)

43 Penrose described what happened in a letter to Jean Leymarie dated 7 April 1966 (copy in ACGB/121/847).

44 *The Eye of Picasso*, Fontana UNESCO Art Books, 1967. Penrose worked on the text from July to November 1966, and it was published simultaneously in several languages in autumn 1967. (Correspondence, drafts, etc., in RPA 596.)

45 'Cher Don Pablo,
Evidement il est pénible de m'en aller sans t'avoir vu et sans la possibilité de deviner avec certitude les raisons. D'abord je ne voudrais pas surtout que ça soit ta santé – j'éspère que tu continues regainer sans retardant tes forces habituelles. Mais je crains que je dois avoir maintenant dans tes yeux la reputation de quelqu'un qui ne viens pas te voir sauf pour te demander quelque chose – malgré que ça ne soit pas pour mon profit personnel – et en effet je dois admettre que cet idée n'est pas sans fondements etant donné des projets que j'ai du initier pour les autres encouragés il faut dire par une generosite rare que tu m'as montré depuis des années.

Enfin à ces projets – Chicago, le tableau pour la vente aux enchères au profit du I.C.A., l'exposition de tes sculptures qu'on reclame à Londres et à New York après la grande exposition de tes oeuvres à Paris – je renonce d'insister etant donné que tous ça t'aggase malgré la perte que ça va occassioner. Au fond pour moi ce n'ai pas ces choses qui comptent et je voudrais me desassocier de ces demandes malgré qu'ils sont d'une tel importance pour les autres et la publique qui t'aime et qu'on ne peut pas les faire sans ta permission.

Pour moi c'est toi et ton bien être qui est essentiel et je t'offre mes excuses si je suis, malgré moi, devenu le symbol du grand emmerdeur.

La proposition fait à moi par l'Unesco de laquelle je t'ai parlé dans ma dernière lettre, est une autre affaire. Il s'agit simplement d'un petit livre qu'ils me demandent à faire sur un aspect de ton oeuvre et j'ai choisit un theme qui m'a preoccupé depuis longtemps – les facons tellement etonnants et divers avec lesquels l'oeil fait son apparence dans tes peintures et tes dessins. Là, evidement, tu as tout fait déjà et ce n'est que pour moi de tracer aussi fidelement que je peux la richesse des apparences et des metamorphoses qui se trouvent partout dans les milliers d'exemplaires.

Enfin, mon cher Pablo, j'éspère que tu ne me verras pas d'un mauvais oeil dans cet exercise et qu'un de ces jours devant tes yeux tu verras ce que je voudais faire à propos de tes yeux.

J'écris ceci avant de prendre l'avion ce soir sur la terrasse de Guy Bernard qui voudrait aussi faire signe de son affection pour toi, toujours spendide et toujours hors-la-loi des autres.

Je embrasse, cher Don Pablo, encore et de tout coeur.

Je te prie d'embraser la très chère J. de ma part.'

(Handwritten draft of a letter to Picasso dated 30 March 1966, sent to Notre-Dame-de-Vie, Mougins, from Antibes; RPA 717.)

46   'Moi aussi j'ai passé de bien bonnes heures avec toi, à l'ombre de ta déception. J'ai admiré ta force de caractère et ta patience angéliques' (letter to Penrose from Guy Bernard dated 12 April 1966; RPA 50). Bernard refers to Picasso as 'notre cher Diable' (our dear Devil) in this letter and as 'Don Diabolus' in a letter to the Penroses dated 1 August 1968 (RPA 50).

47   Handwritten, undated draft of a letter to Picasso, sent to Mougins c. 16 June 1966 (RPA 717).

48   Handwritten draft of a letter to Picasso dated 28 July 1966 (RPA 717).

49   *Head of a Woman*, dated 11 November 1962 [Z.XXIII.74].

50   Penrose suggested 'Cortane' [sic] steel in his letter to William Hartmann of 14 December 1965. On 21 February 1966 Hartmann replied that he had obtained an estimate and was going ahead on this basis. (Both letters in RPA 500.)

51   Penrose enclosed his text, 'Picasso and the Lenin Peace Prize', in a letter to Hartmann dated 13 May 1966 (RPA 500).

52   Letter to Penrose from Hartmann dated 9 September 1966 (RPA 500). A photograph of the maquette is inscribed in Picasso's hand: 'Bon à tirer/ Picasso/ le 9.8.66' (literally, 'passed for press'). Roberto Otero, who was present and took photographs, gives a lively account of Hartmann's visit to Mougins on 8–9 August 1966, when Picasso was shown the architects' final maquette and agreed to the minor adjustments that had proved necessary. It was on this occasion that Picasso not only waived his fee but also donated the original maquette to the Chicago Art Institute (Otero, pp. 45–57). See also note 114 below.

53   The quotations are taken from Penrose's extremely elliptical notes about his visits on 16, 17, 18 and 19 September 1966 [46].

54   Letter to Monroe Wheeler dated 28 September 1966 (ACGB/121/847; RPA 570).

55   Picasso gave the Penroses *Bust of a Seated Woman*, dated 4 June 1962 [Z.XX.250].

56   'Perhaps people shouldn't be permitted to see what I've done. Perhaps it's dangerous for everyone to see it.' 'The Arabs have a [?] law against making images of things.' 'Aquatint has everything. It is richer than paint.' 'I want to make things people won't understand – that I don't understand myself. In drawing lines that mean nothing, one discovers everything, and that's how I like to work! If one draws a nose or an ear, they remain a nose and an ear, nothing more.'

57   Picasso made numerous prints using this technique in August–December 1966 [e.g. Geiser & Baer 1373].

58   'corrections'.

59   'Greetings to the genius!' 'Well, that's what they're saying! I don't know why!'

60   'That's reminiscent of mezzotint, which the English were so good at, especially the artist whose work you showed me in England.' Penrose had shown Picasso John Martin's mezzotint illustrations to Milton's *Paradise Lost*, 1827, which are renowned examples of the technique.

61   Rafael Alberti, 'Los Ojos de Picasso', in *Los 8 nombres de Picasso, y no digo mas que lo no digo*, Barcelona, Kairós, 1970.

62   i.e. 'Todo es Nada': 'All is nothing'.

63   'And the sculpture exhibition in London?' 'Well, I can't refuse you now.'

64   'I don't know. That's for you to decide. You'll tell me what you want.'

65   Presumably a reference to the chapter entitled 'Goya, peintre des regards' in Eugenio d'Ors, *L'art de Goya*, Paris, Delagrave, 1928.

66   'Les nouvelles que tu d'accord pour que l'exposition de sculpture vient à Londres après qu'elle ferme à Paris a été accueillie avec une satisfaction énorme et tu auras bientôt une lettre officielle te remerciant chaleureusement de ta grand générosité en nous permettant un evènement aussi rare et aussi sensationel. On a l'intention de monter ton exposition à la Tate Gallery comme en 1960, parce que la galerie de l'Arts Council qui est en construction en ce moment ne sera pas prête. Et il faut dire que les gens de la Tate sont ravis de l'accueillir. On s'occupera de l'organisation de tout ceci, assurance, emballage soigné, transport etc. avec la même efficacité qu'on a eu pour ton exposition de peinture. D'ailleurs ici à Londres ça sera les mêmes experts qui s'occuperont avec moi de tout celà, donc j'espère vivement que tu n'auras pas le moindre inquiétude.

J'ai parlé aux amis de Musée d'Art Moderne de New York de ton indécision au sujet de l'exposition chez eux, après celà de Londres. Evidemment si jamais tu penses qu'une fois en route il pourrait faire encore une dernière étape à New York, celà les ferait un plaisir fantastique, et Alfred Barr qu'on m'a dit prend sa retraite bientôt sera rajeuni de soixante ans par ces nouvelles, si jamais il les reçoit.

Enfin ça c'est entièrement à toi à décider et je voudrait surtout te remercier de nouveau de tout mon coeur de nous donner un tel privilège. Londres sera ennoblie de ta presence une fois de nouveau. […]'

(Copy of a letter to Picasso dated 8 December 1966; RPA 717.)

67 Copy of a letter to Alfred Barr dated 14 December 1967 (ACGB/121/847).

68 Barr's letter to Penrose of 23 January 1967 gives a detailed description of the 'anxious comedy' of his meeting with Picasso (RPA 570).

69 A small blue pocket notebook inscribed 'Jan 1967' on the cover (RPA 738/21) is filled with notes taken in Paris during this reconnaissance visit, many concerned with the materials and colours used in individual sculptures, others with bibliography and names of collectors. Penrose also listed questions, especially about dating, some of which are annotated with answers.

70 Copy of a letter to Picasso dated 18 January 1967 (RPA 717).

71 'It isn't the picture that is new, it's the artist. The picture is nothing but a passing record of the painter.'

72 The series of drawings with this cast of characters in various combinations dates from 1 January 1967 [e.g. Z.XXVII.415, 416, 425, 428].

73 i.e. drawings for Man with a Sheep, 1943 [S.280], Head of a Woman (Fernande), 1909 [S.24], Figure, 1908 [S.19]. In the event, Picasso lent a few other drawings, too, and Penrose supplemented them with drawings borrowed from other sources. Picasso also lent 31 ceramics, as compared to about 100 loaned to the Petit Palais exhibition.

74 'Picasso', Stedelijk Museum, Amsterdam, 4 March– 30 April 1967.

75 'Mon cher Pablo
    Je suis tormenté depuis plusieurs jours par l'idée categorique que je voudrai t'écrire. Enfin je trouve un moment tranquille pour le faire.
    D'abord comme tu peux imaginer c'est toi qui me preoccupe et comme toujours j'en suis heureux. Tes sculptures sont arrivé à la Tate gallerie. Le transport a été fait avec beaucoup de soin et ils sont en parfait état – mais quel travail! ces hommes ont opérés comme ces araignes qui emballent leurs mouches si soigneusement qu'elles restent bien conservées toute l'hiver. Maintenant c'est des photographes qui sont à l'oeuvre et nous sommes toute un equipe qui s'occupe de l'installation. Pour moi c'est surtout le catalogue et son preface qui me font couler l'encre comme un tanker sur les rochers. Surtout parce que New York m'ont demander que ça soit très remplit – comme un livre copieusement illustré et avec un grand distribution. Je sens l'énorme insuffisance de mes talents pour une tâche tellement grande et que je tiens/ j'ai tellement au coeur.
    En plus nous, notre Institut, nous preparons un dinner dans ton honneur à la Tate le soir avant le vernissage officiel, c'est à dire pour jeudi le 8 Juin et nous avons invité la petite amie de tes rêves, son Altesse Royale la Princesse Margaret de presider en plus elle a acceptée gracieusement et tra la la. Maintenant il ne manquera que toi et ta belle Marquise pour faire un bal de Tate

comme on n'a jamais vu[.] Donc formellement, avec tout le protocol, faux col, etc etc demandé je vous invite et quel joie de miracle ça sera de vous voir arriver tous les deux.
    J'ai envie ces jours-ci si je peut avancer suffisament mon travail de faire un saut à Amsterdam pour revoir cet assemblé encore une fois avant qu'il soit dispersé et peutêtre par la même occasion je prendrait l'avion pour le midi avec l'espoir que tu seras à la maison et peutêtre pret de me recevoir pour cinq minutes. J'ai encore enormement de choses à te raconter mais pour moi c'est tellement plus ageeable de pouvoir de [te] voir en personne et embrasser toi et l'adorable Jacqueline
    Je t'ecrirai de nouveau bientôt.
    En attendant avec Lee nous t'embrassons affectueusement with love.'

(Handwritten draft of a letter to Picasso dated 30 March 1967; RPA 717.)

76 The Board of Trustees of the Tate Gallery declined to purchase Portrait of Uhde at the meeting held on 16 March 1967 (Minutes: TGA/1/3/19). The correspondence with Barr relating to the sale of the painting spans the period 18 March–6 April 1967 (RPA 510).

77 AP 2001, p. 161.

78 See above, Chapter 4, p. 161.

79 See Hartley (2), pp. 120–21.

80 Interview with Joanna Drew conducted by Michael Sweeney on 8 October 1997 (transcript in RPA).

81 See Cabanne (4), pp. 181–82.

82 e.g. Seated Musketeer, dated 19 April 1967 [Z.XXV.337].

83 e.g. Musketeer and Seated Nude, dated 11 April 1967, MP [Z.XXV.334].

84 'Yes, it was bad for weeks. But now I'm better because he is well and has started painting again.'

85 André Breton died on 28 September 1966.

86 John Richardson has suggested (personal communication) that by 'Negus' (the ceremonial title of the Emperor of Ethiopia) Penrose may mean Carlo Ponti, the film producer and Sophia Loren's husband.

87 Brassaï amplifies this jotting. On 5 May 1944 Picasso told him how the iron sculptures came to be damaged: 'The château [de Boisgeloup] was occupied by the French army in the first months of the war, and then by the Wehrmacht. The Germans didn't do any damage. It was the French soldiers of that pre-Blitzkrieg period who amused themselves by balancing my statues on the windowsills. I've redone them, as best I could.' (Brassaï 1967, p. 135).

88 Cement casts of the following sculptures were made in 1937 for the Spanish Pavilion of the Exposition internationale in Paris: Bust of a Woman (Marie-Thérèse), 1931 [S.131]; Head of a Woman, 1931 [S.132]; Head of a Woman, 1931 [S.133]; Woman with a Vase, 1933 [S.135].

89 'What one does now is more dangerous – life is more dangerous.'

90 'Imagine, it would take us at least a day, and then only in good weather, to walk from there to here.' See also RP SB, p. 194, where Picasso's remark is reported.

91 'Why give me all this bother? I've already said, they've got all those forgers in prison, so why not let them do this for me?'

92 Almost certainly 'Cyril Connollys'. Penrose had been a close friend of the critic and writer Cyril Connolly since the late 1930s and must have noticed a certain facial resemblance to Rembrandt and also to the chubby-faced, bewigged figures in Picasso's new paintings.

93 The total attendance was 100,953 (Director's Report, Minutes of the Meeting of the Board of Trustees, 21 September 1967; TGA/1/3/19). The Arts Council had originally predicted only 50,000 (ACGB/121/847).

94 Penrose wrote to Picasso on 18 May and on about 1 June 1967 (copies of both letters in RPA 717).

95 'Londoner's Diary', *Evening Standard*, 2 June 1967. Tickets for the dinner cost 15 guineas, and the proceeds were earmarked for the ICA's 'Nash House Project'.

96 RPA 570.

97 'Londres vaincu stop tes sculptures nous occupent entierement stop princesse captivée stop publique emerveillé. Love Lee Roland' (handwritten draft; RPA 717).

98 *Head of a Woman (Fernande)*, 1909 [S.24].

99 Thus for Robert Melville the exhibition was 'the most marvellous fun palace' and none of the sculptures produced after 1934 were 'serious' works of art ('The Greatest Show on Earth', *New Statesman*, 16 June 1967).

100 Bryan Robertson, 'Picasso at the Tate', *Spectator*, 16 June 1967.

101 Robert Hughes, 'The Corn God on Millbank', *The Observer Review*, 11 June 1967.

102 John Russell, 'Picasso-Sculptor', *The Sunday Times*, 11 June 1967.

103 *Picasso* 1967, p. 8.

104 At the request of the Americans, Penrose expanded his essay for the Museum of Modern Art catalogue. His was not the first study of Picasso's sculpture: that honour goes to Kahnweiler, who wrote a short introduction to the 200-plus magnificent photographs taken by Brassaï (Kahnweiler 1949).

105 godfather.

106 Edouard Dermit, who was Cocteau's companion for the last fifteen years of his life and subsequently his heir. After Cocteau's death (11 October 1963), he married and had two children.

107 These include *The Couple*, dated 10 June 1967, Kunstmuseum Basel [PP.67.238] and *Bust of a Musketeer*, dated 10 June 1967 [Z.XXVII.22].

108 'I paint what I see around me.' The Baptism paintings include *Man Holding a Child*, dated 24 February 1965 [Z.XXV.40].

109 *Nude Man and Woman*, dated 25 October 1965 [Z.XXV.183].

110 chaplain.

111 'Why, there's a hole in it. Look, I can put my hand right into it.'

112 'Jacqueline, you mustn't think that anyone blames you for these inexplicable scenes in front of your friends. Everyone knows that it is he, Don Pablo, who has the most impossible character in the world and that no one can predict his mood from one moment to the next. He is like the wind, like a force of nature, and you, like all the rest of us, are both in admiration before him and also a victim.

He is Notre-Diable-de-Vie [Our-Devil-of-Life] and we love him for it.'

113 Letter to Penrose from William Hartmann dated 28 July 1967 (RPA 500). The monument was constructed by the American Bridge Company Division of U.S. Steel Corporation in Gary, Indiana.

114 RP *SB*, p. 245, and note 52 above. The gift became public knowledge at the time of the inauguration of the monument. (See, e.g., Edward Barry, 'Picasso Sculpture and How it Grew', *Chicago Tribune*, 13 August 1967, p. 2.) Picasso also donated a series of preparatory studies made in January 1964 (Art Institute of Chicago press release, dated 13 March 1968).

115 *Picasso, The Sculptor*, British Film Institute for the ACGB, 1968. Penrose wrote the commentary.

116 Letter to Penrose from Hartmann dated 16 August 1967 (RPA 500).

117 M. W. Newman, 'Hartmann: the man behind our Picasso', *Chicago Daily News*, 15 August 1967.

118 RP *SB*, pp. 243–45.

119 '[…] J'avais toujours compris que cela serait une oeuvre très importante mais de la voir tout d'un coup réalisée dans ces proportions gigantesques et de se trouver à ses pieds au clair de la lune dans cette ville étrange était très émouvant.

J'ai étudié les réactions des gens qui passaient dans la rue et bien des autres, y compris Monsieur le Maire lui-même, et tu as crée dans cette ville un intérêt central qui réunit tout le monde dans une espèce d'étonnement et d'orgeuil d'avoir au centre de la ville un monument tellement fantastique. […]

J'aurais beaucoup aimé venir te voir rapidement pour transmettre un peu de l'enthousiasme que tu as crée, d'abord à New York où l'exposition a un succès fantastique, et où il y avait un moyen de 4000 visiteurs par jour […].'

(Copy of a letter to Picasso dated 31 October 1967; RPA 717.)

Chapter 8 Picasso's Last Years, 1968–1973

1 Penrose mentions this commitment in a letter to Gabriel White dated 28 February 1967 (ACGB/121/847).

2 Penrose's diary notes visits to Notre-Dame-de-Vie on 20, 21 and 22 January 1968 (RPA 743.10).

3 Personal communication from Joanna Drew, 2003.

4 'In the past there was much talk of Art – how serious it is. But for me it's not like that – it's messing about, like what children do – and look at the marvellous things they do.'

5 'Joanna: 'When *Man with a Sheep* was in London I discovered some insect cocoons in clefts in the bronze and I encouraged them to stay quietly there until they reached a warmer climate.'

Picasso: 'Oh, yes. But you know, one day in Vauvenargues, when *Man with a Sheep* was outdoors, I passed my hand over the surface and felt something strange between his legs. When I looked I saw it was a wasps' nest and I took it away – without doing it any harm.'

Joanna: 'Without doing any harm to what isn't there.'
Picasso (surprised): 'You're right – to what isn't there. Yes, usually I pay a lot of attention to the sex – perhaps too much – but more to women's sex than men's. But it's true that I paid no attention to it in *Man with a Sheep*. Perhaps he doesn't need it but in any case I left it unfinished. After making lots of drawings I modelled it very quickly in clay, making lumps of clay for the cheeks and an eye; I rolled the fingers lengthways and fixed them to the hands. It was done so quickly and the armature was so badly made that everything started collapsing. The sheep fell to the ground and the man had to be attached to the steps of the staircase by the neck. But I rescued it and quickly got hold of someone to make a plaster cast.'
Penrose: 'When you made all these drawings, were you thinking of making a painting or a sculpture?'
Picasso: 'Who knows? When one works it's like smoke, and one doesn't know what form it will take.'

6   *Figure*, 1958 [S.544].
7   'People are horrified because a teaspoon got broken. But it isn't a problem – I might just as easily have used a toothbrush for the head.'
8   'Oh, anything will do.'
9   'But not that!'
10 Joanna Drew in an interview conducted by Michael Sweeney on 8 October 1997 (transcript in RPA).
11 The drawing Picasso gave Lee is dated 2 October 1967 and inscribed 'pour Lee Penrose Picasso le 22.1.68' (Scottish National Gallery of Modern Art, Edinburgh). The other is dated 1 January 1968 and inscribed 'Pour Roland Penrose son ami Picasso le 22.1.68' (private collection).
12 'Triton' paints, produced by the firm Van Cauwenberghe. Penrose inscribed the chart 'Paints used by Picasso given to me by him Jan 1968' (RPA 774).
13 The envelope containing them is marked 'Picasso's palettes from Boisgeloup (retained)' (RPA 774).
14 Copy of an undated letter to Picasso sent in mid-February 1968 (RPA 717).
15 'The Obsessive Image 1960–1968', ICA, 10 April–29 May 1968. Mario Amaya is credited as the organiser of the exhibition.
16 RP *SB*, p. 262.
17 *Nude Woman with Man Writing*, 1965 [Z.XXV.110]; *Nude Man and Woman*, 1965 [Z.XXV.107]. Both were lent by the Galerie Louise Leiris, Paris.
18 See RP *SB*, pp. 262–64, and AP 2001, pp. 158–59, 164–65, for personal perspectives on the events that led to Penrose's resignation.
19 For Picasso's increasing isolation, see Cabanne (4), pp. 194–95.
20 'You are one of us.'
21 'I should like to hear Picasso's guitars.'
22 *El entierro del Conde de Orgaz*, published by Gustavo Gili in April 1969 with a preface by Rafael Alberti [Goeppert et al 146]. Picasso's surrealist texts, written in 1957–59, are accompanied by engravings, etchings and aquatints executed in 1966–67.
23 According to his diary, Penrose visited Notre-Dame-de-Vie on 7 October 1968 (RPA 743.10).
24 Geiser & Baer 1496 ff.

25 Pablo Picasso, *Les quatre petites filles: pièce en six actes*, Paris, Gallimard, 1968. Penrose wrote to Leiris to ask him to intervene on 12 November 1968 (copy of letter in RPA 569). By the following January Picasso had given Penrose the green light: a copy of the Gallimard edition is decoratively inscribed 'POUR Rolland [*sic*] Penrose Picasso le 15.1.69' (LMA).
26 On 10 September 1969 Penrose sent the typescript to his literary agent Gillon Aitken (RPA 569). It was published as *The Four Little Girls* by Calder and Boyars in August 1970. For the fiasco over his translation of *Le Désir attrapé par la queue*, see above, Chapter 2, pp. 61–62.
27 'Il nous est arrivé un désastre du premier ordre. […] Lee et moi nous sommes tous les deux désolés, navrés, il n'y a pas de mot.' (Copy of a letter to Picasso dated 9 April 1969; RPA 717.)
28 Letters, press cuttings etc. relating to the theft are in RPA 410.
29 Correspondence exchanged in May 1969 reveals that the Museum of Modern Art also wanted to buy *Still Life* [S.47] but that the Tate Gallery exercised its right to first option (RPA 512).
30 'C'est la geurre des nerfs. La seule chose importante c'est de garder ces nerfs plus intacts que ces miserables voyous.' (Copy of a letter to Picasso dated 21 May 1969; RPA 717.)
31 See the report of the pictures' recovery in *The Times*, 3 July 1969, p. 1, and Penrose's account in RP *SB*, pp. 176–77.
32 'Tout l'Art Squad était venu – c'était comme ces tableaux de la chasse aux fauves avec les chasseurs souriants, fiers et presque avec un pied triomphale sur la tête de la Femme qui Pleure. […] C'était merveilleux de les revoir. La Femme qui Pleure il me semble n'a pas souffert du tout mais il y a un petit trou dans la Nature Morte au Bec de Gaz et les salauds ont enlevé de la Danseuse Nègre le coin en haut à droite, où il y a ta signature. Ceci la police m'a expliqué était le commencement d'un programme envisagé par les voleurs dans lequel j'aurai reçu par la poste à quelques jours d'intervalle de petits morceaux des tableaux.' (Copy of a letter to Picasso dated 8 July 1969; RPA 717.)
33 John Bull, who worked regularly for the Tate Gallery, restored all the pictures damaged in the Hornton Street burglary. (Correspondence in RPA 410.)
34 RP *SB*, p. 179.
35 Edward F. Fry, *Cubism*, New York, McGraw-Hill, and London, Thames & Hudson, 1966. Fry discusses *Les Demoiselles d'Avignon* in detail, pp. 12–16.
36 The first page of the manuscript of *Les quatre petites filles* is dated 'Golfe-Juan 24.11.47', the last 'Vendredi 13 Août 1948 à Vallauris'. Penrose wanted to publish the related drawings with his translation (copy of a letter to Picasso dated 8 July 1969; RPA 717), but Picasso was never able to locate them.
37 The paintings Penrose alludes to in his rapid survey include: *Seated Musketeer Holding a Sword*, dated 19 July 1969 [Z.XXXI.328]; *Reclining Nude*, dated 2 November 1969 [Z.XXXI.488]; *The Kiss*, dated 24 October 1969 [Z.XXXI.475]; *Vase of Flowers on a Table*, dated 28 October 1969 [Z.XXXI.486]; *Seated Man*, dated

4 September 1969 [Z.XXXI.411]; *The Embrace*, dated 19 November 1968 [Z.XXXI.506]; and *Seated Man Holding a Sword and a Flower*, dated 2 August–27 September 1969 [Z.XXXI.449].

38 In a letter sent to Picasso on 29 October 1969 (misdated 'le 29 novembre 1969'; copy in RPA 717), Penrose included a newspaper cutting showing men climbing up the Chicago monument, commenting: 'Qu'est-ce que c'est devenu, trapèze, échelle d'évasion ou cage aux singes? Enfin, ils prennent de l'exercice à Chicago' ('What has become of it – trapeze, escape ladder or monkey cage? Well, they certainly keep fit in Chicago').

39 'Picasso: 347 Engravings, 16.3.1968 to 5.10.1968', ICA, n.d. [March 1970].

40 Copy of a letter to Picasso dated 5 February 1970 (RPA 717).

41 'Il y a évidemment grand remue-ménage sur l'érotisme de certaines gravures, ce qui remet cette exposition dans l'ordre de la grande époque héroïque.' ('The eroticism of certain prints is, of course, creating a commotion, which places this exhibition in the order of the great heroic period.') (Copy of letter to Picasso dated 11 February 1970; RPA 717.)

42 Unsigned article, *Daily Mirror*, 25 February 1970 (RPA 519). At the Galerie Leiris selected visitors were given an envelope with reproductions of the offending prints, whereas the ICA catalogue had an insert bound in at the back. The anxiety within Picasso's entourage about the possible repercussions of exhibiting these prints in Paris is described in Montañés, pp. 59–60, 77–78.

43 'Picasso's Figleaf', *Art and Artists*, March 1970, pp. 12–15. Penrose's original typescript is dated January 1970 (RPA 582). His second essay appeared as 'Picasso's Peepshow', *The Observer Magazine*, 1 March 1970, pp. 30–33. The same arguments are advanced in RP *PLW* 1971, p. 466.

44 See the report of the case in *The Daily Telegraph*, 2 April 1970, p. 19.

45 Edward Lucie-Smith, 'Picasso Senex', *The Sunday Times*, 8 March 1970.

46 Richard Cork, 'The Picasso Mystique and its Flight to Frivolity', *Evening Standard*, 10 March 1970, p. 12.

47 RP *PLW* 1971, p. 462.

48 *The Party for the Madame, c.* 1878, MP, one of twelve monotypes by Degas owned by Picasso.

49 The ornamental dedication reads: 'POUR Rolan[d] Penrose et Pour Lee au[s]si Picasso 13.3.70.' (LMA).

50 RP *PLW* 1971, p. 469.

51 i.e. 'procès', meaning trial.

52 A reference to the 'Calvet affair'. See above, Chapter 3, note 91.

53 'Nous avons loué une chambre à l'Hôtel de France à Mougins pour trois semaines et je vais m'enfermer là pour faire ce chapitre qui a pour but de mettre au point jusqu'à maintenant mon livre sur toi.' (Copy of a letter to Picasso dated 1 May 1970; RPA 717.)

54 'Picasso 1960–1970', Palais des Papes, Avignon, May–September 1970.

55 See Richardson 1999, pp. 299–300.

56 Presumably a reference to the Soviet invasion of Czechoslovakia and repression of the 'Prague Spring' in

the summer of 1968, followed in April 1969 by the forced removal from office of the democratising leader Alexander Dubcek. Penrose was due to go to Prague to lecture on Picasso after leaving Mougins.

57 'He doesn't seem to be like [other people] who are mad, but he is mad all the same. He doesn't seem to be, but he is mad.'

58 Norman Granz had an important collection of Picasso's work.

59 The tapestry copied the huge collage *Women at their Toilette*, 1938, MP [Z.IX.103]. See below, pp. 327–28.

60 *Pierrot and Harlequin*, dated 14 December 1969 [Z.XXXI.544]: it was exhibited in Avignon.

61 The decorated tiles.

62 'We'll see what happens.'

63 Many of Picasso's ceramic sculptures of figures and doves were created with standard, wheel-turned clay pots produced by the Madoura potters.

64 i.e. 'dédicace' (dedication). The highly ornamental inscription on the title-page reads: 'POUR Roland Penrose Picasso le 5.6.70.' A second copy was dedicated on the cover in a simpler style 'POUR Lee'. (Both LMA.) Given Picasso's habitual precision about dating, the visit must have taken place on 5 June, not, as Penrose states, 6 June.

65 For Penrose's earlier contacts with the Brazilian painter-diplomat Cicero Dias, see Chapter 2, p. 48.

66 'Take that to the lavatory.'

67 Among those who had just died was Yvonne Zervos (on 20 January 1970). With her husband Christian, she was the driving-force behind the current exhibition in Avignon.

68 *Harlequin*, dated 12 December 1969 [Z.XXXI.543]. A description of this painting forms the climax of Penrose's account of the exhibition in RP *PLW* 1971, p. 477.

69 This conversation may have taken place on 8 June 1970 – the date of the dedication Picasso made in Penrose's copy of the Avignon catalogue. The drawing on the flyleaf depicts an artist at work.

70 'It is a pity that we don't have a language that unites us. Scientists speak about what they know and I speak about what I know, and we use two different languages. We must learn to understand one another, find a common language.'

71 'No, the Harlequin of '69 [Z.XXXI.543] is more aggressive. He is different from the Harlequin of the Blue period. But he is based on the Harlequin of Shrove Tuesday and the stick he holds is traditional. I was thinking of Cézanne and the gait of the Harlequin in Mardi Gras' (i.e. Cézanne's *Mardi Gras*, 1888, Pushkin Museum, Moscow).

72 The Hidalgos/Noblemen: 'the drawing he has made in my catalogue bears some resemblance to this portrait with a wig of 1898.' (i.e. *Self-Portrait in a Wig*, 1897, MPB [Z.XXI.48].) Penrose may be quoting Jacqueline at this point.

73 e.g. Z.XXXII.84, 94, 111 and 114.

74 *Picasso: eaux-fortes originales pour des textes de Buffon*, Paris, Martin Fabiani, 1942 [Goeppert et al 37]. On 24 January 1943 Picasso decorated Dora Maar's copy with 42 ink and wash drawings. A facsimile edition was published in 1957 (*40 dessins en marge de Buffon*, Paris, Heinz Berggruen). Penrose devoted the first section of the final

chapter of RP *PLW* 1971 (pp. 473–75) to *El entierro del Conde de Orgaz*.

75 The commissions for stained glass windows in the Cathedral at Mézières and for gigantic bronze figures to flank the entrance to a building in New York came to nothing (both mentioned in RP *PLW* 1958, p. 369).

76 The abortive project was for a marble monument to be placed by the old port in Marseille. As a substitute, Nesjar created the concrete monument placed in the Lycée Sud [S.649].

77 Penrose complied with Jacqueline's request (RP *PLW* 1971, pp. 467–69).

78 In 1970 Nesjar made an 8-metre-high concrete enlargement of one of Picasso's sheet-metal heads of *Sylvette* [S.489] for the Bouwcentrum, Rotterdam [S.661]. Picasso gave his approval on 18 November 1969 (see Fairweather, p. 118).

79 *Yo, Picasso*, 1901 [Z.XXI.192].

80 'to my dear friend'.

81 Leymarie's wife.

82 'But there is no difference'. Penrose used this anecdote and quoted Picasso's words exactly in RP *PLW* 1971, p. 465.

83 Julie Lawson.

84 Apart from William Hartmann and his wife, Penrose lists: the sculpture collector Joseph Hirshhorn and his wife; Jacqueline de la Baume-Dürrbach and René Dürrbach, the tapestry-makers referred to disparagingly in Chapter 6, p. 260; the poet, typographer and publisher Ilya Zdanevitch (Iliazd) and his wife; and the Mr. and Mrs. Woodford mentioned in the caption to one of the photographs taken by Lee published in RP *Portrait* 1971 (fig. 310).

85 One wallpaper Picasso used in the cartoon is printed with very detailed maps of the continents.

86 In RP *PLW* 1971, pp. 477–78, Penrose explains this passage: 'During the process of weaving the tapestry Baudouin had brought some of the black and white photostats made for working purposes for Picasso to see. He was at once so pleased with the effect that at his suggestion the Gobelins factory offered to make a second monochrome version of the collage.' The monochrome version, like the first full-colour version, was woven for Picasso, the second full-colour version for the French State.

87 'You're a lawyer. Read that and tell me what you think.'

88 Penrose translated this as 'awkward' in RP *PLW* 1971, p. 478.

89 In *ibid.*, p. 478, Penrose translated this as: 'No. It is I who am awkward. I am always being asked to sign and once I've done so they do what they like. No, I can't sign. They will make as many copies as they want to and I, what do I get? I've already given them quite enough by allowing them to make the tapestry.'

90 Picasso: 'And if I don't sign, what will happen?' Baudouin: 'I shall be in a lot of trouble. They'll ask me what I've done with the tapestry. They may think I've kept it for myself.' Picasso: 'Very well, I shall ask Jacqueline to decide.'

91 Perhaps the baby of 'the French-American couple', Mr. and Mrs. Woodford.

92 In RP *PLW* 1971, p. 479, Penrose translated this as: 'No, I shall not tell you what you ought to do. If I tell you to sign you will not sign, and vice versa. You have made fun of me in this way often enough.' He omitted Jacqueline's final statement, 'I'm saying nothing.'

93 'Well, I shall sign.'

94 'I must explain how it happened, but today you are being too nasty and I shan't tell you anything.'

95 'They are too young to understand. Yes, I am nasty, if it amuses me.'

96 'If it had been a factory, nothing would have been done.'

97 'Me, I just want to work and I don't give a damn about aesthetic reasons.'

98 'We have given it careful consideration and perhaps it will be possible.'

99 'Yes, one needs to have his robust health to be able to appreciate it.'

100 Golding had asked Penrose to obtain some information from Picasso (personal communication, October 2004).

101 Another reference to Françoise Gilot's *Life with Picasso* and the unsuccessful attempt to have the French edition banned.

102 'They want me to hurry up.'

103 '[…] Sera-t-il possible que je te consulte sans deranger Pablo et sans trop t'embeter?
Nous n'avons qu'une petite semaine qui reste dans les montagnes de Mougins mais si tu pourras nous faire savoir nous serons libre à l'instant pour te voir. […]'
(Handwritten draft of an undated letter, which Penrose later dated 'May '70' although it was certainly sent in June; RPA 717.)

104 'J'ai été à la campagne pour trouver la tranquillité qu'il me fallait pour écrire à ton sujet et maintenant après des semaines de lutte acharnée j'espère que j'ai pu dire quelquechose sur les années '60 et ce que s'est passé grâce à toi et autour de toi. Comme toujours c'était fascinant et très difficile, et comme je t'ai promis je voudrais te montrer le manuscrit qui permettra à toi et Jacqueline de me donner votre opinion.' (Copy of a letter to Picasso dated 8 October 1970; RPA 717.)

105 RP *PLW* 1971, pp. 477–79.

106 RP *PLW* 1971, p. 480.

107 Douglas Cooper, 'Profiting from Picasso', *Foylibra*, February 1972, pp. 6–7.

108 Penrose's description of the museum forms part of the conclusion of RP *PLW* 1971 (pp. 481–83).

109 'Picasso in London: A Tribute on his 90th Birthday', ICA, 18 October–7 November 1971. In his brief preface, Penrose noted that the exhibition was both 'a token of the immense esteem' felt for Picasso and also 'a small recognition of the generosity and the encouragement he has shown personally to the ICA'.

110 The drawing is inscribed 'Pour mon ami Roland Penrose. Picasso. le 19.1.71'. Penrose's copy of *El Entierro del Conde de Orgaz* [Goeppert et al 146] is no. 59 out of a total edition of 253.

111 'J'espère que la photo, sous pli séparé, arrivera intact et encore une fois de plus je te remercie pour un dessin qui nous fait tant de joie. Lee en était folle d'admiration quand elle l'a vu.' (Copy of a letter to Picasso dated 16 April 1971; RPA 717.)

112 According to Penrose's diary, the meeting took place on 7 May 1971 (RPA 743.13).

113 The summary of another conversation with the silversmith François Hugo in May–June 1970 (RPA 512) is so elliptical that it has been omitted. It was the basis of the rewritten account of Picasso's collaboration with Hugo in RP *PLW* 1971, p. 416, although Penrose doctored the record by omitting the information that it was Douglas Cooper who brought Hugo and Picasso together: personal animosity got in the way of strict accuracy on this occasion.

114 submissive.

115 On 23 August 1911 the *Mona Lisa* was stolen from the Louvre. Picasso and Apollinaire became implicated when the latter's secretary, Géry Pieret, claimed – falsely – to be the thief. Their situation was precarious because, at the time, they still had in their possession ancient Iberian stone heads which Pieret had stolen from the Louvre in 1907. The whole tragi-comic story is recounted in Richardson 1996, pp. 20–24, 197–205.

116 A photograph taken by Jacqueline on 18 October 1960 (included in RP *Portrait* 1971, fig. 268) shows Picasso and François Hugo holding up the drawings for the vase, which was in fact made in silver and iron, not gold.

117 During this visit Picasso embellished and dedicated various publications to the Penroses, including Roland's translation of *The Four Little Girls* and the latest Galerie Leiris catalogue (*Dessins en noir et en couleurs, 15 décembre 1969–12 janvier 1970*, 23 April–5 June 1971) (LMA).

118 'since I didn't go to bed with him, when there were so many who did.'

119 '[…] d'une façon inadmissible.' (Letter to Penrose from Miguel dated 31 August 1971, sent to 11A Hornton Street, London, from Notre-Dame-de-Vie, Mougins; RPA 717.) Mariano Miguel Montañés, always known as Miguel, had first met Picasso during the war but only became his secretary in May 1968. He and his wife lived in La Californie.

120 Copy of a letter to Miguel dated 10 September 1971, sent to Notre-de-Vie, Mougins (RPA 717).

121 i.e. *Old Steam Boiler in a Corner of the Port*, 1895 [Palau 1981, no. 94]; *The Rape of the Sabines*, 1962 [Z.XXIII.1]; *Musketeer*, 1969 [Z.XXXI.122].

122 'Il me semble maintenant longtemps que je n'ai pas de nouvelles directes de toi, mais quand même je vis tous les jours entièrement entouré de toi, de ta présence qui émane de ton oeuvre et des préparations que nous faisons pour te fêter vers le fin de ce mois. J'espère que tout va bien chez toi, que Jacqueline et toi sont en bonne santé et que tu travailles avec ta force habituelle.

Ici des nouvelles éditions de mes livres sur toi ont disparu chez les imprimeurs pour qu'ils paraissent avant le 25. La BBC a fait un film pour la télévision en couleurs qui dure 70 minutes et dont ils sont fiers. Je l'ai vu et en effet ce n'est pas mal réussi malgré que moi je subis un interview – qui dure à peu près une demie heure – avec un critique d'art, et j'espère que j'ai pu transmettre un peu l'enthousiasme que j'ai pour toi depuis tant d'années.

A l'ICA nous faisons une exposition de toiles, dessins et sculptures de toi prêtés par des collectionneurs de Londres. Ils ont été généreux et nous aurons plus de 40 pièces, commençant avec un très joli petit paysage du port de Malaga de 1895, et finissant avec deux grandes toiles prêtés par Norman Granz, "L'Enlèvement des Sabines" et un "Mousquetaire" de 1969. Dans la soirée du 25 nous allons célébrer ton anniversaire avec une party dans l'exposition, et dans d'autres galeries il y aura une deuxième projection du film de la BBC et un très bon guitariste espagnole.

La présentation des "Quatre Petites Filles" qu'on veut faire aussi a été remise au mois de décembre, pour avoir le temps de faire les préparations nécessaires.

Enfin tu vois qu'on pense à toi et j'espère vivement que ton anniversaire sera un moment de rejouissance pour toi autant que pour nous autres. Je t'enverrai naturellement les livres, les catalogues et tous, aussitôt qu'ils seront sortis, et Lee et moi nous t'embrassons ainsi que la belle Jacqueline, espérant de venir te saluer au mois de novembre.'

(Copy of a letter to Picasso dated 9 October 1971; RPA 717.)

123 See Duncan 1974, pp. 272–77.

124 Cabanne (4), p. 232.

125 Copy of a letter to Picasso dated 11 November 1971 (RPA 717).

126 i.e. 'maquis', meaning underground, as in the Resistance.

127 *Minotaure*, the handsomely produced art journal edited by Albert Skira, became increasingly identified with the Surrealist movement during its life-span, 1933–39.

128 'Picasso: Pintura, Dibujo', Sala Gaspar, Barcelona, October 1971. Celebrations of Picasso's ninetieth birthday provoked disturbances, demonstrations and arrests in Madrid and Barcelona, despite the fact that the Franco government had for some time tried to negotiate the hand-over of *Guernica* and its studies (then still on display in MoMA). The most serious incident was the vandalism of *Vollard Suite* etchings on exhibition at the Galería Theo, Madrid, by the extreme right-wing group Guerrilleros del Cristo Rey (Warriors of Christ the King). (See Hensbergen, pp. 266–73.)

129 Eugenio Arias had been Picasso's barber since 1948. Like Picasso, he was a Communist.

130 Alan Bartlett Shepard Jr., the American astronaut. In 1961 he was the first American to be launched into space and in 1971 commanded the Apollo 14 Lunar Landing Mission. Picasso was fascinated by space travel and watched television programmes about it avidly.

131 *Factory at Horta de Ebro*, 1909, The Hermitage Museum, St Petersburg [DR 279].

132 '[…] Hier soir Londres à fait la connaissance de tes <u>Quatre Petites Filles</u> dans une répétition générale comblée de monde et éblouie par la poésie que ces filles ont pu transmettre par les paroles et par leur beauté naturelle. Ce matin on parle dans les journaux les plus sérieux de cette fantaisie à laquelle les Anglais sont évidemment bien susceptibles.

Enfin tu ne cesses pas de nous étonner. Charles Marowitz le directeur de cette pièce a très bien travaillé et malgré certaines adaptations à cause des difficultés de trouver des chiens volants et suffisament de sang pour noyer toute l'assistance, il a réalisé des effets extrêmement réussis. Le hasard parfois l'a aidé par des effets imprévus comme l'arrivée du chat noir du théâtre sur la scène. Ce qui était bien c'est que les extravagances et la nudité de ces belles jeunes personnes a augmenté plutôt que diminué la poèsie étonnante du texte, et on comprenait entièrement chaque parole, même les plus inattendues, grâce à la diction si claire des petites filles.

Enfin je crois que ça t'aurait amusé et et je peux t'assurer que tout a provoqué une grande enthousiasme parmi l'assistance. Encore on te remercie de tout coeur de nous permettre de joies pareilles.

Je t'enverrai aussitôt que possible le programme qui est très modeste et les photos des filles et de la mise-en-scène, qui était d'ailleurs très simple. Il n'y avait pas de sièges et tout l'espace du théâtre était couvert de gazon rose, bien rembourré, sur lequel les gens étaient assises.

Lee se joint à moi en envoyant à toi et à la belle Jacqueline notre grande affection.

(Copy of a letter to Picasso dated 9 October 1971; RPA 717.) For Charles Marowitz's own memories of the production, see 'Du kitsch, mais c'est adorable', *L'Avant-Scène*, no. 500, August 1972, pp. 28–32. (I am grateful to Kathleen Brunner for drawing my attention to this article.)

133 '[…] Le piece etait un succés enorme dans cette petite théâtre intime qui accomode seulement 150 personnes assises par terre pour chaque seance. Ils ont joué quand même avec salle comblé pour presque deux mois tous les soirs et les filles elles-mêmes se sont tellement amusées que à la fermeture elles ont pleurées qu'elles ne pourrons plus jouer, chanter et reciter tous les soirs ta poésie unique. Il y a une possibilité toujours que on pourrait accepter les invitations qui viennent d'étranger surtout pour la France, mais un autre invitation Yugoslav était consideré trop compliqué. […]' (Copy of a letter to Picasso dated 24 February 1972; RPA 717.)

134 E. L. T. Mesens died on 13 May 1971.

135 Possibly a reference to *Britain's Contribution to Surrealism of the '30s and '40s*, London, Hamet Gallery, 3–27 November 1971.

136 *Landscape*, dated 31 March 1972, MP [Z.XXXIII.331].

137 *Self-Portrait*, dated 30 June 1972, Fuji Television Gallery, Tokyo [Z.XXXIII.435]

138 *Still Life with Steer's Skull*, 1942, Kunstsammlung Nordrhein-Westfalen, Düsseldorf [PP.42.035].

139 Daix 1993, p. 369

140 'Picasso: 172 dessins en noir et en couleurs', Galerie Louise Leiris, Paris, 1 December 1972–13 January 1973. Penrose purchased *Head*, dated 2 July 1972 [Z.XXXIII.436] for 35,000 francs on 9 February 1973 (RPA 520).

141 *Self-Portrait*, 1907, Národni Gallery, Prague [DR 25].

142 RP *SB*, pp. 252–53. A variant of this passage appears in the 'Postscript' in RP *PLW* 1981, p. 484.

143 Copy of a letter to Picasso dated 16 August 1972 (RPA 717).

144 'Picasso: 156 gravures récentes', Galerie Louise Leiris, Paris, 24 January–24 February 1973.

145 '[…] J'ai parle avec Heinni et Zett et nous etions tous d'accord que ce sont probablement les plus beaux dessins que tu as jamais fait. J'attend avec impatience voir le deuxieme exposition qui sera tes gravures.

Nous avons pense beaucoup a toi a Londres le 5 decembre car on a fait un grand reception pour ton arrive en cire parmi toutes l'hierarchie du monde entier. La jeune femme qui fait ces effigies et qui a fait, si tu te rapelle, celui de Rembrandt que tu trouvais pas mal, a finalement reussi faire un ressemblance pas trop mal. Evidement ce n'est pas toi et d'ailleurs ca aura etait encore plus inquietant si c'etait toi. – Surtout a cause de la position ou on t'a place entre le gouvernement Brittanique et la famille Royale[.] A la reception il y avait tout un reunion de tes amis et admirateurs ce qui a cree un atmosphere hallucinant car on voyait tant de tetes qu'on connaissait vrai ou faux. J'ai demande qu'on fasse des photos de toi dans ton nouveau entourage et je pense que tu vas en recevoir bientot. Malheureusement les photos ne sont pas bons a cause de la lumiere qui n'est pas le meme dans laquelle on voit l'effigie en realite. Donc il ne faut pas t'effrayer – c'est quand meme pas si mauvais qu'on craignait et en tout cas on est heureux de t'avoir a Londres.[…]'

(Copy of a letter to Picasso dated 14 December 1972; RPA 717.)

146 According to the entry in his diary, Penrose did not reach Cannes until 1 February 1973. The following day he was in Paris, meeting Jean Leymarie at the Deux Magots (RPA 743.15).

147 'On m'a envoye de Madame Tussauds des photos que tu trouveras ci-joint. Toi en campagnie de notre bonne reine et sa maman, et aussi avec Henry Moore en person. On s'excuse que celui avec la famille royale n'est pas tres reussi, et on va en faire d'autres mais en tout cas peut-etre elles t'amusent.

On a beaucoup pense a toi et beaucoup parle, avec des amis qui sont venus dernierement chez nous. On a eu au ICA un mois francais avec une programme remplie d'evenements serieus et des fois droles. En tout cas ca nous a permi d'avoir une visite de Lucien Clergue qui fait une exposition de ses photos, et Jean Leymarie. Tous les deux sont venus a la ferme et nous n'avons pas cesses de parler a toi. Tout ca a ete bien amusant.

Malgre que je n'ai pas des nouvelles direct de toi recement j'espere que tout va tres bien et que comme d'habitude tu travailles en faisant des splendeurs qu'on verra plus tard. On m'a dit qu'il y aura cette ete encore une exposition a Avignon qu[i] sera arrange par Jacqueline. Ceci est vraiment un nouvelle qui me rejouit beaucoup et je viendrai sans faute avec Lee la voir.

En attendant, Lee et moi nous t'embrassons tres affectueusement, ainsi que la belle Jacqueline.

(Copy of a letter to Picasso dated 23 March 1973; RPA 717.)

148 RP *SB*, p. 255. A variant of this passage appears at the beginning of the 'Postscript' in RP *PLW* 1981, p. 479.

149 According to Penrose's diary, he was in London on the day of Picasso's funeral, 10 April 1973 (RPA 743.15).

150 'I haven't got much longer.'

151 Pablito Picasso, son of Paulo and his first wife, Emilienne. Not permitted to see his grandfather before his death, he drank bleach on the day of the funeral and died after appalling suffering some weeks later.

152 'Pablo Picasso, 1970–1972', Palais des Papes, Avignon, 23 May–23 September 1973.

153 'You've seen the cathedral?'

154 Copy of a letter to Alfred and Margaret Barr dated 14 June 1973 (RPA 46).

155 Duncan 1974, p. 27.

156 RP *PLW* 1981, pp. 480–81.

Epilogue

1 Handwritten notes headed '<u>Avignon</u>' [64].

2 Robert Hughes, 'Picasso's Worst', *Time Magazine*, 18 June 1973, p. 92.

3 Quoted in Richardson 1999, p. 300.

4 Penrose & Golding.

5 'Beauty and the Monster', in *ibid.*, pp. 157–95.

6 'Picasso: The Surrealist Realist. Excerpts from a conversation between Roland Penrose and Dominique Bozo', *Artforum*, September 1980, p. 30.

7 *Woman with a Vase*, 1933–34 [S.135].

8 Daix 1995, p. 239.

9 Penrose was first invited to discuss plans for the museum by Dominique Bozo in a letter dated 23 December 1976 (RPA 533).

10 RP *SB*, p. 272. Correspondence establishes that the committee worked together from 29 May to 2 June 1978 (RPA 533).

11 RP *PLW* 1981. Numerous drafts for this 'postscript' survive. One of the earliest is dated October 1973 (all documents in RPA 593). *Portrait of Picasso* was reissued under the MoMA imprint to coincide with the vast exhibition curated by William Rubin (Rubin 1980).

12 Copy of a letter to Jacqueline Picasso dated 30 January and draft of a letter to her dated 29 December 1980 (RPA 717). Penrose was obliged to make do with a photograph of the cement cast of *Woman with a Vase* outside the Spanish Pavilion at the Exposition Internationale in 1937 (RP *PLW* 1981, plate D2).

13 'Cher Roland,
    Je ne savais pas que Lee nous avait quittés. Je ne sais pas exprimer ma tristesse mais tu sais combien je peux comprendre la tienne.
    Pour ce qui est du Travail tu dois savoir que tout est bloqué, et que je ne suis en mesure de t'aider présentement .
    Je t'embrasse
    Jacqueline'
        (Undated note to Penrose from Jacqueline Picasso; RPA 717.)

14 Penrose wrote twice, unavailingly, to Claude Picasso on 6 November and 20 November 1980 begging him to waive reproduction rights. On 23 December 1980 he wrote to Nicole Laurent at SPADEM appealing against the fees. (Copies of these letters are in RPA 593.)

15 See, for instance, the hostile review by Gabriel Josipovici

('Picasso and Cubism', *London Review of Books*, 16 July–5 August 1981, pp. 17–18) in which Penrose is accused of writing 'part historical romance, part hagiography'.

16 *Picasso: su vida y su obra*, 'Edición definitiva', Barcelona, Argos Vergara, 1981. Translated by Horacio González Trejo. A new French translation, by Jacques Chavy, was published by Flammarion in 1982.

17 Plans for a show of part of the *dation* at the Hayward Gallery were initiated in 1979 (correspondence between Bozo, Penrose and Joanna Drew in RPA 560).

18 Speaking of 'Picasso's Picassos', Joanna Drew said: 'Of course, [Roland] loved it, but Picasso was dead and it wasn't the same as the exhibitions he had organised when he was alive' (interview with Michael Sweeney, 8 October 1997; transcript in RPA).

19 See RP *SB*, pp. 8–9.

20 Deriaz, p. 253. She says she bought postcards and glue for him in Trouville in order to overcome his initial resistance.

21 *A Diane. Souvenir de Trouville*, 1980, reproduced in RP *SB*, p. 294.

22 'Roland Penrose: Collages récents', Galerie Henriette Gomès, Paris, 12 November–30 December 1982; 'Roland Penrose: Recent Collages', The Mayor Gallery, London, 28 November–21 December 1983.

23 Penrose's diary indicates that he flew to the Seychelles on 18 January 1984 and returned to Farley Farm on 9 February. Following a succession of strokes, the entries become increasingly illegible after this point (RPA 743.26).

Appendix 1 Biographical Dictionary

ARAGON, Louis (Louis Andrieux) (1897–1982). French poet and writer. One of the founder-members of the Surrealist movement, he broke definitively with its leader, André Breton, in 1932 over his commitment to Communist orthodoxy. His close association with Picasso developed after the latter joined the Party in 1944 and waned after the Hungary crisis in 1956. In 1939 Aragon married the writer **Elsa Triolet** (1896–1970).

BARR, Alfred H. (1902–1981). American art historian and brilliantly successful first director of the Museum of Modern Art, New York (opened 1929). He organised numerous groundbreaking exhibitions for the Museum, including a major Picasso retrospective in 1939.

BAUDOUIN, Pierre (1921–1970). French artist and teacher, and a close friend of Paul Picasso (q.v.). Appointed in 1946 to teach history of art at the Atelier-Ecole at Aubusson, he became fascinated by the art of tapestry and was responsible for adapting the cartoons and overseeing the fabrication of tapestries designed by leading contemporary artists, including Braque, Calder, Le Corbusier and Picasso.

CLOUZOT, Henri-Georges (1907–1977). French filmmaker. Director of *Le Mystère Picasso*, which won the Prix spécial du Jury at the Cannes Film Festival in 1956.

COCTEAU, Jean (1889–1963). French writer, artist and filmmaker. He first met Picasso in 1915 and collaborated with him on the avant-garde Diaghilev ballet *Parade* (1917). Their friendship cooled during the period when Picasso was close to the Surrealists but became close again after the Liberation. Cocteau was a regular visitor when Picasso settled in Cannes in 1955.

COOPER, Douglas (1911–1984). English art historian and art collector. He wrote several major books about Picasso and curated notable exhibitions during the 1950s and 1960s, when they saw each other regularly in the Midi, where Cooper lived in style in the Château de Castille.

DAIX, Pierre (b. 1922). French writer and art historian. A prominent member of the Communist Party, he became friendly with Picasso during the 1950s and is a leading authority on the artist's life and work.

DERIAZ, Diane (b. 1926). French trapeze artist, who during the late 1940s was the companion of Paul Eluard (q.v.). Her relationship with Penrose began in 1953 and endured until his death.

DREW, Joanna (1929–2003). British arts administrator. She joined the Arts Council of Great Britain in 1952 and became

Director of Exhibitions in 1975. Penrose curated several major exhibitions with her, including groundbreaking retrospectives of Picasso's paintings (1960) and sculpture (1967), both held at the Tate Gallery.

DUNCAN, David Douglas (b. 1916). American photographer for *Life Magazine*, who met Picasso in 1956 and was responsible for some of the most intimate and revealing images of the artist at work and in his various homes in the South of France.

ELUARD, Paul (Eugène Grindel) (1895–1952). French poet. A leading figure in the Surrealist movement until he quarrelled definitively with André Breton in 1938, Eluard met Picasso in the 1920s but became an intimate friend only in 1935. He introduced Penrose to Picasso in 1936. Active in the Resistance during the Occupation, Eluard influenced Picasso's decision to join the Communist Party after the Liberation. Following the death of his second wife **Nusch** (née Maria Benz, 1907–1946), he married **Dominique Laure** (née Odette Lemort, 1914–2000) in 1951.

GILOT, Françoise (b. 1921). French painter. She met Picasso in 1943 and lived with him between 1946 and 1953. Their children, **Claude** and **Paloma**, were born in 1947 and 1949 respectively. Her controversial memoirs, *Life with Picasso*, were published in 1964.

GOLLANCZ, Victor (1893–1967). British publisher, writer, socialist and humanitarian. He formed his own publishing company in 1927 and was one of the founders of the Left Book Club. In 1954 he commissioned Penrose to write a biography of Picasso.

HARTMANN, William (1916–2003). American architect. In 1947 he joined the Chicago branch of the leading architectural practice Skidmore, Owings and Merrill. With Penrose's aid, he persuaded Picasso to design a huge monument in Cor-ten steel for the new Civic Center in Chicago (unveiled 1967).

HUGUÉ, Totote (née Jeanne de Rochette) (d. 1971). Wife of Manolo (Manuel Hugué; 1872–1945), a Catalan sculptor and intimate friend of Picasso's from *c.* 1900 onwards. Picasso was also devoted to their adopted daughter **Rosa (aka Rosita)** (d. 1976).

HUTIN, Catherine (aka Cathy) (b. 1948). Daughter of Jacqueline Picasso (q.v.) by her first husband, André Hutin.

KAHNWEILER, Daniel-Henry (1884–1979). German-born art dealer, publisher and writer. He was Picasso's principal dealer between 1907 and 1914, and again after the end of the

Second World War, through his partnership with his step-daughter Louise Leiris (q.v.).

LEIRIS, Louise (aka Zette) (1900–1986). French art dealer; stepdaughter of Kahnweiler (q.v.) and wife of Michel Leiris (q.v.). As head of the Galerie Louise Leiris, she organised many exhibitions of Picasso's work after the Second World War.

LEIRIS, Michel (1901–1990). French writer and ethnographer. A founder-member of the Surrealist movement, Leiris switched to Georges Bataille's rival *Documents* group in 1929. At around the same time he embarked on an enduring friendship with Picasso.

LEYMARIE, Jean (b. 1919). French art historian, museum curator and writer. He met Picasso during the 1950s and organised the huge *hommage* retrospective held in Paris in 1966–67.

MAAR, Dora (née Theodora Markovitch) (1907–1997). French-born painter and photographer. Through her friendship with Eluard (q.v.), she met Picasso in 1935. Although she never lived with him, their liaison endured until 1944.

OLIVIER, Fernande (1881–1966). An artist's model, she met Picasso in Paris in 1904 and lived with him between 1905 and 1912. Her intimate memoirs, *Picasso et ses amis*, were published in 1933.

PARMELIN, Hélène (1915–1998). French novelist and author of a series of books about Picasso's work and way of life after he moved to the south of France. Like her husband Edouard Pignon (q.v.), she was a prominent figure in the French Communist Party.

PENROSE, Antony (aka Tony) (b. 1947). English farmer and author of several books about his parents, Roland Penrose and Lee Miller, whom he occasionally accompanied on their visits to Picasso during the 1950s and 1960s.

PENROSE, Valentine (née Boué) (1898–1978). French Surrealist poet. She married Roland Penrose in 1925. They were divorced in 1939 but remained close friends until her death.

PICASSO, Jacqueline (née Roque) (1927–1986). Picasso's second wife and mother of Catherine Hutin (q.v.). She met Picasso through her cousin Suzanne Ramié (q.v.) and began living with him in autumn 1954. They were married in 1961.

PICASSO, Olga (née Khokhlova) (1891–1955). Picasso's first wife and mother of Paul (q.v.). A Russian dancer in Diaghilev's ballet company, she met Picasso in Rome in 1917. They married in 1918 and separated in 1935. There was, however, no divorce.

PICASSO, Paul (aka Paulo) (1921–1975). Picasso's son by his first wife, Olga (q.v.). He acted at various times as his father's chauffeur and representative.

PIGNON, Edouard (1905–1993). French artist best known for his social realist paintings. With his wife Hélène Parmelin (q.v.), he was active in the French Communist Party and on intimate terms with Picasso from the Liberation until the latter's death.

RAMIÉ, Georges (1901–1976) and **Suzanne** (1905–1974). Proprietors of the Madoura pottery, which they founded in Vallauris in 1938. Encouraged by Suzanne Ramié, Picasso made his first experimental ceramics at the Madoura works in 1946, the prelude to an exceptionally productive collaboration, which continued (at a progressively slower rate) until 1969.

RICHARDSON, John (b. 1924). English art historian. His ongoing multi-volume *A Life of Picasso* promises to be the definitive biography of the artist, to whom he was introduced in 1949 by his then-partner Douglas Cooper (q.v.).

SABARTÈS, Jaime (1882–1968). Catalan writer and author of several books about Picasso. The two first met in Barcelona in 1898 and in 1935 Sabartès became Picasso's secretary, an association which, with periodic breaks, lasted until Picasso settled in Cannes in 1955. Sabartès was instrumental in establishing the Museu Picasso in Barcelona.

VILATÓ, Lola (1884–1958). Picasso's younger sister. Two of her sons, **Fin** (1916–1969) and **Javier (aka Xavier)** (1921–2000), became painters and lived in exile in France after the defeat of the Republic in the Spanish Civil War.

WALTER, Marie-Thérèse (1909–1977). She met Picasso in January 1927 and soon afterwards secretly became his lover. The birth of their daughter **Maya** in 1935 precipitated the end of Picasso's marriage to Olga (q.v.), but his liaison with Dora Maar (q.v.) prevented the establishment of a permanent family life with her.

ZERVOS, Christian (1899–1970). Greek-born French art historian. He met Picasso in 1926 when he founded the periodical *Cahiers d'Art*. His unbounded admiration for Picasso found expression in numerous essays and a multi-volume catalogue of the complete paintings and drawings.

ZERVOS, Yvonne (1905–1970). French art dealer, and wife and collaborator of Christian Zervos (q.v.). She was responsible for the exhibition of over 200 of Picasso's late paintings and drawings at the Palais des Papes, Avignon, in 1970.

Appendix 2 Roland Penrose's Picasso 'Notebooks'

'Notebooks' are listed below, in broadly chronological order, with their Roland Penrose Archive (RPA) inventory number and a brief description. Letters in square brackets, e.g. [A], have been added where the same RPA inventory number covers more than one 'notebook'. Dimensions are given in centimetres, height before width.

1 RPA 738/1. Lucien Lefebvre Foinet sketchbook with blue, patterned cover; 18 x 13.5. Labelled on front and back: 'June 1953'. Text begins on 1 loose sheet of Farley Farm headed notepaper and continues on sketchbook pages. Many pages unused. Text mainly in pencil; some drawings. Brief excerpts transcribed.

2 RPA 586. Large black Walker's Farringdon Ring Binder; 28.2 x 24.5. Labelled 'IV' on cover and spine. Spine also labelled with list of contents. Binder contains paper of various sizes and types. Text mainly in ink. Only notes of interviews transcribed. Contents dateable 1954–57.

3 RPA 580.02. Four loose sheets of lined paper; 25.3 x 20.2. Text in ink with additions in pencil. Notes headed: 'Vallauris visit Feb 1954'. One short excerpt transcribed.

4 RPA 580.03. Nineteen loose sheets of lined paper; 16 x 9.7. Text in pencil. Notes headed: 'Thurs. 16 Sept 54 Perpignan.' Some cuts in transcription.

5 RPA 580.04 [A]. Two loose sheets of air mail paper; 20.3 x 12.5. Text in pencil with additions in ink. Notes headed: 'Visit to Léger Exhibition at la Maison de la Pensée Française Nov. 1954'.

6 RPA 580.04 [B]. Four loose sheets of lined paper; 18.2 x 10.7. Text in ink. Notes headed: 'Paris. Nov. 54'. Some passages marked with red crayon.

7 RPA 585 [A]. Small black loose leaf binder; 20.3 x 13.5. Binder contains paper of various sizes. Some pages unused. Text in pencil, biro and ink. Contents dateable 1954–57. Some cuts in transcription.

8 RPA 585 [B]. Small black Walker's loose leaf binder; 18.5 x 14.5. Binder contains paper of various sizes. Text mainly in biro and ink. Contents dateable 1954–56. Substantial cuts in transcription.

9 RPA 580.05–08. Seven loose sheets of plain writing paper; 25.2 x 20.2. Text in ink with pencil annotations. Some passages marked with red crayon. Notes headed: 'Visit 16 Feb '55. PARIS'.

10 RPA 587. Green Walker's Kenbury Ring Book; 26 x 23. Binder contains paper of various sizes. Text variously handwritten and typed. Many pages annotated with asterisks, ticks and references to chapters in *Picasso: His Life and Work*. Contents dateable 1954–57. Only a few texts transcribed.

11 RPA 588 [A]. Small notebook with spiral binding and pages printed with a square grid; 12.6 x 8.5. Inscribed on front cover: '1955 Malaga Temboury Madrid'. Text mainly in pencil and ink. Substantial cuts in transcription.

12 RPA 580.09.1. Small red notebook with spiral binding and pages printed with a square grid; 12 x 7.6. Inscribed on front and back covers: 'Barcelona Cannes 1955', and on front cover: 'July 55 (1)'. Text in pencil, biro and ink; some drawings. Some passages marked with red crayon. Some cuts in transcription.

13 RPA 580.09.2. Small blue notebook with spiral binding and pages printed with a square grid; 12 x 7.5. Inscribed on front cover:

'July 1955 Cannes Paris' and 'July 55 (2)'. Many pages unused. Text in pencil, biro and ink. Some passages marked with red chalk. Some cuts in transcription.

14 RPA 580.10. Six loose sheets of lined paper; 25.3 x 20.2. Text in ink. Many passages marked with red crayon or pencil. Notes headed: 'Visit. Cannes. 6 Nov 1955.'

15 RPA 588 [B]. Small green notebook with spiral binding and pages printed with a square grid; 15.5 x 9.4. Text in pencil and ink. Inscribed on front cover: 'Cannes Nov '55. Feb '56. Salmon Toklas.' Some cuts in transcription.

16 RPA 580.11. Seven loose sheets of lined paper; 23.5 x 20.2. Text in ink. Some passages marked with red crayon. Notes dated 21 February–1 March 1956.

17 RPA 588 [C]. Small yellow notebook with spiral binding and pages printed with a square grid; 12.8 x 9. Inscribed on front cover 'Baudouin March 1956'. Some pages unused. Text in pencil and ink. Some passages marked with red crayon. Some cuts in transcription.

18 RPA 564 [A]. One loose sheet of plain writing paper folded in half; 20.2 x 12.7 (folded). Text in ink. Notes headed: 'CLOUZOT – FILM 1st NIGHT Cannes. Visit May 1st to 5th 56.'

19 RPA 564 [B]. Three loose sheets of plain writing paper; 25.3 x 20.2. Text in ink. Contents dateable May 1956.

20 RPA 564 [C]. Four loose pages of lined paper torn from a notebook; 20.3 x 12.7. Text in pencil. Contents dateable May 1956. Some cuts in transcription.

21 RPA 580.12. Small dark blue notebook with spiral binding and pages printed with a square grid; 12.8 x 9. Inscribed on front and back covers: 'Paris Cannes June July 1956'. Many pages torn out. Text mainly in pencil and ink. Some passages marked in red crayon. Some cuts in transcription.

22 RPA 580.13 [A]. Seven loose pages printed with a square grid torn from a notebook; 11.9 x 7.5. Text in ink. Notes headed: '10.12.'56 Cannes.'

23 RPA 580.13 [B]. One loose page printed with a square grid torn from a notebook; 11.9 x 7.5. Text in ink. One passage marked in red crayon. Notes headed: 'Conversation with Dora & Balthus 12 Jan. 57.'

24 RPA 580.14. Seven loose sheets of lined paper; first sheet 26.4 x 20.2, remainder 25.3 x 20.2. Text in ink. Some passages marked with red crayon. Notes headed: 'Visit to Cannes 1st – 15 Ap. 1957.'

25 RPA 580.15. Small notebook with royal blue plastic cover, spiral binding and pages printed with a square grid; 12.6 x 9. Text in pencil and ink; some drawings. Many passages marked with red crayon. Some pages unused. First page of notes headed: 'Cannes 15 Oct. 1957'. Some cuts in transcription.

26 RPA 581/1/1. Small red notebook with spiral binding and pages printed with a square grid; 12.8 x 8.8. Inscribed on front cover: 'Paris. Summer 1958. Cannes.' Text in pencil, biro and ink. Some pages unused, others removed. One passage transcribed.

27 RPA 581/1/2. One loose page printed with a square grid torn from a notebook; 12.8 x 8.8. Text in ink. Some passages marked with green ink. Notes headed: 'Visit to Picasso 22 Ap '59.'

28 RPA 581/1/3. Dark blue notebook with spiral binding and pages printed with a square grid; 15.2 x 9.2. Inscribed on front cover:

'Picasso notes '59 '62 '63'. Text mainly in pencil and ink. Many pages torn out. Some passages marked with green ink. Some cuts in transcription.

29 RPA 581/1/4. One loose page printed with a square grid torn from a notebook; 12.8 x 8.8. Text in pencil, later dated '1959'. List omitted from transcription.

30 RPA 581/1/5. Two loose pages printed with a square grid torn from a notebook; 13 x 8.8. Text in pencil and ink. Some passages marked in red ink. Notes headed: 'Paris 16.12.61'.

31 RPA 581/1/6. Four loose pages printed with a square grid torn from a notebook; 13 x 8.8. Text in pencil and ink. Notes headed: 'June 1962'.

32 RPA 581/1/7. Seven loose pages printed with a square grid torn from a notebook; 12 x 7.6. Text in ink. Notes headed: 'Visit to Picasso. Monday 20 May '63.'

33 RPA 581/1/8. Small yellow notebook with spiral binding and pages printed with a square grid; 12 x 7.5. Inscribed on front cover: 'Picasso '63' and 'P.', and on back cover: 'BARCELONA. MIRO Oct. 1963'. Text mainly in pencil and ink. Notes concerning Picasso transcribed, with some cuts.

34 RPA 581/2/1. Six loose pages printed with a square grid torn from a notebook; 13.3 x 8.3. Text in pencil. Notes headed: 'Visit of 2–7 March 1964'.

35 RPA 581/2/2. One loose page printed with a square grid torn from the same notebook as 36 below; 14 x 8.8. Text in ink. Notes headed: 'Mougins. 3 March '64.'

36 RPA 581/2/3. One loose page printed with a square grid torn from the same notebook as 35 above; 14 x 8.8. Text in pencil. Notes headed: '"Dernier Nouvelles – Premiere Legende ou Incertitude concrete."' Added in red ink on verso: 'Golfe Juan 5 Mars '64'. Text of poem not transcribed.

37 RPA 581/2/4. Three loose pages printed with a square grid torn from a notebook; 13.3 x 8.3. Text in pencil. Notes headed: 'Picasso. 12 May '64'.

38 RPA 581/2/5. Five loose pages printed with a square grid torn from a notebook; 13.3 x 8.3. Text in pencil. Notes kept in an envelope inscribed: 'March May June 1964 Notes on visit to Picasso (Sculpture.)'.

39 RPA 581/2/6. Small red Despé notebook with spiral binding and pages printed with a square grid; 13 x 9.1. Text in pencil, biro and ink. Many pages unused. Inscribed on front cover: 'Mougins Nov '64.' Some cuts in transcription.

40 RPA 565. Small blue notebook with spiral binding and lined pages, 12.2 x 8.2. Text mainly in pencil. Most pages unused. Dateable to 1964–65. Some cuts in transcription.

41 RPA 581/3/1. Four loose sheets of plain writing paper; 25.3 x 20.2. Text typed. Notes headed: '29 Jan. '65 Mougins'. Some cuts in transcription. (A small blue Despé notebook, RPA 581/3/2, inscribed on the front cover 'Mougins Jan '65' is the source of this typescript. It contains a few additional notes, which have not been transcribed.)

42 RPA 581/3/3. Small red Elji notebook with spiral binding and pages printed with a square grid; 13.5 x 8.6. Inscribed on front cover: 'March 1965'. Text in pencil, biro and ink; some drawings. Some pages unused. Most of notebook devoted to Arts Council Tapiès exhibition and plans for ICA. Only notes concerning Picasso transcribed.

43 RPA 581/3/4. Ten loose sheets of plain writing paper; 21 x 13.5. Text in biro. Notes headed: 'Cannes 30 April '65'.

44 RPA 581/3/5. One loose sheet of plain writing paper; 21 x 13.5. Text in biro. Notes headed: 'Sat. 1st May 1.0 N D de V.'

45 RPA 581/3/6. Three loose sheets of plain writing paper; 21 x 13.5. Text in biro. Some passages marked with pencil. Notes headed: 'P. architect. 2 May '65'.

46 RPA 581/4/1. Two loose pages printed with lines, torn from a notebook; 12.4 x 7.9. Text in pencil. Notes headed: 'Visit to Mougins. Sept. 66 on way back from Sardinia'. Brief excerpts transcribed.

47 RPA 581/4/2. Five loose pages printed with a square grid torn from a notebook; 13 x 9. Text in pencil, biro and ink. Notes headed: 'Mougins. Nov. '66 after opening of Paris Exhibitions'. Some cuts in transcription.

48 RPA 581/4/3. One loose page printed with a square grid torn from a notebook; 14 x 8.9. Text in biro. Notes headed: 'Visit 29–30 Jan 1967'.

49 RPA 581/4/4. Four loose pages printed with a square grid torn from a notebook; 14 x 8.9. Text in pencil. Notes headed: '22 Ap. 67'.

50 RPA 581/4/5. Five loose pages printed with a square grid torn from a notebook; 12 x 7.6. Text mainly in pencil. Notes headed: 'Visit to Mougins 11 June '67'.

51 RPA 581/4/6. Two loose pages printed with a square grid torn from a notebook; 14 x 9. Text in pencil. Notes headed: 'PICASSO/ return of sculpture with Joanna Drew/ Mougins 21 Jan 68'.

52 RPA 581/4/7. Two loose pages printed with a square grid, torn from a notebook; 13.5 x 9. Text in pencil. Notes headed: 'N.D. de Vie 21 July '68'.

53 RPA 581/4/8. Three loose pages printed with a square grid, torn from a notebook; 13.5 x 8.8. Text in pencil. Notes headed: 'Visit to Picasso 8–10 Nov '69.'

54 RPA 581/5/1. One loose page printed with a square grid torn from a notebook; 13.4 x 8.8. Text in pencil. Notes headed: 'Visit to Picasso 13.3.70'. (See also 55 below.)

55 RPA 581/5/2. Two loose pages printed with a square grid torn from a notebook; 13.4 x 8.8. Text in pencil. (These notes relate to the same visit as 54 above.) Some cuts in transcription.

56 RPA 581/5/3. Two loose pages printed with a square grid torn from a notebook; 13.4 x 8.8. Text in pencil. Notes headed: 'Mougins 27 May 1970'.

57 RPA 581/5/4. Two loose pages printed with a square grid torn from a notebook; 13.4 x 8.8. Text in ink. Notes headed: 'Mme. Ramié. 1970.'

58 RPA 581/5/5. Small blue notebook with spiral binding and pages printed with a square grid; 12 x 7.4. Inscribed on front cover: 'PICASSO. May–June 1970'. Text mainly in pencil and ink. Some passages marked with red crayon. Many pages unused. Cuts in transcription.

59 RPA 579. One loose page printed with a square grid torn from a notebook; 13.4 x 8.9. Text in pencil, ticked in ink. Notes headed: 'Jean Leymarie'. Dateable to 1970. Cuts in transcription.

60 RPA 738/37. Small pale blue Appunti notebook with spiral binding and pages printed with a square grid; 13.5 x 9.7. Inscribed on front cover: '1970–71 Australia. India. Museo Picasso. Mougins'. Text mainly in pencil and ink. Two brief excerpts transcribed.

61 RPA 581/5/6. Small green notebook with spiral binding and pages printed with a square grid; 14 x 9. Inscribed on front cover: 'Ap. '71* Bordeaux. Mougins. Barcelona.' Text mainly in pencil and ink. Substantial cuts in transcription.

62 RPA 581/5/7. Three loose pages printed with a square grid torn from a notebook; 14 x 8.5. Text mainly in pencil and biro. Notes headed: '26 N. 71 N.D. de Vie'. Some cuts in transcription.

63 RPA 581/5/8. One loose page printed with lines torn from a notebook; 17.4 x 11.4. Text in felt tip pen. Notes headed: 'Picasso 30 June '72.'

64 RPA 554. One loose sheet of lined paper; 25 x 20. Text in ink. Notes headed: 'Visits'. Dateable to 1973.

65 RPA 530. Two loose pages printed with a square grid torn from a notebook; 10.9 x 6.8. Text in pencil. Notes headed: 'Ana Maria Gili 4 June '73'.

Appendix 3   Roland Penrose's Publications on Picasso

Books

Homage to Picasso on his 70th Birthday: Drawings and Watercolours since 1893, London, Lund Humphries, 1951

Portrait of Picasso, London, Lund Humphries, for the Institute of Contemporary Arts, 1956

Portrait of Picasso, New York, The Museum of Modern Art, 1957

Picasso: His Life and Work, London, Victor Gollancz, 1958

Pablo Picasso: Four Themes. The Human Form. Portraits. Landscapes. Still Life, London, Folio Society, 1961

Picasso: Early Years, London, Faber and Faber, 1961. Introduction by R. H. Wilenski

Picasso: Later Years, London, Faber and Faber, 1961. Introduction by R. H. Wilenski

Picasso, Amsterdam, Allert de Lange, and Paris, Editions du Temps, 1961

Picasso: Sculptures, Paris, Fernand Hazan, and London, Methuen, 1965

Picasso at Work: An Intimate Photographic Study by Edward Quinn, London, W. H. Allen & Co., 1965. Introduction and text by Roland Penrose

Pablo Picasso, London, Knowledge Publications/Purnell, 1966

The Eye of Picasso, Fontana UNESCO Art Books, 1967

Picasso, London, Phaidon, 1971

Picasso: His Life and Work, Harmondsworth, Penguin, 1971

Portrait of Picasso, London, Lund Humphries, 1971

Picasso 1881–1973, eds. Roland Penrose and John Golding, London, Paul Elek, 1973. Contains Penrose's essay, 'Beauty and the Monster'. (Second edition: *Picasso in Retrospect*, London, Granada Publishing, 1981.)

Picasso: His Life and Work, London, Granada Publishing, 1981

Scrap Book 1900–1981, London, Thames & Hudson, 1981

Translations

'give tear out twist and kill', *London Bulletin*, nos.15–16, 15 May 1939, p. 3. (Translation of Picasso's text, 'donne arrache tords et tue …'.)

'Picasso Good Master of Liberty', *Homage to Picasso on his 70th Birthday: Drawings and Watercolours since 1893*, London, Lund Humphries, 1951, n.p. (Translation of Paul Eluard's text, 'Picasso bon maître de la liberté'.)

Pablo Picasso, *Desire Caught by the Tail*, London, Calder and Boyars, 1970. (Translation of *Le Désir attrapé par la queue*.)

Pablo Picasso, *The Four Little Girls*, London, Calder and Boyars, 1970. (Translation of *Les quatre petites filles*.)

Exhibition catalogues

Picasso's 'Guernica', with 67 Preparatory Paintings, Sketches and Studies, London, New Burlington Galleries, 4–29 October 1938

Picasso in English Collections, London, London Gallery, 16 May–20 June 1939

Twenty Original Drawings by Picasso, London, London Gallery, 10 May–18 June 1949

Picasso: Drawings and Watercolours since 1893. An Exhibition in Honour of the Artist's 70th Birthday, London, Institute of Contemporary Arts, 11 October–8 December 1951

Picasso Himself, London, Institute of Contemporary Arts, October–December 1956

Picasso, Arts Council of Great Britain, in association with London, Tate Gallery, 16 July–18 September 1960.

Picasso Sculpture, Ceramics, Graphic Art, Arts Council of Great Britain, in association with London, Tate Gallery, 9 June–13 August 1967

The Sculpture of Picasso, New York, The Museum of Modern Art, 11 October 1967–1 January 1968. (Chronology by Alicia Legg.)

Picasso and the Surrealists, From the Collection of Sir Roland Penrose, King's Lynn Festival, Fermoy Art Gallery, 27 July–10 August 1968. Introduction by Roland Penrose.

Picasso: Paintings, Sculpture, Ceramics, Drawings, Graphics, Dublin, Trinity College, 17 May–30 August 1969

Picasso: 347 Engravings, 16.3.1968 to 5.10.1968, London, Institute of Contemporary Arts, n.d. [March 1970]

Picassos in London: A Tribute on his 90th Birthday, London, Institute of Contemporary Arts, 18 October–7 November 1971

Picasso 90 O.R.T. [Organisation for Rehabilitation Through Training]. First viewing of Picasso's 'Portraits Imaginaires', a Suite of 29 Lithographs executed by Marcel Salinas, on the Occasion of Picasso's 90th Birthday and O.R.T.'s 90th Anniversary, London, Institute of Contemporary Arts, 19 October–7 November 1971

Picasso's Picassos: An Exhibition from the Musée Picasso, Paris, Arts Council of Great Britain, London, Hayward Gallery, 17 July–11 October 1981. Contains Penrose's essay, 'The Drawings of Picasso'. Introduction by Timothy Hilton

Articles

'Note', *London Bulletin*, nos.8–9, January–February 1939, p. 59

'Personal Choice: Roland Penrose chooses *Femme assise dans un Fauteuil, Picasso, Paris, 1914*', *Art*, vol. I, no. 8, 3 March 1955, p. 7

'Picasso at home', *The Sunday Times*, 21 October 1956, p. 10

'Picasso: soixante-quinze ans de jeunesse', *L'Oeil*, no. 22, October 1956, pp. 16–31, 50

'Wisdom Exploited', *ICA Bulletin*, no. 140, October 1964, pp. 4–5

'Pablo Picasso, "Les Trois Danseuses (The Three Dancers)",
    1925', *The Tate Gallery Report 1964–65*, London, Her
    Majesty's Stationery Office, 1966, pp. 49–50
'Introduction', in Brassaï, *Picasso and Company*, trans. Francis
    Price, New York, Doubleday, 1966, pp. xi–xvi
'Picasso as sculptor', *The Atlantic Monthly*, October 1967,
    pp. 69–76
'Bildkommentare', in Picasso, *Worte und Gedanken von Pablo
    Picasso*, Basel, Galerie Beyeler, 1967–68
'Dessins récents de Picasso, 1966–1967', *L'Œil*, no. 157,
    January 1968, pp. 18–23
'Picasso's Peepshow', *The Observer Magazine*, 1 March 1970,
    pp. 30–33
'Picasso's Figleaf', *Art and Artists*, vol. 4, no. 12, March 1970,
    pp. 12–15
'Lorsqu'une idée devient sculpture – Thème et variations',
    in *Picasso: l'idée pour une sculpture, thèmes et variations*,
    Lucerne, Galerie Rosengart, July–September 1970
'90 Years in the Life of an Artist', *The Daily Telegraph
    Magazine*, no. 364, 15 October 1971, pp. 40–45
'Enigme, paradoxe et ambiguïté de Picasso', *Le Monde*,
    27 October 1971, p. 17
'Le Thème chrétien', *XXe Siècle*, numéro spécial, 'Hommage à
    Picasso', 1971, pp. 129–30
'Picasso the eagle, with a poet's eye', *The Times*, 12 April 1973,
    p. 18
'Picasso', *The Magazine of the Institute of Contemporary Arts*,
    May 1973, n.p.
'Picasso's Portrait of Kahnweiler', *The Burlington Magazine*,
    vol. CXVI, March 1974, pp. 124–33
'The Riddle of Picasso', in *Picasso: A Loan Exhibition for the
    Benefit of Cancer Care Inc., The National Cancer Foundation*,
    New York, Acquavella Galleries, 15 April–17 May 1975, n.p.
Extracts from *Picasso: His Life and Work*, in *Modern Masters:
    Manet to Matisse*, ed. William S. Lieberman, New York,
    The Museum of Modern Art, 1975, pp. 138, 142, 258.
    (Exhibition also shown in Sydney, Art Gallery of New South
    Wales, and Melbourne, National Gallery of Victoria.)
'Introduction: The Riddle of Picasso', in *Pablo Picasso:
    An Exhibition of Drawings, Prints, Ceramics and Books*,
    Weybridge, Marina Gallery, n.d. [1975]
Untitled text in Japanese and English, *Exposition Picasso Japon
    1977*, Tokyo, Musée de la Ville de Tokyo, 15 October–4
    December 1977, n.p.
'On viewing Picasso', in *Adam: International Review*, nos.
    419–421, 1979, pp. 7–8
'Pablo Picasso', *Enciclopedia universale UNEDI: dizionario
    enciclopedico*, vol. 11, Milan, UNEDI, 1979, p. 80
'Reminiscences' (extracts from *Picasso: His Life and Work*), in
    Picasso from the Musée Picasso, Paris, Minneapolis, Walker
    Art Center, 10 February–30 March 1980, pp. 81–100
'Beauty and the Beast', *The UNESCO Courier*, December 1980,
    pp. 34–37
'The Pick of the Private Picassos', *The Sunday Times Magazine*,
    19 July 1981, pp. 32–43

[Unsigned Editorial], 'A Picasso in its Proper Place', *The Times*,
    11 September 1981, p. 11
'Introduction', in *Picasso and the Theatre*, Brighton, Burstow
    Gallery and Great Hall, Brighton College, 1–30 May 1982,
    pp. 3–4

Open letters

Letter to the Editor, *The Spectator*, 29 October 1937, p. 747
'Picasso Mural', Letter to the Editor, *The Times*, 28 June 1958,
    p. 7
Letter to the Editor, *The Listener*, 11 August 1960, p. 228
'Picasso and Dalí', Letter to the Editor, *The Times*, 28 June
    1980, p. 15

Book reviews

'Picasso's War and Peace', *Arts News and Review*, vol. VI, no. 26,
    22 January 1955, p. 10. (Review of Claude Roy, *Picasso: La
    Guerre et la Paix*, Paris, Editions Cercle d'Art, 1954.)
'The Toreador of Painting', *Art*, 9 March 1956, p. 6. (Review of
    Wilhelm Boeck and Jaime Sabartès, *Picasso*, London,
    Thames & Hudson, 1955.)
'The New Art of Picasso', *Vogue*, vol. 120, no. 7, May 1963,
    pp. 120–24. (Review of Wilhelm Boeck, *Pablo Picasso
    Linocuts*, London, Thames & Hudson, 1963.)
[Untitled], *Museums Journal*, vol. 64, no. 4, March 1965, pp.
    325–27. (Review of Rudolf Arnheim, *Picasso's Guernica:
    The Genesis of a Painting*, London, Faber and Faber, 1964.)
'Chopping Picasso down to size', *New Society*, 11 November
    1965, p. 31. (Review of John Berger, *The Success and Failure
    of Picasso*, Harmondsworth, Penguin, 1965.)

Interviews

'Picasso: genius or hoax?', *Evening Standard*, 19 December
    1945, p. 6. (Roland Penrose in debate with William Gaunt.)
Grace Glueck, 'Roland Penrose: Picasso Persuader', *The New
    York Times*, 15 October 1967, p. 138
'Remembering Picasso: How Don Pablo Lived', *House and
    Garden*, vol. 152, no. 8, August 1980, pp. 102–3, 140–43.
    (Interview with Martin Filler.)
'Picasso: The Surrealist Realist. Excerpts from a conversation
    between Roland Penrose and Dominique Bozo', *Artforum*,
    September 1980, pp. 24–30
'The Connoisseur Interview: Edwin Mullins talks to Sir
    Roland Penrose', *The Connoisseur*, July 1981, p. 157
'Surréalisme: un homme de l'art raconte. Jean-Louis Ferrier
    fait le point avec Roland Penrose', *Le Point*, no. 603, 9 April
    1984, pp. 159–66

Selected films

Picasso, The Sculptor, British Film Institute, for the Arts
    Council of Great Britain, 1968
Picasso in His Time, BBC TV, 1971.

Further Reading

Entries are listed alphabetically by author/editor (in chronological order where there is more than one publication by the same author/editor) or alphabetically by book title as appropriate.

Entries in **bold** refer to abbreviations used in the Notes.

Dawn Ades, *Dada and Surrealism Reviewed*, London, Arts Council of Great Britain, 1978

Agar Eileen Agar (in collaboration with Andrew Lambirth), *A Look at My Life*, London, Methuen, 1988

Alley Ronald Alley, *Catalogue of The Tate Gallery's Collection of Modern Art, other than Works by British Artists*, The Tate Gallery in association with Sotheby Parke Bernet, 1981

André Breton: la beauté convulsive, Paris, Centre Georges Pompidou, Musée National d'Art Moderne, 1991

Dore Ashton, *Picasso on Art: A Selection of Views*, London, Thames & Hudson, 1972

Pierre Assouline, *An Artful Life: A Biography of D. H. Kahnweiler, 1884–1979*, trans. Charles Ruas, New York, Fromm, 1991

Brigitte Baer, 'Seven Years of Printmaking: The Theatre and its Limits', in *Late Picasso: Paintings, Sculpture, Drawings, Prints 1953–1972*, London, Tate Gallery, 1988, pp. 95–135

Baldassari 1994 Anne Baldassari, *Picasso photographe, 1901–1916*, Paris, Réunion des Musées Nationaux, 1994

Baldassari 1997 —, *Picasso and Photography: The Dark Mirror*, trans. Deke Dusinberre, Paris, Flammarion, in association with the Museum of Fine Arts, Houston, 1997

—, *Le Miroir noir: Picasso, sources photographiques 1900–1928*, Paris, Réunion des Musées Nationaux, 1997

Barr 1939 Alfred H. Barr, *Picasso: Forty Years of his Art*, New York, The Museum of Modern Art, 1939

Barr 1946 —, *Picasso: Fifty Years of his Art*, New York, The Museum of Modern Art, 1946

Barr 1951 —, *Matisse: His Art and His Public*, New York, The Museum of Modern Art, 1951

Barr 1986 —, *Defining Modern Art: Selected Writings of Alfred H. Barr, Jr.*, eds Irving Sandler and Amy Newman, New York, Harry N. Abrams, 1986

Cecil Beaton, *Self-Portrait with Friends: The Selected Diaries of Cecil Beaton*, ed. R. Buckle, London, Pimlico, 1991

Clive Bell, *An Account of French Painting*, London, Chatto & Windus, 1931

—, *Old Friends: Personal Recollections*, London, Chatto & Windus, 1956

John Berger, *The Success and Failure of Picasso*, Harmondsworth, Penguin Books, 1965

Marie-Laure Bernadac, 'Picasso 1953–1972: Painting as Model', in *Late Picasso: Paintings, Sculpture, Drawings, Prints 1953–1972*, London, Tate Gallery, 1988, pp. 49–94

Marie-Laure Bernadac and Androula Michael (eds), *Picasso: propos sur l'art*, Paris, Gallimard, 1998

Marie-Laure Bernadac and Christine Piot (eds), *Picasso: Collected Writings*, London, Aurum Press, 1989

Marie-Laure Besnard-Bernadac, Michèle Richet, Hélène Seckel, *The Musée Picasso, Paris: Paintings, Papiers Collés, Picture Reliefs, Sculptures, Ceramics*, Paris, Réunion des Musées Nationaux, 1986

Bloch Georges Bloch, *Pablo Picasso: catalogue de l'œuvre gravé et lithographié*, 5 vols, Berne, Kornfeld and Klipstein, 1968–84

Anthony Blunt, *Picasso's Guernica*, London, Oxford University Press, 1969

Brassaï 1967 Brassaï, *Picasso and Co.*, trans. Francis Price, London, Thames & Hudson, 1967

Brassaï 1999 —, *Conversations with Picasso*, trans. Jane Marie Todd, Chicago and London, Chicago University Press, 1999

Jonathan Brown (ed.), *Picasso and the Spanish Tradition*, New Haven, Yale University Press, 1996

Pierre Cabanne, *Le siècle de Picasso*, vol. 1, *(1881–1912) La naissance du cubisme*, Paris, Denöel, 1975

—, *Le siècle de Picasso*, vol. 2, *(1912–1937) L'époque des métamorphoses*, Paris, Denöel, 1975

—, *Le siècle de Picasso*, vol. 3, *(1937–1955) La guerre*, Paris, Denöel, 1975

Cabanne (4) —, *Le siècle de Picasso*, vol. 4, *(1955–1973) La gloire et la solitude*, Paris, Denöel, 1975

Cahiers d'Art, Paris, 1926–60

Richard Calvocoressi, *Lee Miller: Portraits from a Life*, London, Thames & Hudson, 2002

Mary Ann Caws, *Dora Maar With and Without Picasso: A Biography*, London, Thames & Hudson, 2000

Herschel B. Chipp, *Picasso's Guernica: History, Transformations, Meanings*, Berkeley, University of California Press, 1988

Juan-Eduardo Cirlot, *Picasso: Birth of a Genius*, London, Paul Elek, 1972

Jean Clair (ed.), with Odile Michel, *Picasso 1917–1924: The Italian Journey*, Venice, Palazzo Grassi, 1998

Cooper 1968 Douglas Cooper, *Picasso Theatre*, London, Weidenfeld and Nicolson, 1968

Cooper 1988 Douglas Cooper and the Masters of Cubism, London, Tate Gallery, 1988. Texts by Dorothy M. Kosinski and John Richardson

Cowling & Golding Elizabeth Cowling and John Golding, *Picasso: Sculptor/Painter*, London, Tate Gallery, 1994

Pierre Daix, *La vie de peintre de Pablo Picasso*, Paris, Seuil, 1977

Daix 1993 —, *Picasso: Life and Art*, trans. Olivia Emmet, London, Thames & Hudson, 1993

Daix 1995 —, *Dictionnaire Picasso*, Paris, Robert Laffont, 1995

Pierre Daix and Georges Boudaille, *Picasso: The Blue and Rose Periods*, Greenwich, CT, New York Graphic Society, 1967

Daix & Israël Pierre Daix and Armand Israël, *Pablo Picasso: dossiers de la Préfecture de Police 1901–1940*, Paris, Editions des Catalogues Raisonnés; Moudon, Editions Acatos, 2003

DR Pierre Daix and Joan Rosselet, *Picasso: The Cubist Years, 1907–1916*, trans. Dorothy S. Blair, London, Thames & Hudson, 1979

Deriaz Diane Deriaz, *La tête à l'envers: souvenirs d'un trapéziste chez les poètes, écrit en collaboration avec Gilles Costaz*, Paris, Albin Michel, 1988

Le Dernier Picasso/Late Picasso, Paris, Musée National d'Art Moderne, and London, Tate Gallery, 1988

Desire Pablo Picasso, *Desire Caught by the Tail*, trans. Roland Penrose, London, Calder and Boyars, 1970 (translation of *Le Désir attrapé par la queue*)

David Douglas Duncan, *The Private World of Pablo Picasso*, New York, Ridge Press, 1958

—, *Picasso's Picassos: The Treasures of La Californie*, London, Macmillan & Co., 1961

Duncan 1974 *Goodbye Picasso*, London, Times Books, 1974

Eluard Paul Eluard, *Lettres à Gala 1924–1948*, ed. Pierre Dreyfus, Paris, Gallimard, 1984

Face à l'histoire 1933–1996: L'artiste moderne devant l'évènement historique, Paris, Flammarion, Centre Georges Pompidou, 1996

Fairweather Sally Fairweather, *Picasso's Concrete Sculptures*, New York, Hudson Hills Press, 1982

Michael C. FitzGerald, *Making Modernism: Picasso and the Creation of the Market for Twentieth-Century Art*, New York, Farrar, Straus and Giroux, 1995

Catherine Blanton Freedberg, *The Spanish Pavilion at the Paris World's Fair*, 2 vols, PhD thesis, Harvard University, 1981, and New York, Garland, 1986

Judi Freeman, *Picasso and the Weeping Women: The Years of Marie-Thérèse Walter and Dora Maar*, Los Angeles County Museum of Art, 1994

Susan Grace Galassi, *Picasso's Variations on the Masters: Confrontations with the Past*, New York, Harry N. Abrams, 1996

Gascoyne David Gascoyne, *Journal 1936–1937. Death of an Explorer. Léon Chestov*, London, Enitharmon Press, 1980

Jean-Charles Gateau, *Paul Eluard et la peinture surréaliste (1910–1939)*, Geneva, Librairie Droz, 1982

—, *Eluard, Picasso et la peinture (1936–1952)*, Geneva, Librairie Droz, 1983

Geiser & Baer Bernhard Geiser and Brigitte Baer, *Picasso: Peintre-Graveur*, 7 vols, Berne, Kornfeld, 1986–96

Gilot 1964 Françoise Gilot and Carlton Lake, *Life with Picasso*, Harmondsworth, Penguin, 1966. (First edition: New York, McGraw-Hill, 1964.)

Gilot 2004 Françoise Gilot, *Dans l'arène avec Picasso: entretiens avec Annie Maïllis*, Montpellier, Indigène éditions, 2004

Arnold Glimcher and Marc Glimcher (eds), *Je Suis le Cahier: The Sketchbooks of Picasso*, London, Royal Academy of Arts, 1986

John Golding, 'Picasso and Surrealism', in *Picasso 1881–1973*, London, Paul Elek, 1973, pp. 76–121

—, *Cubism: A History and an Analysis, 1907–1914*, London, Faber and Faber, 1988. (First edition 1959.)

Goeppert et al. Sebastian Goeppert, Herma Goeppert-Frank, Patrick Cramer, *Pablo Picasso: The Illustrated Books. Catalogue Raisonné*, Geneva, Patrick Cramer, 1983

Peggy Guggenheim, *Out of this Century: Confessions of an Art Addict*, London, André Deutsch, 1980

Halliday Nigel Vaux Halliday, *More Than a Bookshop: Zwemmer's and Art in the 20th Century*, London, Philip Wilson, 1991

Hartley (1) Keith Hartley, 'Roland Penrose: private passions for the public good', in *Roland Penrose and Lee Miller: The Surrealist and the Photographer*, Edinburgh, Scottish National Gallery of Modern Art, 2001, pp. 13–29

Hartley (2) —, 'A selected list of works in the collection of Roland Penrose and Lee Miller', in *Roland Penrose and Lee Miller: The Surrealist and the Photographer*, Edinburgh, Scottish National Gallery of Modern Art, 2001, pp. 113–21

Hensbergen Gijs van Hensbergen, 'Guernica': The Biography of a Twentieth-Century Icon*, London, Bloomsbury, 2004

Timothy Hilton, *Picasso*, London, Thames & Hudson, 1975

Homage *Homage to Picasso on his 70th Birthday: Drawings and Watercolours since 1893*, London, Lund Humphries, 1951

Hommage à Pablo Picasso, Paris, Grand Palais and Petit Palais, 1966–67

Kahnweiler 1949 Daniel-Henry Kahnweiler, *The Sculptures of Picasso*, trans. A. D. B. Sylvester, London, Rodney Phillips & Co., 1949. (Original edition: *Les sculptures de Picasso*, Paris, Editions du Chêne, 1949.)

—, *Confessions esthétiques*, Paris, Gallimard, 1963

Daniel-Henry Kahnweiler, with Francis Crémieux, *My Galleries and Painters*, trans. Helen Weaver, London, Thames & Hudson, 1971

Léal Brigitte Léal, *Musée Picasso. Carnets. Catalogue des dessins*, 2 vols, Paris, Réunion des Musées Nationaux, 1996

Brigitte Léal, Christine Piot and Marie-Laure Bernadac, *The Ultimate Picasso*, trans. Molly Stevens and Marjolijn de Jager, New York, Harry N. Abrams, 2000

Leiris Michel Leiris, *Journal 1922–1989*, ed. Jean Jamin, Paris, Gallimard, 1992

London Bulletin, London, 1938–1940

Lord James Lord, *Picasso and Dora: A Memoir*, London, Orion, 1997. (First edition 1993.)

Madeline Laurence Madeline (ed.), *"On est ce que l'on garde!"* *Les archives de Picasso*, Paris, Editions de la Réunion des Musées Nationaux, 2003

André Malraux, *La Tête d'Obsidienne*, Paris, Gallimard, 1974

Marilyn McCully (ed.) *A Picasso Anthology: Documents, Criticism, Reminiscences*, London, Arts Council of Great Britain, 1981

—, *Picasso: The Early Years, 1892–1906*, Washington, National Gallery of Art, 1997

—, *Picasso: Painter and Sculptor in Clay*, London, Royal Academy of Arts, 1998

Melly George Melly, *Don't Tell Sybil: An Intimate Memoir of ELT Mesens*, London, Heinemann, 1997

Isabelle Monod-Fontaine et al., *Daniel-Henry Kahnweiler: marchand, éditeur, écrivain*, Paris, Centre Georges Pompidou, 1984

—, *Donation Louise et Michel Leiris: collection Kahnweiler-Leiris*, Paris, Musée National d'Art Moderne, 1984

Montañés Mariano Miguel Montañés, *Pablo Picasso: les dernières années*, Paris, Editions Assouline, 2004

Mourlot Fernand Mourlot, *Picasso lithographe*, 4 vols, Monte Carlo, Editions du Livre, 1949–64

Museu Picasso: Catàleg de pintura i dibuix, Barcelona, Ajuntament de Barcelona, 1984

Steven A. Nash (ed.) with Robert Rosenblum, *Picasso and the War Years 1937–1945*, London, Thames & Hudson, 1998

Patrick O'Brian, *Picasso: A Biography*, London, Collins, 1976

Olivier 1933 Fernande Olivier, *Picasso et ses amis*, Paris, Stock, 1933

—, *Souvenirs intimes*, ed. Gilbert Krill, Paris, Calmann-Lévy, 1988

Olivier 2001 —, *Loving Picasso: The Private Journal of Fernande Olivier*, ed. Marilyn McCully, trans. Christine Baker and Michael Raeburn, epilogue by John Richardson, New York, Harry N. Abrams, 2001

Oppler Ellen C. Oppler (ed.), *Picasso's Guernica*, New York, W.W. Norton & Co., 1988

Otero Roberto Otero, *Forever Picasso: An Intimate Look at his Last Years*, trans. Elaine Kerrigan, New York, Harry N. Abrams, 1974

Pablo Picasso. Das Spätwerk: Themen 1964–1972, Basel, Kunstmuseum, 1981

Pablo Picasso et Dora Maar: une histoire – des œuvres, photographies de 1906 à 1946, Paris, Maison de la Chimie, 28 October 1998

Palau 1981 Josep Palau i Fabre, *Picasso. Life and Work of the Early Years, 1881–1907*, trans. Kenneth Lyons, London, Phaidon, 1981

—, *Picasso: des ballets au drame (1917–1926)*, trans. Robert Marrast, Cologne, Könemann, 1999

Parmelin 1959 Hélène Parmelin, *Picasso Plain: An Intimate Portrait*, trans. Humphrey Hare, London, Secker and Warburg, 1963. (Original edition: *Picasso sur la place*, Paris, Juillard, 1959.)

Parmelin 1964 —, *Picasso: les dames de Mougins*, Paris, Editions Cercle d'Art, 1964

—, *Voyage en Picasso*, Paris, Robert Laffont, 1980

AP 1985 Antony Penrose, *The Lives of Lee Miller*, London, Thames & Hudson, 1985

AP 1992 — (ed.), *Lee Miller's War: Photographer and Correspondent with the Allies in Europe 1944–45*. Foreword by David E. Scherman. London, Thames & Hudson, 2005. (Original edition: London, Condé Nast Books, 1992.)

AP 2001 —, *Roland Penrose: The Friendly Surrealist. A Memoir*, Munich, London, New York, Prestel, in association with the National Galleries of Scotland, 2001

—, *The Home of the Surrealists: Lee Miller, Roland Penrose and their Circle at Farley Farm*, London, Frances Lincoln, 2001

RP Portrait 1956 Roland Penrose, *Portrait of Picasso*, London, Lund Humphries, for the Institute of Contemporary Arts, 1956

RP PLW 1958 —, *Picasso: His Life and Work*, London, Victor Gollancz, 1958

RP Picasso —, *Picasso*, Amsterdam, Allert de Lange, and Paris, Editions du Temps, 1961

RP Sculptures —, *Picasso: Sculptures*, Paris, Fernand Hazan, and London, Methuen, 1965

RP PLW 1971 —, *Picasso: His Life and Work*, Harmondsworth, Penguin, 1971

RP Portrait 1971 —, *Portrait of Picasso*, London, Lund Humphries, 1971

RP PLW 1981 —, *Picasso: His Life and Work*, London, Granada Publishing, 1981

RP SB —, *Scrap Book 1900–1981*, London, Thames & Hudson, 1981

Penrose & Golding Roland Penrose and John Golding (eds), *Picasso 1881–1973*, London, Paul Elek, 1973

Penrose & Miller Roland Penrose and Lee Miller: *The Surrealist and the Photographer*, Edinburgh, Scottish National Gallery of Modern Art, 2001

Picasso à Antibes, photographies de Michel Sima commentées par Paul Eluard. Introduction par Jaime Sabartès, Paris, René Drouin, 1948

Picasso à l'écran *Picasso à l'écran*, Paris, Centre Georges Pompidou in association with Réunion des Musées Nationaux, 1992

Picasso, jeunesse et genèse: dessins 1893–1905, Paris, Musée Picasso, 1991

Picasso: The Last Years 1963–1973, New York, Solomon R. Guggenheim Museum, 1984

Picasso: peintures 1900–1955, Paris, Musée des Arts Décoratifs, 1955

PP The Picasso Project, *Picasso's Paintings, Watercolours, Drawings and Sculpture: A Comprehensive Illustrated Catalogue 1885–1973*, San Francisco, Alan Wofsy Fine Arts (14 vols to date), 1995–2003

***Picasso* 1967** *Picasso Sculpture, Ceramics, Graphic Art*, Arts Council of Great Britain in association with London, Tate Gallery, 1967

Picasso: toros y toreros, Paris, Réunion des Musées Nationaux, 1993

Picasso: voyage dans l'amitié, Cannes, La Malmaison, 2003

Picasso vu par Brassaï, Paris, Réunion des Musées Nationaux, 1987

Anatoly Podoksik, *Picasso: The Artist's Works in Soviet Museums*, trans. V. Pozner, Leningrad, Aurora Art Publishers, 1989

Quinn *Picasso at Work. An Intimate Photographic Study by Edward Quinn*. Introduction and text by Roland Penrose. London, W. H. Allen & Co., 1965

Ramié Alain Ramié, *Picasso: catalogue de l'œuvre céramique édité 1947–1971*, Vallauris, Galerie Madoura, 1988

Georges Ramié, *Ceramics of Picasso*, Barcelona, Ediciones Polígrafa, 1985

Remy Michel Remy, *Surrealism in Britain*, Aldershot, Ashgate, 1999

Richardson 1991 John Richardson, with the collaboration of Marilyn McCully, *A Life of Picasso*, vol. 1, *1881–1906*, New York, Random House, 1991

Richardson 1996 —, *A Life of Picasso*, vol. 2, *1907–1917: The Painter of Modern Life*, London, Jonathan Cape, 1996

Richardson 1999 John Richardson, *The Sorcerer's Apprentice: Picasso, Provence and Douglas Cooper*, London, Jonathan Cape, 1999

Michèle Richet, *Musée Picasso: catalogue sommaire des collections. Dessins, aquarelles, gouaches, pastels*, Paris, Réunion des Musées Nationaux, 1987

Alexander Robertson et al., *Angels of Anarchy and Machines for Making Clouds: Surrealism in Britain in the Thirties*, Leeds City Art Galleries, 1986

William Rubin, *Dada and Surrealist Art*, London, Thames & Hudson, 1969

—, *Picasso in the Collection of The Museum of Modern Art*, New York, The Museum of Modern Art, 1972

Rubin 1980 —, *Pablo Picasso: A Retrospective*, New York, The Museum of Modern Art, 1980

Rubin 1989 —, *Picasso and Braque: Pioneering Cubism*, New York, The Museum of Modern Art, 1989

— (ed.), *Picasso and Portraiture: Representation and Transformation*, London, Thames & Hudson, 1996

William Rubin, Hélène Seckel, Judith Cousins, *Les Demoiselles d'Avignon*, New York, The Museum of Modern Art, 1994

Frank D. Russell, *Picasso's Guernica: The Labyrinth of Narrative Vision*, Montclair, Allanheld & Schram, 1980

Sabartès 1946 Jaime Sabartès, *Picasso: An Intimate Portrait*, trans. Angel Flores, London, W. H. Allen, 1949. (Original edition: *Picasso: portraits et souvenirs*, Paris, Louis Carré et Maximilien Vox, 1946.)

Sabartès 1954 —, *Picasso: documents iconographiques*, Geneva, Pierre Cailler, 1954

André Salmon, *Souvenirs sans fin*, vol. II, Paris, Gallimard, 1956

Scheler Lucien Scheler, *La grande espérance des poètes, 1940–1945*, Paris, Temps Actuels, 1982

Seckel Hélène Seckel, *Max Jacob et Picasso*, Paris, Réunion des Musées Nationaux, 1994

Seckel-Klein Hélène Seckel-Klein, *Picasso collectionneur*, Paris, Réunion des Musées Nationaux, 1998

Roger-Jean Ségalat, *Album Eluard*, Paris, NRF, 1968

Werner Spies, *Picasso Sculpture, with a Complete Catalogue*, trans. J. Maxwell Brownjohn, London, Thames & Hudson, 1972

—, *Pablo Picasso on the Path to Sculpture*, Munich and New York, Prestel, 1995

Werner Spies (ed.), *Pablo Picasso. Eine Ausstellung zum hundertsten Geburtstag. Werke aus der Sammlung Marina Picasso*, Munich, Haus der Kunst, 1981

S. Werner Spies, with the collaboration of Christine Piot, *Picasso: The Sculptures*, Stuttgart, Hatje Cantz, 2000. (Revised edition of *Picasso: Das plastische Werk*, Stuttgart, Gerd Hatje, 1983.)

Francis Steegmuller, *Cocteau: A Biography*, London, Constable, 1986. (First edition 1970.)

Gertrude Stein, *The Autobiography of Alice B. Toklas*, Harmondsworth, Penguin, 1966. (First edition: New York, Harcourt, Brace, 1933.)

Tabaraud Georges Tabaraud, *Mes années Picasso*, Paris, Plon, 2002

Trevelyan Julian Trevelyan, *Indigo Days*, London, MacGibbon and Kee, 1957

Utley Gertje R. Utley, *Picasso: The Communist Years*, New Haven, Yale University Press, 2000

Vallauris *Vallauris: La Guerre et la Paix: Picasso*, Vallauris, Musée national Picasso, 1998

Antonia Vallentin, *Picasso*, Paris, Albin Michel, 1957

Robert D. Vallette, *Eluard: livre d'identité*, Paris, H. Veyrier, 1983

André Verdet, *Pablo Picasso*, portraits by Roger Hauert, trans. Frances Richardson, Geneva, René Kister, 1956

Carsten-Peter Warncke, *Pablo Picasso 1881–1973*, ed. Ingo F. Walther, 2 vols, Cologne, Benedikt Taschen, 1992

—, *Picasso: Later Years*, London, Faber and Faber, 1961

Z. Christian Zervos, *Pablo Picasso*, 33 vols, Paris, Editions Cahiers d'Art, 1932–78.

Acknowledgments

This book would never have come into existence without the constant support, encouragement and cooperation of Antony Penrose and Richard Calvocoressi. I am deeply grateful to both of them for entrusting me with the absorbing task of selecting and editing the documents which form its main substance, and to Thomas Neurath, head of Thames & Hudson, for never wavering in his commitment to this project. Antony Penrose's books about his parents have been an invaluable source of information and he has answered my many questions with unfailing patience. Selecting the illustrations with him, Arabella Hayes and Carole Callow at the Lee Miller Archives has been a great pleasure.

I owe a particular debt to Michael Sweeney, who was appointed to sort out and catalogue Roland Penrose's books and private papers after his death and did so with consummate good sense, care and tact. He realised instantly that the notes Penrose had dedicated to his visits to Picasso merited publication and his scrupulous transcriptions were the basis for my own. I have further benefited from the numerous interviews he conducted with Penrose's friends during the 1990s and from the generous manner in which he has shared his extensive knowledge with me.

Ann Simpson, Senior Curator of the Archive and Library at the Scottish National Gallery of Modern Art, and her assistants, especially Jane Furness, have been unstintingly supportive and answered innumerable requests with the greatest patience, efficiency and good humour. Without them, my task would have been more daunting and far less enjoyable. Keith Hartley, author of a major study of Penrose's career and art collection, has also been extremely helpful, as have Patrick Elliott, Shona Corner and Janis Adams, his colleagues at the Gallery. Laurence Madeline and Sylvie Fresnault of the Archives Picasso in Paris could not have been more welcoming and cooperative during my periods of study there. I thank them all most warmly.

Many people have generously shared their knowledge or memories with me, including Kathleen Brunner, Bartolomeu Dos Santos, Michael Duffy, Bernard Dütting, Clare Finn, Michèle Griffaut, Antony Griffiths, Charles Marowitz, Anna Monleón and Hilary Rubinstein. I am also profoundly grateful to Marie-Noëlle Delorme, Diane Deriaz, the late Joanna Drew, Gijs von Hensbergen, Julie Lawson, Brigitte Léal, Marilyn McCully and María Teresa Ocaña, to whom I have repeatedly turned for help and advice, and to John Golding and John Richardson, who kindly read the entire book in draft and made invaluable suggestions. Bernard Dod and Julia MacKenzie provided much-needed encouragement at an early stage and Jessie Turner came to my rescue at various points. Michael Bury helped me to sort out my muddled thoughts and patiently put up with my Penrose-Picasso obsession. As ever, my mother gave constant and enthusiastic support.

Finally I should like to thank the exemplary team with whom I have worked at Thames & Hudson: Johanna Neurath, Sarah Praill, Kate Burvill and above all my editor, Jenny Wilson, on whose dedication, wisdom and sense of humour I have so often relied.

Elizabeth Cowling

Picture Credits

Index

Index entries refer to main text only. Numbers in *italics* refer to illustrations.

Agar, Eileen 33, 35
Alberti, Rafael 331
Anderson, Colin 266, 274, 279
Apollinaire, Guillaume 131, 132, 137, 143, 155, 156, 168, 171, 188, 191, 196, 332
Aragon, Louis 51, *53*, 73, 86, 93, 95, 135, 139, 158, 190, 273
Arias, Eugenio 335
Arnera, Hidalgo 247, 256
Arts Council of Great Britain 12, 14, 64, 81, 168, 174, 184, 210, 212, 213, 214, 217, 223, 224, 225, 238, 239, 248, 249, 250, 255, 284, 288, 290, 295, 297, 298, 305, 310
Atlee, Clement 42, *43*
Auric, Georges 162

Bacon, Francis 182, 246, 247, 291
Balthus (Balthasar Klossowski de Rola) 104, 105, 183
Balzac, Honoré de 247, 257
Banting, John 61
Bard, Joseph 33
Barr, Alfred H. 13, 47, 54, 59–60, *68*, 82–84, 94–95, 101–2, 136, 137, 138, 160, 166, 167, 168, 170, 171, 177, 181, 184, 198, 209, 214, 248, 249, 250, 272, 288, 297, 298, 342
Barr, Margaret *68*, 342
Barrey, Fernande 131
Batigne, René 112, 169
Baudelaire, Charles 156, 204
Baudouin, Pierre 87, 89, 90, 93, 112, 158, 159, 162, 244, 245, 326, 327, *327*, 328
Beaumont, Etienne de 226
Beauvoir, Simone de 61, 176
Bell, Clive 99, 100, 101
Bérard, Christian 115
Berger, John 289, 305
Bernal, John Desmond 64, 96, 136, 291
Bernard, Guy 129, 130, 293
Bernier, Georges 72
Bernier, Peggy *53*, 72, 106; *see also* Russell, Rosamond
Besson, Georges 157, 158
Bey, Aziz Eloui 33, 46
Bloch, Henri 138

Blunt, Anthony 37
Boccioni, Umberto 188
Bodkin, Thomas 235
Bonnard, Pierre 105
Bonshons (Bonsons), Jaume Andreu 172
Boué, Valentine 22–24, 25–26, *26*, 27, 46, 76, 98, 113, 116, 246, 247, 339, *339*, 345, 347
Boyesen, Hjahnaar 184
Bozo, Dominique 345, 346
Braque, Georges 22, 61, 78–79, *79*, *80*, 89, 97, 98, 100, 108, 122, 123, 132, 133, 136, 138, 144, 156, 163, 171, 188, 197, 222, 258, 276
Braque, Marcelle 97, 132, 171, 196, 197
Brassaï (Gyula Halász) 16, 55, 61, 165, 230, 279, 282–84
Brauner, Victor 112
Breton, André 24, 28, 32, 37, 39, 67, 130, 137, 138, 190, 300, 301
British Council 14, 54, 98, 175, 182, 223, 224, 238
Brunhoff, Michel de 109
Bull, John 317
Burne-Jones, Edward 117

Callery, Mary 183
Camarasa, Hermengild Anglada 117
Camus, Albert 61
Canals, Ricard 116
Carrington, Leonora 46
Casagemas, Carlos 132
Casanova, Laurent 135, 137, 139, 158, 169
Casas, Ramon 116, 118
Cassou, Jean 226, 256
Castro, Sergio de 193
Cézanne, Paul 105, 134, 215, 222, 244, 261, 263, 271, 276, 324
Chagall, Marc 87, 323
Chaplin, Charlie 140
Char, René 25
Chirico, Giorgio de 30–31, 36
Churchill, Winston 64, 97, 274, 276
Clair, René 139
Clergue, Lucien 315, 341
Clouzot, Henri, *Le Mystère Picasso* 119, 122–23, *124–25*, 128, 134, 135, 160, 161–65, 174
Cocteau, Jean 69, 73, *74*, 87, 95, 100, 101, 108, 113, 132, 135, 143, 190, 192, 247, 306, 315, 331
Coldstream, William 212, 213

Connolly, Cyril (C.C.) 302
Cooper, Douglas 28, 39, 86, 161, 162, 184, 209, 210–14, 215, 217–18, 223, 228–29, 230, 233, 235, 249, 268, 269, 322, 326, 330, 344
Cooper, Gary 166, 167, *167*, 168, 310
Coquiot, Gustave 138
Corot, Jean-Baptiste-Camille 222
Courbet, Gustave 187, 202, 222, 235
Cranach the Elder, Lucas 202
Crane, Walter 117
Crémieux, Janine 257
Crommelynck, Aldo 332–33
Crommelynck, Fernand 104, 256, 257, 302, 315
Crommelynck, Piero 320
Cuttoli, Marie 326

Daix, Françoise 306
Daix, Pierre 215, 271, 272, 273, 306, 337
Dali, Salvador 25
Daumier, Honoré 321
David, Jacques-Louis 144
David, Sylvette 86, 325
De Gaulle, Charles 48, 215, 257, 300
Degas, Edgar 156, 218, 320
Deharme, Lise 131
Delacroix, Eugène 102, 105, 202, 235
Delaunay, Robert 148
Derain, Alice 97, 132, 331
Derain, André 87, 97, 100, 101, 123, 132, 156, 171, 331
Deriaz, Diane 73–74, *75*, 76, 101, 347
Diaghilev, Sergei 99, 100, 101, 131, 132, 191, 212, 226
Dias, Cicero 48, 324
Dickens, Charles 247
Doisneau, Robert *103*
Drew, Joanna 12, *211*, 224, 238, 239, 268, 300, 310–13, *312*, 339
Dubuffet, Jean 149
Duchamp, Marcel 136, 247
Duncan, David Douglas 182, 187, 189, 192, 200, 218, 219, 220, 222, 334, 342
Durio, Paco 187
Duthuit, Marguerite 198
Dyall, Valentine 63, *63*

Effront, Nadine 197
Ehrenburg, Ilya 229, 298
El Greco (Domenikos Theotokopoulos) 109, 202, 204
HRH Queen Elizabeth, the Queen Mother 235, 236, 237, 341
HRH Queen Elizabeth II 235, 236, 237, 257, 341
'Els Quatre Gats' 116, 118, 138

Eluard, Cécile 30, *31*
Eluard, Dominique 218; *see also* Laure, Dominique
Eluard, Nusch 25, *26*, 29, 30, *31*, 33, 37, 40, 50, 51, *52, 53*, 68, 71, 73, 141, 272
Eluard, Paul 22, 24, 25, 27, 29, 30, *31*, 32, 33–34, 37, 38, 39, 40, 41, 44, 47, 48, 50, 51, *52, 53*, 54, 60, 67, 68, 69–70, *70*, 71, 72, 73, 74, 86, 90, 95, 98, 108, 130, 131, 132, 133, 137, 141, 143, 167, 169, 176, 190, 207, 270, 272, 300, 316, 347
Emmer, Luciano 93, 96, 119, 174
Ernst, Dorothea 72
Ernst, Max 12, 24, 32, 35, 44, 46, 48, 72, 140, 144, 240, 291, 337, 345
Errazuriz, Eugenia 131, 141, 184, 189, 332

Feld, Charles 285, 287
Fénéon, Félix 200
Fenosa, Apel·les 87
Fidelin, Ady 33
Foujita, Tsuguharu 131
Franco, Francisco 88, 93, 108, 155, 159, 183, 200, 257, 321
Frechtman, Bernard 61
Freud, Lucian 318
Frua de Angeli, Carlo 263
Fry, Roger 22, 24

Gaffé, René 30–32, 36, 38, 47, 57, 300
Galerie Louise Leiris, Paris 72, 144, 212, 225, 338, 339
Garnelo, José Maria 136
Gascoyne, David 24, 27, 30
Gatti, Ralph 335
Gaudí, Antoni 104, 118, 138
Gauguin, Paul 137, 222, 257
Gaunt, William 55
Gaut, Pierre 284
Gavarni (Sulpice Guillaume Chevalier) 118
Geiser, Bernhard 265, 266, 267
Gheerbrant, Alain 82
Giacometti, Alberto 32, 326
Gili, Ana Maria 322, 324, 337, 342
Gili, Gustavo 315, 337
Gilot, Françoise 16, 54, 57, 61, 68, *70*, 71, 73, *75*, 76, 77, 84, 87, 88, 89, 90, 92, 96, 101, 108, 111, 112–14, 126, 131, 132, 133, 154, 159, 176, 224, 244, 258, 267–70, 271, 284, 287, 289, 294, 321, 323, 325, 329, 330, 346
Gleizes, Albert 156
Golding, John 12, 234–35, 329, 345, 346
Goldscheider, Cécile 193
Gollancz, Victor 13, 14, 82, 95, 99, 174, 198, 199, 206, 207–8, 210, 239, 268

Gouel, Eva 93, 131, 132, 138, 155, 157, 195, 197
Gowing, Lawrence 234
Goya, Francisco José de 204
Granz, Norman 322, 334
Grasset, Bernard 216
Gregory, Eric 57
Gris, Josette 285
Gris, Juan 97, 123, 157
Gross (Hugo), Valentine 190, 331
Guérin, Charles 156
Guttuso, Renato 93, 94

Habasque, Guy 208
Hartmann, William *241*, 248, 250, 252–54, 255, 257, 258, 259, 260, 263, 264, 265, 266, 269, 284, 285, 286, 287, 289, 294, 307, 327, *327*
Haupt, Roland S. *52*
Haviland, Frank 185
Hayter, Stanley William 47, 302
Hirshhorn, Joseph 327, *327*
Huelin y Ruiz Blasco, Ricardo 109, 110
Hughes, Robert 304–5, 344
Hugnet, Georges 198
Hugo, François 331, 332
Hugué, Rosita 77, 89, 90, 92, 114–15, 120
Hugué, Totote 77, 84, 87, 89, 90, 120, 123, 126
Hutin, Catherine (Cathy) 84, 186, 192, 322, 331, 335

Ingres, Jean-Auguste-Dominique 105
Institute of Contemporary Arts, London 12, 14, 56–57, 58, 59, 60, 66, 68, 71, 75, 82, 84, 90, 95, 141, 144, 172, 173, 180, 181, 205–6, *211*, 227, 230, 231, 233, 238, 240, 242, 244, 247, 249, 257, 290–91, 292, 293, 294, 295, 300, 303, 314, 315, 318, 331, 334, 341, 345

Jacob, Max 97, 115, 132, 133, 137, 140, 143, 144, 156, 171, 196, 200
James, Philip 168
Jardot, Maurice 277, *277*
Jarry, Alfred 97, 132, 133, 148, 238
Joliot-Curie, Frédéric 64

Kahnweiler, Daniel-Henry 96, 98, 102, 104, 143, 144, 146, 156, 157, 165, 167, 175, 181, 186, 189, 197, 207, 210, 212, 214, 219, 223, 225, 243, 249, 258, 271, 274, 276, 277, *277*, 278, 288, 291, 292, 298, 328, 329, 340
Keynes, Lydia 99, 100
Keynes, Maynard 22, 99
Khokhlova, Olga 99, 100, 101, 104, 106, 108, 117, 130, 131, 132, 133, 134, 141, 146, 155, 170, 173,

180, 189, 190, 198, 331, 332
Klee, Paul 55, 134, 189, 267
Kootz, Sam 322

Lagut, Irène 131, 132, 155
Lake, Carlton 268, 329
Laporte, Geneviève 113, 176
Larrea, Juan 39, 40, 45
Laure, Dominique 68, 69, 71, 72, 76; *see also* Eluard, Dominique
Laurencin, Marie 196
Lawson, Julie 314, *327*, 339
Lazerme, Jacques de 84, 86, 87, 92, 93, 120, 185
Lazerme, Paule de 84, 86, 88, 89, 90, 92, 120, 169, 185
Le Corbusier (Charles-Edouard Jeanneret) 96, 187
Le Nain, Louis 202, 222, 276
Lefèvre, André 108
Léger, Fernand 96, 162
Leiris, Louise (Zette) 61, 75, 175, 184, 243, 274, 277, 295, 298, 321, 329, 340
Leiris, Michel 61, 175, 176, 182, 184, 270, 274, 277, *277*, 278, 316, 343
Leymarie, Jean 224, 289, 294, 321, 326, 341, 343, 345
Leymarie, Marie Paule 326
Lhote, André 22
Lifar, Serge 212, 320
Loeb, Pierre 189
London Gallery 38–39, 40, 44, 45, 46, 48, 57, 61, 67, 68, 238, 300
Lord, James 177, 180
Loren, Sophia 302

Maar, Dora 25, 29, 30, 33, *34*, 36, 37, 40, 42, 46, 50, 51, 54, 61, 108, 114, 115, 126, 127, 131, 132, 133, 134, 141, 154, 170–71, 176, 177, 183, 188, 189, 197, 219, 237, 270, 272, 325; photographs by *31*, *142*
Madoura factory 58, 84, 147, *167*, 323
Maeght Foundation 267–68, 269, 326
Magritte, René 48
Maillol, Aristide 86, 123
Mallarmé, Stéphane 157, 257
Malraux, André 300, 329
Manolo (Manuel Hugué) 77, 86, 114, 123, 126, 196
Marais, Jean 306
HRH Princess Margaret 236, 237, 257, 299, 303, *304*, 306
Marinetti, Filippo Tommaso 188
Marowitz, Charles 336
Matisse, Henri 54–55, 84, 89, 97, 101, 104, 105, 123, 136, 137, 138, 150, 157–58, 160, 162, 166, 196, 198, 219, 222, 239, 270, 276, 296, 329

Matisse, Pierre 158
Matta (Roberto Matta Echaurren)
156–57
McCarthy, Joseph 72, 95
McEwen, Frank 98, 175
Melly, George 238, 242
Mesens, E. L. T. 31, 38, 39, 44, 45,
46, 47, 48, 50, 56, 57, 67, 238,
300, 302, 337
Mesens, Sybil 69
Metzinger, Jean 136, 156
Michelangelo 96, 149, 201, 280,
344
Miller, Lee 12, 13, 14, 33, 34, 36,
37, 40, 43, 46, 50–51, 52, 53, 57,
60, 62, 63, 65, 66, 68, 72, 73,
74, 75, 76, 77, 78, 82, 84, 88, 95,
101, 110, 115, 119, 131, 141, 146,
161, 163, 166, 175, 178, 184, 186,
189, 191, 194, 205, 207, 215, 223,
224, 231, 242, 243, 249, 252, 257,
259, 263, 264, 266, 268, 269, 272,
274, 275, 284, 290, 293, 295, 300,
301, 302, 310, 313, 314, 316, 321,
323, 326, 327, 331, 336, 337, 345,
346, 347; photographs by 23, 34,
35, 51, 52, 53, 66, 67, 68, 70, 74,
78, 79, 80, 81, 83, 85, 91, 120, 121,
145, 163, 167, 177, 179, 185, 190,
193, 194, 203, 241, 251, 253, 275,
277, 283, 301, 311, 312, 327
Miró, Joan 12, 30–31, 35, 36, 113,
117, 118, 140, 250, 255, 264, 266,
267, 268, 291, 329
Modigliani, Amedeo 276
Moore, Henry 24, 32, 63, 182, 291,
341
Morland, Dorothy 12, 154
Morris, William 117
Moynihan, Rodrigo 64
Muñoz family 87, 88, 89, 162,
186–87
Murphy, Charles 241, 252
Murray, Patsy 77, 183, 184, 339
Musée Picasso, Paris 345, 346
Museu Picasso, Barcelona 314,
320, 321, 330
Museum of Modern Art, New
York 47, 55, 56, 58, 160, 161,
181, 240, 288, 294, 297, 299, 309
Mystère Picasso, Le, see Clouzot,
Henri

Nash, Paul 24
Nesjar, Carl 248, 249, 285, 325
Newton, Eric 42, 54, 208
Nixon, Richard 182
Nonell, Isidre 116, 117

O'Brien, Terry 12
Olivier, Fernande 16, 31, 123, 126,
132, 155, 171, 195–97, 198, 199
Opisso, Ricardo 116

Pallarès, Manuel 107, 178, 188,
313, 326, 336
Pâquerette 131
Parmelin, Hélène 73, 111, 177,
205, 264, 270, 285
Parrot, Louis 48
Pauplin, Christine 150, 162, 173,
329
Peissi, Pierre 193, 195
Pellequer, Max 155
Penrose, Alec 22, 47
Penrose, Antony (Tony) 37, 57,
65, 66, 68, 76, 77, 78, 82, 184,
185, 186, 242, 250, 335;
photograph by 245
Penrose, Beacus 33
Penrose, Lionel 22, 99, 245
Penrose, Roland
Cambridge University 22, 98–99
correspondence with:
Alfred Barr 82–84, 94, 95,
101–2, 160–61, 170–71,
198–99, 248, 297, 342; Lee
Miller 36–37, 40, 43; Pablo
Picasso 38–39, 40–41, 42, 45,
48–50, 51, 57–58, 61–62,
66–67, 69, 70–71, 75, 76,
79–81, 174, 198, 210, 213,
215–16, 220, 224, 227, 229,
230, 233, 235–36, 240–42, 243,
249–50, 255, 257–58, 258–59,
269, 280, 281, 291–92, 292–93,
297, 299, 314, 333–34, 336, 340,
341
photographs by 2, 66, 75, 217,
219
Picasso exhibitions curated by
(in date order):
'Picasso's "Guernica"' (1938–
39) 18, 39–44, 41, 43, 45, 46;
'Picasso: Drawings and
Watercolours since 1893'
(1951) 68–69; 'Picasso
Himself' (1956) 141–43, 144,
163, 165, 172–74, 173, 180;
'Picasso' (1960) 12, 210–14,
211, 215, 217–218, 223–239,
231, 232, 240, 242, 243, 251;
'Picasso Sculpture, Ceramics,
Graphic Art' (1967) 246–58,
272, 284, 288–89, 290, 297–
99, 303–6, 304; 'Picasso: 347
Engravings' (1970) 315,
318–20; 'Picasso's Picassos'
(1981) 235, 346–47
postcard collages by 35–36, 46,
347
publications on Picasso by:
Picasso: His Life and Work
(1958) 13, 14, 15, 17, 25, 26, 32,
33, 64, 82–84, 95, 99, 102, 113,
119, 144, 148, 165, 175, 200,
207–9, 216, 220, 224, 243, 348;
Picasso: His Life and Work
(1971) 13, 95, 256, 270, 319,
326, 330, 331; Picasso: His Life
and Work (1981) 343, 346;
Portrait of Picasso (1956) 14,
165, 170, 172, 174, 180–81, 191,
347; Portrait of Picasso (1971)
14, 321–22, 329, 330, 331; Scrap
Book (1981) 11, 12, 13, 25, 30,
34, 61, 67, 223, 224, 262, 265,
317, 338, 341, 347
residences of:
21 Downshire Hill, London
24, 27, 28, 29, 30, 36, 47, 48;
36 Downshire Hill, London
57, 60; Farley Farm, East Sussex
18, 60, 63, 64, 65, 66, 66, 67, 76,
161, 175, 223, 238, 268, 299,
316, 330, 339, 339, 341, 342,
347; 11A Hornton Street,
London 49, 60, 66, 300
translations of Picasso's writings
by:
Desire Caught by the Tail
60–63, 63, 140, 316, 321; The
Four Little Girls 140, 315–16,
318, 321, 334, 336, 337; other
texts 46, 61
Penrose, Valentine 246; see also
Boué, Valentine
HRH Prince Philip, Duke of
Edinburgh 226–27, 230, 231,
232, 233, 235, 236, 237, 238
Phillips, Ewan 59
Picasso, Bernard 329
Picasso, Claude 57, 62, 65, 85, 86,
87, 90, 92, 112, 119, 159, 244,
289, 320, 322, 323
Picasso, Jacqueline, see Roque,
Jacqueline
Picasso, Maya 24, 108, 113, 124,
125, 128, 131, 132, 133, 146, 176
Picasso, Olga, see Khokhlova, Olga
Picasso, Pablo:
artworks:
Acrobat on a Ball 237
The Blindman's Meal 236
Carafe and Three Bowls 237
Chicago monument 18, 241,
248–57, 258, 260, 261, 263,
264, 265, 266, 269, 271, 273,
284, 285–87, 288, 290, 292,
294, 304, 307–9, 308, 318
The Crane 127
The Crucifixion 191–92
Delacroix's The Women of
Algiers, variations on 102–4,
103, 111, 114, 160, 204
Les Demoiselles d'Avignon
31, 58, 59, 59, 94, 102, 136,
137, 138, 156, 157, 195, 200,
229, 236, 237, 240, 271, 279,
318
Dream and Lie of Franco
etchings 36, 37
The Dryad 237
The Embrace 236
El entierro del Conde de Orgaz,
illustrations in 324, 331, 332
Factory at Horta 237, 336
The Farmer's Wife 237
First Communion 117
Girl with a Mandolin (Fanny
Tellier) 32, 36, 47, 49, 161,
188, 236, 299
The Goat (La chèvre) 159,
217, 217, 218, 219
Grand Air 47
Guernica 29, 32, 33, 36, 37,
39, 40–44, 41, 43, 45, 46, 94,
112, 114, 132, 133, 176, 183,
192, 203, 227, 236, 272, 276,
305, 345
Head of a Woman 303
The Jester 144
Little Girl Skipping 252, 253
Man with a Sheep (L'homme
au mouton; L'homme à
l'agneau) 120, 160, 169, 188,
218, 219, 221, 310, 334
Man with a Violin 32
Manet's Le Déjeuner sur l'herbe
drawings 247
Marseille sculpture project
252, 257, 325
Massacre at Korea (Massacre
de Corée) 177–78, 177, 181,
191
Minotaure period 116, 176,
285
Minotauromachy etching 28
Musketeer 334
Negro Dancer 57, 317
Night Fishing at Antibes 46,
76
Nude with Drapery 237
The Old Jew 237
The Pencil that Talks 44, 300
Portrait of Jacqueline 203
Portrait of Wilhelm Uhde 31,
108, 236, 237, 299, 300, 302
The Rape of the Sabines 334
Science and Charity 117
Seated Musician 179
Self-Portrait (1907) 338
Self-Portrait (1972) 337–38,
339, 339
The Soler Family 236
Still Life (construction) 44,
49
Still Life with Chair Caning
236
Still Life with a Gas Jet 317
Still Life with a Skull 237
Suite 347 315, 318–20
'Temple of Peace' 84, 89–90,
215
The Three Dancers 240, 242,
243, 244, 248, 249, 258, 260,
264, 266, 267, 271–73, 274–
75, 275, 276, 279, 280–81
Three Musicians 236
Two Nudes (Friendship) 237

UNESCO mural 150, 200, 204, 214, 215, 216, 226, 249
Vallauris chapel decoration 150, 170, 215; *see also War and Peace* murals
Velázquez's *Las Meninas*, variations on 199–200, 202, 203, 204, 225, 226, 234, 235, 236, 237, 272, 314
La Vie 236
Vingt Poèmes de Góngora, illustrations in 66
Vollard Suite 305
War and Peace murals 76–77, 93, 112, 169, 226; *see also* Vallauris chapel decoration
Weeping Woman 37, 38, 42, 316, 317
Woman in Green (*La Femme en vert*) 31, 36, 57
Woman Lying in the Sun on the Beach 22, 29–30, 300
The Woman of Arles 71
Woman with a Key (*The Madame*) 77, 78
Woman with a Pushchair 80, 81, 257, 258
Woman with a Vase 345, 346
Woman with Outstretched Arms 249
Woman's Head and Self-Portrait 173, *173*
Women at their Toilette 163, 226, 243, *327*, 330
Women Running on the Beach 236
plays by:
  Le Désir attrapé par la queue 60–62, 140, 315, 316, 320; *Les quatre petites filles* 137, 140, 315, 316, 321, 336
residences of:
  Bateau Lavoir, Paris 96, 97, 115, 140, 146, 156, 195, 196; Château de Boisgeloup, Normandy 29–30, *31*, 60, 97, 105, 150, 173, 188, 284, 302, 313; Château de Vauvenargues, Provence 215, 216, 217, *217*, 218, 220, *220*, 221, 223, 342, 343, 346; La Galloise, Vallauris 61, 62, 71, 73, 76–77, *78*, *79*, *80*, *81*, *85*, 87, 94, 111, 112, 113, 114, 126, 137, 159, 176, 184, *253*, 303; Mas Notre-Dame-de-Vie, Mougins 223, *241*, 245, *245*, 246, 247, 250, *251*, 262, 263, 264, 269, 271, *275*, *277*, *283*, 284, 285, 287, 289, 290, 293, 294, 295, *301*, 306, 310, 311, *312*, 314, 320, 322–24, 326, 327, 329, 330, 331, 332, 333, 334, 335, 337, 339, 341, 342, 343; rue la Boétie, Paris

100, 134, 170, 188, 189; rue des Grands-Augustins, Paris 22, 29, 32, 50, 51–54, *51*, *52*, *53*, 102, 112, 134, 176, 221, 270, 284, 300, 302, 306, 328; Villa La Californie, Cannes *83*, 109, 119, 120–21, *120*, *121*, 122, 126, 128, 130, 135, 140, *145*, 152, 160, 161, *163*, 166, 168, 175, *177*, *179*, 180, 182, 184, 185, *185*, 187, 189, *190*, 191, *193*, *194*, 199, *203*, 212, 215, 216, 217, 218, 219, 223, 227, 228, 242, 243, 329
Picasso, Pablo (Pablito) 329, 342
Picasso, Paloma 57, *85*, 86, 87, 90, 92, 112, 119, 224, 289, 320
Picasso, Paulo 29, *31*, 73, *75*, 77, 89, 90, *91*, 92, 97, 108, 112, 113, 133, 150, 155, 158, 159, 162, 163, 170, 172–73, *173*, 180, 189, 221, 223, 231, 329, 342
Pichot, Ramon 276
Pignon, Edouard 73, *75*, 110, 111, 177, 188, 201, 205, 215
Poiret, Paul 195, 196
Polunin, Vladimir 100
Poussin, Nicolas 202, 337
Prats, Joan 117, 118
Prévert, Jacques 132, 168, 176
Princet, Maurice 100, 156
Pulitzer, Joseph 299

Quinn, Edward 255, 256, 269, 322, 324; photographs by *124–25, 339*

Ramié, Georges 114, 149, 162, 184
Ramié, Suzanne 114, 147, 149, 162, 184, 323, 327, 328
Ray, Man 12, 25, *26*, 33, 74, 141, 143, 337, 345
Raynal, Maurice 97, 114, 115
Read, Herbert 24, 37, 39, 42, 44, 56, *63*, 72, 255, 280
Reeves, Joyce 206, 207, 223
Rembrandt (Harmensz van Rijn) 280, 301, 340
Renoir, Claude 128, 134, 278
Reventós, Ramon, *Deux Contes 10*
Reverdy, Pierre 68
Ribemont-Dessaignes, Georges 207
Richardson, John 15, 162, 177, 212, 215, 230
Richter, Gigi 58
Rimbaud, Arthur 27, 157, 257
Robertson, Bryan 303
Rochas, Marcel 32
Roché, Henri-Pierre 195, 209
Rockefeller, Nelson A. 161
Roque, Jacqueline 11, 14, 77, 84, 86, 87, 88, 89, 90, 92, 93, 97, 104, 119, *120*, 123, 132, 135, 137, 139, 140, *145*, 146, 149, 150, 151, 152,

154, 160–61, 162, 166, 168, 169, 172, 173, 184, 186, 187, 189, 192, 201, 202, 205, 212, 214, 217, 218, 219, 221, 222, 223, 233, 242, 243, 244, 245, 246, 247, 250, 251, *251*, 254, 255, 256, 257, 260, 262, 263, 264, 265, 266, 267, 268, 269, 272, 273, 274, *275*, 284, 285, 286, 287, 289, 294, 295, 302, 306, 307, *312*, 313, 317, 320, 322, 323, 324, 325, 326, 328, 329, 330, 333, 334, 335, 337, 340, 341, 342, 343, 344, 346
Rosenberg, Julius and Ethel 72, 73
Rosenberg, Léonce 189
Rosenberg, Paul 24, 30, 183, 188, 189
Rosengart, Angela 320
Rosengart, Siegfried 320
Rothenstein, John 212, 226, *232*
Rousseau, Henri 87, 120, 133, 136, 148, 156, 180, 256
Roy, Claude 94
Rubinstein, Arthur 214
Rubinstein, Hilary 82, 84, 95, 143
Ruiz y Blasco, José 107, 136, 138, 175, 188, 195
Russell, John 305
Russell, Rosamond 12; *see also* Bernier, Peggy

Sabartès, Jaime 16, 24, 97, 98, 104, 106, 107, 110, 113, 117, 119, 129–30, 141, 143, 146, 147, *147*, 148, 150, 152, 158, 160, 165, 174, 175–76, *179*, 180, 184, 186, 302, 313–14
Sadoul, Georges 162
Sainsère, Olivier 196
Salles, Georges 130, 144–46
Salmon, André 132, 140, 155–56, 196, 200
Sartre, Jean-Paul 61, 176
Sassier, Inès 97, 306, 333
Satie, Erik 186, 190, 191, 257
Scherman, David E. *52*, *53*
Schlossman, Norman *241*, 252
Severini, Gino 188
Shakespeare, William 257, 266
Shchukin Irina 81, 157
Shchukin, Sergei 81, 157
Shepard, Alan Bartlett 335
Simon, Luc 112, 113, 114
Skira, Albert 335
Snowdon, Lord 236, 237, 303, *304*
Sorolla, Joaquín 117
Soto, Angel de 138
Spanish Civil War 25, 26–27, 38, 39, 42, 45, 227
Stein, Gertrude 96, 105, 155, 157, 171–72
Stein, Leo 136, 246
Steinlen, Théophile-Alexandre 118
Stravinsky, Igor 191
Sucre, Josep Maria de 117

Summerskill, Edith 281
Sunyer, Joaquim 116
Sutherland, Graham 97, 291
Sweeney, Michael 18
Sylvester, David 209, 234

Tate Gallery, London 14, 210, 212, 225, 226, 227, 228, 230, *232*, 234, 235, 237, 240, 242, 243, 249, 250, 258, 260, 261, 263, 264, 267, 271, 274, 279, 280, 281, 297, 299, 303, *304*, 316, 325
Tembry, Juan 110
Thomas, Dylan 62–63, *63*
Thompson, John 56, 182
Titian (Tiziano Vecellio) 280, 344
Toklas, Alice B. 123, 155, 157, 171
Tolstoy, Leo 118, 126
Toulouse-Lautrec, Henri de 116, 118
Trevelyan, Julian 42, 47, 61
Triolet, Elsa 51, *53*
Tuck, S. A. 234
Turnbull, William 59
Tzara, Tristan 104, 130

Utrillo, Miquel 136

Valadon, Suzanne 172
Vallentin, Antonina 95, 99, 143, 174, 191, 198, 207
Van Gogh, Vincent 105
Varda, Yanko 24
Velázquez, Diego Rodrigo de Silva y 118, 166, 199, 202, 204, 205, 221, 235, 318
Vilató family 106
  Fin 46, 98, *120*, 173
  Javier (Xavier) 46, 98, *120*
  Lola 27, 103, 107, 115, 117, 118–19, 134
Villon, Jacques 165
Vogue magazine 50, 57, 65
Vollard, Ambroise 108, 132, 133, 196, 197, 217

Walter, Marie-Thérèse 24, 108, 119, 120, 131, 132, 133, 146, 176, 347
Watson, Peter 57
Weelen, Guy 144
West, Rebecca 318
Wheeler, Monroe 294
White, Gabriel 225
White, Sam 228, 229
Wilson, Peter 291
Wright, Buckland 47
Wright, Wilbur 188

Zervos, Christian and Yvonne 25, 26, 27, 116, 165, 259, 260, 262, 263
Zuloaga, Ignacio 257
Zwemmer, Anton 38